THE LETTERS OF JUNIUS

The Letters of
JUNIUS

Edited by

JOHN CANNON

OXFORD
AT THE CLARENDON PRESS
1978

Oxford University Press, Walton Street, Oxford OX2 6DP

OXFORD LONDON GLASGOW
NEW YORK TORONTO MELBOURNE WELLINGTON
IBADAN NAIROBI DAR ES SALAAM LUSAKA CAPE TOWN
KUALA LUMPUR SINGAPORE JAKARTA HONG KONG TOKYO
DELHI BOMBAY CALCUTTA MADRAS KARACHI

British Library Cataloguing in Publication Data

Junius
The letters of Junius. – (Oxford English texts).
Bibl. – Index.
ISBN 0–19–812455–4
1. Cannon, John 2. Series
320. 9'41'072 JN210
Great Britain – Politics and government – 1760–1789

Printed in Great Britain
at the University Press, Oxford
by Vivian Ridler
Printer to the University

STAT NOMINIS UMBRA

Junius' motto from Lucan, *Pharsalia*, i. 135

Stat magni nominis umbra

He stands the shadow of a mighty name

PREFACE

JUNIUS had a low opinion of editors. 'I was not born to be a commentator,' he wrote loftily in his Preface to the collected edition, 'even upon my own works.' One knows what he had in mind. There are editorial tasks that recall Johnson's definition of a lexicographer—'a harmless drudge'. Yet one of the compensations is the insight one is afforded into the meaning of universities as groups of scholars striving to preserve and extend knowledge.

My first thanks are due to my former colleagues in the University of Bristol who received, from time to time, strange inquiries on the subject of Junius, without loss of equanimity. I must particularly mention Professor Stefan Körner, Professor John Vincent, Professor Ronald Grimsley, Professor W. D. Howarth, Mr. S. J. Tester, Mr. J. W. Sherborne, and Mr. B. P. Jones, who gave me much kind assistance on points of detail. I have, as always, leaned heavily on the patience of the staff of the University Library, especially those responsible for inter-library loans. Several years of students have also had to come to terms with Junius and it gives me pleasure to place on record the help and advice I have had from Elizabeth Lyon, Joanna Methuen-Campbell, Nicholas Hervey, and Karen Stagg.

I should also like to thank two colleagues in the University of Newcastle upon Tyne, Mr. Bernard Beckingsale of the Department of History and Dr. A. J. Woodman of the Department of Classics.

Miss S. E. Hearder, of the University Library, Reading, has given me a great deal of assistance, particularly in bibliographical matters: I am much indebted to her.

My work was made much easier by the permission granted by the Librarian of the London Library to use the volumes of the *Public Advertiser* in his charge.

I should also like to acknowledge the help of Miss Mary Williams, the Bristol archivist; Dr. A. Ellegård of the University of Gothenburg; Professor F. Cordasco of Montclair State College, New

Jersey; Mr. John Brooke of the Historical Manuscripts Commission; Dr. Betty Kemp and Dr. J. D. Fleeman of the University of Oxford; Professor Calhoun Winton of the University of South Carolina; Miss Margaret Condon of the Public Record Office; and Mr. E. A. Smith of the University of Reading.

I have much appreciated the kindness of Mr. J. S. G. Simmons and the staff of the Codrington Library at All Souls and I would also like to thank the staff of the following institutions: the Bodleian Library, the Cambridge University Library, the British Library, the Bristol Public Library, the Birmingham University Library, the Exeter City Library, the Institute of Historical Research, the National Register of Archives, the County Record Offices at Taunton, Hereford, Bury St. Edmunds, Dorchester, and Ipswich, and the City of Westminster Archives Department.

CONTENTS

ABBREVIATIONS

Add. MS.	Additional manuscript in the British Library.
Bedford Corr.	*Correspondence of John Russell, fourth Duke of Bedford*, ed. Lord J. Russell, 3 vols., 1842–6.
Burke Corr.	*The correspondence of Edmund Burke*, ed. T. W. Copeland, 1958 onwards.
CJ	*Journals of the House of Commons.*
Ellegård	*A. Ellegård, A statistical method for determining authorship: the Junius letters, 1769–1772*, 1962.
Everett	*The letters of Junius*, ed. C. W. Everett, 1927.
Fortescue	*The correspondence of King George the Third*, ed. Sir J. Fortescue, 6 vols., 1927.
GEC	*The complete peerage*, by G.E.C.
Grafton	*The autobiography and political correspondence of Augustus Henry, third Duke of Grafton*, ed. W. R. Anson, 1898.
Grenville papers	*The Grenville papers*, ed. W. J. Smith, 4 vols., 1852–3.
HMC	Reports of the Royal Commission on historical manuscripts.
Parkes & Merivale	*Memoirs of Sir Philip Francis*, ed. J. Parkes & H. Merivale, 2 vols., 1867.
Parl. Hist.	*The parliamentary history of England from the earliest period to 1803*, 36 vols., 1816.
Pitt. Corr.	*Correspondence of William Pitt, Earl of Chatham*, ed. W. S. Taylor & J. H. Pringle, 4 vols., 1838.
Public & private letters	For easy identification all Junius' letters are numbered. For the letters printed in the *Public Advertiser* and reproduced in the 1772 edition, I have retained Junius' roman numbering and refer to them as public letters. By private letters are meant those, not intended for publication, which passed between Junius and the printer, Junius and Wilkes, and from Junius to Grenville and Lord Chatham: they are given arabic numerals and are printed in Appendices one, two, and three.
State Trials	*A complete collection of state trials*, compiled by T. B. Howell, 1809.

The House of Commons, 1715–54	*The History of Parliament: the House of Commons, 1715–54*, ed. R. R. Sedgwick, 2 vols., 1970.
The House of Commons, 1754–90	*The History of Parliament: the House of Commons, 1754–90*, ed. Sir Lewis Namier & John Brooke, 3 vols., 1964.
Wade	*The letters of Junius*, ed. John Wade, 2 vols., 1850.
Walpole	*Memoirs of the reign of King George the Third*, ed. G. F. Russell Barker, 4 vols., 1894.

INTRODUCTION

THE first letters by the anonymous writer Junius were printed in the *Public Advertiser* at a moment of acute political tension. During the early years of George III's reign there had been a succession of short-lived ministries. Lord Bute's administration, which possessed all the King's confidence, came to an end in April 1763 when his lordship, bruised and exasperated by the miseries of political life, insisted on tendering his resignation. His successor, George Grenville, though a capable administrator, alienated the King by his prolix and tedious harangues and was dismissed in July 1765. The Rockingham ministry lasted a bare twelve months. In the summer of 1766 it seemed that the King might at last have acquired a government with some prospects of stability. Setting aside his distrust of William Pitt—once described as 'a true snake in the grass'—the King agreed to the construction of an administration on a non-party basis, to be composed of men 'eminent above others for their ability and integrity'. Thus was formed Burke's celebrated 'piece of tesselated pavement without cement . . . utterly unsafe to touch and unsure to stand on'.[1]

First Lord of the Treasury in the new ministry was the young Duke of Grafton, though it was understood that Pitt himself, as Lord Privy Seal, would provide the direction and political experience. The government was soon in difficulties. Much of Pitt's popularity in the country disappeared overnight when he accepted a peerage as Earl of Chatham. Worse still, he succumbed within months to a mysterious disorder which prostrated him completely, leaving him quite incapable of conducting business. His ministry, bereft of its leader, carried on as best it could.

The general election of March 1768 resulted in the return of

[1] *The House of Commons, 1754–90*, iii. 298; Edmund Burke, *Speech on American Taxation*, 19 April 1774.

For more detailed accounts of the political situation at this time, see P. Langford, *The first Rockingham administration 1765–1766* (1973), and J. Brooke, *The Chatham administration, 1766–1768* (1956), augmented by J. S. Watson, *The reign of George III, 1760–1815* (1960). The most recent discussion of British policy towards America is to be found in P. D. G. Thomas, *British politics and the Stamp Act crisis* (1975).

John Wilkes, a declared outlaw, for the county of Middlesex and presented the ministers with an awkward problem. Urged on by the King they decided that the return for Middlesex must be quashed, thus providing the opposition with a constitutional issue of great importance. In October 1768, despite the King's entreaties, Lord Chatham resigned, lamenting, with justice, that his infirmities had rendered him 'entirely useless'. With him went Lord Shelburne, a Secretary of State, leaving the ministry, its props breaking one by one, to confront an opposition which, in the King's view, aimed 'at the very vitals of all government'.[1]

Into this situation stepped Junius. His first letter, printed on 21 November 1768, was little regarded by the public and later unacknowledged by the author.[2] It dealt with the issue of the Middlesex election, shortly to be debated by the House of Commons. The beginning was entirely characteristic of Junius in its directness and in the effortless assumption of superiority: 'It will soon be decided by the highest Authority, whether the Justice of our Laws, and the Liberty of our Constitution have been essentially violated in the Person of Mr. Wilkes.' The first of many jeers was directed at the Duke of Grafton, accused of betraying Wilkes's friendship: 'Other Men have been abandoned by their Friends;—Mr. Wilkes alone is oppressed by them.'

Junius' next letter, published on 21 January 1769, was more ambitious—a sustained attack upon the ministers, one by one: 'The finances of a nation, sinking under its debts and expences, are committed to a young nobleman already ruined by play. Introduced to act under the auspices of Lord Chatham, and left at the head of affairs by that nobleman's retreat, he became minister by accident. . . .' Of Lord North, Chancellor of the Exchequer, Junius remarked: 'It may be candid to suppose that he has hitherto voluntarily concealed his talents; intending perhaps to astonish the world, when we least expect it. . . .'[3] But it was his sarcasms

[1] Fortescue, ii, nos. 666 and 707.

[2] The letter was not included by the author in his collected edition, published in 1772, probably because it did not make, in his judgement, an appropriate start to the series. Nevertheless it was signed 'Junius' and has all the hallmarks of genuineness. It is printed in Appendix four, p. 455 below.

[3] This is a good example of the strength and weakness of Junius. It relies for its

against the Commander-in-Chief, the Marquess of Granby—'Nature has been sparing of her gifts to this noble lord'—that led to Junius' success, since they provoked a retort from an army officer, Sir William Draper. The subsequent exchange of letters kindled public interest and established Junius' reputation as a controversialist. Within a few months it was apparent that the author had created a major literary figure. The early letters were issued by Francis Newbery in a collected volume and a little later the author wrote, 'As to Junius . . . this is a Character, which must be kept up with credit.'[1]

Junius' success was by no means instantaneous. His letter of 21 January 1769 was held up by the printer for several days until a backlog of letters to be published had been cleared: Junius suffered the indignity of waiting until Common Sense, Candour, Plain Matter of Fact, and A Surrey Milk-Boy had all had their say. His second letter was also postponed.[2] But the later letters were a considerable commercial success. Henry Sampson Woodfall, printer and owner of the *Public Advertiser*, took care to notify the public in advance. In the early months of 1769 the daily sales of the newspaper were about 3,000 copies. The first letters produced little or no extra demand, but for the sensational letter to the King, printed on 19 December 1769, Woodfall ran off 1,750 additional copies, an increase of nearly 60 per cent. This was an exceptional figure, not to be repeated: nevertheless, 350 extra copies were printed for letters in March 1770, April 1770, and November 1771, 450 extra for the letter of 22 April 1771, 700 extra for the letter to the Duke of Grafton in February 1770, and 750 extra for the letter to Lord Mansfield in November 1770.[3] 'In the present contest between the *Ins* and the *Outs*,' wrote a correspondent in December 1769, 'your Paper is become the principal Theatre where . . . the

effect largely upon the style, insolent and mocking: as a comment it was singularly misguided, since this period in office laid the foundation for Lord North's success. He had unusual gifts for dealing with financial matters.

[1] Private letter no. 6, printed below, p. 352.

[2] *Public Advertiser*, 18 January and 6 February 1769.

[3] The *Public Advertiser's* sales book is Add. MS. 38169. The figures were commented on by C. W. Dilke in the *Athenaeum*, 29 July 1848. *The Gazetteer*, one of the *Public Advertiser's* London rivals, claimed a circulation of 5,000 in December 1770. R. L. Haig, *The Gazetteer, 1735–97: a study in the eighteenth-century English newspaper*, p. 79.

Grand Battles are decided.'[1] One can understand why Junius, nettled at a rumour that no more letters would be forthcoming, observed tartly to the printer, 'it is not your interest to declare that I have done'.[2]

The excitement produced in the political nation by the letters of Junius was intense. Other newspapers and journals reprinted them and inserted paragraphs hinting at the authorship. Supporters sent Junius information that might be of use and begged him to intervene on their behalf. Ministerial hack-writers threatened to unmask him and challenged him to duels, literary and martial. 'If you dare to appear in this paper again,' wrote Poetikastos, 'without any apology for your conduct, I will convince you I am not ignorant of your Person or Residence.'[3] Junius was assailed and defended in some of the most appalling verse ever written:[4]

> Cease, Junius, cease, envenom'd Darts to throw
> From thy dark Corner, like a Coward Foe;
> Such Hell-forg'd Weapons hence to wield Forbear;
> They wound not Granby's Fame, but Britain's Ear.

The government, frustrated in its efforts to track down the author, brought legal actions against several of the printers after the publication of the letter to the King.[5] The weeks after this celebrated letter saw a frenzy of speculation. 'This country', wrote Thomas Whately to George Grenville on 27 December 1769, 'is full of reports about Junius: some say he is a Mr. Lloyd, Chaplain to Lord Shelburne, and that he is in custody.'[6] The readers of the *Exeter*

[1] A Byestander, 2 December 1769.

[2] Private letter no. 44, printed below, p. 378.

[3] *Public Advertiser*, 22 April 1769. Another Junius appeared two days later. I do not know whom Poetikastos assaulted.

[4] 4 August 1769. For the defence, see Lucilius, 17 August 1769.

[5] Henry Sampson Woodfall was tried on 13 June 1770 for seditious libel: the jury returned a verdict of guilty of printing and publishing only. The second trial terminated in Woodfall's acquittal on a technicality. Prosecutions were also commenced against John Almon, bookseller; John Miller, printer of the *London Evening Post*; Charles Say, printer of the *Gazetteer*; George Robinson, printer of the *Independent Chronicle*; Henry Baldwin, printer of the *St. James's Chronicle*. Almon was found guilty; Miller and Baldwin were acquitted; the charges against Say and Robinson seem to have been dropped. *State Trials*, xx. 803–922. The prosecutions were debated in the House of Commons on 27 November 1770; *Parl. Hist.* xvi. 1127–211.

[6] *Grenville Papers*, iv. 500.

Flying Post were regaled with the latest London rumours in hot succession: 'It is now confidently said that Mr. M. a clergyman in Kent about 32 years of age is the author . . . ; that two noblemen of great distinction furnish him with materials. . . .' Its next report hinted at a 'secret junto' and before readers could digest that possibility, they were assured of the 'undoubted fact' that the author was 'Mr. B——e of Ireland'.[1]

It was not to be expected that Junius would be universally admired. The Marquess of Rockingham was understandably nervous about his ferocious ally: the letter to the King, he confided to Dowdeswell, was 'rather too much of a flagellation. I should have liked it better if the turn had not been so directly to have *charged* his Majesty, but to have *conjured him to think*, and no longer to have *been led*. . . .'[2] Sylas Neville and his radical friends, on the other hand, were full of praise: the letter of 28 September 1771 against the Duke of Grafton was 'a most admirable composition'.[3] Government supporters, for the most part, condemned Junius' politics and his style. In the House of Commons Edmund Burke taunted Lord North on the ministry's inability to apprehend the author:[4]

> The myrmidons of the court have been long, and are still, pursuing him in vain. They will not spend their time upon me, or you, or you: no; they disdain such vermin, when the mighty boar of the forest, that has broke through all their toils, is before them. But what will all their efforts avail? No sooner has he wounded one than he lays down another dead at his feet. . . . You crouched, and still crouch, beneath his rage.

Junius' career lasted three years exactly.[5] During that time he produced more than sixty letters, some of them filling several

[1] The clergyman in Kent I take to be the Revd. Edmund Marshal of Charing, Kent, who died 5 May 1797. He was well known as a contributor to newspapers. Since he was admitted to St. John's, Cambridge, in 1749 aged 15, he was about 35 at this time. The two noblemen were, presumably, Lords Chatham and Temple. Though Edmund Burke was constantly suspected of the authorship, in his private letters he strongly denied the charge. *Exeter Flying Post*, 22/9 December 1769.

[2] *Memoirs of the Marquis of Rockingham and his contemporaries*, ed. Earl of Albemarle (1852), ii. 147–8.

[3] *The diary of Sylas Neville, 1767–1788*, ed. B. Cozens-Hardy (1950), 123–4.

[4] *Parl. Hist.* xvi, 1154–5.

[5] That is, dating it by his letters in the collected edition. His first was published 21 January 1769 and the last 21 January 1772. Subsequent letters were published under other names.

columns of the *Public Advertiser*. But the strain of composition soon affected him. 'I really doubt whether I shall write any more under this Signature', he told Woodfall as early as July 1769.[1] After the letter to the King in December 1769 there was a sense of anti-climax, and though he was still capable of devastating passages, the general quality shows some decline. In addition to the fatigue of amassing the materials and polishing the prose, there were great hazards in communicating with the printer and a consciousness at all times of the risks he was running. He was almost completely at the mercy of Woodfall's loyalty: 'I must be more cautious than ever', he wrote during an agitated period in November 1771; 'I am sure I should not survive a Discovery three days . . . I am persuaded you are too honest a man to contribute in any way to my destruction.'[2] Throughout the autumn of 1771 he was extremely busy preparing the letters for a collected edition. But late that year he decided upon a last grand onslaught on Lord Chief Justice Mansfield, accusing him of a deliberate violation of the law of the land on the subject of bail. 'The paper', he wrote to Woodfall, 'is, in *my* opinion, of the highest Stile of Junius and cannot fail to sell.'[3] In fact, it proved a disaster. Abandoning vituperation, at which he was expert, Junius embarked upon a long and tedious legal argument, which was neither entertaining nor convincing. The joy of his literary opponents was unconfined. Philo-Scaevola declared with relish that Junius, 'who has long been languishing under a mortal disease, has at last cut his own throat', and another antagonist wrote that 'the last letter of Junius to Lord Mansfield is universally allowed to be as palpable an act of literary suicide as ever was committed'.[4]

The letter to Mansfield was the last of Junius' writings under that

[1] Private letter no. 5, printed below, p. 351.

[2] Private letter no. 43, p. 376 below. Woodfall's replies to Junius were signalled in a private code in the *Public Advertiser* and left at a pre-arranged coffee-house for collection. If Woodfall had betrayed the name of the rendezvous to the government it would have been an easy matter to have Junius' emissary followed.

[3] Private letter no. 50, printed below, p. 384. Junius had grandiose expectations of the public letter, which was timed to coincide with the opening of the parliamentary session. He wrote to Chatham begging him to attend the House of Lords and move to have Mansfield committed to the Tower.

[4] *Public Advertiser*, 28 January and 6 February 1772.

signature.[1] A week later he turned his attention to Lord Barrington, the Secretary-at-War, and began a series of attacks under the name of Veteran: 'Be careful not to have it known to come from me', he warned the printer.[2] The first letter promised a series of sixteen but Veteran abandoned the chase in March 1772 after five had appeared. Two further attacks under the names of Scotus and Nemesis appeared in May.[3] By this time the collected letters had, after much delay, been given to the public. From May 1772 there were no signs from Junius, either in public or private, until in January 1773 he wrote to Woodfall once more in reply to repeated signals in the *Public Advertiser*. The opposition, he declared, was too divided to be worth supporting. 'In the present state of things, if I were to write again, I must be as silly as any of the horned Cattle, that run mad through the City . . . it is all alike, vile and contemptible.' Woodfall replied, pointing out the East India Company as a new subject.[4] There was no reply. Woodfall's letter was never collected from the coffee-house used for correspondence and at length he reclaimed it. Junius had retreated into darkness.

★ ★ ★

There are several ways in which the letters of Junius may be considered and assessed—as a historical factor in their own right, as a historical source, as a constitutional commentary, and as a literary work.

Junius' immediate political objective was the overthrow of the Grafton administration, which he regarded as dangerously subservient to the King. There can be little doubt that the stinging attacks upon Grafton helped to break his nerve and persuade him to resign. Junius might also claim some responsibility for softening up the ministry and bringing about the crisis of January 1770. Lord Granby, to whom he had directed a specific appeal,[5] abandoned

[1] Or, more strictly, the letter to Lord Camden, which Junius loosely tacked on to the letter to Mansfield.

[2] Private letter no. 53, p. 386 below.

[3] The letters by Veteran, Scotus, and Nemesis are printed in full in Appendix five, where their authenticity is discussed.

[4] Private letters nos. 64 and 65, printed below, pp. 393–6.

[5] Presuming that Junius was also the author of Your Real Friend of 6 May 1769. The matter is discussed in Appendix five, p. 466. It certainly reads like Junius: he concludes, 'I even appeal to your understanding.'

his colleagues early in January and recanted the vote he had previously given on the Middlesex election.[1] Lord Camden, whom Junius had always treated with moderation, was dismissed at the same time, after a speech attacking his fellow ministers; the difficulties in finding an adequate replacement for him as Lord Chancellor led directly to Grafton's resignation. But if Junius did have some share, however indefinable, in bringing down the ministry, it did little good to his political cause. Grafton's successor was Lord North, 'more able, more active, more assiduous, more resolute, and more fitted to deal with mankind'.[2] The opposition melted away and in his last private letter Junius confessed that 'the Cause and the public. Both are given up.'[3]

Nor, at a deeper level of analysis, is it easy to see that the substitution of a Grenville–Rockingham–Chatham ministry for that of Lord North would have been of great historical consequence.[4] Junius believed, or affected to believe, that it was necessary to save the constitution from violation, but the desperate plot to destroy the liberties of the subject existed only in his own mind, and the constitution survived. It has been suggested that Chatham or the Rockinghams might have found a cure for the American troubles:[5] it seems more likely that the American troubles would have torn asunder the fragile unity of the coalition.[6] In the domestic field it is improbable that Chatham's recent and desultory interest in parliamentary reform would have made much progress in face

[1] Granby's attitude is very fully discussed in the biography Sir Lewis Namier contributed to *The House of Commons, 1754–90*. There were of course other pressures on Granby and it is possible that Junius' intervention made it more difficult for him to resign. In November 1769 he wrote that resignation at that time might seem like 'skulking to Junius'.

[2] Horace Walpole to Sir Horace Mann, 30 January 1770; *The Yale edition of Horace Walpole's correspondence* (1967), ed. W. S. Lewis, xxiii. 182.

[3] Private letter no. 64, printed below, p. 393.

[4] Lord Chatham, having resigned in October 1768, returned to the fray wonderfully recovered, appeared in the House of Lords in January 1770 and began an onslaught upon his former colleagues. The Middlesex election issue brought him into a temporary alliance with George Grenville and the Rockinghams.

[5] O. A. Sherrard, *Lord Chatham and America* (1958); I. R. Christie, *Myth and reality in late-eighteenth-century British politics* (1970), 53, 85–6.

[6] One can scarcely conjecture what the American policy of the coalition government might have been. George Grenville had introduced the Stamp Act in 1764; Rockingham repealed it in 1766 but added an act declaratory of British sovereignty; Chatham had been the leading opponent of the Declaratory Act.

of the opposition he was certain to receive from his Rockingham allies.

But although the direct political consequences of Junius' campaign were modest, the by-products were of considerable importance. In 1760 the aristocratic domination of political life, which had grown since 1688, and more particularly since 1714, was at its strongest. Elections were necessary only once every seven years and never had the control exercised over counties and boroughs been tighter. Party differences had almost disappeared. A fierce proscription on reporting of parliamentary debates helped to prevent the creation of an informed public opinion. Within a comparatively brief period the structure began to crack. The resistance of the American colonists was, of course, the most direct challenge to the assumptions on which the old system was based. At home, the spearhead of the attack was Wilkes, but behind him Junius played a significant part. The breakdown of the prosecution of the printers of his letter to the King led in the course of time to a change in the law of libel, whereby juries were allowed to decide on the issue of libel as well as the fact of publication. Secondly, the Junius affair helped to bring about the clash in 1771 between the city of London and the House of Commons, as a result of which the right to publish parliamentary debates was tacitly conceded. These changes increased the area in which public opinion could operate, and Junius drew attention to them in the Dedication of his collected edition: 'Let it be impressed upon your minds, let it be instilled into your children, that the liberty of the press is the *Palladium* of all the civil, political, and religious rights of an Englishman, and that the right of juries to return a general verdict, in all cases whatsoever, is an essential part of our constitution. . . .' It would, of course, be far too much to suggest that the old regime was seriously damaged, but the campaigns of the 1760s and 1770s made breaches in the defences through which, in the nineteenth century, reformers could advance.

As a direct historical source, the letters of Junius are of limited value. The kind of secrets he could pick up were of passing interest only,[1] and though he strove hard to create an impression of omni-

[1] 'By way of intelligence, you may inform the public that Mr. Delafontaine, *for*

science it is clear that much of his information came from newspapers. Junius was always willing to dazzle Woodfall with his superior knowledge: 'depend upon the Assurance *I* give you', he wrote on 16 January 1771, 'that every Man in Administration looks upon War as inevitable.'[1] Woodfall dutifully repeated the tip in his newspaper the following day—but the war did not come. Junius' sketches of contemporaries bear too obviously the marks of rancour to be of much use: though, for effect, he accused Grafton of betraying Wilkes's friendship, there is no reason to disbelieve Grafton's assertion that they had never been on close terms.[2] The world Junius depicts is too full of malevolent and dastardly villains to tell us much except that his own mind was inflamed and suspicious: one would have to search hard to find a historian who believed, with Junius, that the Duke of Bedford aimed at 'absolute power' or that it was the object of Lord Mansfield's existence to undermine the liberties of the subject.[3]

But as a commentator on events Junius can give us the feel of mid-eighteenth-century politics. He shared with many of his contemporaries a deep distrust of both the executive and the judiciary, an almost hysterical regard for the constitution, and a conviction that only extreme watchfulness could preserve it.[4] To read the letters, one by one, is to command a panoramic vista of the politics of the period, though admittedly seen through a distorting lens.

Junius was not merely a factor in promoting the development of

his secret services in the Ally, is appointed Barrack Master to the Savoy.' Private letter no. 16.

1 Private letter no. 28, printed below, p. 367.

2 Grafton, 189.

3 It is true that the language of eighteenth-century newspapers was melodramatic in the extreme, but Junius' private comments suggest an ungovernable temper: 'that Swinney is a wretched but a dangerous fool'; 'That bloody Wretch [Lord Barrington] would never have taken a step, apparently so absurd, if there were [not] some wicked design in it'; 'What an abandoned, prostituted Idiot is your Lord Mayor'. Private letters nos. 5 and 57.

4 Though the consequences of Junius' activities may have been radical, his attitude was defensive and he regarded himself as a victim rather than an aggressor. In public letter no. XLIV, he wrote: 'Our political climate is severely altered; and, without dwelling upon the depravity of modern times, I think no reasonable man will expect that, as human nature is constituted, the enormous influence of the crown should cease to prevail over the virtue of individuals. The mischief lies too deep to be cured by any remedy, less than some great convulsion, which may either carry back the constitution to its original principles, or utterly destroy it.'

the press but a striking indication of the progress it had made since its tentative beginnings in the reign of Anne. By 1770 there were five London daily newspapers and six evening newspapers, as well as several thrice-weeklies: the number of provincial newspapers had risen to more than forty.[1] Advertisements provided most of the revenue and took up a large part of each paper but increasingly popular were readers' letters. The printer of the *Gazetteer* claimed in 1764 to have received 861 letters in four months—i.e. at the rate of roughly 50 a week.[2] Printers occasionally hired writers to get controversies started and encouraged readers to submit their own letters and comments. Letters of interest were reprinted from rival newspapers, and collections of letters on various subjects published as commercial ventures. The success of Junius had to some extent been foreshadowed in the 1760s in the writings of James Scott, under the name of Anti-Sejanus.[3]

By many contemporaries and some later commentators the letters have been much admired as an exposition of the eighteenth-century constitution. This was a claim that Junius himself advanced in his Dedication: 'When kings and ministers are forgotten, when the force and direction of personal satire is no longer understood, and when measures are only felt in their remotest consequences, this book will, I believe, be found to contain principles, worthy to be transmitted to posterity.' That Junius' hopes were not entirely disappointed may be confirmed from an unexpected source. A pocket edition of the letters, once in the possession of Lord Craigavon, first prime minister of Northern Ireland, has inscribed on the flyleaf: 'This book—the property of James Craig—is a guide from which he gained his first knowledge of parliamentary experience.'[4]

[1] S. Morison, *The English newspaper* (1932); R. S. Crane and F. D. Kaye, *A census of British newspapers and periodicals, 1620–1800* (1927); G. A. Cranfield, *The development of the provincial newspaper, 1700–1760* (1962). Essential reading for an understanding of the development of the press is J. Brewer, *Party ideology and popular politics at the accession of George III*, particularly chapters 8 and 11.

[2] Haig, op. cit., p. 71.

[3] Scott's letters, directed against Lord Bute, were originally printed in the *Public Advertiser*. They were included in *A collection of interesting letters*, 1767. More of his letters, under different pseudonyms, appeared in 1770 in *Fugitive political essays*. Brewer prints a valuable bibliography of pamphlet literature.

[4] I am extremely grateful to Mrs. J. R. Vincent for the gift of this small volume.

There is, however, little that is striking or original in Junius' treatment of the constitution, and his gift for vituperation concealed the fact that his political stance was basically a moderate one.[1] Indeed, in the Preface to his collected edition, Junius conceded that the British constitution, though not without blemish, was 'the wisest of human institutions'. In the concluding passages of his letter to the King, which Burke confessed went too far, one feels that Junius was insolent rather than deeply menacing: the King, he wrote, should have before him the fate of the Stuarts— 'The prince who imitates their conduct, should be warned by their example; and while he plumes himself upon the security of his title to the crown, should remember that, as it was acquired by one revolution, it may be lost by another.'[2] Leslie Stephen suggested that Junius was too much the pedant, too wedded to legal precedents, to be capable of any original contribution to political thought:[3]

> Polish was to preserve what was else little worth preservation. For the absence of any speculative thought in Junius's Letters is even more remarkable than in the case of Bolingbroke. Bolingbroke at least aims at being philosophical. Junius makes personal denunciations almost the exclusive substance of his letters. He has no affectation of theory . . . the ferocious onslaught turns generally upon some personal scandal, upon the stories that one duke has been horsewhipped, and another had taken his mistress to the opera; whilst constitutional principles are invoked to injure his enemy, rather than defended at his enemy's cost.

That assessment was not entirely fair to Junius. In one letter Junius went out of his way to deplore undue reliance upon precedent,[4] and if his general stance strikes us as conservative it is because he saw himself as defending the constitution from attack by the crown and its collaborators. The greater part of his output was, in fact, devoted to political and constitutional disputation: if the scurrilous passages remain in the mind, this is as much a commen-

[1] A comparison with either Tom Paine or Major John Cartwright would show how much more radical than Junius they were.

[2] Public letter no. XXXV.

[3] *History of English thought in the eighteenth century* (1876), ii. 200–1.

[4] Footnote to public letter no. XVI, printed on p. 88.

tary upon ourselves as upon Junius. Nevertheless, the question of malice, which Stephen raised, is one that is likely to trouble most readers. That Junius was no more than a railer has been strongly denied and we may readily concede a genuine belief in the cause he had adopted.[1] A more detailed discussion of motive cannot be separated from the problem of authorship and is therefore postponed until Appendix eight. But it is impossible not to discern in the letters the pleasure that the author felt in his own invective. John Horne, in his controversy with Junius, made skilful use of an unguarded expression in one of Junius' replies to hint at the author's less creditable motives: 'Mr. Wilkes is to be supported and assisted in all his attempts (no matter how ridiculous or mischievous his projects) *as long as he continues to be a thorn in the King's side*. The *cause of the country*, it seems, in the opinion of *Junius*, is merely to vex the King. . . .'[2] Support for Horne's suspicions may be found in a private letter from Junius to Wilkes, which previous editors have seen fit to suppress.[3] The Princess Dowager, George III's mother, was dying of cancer of the throat. On 6 November 1771 Junius assured Wilkes that she could not live: 'the odious hypocrite is *in profundis*. Now is your time to torment him with some demonstration from the City . . . think of something.'[4]

One of the fullest statements of Junius' political attitude is to be found in his letter on the Supporters of the Bill of Rights.[5] His whole approach to the question of parliamentary reform was cautious. He warned the Supporters against pompous and inflated language calculated to rouse false hopes: 'let us take care what we attempt. We may demolish the venerable Fabric we intend to repair, and where is the Strength and Virtue to erect a better in its stead?' He had no faith in the abolition of rotten or pocket boroughs—'I am startled at the Idea of so extensive an Amputation'—and argued

[1] J. T. Boulton, 'The Letters of Junius', *Durham University Journal*, March 1962. See also, by the same author, *The language of politics in the age of Wilkes and Burke* (1963), chs. 2 and 4.

[2] Public letter no. LIII.

[3] Add. MS. 30881, f. 30. It is printed in full as private letter no. 82 in Appendix two, p. 435.

[4] In Junius' defence it should be remembered that the eighteenth century was not noted for squeamishness. See Pope's couplet 'On Queen Caroline's Death-bed' in *The poems of Alexander Pope*, ed. John Butt (1954), vi. 390.

[5] Private letter no. 67, printed below, p. 404.

that Parliament had no right to deprive a borough of its representation. Those great industrial towns, like Birmingham and Manchester, which were without representation, should count their blessings: 'You will find the Interruption of Business in those Towns, by the triennial Riots and Cabals of an Election, too dear a price for the nugatory privilege of sending Members to Parliament.' The most he was prepared to envisage was the addition of members to the counties—a proposal recently advocated by Chatham—and the shortening of the term of Parliament from septennial to triennial.[1]

To reach any estimate of Junius' literary quality is difficult. Taste changes and experts disagree. The purity and directness of his style was greatly admired at the time and much imitated.[2] At its best he achieved a kind of savage urbanity, producing an acute inner tension: there is the same contrast between the surface blandness and the fierce passions beneath that we find in some of the writings of Pope and Johnson. He employed irony with great skill. His second letter to Sir William Draper, who had undertaken the defence of Lord Granby with more zeal than adroitness, began: 'I should justly be suspected of acting upon motives of more than common enmity to Lord Granby, if I continued to give you fresh materials or occasion for writing in his defence.'

Yet much of the effect depended upon the situation: 'It is not hard', wrote Johnson, 'to be sarcastic in a mask.'[3] Junius' anonymity allowed him to affect a pose of easy aloofness. 'I cannot descend to an altercation with you in the newspapers', he told John Horne; and although his adversary pointed out how absurd the remark was, coming from Junius, some impression of majesty remained.[4]

[1] A substantial addition to the number of county seats, without any corresponding increase in urban representation, would have strengthened the already dominant landed interest. It was the most conservative proposal imaginable, save perhaps for economical reform.

[2] Coleridge entered his opinion in a copy from the 1797 edition, printed by J. Mundell & Co., preserved in the British Library. The absence of profound thought he considered an advantage: 'The great art of Junius is never to say too much . . . It is impossible to detract from the merit of these letters: they are suited to their purpose, and perfect in their kind. They impel to action, not thought . . .'

[3] *Thoughts on the late transactions respecting Falkland's Islands*, *The Works of Samuel Johnson*, 1825 ed., vi. 205.

[4] Public letter no. LII.

A further complication is that the letters of Junius are variable in quality. It has often been observed that they grow tedious towards the end, when even Junius had exhausted his resources of invective and was forced back upon routine political themes. But, in fact, Junius was at all times an uneven writer, trembling on the brink of disaster. His Dedication to the English Nation concluded with a theatrical flourish which reeks of 'fine writing' and is merely embarrassing. Reminding his readers that they will shortly have a chance to overthrow the accursed system at a general election,[1] he finished:

> If, when the opportunity presents itself, you neglect to do your duty to yourselves and to posterity—to God and to your country—I shall have one consolation left, in common with the meanest and basest of mankind—Civil liberty may still last the life of
>
> JUNIUS

No doubt there are examples of people cutting their throats because their party has lost a general election, but they do not spring readily to mind.

A contemporary discussion of the merits of Junius is recorded in the diary of Sylas Neville, a young radical. Giuseppe Baretti, of whose Tory principles Neville disapproved, complained that Junius' style was abominably laboured: 'he wrote with no ease . . . walked about his chamber and chewed every sentence'. Junius himself admitted on several occasions that he took great pains with composition. There are examples in the letter which Neville was discussing that suggest the kind of thing Baretti may have had in mind. Junius had returned to one of his favourite themes, the character of the Duke of Grafton, who in the summer of 1771 rejoined the ministry as Lord Privy Seal: 'With a rate of abilities which Lord Weymouth very justly looks down upon with contempt, you have done as much mischief to the community as *Cromwell* would have done, if *Cromwell* had been a coward, and as much as *Machiavel*, if *Machiavel* had not known, that an appearance

[1] The people did not, in practice, have any such opportunity. Had 'the system' been a reality rather than a figment of Junius' imagination, the limitations of the representation in the 1770s were too severe to enable public opinion to express itself.

of morals and religion are useful in society.'[1] Here the style is contorted, the grammar faulty, the examples forced and the thought-process muddled.[2]

It is important, too, not to exaggerate Junius' skill as a polemicist, formidable though that was. He excelled at the exposition of political and legal questions: in public letter no. XVI the complicated issues arising from the Middlesex election are analysed with remarkable lucidity and control. But he was quite capable of making false moves in controversy and was evidently embarrassed when his demand for a single instance of the Duke of Bedford's generosity produced several examples. Modestus was convinced that he had got the better of Junius over the Gansell affair and Junius certainly dropped the subject quickly: nor did the exchanges with John Horne in the summer of 1771 end, in my view, to Junius' advantage. The very rare quality he did possess, however, was the ability to kindle excitement. A letter from Junius was felt to be a matter of public importance and each one provoked a flurry of comment and contention: Junius became the standard by which other writers measured themselves and the great adversary whom the fledgelings tried to pull down.

The parts of his letters that have worn best are perhaps those where Junius' touch is lighter—at times almost sportive or playful. As Philo Junius he commented on the scene in the House of Commons when Sir William Blackstone, the celebrated jurisprudent, was refuted on the Middlesex election by George Grenville, who quoted out of his own *Commentaries*:[3]

[1] *Diary of Sylas Neville*, 124; public letter no. LVII.

[2] The remark about Weymouth is a good example of Junius' technique for killing two birds with one stone. But the rest seems to me very contrived. The intention was to blacken Grafton by association with familiar historical villains. But to accuse Grafton of cowardice by means of Cromwell is an absurdity and invites the retort that had Cromwell been a coward he would probably have never been in a position to do either harm or good. 'Appearance' being singular should not have been followed by a plural verb.

[3] Blackstone's *Commentaries on the laws of England* were published from 1765 onwards. On 8 May 1769 he argued in the House that expulsion from Parliament necessarily implied disqualification from re-election. George Grenville pointed out that this cause was not among the nine quoted in the *Commentaries*. Blackstone subsequently amended the passage to take note of the objection, thus leading to the Opposition's toast to 'The *first* edition of Dr. Blackstone's *Commentaries*'. Blackstone is an example of the eminent lawyer uneasy in the House of Commons. Philo Junius description, quoted above, is in public letter no. XIX

The truth of the matter is evidently this. Doctor Blackstone, while he was speaking in the house of commons, never once thought of his Commentaries, until the contradiction was unexpectedly urged, and stared him in the face. Instead of defending himself upon the spot, he sunk under the charge, in an agony of confusion and despair. It is well known that there was a pause of some minutes in the house, from a general expectation that the Doctor would say something in his own defence; but it seems, his faculties were too much overpowered to think of those subtleties and refinements, which have since occurred to him.

Junius' treatment of the choice of the Duke of Grafton to head the non-party ministry in 1766 is an equally good example of the effective use of sarcasm: 'A submissive administration was at last gradually collected from the deserters of all parties, interests and connexions; and nothing remained but to find a leader for these gallant well-disciplined troops. Stand forth, my Lord, for thou art the man.'[1]

A final example of Junius at his most deadly may be found in the private letter to Wilkes on 7 September 1771. His target was the self-importance of the Society of Supporters of the Bill of Rights, which had addressed an appeal to the nation in what Junius considered were bombastic and extravagant terms:

By assuming this false Pomp and Air of Consequence, you either give general Disgust, or, what is infinitely more dangerous, you expose yourselves to be laughed at. The English are a fastidious people, and will not submit to be talked to, in so high a Tone, by a set of private Gentlemen, of whom they know nothing, but that they call themselves *Supporters of the Bill of Rights*.

Here the key word is 'fastidious', chosen with spiteful care.

* * *

The text of the public letters in this edition is based on the collected volumes issued by Woodfall in 1772 and prepared for the press by Junius himself. It seemed better to use these than the text as originally printed in the *Public Advertiser* since the author added

[1] Public letter no. XV.

many important explanatory footnotes, expanded obscure references, and corrected certain misprints and faults of style. Junius was punctilious over his collected edition: 'I weigh every word', he warned the printer, 'and every Alteration, in my Eyes at least, is a blemish.'[1] In Appendix six some indication is given of how the collected edition differed from the letters as they first appeared.

Certain alterations to the 1772 text have, however, been made. It seemed reasonable to accept the small proof corrections which Junius himself noted in private letter no. 60 and to make a few others which escaped his attention.[2] The letter of 22 May 1771 by Philo Junius (an acknowledged signature of Junius himself) was printed twice in the 1772 edition—first as a footnote to public letter no. XX and again as public letter no. XLVI. It seemed unnecessary to follow Junius in this respect and I have printed the letter in its chronological position, drawing the reader's attention to its relevance to public letter no. XX by means of a note. But in those cases in which Junius changed the chronological sequence of the letters, I have followed his order, merely noting the fact.

There are other public letters, certainly by Junius, which are excluded from the main text and printed in Appendix four. His first letter under that signature, dated 21 November 1768, was not included in the collected edition.[3] Although there is no reason to believe that it is spurious, it is hard to see how an editor could go against the deliberate and considered opinion of the author to omit it. Junius also disavowed the ribald letter in reply to Junia, dated 7 September 1769, and it was not included in the collected edition—probably because its tone was so much at variance with the air of dignity he strove to achieve.[4]

[1] Private letter no. 47, printed below, p. 382.

[2] For example, public letter no. XXIII, line forty-two, 'righest peer' should clearly be 'richest peer'.

[3] See p. xiv, n. 2.

[4] It is printed in Appendix four on p. 457. The note asking the printer to disavow it, *subsequent* to publication, was private letter no. 8. It began: 'The last letter you printed was idle and improper and I assure you printed against my own opinion. The Truth is, there are people about me, whom I would wish not to contradict, and who had rather see Junius in the papers ever so improperly, than not at all.' This is a curious remark. At its face value it means that Junius had accomplices and it is difficult to reconcile with the proud boast in the Dedication that 'I am the sole depositary of my own secret, and it shall perish with me.' The tone of the reply to

Also considered in Appendix four is a rather motley group of letters, tracts, and poems attributed to Junius but not included in the 1772 edition. Most of these are clearly spurious. Junius' success was so great that writers were tempted to borrow his name in order to draw attention to their work or to sell a few extra copies. Henry Sampson Woodfall's knowledge of Junius' handwriting enabled him to detect several false Junius letters and occasionally he protested against these attempts to 'impose upon the public'.[1] Other printers were less suspicious or less scrupulous. Junius did not usually bother to have them denied. 'The *London Packet*', he wrote in relation to one such letter of 13 December 1771, 'is not worth our Notice.'[2]

The private correspondence between Junius and the printer, included as Appendix one, was first published in the 1812 edition of the letters, edited by Mason Good. The manuscripts were then in the hands of the Woodfall family and have since been deposited in the British Library. They have been much used in efforts to establish authorship, since Junius was more likely to be unguarded in private letters than in those intended for publication. As evidence, they suffer from the great defect that only two of the sixty-three notes were dated by the author.[3] Mason Good affixed dates to these letters, largely by relating them to signals in the *Public Advertiser*, but with a degree of confidence that was quite unjustified, and without any warning to the reader that many of the attributions were highly conjectural. I have attempted to re-date them from internal evidence and have explained my reasoning in each case so that the interested reader can at least quarrel with my argumentation.

Junia suggests a jolly drinking party one evening and Junius' somewhat prim disavowal suggests the morning after. But if the friend or friends had died before Junius wrote the Dedication, the difficulty is removed. The point is of some consequence in relation to the new evidence on authorship printed by Dame Lucy Sutherland and others in *Bulletin of the Institute of Historical Research*, xlii (1969). The evidence is discussed in Appendix eight, p. 560 below.

[1] *Public Advertiser*, 10 and 23 April 1769.

[2] Private letter no. 48, printed below, p. 383.

[3] Private letter no. 49 was dated 6 January 1772. Private letter no. 45 was dated by Junius 27 November 1770, but was obviously written in 1771. Other letters are partly dated.

The private letters that passed between Junius and John Wilkes, which are of particular importance in assessing Junius' political stance, are also preserved in the British Library. I have printed them as Appendix two, including sections printed before only in part, and one letter completely suppressed by previous editors.[1] This exchange includes the full version of Junius' long letter of 7 September 1771, a part of which he rather incongruously tacked on to the end of the collected edition.

Appendix three contains five letters addressed to George Grenville and to Lord Chatham. Of these, one is unquestionably by Junius.[2] The provenance of the others is of interest since in some of them the writer lays claim to letters published under different pseudonyms.

One of the most tangled editorial problems concerns the public letters which appeared under other names but which have been attributed, on various grounds, to the author of the letters of Junius. Some of these may, without doubt, be accepted. In January 1772 Junius wrote to the printer that he proposed, under another name, to torture 'that bloody wretch', Lord Barrington:[3] letters from Veteran to Barrington duly appeared and may be presumed to be Junius fulfilling his promise. Vindex of 22 February 1771 is also confirmed as a Junius composition by the author's note to the printer.[4] Where it appears extremely likely that the author was indeed Junius, I have given the text in full.[5] But there are many letters under other pseudonyms which have been attributed to Junius on less convincing evidence. I have discussed their authenticity but have not felt under an obligation to print them in full, since they are easily available to scholars in other editions. I am sure this has meant excluding from this edition some letters that were, in fact, written by Junius, but since false attributions have in the past led to a great waste of time and ingenuity, it seemed wiser to err on the side of austerity. The reader is therefore left to con-

[1] Private letter no. 82 of 6 November 1771, referred to previously on p. xxv.

[2] Private letter no. 89 to Chatham, 14 January 1772.

[3] Private letter no. 53.

[4] Private letter no. 34. The text of the letter, in Junius' handwriting, is extant in Add. MS. 27777, f. 13.

[5] In Appendix five.

struct his own case for the validity of any other miscellaneous letters which he wishes to use for polemical purposes.

I have already referred to the signals printed by Woodfall in the *Public Advertiser* as a means of alerting Junius that there were letters or parcels to be collected from the pre-arranged rendezvous. Since these signals are of importance in attempting to date the private letters, I have listed all that I have discovered in Appendix seven. It should be remembered, however, that they are evidence merely that the printer had something to communicate on that date.

Appendix eight attempts to guide the reader through the maze of controversy over the authorship of the letters. I have tried to summarize the evidence as dispassionately as possible, though I do not doubt that my conclusions will appear to some readers woefully wrong-headed.

Junius provided his own footnotes for the 1772 edition. To avoid cluttering the pages of this edition with batteries of footnotes, I have kept mine to the minimum. Biographical references to all persons mentioned in the text are therefore reserved for a special note at the end of the volume. My own footnotes to the letters can then be limited to textual and interpretive points and are printed below the rule: everything above the rule is by Junius.[1] It may be convenient to the reader to observe that Junius used asterisks etc. to mark his footnotes: editorial notes are numbered.[2]

Since the original spelling and punctuation of public and private letters may have some bearing on the question of authorship, no attempt has been made to modernize them, save for the substitution of a modern form for the letter 's' and the elimination of running apostrophes to mark quotations in the text. In the public letters, however, the usage may have as much to do with the compositor as with the author.

[1] I am sure that many readers prefer to have biographical data at the foot of the page and, all things being equal, I share their sentiments. But since the main text was already footnoted by Junius and needed further editorial footnoting, there was an evident risk of producing a crowded and unattractive page. It therefore seemed wiser, on balance, to remove that information which could be placed elsewhere.

[2] Junius frequently placed his asterisks before the sentence to which the note referred.

THE LETTERS OF JUNIUS

THE PUBLIC LETTERS

Junius composed the Dedication and Preface to his collected edition during October 1771, sending them to John Wilkes for comment on 1 November. The theme of the Dedication is that the price of liberty is eternal vigilance. One would have thought that the pointed Dedication to the *English* Nation, coupled with gratuitous attacks upon the Scots in the Preface as time-serving hypocrites, would have been enough to discourage the suggestion that Junius was himself a Scot. It was argued by Lord Campbell, *Lives of the Lord Chancellors* (1846–7), vi. 344, that Junius blundered in his use of the term 'fee-simple', showing that he was not a lawyer.

The Preface is a somewhat strained and laboured composition, in which Junius included those items his readers would expect, such as a fresh attack upon the King. The function of the jury in libel actions, which Junius argued with some skill, was settled by Fox's Libel Act of 1792, 32 George III, c. 60, which declared that 'on every such trial, the jury . . . may give a general verdict of guilty or not guilty upon the whole matter put in issue . . . and shall not be required or directed by the Court or Judge . . . to find the defendant or defendants guilty merely upon the proof of the publication'. This was an important extension of the role of public opinion.

DEDICATION

TO THE

English Nation.

I DEDICATE to You a collection of Letters, written by one of Yourselves for the common benefit of us all. They would never have grown to this size, without your continued encouragement and applause. To me they originally owe nothing, but a healthy, sanguine constitution. Under *Your* care they have thriven. To *You* they are indebted for whatever strength or beauty they possess. When Kings and Ministers are forgotten, when the force and direction of personal satyr is no longer understood, and when measures are only felt in their remotest consequences, this book will, I believe, be found to contain principles, worthy to be transmitted to posterity. When you leave the unimpaired, hereditary freehold to Your children, You do but half Your duty. Both liberty and property are precarious, unless the possessors have sense and spirit enough to defend them.—This is not the language of vanity. If I am a vain man, my gratification lies within a narrow circle. I am the sole depositary of my own secret, and it shall perish with me.

IF an honest, and, I may truly affirm, a laborious zeal for the public service has given me any weight in Your esteem, let me exhort and conjure You never to suffer an invasion of Your political constitution, however minute the instance may appear, to pass by, without a determined, persevering resistance. One precedent creates another.—They soon accumulate, and constitute law. What yesterday was fact, to-day is doctrine. Examples are supposed to justify the most dangerous measures, and where they do not suit exactly, the defect is supplied by analogy.—Be assured that the laws, which protect us in our civil rights, grow out of the constitution, and that they must fall or flourish with it. This is not the cause of faction, or of party, or of any individual, but the common interest of every man in Britain. Although the King should continue to support his present system of government, the period is not very distant, at which You will have the means of redress in your own power. It may be nearer perhaps than any of us expect, and I would warn You to be prepared for it. The King may possibly be advised to dissolve the present parliament a year or two before it expires of course, and precipitate a new election, in hopes of taking the nation by surprize. If such a measure be in agitation, this very caution may defeat or prevent it.[1]

I CANNOT doubt that You will unanimously assert the freedom of election, and vindicate your exclusive right to choose your representatives. But other questions have been started, on which your determination should be equally clear and unanimous. Let it be

[1] This was rather a good guess by Junius. The Parliament was dissolved prematurely with more than six months to run. Despite Junius' warning, the opposition was not prepared: 'This manœuvre of the ministry has taken me very much unaware,' wrote Rockingham to Portland on 1 October 1774. *The House of Commons, 1754–90*, i. 73–4.

impressed upon your minds, let it be instilled into your children, that the liberty of the press is the *Palladium* of all the civil, political, and religious rights of an Englishman, and that the right of juries to return a general verdict, in all cases whatsoever, is an essential part of our constitution, not to be controuled or limited by the judges, nor in any shape questionable by the legislature. The power of King, Lords, and Commons is not an arbitrary power*. They are the trustees, not the owners of the estate. The fee-simple is in US. They cannot alienate, they cannot waste. When we say that the legislature is *supreme*, we mean that it is the highest power known to the constitution;—that it is the highest in comparison with the other subordinate powers established by the laws. In this sense, the word *supreme* is relative, not absolute. The power of the legislature is limited, not only by the general rules of natural justice, and the welfare of the community, but by the forms and principles of our particular constitution. If this doctrine be not true, we must admit, that King, Lords, and Commons have no rule to direct their resolutions, but merely their own will and pleasure. They might unite the legislative and executive power in the same hands, and dissolve the constitution by an act of parliament. But I am persuaded You will not leave it to the choice of seven hundred persons, notoriously corrupted by the crown, whether seven millions of their equals shall be freemen or slaves. The certainty of forfeiting their own rights, when they sacrifice those of the nation,

* This positive denial, of an arbitrary power being vested in the legislature, is not in fact a new doctrine. When the Earl of Lindsey, in the year 1675, brought a bill into the house of lords, *To prevent the dangers, which might arise from persons disaffected to government*, by which an oath and penalty was to be imposed upon the members of both houses, it was affirmed, in a protest signed by twenty three lay-peers, (my lords the bishops were not accustomed to protest) "That the privilege of sitting and voting in parliament was an honour they had by birth, and a right so inherent in them, and inseparable from them, *that nothing could take it away*, but what, by the law of the land, must withal take away their lives, and corrupt their blood."—These noble peers, (whose names are a reproach to their posterity) have, in this instance, solemnly denied the power of parliament to alter the constitution. Under a particular proposition, they have asserted a general truth, in which every man in England is concerned.[1]

[1] The bill referred to demanded an oath of non-resistance from all members of Parliament and office-holders. It was abandoned after a dispute between the two Houses of Parliament. For the protest, see J. E. Thorold Rogers, *A complete collection of the protests of the Lords* (1875), i, no. xxxix.

is no check to a brutal, degenerate mind. Without insisting upon the extravagant concession made to Harry the eighth, there are instances, in the history of other countries, of a formal, deliberate surrender of the public liberty into the hands of the sovereign.[1] If England does not share the same fate, it is because we have better resources, than in the virtue of either house of parliament.

I SAID that the liberty of the press is the *palladium* of all your rights, and that the right of the juries to return a general verdict is part of your constitution. To preserve the whole system, You must correct your legislature. With regard to any influence of the constituent over the conduct of the representative, there is little difference between a seat in parliament for seven years and a seat for life. The prospect of your resentment is too remote; and although the last session of a septennial parliament be usually employed in courting the favour of the people, consider that, at this rate, your representatives have six years for offence, and but one for atonement. A death-bed repentance seldom reaches to restitution. If you reflect that in the changes of administration, which have marked and disgraced the present reign, although your warmest patriots have in their turn been invested with the lawful and unlawful authority of the crown, and though other reliefs or improvements have been held forth to the people, yet that no one man in office has ever promoted or encouraged a bill for shortening the duration of parliaments, but that, (whoever was minister) the opposition to this measure, ever since the septennial act passed, has been constant and uniform on the part of government,—You cannot but conclude, without the possibility of a doubt, that long parliaments are the foundation of the undue influence of the crown. This influence answers every purpose of arbitrary power to the crown, with an expence and oppression to the people, which would be unnecessary in an arbitrary government. The best of our ministers find it the easiest and most compendious mode of conducting the King's affairs; and all ministers have a general interest

[1] If Junius had anything specific in mind, it may have been the legislation permitting Henry VIII to regulate the succession. This is discussed in G. R. Elton, *The Tudor Constitution: documents and commentary* (1960), 2–3. One of the more notable examples in other countries was the promulgation of the Danish *kongelov* in 1665.

in adhering to a system, which of itself is sufficient to support them in office, without any assistance from personal virtue, popularity, labour, abilities, or experience. It promises every gratification to avarice and ambition, and secures impunity.——These are truths unquestionable.—If they make no impression, it is because they are too vulgar and notorious. But the inattention or indifference of the nation has continued too long. You are roused at last to a sense of your danger.—The remedy will soon be in your power. If *Junius* lives, You shall often be reminded of it. If, when the opportunity presents itself, You neglect to do your duty to yourselves and to posterity,—to God and to your country, I shall have one consolation left, in common with the meanest and basest of mankind.—Civil liberty may still last the life of

JUNIUS.

PREFACE.

THE encouragement, given to a multitude of spurious, mangled publications of the letters of *Junius*, persuades me, that a compleat edition, corrected and improved by the author, will be favourably received. The printer will readily acquit me of any view to my own profit. I undertake this troublesome task, merely to serve a man who has deserved well of me, and of the public; and who, on my account, has been exposed to an expensive, tyrannical prosecution. For these reasons, I give to *Mr. Henry Sampson Woodfall*, and to him alone, my right, interest, and property in these letters, as fully and compleatly, to all intents and purposes, as an author can possibly convey his property in his own works to another.

THIS edition contains all the letters of *Junius*, *Philo Junius*, and of *Sir William Draper* and *Mr. Horne* to *Junius*, with their respective dates, and according to the order in which they appeared in the Public Advertiser. The auxiliary part of *Philo Junius* was indispensably necessary to defend or explain particular passages in *Junius*, in answer to plausible objections; but the subordinate character is never guilty of the indecorum of praising his principal. The fraud was innocent, and I always intended to explain it. The notes will be found not only useful, but necessary. References to facts not generally known, or allusions to the current report or opinion of the day, are in a little time unintelligible. Yet the reader will not find himself overloaded with explanations. I was not born to be a commentator, even upon my own works.

IT remains to say a few words upon the liberty of the press. The daring spirit, by which these letters are supposed to be distinguished, seems to require that something serious should be said in their defence. I am no lawyer by profession, nor do I pretend to be more deeply read, than every English gentleman should be in the laws of his country. If therefore the principles I maintain are truly constitutional, I shall not think myself answered, though I should be convicted of a mistake in terms, or of misapplying the language of the law. I speak to the plain understanding of the people, and appeal to their honest, liberal construction of me.

GOOD men, to whom alone I address myself, appear to me to consult their piety as little as their judgment and experience, when they admit the great and essential advantages accruing to society from the freedom of the press, yet indulge themselves in peevish or passionate exclamations against the abuses of it. Betraying an unreasonable expectation of benefits, pure and intire, from any human institution, they in effect arraign the goodness of providence, and confess that they are dissatisfied with the common lot of humanity. In the present instance they really create to their own minds, or greatly exaggerate the evil they complain of. The laws of England provide, as effectually as any human laws can do, for the protection of the subject, in his reputation, as well as in his person and property. If the characters of private men are insulted or injured, a double remedy is open to them, by *action* and *indictment*. If, through indolence, false shame, or indifference, they will not appeal to the laws of their country, they fail in their duty to society, and are unjust to themselves. If, from an unwarrantable distrust of the integrity of juries, they would wish to obtain justice by any mode of proceeding, more summary than a trial by their peers, I do not scruple to affirm, that they are in effect greater enemies to themselves, than to the libeller they prosecute.

WITH regard to strictures upon the characters of men in office and the measures of government, the case is a little different. A considerable latitude must be allowed in the discussion of public affairs, or the liberty of the press will be of no benefit to society. As the indulgence of private malice and personal slander should be checked and resisted by every legal means, so a constant examination into the characters and conduct of ministers and magistrates should be equally promoted and encouraged. They, who conceive that our news papers are no restraint upon bad men, or impediment to the execution of bad measures, know nothing of this country. In that state of abandoned servility and prostitution, to which the undue influence of the crown has reduced the other branches of the legislature, our ministers and magistrates have in reality little punishment to fear, and few difficulties to contend with, beyond the censure of the press, and the spirit of resistance, which it excites among the people. While this censorial power is maintained, to speak in the words of a most ingenious foreigner, both minister and magistrate is compelled, in almost every instance, *to choose between his duty and his reputation.*[1] A dilemma of this kind, perpetually before him, will not indeed work a miracle upon his heart, but it will assuredly operate, in some degree, upon his conduct. At all events, these are not times to admit of any relaxation in the little discipline we have left.

BUT it is alledged, that the licentiousness of the press is carried beyond all bounds of decency and truth;—that our excellent ministers are continually exposed to the public hatred or derision;—that, in prosecutions for libels on government, juries are partial to the popular side; and that, in the most flagrant cases, a verdict cannot be obtained for the King.—If the premises were admitted, I should deny the conclusion. It is not true, that the temper of the times has in general an undue influence over the conduct of juries. On the contrary, many signal instances may be produced of verdicts returned for the King, when the inclinations of the people led strongly to an undistinguishing opposition to government. Witness the cases of *Mr. Wilkes* and *Mr. Almon.*[2] In the late prosecutions of the printers of my address to a great personage, the juries were never fairly dealt with.—*Lord Chief Justice Mansfield*, conscious that

[1] The 'most ingenious foreigner' was Jean Louis de Lolme, whose treatise *Constitution de l'Angleterre* was published in Amsterdam in 1771. The English translation did not appear until 1775. The reference is to a passage in Book II, Chapter xii: *The subject continued—liberty of the press* (1775 edn., pp. 288–9). De Lolme discussed the salutary effects of the vigilance of the press and continued: 'The Juryman knows that his verdict, the Judge that his direction to the Jury, will presently be given out to the Public: and there is no Man in office, but who finds himself compelled, in almost every instance, to choose between his duty, and a surrender of all his former reputation.' See p. 24 n. 1.

[2] John Wilkes had been found guilty before Lord Mansfield in February 1764 of seditious and obscene libel; John Almon, the bookseller, was convicted of libel in June 1770 before the same judge in permitting a copy of the *London Museum*, containing Junius' letter to the King, to be sold in his shop. *State Trials*, xix. 1075–1138; xx. 807–67.

the paper in question contained no treasonable or libellous matter, and that the severest parts of it, however painful to the King or offensive to his servants, were strictly true, would fain have restricted the jury to the finding of special facts, which, as to *guilty* or *not guilty*, were merely indifferent. This particular motive, combined with his general purpose to contract the power of juries, will account for the charge he delivered in *Woodfall*'s trial. He told the jury, in so many words, that they had nothing to determine, except the fact of *printing and publishing*, and whether or no the *blanks*, or *inuendoes* were properly filled up in the information;—but that, whether the defendant had committed a *crime*, or not, was no matter of consideration to twelve men, who yet, upon their oaths, were to pronounce their peer *guilty*, or *not guilty*. When we hear such nonsense delivered from the bench, and find it supported by a laboured train of sophistry, which a plain understanding is unable to follow, and which an unlearned jury, however it may shock their reason, cannot be supposed qualified to refute, can it be wondered that they should return a verdict, perplexed, absurd, or imperfect?—*Lord Mansfield* has not yet explained to the world, why he accepted of a verdict, which the court afterwards set aside as illegal, and which, as it took no notice of the *inuendoes*, did not even correspond with his own charge. If he had known his duty he should have sent the jury back.—I speak advisedly, and am well assured that no lawyer, of character in Westminster-hall, will contradict me. To shew the falsehood of *Lord Mansfield*'s doctrine, it is not necessary to enter into the merits of the paper, which produced the trial. If every line of it were treason, his charge to the jury would still be false, absurd, illegal, and unconstitutional. If I stated the merits of my letter to *the King*, *I should imitate* LORD MANSFIELD, *and** TRAVEL OUT OF THE RECORD. *When*

* The following quotation from a speech delivered by *Lord Chatham* on the eleventh of December, 1770, is taken with exactness. The reader will find it curious in itself, and very fit to be inserted here. "My Lords, The verdict, given in Woodfall's trial, was *guilty of printing and publishing* ONLY; upon which two motions were made in court;—one, in arrest of judgement, by the defendant's council, grounded upon the ambiguity of the verdict;—the other, by the council for the crown, for a rule upon the defendant, to shew cause, why the verdict should not be entered up according to the *legal* import of the words. On both motions, a rule was granted, and soon after the matter was argued before the court of King's Bench. The noble

law and reason speak plainly, we do not want *authority* to direct our understandings. Yet, for the honour of the profession, I am content to oppose one lawyer to another, especially when it happens that the King's Attorney General[1] has virtually disclaimed the doctrine, by which the Chief Justice meant to insure success to the prosecution. The opinion of the plaintiff's council, (however it may be otherwise insignificant) is weighty in the scale of the defendant.—*My Lord Chief Justice De Grey*, who filed the information *ex officio*, is directly with me. If he had concurred in *Lord Mansfield's* doctrine, the trial must have been a very short one. The facts were either admitted by *Woodfall's* council, or easily proved to the satisfaction of the jury. But *Mr. De Grey*, far from thinking he should acquit himself of his duty by barely proving the facts, entered largely, and I confess not without ability, into the demerits of the paper, which he called a *seditious libel*. He dwelt but lightly upon those points, which, (according to Lord Mansfield) were the only matter of consideration to the jury. The criminal intent, the libellous matter, the pernicious tendency of the paper itself, were the topics, on which he principally insisted, and of which, for more

judge, when he delivered the opinion of the court upon the verdict, went regularly through the whole of the proceedings at *Nisi Prius*, as well the evidence that had been given, as his own charge to the jury. This proceeding would have been very proper, had a motion been made of either side for a new trial, because either a verdict given contrary to evidence, or an improper charge by the judge at *Nisi Prius*, is held to be a sufficient ground for granting a new trial. But when a motion is made in arrest of judgement, or for establishing the verdict, by entering it up according to the legal import of the words, it must be on the ground of something appearing *on the face of the record*; and the court, in considering whether the verdict shall be established or not, are so confined to the *record*, that they cannot take notice of any thing that does not appear on the face of it; in the legal phrase, *they cannot travel out of the record*. The noble judge did travel out of the record, and I affirm that his discourse was *irregular*, *extrajudicial*, and *unprecedented*. His apparent motive, for doing what he knew to be wrong, was, that he might have an opportunity of telling the public *extrajudicially*, that the other three judges concurred in the doctrine laid down in his charge."[2]

---

[1] William de Grey was Attorney-General until January 1771 when he became Lord Chief Justice of the Common Pleas. He was succeeded as Attorney-General by Edward Thurlow.

[2] Junius' note is of importance in the controversy over authorship. Lord Chatham's speech was, in fact, delivered on 10 December 1770 and not the 11th; Junius' version is taken, with only slight alterations, from the report given by Phalaris in the *Public Advertiser* of 17 December 1770. See Appendix five, section A, and Appendix eight, pp. 476 and 565–6.

than an hour, he tortured his faculties to convince the jury. If he agreed in opinion with *Lord Mansfield*, his discourse was impertinent, ridiculous, and unreasonable. But, understanding the law as I do, what he said was at least consistent and to the purpose.

IF any honest man should still be inclined to leave the construction of libels to the court, I would intreat him to consider what a dreadful complication of hardships he imposes upon his fellow-subject.—In the first place, the prosecution commences by *information* of an officer of the crown, not by the regular constitutional mode of *indictment* before a grand jury.—As the fact is usually admitted, or in general can easily be proved, the office of the petty jury is nugatory.—The *court* then judges of the nature and extent of the offence, and determines *ad arbitrium*, the *quantum* of the punishment, from a small fine to a heavy one, to repeated whipping, to pillory, and unlimited imprisonment. Cutting off ears and noses *might* still be inflicted by a resolute judge; but I will be candid enough to suppose that penalties, so apparently shocking to humanity, would not be hazarded in these times.—In all other criminal prosecutions, the jury decides upon the fact and the crime in one word, and the court pronounces a *certain* sentence, which is the sentence of the law, not of the judge. If *Lord Mansfield*'s doctrine be received, the jury must either find a verdict of acquittal, contrary to evidence, (which, I can conceive, might be done by very conscientious men, rather than trust a fellow creature to *Lord Mansfield*'s mercy) or they must leave to the court two offices, never but in this instance united, of finding guilty, and awarding punishment.

BUT, says this honest *Lord Chief Justice*, "If the paper be not criminal, the defendant, (tho' found guilty by his peers) is in no danger, for he may move the court in arrest of judgement."—True, my good Lord, but who is to determine upon the motion?—Is not the court still to decide, whether judgement shall be entered up or not; and is not the defendant this way as effectually deprived of judgement by his peers, as if he were tried in a court of civil law, or in the chambers of the inquisition? It is you, my Lord, who then try the crime, not the jury. As to the probable effect of the motion in arrest of judgement, I shall only observe, that no reasonable man would be so eager to possess himself of the invidious power of inflicting punishment, if he were not predetermined to make use of it.

AGAIN;—We are told that judge and jury have a distinct office; that the jury is to find the fact, and the judge to deliver the law.—*De jure respondent judices, de facto jurati.* The *dictam* is true, though not in the sense given to it by *Lord Mansfield.* The jury are undoubtedly to determine the fact, that is, whether the defendant did or did not commit the crime charged against him. The judge pronounces the sentence annexed by law to that fact so found; and if, in the course of the trial, any question of law arises, both the council and the jury must, of necessity, appeal to the judge and leave it to his decision. An *exception*, or *plea in bar* may be allowed by the court; but, when issue is joined, and the jury have received their charge, it is not possible, in the nature of things, for them to separate the law from the fact, unless they think proper to return a *special* verdict.

IT has also been alledged that, although a common jury are sufficient to determine a plain matter of fact, they are not qualified to comprehend the meaning, or to judge of the tendency of a seditious libel. In answer to this objection, (which, if well founded, would prove nothing as to the *strict right* of returning a general verdict) I might safely deny the truth of the assertion. *Englishmen* of that rank, from which juries are usually taken, are not so illiterate as, (to serve a particular purpose) they are now represented. Or, admitting the fact, let a special jury be summoned in all cases of difficulty and importance, and the objection is removed. But the truth is, that if a paper, supposed to be a libel upon government, be so obscurely worded, that twelve common men cannot possibly see the seditious meaning and tendency of it, it is in effect no libel. It cannot inflame the minds of the people, nor alienate their affections from government; for they no more understand what it means, than if it were published in a language unknown to them.

UPON the whole matter, it appears, to *my* understanding, clear beyond a doubt, that if, in any future prosecution for a seditious libel, the jury should bring in a verdict of acquittal not warranted by the evidence, it will be owing to the false and absurd doctrines laid down by *Lord Mansfield*. Disgusted at the odious artifices made use of by the Judge to mislead and perplex them, guarded against his sophistry, and convinced of the falsehood of his assertions, they may perhaps determine to thwart his detestable purpose, and defeat him at any rate. To *him* at least they will do *substantial justice*.—Whereas, if the whole charge, laid in the information, be fairly and honestly submitted to the jury, there is no reason whatsoever to presume that twelve men, upon their oaths, will not decide impartially between the King and the defendant. The numerous instances, in our state-trials, of verdicts recovered for the King, sufficiently refute the false and scandalous imputations thrown by the abettors of *Lord Mansfield* upon the integrity of juries.—But even admitting the supposition that, in times of universal discontent arising from the notorious maladministration of public affairs, a seditious writer should escape punishment, it makes nothing against my general argument. If juries are fallible, to what other tribunal shall we appeal?—If juries cannot safely be trusted, shall we unite the offices of judge and jury, so wisely divided by the constitution, and trust implicitly to *Lord Mansfield*?—Are the judges of the court of King's Bench more likely to be unbiassed and impartial, than twelve yeomen, burgesses, or gentlemen taken indifferently from the county at large?—Or, in short, shall there be *no* decision, until we have instituted a tribunal, from which no possible abuse or inconvenience whatsoever can arise?—If I am not grossly mistaken, these questions carry a decisive answer along with them.

HAVING cleared the freedom of the press from a restraint, equally unnecessary and illegal, I return to the use, which has been made of it in the present publication.

NATIONAL reflections, I confess, are not justified in theory, nor upon any general principles. To know how well they are deserved, and how justly they have been applied, we must have the evidence of facts before us. We must be conversant with the *Scots* in private life, and observe their principles of acting to *us*, and to each other;—the characteristic prudence, the selfish nationality, the indefatigable smile, the persevering assiduity, the everlasting profession of a discreet and moderate resentment.—If the instance were not too important for an experiment, it might not be amiss to confide a little in their integrity.—Without any abstract reasoning upon causes and effects, we shall soon be convinced by *experience*, that the *Scots*, transplanted from their own country, are always a distinct and separate body from the people who receive them. In other settlements, they only love themselves;—in *England*, they cordially love themselves, and as cordially hate their neighbours. For the remainder of their good qualities, I must appeal to the reader's observation, unless he will accept of *my Lord Barrington*'s authority. In a letter to the late *Lord Melcombe*, published by *Mr. Lee*, he expresses himself with a truth and accuracy not very common in his lordship's lucubrations.—"And Cockburne, *like most of his countrymen*, is as abject to those above him, as he is insolent to those below him."[1]—I am far from meaning to impeach the articles of the union. If the true spirit of those articles were religiously adhered to, we should not see such a multitude of Scotch commoners in the lower house, as representatives of English boroughs, while not a single Scotch borough is ever represented by an Englishman. We should not see English peerages given to Scotch ladies, or to the elder sons of Scotch peers, and the number of *sixteen* doubled and trebled by a scandalous evasion of the act of union.—If it should ever be thought advisable to dissolve an act, the violation or observance of which is invariably directed by the advantage and interest of the *Scots*, I shall say very sincerely with Sir Edward Coke. *"When poor England stood alone, and had not the access of another kingdom, and yet had more and as potent enemies as it now hath, yet the King of England prevailed."

SOME opinion may now be expected from me, upon a point of

* Parliamentary History. 7. V. p. 400.[2]

---

[1] I have not succeeded in tracing this letter, which is referred to again in a letter of 4 May 1772 by Scotus, printed in section A of Appendix five.

[2] See p. 329 n. 2.

equal delicacy to the writer, and hazard to the printer.[1] When the character of the chief magistrate is in question, more must be understood, than may safely be expressed. If it be really a part of our constitution, and not a mere *dictum* of the law, *that the King can do no wrong*, it is not the only instance, in the wisest of human institutions, where theory is at variance with practice.—That the sovereign of this country is not amenable to any form of trial, known to the laws, is unquestionable. But exemption from punishment is a singular privilege annexed to the royal character, and no way excludes the possibility of deserving it. How long, and to what extent a King of *England* may be protected by the forms, when he violates the spirit of the constitution, deserves to be considered. A mistake in this matter proved fatal to *Charles* and his son.—For my own part, far from thinking that the King can do no wrong, far from suffering myself to be deterred or imposed upon by the language of forms in opposition to the substantial evidence of truth, if it were my misfortune to live under the inauspicious reign of a prince, whose whole life was employed in one base, contemptible struggle with the free spirit of his people, or in the detestable endeavour to corrupt their moral principles, I would not scruple to declare to him,—"Sir, You alone are the author of the greatest wrong to your subjects and to yourself. Instead of reigning in the hearts of your people, instead of commanding their lives and fortunes thro' the medium of their affections, has not the strength of the crown, whether influence or prerogative, been uniformly exerted, for eleven years together, to support a narrow, pitiful system of government, which defeats itself, and answers no one purpose of real power, profit, or personal satisfaction to You?—With the greatest unappropriated revenue of any prince in Europe, have we not seen You reduced to such vile, and sordid distresses, as would have conducted any other man to a prison?—With a great military, and the greatest naval power in the known world, have not foreign nations repeatedly insulted You with impunity?—Is it not notorious that the vast revenues, extorted from the labour and industry of your subjects, and given You to do honour to

[1] Coleridge recorded his conviction that the paragraph which followed was a 'masterpiece of rhetorical ratiocination'. See p. xxvi n. 2.

Yourself and to the nation, are dissipated in corrupting their representatives?—Are You a prince of the House of Hanover, and do You exclude all the leading Whig families from your councils?—Do you profess to govern according to Law, and is it consistent with that profession, to impart your confidence and affection to those men only, who, though now perhaps detached from the desperate cause of the Pretender, are marked in this country by an hereditary attachment to high and arbitrary principles of government?—Are you so infatuated as to take the sense of your people from the representation of ministers, or from the shouts of a mob, notoriously hired to surround your coach, or stationed at a theatre?—And if You are, in reality, that public Man, that King, that Magistrate, which these questions suppose You to be, is it any answer to your people, to say that, among your domestics You are good-humoured,—that to one lady You are faithful;—that to your children You are indulgent?——Sir, the man, who addresses You in these terms is your best friend. He would willingly hazard his life in defence of your title to the crown; and, if *power* be your object, would still shew You how possible it is for a King of England, by the noblest means, to be the most absolute prince in Europe. You have no enemies, Sir, but those, who persuade You to aim at power without right, and who think it flattery to tell You that the character of King dissolves the natural relation between guilt and punishment."

I CANNOT conceive that there is a heart so callous, or an understanding so depraved, as to attend to a discourse of this nature, and not to feel the force of it. But where is the man, among those who have access to the closet, resolute and honest enough to deliver it. The liberty of the press is our only resource. It will command an audience, when every honest man in the kingdom is excluded. This glorious priviledge may be a security to the King, as well as a resource to his people. Had there been no star-chamber, there would have been no rebellion against Charles the first. The constant censure and admonition of the press would have corrected his conduct, prevented a civil war, and saved him from an ignominious death.—I am no friend to the doctrine of precedents exclusive of right, though lawyers often tell us, that whatever has been once done, may lawfully be done again.

I SHALL conclude this preface with a quotation, applicable to the subject from a foreign writer*, whose essay on the English constitution I beg leave to recommend to the public, as a performance, deep, solid and ingenious.

"IN short, whoever considers what it is, that constitutes the moving principle of what we call great affairs, and the invincible sensibility of man to the opinion of his fellow-creatures, will not hesitate to affirm that, if it were possible for the liberty of the press to exist in a despotic government, and, (what is not less difficult) for it to exist without changing the constitution, this liberty of the press would alone form a counterpoise to the power of the prince. If, for example, in an empire of the East, a sanctuary could be found, which, rendered respectable by the ancient religion of the people, might insure safety to those, who should bring thither their observations of any kind; and that, from thence, printed papers should issue, which, under a certain seal, might be equally respected; and which, in their daily appearance, should examine and freely discuss, the conduct of the Cadis, the Bashaws, the Vizir, the Divan, and the Sultan himself, that would introduce immediately some degree of liberty."

* *Monsieur de Lolme.*[1]

[1] See p. 15 n. 1. This quotation is taken from the end of Book II, Chapter xii. In 1816 Thomas Busby produced a volume entitled *Arguments and Facts*, asserting on the strength of these references and other alleged parallels that de Lolme was the author of the letters of Junius. It is discussed briefly in Appendix eight, p. 546.

LETTERS

OF

JUNIUS, &c.

Junius omitted the letter of 21 November 1768 when compiling the collected edition: it is printed in Appendix four. His decision to begin with the letter of 21 January 1769 was sound. It is one of his best compositions. The general reflections in the introduction serve to create suspense and to invest the writer with an air of judicious authority.

LETTER I.

ADDRESSED TO THE PRINTER OF THE PUBLIC ADVERTISER.

SIR,

21. *January*, 1769.

THE submission of a free people to the executive authority of government is no more than a compliance with laws, which they themselves have enacted. While the national honour is firmly maintained abroad, and while justice is impartially administered at home, the obedience of the subject will be voluntary, chearful, and I might almost say unlimited. A generous nation is grateful even for the preservation of its rights, and willingly extends the respect due to the office of a good prince into an affection for his person. Loyalty, in the heart and understanding of an Englishman, is a rational attachment to the guardian of the laws. Prejudices and passion have sometimes carried it to a criminal length; and, whatever foreigners may imagine, we know that Englishmen have erred as much in a mistaken zeal for particular persons and families, as they ever did in defence of what they thought most dear and interesting to themselves.

IT naturally fills us with resentment, to see such a temper insulted and abused. In reading the history of a free people, whose rights have been invaded, we are interested in their cause. Our own feelings tell us how long they ought to have submitted, and at what moment it would have been treachery to themselves not to have resisted. How much warmer will be our resentment, if experience should bring the fatal example home to ourselves!

THE situation of this country is alarming enough to rouse the attention of every man, who pretends to a concern for the public welfare. Appearances justify suspicion; and, when the safety of a nation is at stake, suspicion is a just ground of enquiry. Let us enter into it with candour and decency. Respect is due to the station of ministers; and, if a resolution must at last be taken, there is none so likely to be supported with firmness, as that which has been adopted with moderation.

THE ruin or prosperity of a state depends so much upon the administration of its government, that, to be acquainted with the merit of a ministry, we need only observe the condition of the people. If we see them obedient to the laws, prosperous in their industry, united at home, and respected abroad, we may reasonably presume that their affairs are conducted by men of experience, abilities and virtue. If, on the contrary, we see an universal spirit of distrust and dissatisfaction, a rapid decay of trade, dissensions in all parts of the empire, and a total loss of respect in the eyes of foreign powers, we may pronounce, without hesitation, that the government of that country is weak, distracted, and corrupt. The multitude, in all countries, are patient to a certain point. Ill-usage may rouse their indignation, and hurry them into excesses, but the original fault is in government. Perhaps there never was an instance of a change, in the circumstances and temper of a whole nation, so sudden and extraordinary as that which the misconduct of ministers has, within these few years, produced in Great Britain. When our gracious sovereign ascended the throne, we were a flourishing and a contented people. If the personal virtues of a king could have insured the happiness of his subjects, the scene could not have altered so entirely as it has done. The idea of uniting all parties, of trying all characters, and distributing the offices of state by rotation, was gracious and benevolent to an extreme, though it has not yet produced the many salutary effects which were intended by it. To say nothing of the wisdom of such a plan, it undoubtedly arose from an unbounded goodness of heart, in which folly had no share. It was not a capricious partiality to new faces;—it was not a natural turn for low intrigue; nor was it the treacherous amusement of double and triple negotiations. No, Sir, it arose from a continued anxiety, in the purest of all possible hearts, for the general welfare. Unfortunately for us, the event has not been answerable to the design. After a rapid succession of changes, we are reduced to that state, which hardly any change can mend. Yet there is no extremity of distress, which of itself ought to reduce a great nation to despair. It is not the disorder but the physician;—it is not a casual concurrence of calamitous circumstances, it is the pernicious hand of government, which alone can make a whole people desperate.

WITHOUT much political sagacity, or any extraordinary depth of observation, we need only mark how the principal departments of the state are bestowed, and look no farther for the true cause of every mischief that befals us.

*THE finances of a nation, sinking under its debts and expences, are committed to a young nobleman already ruined by play. Introduced to act under the auspices of Lord Chatham, and left at the head of affairs by that nobleman's retreat, he became minister by accident; but deserting the principles and professions, which gave him a moment's popularity, we see him, from every honourable engagement to the public, an apostate by design. As for business, the world yet knows nothing of his talents or resolution; unless a wayward, wavering inconsistency be a mark of genius and caprice a demonstration of spirit. It may be said perhaps, that it is

* The Duke of Grafton took the office of Secretary of State, with an engagement to support the Marquis of Rockingham's administration. He resigned however in a little time, under pretence that he could not act without Lord Chatham, nor bear to see Mr. Wilkes abandoned; but that under Lord Chatham he would act in *any* office. This was the signal of Lord Rockingham's dismission. When Lord Chatham came in, the Duke got possession of the Treasury. Reader, mark the consequence![1]

[1] The most recent investigator of these matters, P. Langford, *The first Rockingham administration*, concludes that the resignation of Grafton in April 1766, though weakening the ministry, was not the main cause of its collapse.

his Grace's province, as surely it is his passion, rather to distribute than to save the public money, and that while Lord North is Chancellor of the Exchequer, the First Lord of the Treasury may be as thoughtless and extravagant as he pleases. I hope however he will not rely too much on the fertility of Lord North's genius for finance. His lordship is yet to give us the first proof of his abilities: It may be candid to suppose that he has hitherto voluntarily concealed his talents; intending perhaps to astonish the world, when we least expect it, with a knowledge of trade, a choice of expedients, and a depth of resources, equal to the necessities, and far beyond the hopes of his country. He must now exert the whole power of his capacity, if he would wish us to forget, that, since he has been in office, no plan has been formed, no system adhered to, nor any one important measure adopted for the relief of public credit. If his plan for the service of the current year be not irrevocably fixed on, let me warn him to think seriously of consequences before he ventures to increase the public debt. Outraged and oppressed as we are, this nation will not bear, after a six years peace, to see new millions borrowed, without an eventual diminution of debt, or reduction of interest. The attempt might rouse a spirit of resentment, which might reach beyond the sacrifice of a minister. As to the debt upon the civil list, the people of England expect that it will not be paid without a strict enquiry how it was incurred.[1] If it must be paid by parliament, let me advise the Chancellor of the Exchequer to think of some better expedient than a lottery. To support an expensive war, or in circumstances of absolute necessity, a lottery may perhaps be allowable; but, besides that is at all times the very worst way of raising money upon the people, I think it ill becomes the Royal dignity to have the debts of a King provided for, like the repairs of a country bridge, or a decayed hospital. The management of the King's affairs in the House of Commons cannot be more disgraced than it has been. *A leading minister re-

* This happened frequently to poor Lord North.

[1] Lord North announced in the House of Commons on 28 February 1769 a debt on the civil list of more than £500,000. The House agreed on 2 March to discharge it. *Parl. Hist.* xvi. 598–602. A good account of royal finances is in J. Brooke, *King George III* (1972), ch. 5.

peatedly called down for absolute ignorance;—ridiculous motions ridiculously withdrawn;—deliberate plans disconcerted, and a week's preparation of graceful oratory lost in a moment, give us some, though not adequate idea of Lord North's parliamentary abilities and influence. Yet before he had the misfortune of being Chancellor of the Exchequer, he was neither an object of derision to his enemies, nor of melancholy pity to his friends.

A SERIES of inconsistent measures has alienated the colonies from their duty as subjects, and from their natural affection to their common country. When Mr. Grenville was placed at the head of the Treasury, he felt the impossibility of Great Britain's supporting such an establishment as her former successes had made indispensable, and at the same time of giving any sensible relief to foreign trade, and to the weight of the public debt. He thought it equitable that those parts of the empire, which had benefited most by the expences of the war, should contribute something to the expences of the peace, and he had no doubt of the constitutional right vested in parliament to raise the contribution. But, unfortunately for this country, Mr. Grenville was at any rate to be distressed because he was minister, and Mr. Pitt* and Lord Camden were to be the patrons of America, because they were in opposition. Their declaration gave spirit and argument to the colonies, and while perhaps they meant no more than a ruin of a minister, they in effect divided one half of the empire from the other.

UNDER one administration the stamp act is made; under the second it is repealed; under the third, in spite of all experience, a new mode of taxing the colonies is invented, and a question revived, which ought to have been buried in oblivion. In these circumstances a new office is established for the business of the plantations, and the Earl of Hillsborough called forth, at a most critical season, to govern America.[1] The choice at least announced to us a man of superior

* Yet *Junius* has been called the partizan of Lord Chatham!

[1] A third secretaryship of State for the American Department was created in January 1768.

capacity and knowledge. Whether he be so or not, let his dispatches as far as they have appeared, let his measures as far as they have operated, determine for him. In the former we have seen strong assertions without proof, declamation without argument, and violent censures without dignity or moderation; but neither correctness in the composition, nor judgment in the design. As for his measures, let it be remembered, that he was called upon to conciliate and unite; and that, when he entered into office, the most refractory of the colonies were still disposed to proceed by the constitutional methods of petition and remonstrance. Since that period they have been driven into excesses little short of rebellion. Petitions have been hindered from reaching the throne; and the continuance of one of the principal assemblies rested upon an arbitrary condition*, which, considering the temper they were in, it was impossible they should comply with, and which would have availed nothing as to the general question, if it had been complied with. So violent, and I believe I may call it so unconstitutional an exertion of the prerogative, to say nothing of the weak, injudicious terms in which it was conveyed, gives us as humble an opinion of his lordship's capacity, as it does of his temper and moderation. While we are at peace with other nations, our military force may perhaps be spared to support the Earl of Hillsborough's measures in America. Whenever that force shall be necessarily withdrawn or diminished, the dismission of such a minister will neither console us for his imprudence, nor remove the settled resentment of a people, who, complaining of an act of the legislature, are outraged by an unwarrantable stretch of prerogative, and, supporting their claims by argument, are insulted with declamation.

DRAWING lots would be a prudent and reasonable method of appointing the officers of state, compared to a late disposition of the secretary's office. Lord Rochford was acquainted with the affairs and temper of the southern courts: Lord Weymouth was equally

* That they should retract one of their resolutions, and erase the entry of it.[1]

[1] Hillsborough wrote in 1768 to Francis Bernard, Governor of Massachusetts, that the Assembly must rescind its vote in favour of co-ordinated resistance on pain of dissolution. The Assembly declined to do so and was dissolved on 1 July 1768.

qualified for either department*. By what unaccountable caprice has it happened, that the latter, who pretends to no experience whatsoever, is removed to the most important of the two departments, and the former by preference placed in an office, where his experience can be of no use to him? Lord Weymouth had distinguished himself in his first employment by a spirited, if not judicious conduct. He had animated the civil magistrate beyond the tone of civil authority, and had directed the operations of the army to more than military execution. Recovered from the errors of his youth, from the distraction of play, and the bewitching smiles of Burgundy, behold him exerting the whole strength of his clear, unclouded faculties, in the service of the crown. It was not the heat of midnight excesses, nor ignorance of the laws, nor furious spirit of the house of Bedford: No, Sir, when this respectable minister interposed his authority between the magistrate, and the people, and signed the mandate, on which, for aught he knew, the lives of thousands depended, he did it from the deliberate motion of his heart, supported by the best of his judgment.[1]

IT has lately been a fashion to pay a compliment to the bravery and generosity of the commander in chief†, at the expence of his understanding. They who love him least make no question of his courage, while his friends dwell chiefly on the facility of his disposition. Admitting him to be as brave as a total absence of all feeling and reflection can make him, let us see what sort of merit he

* It was pretended that the Earl of Rochford, while ambassador in France, had quarrelled with the duke of Choiseuïl, and that therefore he was appointed to the Northern department, out of compliment to the French minister.

† The late Lord Granby.

---

[1] Lord Weymouth, as one of the Secretaries of State, wrote on 17 April 1768 to the chairman of the Surrey magistrates advising them to do their duty with firmness and assuring them that military assistance was available if needed. When this was followed by the St. George's Field riot of 10 May, during which troops opened fire on the crowd, killing several, Weymouth's letter was interpreted as an incitement to massacre. John Wilkes obtained a copy of the letter and had it published in the *St. James's Chronicle* of 8/10 December 1768, with offensive interpretive remarks. When examined by the House of Commons on 2 February 1769 Wilkes gloried in 'bringing to light that bloody scroll . . . I shall never deny what I look on as a meritorious action.' *Parl. Hist.* xvi. 543–4.

derives from the remainder of his character. If it be generosity to accumulate in his own person and family a number of lucrative employments; to provide, at the public expence, for every creature that bears the name of Manners; and, neglecting the merit and services of the rest of the army, to heap promotions upon his favourites and dependants, the present commander in chief is the most generous man alive. Nature has been sparing of her gifts to this noble lord; but where birth and fortune are united, we expect the noble pride and independance of a man of spirit, not the servile, humiliating complaisance of a courtier. As to the goodness of his heart, if a proof of it be taken from the facility of never refusing, what conclusion shall we draw from the indecency of never performing? And if the discipline of the army be in any degree preserved, what thanks are due to a man, whose cares, notoriously confined to filling up vacancies, have degraded the office of commander in chief into a broker of commissions!

WITH respect to the navy, I shall only say, that this country is so highly indebted to Sir Edward Hawke, that no expence should be spared to secure to him an honourable and affluent retreat.

THE pure and impartial administration of justice is perhaps the firmest bond to secure a chearful submission of the people, and to engage their affections to government. It is not sufficient that questions of private right or wrong are justly decided, nor that judges are superior to the vileness of pecuniary corruption. Jefferies himself, when the court had no interest, was an upright judge. A court of justice may be subject to another sort of bias, more important and pernicious, as it reaches beyond the interest of individuals, and affects the whole community. A judge under the influence of government, may be honest enough in the decision of private causes, yet a traitor to the public. When a victim is marked out by the ministry, this judge will offer himself to perform the sacrifice. He will not scruple to prostitute his dignity, and betray the sanctity of his office, whenever an arbitrary point is to be carried for government, or the resentment of a court to be gratified.[1]

[1] The reference is to Lord Mansfield.

THESE principles and proceedings, odious and contemptible as they are, in effect are no less injudicious. A wise and generous people are roused by every appearance of oppressive, unconstitutional measures, whether those measures are supported only by the power of government, or masked under the forms of a court of justice. Prudence and self-preservation will oblige the most moderate dispositions to make common cause, even with a man whose conduct they censure, if they see him persecuted in a way, which the real spirit of the laws will not justify. The facts, on which these remarks are founded, are too notorious to require an application.

THIS, Sir, is the detail. In one view behold a nation overwhelmed with debt; her revenues wasted; her trade declining; the affections of her colonies alienated; the duty of the magistrate transferred to the soldiery; a gallant army, which never fought unwillingly but against their fellow subjects, mouldering away for want of the direction of a man of common abilities and spirit; and, in the last instance, the administration of justice become odious and suspected to the whole body of the people. This deplorable scene admits of but one addition—that we are governed by counsels, from which a reasonable man can expect no remedy but poison, no relief but death.

IF, by the immediate interposition of Providence, it were possible for us to escape a crisis so full of terror and despair, posterity will not believe the history of the present times. They will either conclude that our distresses were imaginary, or that we had the good fortune to be governed by men of acknowledged integrity and wisdom: they will not believe it possible that their ancestors could have survived, or recovered from so desperate a condition, while a Duke of Grafton was Prime Minister, a Lord North Chancellor of the Exchequer, a Weymouth and a Hillsborough Secretaries of State, a Granby Commander in Chief, and a Mansfield chief criminal Judge of the kingdom.

JUNIUS.

Junius was fortunate that his letter provoked Sir William Draper to defend Lord Granby. Draper had started on an academic life and for a time held a fellowship at King's College, Cambridge. He then joined the army and had a distinguished career during the Seven Years War. He provided a perfect foil for Junius. Though able enough to maintain a genuine contest, his sputtering indignation and self-important manner put him at a disadvantage in comparison with Junius' easy nonchalance. Draper's letter first appeared in the *St. James's Chronicle* for 28/31 January 1769 and was reprinted in the *Public Advertiser* on 2 February. The date here is that given by Draper.

LETTER II.

TO THE PRINTER OF THE PUBLIC ADVERTISER.

SIR, 26. *January*, 1769.

THE kingdom swarms with such numbers of felonious robbers of private character and virtue, that no honest or good man is safe; especially as these cowardly base assassins stab in the dark, without having the courage to sign their real names to their malevolent and wicked productions. A writer, who signs himself Junius, in the Public Advertiser of the 21st instant, opens the deplorable situation of his country in a very affecting manner; with a pompous parade of his candour and decency, he tells us, that we see dissentions in all parts of the empire, an universal spirit of distrust and dissatisfaction, and a total loss of respect towards us in the eyes of foreign powers. But this writer, with all his boasted candour, has not told us the real cause of the evils he so pathetically enumerates. I shall take the liberty to explain the cause for him. Junius, and such writers as himself, occasion all the mischief complained of, by falsely and maliciously traducing the best characters in the kingdom. For when our deluded people at home, and foreigners abroad, read the poisonous and inflammatory libels that are daily published with impunity, to vilify those who are any way distinguished by their good qualities and eminent virtues: when they find no notice taken of, or reply given to these slanderous tongues and pens, their conclusion is, that both the ministers and the nation have been fairly described; and they act accordingly. I think it therefore the duty of every good citizen to stand forth, and endeavour to undeceive the public, when the vilest arts are made use of to defame and blacken the brightest characters among us. An eminent author affirms it to be almost as criminal to hear a worthy man traduced, without attempting his justification, as to be the author of the calumny against him. For my own part, I think it a sort of misprision of treason against society. No man therefore who knows Lord Granby, can possibly hear so good and great a character most vilely abused, without a warm and just indignation against this Junius, this high-priest of envy, malice, and all uncharitableness, who has endeavoured to sacrifice our beloved commander in chief at the altars of his horrid deities. Nor is the injury done to his lordship alone, but to the whole nation, which may too soon feel the contempt, and consequently the attacks of our late enemies, if they can be induced to believe that the person, on whom the safety of these kingdoms so much depends, is unequal to his high station, and destitute of those qualities which form a good general. One would have thought that his lordship's services in the cause of his country, from the battle of Culloden to his most glorious conclusion of the late war, might have entitled him to common respect and decency at least; but this uncandid indecent writer has gone so far as to turn one of the most amiable men of the age into a stupid, unfeeling, and senseless being; possessed indeed of a personal courage, but void of those essential qualities which distinguish the commander from the common soldier.

A VERY long, uninterrupted, impartial, I will add, a most disinterested friendship with Lord Granby, gives me the right to affirm, that all Junius's assertions are false and scandalous. Lord Granby's courage, though of the brightest and most ardent kind, is among the lowest of his numerous good qualities; he was formed to excel in war by nature's liberality to his mind as well as person. Educated and instructed by his most noble father, and a most spirited as well as excellent scholar, the present bishop of Bangor,[1] he was trained to the nicest sense of honour, and to the truest and noblest sort of pride, that of never doing or suffering a mean action. A sincere love and attachment to his king and country, and to their

[1] John Ewer, Bishop of Llandaff 1761–8; translated to Bangor 1768.

glory, first impelled him to the field, where he never gained aught but honour. He impaired, through his bounty, his own fortune; for his bounty, which this writer would in vain depreciate, is founded upon the noblest of the human affections, it flows from a heart melting to goodness from the most refined humanity. Can a man, who is described as unfeeling, and void of reflection, be constantly employed in seeking proper objects on whom to exercise those glorious virtues of compassion and generosity? The distressed officer, the soldier, the widow, the orphan, and a long list besides, know that vanity has no share in his frequent donations; he gives, because he feels their distresses. Nor has he ever been rapacious with one hand to be bountiful with the other; yet this uncandid Junius would insinuate, that the dignity of the commander in chief is depraved into the base office of a commission broker; that is, Lord Granby bargains for the sale of commissions; for it must have this meaning, if it has any at all. But where is the man living who can justly charge his lordship with such mean practices? Why does not Junius produce him? Junius knows that he has no other means of wounding this hero, than from some missile weapon, shot from an obscure corner: He seeks, as all such defamatory writers do,

——spargere voces
In Vulgum ambiguas——[1]

to raise suspicion in the minds of the people. But I hope that my countrymen will be no longer imposed upon by artful and designing men, or by wretches, who, bankrupts in business, in fame, and in fortune, mean nothing more than to involve this country in the same common ruin with themselves. Hence it is, that they are constantly aiming their dark and too often fatal weapons against those who stand forth as the bulwark of our national safety. Lord Granby was too conspicuous a mark not to be their object. He is next attacked for being unfaithful to his promises and engagements: Where are Junius's proofs? Although I could give some instances, where a breach of promise would be a virtue, especially in the case of those who would pervert the open, unsuspecting moments of convivial mirth, into sly, insidious applications for preferment, or

[1] Virgil, *Aeneid*, ii. 98.

party systems, and would endeavour to surprise a good man, who cannot bear to see any one leave him dissatisfied, into unguarded promises. Lord Granby's attention to his own family and relations is called selfish. Had he not attended to them, when fair and just opportunities presented themselves, I should have thought him unfeeling, and void of reflection indeed. How are any man's friends or relations to be provided for, but from the influence and protection of the patron? It is unfair to suppose that Lord Granby's friends have not as much merit as the friends of any other great man: If he is generous at the public expence, as Junius invidiously calls it, the public is at no more expence for his lordship's friends, than it would be if any other set of men possessed those offices. The charge is ridiculous!

THE last charge against Lord Granby is of a most serious and alarming nature indeed. Junius asserts, that the army is mouldering away for want of the direction of a man of common abilities and spirit. The present condition of the army gives the directest lie to his assertions. It was never upon a more respectable footing with regard to discipline, and all the essentials that can form good soldiers. Lord Ligonier delivered a firm and noble palladium of our safeties into Lord Granby's hands, who has kept it in the same good order in which he received it. The strictest care has been taken to fill up the vacant commissions, with such gentlemen as have the glory of their ancestors to support, as well as their own, and are doubly bound to the cause of their king and country, from motives of private property, as well as publick spirit. The adjutant-general, who has the immediate care of the troops after Lord Granby, is an officer that would do great honour in any service in Europe, for his correct arrangements, good sense and discernment upon all occasions, and for a punctuality and precision which give the most entire satisfaction to all who are obliged to consult him.[1] The reviewing generals, who inspect the army twice a year, have been selected with the greatest care, and have answered the important trust reposed in them in the most laudable manner. Their reports of the condition of the army are much more to be credited

[1] Major-General Edward Harvey.

than those of Junius, whom I do advise, to atone for his shameful aspersions, by asking pardon of Lord Granby and the whole kingdom, whom he has offended by his abominable scandals. In short, to turn Junius's own battery against him, I must assert, in his own words, "that he has given strong assertions without proof, declamation without argument, and violent censures without dignity or moderation."

WILLIAM DRAPER.

Perhaps the most remarkable feature of Junius' reply was the use he made of Draper's observation that Lord Granby 'never gained aught but honour' in the field.

LETTER III.

TO SIR WILLIAM DRAPER, KNIGHT OF THE BATH.

SIR, 7. *February*, 1769.

YOUR defence of Lord Granby does honour to the goodness of your heart. You feel, as you ought to do, for the reputation of your friend, and you express yourself in the warmest language of your passions. In any other cause, I doubt not, you would have cautiously weighed the consequences of committing your name to the licentious discourses and malignant opinions of the world. But here, I presume, you thought it would be a breach of friendship to lose one moment in consulting your understanding; as if an appeal to the public were no more than a military *coup de main*, where a brave man has no rules to follow, but the dictates of his courage. Touched with your generosity, I freely forgive the excesses into which it has led you; and, far from resenting those terms of reproach, which, considering that you are an advocate for decorum, you have heaped upon me rather too liberally, I place them to the account of an honest unreflecting indignation, in which your cooler judgment and natural politeness had no concern. I approve of the spirit, with which you have given your name to the public; and, if it were a proof of any thing but spirit, I should have thought myself bound to follow your example. I should have hoped that even *my* name might carry some authority with it, if I had not seen how very little weight or consideration a printed paper receives even from the respectable signature of Sir William Draper.

YOU begin with a general assertion, that writers, such as I am, are the real cause of all the public evils we complain of. And do you really think, Sir William, that the licentious pen of a political writer is able to produce such important effects? A little calm reflection might have shewn you, that national calamities do not arise from the description, but from the real character and conduct of ministers. To have supported your assertion, you should have proved that the present ministry are unquestionably the *best and brightest* characters of the kingdom; and that, if the affections of the colonies have been alienated, if Corsica has been shamefully abandoned, if commerce languishes, if public credit is threatened with a new debt, and your own Manilla ransom most dishonourably given up, it has all been owing to the malice of political writers, who will not suffer the best and brightest of characters (meaning still the present ministry) to take a single right step for the honour or interest of the nation.[1] But it seems you were a little tender of coming to particulars. Your conscience insinuated to you, that it would be prudent to leave the characters of Grafton, North, Hillsborough, Weymouth, and Mansfield, to shift for themselves; and truly, Sir William, the part you *have* undertaken is at least as much as you are equal to.

WITHOUT disputing Lord Granby's courage, we are yet to learn in what articles of military knowledge nature has been so very liberal to his mind. If you have served with him, you ought to have pointed out some instances of able disposition and well-concerted enterprize, which might fairly be attributed to his capacity as a general. It is you, Sir William, who make your friend appear

[1] The Corsicans, after a long struggle under Pasquale Paoli against the Genoese, were subdued by the French during 1768 and 1769.

In 1762 Draper had led a successful attack upon Manilla, accepting bills for £1 m. instead of plunder. The Spanish government subsequently repudiated the ransom and the British government was obliged to acquiesce. His pamphlet on the subject, published in 1764, was entitled *Colonel Draper's answer to the Spanish arguments . . . respecting payment of the ransom bills for preserving Manilla from pillage and destruction.*

aukward and ridiculous, by giving him a laced suit of tawdry qualifications, which nature never intended him to wear.

YOU say, he has acquired nothing but honour in the field. Is the Ordnance nothing? Are the Blues nothing? Is the command of the army, with all the patronage annexed to it, nothing? Where he got these *nothings* I know not; but you at least ought to have told us where he deserved them.[1]

AS to his bounty, compassion, &c. it would have been but little to the purpose, though you had proved all that you have asserted. I meddle with nothing but his character as commander in chief; and, though I acquit him of the baseness of selling commissions, I still assert that his military cares have never extended beyond the disposal of vacancies; and I am justified by the complaints of the whole army, when I say that, in this distribution, he consults nothing but parliamentary interests, or the gratification of his immediate dependants. As to his servile submission to the reigning ministry, let me ask, whether he did not desert the cause of the whole army, when he suffered Sir Jeffery Amherst to be sacrificed, and what share he had in recalling that officer to the service? Did he not betray the just interest of the army, in permitting Lord Percy to have a regiment? And does he not at this moment give up all character and dignity as a gentleman, in receding from his own repeated declarations in favour of Mr. Wilkes?[2]

IN the two next articles I think we are agreed. You candidly admit, that he often makes such promises as it is a virtue in him to violate, and that no man is more assiduous to provide for his relations at the public expence. I did not urge the last as an abso-

[1] Granby had been Colonel of the Royal Horse Guards (The Blues) since 1758 and Master-General of the Ordnance since 1763.

[2] Sir Jeffery Amherst was responsible for the conquest of Canada during the Seven Years War. He was subsequently appointed Governor of Virginia. His resignation in August 1768 and replacement by Lord Botetourt was the subject of much newspaper comment. Lord Percy had been appointed Colonel of the 5th Foot in 1768 at the age of 25. He was son-in-law to Lord Bute, but according to Horace Walpole owed his promotion to the influence of his father, the Duke of Northumberland; Walpole, iii. 171.

lute vice in his disposition, but to prove that a *careless disinterested spirit* is no part of his character; and as to the other, I desire it may be remembered, that *I* never descended to the indecency of inquiring into his *convivial hours.* It is you, Sir William Draper, who have taken pains to represent your friend in the character of a drunken landlord, who deals out his promises as liberally as his liquor, and will suffer no man to leave his table either sorrowful or sober. None but an intimate friend, who must frequently have seen him in these unhappy, disgraceful moments could have described him so well.

THE last charge, of the neglect of the army, is indeed the most material of all. I am sorry to tell you, Sir William, that, in this article, your first fact is false, and as there is nothing more painful to me than to give a direct contradiction to a gentleman of your appearance, I could wish that, in your future publications, you would pay a greater attention to the truth of your premises, before you suffer your genius to hurry you to a conclusion. Lord Ligonier *did not* deliver the army (which you, in classical language, are pleased to call a palladium) into Lord Granby's hands. It was taken from him much against his inclination, some two or three years before Lord Granby was commander in chief.[1] As to the state of the army, I should be glad to know where you have received your intelligence. Was it in the rooms at Bath, or at your retreat at Clifton? The reports of reviewing generals comprehend only a few regiments in England, which, as they are immediately under the royal inspection, are perhaps in some tolerable order. But do you know any thing of the troops in the West-Indies, the Mediterranean, and North America, to say nothing of a whole army absolutely ruined in Ireland? Inquire a little into facts, Sir William, before you publish your next panegyric upon Lord Granby, and

[1] The position about the Commander-in-Chief was complicated. At the end of the Seven Years War the functions of the office were distributed among three reviewing generals and the salary was not paid. Ligonier certainly regarded himself as having been removed, though he continued to hold the office until August 1766 when he was replaced by Granby. See R. Whitworth, *Field Marshal Lord Ligonier* (1958), 376–87. It is certainly true that Ligonier was reluctant to retire, but, since he was 86 and was rewarded with an earldom, his supersession was not quite as unreasonable as Junius suggested.

believe me you will find there is a fault at head-quarters, which even the acknowledged care and abilities of the adjutant-general cannot correct.

PERMIT me now, Sir William, to address myself personally to you, by way of thanks for the honour of your correspondence. You are by no means undeserving of notice; and it may be of consequence even to Lord Granby to have it determined, whether or no the man, who has praised him so lavishly, be himself deserving of praise. When you returned to Europe, you zealously undertook the cause of that gallant army, by whose bravery at Manilla your own fortune had been established. You complained, you threatened, you even appealed to the public in print. By what accident did it happen, that in the midst of all this bustle, and all these clamours for justice to your injured troops, the name of the Manilla ransom was suddenly buried in a profound, and, since that time, an uninterrupted silence? Did the ministry suggest any motives to you, strong enough to tempt a man of honour to desert and betray the cause of his fellow-soldiers? Was it that blushing ribband, which is now the perpetual ornament of your person? Or was it that regiment, which you afterwards (a thing unprecedented among soldiers) sold to colonel Gisborne? Or was it that government, the full pay of which you are contented to hold, with the half-pay of an Irish colonel?[1] And do you now, after a retreat not very like that of Scipio, presume to intrude yourself, unthought-of, uncalled-for, upon the patience of the public? Are your flatteries of the commander in chief directed to another regiment, which you may again dispose of on the same honourable terms? We know your prudence, Sir William, and I should be sorry to stop your preferment.

JUNIUS.

[1] Draper was a Knight of the Bath, Governor of Great Yarmouth, and had been Colonel of the 16th Regiment of Foot Guards.

Draper's reply, dated 10 February 1769, was first printed in the *St. James's Chronicle* for 14/16 February; the date given here is of its appearance in the *Public Advertiser*.

LETTER IV.

TO JUNIUS.

SIR, 17. *February* 1769.

I RECEIVED Junius's favour last night; he is determined to keep his advantage by the help of his mask; it is an excellent protection, it has saved many a man from an untimely end. But whenever he will be honest enough to lay it aside, avow himself, and produce the face which has so long lurked behind it, the world will be able to judge of his motives for writing such infamous invectives. His real name will discover his freedom and independency, or his servility to a faction. Disappointed ambition, resentment for defeated hopes, and desire of revenge, assume but too often the appearance of public spirit; but be his designs wicked or charitable, Junius should learn that it is possible to condemn measures, without a barbarous and criminal outrage against men. Junius delights to mangle carcases with a hatchet; his language and instrument have a great connexion with Clare-market, and, to do him justice, he handles his weapon most admirably.[1] One would imagine he had been taught to throw it by the savages of America. It is therefore high time for me to step in once more to shield my friend from this merciless weapon, although I may be wounded in the attempt. But I must first ask Junius, by what forced analogy and construction the moments of convivial mirth are made to signify indecency, a violation of engagements, a drunken landlord, and a desire that every one in company should be drunk likewise? He must have culled all the flowers of St. Giles's and Billingsgate to have produced such a piece of oratory. Here the hatchet descends with tenfold vengeance; but, alas! it hurts no one but its master! For Junius must not think to put words into my mouth, that seem too foul even for his own.

[1] Clare Market, near Lincoln's Inn Fields, was noted for the sale of butchers' meat, tripe, and dogs' and cats' food.

My friend's political engagements I know not, so cannot pretend to explain them, or assert their consistency. I know not whether Junius be considerable enough to belong to any party; if he should be so, can he affirm that he has always adhered to one set of men and measures? Is he sure that he has never sided with those whom he was first hired to abuse? Has he never abused those he was hired to praise? To say the truth, most men's politics sit much too loosely about them. But as my friend's military character was the chief object that engaged me in this controversy, to that I shall return.

Junius asks what instances my friend has given of his military skill and capacity as a general? When and where he gained his honour? When he deserved his emoluments? The united voice of the army which served under him, the glorious testimony of prince Ferdinand, and of vanquished enemies, all Germany will tell him. Junius repeats the complaints of the army against parliamentary influence. I love the army too well, not to wish that such influence were less. Let Junius point out the time when it has not prevailed. It was of the least force in the time of that great man, the late duke of Cumberland, who, as a prince of the blood, was able as well as willing to stem a torrent which would have overborne any private subject. In time of war this influence is small. In peace, when discontent and faction have the surest means to operate, especially in this country, and when, from a scarcity of public spirit, the wheels of government are rarely moved, but by the power and force of obligations, its weight is always too great. Yet, if this influence at present has done no greater harm than the placing Earl Percy at the head of a regiment, I do not think that either the rights or best interests of the army are sacrificed and betrayed, or the nation undone. Let me ask Junius, if he knows any one nobleman in the army, who has had a regiment by seniority? I feel myself happy in seeing young noblemen of illustrious name and great property come among us. They are an additional security to the kingdom from foreign or domestic slavery. Junius needs not be told, that should the time ever come, when this nation is to be defended only by those, who have nothing more to lose than their arms and their pay, its danger will be great indeed. A happy mixture of men of quality with soldiers of fortune is always to be wished for. But the main point is still to be contended for, I mean the discipline and condition of the army, and I must still maintain, though contradicted by Junius, that it was never upon a more respectable footing, as to all the essentials that can form good soldiers, than it is at present. Junius is forced to allow that our army at home may be in some tolerable order; yet how kindly does he invite our late enemies to the invasion of Ireland, by assuring them that the army in that kingdom is totally ruined! (The colonels of that army are much obliged to him) I have too great an opinion of the military talents of the lord lieutenant, and of all their diligence and capacity, to believe it.[1] If from some strange, unaccountable fatality, the people of that kingdom cannot be induced to consult their own security, by such an effectual augmentation, as may enable the troops there to act with power and energy, is the commander in chief here to blame? Or is he to blame, because the troops in the Mediterranean, in the West-Indies, in America, labour under great difficulties from the scarcity of men, which is but too visible all over these kingdoms! Many of our forces are in climates unfavourable to British constitutions: their loss is in proportion. Britain must recruit all these regiments from her own emaciated bosom, or, more precariously, by Catholicks from Ireland. We are likewise subject to the fatal drains to the East-Indies, to Senegal, and the alarming emigrations of our people to other countries: Such depopulation can only be repaired by a long peace, or by some sensible bill of naturalization.

I MUST now take the liberty to talk to Junius on my own account. He is pleased to tell me that he addresses himself to me *personally*, I shall be glad to see him. It is his *impersonality* that I complain of, and his invisible attacks; for his dagger in the air is only to be regarded, because one cannot see the hand which holds it; but had it not wounded other people more deeply than myself, I should not have obtruded myself at all on the patience of the public.

[1] George, 4th Viscount Townshend, was Lord Lieutenant of Ireland from 1767 until 1772; at this time he held the rank of major-general.

MARK how a plain tale shall put him down, and transfuse the blush of my ribband into his own cheeks. Junius tells me, that at my return, I zealously undertook the cause of the gallant army, by whose bravery at Manilla my own fortunes were established; that I complained, that I even appealed to the public. I did so; I glory in having done so, as I had an undoubted right to vindicate my own character, attacked by a Spanish memorial, and to assert the rights of my brave companions. I glory likewise, that I have never taken up my pen, but to vindicate the injured. Junius asks by what accident did it happen, that in the midst of all this bustle, and all the clamours for justice to the injured troops, the Manilla ransom was suddenly buried in a profound, and, since that time, an uninterrupted silence? I will explain the cause to the public. The several ministers who have been employed since that time have been very desirous to do justice from two most laudable motives, a strong inclination to assist injured bravery, and to acquire a well deserved popularity to themselves. Their efforts have been in vain. Some were ingenuous enough to own, that they could not think of involving this distressed nation into another war for our private concerns. In short, our rights for the present, are sacrificed to national convenience; and I must confess, that although I may lose five-and-twenty thousand pounds by their acquiescence to this breach of faith in the Spaniards, I think they are in the right to temporize, considering the critical situation of this country, convulsed in every part by poison infused by anonymous, wicked, and incendiary writers. Lord Shelburne will do me the justice to own, that, in September last, I waited upon him with a joint memorial from the admiral Sir S. Cornish and myself, in behalf of our injured companions.[1] His lordship was as frank upon the occasion as other secretaries had been before him. He did not deceive us by giving any immediate hopes of relief.

JUNIUS would basely insinuate, that my silence may have been purchased by my government, by my *blushing* ribband, by my regiment, by the sale of that regiment, and by half-pay as an Irish colonel.

[1] Sir Samuel Cornish had been naval commander at the capture of Manilla.

HIS Majesty was pleased to give me my government, for my service at Madras. I had my first regiment in 1757. Upon my return from Manilla, his Majesty, by Lord Egremont, informed me, that I should have the first vacant red ribband, as a reward for many services in an enterprize, which I had planned as well as executed. The Duke of Bedford and Mr. Grenville confirmed those assurances many months before the Spaniards had protested the ransom bills. To accommodate Lord Clive, then going upon a most important service to Bengal, I waved my claim to the vacancy which then happened. As there was no other vacancy until the Duke of Grafton and Lord Rockingham were joint ministers, I was then honoured with the order, and it is surely no small honour to me, that in such a succession of ministers, they were all pleased to think that I had deserved it; in my favour they were all united. Upon the reduction of the 79th regiment, which had served so gloriously in the East-Indies, his Majesty, unsolicited by me, gave me the 16th of foot as an equivalent. My motives for retiring afterwards are foreign to the purpose; let it suffice, that his Majesty was pleased to approve of them; they are such as no man can think indecent, who knows the shocks that repeated vicissitudes of heat and cold, of dangerous and sickly climates, will give to the best constitutions in a pretty long course of service. I resigned my regiment to colonel Gisborne, a very good officer, for his half-pay, 1200 l. Irish annuity;[1] so that, according to Junius, I have been bribed to say nothing more of the Manilla ransom, and sacrifice those brave men by the strange avarice of accepting three hundred and eighty pounds per ann. and giving up eight hundred! If this be bribery, it is not the bribery of these times. As to my flattery, those who know me will judge of it. By the asperity of Junius's stile, I cannot indeed call him a flatterer, unless he be as a cynick or a mastiff; if he wags his tail, he will still growl, and long to bite. The public will now judge of the credit that ought to be given to Junius's writings, from the falsities that he has insinuated with respect to myself.

WILLIAM DRAPER.

[1] This was a printer's error for £200. The *Public Advertiser* of 22 February 1769 carried a note from Draper correcting the mistake. Junius did not correct it in his 1772 edition.

Coleridge, in the remarks he entered in his own copy of the Letters, considered Junius' reply 'a faultless composition'.

LETTER V.

TO SIR WILLIAM DRAPER, KNIGHT OF THE BATH.

SIR, 21. *February*, 1769.

I SHOULD justly be suspected of acting upon motives of more than common enmity to Lord Granby, if I continued to give you fresh materials or occasion for writing in his defence. Individuals who hate, and the public who despise, have read *your* letters, Sir William, with infinitely more satisfaction than mine. Unfortunately for him, his reputation, like that unhappy country to which you refer me for his last military atchievements, has suffered more by his friends than his enemies. In mercy to him, let us drop the subject. For my own part, I willingly leave it to the public to determine whether your vindication of your friend has been as able and judicious, as it was certainly well intended; and you, I think, may be satisfied with the warm acknowledgments he already owes you for making him the principal figure in a piece, in which, but for your amicable assistance, he might have passed without particular notice or distinction.

IN justice to your friends, let your future labours be confined to the care of your own reputation. Your declaration, that you are happy in seeing young noblemen *come among us*, is liable to two objections. With respect to Lord Percy, it means nothing, for he was already in the army. He was aid de camp to the King, and had the rank of colonel. A regiment therefore could not make him a more military man, though it made him richer, and probably at the expence of some brave, deserving, friendless officer.—The other concerns yourself. After selling the companions of your victory in one instance, and after selling your profession in the other, by what authority do you presume to call yourself a soldier. The plain evidence of facts is superior to all declarations. Before you were appointed to the 16th regiment, your complaints were a distress to government;—from that moment you were silent. The conclusion is inevitable. You insinuate to us that your ill state of health obliged you to quit the service. The retirement necessary to repair a broken constitution would have been as good a reason for not accepting, as for resigning the command of a regiment. There is certainly an error of the press, or an affected obscurity in that paragraph, where you speak of your bargain with colonel Gisborne. Instead of attempting to answer what I do not really understand, permit me to explain to the public what I really know. In exchange for your regiment, you accepted of a colonel's half-pay (at least 220 l. a year) and an annuity of 200 l. for your own and lady Draper's life jointly.——And is this the losing bargain, which you would represent to us, as if you had given up an income of 800 l. a year for 380 l.? Was it decent, was it honourable, in a man who pretends to love the army, and calls himself a soldier, to make a traffic of the royal favour, and turn the highest honour of an active profession into a sordid provision for himself and his family? It were unworthy of me to press you farther. The contempt with which the whole army heard of the manner of your retreat, assures me, that as your conduct was not justified by precedent, it will never be thought an example for imitation.

THE last and most important question remains. When you receive your half pay, do you, or do you not, take a solemn oath, or sign a declaration upon your honour, to the following effect? *That you do not actually hold any place of profit, civil or military, under his Majesty.* The charge which the question plainly conveys against you, is of so shocking a complexion, that I sincerely wish you may be able to answer it well, not merely for the colour of your reputation, but for your own inward peace of mind.

JUNIUS.[1]

[1] This letter as it appeared in the *Public Advertiser* had a postscript: 'I had determined to leave the commander-in-chief in the quiet enjoyment of his friends and the bottle; but Titus deserves an answer, and *shall have* a complete one.' But in private letter no. 45 to Woodfall, Junius instructed him to omit the postscript from the collected edition, presumably because the rejoinder had never been forthcoming. Titus's letter appeared in the *Public Advertiser* on 18 February 1769.

Draper's reply was dated 23 February, printed in the *St. James's Chronicle* of 25/8 February, and reprinted in the *Public Advertiser* of the 27th.

My impression is that, up to this point, Sir William had almost held his own. But in the second paragraph of his reply he made a ludicrous blunder that allowed Junius to deploy all his powers of ridicule.

LETTER VI.

TO JUNIUS.

SIR, 27. *February*, 1769.

I HAVE a very short answer for Junius's important question: I do not either take an oath, or declare upon honour, that I have no *place* of profit, *civil* or military, when I receive the half-pay as an Irish colonel. My most gracious Sovereign gives it me as a pension; he was pleased to think I deserved it. The annuity of 200 l. Irish, and the equivalent for the half-pay together, produces no more than 380 l. per annum, clear of fees and perquisites of office. I receive 167 l. from my government of Yarmouth. Total 547 l. per annum. My conscience is much at ease in these particulars; my friends need not blush for me.

JUNIUS makes much and frequent use of interrogations: they are arms that may be easily turned against himself. I could, by malicious interrogation, disturb the peace of the most virtuous man in the kingdom; I could take the decalogue, and say to one man, Did you never steal? To the next, Did you never commit murder? And to Junius himself, who is putting my life and conduct to the rack, Did you never bear false witness against thy neighbour? Junius must easily see, that unless he affirms to the contrary in his real name, some people who may be as ignorant of him as I am, will be apt to suspect him of having deviated a little from the truth: therefore let Junius ask no more questions. You bite against a file: cease viper.[1]

W. D.

[1] Draper could not resist an academic flourish: the reference is to Aesop, Fable XLIV.

LETTER VII.

TO SIR WILLIAM DRAPER, KNIGHT OF THE BATH.

SIR, 3. *March*, 1769.

AN academical education has given you an unlimited command over the most beautiful figures of speech. Masks, hatchets, racks, and vipers dance through your letters in all the mazes of metaphorical confusion. These are the gloomy companions of a disturbed imagination; the melancholy madness of poetry, without the inspiration. I will not contend with you in point of composition. You are a scholar, Sir William, and, if I am truly informed, you write Latin with almost as much purity as English.[1] Suffer me then, for I am a plain unlettered man, to continue that stile of interrogation, which suits my capacity, and to which, considering the readiness of your answers, you ought to have no objection. Even* Mr. Bingley promises to answer, if put to the torture.

Do you then really think that, if I were to ask a *most virtuous man* whether he ever committed theft, or murder, it would disturb his peace of mind? Such a question might perhaps discompose the gravity of his muscles, but I believe it would little affect the tranquility of his conscience. Examine your own breast, Sir William, and you will discover, that reproaches and enquiries have no power to

* This man, being committed by the court of King's Bench for a contempt, voluntarily made oath, that he would never answer interrogatories, unless he should be put to the torture.[2]

---

[1] In June 1768 Draper had written to Lord Chatham enclosing a long Latin inscription which he intended to erect in the garden of Manilla Hall, Bristol. Through his wife, Chatham modestly declined all but the last four lines. *Pitt. Corr.* iii. 325–30. Draper had taken the sensible precaution of first submitting the Latin to the Provost of Eton, who pruned its excesses.

[2] William Bingley, bookseller and printer, revived Wilkes's *North Briton* and in May 1768 published an attack upon Lord Mansfield. He refused to answer questions put to him on the grounds that he might incriminate himself and was committed to the King's Bench prison for contempt of court, languishing there for nearly two years. On 16 February 1769 he issued a declaration that he would not at any time 'WITHOUT TORTURE, answer to any interrogatory tending to accuse himself'. Junius seems to have regarded Bingley's conduct with some disdain as mock-heroic. See R. R. Rea, *The English press in politics, 1760–1774* (1963), 155–6, 164, 168.

afflict either the man of unblemished integrity, or the abandoned profligate. It is the middle compound character which alone is vulnerable: the man, who, without firmness enough to avoid a dishonourable action, has feeling enough to be ashamed of it.

I THANK you for the hint of the decalogue, and shall take an opportunity of applying it to some of your most virtuous friends in both houses of parliament.

YOU seem to have dropped the affair of your regiment; so let it rest. When you are appointed to another, I dare say you will not sell it either for a gross sum, or for an annuity upon lives.

I AM truly glad (for really, Sir William, I am not your enemy, nor did I begin this contest with you) that you have been able to clear yourself of a crime, though at the expence of the highest indiscretion. You say that your half-pay was given you by way of pension. I will not dwell upon the singularity of uniting in your own person two sorts of provision, which in their own nature, and in all military and parliamentary views, are incompatible; but I call upon you to justify that declaration, wherein you charge your Sovereign with having done an act in your favour notoriously against law. The half-pay, both in Ireland and England, is appropriated by parliament; and if it be given to persons, who, like you, are legally incapable of holding it, it is a breach of law. It would have been more decent in you to have called this dishonourable transaction by its true name; a job to accommodate two persons, by particular interest and management at the castle. What sense must government have had of your services, when the rewards they have given you are only a disgrace to you!

AND now, Sir William, I shall take my leave of you for ever. Motives very different from any apprehension of your resentment, make it impossible you should ever know me. In truth, you have some reason to hold yourself indebted to me. From the lessons I have given you, you may collect a profitable instruction for your future life. They will either teach you so to regulate your conduct, as to be able to set the most malicious inquiries at defiance; or, if that be a lost hope, they will teach you prudence enough not to attract the public attention to a character, which will only pass without censure, when it passes without observation.

JUNIUS.

It has been said, and I believe truly, that it was signified to Sir William Draper, as the request of Lord Granby, that he should desist from writing in his Lordship's defence. Sir William Draper certainly drew *Junius* forward to say more of Lord Granby's character, than he originally intended. He was reduced to the dilemma of either being totally silenced, or of supporting his first letter. Whether Sir William had a right to reduce him to this dilemma, or to call upon him for his name, after a voluntary attack on *his* side, are questions submitted to the candor of the public.—The death of Lord Granby was lamented by *Junius*. He undoubtedly owed some compensations to the public, and seemed determined to acquit himself of them. In private life, he was unquestionably that good man, who, for the interest of his country, ought to have been a great one. *Bonum virum facile dixeris;—magnum libenter.*[1] I speak of him now without partiality;—I never spoke of him with resentment. His mistakes, in public conduct, did not arise either from want of sentiment, or want of judgment, but in general from the difficulty of saying NO to the bad people, who surrounded him.

As for the rest, the friends of Lord Granby should remember, that he himself thought proper to condemn, retract, and disavow, by a most solemn declaration in the House of Commons, that very system of political conduct, which *Junius* had held forth, to the disapprobation of the public.

Draper wrote yet another letter, dated from Clifton 24 April 1769 and published in the *Public Advertiser* of 1 May. It was in reply to An half-pay subaltern but turned aside to attack Junius once more as a man who 'still skulks in the dark, or in the *mean* subterfuge of a mask'. Junius took no notice of it and did not include it in his collected edition, perhaps because he wished to give the impression that Draper had been chased from the field. It is, however, printed in the Piccadilly edition of the letters which came out in 1771.

The controversy over Lord Granby continued between Neocles, An Officer, Titus, Harpocrates, and Draper on 10, 16, 18, 25 February; 1, 2, 3 March; 28 April; and 1 May 1769. But Junius disengaged himself and turned his attention to bigger game—the First Lord of the Treasury.

[1] 'One might easily call him a good man—or even a great one,' Tacitus, *Agricola*, xliv. 2, substituting *dixeris* for *crederes*.

LETTER VIII.

TO THE DUKE OF GRAFTON.

MY LORD, 18. *March*, 1769.

BEFORE you were placed at the head of affairs, it had been a maxim of the English government, not unwillingly admitted by the people, that every ungracious or severe exertion of the prerogative should be placed to the account of the Minister; but that, whenever an act of grace or benevolence was to be performed, the whole merit of it should be attributed to the Sovereign himself*. It was a wise doctrine, my Lord, and equally advantageous to the King and his subjects; for while it preserved that suspicious attention, with which the people ought always to examine the conduct of ministers, it tended at the same time rather to increase than diminish their attachment to the person of their Sovereign. If there be not a fatality attending every measure you are concerned in, by what treachery, or by what excess of folly has it happened, that those ungracious acts, which have distinguished your administration, and which I doubt not were entirely your own, should carry with them a strong appearance of personal interest, and even of personal enmity in a quarter, where no such interest or enmity can be supposed to exist, without the highest injustice and the highest dishonour? On the other hand, by what judicious management have you contrived it, that the only act of mercy, to which you ever advised your Sovereign, far from adding to the lustre of a character, truly gracious and benevolent, should be received with universal disapprobation and disgust? I shall consider it as a ministerial measure, because it is an odious one, and as your measure, my Lord Duke, because you are the minister.[2]

* Les rois ne se sont reservé que les graces. Ils renvoient les condamnations vers leurs officiers. *Montesquieu.*[1]

---

[1] *De l'esprit des lois*, vi. 5: 'Dans quel gouvernement le souverain peut être juge'. The observation, made by the Président de Bellièvre to Louis XIII, should read: 'que les rois ne s'étaient réservé que les grâces, et qu'ils renvoyaient les condamnations vers leurs officiers.'

[2] Edward MacQuirk or M'Quirk, an Irish chairman, was employed by the court party at the Middlesex by-election at Brentford on 8 December 1768. After one

As long as the trial of this chairman was depending, it was natural enough that government should give him every possible encouragement and support. The honourable service for which he was hired, and the spirit with which he performed it, made common cause between your grace and him. The minister, who by secret corruption invades the freedom of elections, and the ruffian, who by open violence destroys that freedom, are embarked in the same bottom. They have the same interests, and mutually feel for each other. To do justice to your Grace's humanity, you felt for Mac Quirk as you ought to do, and if you had been contented to assist him indirectly, without a notorious denial of justice, or openly insulting the sense of the nation, you might have satisfied every duty of political friendship, without committing the honour of your Sovereign, or hazarding the reputation of his government. But when this unhappy man had been solemnly tried, convicted and condemned;—when it appeared that he had been frequently employed in the same services, and that no excuse for him could be drawn either from the innocence of his former life, or the simplicity of his character, was it not hazarding too much to interpose the strength of the prerogative between this felon and the justice of his country*? You ought to have known that an

* *Whitehall, March* 11, 1769. His Majesty has been graciously pleased to extend his royal mercy to Edward M'Quirk, found guilty of the murder of George Clarke, as appears by his royal warrant to the tenor following.

GEORGE R.

WHEREAS a doubt had arisen in Our Royal breast concerning the evidence of the death of George Clarke, from the representations of William Bromfield, Esq; Surgeon, and Solomon Starling, Apothecary; both of whom, as has been represented to Us, attended the deceased before his death, and expressed their opinions that he did not die of the blow he received at Brentford: And whereas it appears to Us, that neither of the said persons were produced as witnesses upon the trial, though the said Solomon Starling had been examined before the Coroner, and the only person called to prove that the death of the said George Clarke was occasioned by the said blow, was John Foot, Surgeon, who never saw the deceased till after his death;

George Clarke had died, apparently from wounds received in a scuffle, MacQuirk and Lawrence Balf were tried for murder. Found guilty by the jury, they were pardoned in March 1769. Since the evidence against Balf had not appeared strong, Junius directed his indignation at the pardon to MacQuirk. A full account of the trial may be found in *Sessions Papers*, 1769: see *British Museum general catalogue of printed books*, vol. 141, 349 under 'The whole proceedings of the Sessions of the Peace . . . for the City of London and County of Middlesex'.

example of this sort was never so necessary as at present; and certainly you must have known that the lot could not have fallen upon a more guilty object. What system of government is this? You are perpetually complaining of the riotous disposition of the lower class of people, yet when the laws have given you the means of making an example, in every sense unexceptionable, and by far the most likely to awe the multitude, you pardon the offence, and are not ashamed to give the sanction of government to the riots you complain of, and even to future murders. You are partial perhaps to the military mode of execution, and had rather see a score of these wretches butchered by the guards, than one of them suffer death by regular course of law. How does it happen, my Lord, that, in *your* hands, even the mercy of the prerogative is cruelty and oppression to the subject?

THE measure it seems was so extraordinary, that you thought

We thought fit thereupon to refer the said representations, together with the report of the Recorder of Our city of London, of the evidence given by Richard and William Beale, and the said John Foot, on the trial of Edward Quirk, otherwise called Edward Kirk, otherwise called Edward M'Quirk, for the Murder of the said Clarke, to the master, wardens, and the rest of the court of examiners of the Surgeons company, commanding them likewise to take such further examination of the said persons so representing, and of said John Foot, as they might think necessary, together with the premisses abovementioned, to form and report to Us their opinion, "Whether it did or did not appear to them, that the said George Clarke died in consequence of the blow he received in the riot at Brentford on the 8th of December last." And the said court of examiners of the Surgeons company having thereupon reported to Us their opinion, "That it did not appear to them that he did;" We have thought proper to extend Our royal mercy to him the said Edward Quirk, otherwise Edward Kirk, otherwise called Edward M'Quirk, and to grant him Our free pardon for the Murder of the said George Clarke, of which he has been found guilty: Our will and pleasure therefore is, That he the said Edward Quirk, otherwise called Edward Kirk, otherwise called Edward M'Quirk, be inserted, for the said Murder, in Our first and next general pardon that shall come out for the poor convicts of Newgate, without any condition whatsoever; and that in the mean time you take bail for his appearance, in order to plead Our said pardon. And for so doing this shall be your warrant.

Given at Our court at St. James's the 10th day of March, 1769, in the ninth year of Our reign.

By his Majesty's command,

ROCHFORD.

To Our trusty and well beloved James Eyre, Esq; Recorder of Our city of London, the Sheriffs of Our said city and county of Middlesex, and all others whom it may concern.

it necessary to give some reasons for it to the public. Let them be fairly examined.

I. YOU say *that Messrs. Bromfield and Starling were not examined at Mac Quirk's trial.* I will tell your Grace why they were not. They must have been examined upon oath; and it was foreseen, that their evidence would either not benefit, or might be prejudicial to the prisoner. Otherwise, is it conceivable that his counsel should neglect to call in such material evidence?

YOU say that *Mr. Foot did not see the deceased until after his death.* A surgeon, my Lord, must know very little of his profession, if, upon examining a wound, or a contusion, he cannot determine whether it was mortal or not.—While the party is alive, a surgeon will be cautious of pronouncing; whereas by the death of the patient, he is enabled to consider both cause and effect in one view, and to speak with a certainty confirmed by experience.

YET we are to thank your Grace for the establishment of a new tribunal. Your *inquisitio post mortem* is unknown to the laws of England, and does honour to your invention. The only material objection to it is, that if Mr. Foot's evidence was insufficient,[1] because he did not examine the wound till after the death of the party, much less can a negative opinion, given by gentlemen who never saw the body of Mr. Clarke, either before or after his decease, authorise you to supersede the verdict of a jury, and the sentence of the law.

NOW, my Lord, let me ask you, Has it never occurred to your Grace, while you were withdrawing this desperate wretch from that justice which the laws had awarded, and which the whole people of England demanded against him, that there is another man, who is the favourite of his country, whose pardon would have been accepted with gratitude, whose pardon would have healed all our divisions? Have you quite forgotten that this man

[1] The *Public Advertiser* prints 'insufficient'; the collected edition 'sufficient'. The first is obviously required.

was once your Grace's friend?[1] Or is it to murderers only that you will extend the mercy of the crown?

THESE are questions you will not answer, Nor is it necessary. The character of your private life, and the uniform tenour of your public conduct, is an answer to them all.

JUNIUS.

There were several answers to Junius' attack. Pro Lege et Rege replied in the *Public Advertiser* of 21 March and a letter by Memnon is printed in the *Gentleman's Magazine*, 1769, 139–40. The most substantial was a pamphlet entitled *A vindication of the Duke of Grafton*. Junius assumed that it had been written by Edward Weston, aged 66. Weston had had a long career as a civil servant and government writer and held the patent for publishing the *London Gazette*. In a letter to the *Public Advertiser* of 14 October 1769 Weston denied authorship of the pamphlet.

LETTER IX.

TO HIS GRACE THE DUKE OF GRAFTON.

MY LORD, 10. *April*, 1769.

I HAVE so good an opinion of your Grace's discernment, that when the author of the vindication of your conduct assures us, that he writes from his own mere motion, without the least authority from your Grace, I should be ready enough to believe him, but for one fatal mark, which seems to be fixed upon every measure, in which either your personal or your political character is concerned.—Your first attempt to support Sir William Proctor ended in the election of Mr. Wilkes; the second ensured success to Mr. Glynn. The extraordinary step you took to make Sir James Lowther Lord Paramount of Cumberland, has ruined his interest in that county for ever.[2] The House List of Directors was cursed

[1] John Wilkes. [2] See note on p. 315.

with the concurrence of government;[1] and even the miserable* Dingley could not escape the misfortune of your Grace's protection.[2] With this uniform experience before us, we are authorised to suspect, that when a pretended vindication of your principles and conduct in reality contains the bitterest reflections upon both, it could not have been written without your immediate direction and assistance. The author indeed calls God to witness for him, with all the sincerity, and in the very terms of an Irish evidence, *to the best of his knowledge and belief*. My Lord, you should not encourage these appeals to heaven. The pious Prince, from whom you are supposed to descend, made such frequent use of them in his public declarations, that at last the people also found it necessary to appeal to heaven in their turn. Your administration has driven us into circumstances of equal distress;—beware at least how you remind us of the remedy.[3]

YOU have already much to answer for. You have provoked this unhappy gentleman to play the fool once more in public life, in spite of his years and infirmities, and to shew us, that, as you yourself are a singular instance of youth without spirit, the man who defends you is a no less remarkable example of age without the

* This unfortunate person had been persuaded by the Duke of Grafton to set up for Middlesex, his Grace being determined to seat him in the House of Commons, if he had but a single vote. It happened unluckily, that he could not prevail upon any one freeholder to put him in nomination.

---

[1] The twenty-four Directors of the East India Company were elected annually. The 'House list' was a panel of candidates sponsored by the Directors, sometimes opposed by a rival list supported by the Court of Proprietors. The election in April 1769 was fiercely contested and the *Gentleman's Magazine*, 211, wrote that it had been decided by 'the most extraordinary piece of jockeyship'. Ten candidates from the House list were elected, nine from the Proprietors' list, and five were double-listed. L. S. Sutherland, *The East India Company in eighteenth century politics* (1952), 33–4 and ch. VII.

[2] Charles Dingley, a saw-mill proprietor, took an active part in city politics on behalf of government. On 8 March 1769 he was knocked down at a meeting called to submit a loyal address to the King; a week later he intended to stand against Wilkes at the Middlesex by-election but was prevented from reaching the hustings. His own account is in *Pitt. Corr.* iii. 352.

[3] The first Duke of Grafton was the natural son of Barbara, Duchess of Cleveland, mistress of Charles II. The Fitzroys were therefore descendants of Charles I and the veiled threat is to the scaffold.

benefits of experience. To follow such a writer minutely would, like his own periods, be a labour without end. The subject too has been already discussed, and is sufficiently understood. I cannot help observing, however, that, when the pardon of Mac Quirk was the principal charge against you, it would have been but a decent compliment to your Grace's understanding, to have defended you upon your own principles. What credit does a man deserve, who tells us plainly, that the facts set forth in the King's proclamation were not the true motives on which the pardon was granted, and that he wishes that those chirurgical reports, which first gave occasion to certain doubts in the royal breast, had not been laid before his Majesty. You see, my Lord, that even your friends cannot defend your actions, without changing your principles, nor justify a deliberate measure of government, without contradicting the main assertion on which it was founded.

THE conviction of Mac Quirk had reduced you to a dilemma, in which it was hardly possible for you to reconcile your political interest with your duty. You were obliged either to abandon an active useful partisan, or to protect a felon from public justice. With your usual spirit, you preferred your interest to every other consideration; and with your usual judgment, you founded your determination upon the only motives, which should not have been given to the public.

I HAVE frequently censured Mr. Wilkes's conduct, yet your advocate reproaches me with having devoted myself to the service of sedition. Your Grace can best inform us, for which of Mr. Wilkes's good qualities you first honoured him with your friendship, or how long it was before you discovered those bad ones in him, at which, it seems, your delicacy was offended. Remember, my Lord, that you continued your connexion with Mr. Wilkes long after he had been convicted of those crimes, which you have since taken pains to represent in the blackest colours of blasphemy and treason. How unlucky is it, that the first instance you have given us of a scrupulous regard to decorum is united with the breach of a moral obligation! For my own part, my Lord, I am proud to affirm, that, if I had been weak enough to form such a friendship, I would never have been base enough to betray it. But, let Mr. Wilkes's character be what it may, this at least is certain, that, circumstanced as he is with regard to the public, even his vices plead for him. The people of England have too much discernment to suffer your Grace to take advantage of the failings of a private character, to establish a precedent by which the public liberty is affected, and which you may hereafter, with equal ease and satisfaction, employ to the ruin of the best men in the kingdom.—Content yourself, my Lord, with the many advantages, which the unsullied purity of your own character has given you over your unhappy deserted friend. Avail yourself of all the unforgiving piety of the court you live in, and bless God that you "are not as other men are; extortioners, unjust, adulterers, or even as this publican." In a heart void of feeling, the laws of honour and good faith may be violated with impunity, and there you may safely indulge your genius. But the laws of England shall not be violated, even by your holy zeal to oppress a sinner; and though you have succeeded in making him a tool, you shall not make him the victim of your ambition.

JUNIUS.

Grafton was defended by Volunteer in the Government's Service, whose letters appeared in the *Public Advertiser* on 14, 17, 18, and 20 April 1769. Crito on 20 April attacked Weston: 'You are a privy counsellor in Ireland, writer of the Gazette, comptroller of the salt office, a clerk of the signet, and a pensioner on the Irish establishment: such is the *Volunteer*.' Junius continued the attack on the same lines.

LETTER X.

TO MR. EDWARD WESTON.

SIR, 21. *April*, 1769.

I SAID you were an old man without the benefit of experience. It seems you are also a volunteer with the stipend of twenty commissions; and at a period when all prospects are at an end, you are still looking forward to rewards, which you cannot enjoy. No man is better acquainted with the bounty of government than you are.

——ton impudence,
Temeraire vieillard, aura sa recompense.[1]

BUT I will not descend to an altercation either with the impotence of your age, or the peevishness of your diseases. Your pamphlet, ingenious as it is, has been so little read, that the public cannot know how far you have a right to give me the lye, without the following citation of your own words.

Page 6—'1. THAT he is persuaded that the motives, which he (Mr. Weston) has alledged, must appear fully sufficient, with or without the opinions of the surgeons.

'2. THAT those very motives MUST HAVE BEEN the foundation, on which the Earl of Rochford thought proper, &c.

'3. THAT he CANNOT BUT REGRET that the Earl of Rochford seems to have thought proper to lay the chirurgical reports before the king, in preference to all the other sufficient motives,' &c.

LET the public determine whether this be defending government on their principles or your own.

THE style and language you have adopted are, I confess, not ill suited to the elegance of your own manners, or to the dignity of the cause you have undertaken. Every common dauber writes rascal and villain under his pictures, because the pictures themselves have neither character nor resemblance. But the works of a master require no index. His features and colouring are taken from nature. The impression they make is immediate and uniform; nor is it possible to mistake his characters, whether they represent the treachery of a minister, or the abused simplicity of a king.

JUNIUS.

[1] Corneille, *Le Cid*, Act I, sc. iii.

Political life in the spring of 1769 was dominated by the issues arising from Wilkes's election for Middlesex in March 1768. On 3 February 1769 the House of Commons voted to expel him. He was re-elected on 16 February without opposition. The Commons declared him again expelled and incapable of re-election. Nevertheless, in March, when Charles Dingley failed to make an appearance, Wilkes was again returned unopposed. He was once more expelled. At the subsequent election, on 13 April 1769, Henry Lawes Luttrell stood as the government candidate and polled 296 votes against 1,143 for Wilkes. Two days later the House of Commons, by 197 to 143, declared Luttrell duly elected.

LETTER XI.

TO HIS GRACE THE DUKE OF GRAFTON.

MY LORD, 24. *April*, 1769.

THE system you seemed to have adopted, when Lord Chatham unexpectedly left you at the head of affairs, gave us no promise of that uncommon exertion of vigour, which has since illustrated your character, and distinguished your administration. Far from discovering a spirit bold enough to invade the first rights of the people, and the first principles of the constitution, you were scrupulous of exercising even those powers, with which the executive branch of the legislature is legally invested. We have not yet forgotten how long Mr. Wilkes was suffered to appear at large, nor how long he was at liberty to canvass for the city and county, with all the terrors of an outlawry hanging over him. Our gracious Sovereign has not yet forgotten the extraordinary care you took of his dignity and of the safety of his person, when, at a crisis which courtiers affected to call alarming, you left the metropolis exposed for two nights together, to every species of riot and disorder. The security of the Royal residence from insult was then sufficiently provided for in Mr. Conway's firmness and Lord Weymouth's discretion; while the prime minister of Great Britain, in a rural retirement, and in the arms of faded beauty, had lost all memory of his Sovereign, his country and himself.[1] In these instances you

[1] The Wilkite riots of 28/29 March 1768. It need hardly be said that Conway was notoriously irresolute and Lord Weymouth imprudent. The 'faded beauty' was Nancy Parsons, later Viscountess Maynard. Compassion was not one of Junius' weaknesses.

might have acted with vigour, for you would have had the sanction of the laws to support you. The friends of government might have defended you without shame, and moderate men, who wish well to the peace and good order of society, might have had a pretence for applauding your conduct. But these it seems were not occasions worthy of your Grace's interposition. You reserved the proofs of your intrepid spirit for trials of greater hazard and importance; and now, as if the most disgraceful relaxation of the executive authority had given you a claim of credit to indulge in excesses still more dangerous, you seem determined to compensate amply for your former negligence; and to balance the non-execution of the laws with a breach of the constitution. From one extreme you suddenly start to the other, without leaving, between the weakness and the fury of the passions, one moment's interval for the firmness of the understanding.

THESE observations, general as they are, might easily be extended into a faithful history of your Grace's administration, and perhaps may be the employment of a future hour. But the business of the present moment will not suffer me to look back to a series of events, which cease to be interesting or important, because they are succeeded by a measure so singularly daring, that it excites all our attention, and engrosses all our resentment.

YOUR patronage of Mr. Luttrell has been crowned with success. With this precedent before you, with the principles on which it was established, and with a future house of commons, perhaps less virtuous than the present, every county in England, under the auspices of the treasury, may be represented as completely as the county of Middlesex. Posterity will be indebted to your Grace for not contenting yourself with a temporary expedient, but entailing upon them the immediate blessings of your administration. Boroughs were already too much at the mercy of government. Counties could neither be purchased nor intimidated. But their solemn determined election may be rejected, and the man they detest may be appointed, by another choice, to represent them in parliament. Yet it is admitted, that the sheriffs obeyed the laws and performed their duty*. The return they made must have been legal and valid, or undoubtedly they would have been censured for making it. With every good-natured allowance for your Grace's youth and inexperience, there are some things which you cannot but know. You cannot but know that the right of the freeholders to adhere to their choice (even supposing it improperly exerted) was as clear and indisputable as that of the house of commons to exclude one of their own members?—nor is it possible for you not to see the wide distance there is between the negative power of rejecting one man, and the positive power of appointing another. The right of expulsion, in the most favourable sense, is no more than the custom of parliament. The right of election is the very essence of the constitution. To violate that right, and much more to transfer it to any other set of men, is a step leading immediately to the dissolution of all government. So far forth as it operates, it constitutes a house of commons, which *does not* represent the people. A house of commons so formed would involve a contradiction and the grossest confusion of ideas; but there are some ministers, my Lord, whose views can only be answered by reconciling absurdities, and making the same proposition, which is false and absurd in argument, true in fact.[1]

THIS measure, my Lord, is however attended with one consequence, favourable to the people, which I am persuaded you did not foresee†. While the contest lay between the ministry and Mr. Wilkes, his situation and private character gave you advantages

* Sir Fletcher Norton, when it was proposed to punish the sheriffs, declared in the house of commons that they, in returning Mr. Wilkes, had done no more than their duty.

† The reader is desired to mark this prophecy.

---

[1] Subsequent cases in which the House of Commons clashed with constituents include Daniel O'Connell's return for county Clare in 1828, Lionel Rothschild's return for London in 1847, David Salomons's for Greenwich in 1851, and Charles Bradlaugh for Northampton in 1880. But perhaps the nearest parallel was in 1960 when Anthony Wedgwood Benn attempted to renounce his succession as 2nd Viscount Stansgate and stood the following year as a candidate for the by-election at Bristol South-East. Though he polled 23,275 votes against 10,231 for Malcolm St. Clair, his Conservative opponent was by the Election Court declared duly elected. It is notable that in each case a change in the law followed.

over him, which common candour, if not the memory of your former friendship, should have forbidden you to make use of. To religious men, you had an opportunity of exaggerating the irregularities of his past life;—to moderate men you held forth the pernicious consequences of faction. Men, who with this character, looked no farther than to the object before them, were not dissatisfied at seeing Mr. Wilkes excluded from parliament. You have now taken care to shift the question; or, rather, you have created a new one, in which Mr. Wilkes is no more concerned than any other English gentleman. You have united this country against you on one grand constitutional point, on the decision of which our existence, as a free people, absolutely depends. You have asserted, not in words but in fact, that the representation in parliament does not depend upon the choice of the freeholders. If such a case can possibly happen once, it may happen frequently; it may happen always:—and if three hundred votes, by any mode of reasoning whatsoever, can prevail against twelve hundred, the same reasoning would equally have given Mr. Luttrell his seat with ten votes, or even with one. The consequences of this attack upon the constitution are too plain and palpable not to alarm the dullest apprehension. I trust you will find, that the people of England are neither deficient in spirit nor understanding, though you have treated them, as if they had neither sense to feel, nor spirit to resent. We have reason to thank God and our ancestors, that there never yet was a minister in this country, who could stand the issue of such a conflict; and with every prejudice in favour of your intentions, I see no such abilities in your Grace, as should entitle you to succeed in an enterprize, in which the ablest and basest of your predecessors have found their destruction. You may continue to deceive your gracious master with false representations of the temper and condition of his subjects. You may command a venal vote, because it is the common established appendage of your office. But never hope that the freeholders will make a tame surrender of their rights, or that an English army will join with you in overturning the liberties of their country. They know that their first duty, as citizens, is paramount to all subsequent engagements, nor will they prefer the discipline or even the honours of their profession to those sacred original rights, which belonged to them before they were soldiers, and which they claim and possess as the birth-right of Englishmen.

RETURN, my Lord, before it be too late, to that easy insipid system, which you first set out with. Take back your mistress;*— the name of friend may be fatal to her, for it leads to treachery and persecution. Indulge the people. Attend Newmarket. Mr. Luttrell may again vacate his seat; and Mr. Wilkes, if not persecuted, will soon be forgotten. To be weak and inactive is safer than to be daring and criminal; and wide is the distance between a riot of the populace and a convulsion of the whole kingdom. You may live to make the experiment, but no honest man can wish you should survive it.

JUNIUS.

On 8 May 1769 the House of Commons, after considering a petition from the Middlesex freeholders, confirmed its decision in favour of Luttrell by 221 votes to 152. Wilkes in the meantime was in prison, having been sentenced to one year and ten months on the original charges concerning No. 45 of the *North Briton* and the Essay on Woman.

LETTER XII.

TO HIS GRACE THE DUKE OF GRAFTON.

MY LORD, 30. *May*, 1769.

IF the measures in which you have been most successful, had been supported by any tolerable appearance of argument, I should have thought my time not ill employed, in continuing to examine your conduct as a minister, and stating it fairly to the public. But when I see questions, of the highest national importance, carried as they have been, and the first principles of the constitution openly violated, without argument or decency, I confess,

* The Duke, about this time, had separated himself from Ann Parsons, but proposed to continue united with her, on some platonic terms of friendship, which she rejected with contempt. His baseness to this woman is beyond description or belief.

I give up the cause in despair. The meanest of your predecessors had abilities sufficient to give a colour to their measures. If they invaded the rights of the people, they did not dare to offer a direct insult to their understanding; and, in former times, the most venal parliaments made it a condition, in their bargain with the minister, that he should furnish them with some plausible pretences for selling their country and themselves. You have had the merit of introducing a more compendious system of government and logic. You neither address yourself to the passions, nor to the understanding, but simply to the touch. You apply yourself immediately to the feelings of your friends, who, contrary to the forms of parliament, never enter heartily into a debate, until they have divided.

RELINQUISHING, therefore, all idle views of amendment to your Grace, or of benefit to the public, let me be permitted to consider your character and conduct merely as a subject of curious speculation.—There is something in both, which distinguishes you not only from all other ministers, but all other men. It is not that you do wrong by design, but that you should never do right by mistake. It is not that your indolence and your activity have been equally misapplied, but that the first uniform principle, or, if I may call it the genius of your life, should have carried you through every possible change and contradiction of conduct, without the momentary imputation or colour of a virtue; and that the wildest spirit of inconsistency should never once have betrayed you into a wise or honourable action. This, I own, gives an air of singularity to your fortune, as well as to your disposition. Let us look back together to a scene, in which a mind like yours will find nothing to repent of. Let us try, my Lord, how well you have supported the various relations in which you stood, to your sovereign, your country, your friends, and yourself. Give us, if it be possible, some excuse to posterity, and to ourselves, for submitting to your administration. If not the abilities of a great minister, if not the integrity of a patriot, or the fidelity of a friend, shew us, at least the firmness of a man.—For the sake of your mistress, the lover shall be spared. I will not lead her into public, as you have done, nor will I insult the memory of departed beauty. Her sex, which alone made her amiable in your eyes, makes her respectable in mine.

THE character of the reputed ancestors of some men, has made it possible for their descendants to be vicious in the extreme, without being degenerate. Those of your Grace, for instance, left no distressing examples of virtue, even to their legitimate posterity, and you may look back with pleasure to an illustrious pedigree, in which heraldry has not left a single good quality upon record to insult or upbraid you. You have better proofs of your descent, my Lord, than the register of a marriage, or any troublesome inheritance of reputation. There are some hereditary strokes of character, by which a family may be as clearly distinguished as by the blackest features of the human face. Charles the First lived and died a hypocrite. Charles the Second was a hypocrite of another sort, and should have died upon the same scaffold. At the distance of a century, we see their different characters happily revived, and blended in your Grace. Sullen and severe without religion, profligate without gaiety, you live like Charles the Second, without being an amiable companion, and, for aught I know, may die as his father did, without the reputation of a martyr.

YOU had already taken your degrees with credit in those schools, in which the English nobility are formed to virtue, when you were introduced to Lord Chatham's protection*. From Newmarket, White's, and the opposition, he gave you to the world with an air of popularity, which young men usually set out with, and seldom preserve:—grave and plausible enough to be thought fit for business; too young for treachery; and, in short, a patriot of no unpromising expectations. Lord Chatham was the earliest object of your political wonder and attachment; yet you deserted him, upon the first hopes that offered of an equal share of power with

* To understand these passages, the reader is referred to a noted pamphlet, called, *The history of the minority*.[1]

---

[1] Wade identified this as Charles Townshend's pamphlet of 1764 entitled *A defence of the minority on the question relating to General Warrants*. It is more likely to have been John Almon's pamphlet of 1765, *The history of the late minority*. Grafton served as Secretary of State for the Northern Department in Rockingham's administration, but resigned in April 1766. By 'the favourite' Junius meant Lord Bute.

Lord Rockingham. When the Duke of Cumberland's first negotiation failed, and when the favourite was pushed to the last extremity, you saved him, by joining with an administration, in which Lord Chatham had refused to engage. Still, however, he was your friend, and you are yet to explain to the world, why you consented to act without him, or why, after uniting with Lord Rockingham, you deserted and betrayed him. You complained that no measures were taken to satisfy your patron, and that your friend, Mr. Wilkes, who had suffered so much for the party, had been abandoned to his fate. They have since contributed, not a little, to your present plenitude of power; yet, I think, Lord Chatham has less reason than ever to be satisfied; and as for Mr. Wilkes, it is, perhaps, the greatest misfortune of his life, that you should have so many compensations to make in the closet for your former friendship with him. Your gracious master understands your character, and makes you a persecutor, because you have been a friend.[1]

LORD Chatham formed his last administration upon principles which you certainly concurred in, or you could never have been placed at the head of the treasury. By deserting those principles, and by acting in direct contradiction to them, in which he found you were secretly supported in the closet, you soon forced him to leave you to yourself, and to withdraw his name from an administration, which had been formed on the credit of it. You had then a prospect of friendships better suited to your genius, and more likely to fix your disposition. Marriage is the point on which every rake is stationary at last; and truly, my Lord, you may well be weary of the circuit you have taken, for you have now fairly travelled through every sign in the political zodiac, from the Scorpion, in which you stung Lord Chatham, to the hopes of a Virgin* in the house of Bloomsbury.[2] One would think that you

* His Grace had lately married Miss Wrottesley, niece of the *Good Gertrude, Duchess of Bedford.*

---

[1] Though for polemical reasons Junius harped on Grafton's former friendship with Wilkes, there is no reason to distrust Grafton's statement that they had never been close friends. Grafton, 189.

[2] Grafton married Elizabeth, da. of the Revd. Sir Richard Wrottesley, Bt., on 24 June 1769. His divorced duchess Anne Liddell had married Lord Upper Ossory

had had sufficient experience of the frailty of nuptial engagements, or, at least, that such a friendship as the Duke of Bedford's, might have been secured to you by the auspicious marriage of your late Dutchess with* his nephew. But ties of this tender nature cannot be drawn too close; and it may possibly be a part of the Duke of Bedford's ambition, after making *her* an honest woman, to work a miracle of the same sort upon your Grace. This worthy Nobleman has long dealt in virtue. There has been a large consumption of it in his own family; and, in the way of traffick, I dare say, he has bought and sold more than half the representative integrity of the nation.

In a political view, this union is not imprudent. The favour of princes is a perishable commodity. You have now a strength sufficient to command the closet; and, if it be necessary to betray one friendship more, you may set even Lord Bute at defiance. Mr. Stuart Mackenzie may possibly remember what use the Duke of Bedford usually makes of his power; and our gracious Sovereign, I doubt not, rejoices at this first appearance of union among his servants.[1] His late Majesty, under the happy influence of a family connexion between his ministers, was relieved from the cares of the government.[2] A more active prince may perhaps observe, with suspicion, by what degrees an artful servant grows upon his master, from the first unlimited professions of duty and attachment, to the painful representation of the necessity of the royal service, and soon, in regular progression, to the humble insolence of dictating in all the obsequious forms of peremptory submission. The interval is carefully employed in forming connexions, creating interests, collecting a party, and laying the foundation of double

* Miss Liddell, after her divorce from the Duke, married Lord Upper Ossory.

---

on 26 March. At the time this letter first appeared, Grafton's second marriage had not taken place: Junius' slightly misleading footnote was added when he was preparing the collected edition in 1771.

[1] In May 1765 George Grenville and the Duke of Bedford insisted on the dismissal of James Stuart Mackenzie from his post of Lord Privy Seal of Scotland, fearing Lord Bute's influence.

[2] Henry Pelham and his brother the Duke of Newcastle were First Lords of the Treasury for fifteen years under George II.

marriages; until the deluded prince, who thought he had found a creature prostituted to his service, and insignificant enough to be always dependent upon his pleasure, finds him at last too strong to be commanded, and too formidable to be removed.

YOUR Grace's public conduct, as a minister, is but the counter part of your private history;—the same inconsistency, the same contradictions. In America we trace you, from the first opposition to the Stamp Act, on principles of convenience, to Mr. Pitt's surrender of the right; then forward to Lord Rockingham's surrender of the fact; then back again to Lord Rockingham's declaration of the right; then forward to taxation with Mr. Townshend; and in the last instance, from the gentle Conway's undetermined discretion, to blood and compulsion with the Duke of Bedford: Yet if we may believe the simplicity of Lord North's eloquence, at the opening of next sessions you are once more to be the patron of America. Is this the wisdom of a great minister? or is it the ominous vibration of a pendulum? Had you no opinion of your own, my Lord? or was it the gratification of betraying every party with which you have been united, and of deserting every political principle, in which you had concurred?

YOUR enemies may turn their eyes without regret from this admirable system of provincial government. They will find gratification enough in the survey of your domestic and foreign policy.

IF, instead of disowning Lord Shelburne, the British court had interposed with dignity and firmness, you know, my Lord, that Corsica would never have been invaded. The French saw the weakness of a distracted ministry, and were justified in treating you with contempt.[1] They would probably have yielded in the first instance, rather than hazard a rupture with this country; but,

[1] Shelburne was for spirited resistance to French intervention; the Bedford group was anxious to avoid war. The conduct of affairs was taken out of his hands and, complaining that he was 'left alone and deserted' by all his colleagues, he resigned in October 1768. Lord Fitzmaurice, *Life of William Earl of Shelburne* (2nd edn., 1912) i. 362–88.

being once engaged, they cannot retreat without dishonour. Common sense foresees consequences, which have escaped your Grace's penetration. Either we suffer the French to make an acquisition, the importance of which you have probably no conception of, or we oppose them by an underhand management, which only disgraces us in the eyes of Europe, without answering any purpose of policy or prudence. From secret, indirect assistance, a transition to some more open decisive measures becomes unavoidable; till at last we find ourselves principal in the war, and are obliged to hazard every thing for an object, which might have originally been obtained without expence or danger. I am not versed in the politics of the north; but this I believe is certain, that half the money you have distributed to carry the expulsion of Mr. Wilkes, or even your secretary's share in the last subscription, would have kept the Turks at your devotion. Was it œconomy, my Lord? or did the coy resistance you have constantly met with in the British senate, make you despair of corrupting the Divan? Your friends indeed have the first claim upon your bounty, but if five hundred pounds a year can be spared in pension to Sir John Moore, it would not have disgraced you to have allowed something to the secret service of the public.[1]

YOU will say perhaps that the situation of affairs at home demanded and engrossed the whole of your attention. Here, I confess, you have been active. An amiable, accomplished prince ascends the throne under the happiest of all auspices, the acclamations and united affections of his subjects. The first measures of his reign, and even the odium of a favourite, were not able to shake their attachment. *Your* services, my Lord, have been more successful. Since you were permitted to take the lead, we have seen the

[1] The affairs of Eastern Europe were in turmoil. War had broken out between the Turks and the Russians in October 1768 and the partition of Poland was imminent. France was traditionally an ally of the Ottoman Empire and retained great influence there. I doubt whether Britain could have gained much sway at Constantinople for £500 p.a., but Junius was making a rhetorical rather than a diplomatic point. His admission that he was 'not versed in the politics of the north' may be believed: Turkish affairs were in the province of the Secretary of State for the Southern Department.

Sir John Moore is identified in public letter no. XIV as a 'broken gambler'.

natural effects of a system of government, at once both odious and contemptible. We have seen the laws sometimes scandalously relaxed, sometimes violently stretched beyond their tone. We have seen the person of the Sovereign insulted; and in profound peace, and with an undisputed title, the fidelity of his subjects brought by his own servants into public question*. Without abilities, resolution, or interest, you have done more than Lord Bute could accomplish with all Scotland at his heels.

YOUR Grace, little anxious perhaps either for present or future reputation, will not desire to be handed down in these colours to posterity. You have reason to flatter yourself that the memory of your administration will survive even the forms of a constitution, which our ancestors vainly hoped would be immortal; and as for your personal character, I will not, for the honour of human nature, suppose that you can wish to have it remembered. The condition of the present times is desperate indeed; but there is a debt due to those who come after us, and it is the historian's office to punish, though he cannot correct. I do not give you to posterity as a pattern to imitate, but as an example to deter; and as your conduct comprehends every thing that a wise or honest minister should avoid, I mean to make you a negative instruction to your successors for ever.

JUNIUS.

Junius' strictures on Grafton produced many counter-attacks from ministerial writers. Poetikastos of 31 May 1769 threatened vague but terrible retribution; Anti-Malagrida of 2 June accused him of being Edmund Burke and declared that he was void of every sense of shame. One of the most persistent was Vindex, who made his first appearance in the *Public Advertiser* on 4 May and contributed at least seventeen more letters by the end of the year. It was difficult for Junius to do combat with these opponents without losing that lofty detachment which was so important an ingredient in his assumed character. His solution was to invent Philo Junius as an ally.

* The wise Duke, about this time, exerted all the influence of government to procure addresses to satisfy the King of the fidelity of his subjects. They came in very thick from *Scotland*; but, after the appearance of this letter, we heard no more of them.

LETTER XIII.

ADDRESSED TO THE PRINTER OF THE PUBLIC ADVERTISER.

SIR, 12. *June*, 1769.

THE Duke of Grafton's Friends, not finding it convenient to enter into a contest with *Junius*, are now reduced to the last melancholy resource of defeated argument, the flat general charge of scurrility and falsehood. As for his stile, I shall leave it to the critics. The truth of his facts is of more importance to the public. They are of such a nature, that I think a bare contradiction will have no weight with any man, who judges for himself. Let us take them in the order in which they appear in his last letter.

1. HAVE not the first rights of the people, and the first principles of the constitution been openly invaded, and the very name of an election made ridiculous by the arbitrary appointment of Mr. Luttrell?

2. DID not the Duke of Grafton frequently lead his mistress into public, and even place her at the head of his table, as if he had pulled down an ancient temple of Venus, and could bury all decency and shame under the ruins?—Is this the man who dares to talk of Mr. Wilkes's morals?

3. IS not the character of his presumptive ancestors as strongly marked in him, as if he had descended from them in a direct legitimate line? The idea of his death is only prophetic; and what is prophecy but a narrative preceding the fact!

4. WAS not Lord Chatham the first who raised him to the rank and post of a minister, and the first whom he abandoned?

5. DID he not join with Lord Rockingham, and betray him?

6. WAS he not the bosom friend of Mr. Wilkes, whom he now pursues to destruction?

7. DID he not take his degrees with credit at Newmarket, White's, and the opposition?

8. AFTER deserting Lord Chatham's principles, and sacrificing his friendship, is he not now closely united with a set of men, who, tho' they have occasionally joined with all parties, have in every different situation, and at all times, been equally and constantly detested by this country?

9. HAS not Sir John Moore a pension of five hundred pounds a year?—This may probably be an acquittance of favours upon the turf; but is it possible for a minister to offer a grosser outrage to a nation, which has so very lately cleared away the beggary of the civil list, at the expence of more than half a million?

10. IS there any one mode of thinking or acting with respect to America, which the Duke of Grafton has not successively adopted and abandoned?

11. IS there not a singular mark of shame set upon this man, who has so little delicacy and feeling as to submit to the opprobrium of marrying a near relation of one who had debauched his wife?—In the name of decency, how are these amiable cousins to meet at their uncle's table?—It will be a scene in Œdipus, without the distress.—Is it wealth, or wit, or beauty,—or is the amorous youth in love?

THE rest is notorious. That Corsica has been sacrificed to the French: that in some instances the laws have been scandalously relaxed, and in others daringly violated; and that the King's subjects have been called upon to assure him of their fidelity, in spite of the measures of his servants.

A WRITER, who builds his arguments upon facts such as these, is not easily to be confuted. He is not to be answered by general assertions, or general reproaches. He may want eloquence to amuse and persuade, but, speaking truth, he must always convince.

PHILO JUNIUS.

Old Noll replied on 19 June 1769 to Junius' letter of the 12th. He observed, with some justice, that far from Grafton deserting Chatham it was the other way round, but his reference to Blackstone gave Junius the opportunity for one of his most stinging rejoinders. Old Noll's letter was reprinted in the *Gentleman's Magazine*, 1769, 331–2. Junius presumed that Grafton's defender was Thomas Bradshaw, secretary to the Treasury and the Duke's man-of-business.

LETTER XIV.

ADDRESSED TO THE PRINTER OF THE PUBLIC ADVERTISER.

SIR, 22. *June*, 1769.

THE name of *Old Noll* is destined to be the ruin of the house of Stuart. There is an ominous fatality in it, which even the spurious descendants of the family cannot escape. Oliver Cromwell had the merit of conducting Charles the first to the block. Your correspondent OLD NOLL appears to have the same design upon the Duke of Grafton. His arguments consist better with the title he has assumed, than with the principles he professes; for though he pretends to be an advocate for the Duke, he takes care to give us the best reasons, why his patron should regularly follow the fate of his presumptive ancestor.—Through the whole course of the Duke of Grafton's life, I see a strange endeavour to unite contradictions, which cannot be reconciled. He marries to be divorced;—he keeps a mistress to remind him of conjugal endearments, and he chooses such friends, as it is virtue in him to desert. If it were possible for the genius of that accomplished president, who pronounced sentence upon Charles the first, to be revived in some modern sycophant*, his Grace I doubt not would by sympathy discover him among the dregs of mankind, and take him for a guide in those paths, which naturally conduct a minister to the scaffold.

THE assertion that two-thirds of the nation approve of the *acceptance* of Mr. Luttrell (for even *Old Noll* is too modest to call it an election) can neither be maintained nor confuted by argument.

* It is hardly necessary to remind the reader of the name of *Bradshaw*.

It is a point of fact, on which every English gentleman will determine for himself. As to lawyers, their profession is supported by the indiscriminate defence of right and wrong, and I confess I have not that opinion of their knowledge or integrity, to think it necessary that they should decide for me upon a plain constitutional question.[1] With respect to the appointment of Mr. Luttrell, the chancellor has never yet given any authentic opinion. Sir Fletcher Norton is indeed an honest, a very honest man; and the Attorney General is *ex officio* the guardian of liberty, to take care, I presume, that it shall never break out into a criminal excess. Doctor Blackstone is Solicitor to the Queen.[2] The Doctor recollected that he had a place to preserve, though he forgot that he had a reputation to lose. We have now the good fortune to understand the Doctor's principles, as well as writings. For the defence of truth, of law, and reason, the Doctor's book may be safely consulted; but whoever wishes to cheat a neighbour of his estate, or to rob a country of its rights, need make no scruple of consulting the Doctor himself.

THE example of the English nobility may, for aught I know, sufficiently justify the Duke of Grafton, when he indulges his genius in all the fashionable excesses of the age; yet, considering his rank and station, I think it would do him more honour to be able to deny the fact, than to defend it by such authority. But if vice itself could be excused, there is yet a certain display of it, a certain outrage to decency, and violation of public decorum, which, for the benefit of society, should never be forgiven. It is not that he kept a mistress at home, but that he constantly attended her abroad.—It is not the private indulgence, but the public insult of which I complain. The name of Miss Parsons would hardly have been known, if the First Lord of the Treasury had not led her in

[1] Old Noll had observed that 'the most eminent lawyers in England, with the Chancellor at their head, declared that the accepting of Mr. Luttrell for member was perfectly legal and constitutional'.

[2] Lord Camden was Chancellor, William de Grey Attorney-General, and Sir Fletcher Norton Chief Justice in Eyre. In addition to taking a prominent part in the ministry's prosecution of Wilkes, Sir William Blackstone had also been legal adviser to Sir James Lowther in the dispute with the Duke of Portland over the Cumberland estates.

triumph through the Opera House, even in the presence of the Queen. When we see a man act in this manner, we may admit the shameless depravity of his heart, but what are we to think of his Understanding?

HIS Grace it seems is now to be a regular domestic man, and as an omen of the future delicacy and correctness of his conduct, he marries a first cousin of the man, who had fixed that mark and title of infamy upon him, which, at the same moment, makes a husband unhappy and ridiculous. The ties of consanguinity may possibly preserve him from the same fate a second time, and as to the distress of meeting, I take for granted the venerable uncle of these common cousins has settled the Etiquette in such a manner, that, if a mistake should happen, it may reach no farther than from *Madame ma femme* to *Madame ma cousine*.

THE Duke of Grafton has always some excellent reason for deserting his friends.—The age and incapacity of Lord Chatham; —the debility of Lord Rockingham;—or the infamy of Mr. Wilkes. There was a time indeed when he did not appear to be quite so well acquainted, or so violently offended with the infirmities of his friends. But now I confess they are not ill exchanged for the youthful, vigorous virtue of the Duke of Bedford;—the firmness of General Conway;—the blunt, or if I may call it, the aukward integrity of Mr. Rigby, and the spotless morality of Lord Sandwich.

IF a late pension to a* broken gambler be an act worthy of commendation, the Duke of Grafton's connexions will furnish him with many opportunities of doing praise-worthy actions; and as he himself bears no part of the expence, the generosity of distributing the public money for the support of virtuous families in distress will be an unquestionable proof of his Grace's humanity.

As to public affairs, *Old Noll* is a little tender of descending to particulars. He does not deny that Corsica has been sacrificed to France, and he confesses that, with regard to America, his patron's measures have been subject to some variation; but then he promises

* Sir John Moore.

wonders of stability and firmness for the future. These are mysteries, of which we must not pretend to judge by experience; and truly, I fear we shall perish in the Desart, before we arrive at the Land of Promise. In the regular course of things, the period of the Duke of Grafton's ministerial manhood should now be approaching. The imbecility of his infant state was committed to Lord Chatham. Charles Townshend took some care of his education at that ambiguous age, which lies between the follies of political childhood, and the vices of puberty. The empire of the passions soon succeeded. His earliest principles and connexions were of course forgotten or despised. The company he has lately kept has been of no service to his morals; and, in the conduct of public affairs, we see the character of his time of life strongly distinguished. An obstinate ungovernable self-sufficiency plainly points out to us that state of imperfect maturity, at which the graceful levity of youth is lost, and the solidity of experience not yet acquired. It is possible the young man may in time grow wiser and reform; but, if I understand his disposition, it is not of such corrigible stuff, that we should hope for any amendment in him, before he has accomplished the destruction of this country. Like other rakes, he may perhaps live to see his error, but not untill he has ruined his estate.

PHILO JUNIUS.

LETTER XV.

TO HIS GRACE THE DUKE OF GRAFTON.

MY LORD, 8. *July*, 1769.

IF nature had given you an understanding qualified to keep pace with the wishes and principles of your heart, she would have made you, perhaps, the most formidable minister that ever was employed, under a limited monarch, to accomplish the ruin of a free people. When neither the feelings of shame, the reproaches of conscience, nor the dread of punishment, form any bar to the designs of a minister, the people would have too much reason to lament their condition, if they did not find some resource in the weakness of his understanding. We owe it to the bounty of providence, that the completest depravity of the heart is sometimes strangely united with a confusion of the mind, which counteracts the most favourite principles, and makes the same man treacherous without art, and a hypocrite without deceiving. The measures, for instance, in which your Grace's activity has been chiefly exerted, as they were adopted without skill, should have been conducted with more than common dexterity. But truly, my Lord, the execution has been as gross as the design. By one decisive step, you have defeated all the arts of writing. You have fairly confounded the intrigues of opposition, and silenced the clamours of faction. A dark, ambiguous system might require and furnish the materials of ingenious illustration; and, in doubtful measures, the virulent exaggeration of party must be employed, to rouse and engage the passions of the people. You have now brought the merits of your administration to an issue, on which every Englishman, of the narrowest capacity, may determine for himself. It is not an alarm to the passions, but a calm appeal to the judgement of the people, upon their own most essential interests. A more experienced minister would not have hazarded a direct invasion of the first principles of the constitution, before he had made some progress in subduing the spirit of the people. With such a cause as yours, my Lord, it is not sufficient that you have the court at your devotion, unless you can find means to corrupt or intimidate the jury. The collective body of the people form that jury, and from *their* decision there is but one appeal.

WHETHER you have talents to support you, at a crisis of such difficulty and danger, should long since have been considered. Judging truly of your disposition, you have perhaps mistaken the extent of your capacity. Good faith and folly have so long been received as synonimous terms, that the reverse of the proposition has grown into credit, and every villain fancies himself a man of abilities. It is the apprehension of your friends, my Lord, that you have drawn some hasty conclusion of this sort, and that a partial reliance upon your moral character has betrayed you beyond the depth of your understanding. You have now carried things too far to retreat. You have plainly declared to the people what they are to expect from the continuance of your administration. It is time for your Grace to consider what you also may expect in return from *their* spirit and *their* resentment.

SINCE the accession of our most gracious Sovereign to the throne, we have seen a system of government, which may well be called a reign of experiments.[1] Parties of all denominations have been employed and dismissed. The advice of the ablest men in this country has been repeatedly called for and rejected; and when the Royal displeasure has been signified to a minister, the marks of it have usually been proportioned to his abilities and integrity. The spirit of the FAVOURITE had some apparent influence upon every administration; and every set of ministers preserved an appearance of duration, as long as they submitted to that influence. But there were certain services to be performed for the Favourite's security, or to gratify his resentments, which your predecessors in office had the wisdom or the virtue not to undertake. The moment this refractory spirit was discovered, their disgrace was determined. Lord Chatham, Mr. Grenville, and Lord Rockingham have successively had the honour to be dismissed for prefering their duty, as servants of the public, to those compliances which were expected from their station. A submissive administration was at last gradually collected from the deserters of all parties, interests, and connexions: and nothing remained but to find a leader for these gallant well-disciplined troops. Stand forth, my Lord, for thou art the man. Lord Bute found no resource of dependence or security in the proud, imposing superiority of Lord Chatham's abilities, the shrewd inflexible judgement of Mr. Grenville, nor in the mild but determined integrity of Lord Rockingham. His views and situation required a creature void of all these properties; and he was forced to go through every division, resolution, composition, and refinement of political chemistry, before he happily arrived at the caput mortuum of vitriol in your Grace. Flat and insipid in your retired state, but brought into action you become vitriol again.

[1] There follows a fairly routine attack upon Lord Bute.

Such are the extremes of alternate indolence or fury, which have governed your whole administration. Your circumstances with regard to the people soon becoming desperate, like other honest servants, you determined to involve the best of masters in the same difficulties with yourself. We owe it to your Grace's well-directed labours, that your Sovereign has been persuaded to doubt of the affections of his subjects, and the people to suspect the virtues of their Sovereign, at a time when both were unquestionable. You have degraded the Royal dignity into a base, dishonourable competition with Mr. Wilkes, nor had you abilities to carry even the last contemptible triumph over a private man, without the grossest violation of the fundamental laws of the constitution and rights of the people. But these are rights, my Lord, which you can no more annihilate, than you can the soil to which they are annexed. The question no longer turns upon points of national honour and security abroad, or on the degrees of expedience and propriety of measures at home. It was not inconsistent that you should abandon the cause of liberty in another country,[1] which you had persecuted in your own; and in the common arts of domestic corruption, we miss no part of Sir Robert Walpole's system except his abilities. In this humble imitative line, you might long have proceeded, safe and contemptible. You might probably never have risen to the dignity of being hated, and even have been despised with moderation. But it seems you meant to be distinguished, and, to a mind like yours, there was no other road to fame but by the destruction of a noble fabric, which you thought had been too long the admiration of mankind. The use you have made of the military force introduced an alarming change in the mode of executing the laws. The arbitrary appointment of Mr. Luttrell invades the foundation of the laws themselves, as it manifestly transfers the right of legislation from those whom the people have chosen, to those whom they have rejected. With a succession of such appointments, we may soon see a house of commons collected, in the choice of which the other towns and counties of England will have as little share as the devoted county of Middlesex.

[1] Corsica. Junius believed in making a little go a long way and like a good polemicist was not ashamed to repeat himself.

YET I trust your Grace will find that the people of this country are neither to be intimidated by violent measures, nor deceived by refinements. When they see Mr. Luttrell seated in the house of commons by mere dint of power, and in direct opposition to the choice of a whole county, they will not listen to those subtleties, by which every arbitrary exertion of authority is explained into the law and privilege of parliament. It requires no persuasion of argument, but simply the evidence of the senses, to convince them, that to transfer the right of election from the collective to the representative body of the people, contradicts all those ideas of a house of commons, which they have received from their forefathers, and which they had already, though vainly perhaps, delivered to their children. The principles, on which this violent measure has been defended, have added scorn to injury, and forced us to feel, that we are not only oppressed but insulted.

WITH what force, my Lord, with what protection, are you prepared to meet the united detestation of the people of England? The city of London has given a generous example to the kingdom, in what manner a king of this country ought to be addressed; and I fancy, my Lord, it is not yet in your courage to stand between your Sovereign and the addresses of his subjects.[1] The injuries you have done this country are such as demand not only redress, but vengeance. In vain shall you look for protection to that venal vote, which you have already paid for—another must be purchased; and to save a minister, the house of commons must declare themselves not only independent of their constituents, but the determined enemies of the constitution. Consider, my Lord, whether this be an extremity to which their fears will permit them to advance; or, if *their* protection should fail you, how far you are authorised to rely upon the sincerity of those smiles, which a pious court lavishes without reluctance upon a libertine by profession. It is not indeed the least of the thousand contradictions which attend you, that a man, marked to the world by the grossest violation of all

[1] The liverymen of the city of London petitioned in June 1769, complaining of 'intolerable grievances'. Their petition is printed in the *Gentleman's Magazine*, 1769, 329–30. After some delays the King received it on 5 July, pointedly snubbing the Lord Mayor.

ceremony and decorum, should be the first servant of a court, in which prayers are morality, and kneeling is religion. Trust not too far to appearances, by which your predecessors have been deceived, though they have not been injured. Even the best of princes may at last discover, that this is a contention, in which every thing may be lost, but nothing can be gained; and as you became minister by accident, were adopted without choice, trusted without confidence, and continued without favour, be assured that, whenever an occasion presses, you will be discarded without even the forms of regret. You will then have reason to be thankful, if you are permitted to retire to that seat of learning, which, in contemplation of the system of your life, the comparative purity of your manners with those of their high steward, and a thousand other recommending circumstances, has chosen you to encourage the growing virtue of their youth, and to preside over their education.[1] Whenever the spirit of distributing prebends and bishopricks shall have departed from you, you will find that learned seminary perfectly recovered from the delirium of an installation, and, what in truth it ought to be, once more a peaceful scene of slumber and thoughtless meditation. The venerable tutors of the university will no longer distress your modesty, by proposing you for a pattern to their pupils. The learned dulness of declamation

[1] The University of Cambridge, of which the Duke had been elected Chancellor in November 1768 on the death of the Duke of Newcastle.

But in his comparison Junius made an odd mistake. He was obviously under the impression that the High Steward was Lord Sandwich, opprobriously known as Jemmy Twitcher for his hypocritical denunciation of Wilkes's morals. Junius' editors, not surprisingly, followed him and identified Sandwich as the man intended. But the High Steward was, in fact, the 2nd Earl of Hardwicke, a worthy and blameless character—'a bookish man, conversant only with parsons', according to Horace Walpole.

The contest between Hardwicke and Sandwich in 1764 for the high stewardship became the occasion of a superb university convulsion. Walpole described Sandwich as making the greatest possible exertions: 'There was not a corner of England, nay not the Isle of Man, unransacked by him for votes. He ferreted out the mad, the lame, the diseased, from their poor retreats and imported them into the University.' The outcome was a dead heat which, on appeal, was decided in favour of Hardwicke, who held the post until his death in 1790. To compound the confusion *GEC* muddles the contest with that in 1749 when the 1st Earl of Hardwicke was returned unopposed.

Though the point is not of great importance, it does suggest that Junius was not a Cambridge man. Lord Sandwich had taken a prominent part in the installation of the Duke a week before this letter was printed, and that may have caused the confusion.

will be silent; and even the venal muse, though happiest in fiction, will forget your virtues.[1] Yet, for the benefit of the succeeding age, I could wish that your retreat might be deferred, until your morals shall happily be ripened to that maturity of corruption, at which the worst examples cease to be contagious.

JUNIUS.

In June 1769 a ministerial writer published *The case of the election for the county of Middlesex considered*, in which he argued that the House of Commons had undisputed jurisdiction over its own membership and over the qualifications of electors and elected. To admit that right but to deny that the House had the power to declare an expelled member incapable of re-election would be absurd since it would deprive the House of the means of enforcing its decision. 'Incapacity', asserted the writer, 'is the necessary effect of expulsion.' The votes of those freeholders who polled for Wilkes were therefore thrown away and Henry Lawes Luttrell rightly declared elected. The pamphlet was generally attributed to Jeremiah Dyson, a Lord of the Treasury, though the British Library catalogue also attributes it to Sir William Blackstone.

LETTER XVI.

TO THE PRINTER OF THE PUBLIC ADVERTISER.

SIR, 19. *July*, 1769.

A GREAT deal of useless argument might have been saved, in the political contest, which has arisen from the expulsion of Mr. Wilkes, and the subsequent appointment of Mr. Luttrell, if the question had been once stated with precision, to the satisfaction of each party, and clearly understood by them both. But in this, as

[1] The installation of Grafton as Chancellor on 1 July 1769 was a grand affair, attended by the Archbishop of Canterbury, the Duke of Bedford, and many peers. The new chancellor was bombarded with Latin and English verses in his honour. Thomas Gray, appointed Professor of Modern History the previous year, responded with an 'Ode to Music'. Although claiming that the University 'no vulgar praise, no venal incense flings', he was not above a gentle reminder:

Thy liberal heart, thy judging eye,
The flower unheeded shall descry,
And bid it round Heaven's altars shed
The fragrance of its blushing head.

in almost every other dispute, it usually happens that much time is lost in referring to a multitude of cases and precedents, which prove nothing to the purpose, or in maintaining propositions, which are either not disputed, or, whether they be admitted or denied, are entirely indifferent as to the matter in debate; until at last the mind, perplexed and confounded with the endless subtleties of controversy, loses sight of the main question, and never arrives at truth. Both parties in the dispute are apt enough to practise these dishonest artifices. The man, who is conscious of the weakness of his cause, is interested in concealing it: and, on the other side, it is not uncommon to see a good cause mangled by advocates, who do not know the real strength of it.

I SHOULD be glad to know, for instance, to what purpose, in the present case, so many precedents have been produced to prove, that the house of commons have a right to expel one of their own members; that it belongs to them to judge of the validity of elections; or that the law of parliament is part of the law of the land*? After all these propositions are admitted, Mr. Luttrell's right to his seat will continue to be just as disputable as it was before. Not one of them is at present in agitation. Let it be admitted that the house of commons were authorised to expel Mr. Wilkes; that they are the proper court to judge of elections, and that the law of parliament is binding upon the people; still it remains to be enquired whether the house, by their resolution in favour of Mr. Luttrell, have or have not truly declared that law. To facilitate this enquiry, I would have the question cleared of all foreign or indifferent matter. The following state of it will probably be thought a fair one by both parties; and then I imagine there is no gentleman in this country, who will not be capable of forming a judicious and true opinion upon it. I take the question to be strictly this: "Whether or no it be the known, established law of parliament, that the expulsion of a member of the house of commons of itself creates in him such an incapacity to be re-elected, that, at a subsequent

* The reader will observe that these admissions are made, not as of truths unquestionable, but for the sake of argument, and in order to bring the real question to issue.

election, any votes given to him are null and void, and that any other candidate, who, except the person expelled, has the greatest number of votes, ought to be the sitting member."

TO prove that the affirmative is the law of parliament, I apprehend it is not sufficient for the present house of commons to declare it to be so. We may shut our eyes indeed to the dangerous consequences of suffering one branch of the legislature to declare new laws, without argument or example, and it may perhaps be prudent enough to submit to authority; but a mere assertion will never convince, much less will it be thought reasonable to prove the right by the fact itself. The ministry have not yet pretended to such a tyranny over our minds. To support the affirmative fairly, it will either be necessary to produce some statute, in which that positive provision shall have been made, that specific disability clearly created, and the consequences of it declared; or, if there be no such statute, the custom of parliament must then be referred to, and some case or cases*, strictly in point, must be produced, with the decision of the court upon them; for I readily admit that the custom of parliament, once clearly proved, is equally binding with the common and statute law.

THE consideration of what may be reasonable or unreasonable makes no part of this question. We are enquiring what the law is, not what it ought to be. Reason may be applied to shew the impropriety or expedience of a law, but we must have either statute or precedent to prove the existence of it. At the same time I do not mean to admit that the late resolution of the house of commons is defensible on general principles of reason, any more than in law. This is not the hinge on which the debate turns.

SUPPOSING therefore that I have laid down an accurate state of the question, I will venture to affirm, 1st, That there is no statute, existing by which that specific disability, which we speak of, is created. If there be, let it be produced. The argument will then be at an end.

* Precedents, in opposition to principles, have little weight with *Junius*; but he thought it necessary to meet the ministry, upon their own ground.

2dly, THAT there is no precedent in all the proceedings of the house of commons which comes entirely home to the present case, viz. "where an expelled member has been returned again, and another candidate, with an inferior number of votes, has been declared the sitting member." If there be such a precedent, let it be given to us plainly, and I am sure it will have more weight than all the cunning arguments which have been drawn from inferences and probabilities.

THE ministry, in that laborious pamphlet which I presume contains the whole strength of the party, have declared*, "That Mr. Walpole's was the first and only instance, in which the electors of any county or borough had returned a person expelled to serve in the same parliament." It is not possible to conceive a case more exactly in point.[1] Mr. Walpole was expelled, and, having a majority of votes at the next election, was returned again. The friends of Mr. Taylor, a candidate set up by the ministry, petitioned the house that he might be the sitting member. Thus far the circumstances tally exactly, except that our house of commons saved Mr. Luttrell the trouble of petitioning. The point of law however was the same. It came regularly before the house, and it was their business to determine upon it. They did determine it, for they declared Mr. Taylor *not duly elected.* If it be said that they meant this resolution as matter of favour and indulgence to the borough, which had retorted Mr. Walpole upon them, in order that the burgesses, knowing what the law was, might correct their error, I answer,

I. THAT it is a strange way of arguing to oppose a supposition, which no man can prove, to a fact which proves itself.

II. THAT if this were the intention of the house of commons, it must have defeated itself. The burgesses of Lynn could never have known their error, much less could they have corrected it by any

* *Case of the Middlesex election considered*, page 38.

[1] The decisions of the House of Commons in the case of Samuel Taylor and Robert Walpole are in *CJ* xvii. 29–31, 128. The election of 11 February 1712 for King's Lynn was declared void and a new election held, at which John Turner was returned.

instruction they received from the proceedings of the house of commons. They might perhaps have foreseen, that, if they returned Mr. Walpole again, he would again be rejected; but they never could infer, from a resolution by which the candidate with the fewest votes was declared *not duly elected*, that, at a future election, and in similar circumstances, the house of commons would reverse their resolution, and receive the same candidate as duly elected, whom they had before rejected.

THIS indeed would have been a most extraordinary way of declaring the law of parliament, and what I presume no man, whose understanding is not at cross purposes with itself, could possibly understand.

IF, in a case of this importance, I thought myself at liberty to argue from suppositions rather than from facts, I think the probability, in this instance, is directly the reverse of what the ministry affirm; and that it is much more likely that the house of commons at that time would rather have strained a point in favour of Mr. Taylor, than that they would have violated the law of parliament, and robbed Mr. Taylor of a right legally vested in him, to gratify a refractory borough, which, in defiance of them, had returned a person branded with the strongest mark of the displeasure of the house.

BUT really, Sir, this way of talking, for I cannot call it argument, is a mockery of the common understanding of the nation, too gross to be endured. Our dearest interests are at stake. An attempt has been made, not merely to rob a single county of its rights, but, by inevitable consequence, to alter the constitution of the house of commons. This fatal attempt has succeeded, and stands as a precedent recorded for ever. If the ministry are unable to defend their cause by fair argument founded on facts, let them spare us at least the mortification of being amused and deluded like children. I believe there is yet a spirit of resistance in this country, which will not submit to be oppressed; but I am sure there is a fund of good sense in this country, which cannot be deceived.

JUNIUS.

Sir William Blackstone, Solicitor-General to the Queen, published a defence of his conduct under the title *A speech without doors upon the subject of a vote given on the 9th. day of May 1769*. He maintained that 'the principle upon which I voted was this, that in all cases of election by a majority of votes, wherever the candidate for whom the most votes are given, appears to have been, at the time of the election, under a *known legal incapacity*, the person who had the next greatest number of votes ought to be considered as the person duly elected'.

The letter by G. A. appeared in the *Public Advertiser* of 28 July. It asked why the existing House of Commons could not establish precedents: 'Are things wrong merely because they were never done before?' For the Aylesbury election case of 1703–4, see *CJ* xiv.

LETTER XVII.

TO THE PRINTER OF THE PUBLIC ADVERTISER.

SIR, 1. *August*, 1769.

IT will not be necessary for *Junius* to take the trouble of answering your correspondent G. A. or the quotation from a speech without doors, published in your paper of the 28th of last month. The speech appeared before *Junius*'s letter, and as the author seems to consider the great proposition, on which all his argument depends, viz. *that Mr. Wilkes was under that known legal incapacity, of which Junius speaks* as a point granted, his speech is, in no shape, an answer to *Junius*, for this is the very question in debate.

As to G. A. I observe first, that if he did not admit *Junius*'s state of the question, he should have shewn the fallacy of it, or given us a more exact one;—secondly, that, considering the many hours and days, which the ministry and their advocates have wasted, in public debate, in compiling large quartos, and collecting innumerable precedents, expressly to prove that the late proceedings of the house of commons are warranted by the law, custom, and practice of parliament, it is rather an extraordinary supposition, to be made by one of their own party even for the sake of argument, *that no such statute, no such custom of parliament, no such case in point can be produced.* G. A. may however make the supposition with safety. It contains nothing, but literally the fact, except that there is a case exactly in point, with a decision of the house, diametrically opposite to that which the present house of commons came to in favour of Mr. Luttrell.

THE ministry now begin to be ashamed of the weakness of their cause, and, as it usually happens with falsehood, are driven to the necessity of shifting their ground, and changing their whole defence. At first we were told that nothing could be clearer than that the proceedings of the house of commons were justified by the known law and uniform custom of parliament. But now it seems, if there be no law, the house of commons have a right to make one, and if there be no precedent, they have a right to create the first; —for this I presume is the amount of the questions proposed to *Junius*. If your correspondent had been at all versed in the law of parliament, or generally in the laws of this country, he would have seen that this defence is as weak and false as the former.

THE privileges of either house of parliament, it is true, are indefinite, that is, they have not been described or laid down in any one code or declaration whatsoever; but whenever a question of privilege has arisen, it has invariably been disputed or maintained upon the footing of precedents alone*. In the course of the proceedings upon the Aylsbury election, the house of lords resolved, "That neither house of parliament had any power, by any vote or declaration, to create to themselves any new privilege that was not warranted by the known laws and customs of parliament." And to this rule the house of commons, though otherwise they had acted in a very arbitrary manner, gave their assent, for they affirmed that they had guided themselves by it, in asserting their privileges.—Now, Sir, if this be true with respect to matters of privilege, in which the house of commons, individually and as a body, are principally concerned, how much more strongly will it hold against any pretended power in that house, to create or de-

* This is still meeting the ministry upon their own ground; for, in truth, no precedents will support either natural injustice, or violation of positive right.

clare a new law, by which not only the rights of the house over their own member, and those of the member himself are concluded, but also those of a third and separate party, I mean the freeholders of the kingdom. To do justice to the ministry, they have not yet pretended that any one or any two of the three estates have power to make a new law, without the concurrence of the third. They know that a man who maintains such a doctrine, is liable, by statute, to the heaviest penalties. They do not acknowledge that the house of commons have assumed a *new* privilege, or declared a *new* law.—On the contrary, they affirm that their proceedings have been strictly conformable to and founded upon the ancient law and custom of parliament. Thus therefore the question returns to the point, at which *Junius* had fixed it, viz. *Whether or no this be the law of parliament.* If it be not, the house of commons had no legal authority to establish the precedent; and the precedent itself is a mere fact, without any proof of right whatsoever.

YOUR correspondent concludes with a question of the simplest nature: *Must a thing be wrong, because it has never been done before?* No. But admitting it were proper to be done, that alone does not convey an authority to do it. As to the present case, I hope I shall never see the time, when not only a single person, but a whole county, and in effect the entire collective body of the people may again be robbed of their birthright by a vote of the house of commons. But if, for reasons which I am unable to comprehend, it be necessary to trust that house with a power so exorbitant and so unconstitutional, at least let it be given to them by an act of the legislature.

PHILO JUNIUS.

It is not clear whether Junius reprinted the next letter out of its chronological order inadvertently or because it enabled the argument over the Wilkes case to proceed more coherently. Two further pamphlets devoted to the issue were *The question stated* by Sir William Meredith for the opposition and *An answer to the question stated.* The latter was attributed by Junius to Blackstone; the *Monthly Review*, 1769, ii. 77 concurs, though the British Library catalogue attributes it to the Revd. Nathaniel Forster.

LETTER XVIII.

TO SIR WILLIAM BLACKSTONE, SOLICITOR GENERAL TO HER MAJESTY.

SIR, 29. *July*, 1769.

I SHALL make you no apology for considering a certain pamphlet, in which your late conduct is defended, as written by yourself. The personal interest, the personal resentments, and above all, that wounded spirit, unaccustomed to reproach, and I hope not frequently conscious of deserving it, are signals which betray the author to us as plainly as if your name were in the title-page. You appeal to the public in defence of your reputation. We hold it, Sir, that an injury offered to an individual is interesting to society. On this principle the people of England made common cause with Mr. Wilkes. On this principle, if *you* are injured, they will join in your resentment. I shall not follow you through the insipid form of a third person, but address myself to you directly.

YOU seem to think the channel of a pamphlet more respectable and better suited to the dignity of your cause, than that of a news-paper. Be it so. Yet if news papers are scurrilous, you must confess they are impartial. They give us, without any apparent preference, the wit and argument of the ministry, as well as the abusive dulness of the opposition. The scales are equally poised. It is not the printer's fault if the greater weight inclines the balance.

YOUR pamphlet then is divided into an attack upon Mr. Grenville's character, and a defence of your own. It would have been more consistent perhaps with your professed intention, to have confined yourself to the last. But anger has some claim to indulgence, and railing is usually a relief to the mind. I hope you have found benefit from the experiment. It is not my design to enter into a formal vindication of Mr. Grenville, upon his own principles. I have neither the honour of being personally known to him, nor do I pretend to be completely master of all the facts. I need not run the risque of doing an injustice to his opinions, or to his conduct, when your pamphlet alone carries, upon the face of it, a full vindication of both.

YOUR first reflection, is, that Mr. Grenville* was, of all men, the person, who should not have complained of inconsistence with regard to Mr. Wilkes. This, Sir, is either an unmeaning sneer, a peevish expression of resentment, or, if it means any thing, you plainly beg the question; for whether his parliamentary conduct with regard to Mr. Wilkes has or has not been inconsistent, remains yet to be proved. But it seems he received upon the spot a sufficient chastisement for exercising *so unfairly* his talents of misrepresentation. You are a lawyer, Sir, and know better than I do, upon what particular occasions a talent for misrepresentation may be *fairly* exerted; but to punish a man a second time, when he has been once sufficiently chastised, is rather too severe. It is not in the laws of England; it is not in your own commentaries, nor is it yet, I believe in the new law you have revealed to the house of commons. I hope this doctrine has no existence but in your own heart. After all, Sir, if you had consulted that sober discretion, which you seem to oppose with triumph to the honest jollity of a tavern, it might have occurred to you that, although you could have succeeded in fixing a charge of inconsistence upon Mr. Grenville, it would not have tended in any shape to exculpate yourself.

YOUR next insinuation, that Sir William Meredith had hastily adopted the false glosses of his new ally, is of the same sort with the first. It conveys a sneer as little worthy of the gravity of your character, as it is useless to your defence. It is of little moment to the public to enquire, by whom the charge was conceived, or by whom it was adopted. The only question we ask is, whether or no it be true. The remainder of your reflections upon Mr. Grenville's conduct destroy themselves. He could not possibly come prepared to traduce your integrity to the house. He could not foresee that you would even speak upon the question, much less could he foresee that you would maintain a direct contradiction of that doctrine,

* Mr. Grenville had quoted a passage from the Doctor's excellent commentaries, which directly contradicted the doctrine maintained by the Doctor in the house of commons.

which you had solemnly, disinterestedly, and upon soberest reflection delivered to the public. He came armed indeed with what he thought a respectable authority, to support what he was convinced was the cause of truth, and I doubt not he intended to give you, in the course of the debate, an honourable and public testimony of his esteem. Thinking highly of his abilities, I cannot however allow him the gift of divination. As to what you are pleased to call a plan coolly formed to impose upon the house of commons, and his producing it without provocation at midnight, I consider it as the language of pique and invective, therefore unworthy of regard. But, Sir, I am sensible I have followed your example too long, and wandered from the point.

THE quotation from your commentaries is matter of record. It can neither be *altered* by your friends, nor misrepresented by your enemies; and I am willing to take your own word for what you have said in the house of commons. If there be a real difference between what you have written and what you have spoken, you confess that your book ought to be the standard. Now, Sir, if words mean any thing, I apprehend that, when a long enumeration of disqualifications (whether by statute or the custom of parliament) concludes with these general comprehensive words, "but subject to these restrictions and disqualifications, *every* subject of the realm is eligible of common right," a reader of plain understanding, must of course rest satisfied that no species of disqualification whatsoever had been omitted. The known character of the author, and the apparent accuracy with which the whole work is compiled, would confirm him in his opinion; nor could he possibly form any other judgment, without looking upon your commentaries in the same light in which you consider those penal laws, which though not repealed, are fallen into disuse, and are now in effect A SNARE TO THE UNWARY*.

YOU tell us indeed that it was not part of your plan to specify any temporary incapacity, and that you could not, without a spirit of prophecy, have specified the disability of a private individual,

* If, in stating the law upon any point, a judge deliberately affirms that he has included *every* case, and it should appear that he has purposely omitted a material case, he does in effect lay a snare for the unwary.

subsequent to the period at which you wrote. What your plan was I know not; but what it should have been, in order to complete the work you have given us, is by no means difficult to determine. The incapacity, which you call temporary, may continue seven years; and though you might not have foreseen the particular case of Mr. Wilkes, you might and should have foreseen the possibility of *such* a case, and told us how far the house of commons were authorized to proceed in it by the law and custom of parliament. The freeholders of Middlesex would then have known what they had to trust to, and would never have returned Mr. Wilkes, when colonel Luttrell was a candidate against him. They would have chosen some indifferent person, rather than submit to be represented by the object of their contempt and detestation.

YOUR attempt to distinguish between disabilities, which affect whole classes of men, and those which affect individuals only, is really unworthy of your understanding. Your commentaries had taught me that, although the instance, in which a penal law is exerted, be particular, the laws themselves are general. They are made for the benefit and instruction of the public, though the penalty falls only upon an individual. You cannot but know, Sir, that what was Mr. Wilkes's case yesterday may be your's or mine tomorrow, and that consequently the common right of every subject of the realm is invaded by it. Professing therefore to treat of the constitution of the house of commons, and of the laws and customs relative to that constitution, you certainly were guilty of a most unpardonable omission in taking no notice of a right and privilege of the house, more extraordinary and more arbitrary than all the others they possess put together. If the expulsion of a member, not under any legal disability, of itself creates in him an incapacity to be elected, I see a ready way marked out, by which the majority may at any time remove the honestest and ablest men who happen to be in opposition to them. To say that they *will not* make this extravagant use of their power, would be a language unfit for a man so learned in the laws as you are. By your doctrine, Sir, they *have* the power, and laws you know are intended to guard against what men *may* do, not to trust to what they *will* do.

UPON the whole, Sir, the charge against you is of a plain, simple nature: It appears even upon the face of your own pamphlet. On the contrary, your justification of yourself is full of subtlety and refinement, and in some places not very intelligible. If I were personally your enemy, I should dwell, with a malignant pleasure, upon those great and useful qualifications, which you certainly possess, and by which you once acquired, though they could not preserve to you the respect and esteem of your country. I should enumerate the honours you have lost, and the virtues you have disgraced: but having no private resentments to gratify, I think it sufficient to have given my opinion of your public conduct, leaving the punishment it deserves to your closet and to yourself.

JUNIUS.

Publius' letter appeared in the *St. James's Chronicle* for 8/10 August 1769 and accused Junius of disingenuousness: 'Did you expect to find . . . a list of all such possible or imaginable cases as might call for the severest inflictions from the authority of the House?' He afforded Philo Junius the chance to draw his brilliant little sketch of Blackstone's discomfiture.

Philo Junius appears to have confused the newspaper in which Publius' letter was printed. When editing the correspondence for the 1772 edition Junius decided, rather incongruously, to attach the long postscript added by Blackstone to his pamphlet in reply to Junius' letter of 19 July.

LETTER XIX.

ADDRESSED TO THE PRINTER OF THE PUBLIC ADVERTISER.

SIR, 14. *August*, 1769.

A CORRESPONDENT of the St. James's Evening Post first wilfully misunderstands Junius, then censures him for a bad reasoner. Junius does not say that it was incumbent upon Doctor Blackstone to foresee and state the crimes, for which Mr. Wilkes was expelled. If, by a spirit of prophecy, he had even done so, it would have been nothing to the purpose. The question is, not for what particular offences a person may be expelled, but generally whether by the law of parliament expulsion alone creates a disqualification. If the affirmative be the law of parliament, Doctor Blackstone might and should have told us so. The question is not confined to this or that particular person, but forms one great general branch of disqualification, too important in itself, and too extensive in its consequences, to be omitted in an accurate work expressly treating of the law of parliament.

THE truth of the matter is evidently this. Doctor Blackstone, while he was speaking in the house of commons, never once thought of his Commentaries, until the contradiction was unexpectedly urged, and stared him in the face. Instead of defending himself upon the spot, he sunk under the charge, in an agony of confusion and despair. It is well known that there was a pause of some minutes in the house, from a general expectation that the Doctor would say something in his own defence; but it seems, his faculties were too much overpowered to think of those subtleties and refinements, which have since occurred to him. It was then Mr. Grenville received that severe chastisement, which the Doctor mentions with so much triumph. *I wish the honourable gentleman, instead of shaking his head, would shake a good argument out of it.* If to the elegance, novelty, and bitterness of this ingenious sarcasm, we add the natural melody of the amiable Sir Fletcher Norton's pipe, we shall not be surprised that Mr. Grenville was unable to make him any reply.

As to the Doctor, I would recommend it to him to be quiet. If not, he may perhaps hear again from Junius himself.

PHILO JUNIUS.

Postscript to a Pamphlet intitled, 'An Answer to the Question stated.' Supposed to be written by Dr. Blackstone, Solicitor to the Queen, in answer to Junius's Letter.

SINCE these papers were sent to the press, a writer in the public papers, who subscribes himself Junius, has made a feint of bringing this question to a short issue. Though the foregoing observations contain in my opinion, at least, a full refutation of all that this writer has offered, I shall, however, bestow a very few words upon him. It will cost me very little trouble to unravel and expose the sophistry of his argument.

'I TAKE the question, says he, to be strictly this: Whether or no it be the known established law of parliament, that the expulsion of a member of the house of commons of itself creates in him such an incapacity to be re-elected, that, at a subsequent election, any votes given to him are null and void; and that any other candidate, who, except the person expelled, has the greatest number of votes, ought to be the sitting member.'

WAVING for the present any objection I may have to this state of the question, I shall venture to meet our champion upon his own ground; and attempt to support the affirmative of it, in one of the two ways, by which he says it can be alone fairly supported. 'If there be no statute, says he, in which the specific disability is clearly created, &c. (and we acknowledge there is none) the custom of parliament must then be referred to, and some case or cases, strictly in point, must be produced, with the decision of the court upon them.' Now I assert, that this has been done. Mr. Walpole's case is strictly in point, to prove that expulsion creates absolute incapacity of being re-elected. This was the clear decision of the house upon it; and was a full declaration, that incapacity was the necessary consequence of expulsion. The law was as clearly and firmly fixed by this resolution, and is as binding in every subsequent case of expulsion, as if it had been declared by an express statute, "That a member expelled by a resolution of the house of commons shall be deemed incapable of being re-elected." Whatever doubt then there might have been of the law before Mr. Walpole's case, with respect to the full operation of a vote of expulsion, there can be none now. The decision of the house upon this case is strictly in point to prove, that expulsion creates absolute incapacity in law of being re-elected.

BUT incapacity in law in this instance must have the same operation and effect with incapacity in law in every other instance.

Now, incapacity of being re-elected implies in its very terms, that any votes given to the incapable person, at a subsequent election, are null and void. This is its necessary operation, or it has no operation at all. It is *vox et prœterea nihil.*[1] We can no more be called upon to prove this proposition, than we can to prove that a dead man is not alive, or that twice two are four. When the terms are understood, the proposition is self-evident.

LASTLY, It is in all cases of election, the known and established law of the land, grounded upon the clearest principles of reason and common sense, that if the votes given to one candidate are null and void, they cannot be opposed to the votes given to another candidate. They cannot affect the votes of such candidate at all. As they have, on the one hand, no positive quality to add or establish, so have they, on the other hand, no negative one to substract or destroy. They are, in a word, a mere non-entity. Such was the determination of the house of commons in the Malden and Bedford elections; cases strictly in point to the present question, as far as they are meant to be in point.[2] And to say, that they are not in point, in all circumstances, in those particularly which are independent of the proposition which they are quoted to prove, is to say no more than that Malden is not Middlesex, nor Serjeant Comyns Mr. Wilkes.

LET us see then how our proof stands. Expulsion creates incapacity; incapacity annihilates any votes given to the incapable person. The votes given to the qualified candidate stand upon their own bottom, firm, and untouched, and can alone have effect. This, one would think, would be sufficient. But we are stopped short, and told, that none of our precedents come home to the present case; and are challenged to produce "a precedent in all the proceedings

[1] i.e. a voice and nothing more.

[2] In 1715 the House of Commons found against John Comyns, member for Maldon, on the grounds that he had refused to take the oath that he possessed the necessary qualifications and seated Samuel Tufnell who had received fewer votes; *CJ* xviii. 24, 126–9. In April 1728 it considered a disputed election for Bedford, found Samuel Ongley 'incapable of claiming to sit' because of a place in the Customs, and awarded the seat to John Orlebar; *CJ* xxi. 34, 50, 138–9.

of the house of commons that does come home to it, viz. *where an expelled member has been returned again, and another candidate, with an inferior number of votes, has been declared the sitting member.*"

INSTEAD of a precedent, I will beg leave to put a case; which, I fancy, will be quite as decisive to the present point. Suppose another Sacheverel, (and every party must have its Sacheverel) should, at some future election, take it into his head to offer himself a candidate for the county of Middlesex.[1] He is opposed by a candidate, whose coat is of a different colour; but however of a very good colour. The divine has an indisputable majority; nay, the poor layman is absolutely distanced. The sheriff, after having had his conscience well informed by the reverend casuist, returns him, as he supposes, duly elected. The whole house is in an uproar, at the apprehension of so strange an appearance amongst them. A motion however is at length made, that the person was incapable of being elected, that his election therefore is null and void, and that his competitor ought to have been returned. No, says a great orator, First, shew me your law for this proceeding. "Either produce me a statute, in which the specific disability of a clergyman is created; or, produce me a precedent *where a clergyman has been returned, and another candidate, with an inferior number of votes, has been declared the sitting member.*" No such statute, no such precedent to be found. What answer then is to be given to this demand? The very same answer which I will give to that of Junius: That there is more than one precedent in the proceedings of the house—"where an incapable person has been returned, and another candidate, with an inferior number of votes, has been declared the sitting member; and that this is the known and established law, in all cases of incapacity, from whatever cause it may arise."

I SHALL now therefore beg leave to make a slight amendment

[1] Dr. Henry Sacheverell, a Tory clergyman, was impeached in 1710 for a sermon attacking the practice of occasional conformity. Blackstone introduced him here merely as a dramatic illustration of the simple point that there was no statute disqualifying clerics from membership of the House of Commons. After the return of John Horne Tooke for Old Sarum in 1801, the matter was cleared up by *An act to remove doubts respecting the eligibility of persons in Holy Orders to sit in the House of Commons*, 41 George III, c. 63.

to Junius's state of the question, the affirmative of which will then stand thus:

"IT is the known and established law of parliament, that the expulsion of any member of the house of commons creates in him an incapacity of being re-elected; that any votes given to him at a subsequent election are, in consequence of such incapacity, null and void; and that any other candidate, who, except the person rendered incapable, has the greatest number of votes, ought to be the sitting member."

BUT our business is not yet quite finished. Mr. Walpole's case must have a re-hearing. "It is not possible, says this writer, to conceive a case more exactly in point. Mr. Walpole was expelled, and having a majority of votes at the next election, was returned again. The friends of Mr. Taylor, a candidate set up by the ministry, petitioned the house that he might be the sitting member. Thus far the circumstances tally exactly, except that our house of commons saved Mr. Luttrell the trouble of petitioning. The point of law, however, was the same. It came regularly before the house, and it was their business to determine upon it. They did determine it; for they declared Mr. Taylor *not duly elected*."

INSTEAD of examining the justness of this representation, I shall beg leave to oppose against it my own view of this case, in as plain a manner and as few words as I am able.

IT was the known and established law of parliament, when the charge against Mr. Walpole came before the house of commons, that they had power to expel, to disable, and to render incapable for offences. In virtue of this power they expelled him.

HAD they, in the very vote of expulsion, adjudged him, in terms, to be incapable of being re-elected, there must have been at once an end with him. But though the right of the house, both to expel, and adjudge incapable, was clear and indubitable, it does not appear to me, that the full operation and effect of a vote of expulsion singly was so. The law in this case had never been expressly declared. There had been no event to call up such a declaration. I trouble not myself with the grammatical meaning of the word expulsion. I regard only its legal meaning. This was not, as I think, precisely fixed. The house thought proper to fix it, and explicitly to declare the full consequences of their former vote, before they suffered these consequences to take effect. And in this proceeding they acted upon the most liberal and solid principles of equity, justice and law. What then did the burgesses of Lynn collect from the second vote? Their subsequent conduct will tell us: it will with certainty tell us, that they considered it as decisive against Mr. Walpole; it will also, with equal certainty, tell us, that, upon supposition that the law of election stood then, as it does now, and that they knew it to stand thus, they inferred, "that at a future election, and in case of a similar return, the house would receive the same candidate, as duly elected, whom they had before rejected." They could infer nothing but this.

IT is needless to repeat the circumstance of dissimilarity in the present case. It will be sufficient to observe, that as the law of parliament, upon which the house of commons grounded every step of their proceedings, was clear beyond the reach of doubt, so neither could the freeholders of Middlesex be at a loss to foresee what must be the inevitable consequence of their proceedings in opposition to it. For upon every return of Mr. Wilkes, the house made enquiry, whether any votes were given to any other candidate?

BUT I could venture, for the experiment's sake, even to give this writer the utmost he asks; to allow the most perfect similarity throughout in these two cases; to allow, that the law of expulsion was quite as clear to the burgesses of Lynn, as to the freeholders of Middlesex. It will, I am confident, avail his cause but little. It will only prove, that, the law of election at that time was different from the present law. It will prove, that, in all cases of an incapable candidate returned, the law then was, that the whole election should be void. But now we know that this is not law. The cases of

Malden and Bedford were, as has been seen, determined upon other and more just principles. And these determinations are, I imagine, admitted on all sides, to be law.

I WOULD willingly draw a veil over the remaining part of this paper. It is astonishing, it is painful, to see men of parts and ability, giving into the most unworthy artifices, and descending so much below their true line of character. But if they are not the dupes of their sophistry, (which is hardly to be conceived) let them consider that they are something much worse.

THE dearest interests of this country are its laws and its constitution. Against every attack upon these, there will, I hope, be always found amongst us the firmest *spirit of resistance*; superior to the united efforts of faction and ambition. For ambition, though it does not always take the lead of faction, will be sure in the end to make the most fatal advantage of it, and draw it to its own purposes. But, I trust, our day of trial is yet far off; and there is *a fund of good sense in this country, which cannot long be deceived*, by the arts either of false reasoning or false patriotism.

Of Letter XX Junius wrote to the printer: 'I am not capable of writing any thing more finished.'; Private letter no. 7. It is an answer to the Blackstone argument given as the postscript to the previous letter.

LETTER XX.

TO THE PRINTER OF THE PUBLIC ADVERTISER.

SIR, 8. *August* 1769.

THE gentleman, who has published an answer to Sir William Meredith's pamphlet, having honoured me with a postscript of six quarto pages, which he moderately calls, bestowing a *very* few words upon me, I cannot, in common politeness, refuse him a reply. The form and magnitude of a quarto imposes upon the mind; and men, who are unequal to the labour of discussing an intricate argument, or wish to avoid it, are willing enough to suppose, that much has been proved, because much has been said. Mine, I confess, are humble labours. I do not presume to instruct the learned, but simply to inform the body of the people; and I prefer that channel of conveyance, which is likely to spread farthest among them. The advocates of the ministry seem to me to write for fame, and to flatter themselves, that the size of their works will make them immortal. They pile up reluctant quarto upon solid folio, as if their labours, because they are gigantic, could contend with truth and heaven.

THE writer of the volume in question meets me upon my own ground. He acknowledges there is no statute, by which the specific disability we speak of is created, but he affirms, that the custom of parliament has been referred to, and that a case strictly in point has been produced, with the decision of the court upon it.—I thank him for coming so fairly to the point. He asserts, that the case of Mr. Walpole is strictly in point to prove that expulsion creates an absolute incapacity of being re-elected; and for this purpose he refers generally to the first vote of the house upon that occasion, without venturing to recite the vote itself. The unfair, disingenuous artifice of adopting that part of a precedent, which seems to suit his purpose, and omitting the remainder, deserves some pity, but cannot excite my resentment. He takes advantage eagerly of the first resolution, by which Mr. Walpole's incapacity is declared; but as to the two following, by which the candidate with the fewest votes was declared "not duly elected," and the election itself vacated, I dare say he would be well satisfied, if they were for ever blotted out of the journals of the house of commons. In fair argument, no part of a precedent should be admitted, unless the whole of it be given to us together. The author has divided his precedent, for he knew, that, taken together, it produced a consequence directly the reverse of that, which he endeavours to draw from a vote of expulsion. But what will this honest person say, if I take him at his word, and demonstrate to him, that the house of commons never meant to found Mr. Walpole's incapacity upon his expulsion only? What subterfuge will then remain?

LET it be remembered that we are speaking of the intention of men, who lived more than half a century ago, and that such intention can only be collected from their words and actions, as they are delivered to us upon record. To prove their designs by a supposition of what they would have done, opposed to what they actually did, is mere trifling and impertinence. The vote, by which Mr. Walpole's incapacity was declared, is thus expressed, "That Robert Walpole, Esq: having been this session of parliament committed a prisoner to the Tower, and expelled this house for a breach of trust in the execution of his office, and notorious corruption when secretary at war, was and is incapable of being elected a member to serve in this present parliament*." Now, Sir, to my understanding, no proposition of this kind can be more evident, than that the house of commons, by this very vote, themselves understood, and meant to declare, that Mr. Walpole's incapacity arose from the crimes he had committed, not from the punishment the house annexed to them. The high breach of trust, the notorious corruption are stated in the strongest terms. They do not tell us that he was incapable because he was expelled, but because he had been guilty of such offences as justly rendered him unworthy of a seat in parliament. If they had intended to fix the disability upon his expulsion alone, the mention of his crimes in the same vote would have been highly improper. It could only perplex the minds of the electors, who, if they collected any thing from so confused a declaration of the law of parliament, must have concluded that their representative had been declared incapable because he was highly guilty, not because he had been punished. But even admitting them to have understood it in the other sense, they must then, from

* It is well worth remarking, that the compiler of a certain quarto, called *The case of the last election for the county of Middlesex considered*, has the impudence to recite this very vote, in the following terms, vide page 11, "Resolved, that Robert Walpole, Esq; having been that session of parliament expelled the house, was and is incapable of being elected a member to serve in the present parliament." There cannot be a stronger positive proof of the treachery of the compiler, nor a stronger presumptive proof that he was convinced that the vote, if truly recited, would overturn his whole argument.

the very terms of the vote, have united the idea of his being sent to the Tower with that of his expulsion, and considered his incapacity as the joint effect of both.[1]

I DO not mean to give an opinion upon the justice of the proceedings of the house of commons with regard to Mr. Walpole; but certainly, if I admitted their censure to be well founded, I could no way avoid agreeing with them in the consequence they drew from it. I could never have a doubt, in law or reason, that a man, convicted of a high breach of trust, and of a notorious corruption, in the execution of a public office, was and ought to be incapable of sitting in the same parliament. Far from attempting to invalidate that vote, I should have wished that the incapacity declared by it could legally have been continued for ever.

NOW, Sir, observe how forcibly the argument returns. The house of commons, upon the face of their proceedings, had the strongest motives to declare Mr. Walpole incapable of being re-elected. They thought such a man unworthy to sit among them;—To that point they proceeded no farther; for they respected the rights of the people, while they asserted their own. They did not infer, from Mr. Walpole's incapacity, that his opponent was duly elected; on the contrary they declared Mr. Taylor "Not duly elected," and the election itself void.

SUCH, however, is the precedent, which my honest friend assures us is strictly in point to prove, that expulsion of itself creates an incapacity of being elected. If it had been so, the present house of commons should at least have followed strictly the example before them, and should have stated to us, in the same vote, the crimes for which they expelled Mr. Wilkes; whereas they resolve simply, that, "having been expelled, he was and is incapable." In this proceeding I am authorized to affirm, they have

[1] When editing his material for the 1772 volumes Junius seems to have become somewhat confused. He had previously changed the chronological order of the letters in a rather bewildering fashion. At this point he quoted the letter of Philo Junius of 22 May 1771 as a footnote but printed it again as Letter XLVI. Here it is included in its chronological position on p. 239.

neither statute, nor custom, nor reason, nor one single precedent to support them. On the other side, there is indeed a precedent so strongly in point, that all the inchanted castles of ministerial magic fall before it. In the year 1698, (a period which the rankest Tory dare not except against) Mr. Wollaston was expelled, re-elected, and admitted to take his seat in the same parliament.[1] The ministry have precluded themselves from all objections drawn from the cause of his expulsion, for they affirm absolutely, that expulsion of itself creates the disability. Now, Sir, let sophistry evade, let falsehood assert, and impudence deny—here stands the precedent, a land-mark to direct us through a troubled sea of controversy, conspicuous and unremoved.

I HAVE dwelt the longer upon the discussion of this point, because, in *my* opinion, it comprehends the whole question. The rest is unworthy of notice. We are enquiring whether incapacity be or not be created by expulsion. In the cases of Bedford and Malden, the incapacity of the persons returned, was matter of public notoriety, for it was created by act of parliament. But, really, Sir, my honest friend's suppositions are as unfavourable to him as his facts. He well knows that the clergy, besides that they are represented in common with their fellow-subjects, have also a separate parliament of their own?——that their incapacity to sit in the house of commons has been confirmed by repeated decisions of the house, and that the law of parliament, declared by those decisions, has been for above two centuries notorious and undisputed. The author is certainly at liberty to fancy cases, and make whatever comparisons he thinks proper; his suppositions still continue as distant from fact, as his wild discourses are from solid argument.

THE conclusion of his book is candid to extreme. He offers to grant me all I desire. He thinks he may safely admit that the case of Mr. Walpole makes directly against him, for it seems he has one grand solution *in petto*[2] for all difficulties. *If*, says he, *I were to allow*

[1] Richard Wollaston or Woolaston was returned for Whitchurch in July 1698. Expelled on 20 February 1699 as Receiver of the Duty on Houses, he was re-elected on 7 March. *CJ* xii. 519; *Official return of members of Parliament* (1878), i. 583.

[2] i.e. held in reserve.

all this, it will only prove, that the law of election was different, in Queen Anne's time, from what it is at present.

THIS indeed is more than I expected. The principle, I know, has been maintained in fact, but I never expected to see it so formally declared. What can he mean? does he assume this language to satisfy the doubts of the people, or does he mean to rouse their indignation; are the ministry daring enough to affirm, that the house of commons have a right to make and unmake the law of parliament at their pleasure?—Does the law of parliament, which we are so often told is the law of the land;—does the common right of every subject of the realm depend upon an arbitrary capricious vote of one branch of the legislature?—The voice of truth and reason must be silent.

THE ministry tell us plainly that this is no longer a question of right, but of power and force alone. What was law yesterday is not law to-day: and now it seems we have no better rule to live by than the temporary discretion and fluctuating integrity of the house of commons.

PROFESSIONS of patriotism are become stale and ridiculous. For my own part, I claim no merit from endeavouring to do a service to my fellow-subjects. I have done it to the best of my understanding; and, without looking for the approbation of other men, my conscience is satisfied. What remains to be done concerns the collective body of the people. They are now to determine for themselves, whether they will firmly and constitutionally assert their rights; or make an humble, slavish surrender of them at the feet of the ministry. To a generous mind there cannot be a doubt. We owe it to our ancestors to preserve entire these rights, which they have delivered to our care: we owe it to our posterity, not to suffer their dearest inheritance to be destroyed. But if it were possible for us to be insensible of these sacred claims, there is yet an obligation binding upon ourselves, from which nothing can acquit us,—a personal interest, which we cannot surrender. To alienate even our own rights, would be a crime as much more enormous than suicide, as a life of civil security and freedom is superior to a bare existence; and if life be the bounty of heaven, we scornfully reject the noblest part of the gift, if we consent to surrender that certain rule of living, without which the condition of human nature is not only miserable, but contemptible.

JUNIUS.

Junius was answered the following day by Anti-Junius, who protested that the House of Commons was not obliged to act upon precedent without considering whether it was reasonable. 'Parliament is a Court of Equity, and consequently may, nay ought to contradict even the spirit of any particular precedent if it clashes and disagrees with the general spirit of all the precedents before them.'

LETTER XXI.

TO THE PRINTER OF THE PUBLIC ADVERTISER.

SIR, 22. *August*, 1769.

I MUST beg of you to print a few lines, in explanation of some passages in my last letter, which I see have been misunderstood.

1. WHEN I said, that the house of commons never meant to found Mr. Walpole's incapacity on his expulsion *only*, I meant no more than to deny the general proposition, that expulsion *alone* creates the incapacity. If there be any thing ambiguous in the expression, I beg leave to explain it by saying, that, in my opinion, expulsion neither creates, nor in any part contributes to create the incapacity in question.

2. I CAREFULLY avoided entering into the merits of Mr. Walpole's case. I did not enquire, whether the house of commons acted justly, or whether they truly declared the law of parliament. My remarks went only to their apparent meaning and intention, as it stands declared in their own resolution.

3. I NEVER meant to affirm, that a commitment to the Tower created a disqualification. On the contrary, I considered that idea as an absurdity, into which the ministry must inevitably fall, if they reasoned right upon their own principles.

THE case of Mr. Wollaston speaks for itself. The ministry assert that *expulsion alone* creates an absolute, complete incapacity to be re-elected to sit in the same parliament. This proposition they have uniformly maintained, without any condition or modification whatsoever. Mr. Wollaston was expelled, re-elected, and admitted to take his seat in the same parliament.—I leave it to the public to determine, whether this be a plain matter of fact, or mere nonsense or declamation.

JUNIUS.

Whether it was altogether wise for Junius to become so involved in one issue may be doubted. Junius himself seems to have had some misgivings since he wrote about this time to Woodfall in private letter no. 6: 'As to Junius, I must wait for fresh Matter, as this is a Character, which must be kept up with credit.'

LETTER XXII.

TO THE PRINTER OF THE PUBLIC ADVERTISER.

4. *Sept.* 1769.

ARGUMENT against FACT; or, A new system of political Logic, by which the ministry have demonstrated, to the satisfaction of their friends, that expulsion alone creates a complete incapacity to be re-elected; *alias*, that a subject of this realm may be robbed of his common right, by a vote of the house of commons.

FIRST FACT.

MR. *Wollaston, in* 1698, *was expelled, re-elected, and admitted to take his seat.*

ARGUMENT.

As this cannot conveniently be reconciled with our general proposition, it may be necessary to shift our ground, and look back to the *cause* of Mr. Wollaston's expulsion. From thence it will appear clearly that, "although he was expelled, he had not rendered himself a culprit too ignominious to sit in parliament, and that having resigned his employment, he was no longer incapacitated by law." *Vide Serious Considerations, page* 23.[1] Or thus, "The house, somewhat *inaccurately*, used the word EXPELLED; they should have called it AMOTION." *Vide Mungo's case considered, page* 11.[2] Or in short, if these arguments should be thought insufficient, we may fairly deny the fact. For example; "I affirm that he was not re-elected. The same Mr. Wollaston, who was expelled, was not again elected. The same individual, if you please, walked into the house, and took his seat there, but the same person in law was not admitted a member of that parliament, from which he had been discarded." *Vide Letter to Junius, page* 12.[3]

SECOND FACT.

Mr. Walpole having been committed to the Tower, and expelled for a high breach of trust and notorious corruption in a public office, was declared incapable, &c.

ARGUMENT.

FROM the terms of this vote, nothing can be more evident than that the house of commons meant to fix the incapacity upon the punishment, and not upon the crime; but lest it should appear in a different light to weak, uninformed persons, it may be adviseable to gut the resolution, and give it to the public, with all possible solemnity, in the following terms, viz. "Resolved, that Robert Walpole, Esq; having been that session of parliament expelled the house, was and is incapable of being elected member to serve in that present parliament." *Vide Mungo, on the use of quotations, page* 11.

N. B. THE author of the answer to Sir William Meredith seems to have made use of Mungo's quotation, for in page 18, he assures

[1] *Serious considerations on a late very important decision of the House of Commons*, printed by S. Bladon. Reviewed in *Gentleman's Magazine*, 1769, 309 and 405.

[2] In debate on 26 January 1769 Isaac Barré christened Dyson 'Mungo' in reference to his readiness to act as general factotum to the ministry. This was the name of a black slave in Isaac Bickerstaffe's *The Padlock* (1768).

[3] *A letter to Junius*. By the author of *The answer to the question stated*. I have not traced a copy of this pamphlet but it is briefly reviewed in the *Gentleman's Magazine*, 1769, 405.

us, "That the declaratory vote of the 17th of February, 1769, was indeed a literal copy of the resolution of the house in Mr. Walpole's case."

THIRD FACT.

His opponent, Mr. Taylor, having the smallest number of votes at the next election, was declared NOT DULY ELECTED.

ARGUMENT.

THIS fact we consider as directly in point to prove that Mr. Luttrell ought to be the sitting member, for the following reasons. "The burgesses of Lynn could draw no other inference from this resolution, but this, that at a future election, and in case of a similar return, the house would receive the same candidate as duly elected, whom they had before rejected." *Vide Postscript to Junius, p.* 37. Or thus: "This their resolution leaves no room to doubt what part they *would* have taken, if, upon a subsequent re-election of Mr. Walpole, there had been any other candidate in competition with him. For, by their vote, they could have no other intention than to admit such other candidate." *Vide Mungo's case considered, p.* 39. Or take it in this light.—The burgesses of Lynn having, in defiance of the house, retorted upon them a person, whom they had branded with the most ignominious marks of their displeasure, were thereby so well intitled to favour and indulgence, that the house could do no less than rob Mr. Taylor of a right legally vested in him, in order that the burgesses might be apprised of the law of parliament; which law the house took a very direct way of explaining to them, by resolving that the candidate with the fewest votes was not duly elected:—"And was not this much more equitable, more in the spirit of that equal and substantial justice, which is the end of all law, than if they had violently adhered to the strict maxims of law?" *Vide Serious Considerations, p.* 33 *and* 34. "And if the present house of commons had chosen to follow the spirit of this resolution, they would have received and established the candidate with the fewest votes." *Vide Answer to Sir W. M. p.* 18.

PERMIT me now, Sir, to shew you that the worthy Dr. Blackstone sometimes contradicts the ministry as well as himself. The

Speech without doors asserts, page 9, "that the legal effect of an incapacity, founded on a judicial determination of a complete court, is precisely the same as that of an incapacity created by act of parliament." Now for the Doctor.—*The law and the opinion of the judge are not always convertible terms, or one and the same thing; since it sometimes may happen that the judge may mistake the law.* Commentaries, Vol. I. p. 71.

THE answer to Sir W. M. asserts, page 23, "That the returning officer is not a judicial, but a purely ministerial officer. His return is no judicial act."—At 'em again, Doctor. *The Sheriff, in his judicial capacity is to hear and determine causes of* 40 *shillings value and under in his county court. He has also a judicial power in divers other civil cases. He is likewise to decide the elections of knights of the shire (subject to the control of the house of commons), to judge of the qualification of voters, and to return such as he shall* DETERMINE *to be duly elected.* Vide Commentaries, page 332. Vol. I.

WHAT conclusion shall we draw from such facts, and such arguments, such contradictions? I cannot express my opinion of the present ministry more exactly than in the words of Sir Richard Steele, "that we are governed by a set of drivellers, whose folly takes away all dignity from distress, and makes even calamity ridiculous."[1]

PHILO JUNIUS.

John Russell, 4th Duke of Bedford, at the age of 60 was almost blind and near the end of a long political life, in which he had held office as Secretary of State, Lord Lieutenant of Ireland, and Lord President of the Council. He had also been special ambassador to France to conduct the peace settlement in 1762 and it was the firm belief of the radicals that he had betrayed the interests of his country. His supporters had a reputation for unsqueamish rapacity: in fact their political attitude was unusually coherent since they

[1] I have not been able to find this reference. Heron in 1802 identified it as from a pamphlet written jointly by Steele and Walpole on the South Sea crisis but did not give the title. Subsequent editors, like Wade, merely changed the word order of Heron's note. I am obliged to Professor Calhoun Winton, author of *Captain Steele* and *Sir Richard Steele, M.P.*, for help in trying to track down the precise reference.

advocated authority and firm government at home and in the American colonies. In December 1767 they coalesced with Grafton, bringing much-needed strength to his administration: Weymouth, Gower, Sandwich, and Richard Rigby took office. Junius wrote to Woodfall of this letter (in private letter no. 9) 'I mean to make it worth printing', and certainly it is one of his most spiteful productions, dredging up and distorting forgotten episodes in the hope of discrediting or wounding the Duke.

LETTER XXIII.

TO HIS GRACE THE DUKE OF BEDFORD.

MY LORD, 19. *Sept.* 1769.

YOU are so little accustomed to receive any marks of respect or esteem from the public, that if, in the following lines, a compliment or expression of applause should escape me, I fear you would consider it as a mockery of your established character, and perhaps an insult to your understanding. You have nice feelings, my Lord, if we may judge from your resentments. Cautious therefore of giving offence, where you have so little deserved it, I shall leave the illustration of your virtues to other hands. Your friends have a privilege to play upon the easiness of your temper, or possibly they are better acquainted with your good qualities than I am. You have done good by stealth. The rest is upon record. You have still left ample room for speculation, when panegyric is exhausted.

YOU are indeed a very considerable man. The highest rank;—a splendid fortune; and a name, glorious till it was yours, were sufficient to have supported you with meaner abilities than I think you possess. From the first, you derive a constitutional claim to respect; from the second, a natural extensive authority;—the last created a partial expectation of hereditary virtues. The use you have made of these uncommon advantages might have been more honourable to yourself, but could not be more instructive to mankind. We may trace it in the veneration of your country, the choice of your friends, and in the accomplishment of every sanguine hope, which the public might have conceived from the illustrious name of Russel.

THE eminence of your station gave you a commanding prospect of your duty. The road, which led to honour, was open to your view. You could not lose it by mistake, and you had no temptation to depart from it by design. Compare the natural dignity and importance of the richest peer of England;—the noble independence, which he might have maintained in parliament, and the real interest and respect, which he might have acquired, not only in parliament, but through the whole kingdom; compare these glorious distinctions with the ambition of holding a share in government, the emoluments of a place, the sale of a borough, or the purchase of a corporation; and though you may not regret the virtues, which create respect, you may see with anguish, how much real importance and authority you have lost. Consider the character of an independent virtuous Duke of Bedford; imagine what he might be in this country, then reflect one moment upon what you are. If it be possible for me to withdraw my attention from the fact, I will tell you in theory what such a man might be.

CONSCIOUS of his own weight and importance, his conduct in parliament would be directed by nothing but the constitutional duty of a peer. He would consider himself as a guardian of the laws. Willing to support the just measures of government, but determined to observe the conduct of the minister with suspicion, he would oppose the violence of faction with as much firmness, as the encroachments of prerogative. He would be as little capable of bargaining with the minister for places for himself, or his dependants, as of descending to mix himself in the intrigues of opposition. Whenever an important question called for his opinion in parliament, he would be heard, by the most profligate minister, with deference and respect. His authority would either sanctify or disgrace the measures of government.—The people would look up to him as to their protector, and a virtuous prince would have one honest man in his dominions, in whose integrity and judgment he might safely confide. *If it should be the will of providence

* The Duke lately lost his only son, by a fall from his horse.[1]

[1] Lord Tavistock, by all accounts a pleasant and able young man, died on 22 March 1767. Junius claimed that his parents behaved with callous indifference. Horace Walpole's account was that the Duke was greatly afflicted but incurred

to afflict him with a domestic misfortune, he would submit to the stroke, with feeling, but not without dignity. He would consider the people as his children, and receive a generous heart-felt consolation, in the sympathising tears, and blessings of his country.

YOUR Grace may probably discover something more intelligible in the negative part of this illustrious character. The man I have described would never prostitute his dignity in parliament by an indecent violence either in opposing or defending a minister. He would not at one moment rancorously persecute, at another basely cringe to the favourite of his Sovereign. After outraging the royal dignity with peremptory conditions, little short of menace and hostility, he would never descend to the humility of soliciting an interview* with the favourite, and of offering to recover, at any price, the honour of his friendship. Though deceived perhaps in his youth, he would not, through the course of a long life, have invariably chosen his friends from among the most profligate of mankind. His own honour would have forbidden him from mixing his private pleasures or conversation with jockeys, gamesters, blasphemers, gladiators, or buffoons. He would then have never felt, much less would he have submitted to the dishonest necessity of engaging in the interests and intrigues of his dependants, of supplying their vices, or relieving their beggary, at the expence of his country. He would not have betrayed such ignorance, or such contempt of the constitution, as openly to avow, in a court of

* At this interview, which passed at the house of the late Lord Eglingtoun, Lord Bute told the Duke that he was determined never to have any connexion with a man, who had so basely betrayed him.[1]

censure by voting at India House a fortnight later. Walpole's comment on Junius seems eminently just: 'Of flint must the heart have been that could think such a domestic stroke a proper subject for insult.' Walpole, ii. 313–14. David Hume wrote to the Marquise de Barbentane, 13 March 1767: 'No body believes that the Duke would survive his Son's Death'. *The letters of David Hume*, ed. J. Y. T. Greig (1932), ii. 128.

[1] The meeting referred to took place on 12 February 1766. The version in Walpole, ii. 209 supports that of Junius: not surprisingly, rather different accounts are given by George Grenville in *Grenville papers*, iii. 362–3 and by the Duke of Bedford in *Bedford Corr.* iii. 328–9.

justice, the* purchase and sale of a borough. He would not have thought it consistent with his rank in the state, or even with his personal importance, to be the little tyrant of a little corporation†. He would never have been insulted with virtues, which he had laboured to extinguish, nor suffered the disgrace of a mortifying defeat, which has made him ridiculous and contemptible, even to the few by whom he was not detested.—I reverence the afflictions of a good man,—his sorrows are sacred. But how can we take part in the distresses of a man, whom we can neither love nor esteem; or feel for a calamity, of which he himself is insensible? Where was the father's heart, when he could look for, or find an immediate consolation for the loss of an only son, in consultations and bargains for a place at court, and even in the misery of balloting at the India house!

ADMITTING then that you have mistaken or deserted those honourable principles, which ought to have directed your conduct; admitting that you have as little claim to private affection as to public esteem, let us see with what abilities, with what degree of judgment you have carried your own system into execution. A great man, in the success and even in the magnitude of his crimes, finds a rescue from contempt. Your Grace is every way unfortunate. Yet I will not look back to those ridiculous scenes, by which in your earlier days, you thought it an honour to be distinguished‡;

* In an answer in Chancery, in a suit against him to recover a large sum paid him by a person, whom he had undertaken to return to parliament, for one of his Grace's boroughs. He was compelled to repay the money.[1]

† Of Bedford, where the tyrant was held in such contempt and detestation, that, in order to deliver themselves from him, they admitted a great number of strangers to the freedom. To make his defeat truly ridiculous, he tried his whole strength against Mr. *Horne*, and was beaten upon his own ground.[2]

‡ Mr. Heston Homphrey, a country Attorney, horsewhipped the Duke, with equal justice, severity, and perseverance, on the Course at Litchfield. *Rigby* and *Lord Trentham* were also cudgelled in a most exemplary manner. This gave rise to the following story: "When the late King heard that Sir Edward Hawke had given

[1] I have not succeeded in tracing the case to which Junius referred. It is not included in the Chancery suits in *English reports*, but these are incomplete.

[2] This was one of the very few electoral victories gained, under Horne's leadership, by the Society of Supporters of the Bill of Rights, originally established to pay Wilkes's debts; *The House of Commons, 1754–90*, i. 206–7; John Cannon, *Parliamentary reform, 1640–1832* (1973), ch. 3.

—the recorded stripes, the public infamy, your own sufferings, or Mr. Rigby's fortitude. These events undoubtedly left an impression, though not upon your mind.[1] To such a mind, it may perhaps be a pleasure to reflect, that there is hardly a corner of any of his Majesty's kingdoms, except France, in which, at one time or other, your valuable life has not been in danger. Amiable man! we see and acknowledge the protection of Providence, by which you have so often escaped the personal detestation of your fellow-subjects, and are still reserved for the public justice of your country.

YOUR history begins to be important at that auspicious period, at which you were deputed to represent the Earl of Bute, at the court of Versailles. It was an honourable office, and executed with the same spirit, with which it was accepted. Your patrons wanted an ambassador, who would submit to make concessions, without daring to insist upon any honourable condition for his Sovereign. Their business required a man, who had as little feeling for his own dignity as for the welfare of his country; and they found him in the first rank of the nobility. Belleisle, Goree, Guadeloupe, St. Lucia, Martinique, the Fishery, and the Havanna, are glorious monuments of your Grace's talents for negotiation. My Lord, we are too well

the French a *drubbing*, his Majesty, who had never received that kind of chastisement, was pleased to ask Lord Chesterfield the meaning of the word.—Sir, says Lord Chesterfield, the meaning of the word—but here comes the Duke of Bedford, who is better able to explain it to your Majesty than I am."

---

[1] Junius worked hard to get this jeer made: on two separate occasions (in private letters nos. 41 and 44) he asked the printer to find out the date of the incident—presumably neither Junius nor Woodfall could recall it. The name of the perpetrator is misquoted: it should be Jeston Homphrey. The episode happened at Lichfield races in September 1747—a mere 22 years before. Bedford and his friends were jostled and assaulted by a Tory/Jacobite group, incensed at what they considered the apostasy of Lord Gower (Bedford's father-in-law). They were subsequently prosecuted at Staffordshire Assizes. *Notes & Queries*, 11th series, iii. 375; *Gentleman's Magazine*, 1748, 378; *The House of Commons, 1715–54*, i. 319. The degree of bitterness felt towards Gower at the time may be judged by Johnson's suggested dictionary definition of 'Renegade': 'one who deserts to the enemy—*sometimes we say a GOWER*;' Boswell's *Life of Johnson*, ed. G. B. Hill (revd. edn., 1934), i. 296. The events at Lichfield are recorded in caricature prints Nos. 2863, 2864 and 2865, listed in *Catalogue of Prints and Drawings in the British Museum*, Division I, *Political and Personal Satires*, ed. F. G. Stephens (1877), vol. iii, part i, 1734–1750.

acquainted with your pecuniary character, to think it possible that so many public sacrifices should have been made, without some private compensations. Your conduct carries with it an internal evidence, beyond all the legal proofs of a court of justice. Even the callous pride of Lord Egremont was alarmed.* He saw and felt his own dishonour in corresponding with you; and there certainly was a moment, at which he meant to have resisted, had not a fatal lethargy prevailed over his faculties, and carried all sense and memory away with it.

I WILL not pretend to specify the secret terms on which you were invited to support an† administration which Lord Bute pretended to leave in full possession of their ministerial authority, and perfectly masters of themselves. He was not of a temper to relinquish power, though he retired from employment. Stipulations were certainly made between your Grace and him, and certainly violated. After two years submission, you thought you had collected a strength sufficient to controul his influence, and that it was your turn to be a tyrant, because you had been a slave. When you found yourself mistaken in your opinion of your gracious Master's firmness, disappointment got the better of all your humble discretion, and carried you to an excess of outrage to his person, as distant from true spirit, as from all decency and respect‡. After robbing him of the rights of a King, you would not permit him to preserve the honour of a gentleman.[1] It was then Lord Weymouth was

* This man, notwithstanding his pride and tory principles, had some English stuff in him. Upon an official letter he wrote to the Duke of Bedford, the Duke desired to be recalled, and it was with the utmost difficulty that Lord Bute could appease him.

† Mr. Grenville, Lord Halifax, and Lord Egremont.

‡ The ministry having endeavoured to exclude the Dowager out of the regency bill, the Earl of Bute determined to dismiss them. Upon this the Duke of Bedford demanded an audience of the——, reproached him in plain terms, with his duplicity, baseness, falsehood, treachery, and hypocrisy,——repeatedly gave him the lye, and left him in convulsions.

---

[1] The Duke of Bedford's audience with the King was on 12 June 1765. By his own account (*Bedford Corr.* iii. 286–8) there was some plain speaking: 'whether his countenance and support had not been promised them? whether this promise had been kept? but on the contrary, whether all those who are our most bitter enemies had not been countenanced by him (the King) in public?' The King complained to

nominated to Ireland, and dispatched (we well remember with what indecent hurry) to plunder the treasury of the first fruits of an employment which you well knew he was never to execute*.[1]

THIS sudden declaration of war against the favourite might have given you a momentary merit with the public, if it had either been adopted upon principle, or maintained with resolution. Without looking back to all your former servility, we need only observe your subsequent conduct, to see upon what motives you acted. Apparently united with Mr. Grenville, you waited until Lord Rockingham's feeble administration should dissolve in its own weakness.—The moment their dismission was suspected, the moment you perceived that another system was adopted in the closet, you thought it no disgrace to return to your former dependance, and solicit once more the friendship of Lord Bute. You begged an interview, at which he had spirit enough to treat you with contempt.

IT would now be of little use to point out, by what a train of weak, injudicious measures, it became necessary, or was thought so, to call you back to a share in the administration†. The friends, whom you did not in the last instance desert, were not of a character to add strength or credit to government; and at that time your alliance with the Duke of Grafton was, I presume, hardly foreseen. We must look for other stipulations, to account for that sudden resolution of the closet, by which three of your dependants‡

* He received three thousand pounds for plate and equipage money.

† When Earl Gower was appointed President of the council, the King, with his usual sincerity, assured him, that he had not had one happy moment, since the Duke of Bedford left him.

‡ Lord Gower, Weymouth, and Sandwich.

Lord Northington of the indignation he felt at 'so very offensive a declaration'; J. Brooke, *King George III*, 120–1. Junius' concern at such insolence to the King did not last. *Bedford Corr.* iii. 98–218 deals with Bedford's embassy. Bedford's letter to Bute, 20 September 1762, is printed on p. 116.

[1] Lord Weymouth was appointed Lord Lieutenant on 29 May 1765 but resigned in July when the Grenville ministry was dismissed. Weymouth's financial difficulties were mentioned in Grenville's diary for 12 May; *Grenville papers*, iii. 163.

(whose characters, I think, cannot be less respected than they are) were advanced to offices, through which you might again controul the minister, and probably engross the whole direction of affairs.

THE possession of absolute power is now once more within your reach. The measures you have taken to obtain and confirm it, are too gross to escape the eyes of a discerning judicious prince. His palace is besieged; the lines of circumvallation are drawing round him; and unless he finds a resource in his own activity, or in the attachment of the real friends of his family, the best of princes must submit to the confinement of a state prisoner, until your Grace's death, or some less fortunate event shall raise the siege. For the present, you may safely resume that stile of insult and menace, which even a private gentleman cannot submit to hear without being contemptible. Mr. Mackenzie's history is not yet forgotten, and you may find precedents enough of the mode, in which an imperious subject may signify his pleasure to his Sovereign.[1] Where will this gracious monarch look for assistance, when the wretched Grafton could forget his obligations to his master, and desert him for a hollow alliance with *such* a man as the Duke of Bedford!

LET us consider you, then, as arrived at the summit of worldly greatness: let us suppose, that all your plans of avarice and ambition are accomplished, and your most sanguine wishes gratified in the fear, as well as the hatred of the people: Can age itself forget that you are now in the last act of life? Can grey hairs make folly venerable? and is there no period to be reserved for meditation and retirement? For shame! my Lord: let it not be recorded of you, that the latest moments of your life were dedicated to the same unworthy pursuits, the same busy agitations, in which your youth and manhood were exhausted. Consider, that, although you cannot disgrace your former life, you are violating the character of age, and exposing the impotent imbecility, after you have lost the vigour of the passions.

[1] The dismissal of James Stuart Mackenzie, younger brother of Lord Bute, was one of the conditions Grenville and Bedford insisted upon in May 1765 when the King had failed to form an alternative administration.

YOUR friends will ask, perhaps, Whither shall this unhappy old man retire? Can he remain in the metropolis, where his life has been so often threatened, and his palace so often attacked? If he returns to Wooburn, scorn and mockery await him. He must create a solitude round his estate, if he would avoid the face of reproach and derision. At Plymouth, his destruction would be more than probable; at Exeter, inevitable. No honest Englishman will ever forget his attachment, nor any honest Scotchman forgive his treachery to Lord Bute. At every town he enters, he must change his liveries and name. Which ever way he flies, the *Hue and Cry* of the country pursues him.[1]

IN another kingdom indeed, the blessings of his administration have been more sensibly felt; his virtues better understood; or at worst, they will not, for him alone, forget their hospitality.—As well might VERRES have returned to Sicily.[2] You have twice escaped, my Lord; beware of a third experiment. The indignation of a whole people, plundered, insulted, and oppressed as they have been, will not always be disappointed.

IT is in vain therefore to shift the scene. You can no more fly from your enemies than from yourself. Persecuted abroad, you look into your own heart for consolation, and find nothing but reproaches and despair. But, my Lord, you may quit the field of business, though not the field of danger; and though you cannot be safe, you may cease to be ridiculous. I fear you have listened too long to the advice of those pernicious friends, with whose interests you have sordidly united your own, and for whom you have sacrificed every thing that ought to be dear to a man of honour. They are still base enough to encourage the follies of your age, as they once

1 After the Peace of Paris, the Duke of Bedford suffered considerably at the hands of the mob. In May 1765 he was struck on the head by a large stone thrown into his carriage and his house in Bloomsbury Square subjected to a determined attack. In the summer of 1769, while visiting Devon in his capacity as Lord Lieutenant, he was menaced by a Wilkite mob outside Exeter Cathedral and assaulted in the streets of Honiton. Junius used these incidents with some skill to depict a man hounded from human society.

2 Gaius Verres was prosecuted by Cicero in 70 B.C. for extortion and oppression during his term as Governor of Sicily.

did the vices of your youth. As little acquainted with the rules of decorum, as with the laws of morality, they will not suffer you to profit by experience, nor even to consult the propriety of a bad character. Even now they tell you, that life is no more than a dramatic scene, in which the hero should preserve his consistency to the last, and that as you lived without virtue, you should die without repentance.

JUNIUS.

Woodfall appears to have printed the letter to the Duke of Bedford with some misgivings, and Junius wrote in private letter no. 10 to reassure him: 'You have nothing to fear from the Duke of Bedford. I reserve some things expressly to awe him, in case he should think of bringing you before the House of Lords. I am sure I can threaten him privately with such a Storm as would make him tremble even in his grave.'

These remarks may, of course, be mere bombast, designed to amaze the printer. If there is any substance in them, it may be that Junius was in communication with Dr. Musgrave of Exeter, who had just published sensational accusations that the Duke and his colleagues had taken bribes from France at the peace settlement. Later in 1769, over Hine's case, Junius appeared to have some knowledge of Exeter affairs. It may also be significant that when Musgrave was examined by the House of Commons and his assertions shown to be ridiculous, Junius defended him with spirit.

The reappearance of Sir William Draper, following the publication by Francis Newbery in July of a pirate edition of the letters under the title *The political contest*, cannot have been welcome to Junius. Draper seemed as indignant as if he had read Junius' letter of 7 February for the first time and issued a formal challenge to a duel. Draper's letter was printed in the *Public Advertiser* on 20 September 1769.

LETTER XXIV.

TO JUNIUS.

SIR, 14. *September*, 1769.

HAVING accidentally seen a *republication* of your letters, wherein you have been pleased to *assert*, that I had *sold* the companions of my success; I am again obliged to declare the said assertion to be a most *infamous* and *malicious falsehood*; and I *again* call upon you to stand forth, avow yourself, and *prove* the charge. If you can make it out to the satisfaction of any one man in the kingdom, I will be content to be thought the worst man in it; if you do not, what must the nation think of you? *Party* has nothing to do in this affair: you have made a personal attack upon my honour, defamed me by a most vile calumny, which might possibly have sunk into oblivion, had not such uncommon pains been taken to renew and perpetuate this scandal, chiefly because it has been told in good language: for I give you full credit for your elegant diction, well turned periods, and attic wit; but wit is oftentimes false, though it may appear brilliant; which is exactly the case of your *whole performance*. But, Sir, I am obliged in the most *serious* manner to accuse you of being guilty of *falsities*. You have said the thing that is *not*. To support your story, you have recourse to the following *irresistible* argument: "You *sold* the companions of your victory, because when the 16th regiment was given to *you*, you was *silent*." The conclusion is inevitable. I believe that such *deep* and *acute reasoning* could only come from such an extraordinary writer as *Junius*. But unfortunately for you, the *premises* as well as the *conclusion* are absolutely *false*. Many applications have been made to the ministry on the subject of the Manilla Ransom *since* the time of my being colonel of that regiment. As I have for some years quitted London, I was obliged to have recourse to the honourable Colonel Monson and Sir Samuel Cornish to *negotiate* for me; in the last autumn, I personally delivered a memorial to the Earl of Shelburne at his seat in Wiltshire. As you have told us of your importance, that you are a person of *rank* and *fortune*, and above a *common* bribe, you may in all probability be not *unknown* to his lordship, who can satisfy you of the truth of what I say.[1] But I shall now take the liberty, Sir, to seize your battery, and turn it against yourself. If your puerile and tinsel logic could carry the least weight or conviction with it, how must you stand affected by the *inevitable conclusion*, as you are pleased to term it? According to *Junius*, *Silence* is *Guilt*. In many of the public papers, you have been called in the most direct and offensive terms a *liar* and a *coward*.

[1] Junius used these phrases in a short letter of 12 April 1769 which he did not include in the collected edition. It is printed in Appendix four, p. 456.

When did you reply to these foul accusations? You have been quite *silent*; quite chop-fallen: therefore, *because* you was *silent*, the nation has a right to pronounce you to be both a liar and a coward from your own argument: but, Sir, I will give you fair-play; will afford you an opportunity to wipe off the first appellation; by desiring the proofs of your charge against me. Produce them! To wipe off the last, produce *yourself*. People cannot bear any longer your *Lion's skin*, and the despicable *imposture* of the *old Roman name* which you have *affected*. For the future assume the name of some *modern*★ bravo and dark assassin: let your appellation have some affinity to your practice. But if I must *perish*, *Junius*, let me *perish* in the face of day; be for *once* a generous and open enemy. I allow that gothic *appeals* to cold iron are no better proofs of a man's honesty and veracity than hot iron and burning ploughshares are of *female chastity:* but a soldier's honour is as delicate as a woman's; it must not be suspected; you have dared to throw more than a suspicion upon mine: you cannot but know the consequences, which even the meekness of Christianity would pardon me for, after the injury you have done me.

WILLIAM DRAPER.

LETTER XXV.

Hæret lateri lethalis arundo.[1]

TO SIR WILLIAM DRAPER, K. B.

SIR, 25. *September*, 1769.

AFTER so long an interval, I did not expect to see the debate revived between us. My answer to your last letter shall be short; for I write to you with reluctance, and I hope we shall now conclude our correspondence for ever.

★ Was *Brutus* an *ancient* bravo and dark assassin; or does Sir W. D. think it criminal to stab a tyrant to the heart?

---

[1] The deadly shaft stuck fast in [his] side. Virgil, *Aeneid*, iv. 73.

HAD you been originally and without provocation attacked by an anonymous writer, you would have some right to demand his name. But in this cause you are a volunteer. You engaged in it with the unpremeditated gallantry of a soldier. You were content to set your name in opposition to a man, who would probably continue in concealment. You understood the terms upon which we were to correspond, and gave at least a tacit assent to them. After voluntarily attacking me under the character of Junius, what possible right have you to know me under any other? Will you forgive me if I insinuate to you, that you foresaw some honour in the apparent spirit of coming forward in person, and that you were not quite indifferent to the display of your literary qualifications?

YOU cannot but know that the republication of my letters was no more than a catchpenny contrivance of a printer, in which it was impossible I should be concerned, and for which I am no way answerable. At the same time I wish you to understand, that if I do not take the trouble of reprinting these papers, it is not from any fear of giving offence to Sir William Draper.

YOUR remarks upon a signature, adopted merely for distinction, are unworthy of notice; but when you tell me I have submitted to be called a liar and a coward, I must ask you in my turn, whether you seriously think it any way incumbent upon me to take notice of the silly invectives of every simpleton, who writes in a newspaper; and what opinion you would have conceived of my discretion, if I had suffered myself to be the dupe of so shallow an artifice?

YOUR appeal to the sword, though consistent enough with your late profession, will neither prove your innocence nor clear you from suspicion.——Your complaints with regard to the Manilla ransom were, for a considerable time, a distress to government. You were appointed (greatly out of your turn) to the command of a regiment, and *during that administration* we heard no more of Sir William Draper. The facts, of which I speak, may indeed be variously accounted for, but they are too notorious to be denied;

and I think you might have learnt at the university, that a false conclusion is an error in argument, not a breach of veracity. Your solicitations, I doubt not, were renewed under *another* administration. Admitting the fact, I fear an indifferent person would only infer from it, that experience had made you acquainted with the benefits of complaining. Remember, Sir, that you have yourself confessed, that, *considering the critical situation of this country, the ministry are in the right to temporise with Spain.* This confession reduces you to an unfortunate dilemma. By renewing your solicitations, you must either mean to force your country into a war at a most unseasonable juncture; or, having no view or expectation of that kind, that you look for nothing but a private compensation to yourself.

AS to me, it is by no means necessary that I should be exposed to the resentment of the worst and the most powerful men in this country, though I may be indifferent about yours. Though *you* would fight, there are others who would assassinate.

BUT after all, Sir, where is the injury? You assure me, that my logic is puerile and tinsel, that it carries not the least weight or conviction, that my premises are false and my conclusions absurd. If this be a just description of me, how is it possible for such a writer to disturb your peace of mind, or to injure a character so well established as yours? Take care, Sir William, how you indulge this unruly temper, lest the world should suspect that conscience has some share in your resentments. You have more to fear from the treachery of your own passions, than from any malevolence of mine.

I BELIEVE, Sir, you will never know me. A considerable time must certainly elapse before we are personally acquainted. You need not, however, regret the delay, or suffer an apprehension that any length of time can restore you to the Christian meekness of your temper, and disappoint your present indignation. If I understand your character, there is in your own breast a repository, in which your resentments may be safely laid up for future occasions, and preserved without the hazard of diminution. The *Odia in longum jaciens, quae reconderet, auctaque promeret,* I thought had only belonged to the worst character of antiquity. The text is in Tacitus;—you know best where to look for the commentary.[1]

JUNIUS.

Draper's reply was dated 2 October by the author and appeared in the *Public Advertiser* of 7 October 1769.

LETTER XXVI.

A WORD AT PARTING TO JUNIUS.

*SIR, 7. *October*, 1769.

AS you have not favoured me with either of the *explanations* demanded of you, I can have nothing more to say to you upon my *own* account. Your mercy to me, or tenderness for yourself, has been very great. The public will judge of your *motives*. If your excess of modesty forbids you to produce either the proofs, or yourself, I will excuse it. Take courage; I have not the temper of Tiberius, any more than the rank or power. You, indeed, are a tyrant of another sort, and upon your political bed of torture can excruciate any subject, from a first minister down to such a grub or butterfly as myself; like another detested tyrant of antiquity, can make the wretched sufferer fit the bed, if the bed will not fit the sufferer, by

* *Measures and not men* is the common cant of affected moderation;—a base, counterfeit language, fabricated by knaves, and made current among fools. Such gentle censure is not fitted to the present, degenerate state of society. What does it avail to expose the absurd contrivance, or pernicious tendency of measures, if the man, who advises or executes, shall be suffered not only to escape with impunity, but even to preserve his power, and insult us with the favour of his Sovereign! I would recommend to the reader the whole of Mr. Pope's letter to Doctor Arbuthnot, dated 26. July, 1734. from which the following is an extract. "To reform and not to chastise I am afraid, is impossible; and that the best precepts, as well as the best laws, would prove of small use, if there were no examples to inforce them. To attack vices in the abstract, without touching persons, may be safe fighting indeed, but it is fighting with shadows. My greatest comfort and encouragement to proceed has been to see that those, who have no shame, and not fear of any thing else, have appeared touched by my satires."

---

[1] Bottling up his malice to be brought forth with increased violence. Tacitus, *Annals*, i. 69. The reference was to Tiberius.

disjointing or tearing the trembling limbs until they are stretched to its extremity. But courage, constancy, and patience, under torments, have sometimes caused the most hardened monsters to relent, and forgive the object of their cruelty. You, Sir, are determined to try all that human nature can endure, until she expires: else, was it possible that you could be the author of that most inhuman letter to the Duke of Bedford, I have read with astonishment and horror? Where, Sir, where were the feelings of your own heart, when you could upbraid a most affectionate father with the loss of his only and most amiable son? Read over again those cruel lines of yours, and let them wring your very soul! Cannot political questions be discussed without descending to the most odious personalities? Must you go wantonly out of your way to torment declining age, because the Duke of Bedford may have quarrelled with those whose cause and politics you espouse? For shame! for shame! As you have *spoke daggers* to him, you may justly dread the *use* of them against your own breast, did a want of courage, or of noble sentiments, stimulate him to such mean revenge. He is above it; he is brave. Do you fancy that your own base arts have infected our whole island? But your own reflections, your own conscience, must and will, if you have any spark of humanity remaining, give him most ample vengeance. Not all the power of words with which you are so graced, will ever wash out, or even palliate this foul blot in your character. I have not time at present to dissect your letter so minutely as I could wish, but I will be bold enough to say, that it is (as to reason and argument) the most extraordinary piece of *florid impotence* that was ever imposed upon the eyes and ears of the too credulous and deluded mob.[1] It accuses the Duke of Bedford of high treason. Upon what foundation? You tell us, "that the Duke's *pecuniary character* makes it more than *probable*, that he could not have made such sacrifices at the peace, without *some private compensations*; that his conduct carried with it an interior evidence, beyond all the legal proofs of a court of justice."

[1] Another of Sir William's academic flourishes. 'Florid impotence' is a quotation from Pope's *Epistle to Dr. Arbuthnot*, line 317. Pope's victim was John, Lord Hervey, under the name of *Sporus*.

My academical education, Sir, bids me tell you that it is necessary to establish the truth of your first proposition, before you presume to draw inferences from it. First prove the avarice, before you make the rash, hasty, and most wicked conclusion. This father, *Junius*, whom you call avaricious, allowed that son eight thousand pounds a year. Upon his most unfortunate death, which your usual good-nature took care to remind him of, he greatly increased the jointure of the afflicted lady, his widow. Is this avarice? Is this doing good by *stealth*? It is upon record.

If exact order, method, and true œconomy as a master of a family; if splendor and just magnificence, without wild waste and thoughtless extravagance, may constitute the character of an avaricious man, the Duke is guilty. But for a moment let us admit that an ambassador may love money too much; what proof do you give that he has taken any to betray his country? Is it hearsay; or the evidence of letters, or ocular; or the evidence of those concerned in this black affair? Produce your authorities to the public. It is a most impudent kind of sorcery to attempt to blind us with the smoke, without convincing us that the fire has existed. You first brand him with a vice that he is free from, to render him odious and suspected. Suspicion is the foul weapon with which you make all your chief attacks; with that you stab. But shall one of the first subjects of the realm be ruined in his fame; shall even his life be in constant danger, from a charge built upon such sandy foundations? Must his house be besieged by lawless ruffians, his journies impeded, and even the asylum of an altar be insecure, from assertions so base and false? Potent as he is, the Duke is amenable to justice; if guilty, punishable. The parliament is the high and solemn tribunal for matters of such great moment. To that be they submitted. But I hope also that some notice will be taken of, and some punishment inflicted upon, false accusers, especially upon such, *Junius*, who are *wilfully false*. In any truth I will agree even with *Junius*; will agree with him that it is highly unbecoming the dignity of Peers to tamper with boroughs. Aristocracy is as fatal as democracy. Our constitution admits of neither. It loves a King, Lords, and Commons really chosen by the unbought suffrages of a free people. But if corruption only shifts hands; if the wealthy commoner gives the bribe, instead of the potent Peer, is the state better served by this exchange? Is the real emancipation of the borough effected, because new parchment bonds may possibly supersede the old? To say the truth, wherever such practices prevail, they are equally criminal to and destructive of our freedom.

THE rest of your declamation is scarce worth considering, excepting for the elegance of the language. Like Hamlet in the play, you produce two pictures: you tell us, that one is not like the Duke of Bedford; then you bring a most hideous caricatura, and tell us of the resemblance; but *multum abludit imago.*[1]

ALL your long tedious accounts of the ministerial quarrels, and the intrigues of the cabinet, are reducible to a few short lines; and to convince you, Sir, that I do not mean to flatter any minister, either past or present, these are my thoughts: they seem to have acted like lovers, or children; have* pouted, quarrelled, cried, kissed, and been friends again, as the objects of desire, the ministerial rattles, have been put into their hands. But such proceedings are very unworthy of the gravity and dignity of a great nation. We do not want men of abilities; but we have wanted steadiness; we want unanimity: your letters, *Junius*, will not contribute thereto. You may one day expire by a flame of your own kindling. But it is my humble opinion that lenity and moderation, pardon and oblivion, will disappoint the efforts of all the seditious in the land, and extinguish their wide spreading fires. I have lived with this sentiment; with this I shall die.

WILLIAM DRAPER.

* Sir William gives us a pleasant account of men, who, in *his* opinion at least, are the best qualified to govern an empire.

---

[1] 'The image does not much disagree with you'—i.e. fits you well. Horace, *Satires*, II. iii. 320.

LETTER XXVII.

TO THE PRINTER OF THE PUBLIC ADVERTISER.

SIR, 13. *October*, 1769.

IF Sir William Draper's bed be a bed of torture, he has made it for himself. I shall never interrupt his repose. Having changed the subject, there are parts of his last letter not undeserving of a reply. Leaving his private character and conduct out of the question, I shall consider him merely in the capacity of an author, whose labours certainly do no discredit to a news-paper.

WE say, in common discourse, that a man may be his own enemy, and the frequency of the fact makes the expression intelligible. But that a man should be the bitterest enemy of his friends, implies a contradiction of a peculiar nature. There is something in it, which cannot be conceived without a confusion of ideas, nor expressed without a solecism in language. Sir William Draper is still that fatal friend Lord Granby found him. Yet I am ready to do justice to his generosity; if indeed it be not something more than generous, to be the voluntary advocate of men, who think themselves injured by his assistance, and to consider nothing in the cause he adopts, but the difficulty of defending it. I thought however he had been better read in the history of the human heart, than to compare or confound the tortures of the body with those of the mind. He ought to have known, though perhaps it might not be his interest to confess, that no outward tyranny can reach the mind. If conscience plays the tyrant, it would be greatly for the benefit of the world that she were more arbitrary, and far less placable, than some men find her.

BUT it seems I have outraged the feelings of a father's heart.——Am I indeed so injudicious? Does Sir William Draper think I would have hazarded my credit with a generous nation, by so gross a violation of the laws of humanity? Does he think I am so little acquainted with the first and noblest characteristic of Englishmen? Or how will he reconcile such folly with an understanding so full of artifice as mine? Had *he* been a father, he would have been but little offended with the severity of the reproach, for his mind would have been filled with the justice of it. He would have seen that I did not insult the feelings of a father, but the father who felt nothing. He would have trusted to the evidence of his own paternal heart, and boldly denied the possibility of the fact, instead of defending it. Against whom then will his honest indignation be directed, when I assure him, that this whole town beheld the Duke of Bedford's conduct, upon the death of his son, with horror and astonishment. Sir William Draper does himself but little honour in opposing the general sense of his country. The people are seldom wrong in their opinions,—in their sentiments they are never mistaken. There may be a vanity perhaps in a singular way of thinking;—but when a man professes a want of those feelings, which do honour to the multitude, he hazards something infinitely more important than the character of his understanding. After all, as Sir William may possibly be in earnest in his anxiety for the Duke of Bedford, I should be glad to relieve him from it. He may rest assured this worthy nobleman laughs, with equal indifference, at *my* reproaches, and Sir William's distress about him. But here let it stop. Even the Duke of Bedford, insensible as he is, will consult the tranquillity of his life, in not provoking the moderation of my temper. If, from the profoundest contempt, I should ever rise into anger, he should soon find, that all I have already said of him was lenity and compassion.

OUT of a long catalogue, Sir William Draper has confined himself to the refutation of two charges only. The rest he had not time to discuss; and indeed it would have been a laborious undertaking. To draw up a defence of such a series of enormities, would have required a life at least as long as that, which has been uniformly employed in the practice of them. The public opinion of the Duke of Bedford's extreme œconomy is, it seems, entirely without foundation. Though not very prodigal abroad, in his own family at least, he is regular and magnificent. He pays his debts, abhors a beggar, and makes a handsome provision for his son. His charity has improved upon the proverb, and ended where it began.

Admitting the whole force of this single instance of his domestic generosity (wonderful indeed, considering the narrowness of his fortune, and the little merit of his only son) the public may still perhaps be dissatisfied, and demand some other less equivocal proofs of his munificence. Sir William Draper should have entered boldly into the detail—of indigence relieved—of arts encouraged—of science patronized; men of learning protected, and works of genius rewarded;—in short, had there been a single instance, besides Mr. Rigby*, of blushing merit brought forward by the duke, for the service of the public, it should not have been omitted.[1]

I WISH it were possible to establish my inference with the same certainty, on which I believe the principle is founded. My conclusion however was not drawn from the principle alone. I am not so unjust as to reason from one crime to another; though I think, that, of all the vices, avarice is most apt to taint and corrupt the heart. I combined the known temper of the man with the extravagant concessions made by the ambassador; and though I doubt not sufficient care was taken to leave no document of any treasonable negociation, I still maintain that the conduct† of this minister carries with it an internal and convincing evidence against him. Sir William Draper seems not to know the value or force of such a proof. He will not permit us to judge of the motives of men, by the manifest tendency of their actions, nor by the notorious character of their minds. He calls for papers and witnesses, with a triumphant security, as if nothing could be true, but what could be proved in a court of justice. Yet a religious man might have remembered,

* This gentleman is supposed to have the same idea of *blushing*, that a man blind from his birth, has of scarlet or sky-blue.

† If Sir W. D. will take the trouble of looking into Torcy's Memoirs, he will see with what little ceremony a bribe may be offered to a Duke, and with what little ceremony it was *only not accepted*.[2]

---

[1] Wraxall wrote of Richard Rigby that 'the *lumen purpureum* which beamed from his suffused features served as a comment on the text of Junius'. *The historical and the posthumous memoirs*, ed. H. B. Wheatley (1884), i. 421.

[2] An attempt to bribe the Duke of Marlborough in May 1709 is recounted in *Mémoires de marquis de Torcy, pour servir à l'histoire des négociations depuis le Traité de Riswick jusqu'à la Paix d'Utrecht*. An English translation was published in 1757. The matter is discussed in W. S. Churchill, *Marlborough: his life and times*, iv. 62–72.

upon what foundation some truths, most interesting to mankind, have been received and established. If it were not for the internal evidence, which the purest of religions carries with it, what would have become of his once well-quoted decalogue, and of the meekness of his Christianity?

THE generous warmth of his resentment makes him confound the order of events. He forgets that the insults and distresses which the Duke of Bedford has suffered, and which Sir William has lamented with many delicate touches of the true pathetic, were only recorded in my letter to his Grace, not occasioned by it. It was a simple, candid narrative of facts; though, for aught I know, it may carry with it something prophetic. His Grace undoubtedly has received several ominous hints; and I think, in certain circumstances, a wise man would do well to prepare himself for the event.

BUT I have a charge of a heavier nature against Sir William Draper. He tells us that the Duke of Bedford is amenable to justice;—that parliament is a high and solemn tribunal; and that, if guilty, he may be punished by due course of law; and all this, he says, with as much gravity as if he believed one word of the matter. I hope indeed, the day of impeachments will arrive, before this nobleman escapes out of life;—but to refer us to that mode of proceeding now, with such a ministry, and such a house of commons as the present, what is it, but an indecent mockery of the common sense of the nation? I think he might have contented himself with defending the greatest enemy, without insulting the distresses of his country.

HIS concluding declaration of his opinion, with respect to the present condition of affairs, is too loose and undetermined to be of any service to the public. How strange is it that this gentleman should dedicate so much time and argument to the defence of worthless or indifferent characters, while he gives but seven solitary lines to the only subject, which can deserve his attention, or do credit to his abilities.

JUNIUS.

Junius' challenge for a single instance of the Duke of Bedford's generosity was taken up. A letter from Mrs. Griffiths, signed Frances, was printed in the *Public Advertiser* of 17 October 1769 and another from Lieutenant Jere. Mears on the 20th. Both testified to acts of kindness by the Duke. Junius' reply to the former is perhaps the feeblest retort he ever made.

LETTER XXVIII.

TO THE PRINTER OF THE PUBLIC ADVERTISER.

SIR, 20. *October* 1769.

I VERY sincerely applaud the spirit with which a lady has paid the debt of gratitude to her benefactor. Though I think she has mistaken the point, she shews a virtue which makes her respectable. The question turned upon the personal generosity or avarice of a man, whose private fortune is immense. The proofs of his munificence must be drawn from the uses, to which he has applied that fortune. I was not speaking of a Lord Lieutenant of Ireland, but of a rich English duke, whose wealth gave him the means of doing as much good in this country, as he derived from his power in another. I am far from wishing to lessen the merit of this single benevolent action;—perhaps it is the more conspicuous from standing alone. All I mean to say is, that it proves nothing in the present argument.

JUNIUS.

Junius' next adversary, Modestus, began writing in the *Gazetteer and New Daily Advertiser* on 25 September. Charles Green Say, the editor of that newspaper, claimed in a petition to government that he had hired Modestus to combat Junius. *Calendar of Home Office papers, 1770–2*, no. 143. Wade identified Modestus as John Dalrymple, but John Cleland, author of *Fanny Hill* (1750), is also said to have contributed under that name.

When preparing the collected edition Junius once again changed the chronological order of the letters. As Philo Junius, he here replied to Modestus of the 16th October, which asserted that the absurdities and solecisms of Junius' previous letter revealed him to be an Irishman—'The muddiest head from the muddiest bog in Ireland'.

LETTER XXIX.

ADDRESSED TO THE PRINTER OF THE PUBLIC ADVERTISER.

SIR, 19. *October* 1769.

I AM well assured that *Junius* will never descend to a dispute with such a writer as *Modestus* (whose letter appeared in the Gazetteer of Monday) especially as the dispute must be chiefly about words. Notwithstanding the partiality of the Public, it does not appear that *Junius* values himself upon any superior skill in composition, and I hope his time will always be more usefully employed than in the trifling refinements of verbal criticism. *Modestus*, however, shall have no reason to triumph in the silence and moderation of *Junius*. If he knew as much of the propriety of language, as I believe he does of the facts in question, he would have been as cautious of attacking *Junius* upon his composition, as he seems to be of entering into the subject of it; yet after all, the last is the only article of any importance to the public.

I DO not wonder at the unremitted rancour with which the Duke of Bedford and his adherents invariably speak of a nation, which we well know has been too much injured to be easily forgiven. But why must *Junius* be an Irishman?—*The absurdity of his writings betrays him.*—Waving all consideration of the insult offered by *Modestus* to the declared judgment of the people (they may well bear this among the rest) let us follow the several instances and try whether the charge be fairly supported.

FIRST then,—the leaving a man to enjoy such repose as he can find upon a bed of torture, is severe indeed; perhaps too much so, when applied to such a trifler as Sir William Draper; but there is nothing absurd either in the idea or expression. *Modestus* cannot distinguish between a sarcasm and a contradiction.

2. I AFFIRM with *Junius*, that it is the *frequency* of the fact, which alone can make us comprehend how a man can be his own enemy. We should never arrive at the complex idea conveyed by those

words, if we had only seen one or two instances of a man acting to his own prejudice. Offer the proposition to a child, or a man unused to compound his ideas, and you will soon see how little either of them understand you. It is not a simple idea arising from a single fact, but a very complex idea arising from many facts well observed, and accurately compared.

3. MODESTUS could not, without great affectation, mistake the meaning of *Junius*, when he speaks of a man who is the bitterest enemy of his friends. He could not but know, that *Junius* spoke, not of a false or hollow friendship, but of a real intention to serve, and that intention producing the worst effects of enmity. Whether the description be strictly applicable to Sir William Draper is another question. *Junius* does not say that it is more *criminal* for a man to be the enemy of his friends than his own, though he might have affirmed it with truth. In a moral light a man may certainly take greater liberties with himself than with another. To sacrifice ourselves merely is a weakness we may indulge in, if we think proper, for we do it at our own hazard and expence; but, under the pretence of friendship, to sport with the reputation, or sacrifice the honour of another, is something worse than weakness; and if, in favour of the foolish intention, we do not call it a crime, we must allow at least that it arises from an overweening, busy, meddling impudence.—*Junius* says only, and he says truly, that it is more extraordinary, that it involves a greater contradiction than the other; and is it not a maxim received in life, that in general we can determine more wisely for others than for ourselves? The reason of it is so clear in argument, that it hardly wants the confirmation of experience. Sir William Draper, I confess, is an exception to the general rule, though not much to his credit.

4. IF this gentleman will go back to his Ethicks, he may perhaps discover the truth of what *Junius* says, *that no outward tyranny can reach the mind.* The tortures of the body may be introduced by way of ornament or illustration to represent those of the mind, but strictly there is no similitude between them. They are totally different both in their cause and operation. The wretch, who suffers

upon the rack, is merely passive; but when the mind is tortured, it is not at the command of any outward power. It is the sense of guilt which constitutes the punishment, and creates that torture with which the guilty mind acts upon itself.

5. HE misquotes what *Junius* says of conscience, and makes the sentence ridiculous, by making it his own.

SO much for composition. Now for fact.—*Junius* it seems has mistaken the duke of Bedford. His Grace had all the proper feelings of a father, though he took care to suppress the appearance of them. Yet it was an occasion, one would think, on which he need not have been ashamed of his grief;—on which less fortitude would have done him more honour. I can conceive indeed a benevolent motive for his endeavouring to assume an air of tranquillity in his own family, and I wish I could discover any thing, in the rest of his character, to justify my assigning that motive to his behaviour. But is there no medium? Was it necessary to appear abroad, to ballot at the India-house, and make a public display, tho' it were only of an apparent insensibility?—I know we are treading on tender ground, and *Junius*, I am convinced, does not wish to urge this question farther. Let the friends of the Duke of Bedford observe that humble silence, which becomes their situation. They should recollect that there are still some facts in store, at which human nature would shudder. I shall be understood by those whom it concerns, when I say that these facts go farther than to the Duke*.

IT is not inconsistent to suppose that a man may be quite indifferent about one part of a charge, yet severely stung with

* Within a fortnight after Lord Tavistock's death, the venerable *Gertrude* had a route at Bedford-house. The good Duke (who had only sixty thousand pounds a year) ordered an inventory to be taken of his son's wearing apparel, down to his slippers, sold them all, and put the money in his pocket. The amiable Marchioness, shocked at such brutal, unfeeling avarice, gave the value of the cloaths, to the Marquis's servant, out of her own purse. That incomparable woman did not long survive her husband. When she died, the Duchess of Bedford treated her as the Duke had treated his only son. She ordered every gown and trinket to be sold, and pocketed the money.—These are the monsters, whom Sir William Draper comes forward to defend.—May God protect *me* from doing any thing that may require such defence, or deserve such friendship!

another, and though he feels no remorse, that he may wish to be revenged. The charge of insensibility carries a reproach indeed, but no danger with it.—*Junius* had said, *there are others who would assassinate. Modestus*, knowing his man, will not suffer the insinuation to be divided, but fixes it all upon the Duke of Bedford.

WITHOUT determining upon what evidence *Junius* would *choose to be condemned*, I will venture to maintain, in opposition to *Modestus*, or to Mr. Rigby (who is certainly not *Modestus*) or any other of the Bloomsbury gang, that the evidence against the Duke of Bedford is as strong as any presumptive evidence can be. It depends upon a combination of facts and reasoning, which require no confirmation from the anecdote of the Duke of Marlborough. This anecdote was referred to merely to shew how ready a great man may be to receive a great bribe; and if *Modestus* could read the original, he would see that the expression, *only not accepted*, was probably the only one in our language that exactly fitted the case. The bribe, offered to the Duke of Marlborough, was not refused.

I CANNOT conclude without taking notice of this honest gentleman's learning, and wishing he had given us a little more of it. When he accidentally found himself so near speaking truth, it was rather unfair of him to leave out the *non potuisse refelli*. As it stands, the *pudet hæc opprobria* may be divided equally between Mr. Rigby and the Duke of Bedford. Mr. Rigby, I take for granted, will assert his natural right to the modesty of the quotation, and leave all the opprobrium to his Grace.[1]

PHILO JUNIUS.

Before the echoes of his last assault had died away, Junius began a fresh one. On 21 September 1769 Major-General William Gansell was arrested in Piccadilly for debt. He was subsequently rescued by men from the Horse Guards, though he later gave himself up. What might have seemed no more than an isolated incident became, under Junius' scrutiny, a warning of the danger of military rule and an indication that the ministers cared little for the niceties of the constitution.

[1] Pudet haec opprobria nobis et dici potuisse et non potuisse refelli, Ovid, *Metamorphoses*, i. 758–9: 'One is ashamed that such an insult should have been uttered but not refuted'. Modestus in his letter had quoted the first four words.

LETTER XXX.

TO THE PRINTER OF THE PUBLIC ADVERTISER.

SIR, 17. *October*, 1769.

IT is not wonderful that the great cause, in which this country is engaged, should have roused and engrossed the whole attention of the people. I rather admire the generous spirit, with which they feel and assert their interest in this important question, than blame them for their indifference about any other. When the constitution is openly invaded, when the first original right of the people, from which all laws derive their authority, is directly attacked, inferior grievances naturally lose their force, and are suffered to pass by without punishment or observation. The present ministry are as singularly marked by their fortune, as by their crimes. Instead of atoning for their former conduct by any wise or popular measure, they have found, in the enormity of one fact, a cover and defence for a series of measures, which must have been fatal to any other administration. I fear we are too remiss in observing the whole of their proceedings. Struck with the principal figure, we do not sufficiently mark in what manner the canvass is filled up. Yet surely it is not a less crime, nor less fatal in its consequences, to encourage a flagrant breach of the law by a military force, than to make use of the forms of parliament to destroy the constitution.— The ministry seem determined to give us a choice of difficulties, and, if possible, to perplex us with the multitude of their offences. The expedient is worthy of the Duke of Grafton. But though he has preserved a gradation and variety in his measures, we should remember that the principle is uniform. Dictated by the same spirit, they deserve the same attention. The following fact, though of the most alarming nature, has not yet been clearly stated to the public, nor have the consequences of it been sufficiently understood. Had I taken it up at an earlier period, I should have been accused of an uncandid, malignant precipitation, as if I watched for an unfair advantage against the ministry, and would not allow them a reasonable time to do their duty. They now stand without excuse. Instead of employing the leisure they have had, in a strict examination of the offence, and punishing the offenders, they seem to have considered *that* indulgence as a security to them, that, with a little time and management, the whole affair might be buried in silence, and utterly forgotten.

*A MAJOR general of the army is arrested by the sheriffs officers for a considerable debt. He persuades them to conduct him to the Tilt-yard in St. James's Park, under some pretence of business, which it imported him to settle before he was confined.[1] He applies to a serjeant, not immediately on duty, to assist with some of his companions in favouring his escape. He attempts it. A bustle ensues. The bailiffs claim their prisoner. †An officer of the guards, not then on duty, takes part in the affair, applies to the ‡lieutenant commanding the Tilt-yard guard, and urges him to turn out his guard to relieve a general officer. The lieutenant declines interfering in person, but stands at a distance, and suffers the business to be done. The officer takes upon himself to order out the guard. In a moment they are in arms, quit their guard, march, rescue the general, and drive away the sheriffs officers, who, in vain represent their right to the prisoner, and the nature of the arrest. The soldiers first conduct the general into the guard-room, then escort him to a place of safety, with bayonets fixed, and in all the forms of military triumph. I will not enlarge upon the various circumstances which attended this atrocious proceeding. The personal injury received by the officers of the law in the execution of their duty, may perhaps be atoned for by some private compensation. I consider nothing but the wound, which has been given to the law itself, to which no remedy has been applied, no satisfaction made. Neither is it my design to dwell upon the misconduct of the parties concerned, any farther than is necessary to shew the behaviour of the ministry in its true light. I would make every compassionate allowance for the infatuation of the prisoner, the false and criminal discretion of one officer, and the madness of another. I would leave the ignorant

* Major General Gansel. † Lieutenant Dodd.
‡ Lieutenant Garth.

[1] The Horse Guards was built on the site of the old Tiltyard, used in Tudor times for weapon training and tournaments.

soldiers entirely out of the question. They are certainly the least guilty, though they are the only persons who have yet suffered, even in the appearance of punishment.* The fact itself, however atrocious, is not the principal point to be considered. It might have happened under a more regular government, and with guards better disciplined than ours. The main question is, in what manner have the ministry acted on this extraordinary occasion. A general officer calls upon the king's own guard, then actually on duty, to rescue him from the laws of his country; yet at this moment he is in a situation no worse, than if he had not committed an offence, equally enormous in a civil and military view.—A lieutenant upon duty designedly quits his guard, and suffers it to be drawn out by another officer, for a purpose, which he well knew (as we may collect from an appearance of caution, which only makes his behaviour the more criminal) to be in the highest degree illegal. Has this gentleman been called to a court martial to answer for his conduct? No. Has it been censured? No. Has it been in any shape inquired into? No.—Another lieutenant, not upon duty, nor even in his regimentals, is daring enough to order out the king's guard, over which he had properly no command, and engages them in a violation of the laws of his country, perhaps the most singular and extravagant that ever was attempted.—What punishment has *he* suffered? Literally none. Supposing he should be prosecuted at common law for the rescue, will that circumstance, from which the ministry can derive no merit, excuse or justify their suffering so flagrant a breach of military discipline to pass by unpunished, and unnoticed? Are they aware of the outrage offered to their sovereign, when his own proper guard is ordered out to stop by main force, the execution of his laws? What are we to conclude from so scandalous a neglect of their duty, but that they have other views, which can only be answered by securing the attachment of the guards? The minister would hardly be so cautious of offending them, if he did not mean, in due time, to call for their assistance.

WITH respect to the parties themselves, let it be observed, that these gentlemen are neither young officers, nor very young men.

* A few of them were confined.

Had they belonged to the unfledged race of ensigns, who infest our streets, and dishonor our public places, it might perhaps be sufficient to send them back to that discipline, from which their parents, judging lightly from the maturity of their vices, had removed them too soon. In this case, I am sorry to see, not so much the folly of youth, as the spirit of the corps, and the connivance of government. I do not question that there are many brave and worthy officers in the regiments of guards. But considering them as a corps, I fear, it will be found that they are neither good soldiers, nor good subjects. Far be it from me to insinuate the most distant reflection upon the army. On the contrary, I honour and esteem the profession; and if these gentlemen were better soldiers, I am sure they would be better subjects. It is not that there is any internal vice or defect in the profession itself, as regulated in this country, but that it is the spirit of this particular corps, to despise their profession, and that while they vainly assume the lead of the army, they make it matter of impertinent comparison and triumph over the bravest troops in the world (I mean our marching regiments) that *they* indeed stand upon higher ground, and are privileged to neglect the laborious forms of military discipline and duty. Without dwelling longer upon a most invidious subject, I shall leave it to military men, who have seen a service more active than the parade, to determine whether or no I speak truth.[1]

HOW far this dangerous spirit has been encouraged by government, and to what pernicious purposes it may be applied hereafter, well deserves our most serious consideration. I know indeed, that when this affair happened, an affectation of alarm ran through the ministry. Something must be done to save appearances. The case was too flagrant to be passed by absolutely without notice. But how have they acted? Instead of ordering the officers concerned, (and who, strictly speaking, are alone guilty,) to be put under arrest, and brought to trial, they would have it understood, that they did their duty completely, in confining a serjeant and four

[1] Junius returned to this subject in his letter to the King of 19 December 1769. There was much resentment of the privileged position of the Guards regiments, in which chances of promotion were much better than average. See Junius' note on p. 169.

private soldiers, until they should be demanded by the civil power; so that while the officers, who ordered or permitted the thing to be done, escape without censure, the poor men who obeyed those orders, who in a military view are no way responsible for what they did, and who for that reason have been discharged by the civil magistrates, are the only objects whom the ministry have thought proper to expose to punishment. They did not venture to bring even these men to a court martial, because they knew their evidence would be fatal to some persons, whom they were determined to protect. Otherwise, I doubt not, the lives of these unhappy, friendless soldiers would long since have been sacrificed without scruple to the security of their guilty officers.

I HAVE been accused of endeavouring to enflame the passions of the people.—Let me now appeal to their understanding. If there be any tool of administration daring enough to deny these facts, or shameless enough to defend the conduct of the ministry, let him come forward. I care not under what title he appears. He shall find me ready to maintain the truth of my narrative, and the justice of my observations upon it, at the hazard of my utmost credit with the public.

UNDER the most arbitrary governments, the common administration of justice is suffered to take its course. The subject, though robbed of his share in the legislature, is still protected by the laws. The political freedom of the English constitution was once the pride and honour of an Englishman. The civil equality of the laws preserved the property, and defended the safety of the subject. Are these glorious privileges the birthright of the people, or are we only tenants at the will of the ministry?—But that I know there is a spirit of resistance in the hearts of my countrymen, that they value life, not by its conveniences, but by the independance and dignity of their condition, I should, at this moment, appeal only to their discretion. I should persuade them to banish from their minds all memory of what we were; I should tell them this is not a time to remember that we were Englishmen; and give it as my last advice, to make some early agreement with the minister, that since it has pleased him to rob us of those political rights, which once distinguished the inhabitants of a country, where honour was happiness, he would leave us at least the humble, obedient security of citizens, and graciously condescend to protect us in our submission.

JUNIUS.

Once more Junius was engulfed in a storm of controversy. Plato, on 26 October 1769, accused him of vindictiveness towards Gansell; An Old Soldier, 7 November, complained that he was 'catching at any thing to find fault'. But the most sustained criticism came once more from Modestus in a letter to the *Gazetteer and New Daily Advertiser* of 20 October: 'the time was, when the escape of an unfortunate officer from a bailiff, would not have been wrought up into a charge against government . . . but a Minister was to be wounded, and provided this could be done, no matter through whose side the weapon struck.'

Junius defended himself under the name Moderatus and included the letter in his collected edition, attributing it to Philo Junius.

LETTER XXXI.

TO THE PRINTER OF THE PUBLIC ADVERTISER.

SIR, *November* 14, 1769.

THE variety of remarks, which have been made upon the last letter of *Junius*, and my own opinion of the Writer, who, whatever may be his faults, is certainly not a weak man, have induced me to examine, with some attention, the subject of that letter. I could not persuade myself that, while he had plenty of important materials, he would have taken up a light or trifling occasion to attack the Ministry; much less could I conceive that it was his intention to ruin the officers concern'd in the rescue of general Gansel, or to injure the general himself. These are little objects, and can no way contribute to the great purposes he seems to have in view by addressing himself to the publick.—Without considering the ornamented stile he has adopted, I determined to look farther into the matter, before I decided upon the merits of his letter. The first step I took was to enquire into the truth of the facts; for if these were either false or misrepresented, the most artful exertion of his understanding, in reasoning upon them, would only be a disgrace to him.—Now, Sir, I have found every circumstance stated by *Junius* to be literally true. General Gansel persuaded the bailiffs to conduct him to the parade, and certainly solicited a Corporal and other Soldiers to assist him in making his escape. Captain Dodd did certainly apply to Captain Garth for the assistance of his guard.[1] Captain Garth declined appearing himself, but stood aloof, while the other took upon him to order out the King's guard, and by main force rescued the General. It is also strictly true, that the General was escorted by a file of musqueteers to a place of security.—These are facts, Mr. Woodfall, which I promise you no gentleman in the guards will deny. If all or any of them are false, why are they not contradicted by the parties themselves? However secure against military censure, they have yet a character to lose, and surely, if they are innocent, it is not beneath them to pay some attention to the opinion of the public.

THE force of *Junius*'s Observations upon these facts cannot be better marked, than by stating and refuting the objections which have been made to them. One writer says, "Admitting the officers have offended, they are punishable at common law, and will you have a British subject punished twice for the same offence?"—I answer that they have committed two offences, both very enormous, and violated two laws. The rescue is one offence, the flagrant breach of discipline another, and hitherto it does not appear that they have been punished, or even censured for either. Another gentleman lays much stress upon the calamity of the case, and, instead of disproving facts, appeals at once to the compassion of the public. This idea, as well as the insinuation *that depriving the parties of their commissions would be an injury to their creditors*, can only refer to General Gansel. The other officers are in no distress, therefore, have no claim to compassion, nor does it appear, that their creditors,

[1] The confusion about the rank of these men arises from the fact that Guards officers were entitled to higher rank in the army. Hence Guards lieutenants held the army rank of captain.

if they have any, are more likely to be satisfied by their continuing in the guards. But this sort of plea will not hold in any shape. Compassion to an offender, who has grossly violated the laws, is in effect a cruelty to the peaceable subject who has observed them; and, even admitting the force of any alleviating circumstances, it is nevertheless true, that, in this instance, the royal compassion has interposed too soon. The legal and proper mercy of a King of England may remit the punishment, but ought not to stop the trial.

BESIDES these particular objections, there has been a cry raised against *Junius* for his malice and injustice in attacking the ministry upon an event, which they could neither hinder nor foresee. This, I must affirm, is a false representation of his argument. He lays no stress upon the event itself, as a ground of accusation against the ministry, but dwells entirely upon their subsequent conduct. He does not say that they are answerable for the offence, but for the scandalous neglect of their duty, in suffering an offence, so flagrant, to pass by without notice or inquiry. Supposing them ever so regardless of what they owe to the public, and as indifferent about the opinion as they are about the interests of their country, what answer, as officers of the crown, will they give to *Junius*, when he asks them, *Are they aware of the outrage offered to their Sovereign, when his own proper guard is ordered out to stop, by main force, the execution of his laws?*—And when we see a ministry giving such a strange unaccountable protection to the officers of the guards, is it unfair to suspect, that they have some secret and unwarrantable motives for their conduct? If they feel themselves injured by such a suspicion, why do they not immediately clear themselves from it, by doing their duty? For the honour of the guards, I cannot help expressing another suspicion, that, if the commanding officer had not received a secret injunction to the contrary, he would, in the ordinary course of his business, have applied for a court martial to try the two subalterns; the one for quitting his guard;—the other for taking upon him the command of the guard, and employing it in the manner he did. I do not mean to enter into or defend the severity, with which *Junius* treats the guards. On the contrary, I will suppose, for a moment, that they deserve a very different character. If this be true, in what light will they consider the conduct of the two subalterns, but as a general reproach and disgrace to the whole corps? And will they not wish to see them censured in a military way, if it were only for the credit and discipline of the Regiment.

UPON the whole, Sir, the Ministry seem to me to have taken a very improper advantage of the good-nature of the public, whose humanity, they found, considered nothing in this affair but the distress of General Gansel. They would persuade us that it was only a common rescue by a few disorderly soldiers, and not the formal deliberate act of the king's guard, headed by an officer, and the public has fallen into the deception. I think, therefore, we are obliged to *Junius* for the care he has taken to inquire into the facts, and for the just commentary with which he has given them to the world.—For my own part, I am as unwilling as any man to load the unfortunate; but, really, Sir, the precedent, with respect to the guards, is of a most important nature, and alarming enough (considering the consequences with which it may be attended) to deserve a parliamentary inquiry: when the guards are daring enough, not only to violate their own discipline, but publicly and with the most atrocious violence to stop the execution of the laws, and when such extraordinary offences pass with impunity, believe me, Sir, the precedent strikes deep.

PHILO JUNIUS.

In his letter of 17 October on General Gansell Junius had challenged anyone 'shameless enough to defend the conduct of the ministry' to come forward: 'He shall find me ready to maintain the truth of my narrative.' He did not, however, reply under the name of Junius to Modestus's defence of 20 October and that writer reminded him of his promise: 'It is time, Junius, you should think of the challenge you gave.' Modestus's letter was reprinted in the *Gentleman's Magazine*, 1769, 537–8.

Junius' reply, when it came, seemed half-hearted and Modestus wrote in the *Gazetteer* of 18 November claiming victory: 'Had I not imagined you capable of making a better defence, you had never been attacked by me.'

LETTER XXXII.

TO THE PRINTER OF THE PUBLIC ADVERTISER.

SIR, 15. *Nov.* 1769.

I ADMIT the claim of a gentleman, who publishes in the Gazetteer under the name of *Modestus*. He has some right to expect an answer from me; though, I think, not so much from the merit or importance of his objections, as from my own voluntary engagement. I had a reason for not taking notice of him sooner, which, as he is a candid person, I believe he will think sufficient. In my first letter, I took for granted, from the time which had elapsed, that there was no intention to censure, nor even to try the persons concerned in the rescue of General Gansel; but *Modestus* having since either affirmed, or strongly insinuated, that the offenders might still be brought to a legal trial, any attempt to prejudge the cause, or to prejudice the minds of a jury, or a court martial, would be highly improper.

A MAN, more hostile to the ministry than I am, would not so often remind them of their duty. If the Duke of Grafton will not perform the duty of his station, why is he minister?—I will not descend to a scurrilous altercation with any man: but this is a subject too important to be passed over with silent indifference. If the gentlemen, whose conduct is in question, are not brought to a trial, the Duke of Grafton shall hear from me again.

THE motives on which I am supposed to have taken up this cause, are of little importance, compared with the facts themselves, and the observations I have made upon them. Without a vain profession of integrity, which, in these times might justly be suspected, I shall shew myself in effect a friend to the interests of my countrymen, and leave it to them to determine, whether I am moved by a personal malevolence to three private gentlemen, or merely by a hope of perplexing the ministry, or whether I am animated by a just and honourable purpose of obtaining a satisfaction to the laws of this country, equal, if possible, to the violation they have suffered.

JUNIUS.

Junius now abandoned the Gansell affair, at least under that pseudonym. It was carried on throughout the rest of November by Modestus and Y.Y. on the government side, and X.X., who may have been Junius, for the opposition. Their letters are discussed in Appendix Five and were printed by Wade, ii. 284–92.

The new subject was the prosecution commenced by the government against Samuel Vaughan for attempted bribery. Vaughan was a West Indian merchant who had played a prominent part in city politics on the radical side: on 8 March 1769 he had taken over the meeting at which Charles Dingley and the supporters of the government were defeated. In the summer of 1769 he was foolish enough to write to Grafton offering £5,000 for the reversion of an office in Jamaica. Grafton set in train a prosecution. The affair was mentioned in the *Public Advertiser* as early as 16 August by Q in the Corner, which may have been one of Junius' other pseudonyms. Vaughan in desperation made contact with Junius through the printer (private letter no. 11). But on 27 November Lord Mansfield in King's Bench summed up strongly against Vaughan, calling his letter 'a daring attempt at bribery', and the rule was made absolute. At the end of the month Junius intervened with devastating effect.

LETTER XXXIII.

TO HIS GRACE THE DUKE OF GRAFTON.

MY LORD, 29. *Nov.* 1769.

THOUGH my opinion of your Grace's integrity was but little affected by the coyness with which you received Mr. Vaughan's proposals, I confess I give you some credit for your discretion. You had a fair opportunity of displaying a certain delicacy, of which you had not been suspected; and you were in the right to make use of it. By laying in a moderate stock of reputation, you undoubtedly meant to provide for the future necessities of your character, that with an honourable resistance upon record, you might safely indulge your genius, and yield to a favourite inclination with security. But you have discovered your purposes too soon; and, instead of the modest reserve of virtue, have shewn us the termagant chastity of a prude, who gratifies her passions with distinction, and prosecutes one lover for a rape, while she solicits the lewd embraces of another.

YOUR cheek turns pale; for a guilty conscience tells you, you are undone.—Come forward, thou virtuous minister, and tell the world by what interest Mr. Hine has been recommended to so extraordinary a mark of his Majesty's favour; what was the price of the patent he has bought, and to what honourable purpose the purchase money has been applied. Nothing less than many thousands could pay Colonel Burgoyne's expences at Preston. Do you dare to prosecute such a creature as Vaughan, while you are basely setting up the Royal Patronage to auction? Do you dare to complain of an attack upon your own honour, while you are selling the favours of the crown, to raise a fund for corrupting the morals of the people? And, do you think it possible such enormities should escape without impeachment? It is indeed highly your interest to maintain the present house of commons. Having sold the nation to you in gross, they will undoubtedly protect you in the detail; for while they patronize your crimes, they feel for their own.

JUNIUS.

In the face of this accusation the ministry maintained a discreet silence. Early in December, Junius wrote to the printer (private letter no. 14) that he had saved Vaughan already, 'and really without intending it. The facts are all literally true.'

LETTER XXXIV.

TO HIS GRACE THE DUKE OF GRAFTON.

MY LORD, 12. *Dec.* 1769.

I FIND with some surprise, that you are not supported as you deserve. Your most determined advocates have scruples about them, which you are unacquainted with; and, though there be nothing too hazardous for your Grace to engage in, there are some things too infamous for the vilest prostitute of a news-paper to defend*. In what other manner shall we account for the profound, submissive silence, which you and your friends have observed upon a charge, which called immediately for the clearest refutation, and would have justified the severest measures of resentment? I did not attempt to blast your character by an indirect, ambiguous insinuation, but candidly stated to you a plain fact, which struck directly at the integrity of a privy counsellor, of a first commissioner of the treasury, and of a leading minister, who is supposed to enjoy the first share in his Majesty's confidence†.[1] In every one of these capacities I employed the most moderate terms to charge you with treachery to your Sovereign, and breach of trust in your office. I accused you of having sold a patent place in the collection of the customs at Exeter, to one Mr. Hine, who, unable or unwilling to deposit the whole purchase-money himself, raised part of it by contribution, and has now a certain Doctor Brooke quartered upon the salary for one hundred pounds a year.—No sale by the candle was ever conducted with greater formality.—I affirm that the price, at which the place was knocked down (and which, I have good reason to think, was not less than three thousand five hundred pounds) was, with your connivance and consent, paid to Colonel Burgoyne, to reward him, I presume, for the decency of his deportment at Preston; or to reimburse him, perhaps, for the fine of one thousand pounds, which, for that very deportment, the court of King's Bench thought proper to set upon him.—It is

* From the publication of the preceding to this date, not one word was said in defence of the infamous Duke of Grafton. But vice and impudence soon recovered themselves, and the sale of the royal favour was openly avowed and defended. We acknowledge the piety of St. James's; but what is become of *his* morality?

† And by the same means preserves it to this hour.

---

[1] Although the Duke of Grafton resigned in January 1770, he had rejoined the administration by the time Junius came to write the footnote in the autumn of 1771.

There can be little doubt that reticence was deliberate ministerial policy. When Grafton was once more attacked by Junius in September 1771, Thomas Bradshaw advised him not to reply—otherwise 'this use will be made of it—why was no direct contradiction given to any part of Hine's case?' 30 September 1771, Grafton MSS. 966, Bury St. Edmunds.

not often that the chief justice and the prime minister are so strangely at variance in their opinions of men and things.[1]

I THANK God there is not in human nature a degree of impudence daring enough to deny the charge I have fixed upon you. *Your courteous secretary, your confidential architect†, are silent as the grave. Even Mr. Rigby's countenance fails him. He violates his second nature, and blushes whenever he speaks of you.—Perhaps the noble Colonel himself will relieve you. No man is more tender of his reputation. He is not only nice, but perfectly sore in every thing that touches his honour. If any man, for example, were to accuse him of taking his stand at a gaming-table, and watching, with the soberest attention, for a fair opportunity of engaging a drunken young nobleman at piquet, he would undoubtedly consider it as an infamous aspersion upon his character, and resent it like a man of honour.[2] Acquitting him therefore of drawing a regular and splendid subsistence from any unworthy practices, either in his own house or elsewhere, let me ask your Grace, for what military merits you have been pleased to reward him with military government? He had a regiment of dragoons, which one would imagine, was at least an equivalent for any services he ever performed. Besides, he is but a young officer considering his preferment, and, except in his activity at Preston, not very conspicuous in his profession. But it seems, the sale of a civil employment was not sufficient, and military governments, which were intended for the support of worn out veterans, must be thrown into the scale, to defray the

* Tommy Bradshaw.

† Mr. Taylor. He and George Ross, (the Scotch agent and worthy confidante of Lord Mansfield) managed the business.[3]

---

[1] John Burgoyne's contest for Preston at the general election of 1768 was described in *The House of Commons 1754–90*, ii. 142 as 'one of the most violent elections of the century'. Grafton was certainly anxious to recompense Burgoyne 'on account of an expensive attack he has made in a part of the country the least affected to Government, and which has cost him a sum which I dare hardly name'. It cost him a further £1,000 fine in May 1769. Burgoyne's appointment as Governor of Fort William was announced early in December, just before this letter was written.

[2] Walpole wrote that this insinuation of sharp practice was considered unfair 'as he was never supposed to do more than play very well'. Walpole to Mason, 5 October 1777, *Yale Edition*, vol. 28, 336–7.

[3] I should perhaps remind the reader that all persons mentioned in the text are included in the biographical references at the end of the volume.

extensive bribery of a contested election. Are these the steps you take to secure to your Sovereign the attachment of his army? With what countenance dare you appear in the royal presence, branded as you are with the infamy of a notorious breach of trust? With what countenance can you take your seat at the treasury-board or in council, when you feel that every circulating whisper is at your expence alone, and stabs you to the heart? Have you a single friend in parliament so shameless, so thoroughly abandoned, as to undertake your defence? You know, my Lord, that there is not a man in either house, whose character, however flagitious, would not be ruined by mixing his reputation with yours; and does not your heart inform you, that you are degraded below the condition of a man, when you are obliged to bear these insults with submission, and even to thank me for my moderation?

WE are told, by the highest judicial authority, that Mr. Vaughan's offer to purchase the reversion of a patent in Jamaica (which he was otherwise sufficiently entitled to) amounted to a high misdemeanour. Be it so: and if he deserves it, let him be punished. But the learned judge might have had a fairer opportunity of displaying the powers of his eloquence. Having delivered himself with so much energy upon the criminal nature, and dangerous consequences of any attempt to corrupt a man in your Grace's station, what would he have said to the minister himself, to that very privy counsellor, to that first commissioner of the treasury, who does not wait for, but impatiently solicits the touch of corruption; who employs the meanest of his creatures in these honourable services, and, forgetting the genius and fidelity of his secretary, descends to apply to his house-builder for assistance?

THIS affair, my Lord, will do infinite credit to government, if, to clear your character, you should think proper to bring it into the house of Lords, or into the court of King's Bench.——But, my Lord, you dare not do either.

JUNIUS.

A little before the publication of this and the preceding letter, the chaste Duke of Grafton had commenced a prosecution against Mr. Samuel Vaughan, for endeavouring to corrupt his integrity by an office of five thousand pounds for a patent place in

Jamaica.[1] A rule to shew cause, why an information should not be exhibited against Vaughan for certain misdemeanors, being granted by the Court of King's Bench, the matter was solemnly argued on the 27. of November, 1769, and, by the unanimous opinion of the four judges, the rule was made absolute. The pleadings and speeches were accurately taken in short-hand and published. The whole of Lord Mansfield's speech, and particularly the following extracts from it, deserve the reader's attention. "A practice of the kind complained of here is certainly dishonourable and scandalous.—If a man, standing under the relation of an officer under the King, or of a person in whom the King puts confidence, or of a minister, takes money for the use of that confidence the King puts in him, he basely betrays the King,—he basely betrays his trust.—If the King sold the office, it would be acting contrary to the trust the constitution hath reposed in him. The constitution does not intend the crown should sell those offices, to raise a revenue out of them.—Is it possible to hesitate, whether this would not be criminal in the Duke of Grafton;—contrary to his duty as a privy councillor;—contrary to his duty as a minister—contrary to his duty as a subject.—His advice should be free according to his judgement;—It is the duty of his office;—he has sworn to it."—Notwithstanding all this, the chaste Duke of Grafton certainly sold a patent place to Mr. Hine for three thousand five hundred pounds; and, for so doing, is now Lord Privy Seal to the chaste George, with whose piety we are perpetually deafened. If the house of commons had done their duty, and impeached the black Duke for this most infamous breach of trust, how woefully must poor, honest Mansfield have been puzzled! His embarassment would have afforded the most ridiculous scene, that ever was exhibited. To save the worthy judge from this perplexity, and the no less worthy Duke from impeachment, the prosecution against *Vaughan* was, immediately dropped upon my discovery and publication of the Duke's treachery. The suffering this charge to pass, without any inquiry, fixes shameless prostitution upon the face of the house of commons, more strongly than even the Middlesex election—Yet the licentiousness of the press is complained of![2]

'The affair of Hine's patent makes a great noise,' wrote Thomas Whately on 19 December, *Grenville papers*, iv. 495. Junius' charges eventually stung ministerial writers into action. On 14 December, in the *Public Advertiser*, Justice denied that there was anything improper in the transaction unless it could be shown that the Duke had pocketed the money; in a second letter, dated 26 December, he asserted that Hine had been appointed before the general election. From Cambridge, John Symons, a lawyer and Fellow of Peterhouse, submitted a long and tedious defence of the ministry published in the *Gazetteer* 16–17 December, and reprinted in the *Gentleman's Magazine*, 1769, 622–6. His reward was gratifyingly swift: in 1771 he was appointed Regius Professor of Modern History in succession to Thomas Gray and the following year was made Recorder of Bury St. Edmunds, where Grafton had influence. The dispute over Hine's case is a further example of the

[1] Junius presumably intended 'offer' rather than 'office'.

[2] Vaughan published two pamphlets defending his actions—*A refutation of a false aspersion first thrown out in the Public Ledger* (1769) and *An appeal to the public in a narrative of his negotiation with the Duke of Grafton* (1770).

changing attitude towards public office: what to Junius seemed evident jobbery was to others a perfectly unremarkable and traditional practice.

In the meantime Junius moved on to a fresh subject which, he told Woodfall, would be 'a capital and I hope a final Piece'. (Private letter no. 14.) This was the famous attack upon the King, described by Horace Walpole as 'the most daring insult ever offered to a prince but in times of open rebellion'. Walpole, iii. 266. Though for the most part Junius adhered to the convention that George III had been misled by his ministers, he came nearer than ever before to charging the King with personal responsibility for the events of his reign.

LETTER XXXV.

TO THE PRINTER OF THE PUBLIC ADVERTISER.

19. *December*, 1769.

When the complaints of a brave and powerful people are observed to encrease in proportion to the wrongs they have suffered; when, instead of sinking into submission, they are roused to resistance, the time will soon arrive at which every inferior consideration must yield to the security of the Sovereign, and to the general safety of the state. There is a moment of difficulty and danger, at which flattery and falshood can no longer deceive, and simplicity itself can no longer be misled. Let us suppose it arrived. Let us suppose a gracious, well-intentioned prince, made sensible at last of the great duty he owes to his people, and of his own disgraceful situation; that he looks round him for assistance, and asks for no advice, but how to gratify the wishes, and secure the happiness of his subjects. In these circumstances, it may be matter of curious SPECULATION to consider, if an honest man were permitted to approach a King, in what terms he would address himself to his Sovereign. Let it be imagined, no matter how improbable, that the first prejudice against his character is removed, that the ceremonious difficulties of an audience are surmounted, that he feels himself animated by the purest and most honourable affections to his King and country, and that the great person, whom he addresses, has spirit enough to bid him speak freely, and understanding enough to listen to him with attention. Unacquainted with the vain impertinence of forms, he would deliver his sentiments with dignity and firmness, but not without respect.

SIR,

IT is the misfortune of your life, and originally the cause of every reproach and distress, which has attended your government, that you should never have been acquainted with the language of truth, until you heard it in the complaints of your people. It is not, however, too late to correct the error of your education. We are still inclined to make an indulgent allowance for the pernicious lessons you received in your youth, and to form the most sanguine hopes from the natural benevolence of your disposition*.[1] We are far from thinking you capable of a direct, deliberate purpose to invade those original rights of your subjects, on which all their civil and political liberties depend. Had it been possible for us to entertain a suspicion so dishonourable to your character, we should long since have adopted a style of remonstrance very distant from the humility of complaint. The doctrine inculcated by our laws, *That the King can do no wrong*, is admitted without reluctance. We separate the amiable, good-natured prince from the folly and treachery of his servants, and the private virtues of the man from the vices of his government. Were it not for this just distinction, I know not whether your Majesty's condition, or that of the English nation, would deserve most to be lamented. I would pre-

* The plan of tutelage and future dominion over the heir apparent, laid many years ago at Carlton-house between the Princess Dowager and her favourite the Earl of Bute, was as gross and palpable, as that, which was concerted between Anne of Austria and Cardinal Mazarin, to govern Lewis the Fourteenth, and in effect to prolong his minority until the end of their lives. That prince had strong natural parts, and used frequently to blush for his own ignorance and want of education, which had been wilfully neglected by his mother and her minion. A little experience however soon shewed him how shamefully he had been treated, and for what infamous purposes he had been kept in ignorance. Our great Edward too, at an early period, had sense enough to understand the nature of the connection between his abandoned mother, and the detested Mortimer. But, since that time, human nature, we may observe, is greatly altered for the better. Dowagers may be chaste, and minions may be honest. When it was proposed to settle the present King's household as Prince of Wales, it is well known that the Earl of Bute was forced into it, in direct contradiction to the late King's inclination. *That* was the salient point, from which all the mischiefs and disgraces of the present reign, took life and motion. From that moment, Lord Bute never suffered the Prince of Wales to be an instant out of his sight.—We need not look farther.

---

[1] For a less partisan account of the King's early upbringing, see J. Brooke, *King George III*, chs. 2 and 3.

pare your mind for a favourable reception of truth, by removing every painful, offensive idea of personal reproach. Your subjects, Sir, wish for nothing but that, as *they* are reasonable and affectionate enough to separate your person from your government, so *you*, in your turn, should distinguish between the conduct, which becomes the permanent dignity of a King, and that which serves only to promote the temporary interest and miserable ambition of a minister.

YOU ascended the throne with a declared, and, I doubt not, a sincere resolution of giving universal satisfaction to your subjects. You found them pleased with the novelty of a young prince, whose countenance promised even more than his words, and loyal to you not only from principle, but passion. It was not a cold profession of allegiance to the first magistrate, but a partial, animated attachment to a favourite prince, the native of their country. They did not wait to examine your conduct, nor to be determined by experience, but gave you a generous credit for the future blessings of your reign, and paid you in advance the dearest tribute of their affections. Such, Sir, was once the disposition of a people, who now surround your throne with reproaches and complaints. Do justice to yourself. Banish from your mind those unworthy opinions, with which some interested persons have laboured to possess you. Distrust the men, who tell you that the English are naturally light and inconstant;—that they complain without a cause. Withdraw your confidence equally from all parties: from ministers, favourites, and relations; and let there be one moment in your life, in which you have consulted your own understanding.

WHEN you affectedly renounced the name of Englishman, believe me, Sir, you were persuaded to pay a very ill-judged compliment to one part of your subjects, at the expence of another.[1] While the natives of Scotland are not in actual rebellion, they are undoubtedly intitled to protection; nor do I mean to condemn the policy of giving some encouragement to the novelty of their affections for

[1] The King's first speech to Parliament had included the sentiment, 'Born and educated in this country, I glory in the name of Britain.'

the house of Hanover. I am ready to hope for every thing from their new-born zeal, and from the future steadiness of their allegiance. But hitherto they have no claim to your favour. To honour them with a determined predilection and confidence, in exclusion of your English subjects, who placed your family, and in spite of treachery and rebellion, have supported it upon the throne, is a mistake too gross, even for the unsuspecting generosity of youth. In this error we see a capital violation of the most obvious rules of policy and prudence. We trace it, however, to an original bias in your education, and are ready to allow for your inexperience.[1]

To the same early influence we attribute it, that you have descended to take a share not only in the narrow views and interests of particular persons, but in the fatal malignity of their passions. At your accession to the throne, the whole system of government was altered, not from wisdom or deliberation, but because it had been adopted by your predecessor. A little personal motive of pique and resentment was sufficient to remove the ablest servants of the crown*; but it is not in this country, Sir, that such men can be dishonoured by the frowns of a King. They were dismissed, but could not be disgraced. Without entering into a minuter discussion of the merits of the peace, we may observe, in the imprudent hurry with which the first overtures from France were accepted, in the conduct of the negotiation, and terms of the treaty, the strongest marks of that precipitate spirit of concession, with which a certain part of your subjects have been at all times ready to purchase a peace with the natural enemies of this country. On *your* part we are satisfied that every thing was honourable and sincere, and if England was sold to France, we doubt not that your Majesty was

* One of the first acts of the present reign was to dismiss Mr. Legge, because he had some years before refused to yield his interest in Hampshire to a Scotchman recommended by Lord Bute. This was the reason publicly assigned by his Lordship.[2]

---

[1] Junius hints at the influence of Lord Bute, who was Groom of the Stole when George was Prince of Wales: he had been the prince's tutor from 1755 onwards.

[2] Henry Legge was Chancellor of the Exchequer until dismissed in March 1761. The political situation in Hampshire is explained in *The House of Commons, 1754–90*, iii. 31.

equally betrayed. The conditions of the peace were matter of grief and surprise to your subjects, but not the immediate cause of their present discontent.

HITHERTO, Sir, you had been sacrificed to the prejudices and passions of others. With what firmness will you bear the mention of your own?

A MAN, not very honourably distinguished in the world, commences a formal attack upon your favourite, considering nothing, but how he might best expose his person and principles to detestation, and the national character of his countrymen to contempt.[1] The natives of that country, Sir, are as much distinguished by a peculiar character, as by your Majesty's favour. Like another chosen people, they have been conducted into the land of plenty, where they find themselves effectually marked, and divided from mankind. There is hardly a period, at which the most irregular character may not be redeemed. The mistakes of one sex find a retreat in patriotism; those of the other in devotion. Mr. Wilkes brought with him into politics the same liberal sentiments, by which his private conduct had been directed, and seemed to think, that, as there are few excesses, in which an English gentleman may not be permitted to indulge, the same latitude was allowed him in the choice of his political principles, and in the spirit of maintaining them.—I mean to state, not entirely to defend his conduct. In the earnestness of his zeal, he suffered some unwarrantable insinuations to escape him. He said more than moderate men would justify; but not enough to entitle him to the honour of your Majesty's personal resentment. The rays of Royal indignation, collected upon him, served only to illuminate, and could not consume. Animated by the favour of the people on one side, and heated by persecution on the other, his views and sentiments changed with his situation. Hardly serious at first, he is now an enthusiast. The coldest bodies warm with opposition, the hardest sparkle in collision. There is a holy mistaken zeal in politics as well as religion. By persuading

[1] The reference is to Wilkes, whose newspaper, the *North Briton*, specialized in anti-Scottish jokes.

others, we convince ourselves. The passions are engaged, and create a maternal affection in the mind, which forces us to love the cause, for which we suffer.—Is this a contention worthy of a King? Are you not sensible how much the meanness of the cause gives an air of ridicule to the serious difficulties into which you have been betrayed? the destruction of one man has been now, for many years, the sole object of your government, and if there can be any thing still more disgraceful, we have seen, for such an object, the utmost influence of the executive power, and every ministerial artifice exerted without success. Nor can you ever succeed, unless *he* should be imprudent enough to forfeit the protection of those laws, to which you owe your crown, or unless your ministers should persuade you to make it a question of force alone, and try the whole strength of government in opposition to the people. The lessons *he* has received from experience, will probably guard him from such excess of folly; and in your Majesty's virtues we find an unquestionable assurance that no illegal violence will be attempted.

FAR from suspecting you of so horrible a design, we would attribute the continued violation of the laws, and even this last enormous attack upon the vital principles of the constitution, to an ill-advised, unworthy, personal resentment. From one false step you have been betrayed into another, and as the cause was unworthy of you, your ministers were determined that the prudence of the execution should correspond with the wisdom and dignity of the design. They have reduced you to the necessity of choosing out of a variety of difficulties;—to a situation so unhappy, that you can neither do wrong without ruin, nor right without affliction. These worthy servants have undoubtedly given you many singular proofs of their abilities. Not contented with making Mr. Wilkes a man of importance, they have judiciously transferred the question, from the rights and interests of one man, to the most important rights and interests of the people, and forced your subjects, from wishing well to the cause of an individual, to unite with him in their own. Let them proceed as they have begun, and your Majesty need not doubt that the catastrophe will do no dishonour to the conduct of the piece.

THE circumstances to which you are reduced, will not admit of a compromise with the English nation. Undecisive, qualifying measures will disgrace your government still more than open violence, and, without satisfying the people, will excite their contempt. They have too much understanding and spirit to accept of an indirect satisfaction for a direct injury. Nothing less than a repeal, as formal as the resolution itself, can heal the wound, which has been given to the constitution, nor will any thing less be accepted. I can readily believe that there is an influence sufficient to recall that pernicious vote. The house of commons undoubtedly consider their duty to the crown as paramont to all other obligations. To *us* they are only indebted for an accidental existence, and have justly transferred their gratitude from their parents to their benefactors;—from those, who gave them birth, to the minister, from whose benevolence they derive the comforts and pleasures of their political life;—who has taken the tenderest care of their infancy, and relieves their necessities without offending their delicacy. But, if it were possible for their integrity to be degraded to a condition so vile and abject, that, compared with it, the present estimation they stand in is a state of honour and respect, consider, Sir, in what manner you will afterwards proceed. Can you conceive that the people of this country will long submit to be governed by so flexible a house of commons! It is not in the nature of human society, that any form of government, in such circumstances, can long be preserved. In ours, the general contempt of the people is as fatal as their detestation. Such, I am persuaded, would be the necessary effect of any base concession made by the present house of commons, and, as a qualifying measure would not be accepted, it remains for you to decide whether you will, at any hazard, support a set of men, who have reduced you to this unhappy dilemma, or whether you will gratify the united wishes of the whole people of England by dissolving the parliament.

TAKING it for granted, as I do very sincerely, that you have personally no design against the constitution, nor any view inconsistent with the good of your subjects, I think you cannot hesitate long upon the choice, which it equally concerns your interest, and your honour to adopt. On one side, you hazard the affections of all your English subjects; you relinquish every hope of repose to yourself, and you endanger the establishment of your family for ever. All this you venture for no object whatsoever, or for such an object, as it would be an affront to you to name. Men of sense will examine your conduct with suspicion; while those who are incapable of comprehending to what degree they are injured, afflict you with clamours equally insolent and unmeaning. Supposing it possible that no fatal struggle should ensue, you determine at once to be unhappy, without the hope of a compensation either from interest or ambition. If an English King be hated or despised, he *must* be unhappy; and this perhaps is the only political truth, which he ought to be convinced of without experiment. But if the English people should no longer confine their resentment to a submissive representation of their wrongs; if, following the glorious example of their ancestors, they should no longer appeal to the creature of the constitution, but to that high Being, who gave them the rights of humanity, whose gifts it were sacrilege to surrender, let me ask you, Sir, upon what part of your subjects would you rely for assistance?

THE people of Ireland have been uniformly plundered and oppressed. In return, they give you every day fresh marks of their resentment. They despise the miserable governor you have sent them*, because he is the creature of Lord Bute; nor is it from any natural confusion in their ideas, that they are so ready to confound the original of a King with the disgraceful representation of him.

THE distance of the Colonies would make it impossible for them to take an active concern in your affairs, if they were as well affected to your government as they once pretended to be to your person. They were ready enough to distinguish between *you* and your ministers. They complained of an act of the legislature, but traced the origin of it no higher than to the servants of the crown: They pleased themselves with the hope that their Sovereign, if not

* Viscount Townshend, sent over on the plan of being resident governor. The history of his ridiculous administration shall not be lost to the public.

favourable to their cause, at least was impartial. The decisive, personal part you took against them, has effectually banished that first distinction from their minds*. They consider you as united with your servants against America, and know how to distinguish the Sovereign and a venal parliament on one side, from the real sentiments of the English people on the other. Looking forward to independence, they might possibly receive you for their King; but, if ever you retire to America, be assured they will give you such a covenant to digest, as the presbytery of Scotland would have been ashamed to offer to Charles the second. They left their native land in search of freedom, and found it in a desart. Divided as they are into a thousand forms of policy and religion, there is one point in which they all agree:—they equally detest the pageantry of a King, and the supercilious hypocrisy of a bishop.

It is not then from the alienated affections of Ireland or America, that you can reasonably look for assistance; still less from the people of England, who are actually contending for their rights, and in this great question, are parties against you. You are not however, destitute of every appearance of support: You have all the Jacobites, Non-jurors, Roman Catholics, and Tories of this country, and all Scotland without exception. Considering from what family you are descended, the choice of your friends has been singularly directed; and truly, Sir, if you had not lost the whig interest of England, I should admire your dexterity in turning the hearts of your enemies. Is it possible for you to place any confidence in men, who, before they are faithful to you, must renounce every opinion, and betray every principle, both in church and state, which they inherit from their ancestors, and are confirmed in by their education? whose numbers are so inconsiderable, that they have long since been obliged to give up the principles and language which distinguish them as a party, and to fight under the banners of their enemies?

* In the King's speech of 8. November, 1768, it was declared "That the spirit of faction had broken out a fresh in some of the colonies, and, in one of them, proceeded to acts of violence and resistance to the execution of the laws;—that Boston was in a state of disobedience to all law and government, and had proceeded to measures subversive of the constitution, and attended with circumstances, that manifested a disposition to throw off their dependance on Great Britain."

Their zeal begins with hypocrisy, and must conclude in treachery. At first they deceive; at last they betray.

As to the Scotch, I must suppose your heart and understanding so biassed, from your earliest infancy, in their favour, that nothing less than *your own* misfortunes can undeceive you. You will not accept of the uniform experience of your ancestors; and when once a man is determined to believe, the very absurdity of the doctrine confirms him in his faith. A bigoted understanding can draw a proof of attachment to the house of Hanover from a notorious zeal for the house of Stuart, and find an earnest of future loyalty in former rebellions. Appearances are however in their favour; so strongly indeed, that one would think they had forgotten that you are their lawful King, and had mistaken you for a pretender to the crown. Let it be admitted then that the Scotch are as sincere in their present professions, as if you were in reality not an Englishman, but a Briton of the North. You would not be the first prince, of their native country, against whom they have rebelled, nor the first whom they have basely betrayed. Have you forgotten, Sir, or has your favourite concealed from you that part of our history, when the unhappy Charles, (and he too had private virtues) fled from the open, avowed indignation of his English subjects, and surrendered himself at discretion to the good faith of his own countrymen. Without looking for support in their affections as subjects, he applied only to their honour as gentlemen, for protection. They received him as they would your Majesty, with bows, and smiles, and falshood, and kept him until they had settled their bargain with the English parliament; then basely sold their native king to the vengeance of his enemies. This, Sir, was not the act of a few traitors, but the deliberate treachery of a Scotch parliament, representing the nation. A wise prince might draw from it two lessons of equal utility to himself. On one side he might learn to dread the undisguised resentment of a generous people, who dare openly assert their rights, and who, in a just cause are ready to meet their Sovereign in the field. On the other side, he would be taught to apprehend something far more formidable;—a fawning treachery, against which no prudence can guard, no courage can defend. The insidious smile upon the cheek would warn him of the canker in the heart.

FROM the uses, to which one part of the army has been too frequently applied, you have some reason to expect, that there are no services they would refuse. Here too we trace the partiality of your understanding. You take the sense of the army from the conduct of the guards, with the same justice with which you collect the sense of the people from the representations of the ministry. Your marching regiments, Sir, will not make the guards their example either as soldiers or subjects. They feel and resent, as they ought to do, that invariable, undistinguishing favour with which the guards are treated;* while those gallant troops, by whom every hazardous, every laborious service is performed, are left to perish in garrisons abroad, or pine in quarters at home, neglected and forgotten. If they had no sense of the great original duty they owe their country, their resentment would operate like patriotism, and leave your cause to be defended by those, to whom you have lavished the rewards and honours of their profession. The Prætorian Bands, enervated and debauched as they were, had still strength enough to awe the Roman populace: but when the distant legions took the alarm, they marched to Rome, and gave away the empire.

ON this side then, which ever way you turn your eyes, you see nothing but perplexity and distress. You may determine to support the very ministry who have reduced your affairs to this deplorable situation: you may shelter yourself under the forms of a parliament, and set your people at defiance. But be assured, Sir, that such a resolution would be as imprudent as it would be odious. If it did not immediately shake your establishment, it would rob you of your peace of mind for ever.

* The number of commissioned officers in the guards are to the marching regiments as *one* to eleven;—the number of regiments given to the guards, compared with those given to the line, is about three to one, at a moderate computation; consequently the partiality in favour of the guards is as thirty-three to one.—So much for the officers.—The private men have four-pence a day to subsist on; and five hundred lashes, if they desert. Under this punishment, they frequently expire. With these encouragements, it is supposed, they may be depended upon, whenever a certain person thinks it necessary to butcher his *fellow subjects*.

ON the other, how different is the prospect! How easy, how safe and honourable is the path before you! The English nation declare they are grossly injured by their representatives, and solicit your Majesty to exert your lawful prerogative, and give them an opportunity of recalling a trust, which, they find, has been scandalously abused. You are not to be told that the power of the house of commons is not original, but delegated to them for the welfare of the people, from whom they received it. A question of right arises between the constituent and the representative body. By what authority shall it be decided? Will your Majesty interfere in a question in which you have properly no immediate concern.—It would be a step equally odious and unnecessary. Shall the lords be called upon to determine the rights and privileges of the commons?—They cannot do it without a flagrant breach of the constitution. Or will you refer it to the judges?—They have often told your ancestors, that the law of parliament is above them. What party then remains, but to leave it to the people to determine for themselves? They alone are injured; and since there is no superior power, to which the cause can be referred, they alone ought to determine.

I DO not mean to perplex you with a tedious argument upon a subject already so discussed, that inspiration could hardly throw a new light upon it. There are, however, two points of view, in which it particularly imports your Majesty to consider, the late proceedings of the house of commons. By depriving a subject of his birthright, they have attributed to their own vote an authority equal to an act of the whole legislature; and, tho' perhaps not with the same motives, have strictly followed the example of the long parliament, which first declared the regal office useless, and soon after with as little ceremony, dissolved the house of lords. The same pretended power, which robs an English subject of his birthright, may rob an English King of his crown. In another view, the resolution of the house of commons, apparently not so dangerous to your Majesty, is still more alarming to your people. Not contented with divesting one man of his right, they have arbitrarily conveyed that right to another. They have set aside a return as illegal, without daring to censure those officers, who were particularly apprized of Mr. Wilkes's incapacity, not only by the declaration of the house, but expressly by the writ directed to them, and, who nevertheless returned him as duly elected. They have rejected the majority of votes, the only criterion, by which our laws judge of the sense of the people; they have transferred the right of election from the collective to the representative body; and by these acts, taken separately or together, they have essentially altered the original constitution of the house of commons. Versed, as your Majesty undoubtedly is, in the English history, it cannot easily escape you, how much it is your interest, as well as your duty to prevent one of the three estates from encroaching upon the province of the other two, or assuming the authority of them all. When once they have departed from the great constitutional line, by which all their proceedings should be directed, who will answer for their future moderation? Or what assurance will they give you, that, when they have trampled upon their equals, they will submit to a superior? Your Majesty may learn hereafter, how nearly the slave and tyrant are allied.

SOME of your council, more candid than the rest, admit the abandoned profligacy of the present house of commons, but oppose their dissolution upon an opinion, I confess not very unwarrantable that their successors, would be equally at the disposal of the treasury. I cannot persuade myself that the nation will have profited so little by experience. But if that opinion were well founded, you might then gratify our wishes at an easy rate, and appease the present clamour against your government, without offering any material injury to the favourite cause of corruption.

YOU have still an honourable part to act. The affections of your subjects may still be recovered. But before you subdue *their* hearts, you must gain a noble victory over your own. Discard those little, personal resentments, which have too long directed your public conduct. Pardon this man the remainder of his punishment, and if resentment still prevails, make it, what it should have been long since, an act, not of mercy, but contempt. He will soon fall back into his natural station,—a silent senator, and hardly supporting the weekly eloquence of a news paper. The gentle breath of peace would leave him on the surface, neglected and unremoved. It is only the tempest, that lifts him from his place.[1]

WITHOUT consulting your minister, call together your whole council. Let it appear to the public that you can determine and act for yourself. Come forward to your people. Lay aside the wretched formalities of a King, and speak to your subjects with the spirit of a man, and in the language of a gentleman. Tell them you have been fatally deceived. The acknowledgement will be no disgrace, but rather an honour to your understanding. Tell them you are determined to remove every cause of complaint against your government; that you will give your confidence to no man, who does not possess the confidence of your subjects; and leave it to themselves to determine, by their conduct at a future election, whether or no it be in reality the general sense of the nation, that their rights have been arbitrarily invaded by the present house of commons, and the constitution betrayed. They will then do justice to their representatives and to themselves.

THESE sentiments, Sir, and the stile they are conveyed in, may be offensive, perhaps, because they are new to you. Accustomed to the language of courtiers, you measure their affections by the vehemence of their expressions; and, when they only praise you indirectly, you admire their sincerity. But this is not a time to trifle with your fortune. They deceive you, Sir, who tell you that you have many friends, whose affections are founded upon a principle of personal attachment. The first foundation of friendship is not the power of conferring benefits, but the equality with which they are received, and *may* be returned. The fortune, which made you a King, forbad you to have a friend. It is a law of nature which cannot be violated with impunity. The mistaken prince, who looks for friendship, will find a favourite, and in that favourite the ruin of his affairs.

[1] Wilkes did not forget this unflattering portrait and in September 1771 wrote to Junius ruefully: 'I am satisfied that Junius now means me well . . . He has poured balm into my wounds, the deepest of which, I sigh when I recollect, were made by that now friendly hand.' Private letter no. 70.

THE people of England are loyal to the house of Hanover, not from a vain preference of one family to another, but from a conviction that the establishment of that family was necessary to the support of their civil and religious liberties. This, Sir, is a principle of allegiance equally solid and rational;—fit for Englishmen to adopt, and well worthy of your Majesty's encouragement. We cannot long be deluded by nominal distinctions. The name of Stuart, of itself, is only contemptible;—armed with the Sovereign authority, their principles are formidable. The Prince, who imitates their conduct, should be warned by their example; and while he plumes himself upon the security of his title to the crown, should remember that, as it was acquired by one revolution, it may be lost by another.

JUNIUS.

January 1770 produced a violent political convulsion. At the beginning of the parliamentary session the Lord Chancellor, Camden, attacked his own colleagues over their conduct of the Wilkes affair and was dismissed. Out at the same time went Lord Huntingdon, Groom of the Stole, Lord Coventry, and the Dukes of Manchester and Beaufort. Lord Granby resigned his post of Commander-in-Chief on the 17th. Charles Yorke, who had accepted with great uneasiness the seal in succession to Camden, died three days later, some said by his own hand. On the 20th, John Dunning resigned as Solicitor-General and James Grenville as Joint Vice-Treasurer of Ireland. The ministry was evidently falling to pieces and there was a marked reluctance among newcomers to commit themselves to its support. Grafton confided to Conway that 'his head turned, that he could not bear it'. On the 27th he resigned and Lord North, after considerable pressure, was induced to accept the lead as First Lord of the Treasury. 'Nothing', wrote Horace Walpole, 'could be more distressful than the situation into which the Duke of Grafton had brought the King and in which he abandoned him.' Walpole, iv. 50.

LETTER XXXVI.

TO HIS GRACE THE DUKE OF GRAFTON.

MY LORD, 14. *Feb.* 1770.

IF I were personally your enemy, I might pity and forgive you. You have every claim to compassion, that can arise from misery and distress. The condition you are reduced to would disarm a private enemy of his resentment, and leave no consolation to the most vindictive spirit, but that such an object, as you are, would disgrace the dignity of revenge. But in the relation you have borne to this country, you have no title to indulgence; and if I had followed the dictates of my own opinion, I never should have allowed you the respit of a moment. In your public character, you have injured every subject of the empire; and though an individual is not authorised to forgive the injuries done to society, he is called upon to assert his separate share in the public resentment. I submitted however to the judgment of men, more moderate, perhaps more candid than myself. For my own part, I do not pretend to understand those prudent forms of decorum, those gentle rules of discretion, which some men endeavour to unite with the conduct of the greatest and most hazardous affairs. Engaged in the defence of an honourable cause, I would take a decisive part.—I should scorn to provide for a future retreat, or to keep terms with a man, who preserves no measures with the public. Neither the abject submission of deserting his post in the hour of danger, nor even the *sacred shield of cowardice should protect him. I would pursue him through life, and try the last exertion of my abilities to preserve the perishable infamy of his name, and make it immortal.

WHAT then, my Lord, is this the event of all the sacrifices you have made to Lord Bute's patronage, and to your own unfortunate ambition? Was it for this you abandoned your earliest friendships, —the warmest connexions of your youth, and all those honourable engagements, by which you once solicited, and might have acquired the esteem of your country? Have you secured no recompence for such a waste of honour?—Unhappy man! what party will receive the common deserter of all parties? Without a client to flatter, without a friend to console you, and with only one companion from the honest house of Bloomsbury, you must now retire into a dreadful solitude. At the most active period of life, you must quit the

* ——*Sacro tremuere timore.* Every coward pretends to be planet-struck.[1]

[1] Possibly a reminiscence of Silius Italicus, *Punica*, iii. 31—sacro implevere timore: 'they were filled with an aweful fear'.

busy scene, and conceal yourself from the world, if you would hope to save the wretched remains of a ruined reputation. The vices operate like age,—bring on disease before its time, and in the prime of youth leave the character broken and exhausted.[1]

YET your conduct has been mysterious, as well as contemptible. Where is now that firmness, or obstinacy so long boasted of by your friends, and acknowledged by your enemies? We were taught to expect, that you would not leave the ruin of this country to be compleated by other hands, but were determined either to gain a decisive victory over the constitution, or to perish bravely at least behind the last dike of the prerogative. You knew the danger, and might have been provided for it. You took sufficient time to prepare for a meeting with your parliament, to confirm the mercenary fidelity of your dependants, and to suggest to your Sovereign a language suited to his dignity at least, if not to his benevolence and wisdom. Yet, while the whole kingdom was agitated with anxious expectation upon one great point, you meanly evaded the question, and, instead of the explicit firmness and decision of a King, gave us nothing but the misery of a ruined* grazier, and the whining piety of a Methodist.[2] We had reason to expect, that notice would have been taken of the petitions which the king has received from the English nation; and although I can conceive some personal motives for not yielding to them, I can find none, in common prudence or decency, for treating them with contempt. Be assured, my Lord, the English people will not tamely submit to this unworthy treatment;—they had a right to be heard, and their petitions, if not

* There was something wonderfully pathetic in the mention of the horned cattle.

---

[1] Junius had trouble with this image and even in its revised form it is awkward. The original version, in the *Public Advertiser*, read: 'The Vices never fail of their Effect. They operate like Age—bring on Dishonour before its Time, and in the Prime of Youth leave the Character broken and exhausted.'

[2] The King's Speech, delivered on 9 January 1770, began: 'It is with much concern that I find myself obliged to open the session of Parliament, with acquainting you, that the distemper among the Horned Cattle has lately broke out in this kingdom . . .' There was no direct reference to the Middlesex election issue. The rest was rather general exhortation to 'cultivate that spirit of harmony, which beomes those who have but one common object in their view'. *Parl. Hist.* xvi. 642–3.

granted, deserved to be considered. Whatever be the real views and doctrine of a court, the Sovereign should be taught to preserve some forms of attention to his subjects, and if he will not redress their grievances, not to make them a topic of jest and mockery among lords and ladies of the bedchamber. Injuries may be atoned for and forgiven; but insults admit of no compensation. They degrade the mind in its own esteem, and force it to recover its level by revenge. This neglect of the petitions was however a part of your original plan of government, nor will any consequences it has produced account for your deserting your Sovereign, in the midst of that distress, in which you and your* new friends had involved him. One would think, my Lord, you might have taken this spirited resolution before you had dissolved the last of those early connexions, which once, even in your own opinion, did honour to your youth;—before you had obliged Lord Granby to quit a service he was attached to;—before you had discarded one chancellor, and killed another. To what an abject condition have you laboured to reduce the best of princes, when the unhappy man, who yields at last to such personal instance and solicitation, as never can be fairly employed against a subject, feels himself degraded by his compliance, and is unable to survive the disgraceful honours which his gracious Sovereign had compelled him to accept. He was a man of spirit, for he had a quick sense of shame, and death has redeemed his character. I know your Grace too well to appeal to your feelings upon this event; but there is another heart, not yet, I hope, quite callous to the touch of humanity, to which it ought to be a dreadful lesson for ever.†

NOW, my Lord, let us consider the situation to which you have conducted, and in which you have thought it adviseable to abandon

* The Bedford party.

† The most secret particulars of this detestable transaction shall, in due time, be given to the public. The people shall know what kind of man they have to deal with.[1]

---

[1] Junius did not keep this promise to discuss the circumstances of Charles Yorke's death. At an audience on 17 January the King was said to have threatened to make sure that Yorke should never be Chancellor if he did not at once accept. *The House of Commons, 1754–90*, iii. 677–8.

your royal master. Whenever the people have complained, and nothing better could be said in defence of the measures of government, it has been the fashion to answer us, though not very fairly, with an appeal to the private virtues of your Sovereign. "Has he not, to relieve the people, surrendered a considerable part of his revenue?—Has he not made the judges independent, by fixing them in their places for life?"—My Lord, we acknowledge the gracious principle, which gave birth to these concessions, and have nothing to regret, but that it has never been adhered to. At the end of seven years, we are loaded with a debt of above five hundred thousand pounds upon the civil list, and we now see the Chancellor of Great Britain tyrannically forced out of his office, not for want of abilities, not for want of integrity, or of attention to his duty, but for delivering his honest opinion in parliament, upon the greatest constitutional question, that has arisen since the revolution.—We care not to whose private virtues you appeal; the theory of such a government is falsehood and mockery;—the practice is oppression. You have laboured then (though I confess to no purpose) to rob your master of the only plausible answer, that ever was given in defence of his government,—of the opinion, which the people had conceived of his personal honour and integrity.—The Duke of Bedford was more moderate than your Grace. He only forced his master to violate a solemn promise made to an* individual. But you, my Lord, have successfully extended your advice to every political, every moral engagement, that could bind either the magistrate or the man. The condition of a King is often miserable, but it required your Grace's abilities to make it contemptible.—You will say perhaps that the faithful servants, in whose hands you have left him, are able to retrieve his honour, and to support his government. You have publicly declared, even since your resignation, that you approved of their measures, and admired their conduct,—particularly that of the Earl of Sandwich. What a pity it is, that, with all this appearance, you should think it necessary to separate yourself from such amiable companions. You forget, my Lord, that while

* Mr. Stuart Mackenzie.[1]

---

[1] See p. 71 n. 1.

you are lavish in the praise of men whom you desert, you are publicly opposing your conduct to your opinions, and depriving yourself of the only plausible pretence you had for leaving your Sovereign overwhelmed with distress; I call it plausible, for, in truth, there is no reason whatsoever, less than the frowns of your master, that could justify a man of spirit for abandoning his post at a moment so critical and important? It is in vain to evade the question. If you will not speak out, the public have a right to judge from appearances. We are authorized to conclude, that you either differed from your colleagues, whose measures you still affect to defend, or that you thought the administration of the King's affairs no longer tenable. You are at liberty to choose between the hypocrite and the coward. Your best friends are in doubt which way they shall incline. Your country unites the characters, and gives you credit for them both. For my own part, I see nothing inconsistent in your conduct. You began with betraying the people, —you conclude with betraying the King.

IN your treatment of particular persons, you have preserved the uniformity of your character. Even Mr. Bradshaw declares, that no man was ever so ill used as himself.[1] As to the provision* you have made for his family, he was intitled to it by the house he lives in. The successor of one Chancellor might well pretend to be the rival of another. It is the breach of private friendship which touches

* A pension of 1500 *l.* per annum, insured upon the 4 1-half per cents, (he was too cunning to trust to Irish security) for the lives of himself and all his sons. This gentleman, who a very few years ago was clerk to a contractor for forage, and afterwards exalted to a petty post in the war office, thought it necessary (as soon as he was appointed Secretary to the Treasury) to take that great house in Lincoln's-Inn-Fields, in which the Earl of Northington had resided, while he was Lord High Chancellor of Great Britain. As to the pension, Lord North very solemnly assured the house of commons, that no pension was ever so well deserved as Mr. Bradshaw's— N. B. Lord Camden and Sir Jeffery Amherst are not near so well provided for, and Sir Edward Hawke, who saved the state, retires with two thousand pounds a year, on the Irish establishment, from which he in fact receives less than Mr. Bradshaw's pension.

---

[1] Horace Walpole, in his account of the Duke's resignation, wrote that Grafton had told Conway, 'I am betrayed by my own confidential secretary, Bradshaw.' Walpole, iv. 45. But Bradshaw and Grafton appear to have remained on good terms afterwards: he resigned his post as Secretary to the Treasury soon after Grafton went and did not resume office until Grafton rejoined the ministry.

Mr. Bradshaw; and to say the truth, when a man of his rank and abilities had taken so active a part in your affairs, he ought not to have been let down at last with a miserable pension of fifteen hundred pounds a year. Colonel Luttrell, Mr. Onslow, and Governor Burgoyne, were equally engaged with you, and have rather more reason to complain than Mr. Bradshaw. These are men, my Lord, whose friendship you should have adhered to on the same principle, on which you deserted Lord Rockingham, Lord Chatham, Lord Camden, and the Duke of Portland. We can easily account for your violating your engagements with men of honour, but why should you betray your natural connexions? Why separate yourself from Lord Sandwich, Lord Gower, and Mr. Rigby, or leave the three worthy gentlemen abovementioned to shift for themselves? With all the fashionable indulgence of the times, this country does not abound in characters like theirs; and you may find it a difficult matter to recruit the black catalogue of your friends.

THE recollection of the royal patent you sold to Mr. Hine, obliges me to say a word in defence of a man whom you have taken the most dishonourable means to injure.[1] I do not refer to the sham prosecution which you affected to carry on against him. On that ground, I doubt not he is prepared to meet you with tenfold recrimination, and set you at defiance. The injury you had done him affects his moral character.[2] You knew that the offer to purchase the reversion of a place, which has heretofore been sold under a decree of the court of Chancery, however imprudent in his situation, would no way tend to cover him with that sort of guilt which you wished to fix upon him in the eyes of the world. You laboured then, by every species of false suggestion, and even by publishing counterfeit letters, to have it understood that he had proposed terms of accommodation to you, and had offered to abandon his principles, his party, and his friends.[3] You consulted your own

[1] Samuel Vaughan. See public letter no. XXXIII.

[2] The *Public Advertiser* reads 'the injury you *have* done him', which seems more appropriate. Vaughan had been expelled from the Society of Supporters of the Bill of Rights as an apostate.

[3] The first spurious letter appeared in August; the second was published in the *London Evening Post*, 30 November, and reprinted in the *Public Advertiser* of 1 December.

breast for a character of consummate treachery, and gave it to the public for that of Mr. Vaughan. I think myself obliged to do this justice to an injured man, because I was deceived by the appearances thrown out by your Grace, and have frequently spoken of his conduct with indignation. If he really be, what I think him, honest, though mistaken, he will be happy in recovering his reputation, though at the expence of his understanding. Here, I see, the matter is likely to rest. Your Grace is afraid to carry on the prosecution. Mr. Hine keeps quiet possession of his purchase; and Governor Burgoyne, relieved from the apprehension of refunding the money, sits down, for the remainder of his life, INFAMOUS AND CONTENTED.

I BELIEVE, my Lord, I may now take my leave of you for ever. You are no longer that resolute minister, who had spirit to support the most violent measures; who compensated for the want of good and great qualities, by a brave determination, (which some people admired and relied on) to maintain himself without them. The reputation of obstinacy and perseverance might have supplied the place of all the absent virtues. You have now added the last negative to your character, and meanly confessed that you are destitute of the common spirit of a man. Retire then, my Lord, and hide your blushes from the world; for, with such a load of shame, even BLACK may change its colour. A mind such as yours, in the solitary hours of domestic enjoyment, may still find topics of consolation. You may find it in the memory of violated friendship; in the afflictions of an accomplished prince, whom you have disgraced and deserted, and in the agitations of a great country, driven, by your councils, to the brink of destruction.

THE palm of ministerial firmness is now transferred to Lord North. He tells us so himself, with the plenitude of the *ore rotundo**;

* This eloquent person has got as far as the *discipline* of Demosthenes. He constantly speaks with pebbles in his mouth, to improve his articulation.[1]

---

[1] Horace Walpole also gives an unflattering account of North's oratorical style: 'a wide mouth, thick lips . . . and a deep untunable voice, which, instead of modulating, he enforced with unnecessary pomp.' Walpole, iv. 52. North compensated for these defects by common sense and affability and Junius constantly underestimated him.

and I am ready enough to believe, that, while he can keep his place, he will not easily be persuaded to resign it. Your Grace was the firm minister of yesterday: Lord North is the firm minister of today. Tomorrow, perhaps, his Majesty, in his wisdom, may give us a rival for you both. You are too well acquainted with the temper of your late allies, to think it possible that Lord North should be permitted to govern this country. If we may believe common fame, they have shewn him their superiority already. His Majesty is indeed too gracious to insult his subjects, by chusing his first minister from among the domestics of the Duke of Bedford. That would have been too gross an outrage to the three kingdoms. Their purpose, however, is equally answered by pushing forward this unhappy figure, and forcing it to bear the odium of measures, which they in reality direct. Without immediately appearing to govern, they possess the power, and distribute the emoluments of government as they think proper. They still adhere to the spirit of that calculation, which made Mr. Luttrell representative of Middlesex. Far from regretting your retreat, they assure us very gravely, that it increases the real strength of the ministry. According to this way of reasoning, they will probably grow stronger, and more flourishing, every hour they exist: for I think there is hardly a day passes in which some one or other of his majesty's servants does not leave them to improve by the loss of his assistance. But, alas! their countenances speak a different language. When the members drop off, the main body cannot be insensible of its approaching dissolution. Even the violence of their proceedings is a signal of despair. Like broken tenants, who have had warning to quit the premises, they curse their landlord, destroy the fixtures, throw every thing into confusion, and care not what mischief they do to the estate.

JUNIUS.

In the autumn of 1769 the opposition instituted a widespread petitioning campaign on the subject of the Middlesex election. There was some disagreement whether the petitions should be submitted to a House of Commons which, in the view of the petitioners, had shown itself hopelessly corrupt, or direct to the King. The city of London, where William Beckford was serving a second term as Lord Mayor, was in the van of the movement and on 6th March the liverymen adopted a fiercely worded remonstrance, complaining that a 'secret and malign influence' had robbed the people of their rights and demanding the dissolution of Parliament. The King's retort on 14 March was that the remonstrance was disrespectful to him personally, injurious to Parliament, and irreconcilable with the principles of the constitution. Junius was in a state of great agitation: 'now is the crisis', he told Woodfall on Saturday, 17 March, and the following day he assured the printer that 'Lord Chatham is determined to go to the Hall to support the Westminster remonstrance. I have no doubt that we shall conquer them at last.' Private letters nos. 21 and 22. See p. 184 n. 1.

LETTER XXXVII.

TO THE PRINTER OF THE PUBLIC ADVERTISER.

SIR, 19. *March*, 1770.

I BELIEVE there is no man, however indifferent about the interests of this country, who will not readily confess that the situation, to which we are now reduced, whether it has arisen from the violence of faction, or from an arbitrary system of government, justifies the most melancholy apprehensions, and calls for the exertion of whatever wisdom or vigour is left among us. The King's answer to the remonstrance of the city of London, and the measures since adopted by the ministry, amount to a plain declaration, that the principle, on which Mr. Luttrell was seated in the house of commons, is to be supported in all its consequences, and carried to its utmost extent. The same spirit, which violated the freedom of election, now invades the declaration and bill of rights, and threatens to punish the subject for exercising a privilege, hitherto undisputed, of petitioning the crown. The grievances of the people are aggravated by insults; their complaints not merely disregarded, but checked by authority; and every one of those acts, against which they remonstrated, confirmed by the King's decisive approbation. At such a moment, no honest man will remain silent or inactive. However distinguished by rank or property, in the rights of freedom we are all equal. As we are Englishmen, the least considerable man among us has an interest equal to the proudest nobleman, in the laws and constitution of his country, and is equally called upon to make a generous contribution in support of them;—whether it be the heart to conceive, the understanding to direct, or the hand to execute. It is a common cause, in which we are all interested, in which we should all be engaged. The man who deserts it at this alarming crisis, is an enemy to his country, and, what I think of infinitely less importance, a traitor to his Sovereign. The subject, who is truly loyal to the chief magistrate, will neither advise nor submit to arbitrary measures. The city of London have given an example, which, I doubt not, will be followed by the whole kingdom. The noble spirit of the metropolis is the lifeblood of the state, collected at the heart: from that point it circulates, with health and vigour, through every artery of the constitution. The time is come, when the body of the English people must assert their own cause: conscious of their strength, and animated by a sense of their duty, they will not surrender their birthright to ministers, parliaments, or kings.

THE city of London have expressed their sentiments with freedom and firmness; they have spoken truth boldly; and, in whatever light their remonstrance may be represented by courtiers, I defy the most subtle lawyer in this country to point out a single instance, in which they have exceeded the truth. Even that assertion, which we are told is most offensive to parliament, in the theory of the English constitution, is strictly true. If any part of the representative body be not chosen by the people, that part vitiates and corrupts the whole. If there be a defect in the representation of the people, that power, which alone is equal to the making of the laws in this country, is not complete, and the acts of parliament under that circumstance, are not the acts of a pure and entire legislature. I speak of the theory of our constitution; and whatever difficulties or inconveniencies may attend the practice, I am ready to maintain, that, as far as the fact deviates from the principle, so far the practice is vicious and corrupt. I have not heard a question raised upon any other part of the remonstrance. That the principle, on which the Middlesex election was determined, is more pernicious in its effects, than either the levying of ship-money, by Charles the First, or the suspending power assumed by his son, will hardly be disputed by any man who understands or wishes well to the English constitution. It is not an act of open violence done by the King, or any direct or palpable breach of the laws attempted by his minister, that can ever endanger the liberties of this country. Against such a King or minister the people would immediately take the alarm, and all the parties unite to oppose him. The laws may be grossly violated in particular instances, without any direct attack upon the whole system. Facts of that kind stand alone; they are attributed to necessity, not defended by principle. We can never be really in danger, until the forms of parliament are made use of to destroy the substance of our civil and political liberties;—until parliament itself betrays its trust, by contributing to establish new principles of government, and employing the very weapons committed to it by the collective body, to stab the constitution.

As for the terms of the remonstrance, I presume it will not be affirmed, by any person less polished than a gentleman usher, that this is a season for compliments.[1] Our gracious King indeed is abundantly civil to himself. Instead of an answer to a petition, his majesty, very gracefully pronounces his own panegyric;[2] and I confess, that, as far as his personal behaviour, or the royal purity of his intentions is concerned, the truth of those declarations, which the minister has drawn up for his master, cannot decently be disputed. In every other respect, I affirm, that they are absolutely unsupported, either in argument or fact. I must add too, that supposing the speech were otherwise unexceptionable, it is not a direct answer to the petition of the city. His Majesty is pleased to say, that he is always ready to receive the requests of his subjects; yet the sheriffs were twice sent back with an excuse, and it was

1 The text of the remonstrance is given in *Parl. Hist.* xvi. 893–5 and in the *Gentleman's Magazine*, 1770, 110–11.

2 'I have ever made the law of the land the rule of my conduct, esteeming it my chief glory to reign over a free people: with this view I have always been careful, as well to execute faithfully the trust reposed in me, as to avoid even the appearance of invading any of those powers which the constitution has placed in other hands . . . while I act upon these principles, I shall have a right to expect, and I am confident I shall continue to receive, the steady and affectionate support of my people.' *Gentleman's Magazine*, 1770, 113.

certainly debated in council whether or no the magistrates of the city of London should be admitted to an audience. Whether the remonstrance be or be not injurious to parliament, is the very question between the parliament and the people, and such a question as cannot be decided by the assertion of a third party, however respectable. That the petitioning for a dissolution of parliament is irreconcileable with the principles of the constitution is a new doctrine. His Majesty perhaps has not been informed, that the house of commons themselves have, by a formal resolution, admitted it to be the right of the subject.[1] His Majesty proceeds to assure us that he has made the laws the rule of his conduct.—Was it in ordering or permitting his ministers to apprehend Mr. Wilkes by a general warrant?—Was it in suffering his ministers to revive the obsolete maxim of *nullum tempus* to rob the Duke of Portland of his property, and thereby give a decisive turn to a county election? —Was it in erecting a chamber consultation of surgeons, with authority to examine into and supersede the legal verdict of a jury? Or did his Majesty consult the laws of this country, when he permitted his secretary of state to declare, that whenever the civil magistrate is trifled with, a military force must be sent for, *without the delay of a moment*, and effectually employed? Or was it in the barbarous exactness with which this illegal, inhuman doctrine was carried into execution?—If his Majesty had recollected these facts, I think he would never have said, at least with any reference to the measures of his government, that he had made the laws the rule of his conduct. To talk of preserving the affections, or relying on the support of his subjects, while he continues to act upon these principles, is indeed paying a compliment to their loyalty, which I hope they have too much spirit and understanding to deserve.[2]

HIS Majesty, we are told, is not only punctual in the performance of his own duty, but careful not to assume any of those powers

[1] In the proceedings on the Kentish petition, 26 February 1701; *CJ* xiii. 767; *Parl. Hist.* v. 1340.

[2] The controversy over the Duke of Portland's property is explained in n. 1 on p. 315. The 'consultation of surgeons' is a reference to MacQuirk's case, discussed by Junius in public letters nos. VIII and IX. Lord Weymouth was the Secretary of State accused of encouraging the magistrates to butcher demonstrators: see note to public letter no. I on p. 31.

which the constitution has placed in other hands. Admitting this last assertion to be strictly true, it is no way to the purpose. The city of London have not desired the King to assume a power placed in other hands. If they had, I should hope to see the person, who dared to present such a petition, immediately impeached. They solicit their Sovereign to exert that constitutional authority, which the laws have vested in him, for the benefit of his subjects. They call upon him to make use of his lawful prerogative in a case, which our laws evidently supposed might happen, since they have provided for it by trusting the Sovereign with a discretionary power to dissolve the parliament. This request will, I am confident, be supported by remonstrances from all parts of the kingdom. His Majesty will find at last, that this is the sense of his people, and that it is not his interest to support either ministry or parliament, at the hazard of a breach with the collective body of his subjects.—That he is the King of a free people, is indeed his greatest glory. That he may long continue the King of a free people, is the second wish that animates my heart. The first is, THAT THE PEOPLE MAY BE FREE.*

JUNIUS.

At this point the opposition began to falter. In the House of Commons many of the Rockingham party were embarrassed by the violence of the language used in the remonstrance, and a loyal address to the King was carried on 20 March by the overwhelming majority of 248 votes against 94. A Westminster petition similar to that from the city of London was voted on 28 March and presented the same day, but Lord Chatham did not, after all, attend, pleading gout. The following day Calcraft reported to Chatham that Beckford and 'the leading people of Middlesex' were greatly offended at the lack of support: 'they lay the whole of this mischief to the Rockingham party'. *Pitt. Corr.* iii. 436. The main beneficiary of all this was Lord North, who handled the situation with firmness and moderation.

* When his Majesty had done reading his speech, the Lord Mayor, &c. had the honour of kissing his Majesty's hand; after which, as they were withdrawing, his Majesty instantly turned round to his courtiers, *and burst out a laughing*.

Nero fiddled, while Rome was burning. JOHN HORNE.[1]

1 Horne's remark appeared in the *Public Advertiser* of 15 March 1770. Threatened with prosecution he withdrew, declaring that 'Nero did *not* fiddle while Rome was burning'.

LETTER XXXVIII.

TO THE PRINTER OF THE PUBLIC ADVERTISER.

SIR, 3. *April*, 1770.

IN my last letter I offered you my opinion of the truth and propriety of his Majesty's answer to the city of London, considering it merely as the speech of a minister, drawn up in his own defence, and delivered, as usual, by the chief magistrate. I would separate, as much as possible, the King's personal character and behaviour from the acts of the present government. I wish it to be understood that his Majesty had in effect no more concern in the substance of what he said, than Sir James Hodges had in the remonstrance, and that as Sir James, in virtue of his office, was obliged to speak the sentiments of the people,[1] his Majesty might think himself bound, by the same official obligation, to give a graceful utterance to the sentiments of his minister. The cold formality of a well repeated lesson is widely distant from the animated expression of the heart.

THIS distinction, however, is only true with respect to the measure itself. The consequences of it reach beyond the minister, and materially affect his Majesty's honour. In their own nature they are formidable enough to alarm a man of prudence, and disgraceful enough to afflict a man of spirit. A subject, whose sincere attachment to his Majesty's person and family is founded upon rational principles, will not, in the present conjuncture, be scrupulous of alarming, or even of afflicting his Sovereign. I know there is another sort of loyalty, of which his Majesty has had plentiful experience. When the loyalty of Tories, Jacobites, and Scotchmen, has once taken possession of an unhappy Prince, it seldom leaves him without accomplishing his destruction. When the poison of their doctrines has tainted the natural benevolence of his disposition, when their insidious counsels have corrupted the *stamina* of his government, what antidote can restore him to his political health and honour, but the firm sincerity of his English subjects?

[1] Sir James Hodges was common clerk of the city of London.

It has not been usual in this country, at least since the days of Charles the first, to see the sovereign personally at variance, or engaged in a direct altercation with his subjects. Acts of grace and indulgence are wisely appropriated to him, and should constantly be performed by himself. He never should appear but in an amiable light to his subjects. Even in France, as long as any ideas of a limited monarchy were thought worth preserving, it was a maxim, that no man should leave the royal presence discontented. They have lost or renounced the moderate principles of their government, and now, when their parliaments venture to remonstrate, the tyrant comes forward, and answers absolutely for himself.[1] The spirit of their present constitution requires that the King should be feared, and the principle, I believe, is tolerably supported by the fact. But in our political system, the theory is at variance with the practice, for the King should be beloved. Measures of greater severity may, indeed, in some circumstances, be necessary; but the minister who advises, should take the execution and odium of them entirely upon himself. He not only betrays his master, but violates the spirit of the English constitution, when he exposes the chief magistrate to the personal hatred or contempt of his subjects. When we speak of the firmness of government, we mean an uniform system of measures, deliberately adopted, and resolutely maintained by the servants of the crown, not a peevish asperity in the language or behaviour of the sovereign. The government of a weak, irresolute monarch may be wise, moderate, and firm;—that of an obstinate capricious prince, on the contrary, may be feeble, undetermined and relaxed. The reputation of public measures depends upon the minister, who is responsible, not upon the King, whose private opinions are not supposed to have any weight against the advice of his counsel, whose personal authority should therefore never be interposed in public affairs.—This, I believe, is true, constitutional doctrine. But for a moment let us suppose it false.

[1] France, in 1770, was at the beginning of a great crisis over the role of the Paris Parlement. Louis XV and his minister Maupeou were attempting to curtail its powers in order to introduce financial and administrative reforms. In 1766, at a *lit de justice*, the King declared that 'it is in my person that sovereign power resides . . . to me alone belongs the legislative power.' The Parlement retorted that it constituted the only remaining barrier to royal despotism in France.

Let it be taken for granted, that an occasion may arise, in which a King of England shall be compelled to take upon himself the ungrateful office of rejecting the petitions, and censuring the conduct of his subjects; and let the City remonstrance be supposed to have created so extraordinary an occasion. On this principle, which I presume no friend of administration will dispute, let the wisdom and spirit of the ministry be examined. They advise the King to hazard his dignity, by a positive declaration of his own sentiments?—they suggest to him a language full of severity and reproach. What follows? When his Majesty had taken so decisive a part in support of his ministry and parliament, he had a right to expect from them a reciprocal demonstration of firmness in their own cause, and of their zeal for his honour. He had reason to expect (and such, I doubt not, were the blustering promises of Lord North) that the persons, whom he had been advised to charge with having failed in their respect to him, with having injured parliament, and violated the principles of the constitution, should not have been permitted to escape without some severe marks of the displeasure and vengeance of parliament. As the matter stands, the minister, after placing his sovereign in the most unfavourable light to his subjects, and after attempting to fix the ridicule and odium of his own precipitate measures upon the royal character, leaves him a solitary figure upon the scene, to recall, if he can, or to compensate, by future compliances, for one unhappy demonstration of ill-supported firmness, and ineffectual resentment. As a man of spirit, his Majesty cannot but be sensible, that the lofty terms in which he was persuaded to reprimand the city, when united with the silly conclusion of the business, resemble the pomp of a mock-tragedy, where the most pathetic sentiments, and even the sufferings of the hero are calculated for derision.

SUCH has been the boasted firmness and consistency of a minister,* whose appearance in the house of commons was thought essential to the King's service;—whose presence was to influence

* This graceful minister is oddly constructed. His tongue is a little too big for his mouth, and his eyes a great deal too big for their sockets. Every part of his person sets natural proportion at defiance. At this present writing, his head is supposed to be much too heavy for his shoulders.

every division;—who had a voice to persuade, an eye to penetrate, a gesture to command.[1] The reputation of these great qualities has been fatal to his friends. The little dignity of Mr. Ellis has been committed. The mine was sunk;—combustibles provided, and Welbore Ellis, the Guy Faux of the fable, waited only for the signal of command. All of a sudden the country gentlemen discover how grossly they have been deceived;—the minister's heart fails him, the grand plot is defeated in a moment, and poor Mr. Ellis and his motion taken into custody. From the event of Friday last, one would imagine, that some fatality hung over this gentleman.[2] Whether he makes or suppresses a motion, he is equally sure of his disgrace. But the complexion of the times will suffer no man to be vice-treasurer of Ireland with impunity*.

I DO not mean to express the smallest anxiety for the minister's reputation. He acts separately for himself, and the most shameful inconsistency may perhaps be no disgrace to him. But when the Sovereign, who represents the majesty of the state, appears in

* About this time, the courtiers talked of nothing but a bill of pains and penalties against the Lord Mayor and Sheriffs, or impeachment at the least. Little *Mannikin Ellis* told the King that, if the business were left to his management, he would engage to do wonders. It was thought very odd that a motion of so much importance should be intrusted to the most contemptible little piece of machinery in the whole kingdom. His honest zeal however was disappointed. The minister took fright, and at the very instant that little Ellis was going to open, sent him an order to sit down. All their magnanimous threats ended in a ridiculous vote of censure, and a still more ridiculous address to the King. This shameful desertion so afflicted the generous mind of George the Third, that he was obliged to live upon potatoes for three weeks, to keep off a malignant fever.—Poor man!—*quis talia fando temperet a lacrymis!*[3]

---

[1] Lord North. Junius' footnote is worth attention as an example of the puerility to which he could sink on occasions.

[2] On Friday, 30 March 1770 the House of Commons debated George Grenville's bill for a new method of considering election disputes. Welbore Ellis, for the government, moved its rejection but was beaten by 185 votes to 123. North consequently withdrew his opposition and the measure became law. *Parl. Hist.* xvi. 916–23.

[3] Fortunately the evidence exists to correct Junius' burlesque account of the government's tactics. The King wrote to North in the afternoon of 18 March commending the resolutions which were to be moved in the House of Commons and specifically approving the decision not to attempt measures against the Lord Mayor and Sheriff. He added that the opposition relied upon the court's showing severity in order to close ranks. Fortescue, ii, no. 769. One of Junius' most serious defects as a politician was to be persuaded by his own writings into persistently underestimating his opponents. The Latin is from Virgil, *Aeneid*, ii. 6: 'Who could talk of such things and refrain from tears?'

person, his dignity should be supported. The occasion should be important;—the plan well considered;—the execution steady and consistent. My zeal for his Majesty's real honour compels me to assert, that it has been too much the system of the present reign, to introduce him personally, either to act for, or to defend his servants. They persuade him to do what is properly *their* business, and desert him in the midst of it*. Yet this is an inconvenience, to which he must for ever be exposed, while he adheres to a ministry divided among themselves, or unequal in credit and ability to the great task they have undertaken. Instead of reserving the interposition of the royal personage, as the last resource of government, their weakness obliges them to apply it to every ordinary occasion, and to render it cheap and common in the opinion of the people. Instead of supporting their master, they look to *him* for support; and, for the emoluments of remaining one day more in office, care not how much his sacred character is prostituted and dishonoured.

If I thought it possible for this paper to reach the closet, I would venture to appeal at once to his Majesty's judgement. I would ask him, but in the most respectful terms, "As you are a young man, Sir, who ought to have a life of happiness in prospect;—as you are a husband;—as you are a father, [your filial duties I own have been religiously performed] is it *bona fide* for your interest or your honor to sacrifice your domestic tranquillity, and to live in a perpetual disagreement with your people, merely to preserve such a chain of beings as North, Barrington, Weymouth, Gower, Ellis, Onslow, Rigby, Jerry Dyson, and Sandwich? Their very names are a satire upon all government, and I defy the gravest of your chaplains to read the catalogue without laughing."

For my own part, Sir, I have always considered addresses from parliament as a fashionable, unmeaning formality. Usurpers, ideots, and tyrants have been successively complimented with almost the same professions of duty and affection. But let us suppose them to

* After a certain person had succeeded in cajolling Mr. Yorke, he told the Duke of Grafton, with a witty smile, "My Lord, you may kill the next Percy yourself."—N. B. He had but that instant wiped the tears away, which overcame Mr. Yorke.

mean exactly what they profess. The consequences deserve to be considered. Either the sovereign is a man of high spirit and dangerous ambition, ready to take advantage of the treachery of his parliament, ready to accept of the surrender they make him of the public liberty;—or he is a mild, undesigning prince, who, provided they indulge him with a little state and pageantry, would of himself intend no mischief. On the first supposition, it must soon be decided by the sword, whether the constitution should be lost or preserved. On the second, a prince no way qualified for the execution of a great and hazardous enterprize, and without any determined object in view, may nevertheless be driven into such desperate measures, as may lead directly to his ruin, or disgrace himself by a shameful fluctuation between the extremes of violence at one moment, and timidity at another. The minister perhaps may have reason to be satisfied with the success of the present hour, and with the profits of his employment. He is the tenant of the day, and has no interest in the inheritance. The sovereign himself is bound by other obligations, and ought to look forward to a superior, a permanent interest. His paternal tenderness should remind him, how many hostages he has given to society.[1] The ties of nature come powerfully in aid of oaths and protestations. The father, who considers his own precarious state of health, and the possible hazard of a long minority, will wish to see the family estate free and unincumbered.* What is the dignity of the crown, though it were really maintained;—what is the honour of parliament, supposing it could exist without any foundation of integrity and justice;—or what is the vain reputation of firmness, even if the scheme of the government were uniform and consistent, compared with the heartfelt affections of the people, with the happiness and security of the royal family, or even with the grateful acclamations of the populace! Whatever style of contempt may be adopted by ministers or

* Every true friend of the House of Brunswick sees with affliction, how rapidly some of the principal branches of the family have dropped off.[2]

---

[1] The score was 6 not out at the time Junius wrote; the final score was 15.

[2] The King's uncle, the Duke of Cumberland, died in 1765 at the age of 44. During the 1760s the King also lost two brothers, the Duke of York and Prince Frederick, and a sister, Princess Louisa.

parliaments, no man sincerely despises the voice of the English nation. The house of commons are only interpreters, whose duty it is to convey the sense of the people faithfully to the crown. If the interpretation be false or imperfect, the constituent powers are called upon to deliver their own sentiments. Their speech is rude, but intelligible;—their gestures fierce, but full of explanation. Perplexed by sophistries, their honest eloquence rises into action. Their first appeal was to the integrity of their representatives:—the second to the King's justice;—the last argument of the people, whenever they have recourse to it, will carry more perhaps than persuasion to parliament, or supplication to the throne.

JUNIUS.

Parliament was prorogued on Saturday, 19 May. Junius' next letter was a grand review of the state of the nation.

LETTER XXXIX.

TO THE PRINTER OF THE PUBLIC ADVERTISER.

SIR, 28. *May* 1770.

WHILE parliament was sitting, it would neither have been safe, nor perhaps quite regular, to offer any opinion to the public, upon the justice or wisdom of their proceedings. To pronounce fairly upon their conduct, it was necessary to wait until we could consider, in one view, the beginning, progress, and conclusion of their deliberations. The cause of the public was undertaken and supported by men, whose abilities and united authority, to say nothing of the advantageous ground they stood on, might well be thought sufficient to determine a popular question in favour of the people. Neither was the house of commons so absolutely engaged in defence of the ministry, or even of their own resolutions, but that *they* might have paid some decent regard to the known disposition of their constituents, and, without any dishonour to their firmness, might have retracted an opinion too hastily adopted, when they saw the alarm it had created, and how strongly it was opposed by the general sense of the nation. The ministry too would have consulted their own immediate interest, in making some concession satisfactory to the moderate part of the people. Without touching the fact, they might have consented to guard against, or give up the dangerous principle, on which it was established. In this state of things, I think it was highly improbable at the beginning of the session, that the complaints of the people upon a matter, which, in *their* apprehension at least, immediately affected the life of the constitution, would be treated with as much contempt by their own representatives, and by the house of lords, as they had been by the other branch of the legislature. Despairing of their integrity, we had a right to expect something from their prudence, and something from their fears. The Duke of Grafton certainly did not foresee to what an extent the corruption of a parliament might be carried. He thought, perhaps, that there was still some portion of shame or virtue left in the majority of the house of commons, or that there was a line in public prostitution, beyond which they would scruple to proceed. Had the young man been a little more practised in the world, or had he ventured to measure the characters of other men by his own, he would not have been so easily discouraged.

THE prorogation of parliament naturally calls upon us to review their proceedings, and to consider the condition in which they have left the kingdom. I do not question but they have done what is usually called the King's business, much to his Majesty's satisfaction.[1] We have only to lament, that, in consequence of a system introduced or revived in the present reign, this kind of merit should be very consistent with the neglect of every duty they owe to the nation. The interval between the opening of the last and close of the former session was longer than usual.[2] Whatever were the views of the minister in deferring the meeting of parliament, sufficient time was certainly given to every member of the house of

[1] In his prorogation speech the King declared to the Lords and Commons that 'the temper with which you have conducted all your proceedings, has given me great satisfaction, and I promise myself the happiest effects from the firmness as well as the moderation which you have manifested in the very critical circumstances which have attended your late deliberations.'

[2] Parliament stood prorogued from 14 July 1769 until 9 January 1770. This was the longest period of prorogation since the session of 1764/5.

commons, to look back upon the steps he had taken, and the consequences they had produced. The zeal of party, the violence of personal animosities, and the heat of contention had leisure to subside. From that period, whatever resolution they took was deliberate and prepense. In the preceding session, the dependents of the ministry had affected to believe, that the final determination of the question would have satisfied the nation, or at least put a stop to their complaints; as if the certainty of an evil could diminish the sense of it, or the nature of injustice could be altered by decision. But they found the people of England were in a temper very distant from submission; and, although it was contended that the house of commons could not themselves reverse a resolution, which had the force and effect of a judicial sentence, there were other constitutional expedients, which would have given a security against any similar attempts for the future. The general proposition, in which the whole country had an interest, might have been reduced to a particular fact, in which Mr. Wilkes and Mr. Luttrell would alone have been concerned. The house of lords might interpose;—the King might dissolve the parliament;—or, if every other resource failed, there still lay a grand constitutional writ of error, in behalf of the people, from the decision of one court to the wisdom of the whole legislature. Every one of these remedies has been successively attempted. The people performed *their* part with dignity, spirit, and perseverance. For many months his Majesty heard nothing from his people but the language of complaint and resentment;—unhappily for this country, it was the daily triumph of his courtiers that he heard it with an indifference approaching to contempt.

THE house of commons having assumed a power unknown to the constitution, were determined not merely to support it in the single instance in question, but to maintain the doctrine in its utmost extent, and to establish the fact as a precedent in law, to be applied in whatever manner his Majesty's servants should hereafter think fit. Their proceedings upon this occasion are a strong proof that a decision, in the first instance illegal and unjust, can only be supported by a continuation of falsehood and injustice. To support their former resolutions, they were obliged to violate some of the best known and established rules of the house. In one instance they went so far as to declare, in open defiance of truth and common sense, that it was not the rule of the house to divide a complicated question, at the request of a member*.[1] But after trampling upon the laws of the land, it was not wonderful that they should treat the private regulations of their own assembly with equal disregard. The speaker, being young in office, began with pretended ignorance, and ended with deciding for the ministry.[2] We were not surprized at the decision; but he hesitated and blushed at his own baseness, and every man was astonished†.

THE interest of the public was vigorously supported in the house of lords. Their right to defend the constitution against an incroachment of the other estates, and the necessity of exerting it at this period, was urged to them with every argument, that could be supposed to influence the heart or the understanding. But it soon appeared, that they had already taken their part, and were

* This extravagant resolution appears in the Votes of the house; but, in the minutes of the committees, the instances of resolutions contrary to law and truth, or of refusals to acknowledge law and truth when proposed to them, are innumerable.

† When the King first made it a measure of his government to destroy Mr. Wilkes, and when for this purpose it was necessary to run down privilege, Sir Fletcher Norton, with his usual prostituted effrontery, assured the house of commons, that he should regard one of their votes, no more than a resolution of so many drunken porters. This is the very Lawyer, whom Ben Jonson describes in the following lines:[3]

"Gives forked counsel; takes provoking gold,
On either hand, and puts it up.
So wise, so grave, of so perplex'd a tongue,
And *loud* withal, that would not wag, nor scarce
Lie still without *a fee*."

[1] On 16 February 1770 the committee on the state of the nation reported that in matters of election the House was bound to judge by the law of the land and that the expulsion and incapacity to serve of John Wilkes was agreeable to the law of the land. Three days later, Sir William Meredith, one of the opposition, moved that it was the rule of the House that complicated questions might be divided. The motion was rejected by 243 votes to 174. *CJ* xxxii. 710; *Parl. Hist.* xvi. 807–13.

[2] Sir Fletcher Norton succeeded Sir John Cust as Speaker in January 1770. On 16 February he was involved in a violent altercation with Sir William Meredith. *CJ* xxxii. 707–8.

[3] *Volpone*, Act I, sc. iii.

determined to support the house of commons, not only at the expence of truth and decency, but even by a surrender of their own most important rights. Instead of performing that duty which the constitution expected from them, in return for the dignity and independence of their station, in return for the hereditary share it has given them in the legislature, the majority of them made common cause with the other house in oppressing the people, and established another doctrine as false in itself, and if possible more pernicious to the constitution, than that on which the Middlesex election was determined. By resolving, "that they had no right to impeach a judgment of the house of commons in any case whatsoever, where that house has a competent jurisdiction,"[1] they in effect gave up that constitutional check and reciprocal controul of one branch of the legislature over the other, which is perhaps the greatest and most important object provided for by the division of the whole legislative power into three estates; and now, let the judicial decisions of the house of commons be ever so extravagant, let their declarations of the law be ever so flagrantly false, arbitrary, and oppressive to the subject, the house of lords have imposed a slavish silence upon themselves;—they cannot interpose,—they cannot protect the subject,—they cannot defend the laws of their country. A concession so extraordinary in itself, so contradictory to the principles of their own institution, cannot but alarm the most unsuspecting mind. We may well conclude, that the lords would hardly have yielded so much to the other house, without the certainty of a compensation, which can only be made to them at the expence of the people*. The arbitrary power they have assumed of imposing fines and committing, during pleasure, will now be exercised in its full extent. The house of commons are too much in their debt to question or interrupt their proceedings. The crown too, we may be well assured, will lose nothing in this new distribution of power. After declaring, that to petition for

* The man who resists and overcomes this iniquitous power, assumed by the lords, must be supported by the whole people. We have the laws of our side, and want nothing but an intrepid leader. When such a man stands forth, let the nation look to it. It is not *his* cause, but our own.

---

1 2 February 1770, *Parl. Hist.* xvi. 823–9.

a dissolution of parliament is irreconcileable with the principles of the constitution, his Majesty has reason to expect that some extraordinary compliment will be returned to the Royal prerogative. The three branches of the legislature seem to treat their separate rights and interests as the Roman Triumvirs did their friends. They reciprocally sacrifice them to the animosities of each other, and establish a detestable union among themselves, upon the ruin of the laws and liberty of the commonwealth.

THROUGH the whole proceedings of the house of commons in this session, there is an apparent, a palpable consciousness of guilt, which has prevented their daring to assert their own dignity, where it has been immediately and grossly attacked. In the course of Doctor Musgrave's examination, he said every thing that can be conceived mortifying to individuals, or offensive to the house. They voted his information frivolous, but they were awed by his firmness and integrity, and sunk under it.* The terms, in which the sale of a patent to Mr. Hine were communicated to the public, naturally called for a parliamentary enquiry. The integrity of the house of commons was directly impeached; but they had not courage to move in their own vindication, because the enquiry would have been fatal to Colonel Burgoyne, and the Duke of Grafton. When Sir George Savile branded them with the name of traitors to their constituents, when the Lord Mayor, the Sheriffs, and Mr. Trecothick, expressly avowed and maintained every part of the city remonstrance, why did they tamely submit to be insulted? Why did they not immediately expel those refractory members? Conscious

* The examination of this firm, honest man, is printed for *Almon*. The reader will find it a most curious, and a most interesting tract. Doctor Musgrave, with no other support but truth, and his own firmness, resisted, and overcame the whole house of commons.[1]

[1] Junius must have been alone in his interpretation. On 12 August 1769 Dr. Samuel Musgrave, an Exeter physician, revived the old story that British negotiators at the Paris settlement had been bribed to betray their country. He named the Chevalier D'Eon as a key witness. When the Chevalier denied any knowledge of the affair, opposition writers insinuated that he too had been bribed. On 29 January 1770 Dr. Musgrave was examined before the House of Commons and his assertions voted frivolous and without foundation. No action was taken against him since it seemed clear that he was a well-meaning fool, taken in by tavern gossip. *Gentleman's Magazine*, 1769, 429–33, 585–7; *Parl. Hist.* xvi. 763–85.

of the motives, on which they had acted, they prudently preferred infamy to danger, and were better prepared to meet the contempt, than to rouze the indignation of the whole people. Had they expelled those five members, the consequences of the new doctrine of incapacitation would have come immediately home to every man. The truth of it would then have been fairly tried, without any reference to Mr. Wilkes's private character, or the dignity of the house, or the obstinacy of one particular county. These topics, I know, have had their weight with men, who affecting a character of moderation, in reality consult nothing but their own immediate ease;—who are weak enough to acquiesce under a flagrant violation of the laws, when it does not directly touch themselves, and care not what injustice is practised upon a man, whose moral character they piously think themselves obliged to condemn. In any other circumstances, the house of commons must have forfeited all credit and dignity, if, after such gross provocation, they had permitted those five gentlemen to sit any longer among them. We should then have seen and felt the operation of a precedent, which is represented to be perfectly barren and harmless. But there is a set of men in this country, whose understandings measure the violation of law, by the magnitude of the instance, not by the important consequences, which flow directly from the principle, and the minister, I presume, did not think it safe to quicken their apprehensions too soon. Had Mr. Hampden reasoned and acted like the moderate men of these days, instead of hazarding his whole fortune in a law-suit with the crown, he would have quietly paid the twenty shillings demanded of him,—the Stuart family would probably have continued upon the throne, and, at this moment, the imposition of ship-money would have been an acknowledged prerogative of the crown.

WHAT then has been the business of the session, after voting the supplies, and confirming the determination of the Middlesex election? The extraordinary prorogation of the Irish parliament, and the just discontents of that kingdom, have been passed by without notice.[1] Neither the general situation of our Colonies,

[1] The term of office of Lord Townshend as Lord Lieutenant of Ireland was eventful. The government wished to augment the Irish army to 15,000 men, an increase of

nor that particular distress which forced the inhabitants of Boston to take up arms in their defence, have been thought worthy of a moment's consideration. In the repeal of those acts, which were most offensive to America, the parliament have done every thing, but remove the offence. They have relinquished the revenue, but judiciously taken care to preserve the contention. It is not pretended that the continuation of the tea duty is to produce any direct benefit whatsoever to the mother country. What is it then but an odious, unprofitable exertion of a speculative right, and fixing a badge of slavery upon the Americans, without service to their masters? But it has pleased God to give us a ministry and a parliament, who are neither to be persuaded by argument, nor instructed by experience.[1]

LORD North, I presume, will not claim an extraordinary merit from any thing he has done this year in the improvement or application of the revenue. A great operation, directed to an important object, though it should fail of success, marks the genius and elevates the character of a minister. A poor contracted understanding deals in little schemes, which dishonour him if they fail, and do him no credit when they succeed. Lord North had fortunately the means in his possession of reducing all the four per cents at once. The failure of his first enterprize in finance is not half so disgraceful to his reputation as a minister, as the enterprize itself is injurious to the public. Instead of striking one decisive blow, which would have cleared the market at once, upon terms proportioned to the price of the four per cents six weeks ago, he has tampered with a

some 3,000 over the usual peace-time establishment. In exchange it permitted the Octennial Bill to be passed, thus limiting the duration of Irish Parliaments for the first time (other than by the death of the monarch). But Irish aspirations were far from satisfied, and after the general election of 1768 a fresh dispute broke out over the right of the English Privy Council to originate money bills. On 26 December 1769 Townshend entered a formal protest in the Journals of both Houses and prorogued Parliament for fourteen months.

[1] Lord North inherited a situation in America much inflamed by Charles Townshend's decision to impose duties on tea, glass, paper, printer's colours, and red and white lead. The Grafton cabinet resolved in May 1769 to repeal all the duties except that on tea, which was preserved partly to maintain the principle of taxation. North continued the policy. The intention was to find some middle course that might be acceptable to both American and British opinion.

pitiful portion of a commodity, which ought never to have been touched but in gross;—he has given notice to the holders of that stock, of a design formed by government to prevail upon them to surrender it by degrees, consequently has warned them to hold up and inhance the price;—so that the plan of reducing the four per cents must either be dropped entirely, or continued with an increasing disadvantage to the public. The minister's sagacity has served to raise the value of the thing he means to purchase, and to sink that of the three per cents, which it is his purpose to sell. In effect, he has contrived to make it the interest of the proprietor of four per cents to sell out and buy three per cents in the market, rather than subscribe his stock upon any terms, that can possibly be offered by government.[1]

THE state of the nation leads us naturally to consider the situation of the King. The prorogation of parliament has the effect of a temporary dissolution. The odium of measures adopted by the collective body sits lightly upon the separate members, who composed it. They retire into summer quarters, and rest from the disgraceful labours of the campaign. But as for the Sovereign, *it is not so with him*. HE has a permanent existence in this country; HE cannot withdraw himself from the complaints, the discontents, the reproaches of his subjects. They pursue him to his retirement, and invade his domestic happiness, when no address can be obtained from an obsequious parliament to encourage or console him. In other times, the interest of the King and people of England was, as it ought to be, entirely the same. A new system has not only been adopted in fact, but professed upon principle. Ministers are no longer the public servants of the state, but the private domestics of the Sovereign. *One particular class of men are permitted to call

* "An ignorant, mercenary, and servile crew; unanimous in evil, diligent in

---

[1] A detailed and apparently authoritative refutation of Junius' criticisms was supplied by Varro in the *Public Advertiser* of 18 August. Noting that only half of the limited subscription had been taken up, he denied that it would have been possible for the minister to have wiped out all the four per cents: 'I must confess, that I do not see the force of this reasoning. Two millions and an half could not be reduced at a certain price, therefore 20,240,000£ might have been reduced at the same rate. In what university did the doughty writer learn his logic?' Varro argued that North's transaction had saved the country £204,000.

themselves the King's friends, as if the body of the people were the King's enemies; or as if his Majesty looked for a resource or consolation, in the attachment of a few favourites, against the general contempt and detestation of his subjects. Edward, and Richard the second, made the same distinction between the collective body of the people, and a contemptible party who surrounded the throne. The event of their mistaken conduct might have been a warning to their successors. Yet the errors of those princes were not without excuse. They had as many false friends, as our present gracious Sovereign, and infinitely greater temptations to seduce them. They were neither sober, religious, nor demure. Intoxicated with pleasure, they wasted their inheritance in pursuit of it. Their lives were like a rapid torrent, brilliant in prospect, though useless or dangerous in its course. In the dull, unanimated existence of other princes, we see nothing but a sickly, stagnant water, which taints the atmosphere without fertilizing the soil.—The morality of a King is not to be measured by vulgar rules. His situation is singular. There are faults which do him honour, and virtues that disgrace him. A faultless, insipid equality in his character, is neither capable of vice nor virtue in the extreme; but it secures his submission to those persons, whom he has been accustomed to respect, and makes him a dangerous instrument of *their* ambition. Secluded from the world, attached from his infancy to one set of persons, and one set of ideas, he can neither open his heart to new connexions, nor his mind to better information. A character of this sort is the soil fittest to produce that obstinate bigotry in politics and religion, which begins with a meritorious sacrifice of the understanding, and finally conducts the monarch and the martyr to the block.

AT any other period, I doubt not, the scandalous disorders, which have been introduced into the government of all the dependencies in the Empire, would have rouzed the attention of the public.

mischief, variable in principles, constant to flattery, talkers for liberty, but slaves to power;—stiling themselves the court party, and the prince's only friends." *Davenant.*[1]

---

[1] *The political and commercial works of Charles D'Avenant*, ed. Sir Charles Whitworth (1771), ii. 305: 'Of private men's duty in the administration of public affairs.'

The odious abuse and prostitution of the prerogative at home,—the unconstitutional employment of the military,—the arbitrary fines and commitments by the house of lords, and court of king's bench;—the mercy of a chaste and pious Prince extended chearfully to a wilful murderer, because that murderer is the brother of a common prostitute*, would, I think, at any other time, have excited universal indignation. But the daring attack upon the constitution, in the Middlesex election, makes us callous and indifferent to inferior grievances. No man regards an eruption upon the surface, when the noble parts are invaded, and he feels a mortification approaching to his heart. The free election of our representatives in parliament comprehends, because it is, the source and security of every right and privilege of the English nation. The ministry have realised the compendious ideas of Caligula.[1] They know that the liberty, the laws, and property of an Englishman have in truth but one neck, and that to violate the freedom of election strikes deeply at them all.

JUNIUS.

LETTER XL.

TO LORD NORTH

MY LORD, 22. *Aug.* 1770.

MR. Luttrell's services were the chief support and ornament of the Duke of Grafton's administration. The honour of

* Miss Kennedy.[2]

---

[1] According to Suetonius, *Gaius Caligula*, xxx. 2, the Emperor wished that the Roman people had but a single neck.

[2] John Bigby, a watchman, was murdered in a drunken scuffle on Westminster Bridge by Patrick and Matthew Kennedy. They were tried at the Old Bailey in February 1770 and sentenced to death, but subsequently pardoned on condition of transportation. The widow of the deceased then lodged an appeal but, according to reports, was persuaded to withdraw it on payment of £350 compensation. George Selwyn, Lord Palmerston, Lord Spencer, Lord Fife, and John St. John were among those who intervened on behalf of the Kennedy brothers; Horace Walpole reported that their 'handsome sister' Kitty was kept by 'two young men of quality'. In 1781 William Fawkener wrote nonchalantly to Lord Carlisle: 'The Kennedy died last week, and John St. John is gone out of town, I hear, in great affliction: it is one of the luckiest events that could have happened for him, as she was a great expense to him.' *HMC Carlisle*, 533; *Annual Register*, 1770, 74–5, 109, 118, 161; J. H. Jesse, *George Selwyn and his contemporaries*, ii. 384–92; Walpole, iv. 110–11.

rewarding them was reserved for your Lordship. The Duke, it seems, had contracted an obligation he was ashamed to acknowledge, and unable to acquit. You, my Lord, had no scruples. You accepted the succession with all its incumbrances, and have paid Mr. Luttrell his legacy, at the hazard of ruining the estate.

WHEN this accomplished youth declared himself the champion of government, the world was busy in enquiring what honours or emoluments could be a sufficient recompence, to a young man of his rank and fortune, for submitting to mark his entrance into life with the universal contempt and detestation of his country.—His noble father had not been so precipitate.—To vacate his seat in parliament;—to intrude upon a county in which he had no interest or connexion;—to possess himself of another man's right, and to maintain it in defiance of public shame as well as justice, bespoke a degree of zeal or of depravity, which all the favour of a pious Prince could hardly requite. I protest, my Lord, there is in this young man's conduct, a strain of prostitution, which, for its singularity, I cannot but admire. He has discovered a new line in the human character;—he has degraded even the name of Luttrell, and gratified his father's most sanguine expectations.

THE Duke of Grafton, with every possible disposition to patronise this kind of merit, was contented with pronouncing Colonel Luttrell's panegyric.[1] The gallant spirit, the disinterested zeal of the young adventurer, were echoed through the house of lords. His Grace repeatedly pledged himself to the house, as an evidence of the purity of his friend Mr. Luttrell's intentions;—that he had engaged without any prospect of personal benefit, and that the idea of compensation would mortally offend him*. The noble Duke could hardly be in earnest; but he had lately quitted his employment, and began to think it necessary to take some care of his reputation. At that very moment the Irish negociation was probably

* He now says that his great object is the rank of Colonel, and that he *will* have it.

---

1 In the debate of 1 May 1770, *Parl. Hist.* xvi. 965.

begun.—Come forward, thou worthy representative of Lord Bute, and tell this insulted country, who advised the King to appoint Mr. Luttrell, ADJUTANT-GENERAL to the army in Ireland. By what management was Colonel Cuninghame prevailed on to resign his employment, and the obsequious Gisborne to accept of a pension for the government of Kinsale*?

WAS it an original stipulation with the Princess of Wales, or does he owe his preferment to your Lordship's partiality, or to the Duke of Bedford's friendship? My Lord, though it may not be possible to trace this measure to its source, we can follow the stream, and warn the country of its approaching destruction. The English nation must be rouzed, and put upon its guard. Mr. Luttrell has already shewn us how far he may be trusted, whenever an open attack is to be made upon the liberties of this country. I do not doubt that there is a deliberate plan formed.—Your Lordship best knows by whom;—the corruption of the legislative body on this side—a military force on the other—and then, *Farewell to England!* It is impossible that any minister shall dare to advise the King to place such a man as Luttrell in the confidential post of Adjutant-general, if there were not some secret purpose in view, which only such a man as Luttrell is fit to promote. The insult offered to the army in general is as gross as the outrage intended to the people of England. What! Lieutenant-colonel Luttrell, Adjutant-general of an army of sixteen thousand men! one would think his Majesty's campaigns at Blackheath and Wimbledon might have taught him better.[1]—I cannot help wishing General Harvey joy of a colleague,

* This infamous transaction ought to be explained to the public. Colonel Gisborne was quarter-master-general in Ireland. Lord Townshend persuades him to resign to a Scotch officer, one Fraser, and gives him the government of Kinsale.—Colonel Cuninghame was Adjutant-general in Ireland. Lord Townshend offers him a pension, to induce him to resign to Luttrell. Cuninghame treats the offer with contempt. What's to be done? poor Gisborne must move once more.—He accepts of a pension of 500 l. a year, until a government of greater value shall become vacant. Colonel Cuninghame is made Governor of Kinsale; and Luttrell, at last, for whom the whole machinery is put in motion, becomes Adjutant-general, and in effect takes the command of the army in Ireland.

---

[1] Blackheath and Wimbledon common were used for reviews. The King had been present on 16 April 1770 at a review of the light horse on Wimbledon common, in which a trooper was accidentally wounded. *Gentleman's Magazine*, 1770, 188.

who does so much honour to the employment.—But, my Lord, this measure is too daring to pass unnoticed, too dangerous to be received with indifference or submission. You shall not have time to new-model the Irish army. They will not submit to be garbled by Colonel Luttrell. As a mischief to the English constitution, (for he is not worth the name of enemy) they already detest him. As a boy, impudently thrust over their heads, they will receive him with indignation and contempt.—As for you, my Lord, who perhaps are no more than the blind, unhappy instrument of Lord Bute and her Royal Highness the Princess of Wales, be assured that you shall be called upon to answer for the advice, which has been given, and either discover your accomplices, or fall a sacrifice to their security.

JUNIUS.

In the course of the summer of 1770 the government commenced prosecutions against several printers and booksellers for publishing or selling Junius' letter to the King. John Almon was found guilty and held over for sentence; Woodfall, on 13 June, was found guilty of printing and publishing only; John Miller and Henry Baldwin were acquitted; and the prosecutions against Charles Say and George Robinson were dropped. All the cases were heard in King's Bench before Lord Chief Justice Mansfield. Junius' letter may have been intended to prepare the ground for the debates on the administration of justice which took place after Parliament reassembled on 13 November. The previous day Junius wrote to the printer in private letter no. 24: 'The inclosed, though begun within these few days, has been greatly laboured. It is very correctly copied, and I beg you will take care that it be literally printed as it stands. I don't think you run the least Risque. We have got the Rascal down. Let us strangle him if it be possible.'

Horace Walpole commented to Mann on 15 November that this letter was 'the most outrageous I suppose ever published against so high a magistrate by name'. *Yale Edition*, vol. 23, 247.

LETTER XLI.

TO THE RIGHT HONOURABLE LORD MANSFIELD.

MY LORD, 14. *November* 1770.

THE appearance of this letter will attract the curiosity of the public, and command even your Lordship's attention. I am considerably in your debt, and shall endeavour, once for all, to balance the account. Accept of this address, my Lord, as a prologue to more important scenes, in which you will probably be called upon to act or suffer.

YOU will not question my veracity, when I assure you that it has not been owing to any particular respect for your person that I have abstained from you so long. Besides the distress and danger with which the press is threatened, when your lordship is party, and the party is to be judge, I confess I have been deterred by the difficulty of the task. Our language has no term of reproach, the mind has no idea of detestation, which has not already been happily applied to you, and exhausted.—Ample justice has been done by abler pens than mine to the separate merits of your life and character. Let it be *my* humble office to collect the scattered sweets, till their united virtue tortures the sense.

PERMIT me to begin with paying a just tribute to Scotch sincerity, wherever I find it. I own I am not apt to confide in the professions of gentlemen of that country, and when they smile, I feel an involuntary emotion to guard myself against mischief. With this general opinion of an ancient nation, I always thought it much to your lordship's honour, that, in your earlier days, you were but little infected with the prudence of your country. You had some original attachments, which you took every proper opportunity to acknowledge. The liberal spirit of youth prevailed over your native discretion. Your zeal in the cause of an unhappy prince was expressed with the sincerity of wine, and some of the solemnities of religion.* This I conceive, is the most amiable point of view, in

* THIS man was always a rank Jacobite. Lord Ravensworth produced the most satisfactory Evidence of his having frequently drank the Pretender's health upon his knees.[1]

[1] Lord Ravensworth was examined by a committee of the Privy Council on 15 February 1753 in connection with his allegations against Mansfield. It found them to be scandalous and malicious. The best account is in J. Brooke, *King George III*, 35–8. It is clear from a letter quoted in *The House of Commons, 1715–54*, ii. 285–6 that Mansfield had professed Jacobite sympathies while at Oxford. Lord Chesterfield commented to Solomon Dayrolles on 6 April 1753: 'Lord Ravensworth's conduct was

which your character has appeared. Like an honest man, you took that part in politics, which might have been expected from your birth, education, country and connexions. There was something generous in your attachment to the banished house of Stuart. We lament the mistakes of a good man, and do not begin to detest him until he affects to renounce his principles. Why did you not adhere to that loyalty you once professed? Why did you not follow the example of your worthy brother?* With him, you might have shared in the honour of the Pretender's confidence—with him, you might have preserved the integrity of your character, and England, I think, might have spared you without regret. Your friends will say, perhaps, that altho' you deserted the fortune of your liege Lord, you have adhered firmly to the principles which drove his father from the throne;—that without openly supporting the person, you have done essential service to the cause, and consoled yourself for the loss of a favourite family by reviving and establishing the maxims of their government. This is the way, in which a Scotchman's understanding corrects the error of his heart.—My lord, I acknowledge the truth of the defence, and can trace it through all your conduct. I see through your whole life, one uniform plan to enlarge the power of the crown, at the expence of the liberty of the subject. To this object, your thoughts, words and actions have been constantly directed. In contempt or ignorance of the common law of England, you have made it your study to introduce into the court, where you preside, maxims of jurisprudence unknown to Englishmen. The Roman code, the law of nations, and the opinion of foreign civilians, are your perpetual theme;—but whoever heard you mention Magna Charta or the Bill of Rights with approbation or respect? By such treacherous

* CONFIDENTIAL Secretary to the late Pretender. This circumstance confirmed the friendship between the brothers.[1]

---

merely the result of honest, wrongheaded Whig zeal . . . no reasonable man, I believe, thinks them Jacobites now, whatever they may have been formerly.' *Letters of Philip Dormer Stanhope, 4th Earl of Chesterfield*, ed. B. Dobrée (1932), v. 2014. See also *Parl. Hist.* xiv. 1294–7.

[1] James Murray was an active Jacobite all his life and was created Earl of Dunbar in the Jacobite peerage. He was Secretary of State to the Pretender from 1727 to 1747.

arts, the noble simplicity and free spirit of our Saxon laws were first corrupted. The Norman conquest was not compleat, until Norman lawyers had introduced their laws, and reduced slavery to a system.—This one leading principle directs your interpretation of the laws, and accounts for your treatment of juries. It is not in political questions only (for there the courtier might be forgiven) but let the cause be what it may, your understanding is equally on the rack, either to contract the power of the jury, or to mislead their judgment. For the truth of this assertion, I appeal to the doctrine you delivered in Lord Grosvenor's cause.[1] An action for criminal conversation being brought by a peer against a prince of the blood, you were daring enough to tell the jury that, in fixing the damages, they were to pay no regard to the quality or fortune of the parties;—that it was a trial between A. and B.—that they were to consider the offence in a moral light only, and give no greater damages to a peer of the realm, than to the meanest mechanic. I shall not attempt to refute a doctrine, which, if it was meant for law, carries falshood and absurdity upon the face of it; but, if it was meant for a declaration of your political creed, is clear and consistent. Under an arbitrary government, all ranks and distinctions are confounded. The honour of a nobleman is no more considered than the reputation of a peasant, for, with different liveries, they are equally slaves.

EVEN in matters of private property, we see the same byass and inclination to depart from the decisions of your predecessors, which you certainly ought to receive as evidence of the common law. Instead of those certain, positive rules, by which the judgment of a court of law should invariably be determined, you have fondly introduced your own unsettled notions of equity and substantial

[1] An account of this case is given in the *Gentleman's Magazine*, 1770, 314–19. Lord Grosvenor's action for damages against the Duke of Cumberland, younger brother of the King, was heard in King's Bench on 5 July 1770. According to Horace Walpole, the public was more shocked by the Duke's spelling than his morals: 'His Royal Highness's diction and learning scarce exceeded that of a cabin boy.' Alexander Wedderburn, for Lord Grosvenor, insisted that the Duke's rank was an aggravation of the offence and asked for £100,000 damages. Mansfield told the jury to give 'adequate recompense to the party injured and not give a sum as a punishment', whereupon they awarded £10,000.

justice. Decisions given upon such principles do not alarm the public so much as they ought, because the consequence and tendency of each particular instance, is not observed or regarded. In the mean time the practice gains ground; the court of King's Bench becomes a court of equity, and the judge, instead of consulting strictly the law of the land, refers only to the wisdom of the court, and to the purity of his own conscience. The name of Mr. Justice Yates, will naturally revive in your mind some of those emotions of fear and detestation, with which you always beheld him. That great lawyer, that honest man, saw your whole conduct in the light that I do. After years of ineffectual resistance to the pernicious principles introduced by your Lordship, and uniformly supported by your *humble friends* upon the bench, he determined, to quit a court, whose proceedings and decisions he could neither assent to with honour, nor oppose with success.[1]

*THE injustice done to an Individual is sometimes of service to the public. Facts are apt to alarm us more than the most dangerous principles. The sufferings and firmness of a Printer have roused the public attention. You knew and felt that your conduct would not bear a parliamentary inquiry, and you hoped to escape it by the meanest, the basest sacrifice of dignity and consistency, that ever was made by a great magistrate. Where was your firmness, where was that vindictive spirit, of which we have seen so many examples, when a man, so inconsiderable as Bingley, could force you to confess, in the face of this country, that, for two years together, you had illegally deprived an English subject of his liberty, and that he had triumphed over you at last? Yet I own, my lord, that your's is not an uncommon character. Women, and men like women, are timid, vindictive, and irresolute. Their passions counteract each other, and make the same creature, at one moment hateful, at another

* THE oppression of an obscure individual gave birth to the famous *Habeas Corpus* Act of 31. Car. 2. which is frequently considered as another Magna Charta of the Kingdom. *Blackstone*, 3. 135.

[1] Sir Joseph Yates was appointed a judge in King's Bench in 1764. It seems clear that he found Mansfield a difficult colleague and in February 1770 transferred to Common Pleas. He died in June 1770 at the age of 48.

contemptible. I fancy, my Lord, some time will elapse before you venture to commit another Englishman for refusing to answer interrogatories.*

THE doctrine you have constantly delivered, in cases of libel, is another powerful evidence of a settled plan to contract the legal power of juries, and to draw questions, inseparable from fact, within the *arbitrium* of the court. Here, my Lord, you have fortune of your side. When you invade the province of the jury, in matter of libel, you, in effect, attack the liberty of the press, and with a single stroke, wound two of your greatest enemies.—In some instances you have succeeded, because jurymen are too often ignorant of their own rights, and too apt to be awed by the authority of a chief justice. In other criminal prosecutions, the malice of the design is confessedly as much the subject of consideration to a jury, as the certainty of the fact. If a different doctrine prevails in the case of libels, why should it not extend to *all* criminal cases?—Why not to capital offences? I see no reason (and I dare say you will agree with me that there is no good one) why the life of the subject should be better protected against you, than his liberty or property. Why should you enjoy the full power of pillory, fine, and imprisonment, and not be indulged with hanging or transportation? With your Lordship's fertile genius and merciful disposition, I can conceive such an exercise of the power you have, as could hardly be aggravated by that which you have not.

BUT, my Lord, since you have laboured, (and not unsuccessfully) to destroy the substance *of the trial*, why should you suffer

* BINGLEY was committed for contempt in not submitting to be examined: He lay in prison two years, until the Crown thought the matter might occasion some serious complaint, and therefore he was let out, in the same contumelious state he had been put in, with all his sins about him, unannointed and unannealed.—There was much coquetry between the Court and the Attorney General, about who should undergo the ridicule of letting him escape.—*Vide another Letter to* ALMON, *p.* 189.[1]

---

[1] See p. 51, n. 2. In 1764 Almon published *An enquiry into the doctrine, recently propagated, concerning Libels, Warrants and the Seizure of Papers . . . in a letter to Mr. Almon from the Father of Candor*. The 1770 pamphlet was entitled *Another letter to Mr. Almon in matter of Libel.*

the form of the *verdict* to remain? Why force twelve honest men, in palpable violation of their oaths, to pronounce their fellow-subject a *guilty* man, when, almost at the same moment, you forbid their enquiring into the only circumstance, which in the eye of law and reason, constitutes guilt—the malignity or innocence of his intentions?—But I understand your Lordship.—If you could succeed in making the trial by jury useless and ridiculous, you might then with greater safety introduce a bill into parliament for enlarging the jurisdiction of the court, and extending your favourite trial by interrogatories to every question, in which the life or liberty of an Englishman is concerned.*

YOUR charge to the jury, in the prosecution against Almon and Woodfall, contradicts the highest legal authorities, as well as the plainest dictates of reason. In Miller's cause, and still more expressly in that of Baldwin, you have proceeded a step farther, and grossly contradicted yourself.—You may know perhaps, though I do not mean to insult you by an appeal to your experience, that the language of truth is uniform and consistent. To depart from it safely, requires memory and discretion. In the two last trials, your charge to the jury began, as usual, with assuring them that they had nothing to do with the law,—that they were to find the bare fact, and not concern themselves about the legal inferences drawn from it, or the degree of the defendant's guilt.—Thus far you were consistent with your former practice.—But how will you account for the conclusion? You told the jury that, "if, after all, they would

* The philosophical poet, doth notably describe the damnable and damned proceedings of the Judge of Hell,

> "Gnossius hæc Rhadamanthus habet durissima regna,
> Castigatque, auditque dolos, *subigitque fateri.*"

First he punisheth, and *then* he heareth: and lastly compelleth to confess, and makes and mars laws at his pleasure; like as the Centurion, in the holy history did to St. Paul, for the text saith, "Centurio apprehendi Paulum jussit, & se catenis eligari, et *tunc* INTERROGABAT, quis fuisset, & quid fecisset;" but good Judges and Justices abhor these Courses. *Coke* 2. *Inst.* 55.[1]

---

[1] The 'philosophical poet' was of course Virgil, and the reference is to *Aeneid*, vi. 566–7: 'Here Rhadamanthus has his severe jurisdiction, He punishes, and hears wrong-doing and forces confessions . . .' The whole note, including the quotation from the Acts of the Apostles, is borrowed from Sir Edward Coke.

take upon themselves to determine the law, *they might do it*, but they must be very sure that they determined according to law, for it touched their consciences, and they acted at their peril."—If I understand your first proposition, you meant to affirm, that the jury were not competent judges of the law in the criminal case of a libel —that it did not fall within *their* jurisdiction; and that, with respect to *them*, the malice or innocence of the defendants intentions would be a question *coram non judice*.—But the second proposition clears away your own difficulties, and restores the jury to all their judicial capacities. *You make the competence of the court to depend upon the legality of the decision. In the first instance you deny the power absolutely. In the second, you admit the power, provided it be legally exercised. Now, my Lord, without pretending to reconcile the distinctions of Westminster-hall with the simple information of common-sense, or the integrity of fair argument, I shall be understood by your Lordship, when I assert that, if a jury or any other court of judicature (for jurors are judges) have no right to entertain a cause, or question of law, it signifies nothing whether their decision be or be not according to law. Their decision is in itself a mere nullity: the parties are not bound to submit to it; and, if the jury run any risque of punishment, it is not for pronouncing a corrupt or illegal verdict, but for the illegality of meddling with a point, on which they have no legal authority to decide.†

* Directly the reverse of the doctrine he constantly maintained in the house of lords and elsewhere, upon the decision of the Middlesex election. He invariably asserted that the decision must be *legal*, because the court was *competent*; and never could be prevailed on to enter farther into the question.[1]

† These iniquitous prosecutions cost the best of princes six thousand pounds, and ended in the total defeat and disgrace of the prosecutors. In the course of one of them Judge Aston had the unparallelled impudence to tell Mr. Morris (a gentleman of unquestionable honour and integrity, and who was then giving his evidence on oath) that *he should pay very little regard to any affidavit he should make.*[2]

---

[1] One of the clearest discussions of this question is to be found in the debate of 6 December 1770 on the administration of criminal justice. John Glynn denied that it was the law of the land that juries were not to judge of intention but to confine themselves to the fact of publication. *Parl. Hist.* xvi. 1211–1301.

[2] At his trial John Almon produced several affidavits to exculpate himself, among them one from Robert Morris, secretary to the Society of Supporters of the Bill of Rights. When sentencing Almon on 28 November, Mr. Justice Aston declared he

I CANNOT quit this subject without reminding your Lordship of the name of Mr. Benson. Without offering any legal objection, you ordered a special juryman to be set aside in a cause, where the King was prosecutor. The novelty of the fact required explanation. Will you condescend to tell the world by what law or custom you were authorised to make a peremptory challenge of a juryman? The parties indeed have this power, and perhaps your Lordship, having accustomed yourself to unite the characters of judge and party, may claim it in virtue of the new capacity you have assumed, and profit by your own wrong. The time, within which you might have been punished for this daring attempt to pack a jury, is, I fear, elapsed; but no length of time shall erase the record of it.

THE mischiefs you have done this country, are not confined to your interpretation of the laws. You are a minister, my Lord, and, as such, have long been consulted. Let us candidly examine what use you have made of your ministerial influence. I will not descend to little matters, but come at once to those important points, on which your resolution was waited for, on which the expectation of your opinion kept a great part of the nation in suspence.—A constitutional question arises upon a declaration of the law of parliament, by which the freedom of election, and the birthright of the subject were supposed to have been invaded.—The King's servants are accused of violating the constitution.—The nation is in a ferment.—The ablest men of all parties engage in the question, and exert their utmost abilities in the discussion of it.—What part has the honest Lord Mansfield acted? As an eminent judge of the law, his opinion would have been respected.—As a peer, he had a right to demand an audience of his Sovereign, and inform him that his ministers were pursuing unconstitutional measures.—Upon other occasions, my Lord, you have no difficulty in finding your way into the closet. The pretended neutrality of belonging to no party, will not save your reputation. In questions merely political, an honest man may stand neuter. But the laws and constitution are

would 'not pay any regard' to Morris's testimony, hinting that it was partisan. *State Trials*, xx. 843–8. The diaries of Robert Morris have been edited by J. E. Ross under the title *Radical Adventurer* (1971).

the general property of the subject; not to defend is to relinquish;—and who is there so senseless as to renounce his share in a common benefit, unless he hopes to profit by a new division of the spoil. As a lord of parliament, you were repeatedly called upon to condemn or defend the new law declared by the house of commons. You affected to have scruples, and every expedient was attempted to remove them.—The question was proposed and urged to you in a thousand different shapes.—Your prudence still supplied you with evasion;—your resolution was invincible. For my own part, I am not anxious to penetrate this solemn secret.[1] I care not to whose wisdom it is intrusted, nor how soon you carry it with you to your grave*. You have betrayed your opinion by the very care you have taken to conceal it. It is not from Lord Mansfield that we expect any reserve in declaring his real sentiments in favour of government, or in opposition to the people; nor is it difficult to account for the motions of a timid, dishonest heart, which neither has virtue enough to acknowledge truth, nor courage to contradict it.—Yet you continue to support an administration which you know is universally odious, and which, on some occasions, you yourself speak of with contempt. You would fain be thought to take no share in government, while, in reality, you are the main spring of the machine.—Here too we trace the *little*, prudential policy of a Scotchman.—Instead of acting that open, generous part, which becomes your rank and station, you meanly skulk into the closet and give your Sovereign such advice, as you have not spirit to avow or defend. You secretly ingross the power, while you decline the title of minister; and though you dare not be Chancellor, you know how to secure the emoluments of the office.—Are the seals to be for ever in commission, that you may enjoy five thousand pounds a year?—I beg pardon, my Lord;—your fears have interposed at last, and forced you to resign.—The odium of continuing

* He said in the house of lords, that he believed he should carry his opinion with him to the grave. It was afterwards reported that he had intrusted it, in special confidence, to the ingenious Duke of Cumberland.

[1] Mansfield held the perfectly respectable view that, since the Commons were the undisputed judges of their own composition, any expression of the Lords' opinion would be improper. He supported a motion to that effect on 2 February 1770.

speaker of the house of lords, upon such terms, was too formidable to be resisted. What a multitude of bad passions are forced to submit to a constitutional infirmity! But though you have relinquished the salary, you still assume the rights of a minister.—Your conduct, it seems, must be defended in parliament.—For what other purpose is your wretched friend, that miserable serjeant, posted to the house of commons? Is it in the abilities of Mr. Leigh to defend the great Lord Mansfield?—Or is he only the punch of the puppet-shew, to speak as he is prompted, by the CHIEF JUGGLER behind the curtain*?

IN public affairs, my Lord, cunning, let it be ever so well wrought, will not conduct a man honourably through life. Like bad money, it may be current for a time, but it will soon be cried down. It cannot consist with a liberal spirit, though it be sometimes united with extraordinary qualifications. When I acknowledge your abilities, you may believe I am sincere. I feel for human nature, when I see a man, so gifted as you are, descend to such vile practise.—Yet do not suffer your vanity to console you too soon. Believe me, my good Lord, you are not admired in the same degree, in which you are detested. It is only the partiality of your friends, that balances the defects of your heart with the superiority of your understanding. No learned man, even among your own tribe, thinks you qualified to preside in a court of common law. Yet it is confessed that, under *Justinian*, you might have made an incomparable *Prætor*.—It is remarkable enough, but I hope not ominous, that the laws you understand best, and the judges you affect to admire most, flourished in the decline of a great empire, and are supposed to have contributed to its fall.

HERE, my Lord, it may be proper for us to pause together.—It is not for my own sake that I wish you to consider the delicacy of your situation. Beware how you indulge the first emotions of your

* This paragraph gagged poor *Leigh*. I really am concerned for the man, and wish it were possible to open his mouth. . . . He is a very pretty orator.[1]

1 Richard Leigh was brought into the House of Commons on the government interest for East Looe in October 1770. He died in March 1772.

resentment. This paper is delivered to the world, and cannot be recalled. The persecution of an innocent printer cannot alter facts, nor refute arguments.—Do not furnish me with farther materials against yourself.—An honest man, like the true religion, appeals to the understanding, or modestly confides in the internal evidence of his conscience. The impostor employs force instead of argument, imposes silence where he cannot convince, and propagates his character by the sword.

JUNIUS.

Junius wrote nothing under that signature for another ten weeks. But he seems to have been very active under other pseudonyms. Letters from Testis and Testiculus attacking Lord Barrington, the Secretary-at-War, appeared on 19 and 24 November. On reports that the Duke of Grafton was to rejoin the ministry, Junius revived his old name of Domitian, publishing letters on 8 and 24 December and on 17 January threatening more revelations about the Hine case. On 17 December Phalaris replied to a defence of Lord Mansfield by Nerva; since Junius subsequently quoted extensively from Phalaris in his collected edition, it is probable that this was another of his enterprises. These letters are discussed in Appendix Five.

In the course of December and January there was a very sharp war scare. In June 1770 an English naval force in the Falkland Islands was unceremoniously bundled out by a superior Spanish squadron. Strong diplomatic representations were made, and on 16 January 1771 Junius wrote to the printer (private letter no. 28) that 'every man in administration looks upon war as inevitable'. But on 25 January the ministers laid before both houses the terms of a settlement whereby the King of Spain agreed to restore the territory while reserving the matter of sovereignty. In the House of Commons Colonel Barré at once declared that the honour of the nation had been stabbed to the heart.

LETTER XLII.

TO THE PRINTER OF THE PUBLIC ADVERTISER.

SIR, *January* 30, 1771.

IF we recollect in what manner the *King's Friends* have been constantly employed, we shall have no reason to be surprised at any condition of disgrace, to which the once-respected name of

Englishmen may be degraded. His Majesty has no cares, but such as concern the laws and constitution of this country. In his Royal breast there is no room left for resentment, no place for hostile sentiments against the natural enemies of his crown. The system of government is uniform.—Violence and oppression at home can only be supported by treachery and submission abroad. When the civil rights of the people are daringly invaded on one side, what have we to expect, but that their political rights should be deserted and betrayed, in the same proportion, on the other? The plan of domestic policy, which has been invariably pursued, from the moment of his present Majesty's accession, engrosses all the attention of his servants. They know that the security of their places depends upon their maintaining, at any hazard, the secret system of the closet. A foreign war might embarrass, an unfavourable event might ruin the minister, and defeat the deep-laid scheme of policy, to which he and his associates owe their employments. Rather than suffer the execution of that scheme to be delayed or interrupted, the King has been advised to make a public surrender, a solemn sacrifice, in the face of all Europe, not only of the interests of his subjects, but of his own personal reputation, and of the dignity of that crown, which his predecessors have worn with honour. These are strong terms, Sir, but they are supported by fact and argument.

THE King of Great-Britain had been for some years in possession of an island, to which, as the ministry themselves have repeatedly asserted, the Spaniards had no claim of right. The importance of the place is not in question. If it were, a better judgment might be formed of it from the opinion of Lord Anson and Lord Egmont, and from the anxiety of the Spaniards, than from any fallacious insinuations thrown out by men, whose interest it is to undervalue that property, which they are determined to relinquish.[1] The pretensions of Spain were a subject of negotiation between the two courts. They had been discussed, but not admitted. The King of

[1] The need for such a base had been suggested in the account published in 1748 of Anson's great voyage round the world. Lord Egmont was First Lord of the Admiralty when Commodore Byron's expedition was sent out in 1764 and the chief settlement was named after him.

Spain, in these circumstances, bids adieu to amicable negotiation, and appeals directly to the sword. The expedition against Port Egmont does not appear to have been a sudden ill-concerted enterprise. It seems to have been conducted not only with the usual military precautions, but in all the forms and ceremonies of war. A frigate was first employed to examine the strength of the place. A message was then sent, demanding immediate possession, in the Catholic King's name, and ordering our people to depart. At last a military force appears, and compels the garrison to surrender. A formal capitulation ensues, and his Majesty's ship, which might at least have been permitted to bring home his troops immediately, is detained in port twenty days, and her rudder forcibly taken away. This train of facts carries no appearance of the rashness or violence of a Spanish governor. On the contrary, the whole plan seems to have been formed and executed, in consequence of deliberate orders, and a regular instruction from the Spanish court. Mr. Bucarelli is not a pirate, nor has he been treated as such by those who employed him. I feel for the honour of a gentleman, when I affirm that our King owes him a signal reparation.—Where will the humiliation of this country end! A King of Great Britain, not contented with placing himself upon a level with a Spanish governor, descends so low as to do a notorious injustice to that governor. As a salvo for his own reputation, he has been advised to traduce the character of a brave officer, and to treat him as a common robber, when he knew with certainty that Mr. Bucarelli had acted in obedience to his orders, and had done no more than his duty. Thus it happens in private life, with a man who has no spirit nor sense of honour.—One of his equals orders a servant to strike him.—Instead of returning the blow to the master, his courage is contented with throwing an aspersion, equally false and public, upon the character of the servant.

THIS short recapitulation was necessary to introduce the consideration of his Majesty's speech, of 13. November, 1770, and the subsequent measures of government. The excessive caution, with which the speech was drawn up, had impressed upon me an early conviction, that no serious resentment was thought of, and that the conclusion of the business, whenever it happened, must, in some degree, be dishonourable to England. There appears through the whole speech a guard and reserve in the choice of expression, which shews how careful the ministry were not to embarrass their future projects by any firm or spirited declaration from the throne. When all hopes of peace are lost, his Majesty tells his parliament, that he is preparing,—not for barbarous war, but (with all his mother's softness,) *for a different Situation.*[1]—An open hostility, authorised by the Catholic King, is called *an act of a governor*. This act, to avoid the mention of a regular siege and surrender, passes under the piratical description of *seizing by force*; and the thing taken is described, not as a part of the King's territory or proper dominion, but merely as a *possession*, a word expressly chosen in contradistinction to, and exclusion of the idea of *right*, and to prepare us for a future surrender both of the right and of the possession. Yet this speech, Sir, cautious and equivocal as it is, cannot, by any sophistry, be accommodated to the measures, which have since been adopted. It seemed to promise, that whatever might be given up by secret stipulation, some care would be taken to save appearances to the public. The event shews us, that to depart, in the minutest article, from the nicety and strictness of punctilio, is as dangerous to national honour, as to female virtue. The woman, who admits of one familiarity, seldom knows where to stop, or what to refuse; and when the counsels of a great country give way in a single instance,—when they once are inclined to submission, every step accelerates the rapidity of the descent. The ministry themselves, when they framed the speech, did not foresee, that they should ever accede to such an accommodation, as they have since advised their master to accept of.

THE King says, *The honour of my crown and the rights of my people are deeply affected.* The Spaniard, in his reply, says, *I give you back possession, but I adhere to my claim of prior right, reserving the assertion of it for a more favourable opportunity.*

[1] In the newspaper version, this sentence was followed by: 'It would indeed be happy for this Country, if the Lady I speak of were obliged to prepare herself for a different Situation.' In the 1772 edition, it was omitted. See Appendix Six, p. 532.

THE speech says, *I made an immediate demand of satisfaction, and, if that fails, I am prepared to do myself justice.* This immediate demand must have been sent to Madrid on the 12th of September, or in a few days after. It was certainly refused, or evaded, and the King *has not* done himself justice.—When the first magistrate speaks to the nation, some care should be taken of his apparent veracity.

THE speech proceeds to say, *I shall not discontinue my preparations until I have received proper reparation for the injury.* If this assurance may be relied on, what an enormous expence is entailed, *sine die*, upon this unhappy country! Restitution of a possession, and reparation of an injury are as different in substance, as they are in language. The very act of restitution may contain, as in this instance it palpably does, a shameful aggravation of the injury. A man of spirit does not measure the degree of an injury by the mere positive damage he has sustained. He considers the principle on which it is founded; he resents the superiority asserted over him; and rejects with indignation the claim of right, which his adversary endeavours to establish, and would force him to acknowledge.

THE motives, on which the Catholic King makes restitution, are, if possible, more insolent and disgraceful to our Sovereign, than even the declaratory condition annexed to it. After taking four months to consider, whether the expedition was undertaken by his own orders or not, he condescends to disavow the enterprize, and to restore the island,—not from any regard to justice;—not from any regard he bears to his Britannic Majesty, but merely *from the persuasion, in which he is, of the pacific sentiments of the King of Great Britain.*—At this rate, if our King had discovered the spirit of a man,—if he had made a peremptory demand of satisfaction, the King of Spain would have given him a peremptory refusal. But why this unseasonable, this ridiculous mention of the King of Great Britain's pacific intentions? Have they ever been in question? Was *He* the aggressor? Does he attack foreign powers without provocation? Does he even resist, when he is insulted? No, Sir, if any ideas of strife or hostility have entered his royal mind, they have a very different direction. The enemies of England have nothing to fear from them.

AFTER all, Sir, to what kind of disavowal has the King of Spain at last consented? Supposing it made in proper time, it should have been accompanied with instant restitution; and if Mr. Bucarelli acted without orders, he deserved death. Now, Sir, instead of immediate restitution, we have a four months negociation, and the officer, whose act is disavowed, returns to court, and is loaded with honours.

IF the actual situation of Europe be considered, the treachery of the King's servants, particularly of Lord North, who takes the whole upon himself, will appear in the strongest colours of aggravation. Our allies were masters of the Mediterranean. The King of France's present aversion from war, and the distraction of his affairs are notorious. He is now in a state of war with his people.[1] In vain did the Catholic King solicit him to take part in the quarrel against us. His finances were in the last disorder, and it was probable that his troops might find sufficient employment at home. In these circumstances, we might have dictated the law to Spain. There are no terms, to which she might not have been compelled to submit. At the worst, a war with Spain alone, carries the fairest promise of advantage. One good effect at least would have been immediately produced by it. The desertion of France would have irritated her ally, and in all probability have dissolved the family compact. The scene is now fatally changed. The advantage is thrown away. The most favourable opportunity is lost.—Hereafter we shall know the value of it. When the French King is reconciled to his subjects; when Spain has compleated her preparations; when the collected strength of the house of Bourbon attacks us at once, the King himself will be able to determine upon the wisdom or imprudence of his present conduct.[2] As far as the probability of argument extends, we may safely pronounce, that a

[1] See p. 188 n. 1. In January 1771 the recalcitrant magistrates were ordered into exile and the crown prepared to establish new law courts to carry out the work of the Parlement.

[2] In the most recent examination of this affair, N. Tracy, 'The Falkland Islands crisis of 1770; use of naval force', *English Historical Review*, xc. 40–75, concurs with Junius that the British missed an opportunity to crush an isolated Spain and prevent, or retard, a united Bourbon war of revenge.

conjuncture, which threatens the very being of this country, has been wilfully prepared and forwarded by our own ministry. How far the people may be animated to resistance under the present administration, I know not; but this I know with certainty, that, under the present administration, or if any thing like it should continue, it is of very little moment whether we are a conquered nation or not*.

HAVING travelled thus far in the high road of matter of fact, I may now be permitted to wander a little into the field of imagination. Let us banish from our minds the persuasion that these events have really happened in the reign of the best of princes. Let us consider them as nothing more than the materials of a fable, in which we may conceive the Sovereign of some other country to be concerned. I mean to violate all the laws of probability, when I suppose that this imaginary King, after having voluntarily disgraced himself in the eyes of his subjects, might return to a sense of his dishonour;—that he might perceive the snare laid for him by his ministers, and feel a spark of shame kindling in his breast.—The part he must then be obliged to act, would overwhelm him with confusion. To his parliament he must say, *I called you together to receive your advice, and have never asked your opinion.*—To the merchant,—*I have distressed your commerce; I have dragged your seamen out of your ships, I have loaded you with a grievous weight of insurances.*—To the landholder,—*I told you war was too probable, when I was determined to submit to any terms of accommodation; I extorted new taxes from you before it was possible they could be wanted, and am now unable to account for the application of them.*—To the public creditor,—*I have*

* The King's acceptance of the Spanish Ambassador's declaration, is drawn up in barbarous French, and signed by the Earl of Rochford. This diplomatic Lord has spent his life in the study and practice of *Etiquettes*, and is supposed to be a profound master of the ceremonies. I will not insult him by any reference to grammar or common sense, if he were even acquainted with the common forms of his office, I should think him as well qualified for it, as any man in his Majesty's service.—The reader is requested to observe Lord Rochford's method of authenticating a public instrument. "En foi de quoi, *moi* soussigné, un des principaux Secretaires d'Etat S. M. B. *ai* signé la presente de ma signature ordinaire, et icelle fait apposer le cachet de *nos* Armes." In three lines there are no less than seven false concords. But the man does not even know the stile of his office;—If he had known it, he would have said "*nous*, soussigné Secretaire d'Etat de S. M. B. avons signé *&c.*"

delivered up your fortunes a prey to foreigners and to the vilest of your fellow subjects. Perhaps this repenting Prince might conclude with one general acknowledgement to them all,—*I have involved every rank of my subjects in anxiety and distress, and have nothing to offer you in return, but the certainty of national dishonour, an armed truce, and peace without security.*

IF these accounts were settled, there would still remain an apology to be made to his navy and to his army. To the first he would say, *you were once the terror of the world. But go back to your harbours. A man dishonoured, as I am, has no use for your service.* It is not probable that he would appear again before his soldiers, even in the pacific ceremony of a review*. But wherever he appeared, the humiliating confession would be extorted from him. *I have received a blow,—and had not spirit to resent it. I demanded satisfaction, and have accepted a declaration, in which the right to strike me again is asserted and confirmed.* His countenance at least would speak this language, and even his guards would blush for him.

BUT to return to our argument.—The ministry, it seems, are labouring to draw a line of distinction between the honour of the crown and the rights of the people. This new idea has yet been only started in discourse, for in effect both objects have been equally sacrified. I neither understand the distinction, nor what use the ministry propose to make of it. The King's honour is that of his people. *Their* real honour and real interest are the same.—I am not contending for a vain punctilio. A clear, unblemished character comprehends not only the integrity that will not offer, but the spirit that will not submit to an injury; and whether it belongs to an individual or to a community, it is the foundation of peace, of independance, and of safety. Private credit is wealth;—public honour is security.—The feather that adorns the royal bird, supports his flight. Strip him of his plumage and you fix him to the earth.

JUNIUS.

* A Mistake. He appears before them every day, with the mark of a blow upon his face. . . . *proh pudor!*

Junius' views were combated in the *Public Advertiser* of 4 February 1771 by a ministerial writer under the name of Anti-Junius. The government also persuaded Dr. Johnson to produce a pamphlet entitled *Thoughts on the late transactions respecting Falkland's Islands.* In it he launched a strong attack upon Junius himself: 'He has sometimes sported with lucky malice; but to him that knows his company, it is not hard to be sarcastic in a mask . . . When he had once provided for his safety by impenetrable secrecy, he had nothing to combat but truth and justice.'

Junius was pleased with the result of public letter no. XLII which, he assured Woodfall, 'has a great effect'. In an attempt to force the ministers to open the House of Lords to the public when Chatham raised the matter of the settlement on 5 February, Junius induced Woodfall to place hints in his newspaper (private letter no. 29). They failed in their intention and the public was excluded from the debate.

LETTER XLIII.

TO THE PRINTER OF THE PUBLIC ADVERTISER.

SIR, *6. February*, 1771

I HOPE your correspondent *Junius* is better employed than in answering or reading the criticisms of a news-paper. This is a task, from which, if he were inclined to submit to it, his friends ought to relieve him. Upon this principle, I shall undertake to answer Anti-Junius; more, I believe, to his conviction than to his satisfaction. Not daring to attack the main body of *Junius*'s last letter, he triumphs in having, as he thinks, surprised an out-post, and cut off a detached argument, a mere straggling proposition. But even in this petty warfare, he shall find himself defeated.

JUNIUS does not speak of the Spanish *nation* as the *natural enemies* of England. He applies that description with the strictest truth and justice, to the Spanish *Court*. From the moment, when a Prince of the House of Bourbon ascended that throne, their whole system of government was inverted and became hostile to this country. Unity of possession introduced a unity of politics, and Lewis the fourteenth had reason when he said to his grandson, "*The Pyrenees are removed.*" The History of the present century is one continued confirmation of the prophecy.

THE Assertion "*That violence and oppression at home can only be supported by treachery and submission abroad,*" is applied to a free people, whose rights are invaded, not to the government of a country, where despotic, or absolute power is confessedly vested in the prince; and with this application, the assertion is true. An absolute monarch having no points to carry at home, will naturally maintain the honour of his crown in all his transactions with foreign powers. But if we could suppose the Sovereign of a free nation, possessed with a design to make himself absolute, he would be inconsistent with himself if he suffered his projects to be interupted or embarrassed by a foreign war; unless that war tended, as in some cases it might, to promote his principal design. Of the three exceptions to this general rule of conduct, (quoted by Anti-Junius) that of Oliver Cromwell is the only one in point. Harry the Eighth, by the submission of his parliament, was as absolute a prince as Lewis the Fourteenth. Queen Elizabeth's government was not oppressive to the people; and as to her foreign wars, it ought to be considered that they were *unavoidable.* The national honour was not in question. She was compelled to fight in defence of her own person and of her title to the crown. In the common course of selfish policy,[1] Oliver Cromwell should have cultivated the friendship of foreign powers, or at least have avoided disputes with them, the better to establish his tyranny at home. Had he been only a bad man, he would have sacrificed the honour of the nation to the success of his domestic policy. But, with all his crimes, he had the spirit of an Englishman. The conduct of such a man must always be an exception to vulgar rules. He had abilities sufficient to reconcile contradictions, and to make a great nation at the same moment unhappy and formidable. If it were not for the respect I bear the minister, I could name a man, who, without one grain of understanding, can do half as much as Oliver Cromwell.

WHETHER or no there be a *secret system* in the closet, and what may be the object of it, are questions, which can only be deter-

[1] Junius wrote in the *Public Advertiser* of 7 February 1771 correcting 'cause' to 'course'. See p. 458. Curiously, he did not remember to correct it when preparing the collected edition.

mined by appearances, and on which every man must decide for himself.

THE whole plan of *Junius*'s letter proves that he himself makes no distinction between the real honour of the crown and the real interest of the people. In the climax, to which your correspondent objects, *Junius* adopts the language of the Court, and, by that conformity, gives strength to his argument. He says that, "*the King has not only sacrificed the interests of his people, but,* (what was likely to touch him more nearly,) *his personal reputation and the dignity of his crown.*"

THE queries, put by *Anti-Junius*, can only be answered by the ministry.[1] Abandoned as they are, I fancy they will not confess that they have for so many years, maintained possession of another man's property. After admitting the assertion of the ministry—viz. *that the Spaniards had no rightful claim*, and after justifying them for saying so;—it is *his* business not *mine*, to give us some good reason for their *suffering the pretensions of Spain to be a subject of negotiation.* He admits the facts;—let him reconcile them if he can.

THE last paragraph brings us back to the original question, whether the Spanish declaration contains such a satisfaction as the King of Great Britain ought to have accepted. This was the field, upon which he ought to have encountered *Junius* openly and fairly. But here he leaves the argument, as no longer defensible. I shall therefore conclude with one general admonition to my fellow subjects;—that, when they hear these matters debated, they should not suffer themselves to be misled by general declamations upon the conveniences of peace, or the miseries of war. Between peace and war, abstractedly, there is not, there cannot be a question in the mind of a rational being. The real questions are, *Have we any security that the peace we have so dearly purchased will last a twelvemonth?* and, if not,—*have we, or have we not, sacrificed the fairest opportunity of making war with advantage?*

PHILO JUNIUS.

[1] Anti-Junius had asked of Britain's claim to the Falkland Islands: 'how that possession was acquired? Whether there was any previous possession of it by any other nation? Whether the right of possession of islands . . . may not, in many cases, depend upon their natural situation?'

The government's settlement of the Falkland Islands dispute was debated in the House of Commons on 13 February and approved by 271 votes to 157: in the Lords the following day the ministry won by 107 votes to 38. Junius' continued interest in the affair was shown under the guise of Vindex. His first letter under that name contained such direct charges of cowardice against the King that Woodfall refused to print it on the grounds that it would 'render me liable to very severe reprehension'. An abbreviated version was published on 22 February. In a second letter of 6 March Vindex took issue with Lauchlin Macleane over some remarks he had made in the debate of 13 February. The Vindex letters are printed in full on pp. 487–9.

Junius' next letter was concerned with a different subject. The House of Commons had long maintained a fierce if fitful prohibition of the publication of its debates. Nevertheless public interest was so great that printers sought ingenious means of avoiding the issue of privilege. For many years the *Gentleman's Magazine* carried reports thinly disguised as debates in the Senate of Lilliput. In 1770 its reports of the Lords' debates were described as 'proceedings in the upper chamber of a great assembly' and the Commons' debates were given as discussions in 'a new political society'. In February 1771 George Onslow, the member for Guildford, persuaded the House to launch one of its periodic counter-attacks. But when the messenger from the Serjeant-at-Arms attempted to arrest John Miller, publisher of the *London Evening Post*, he was taken before Wilkes, acting as an Alderman, who imprisoned him for assault. The Lord Mayor of London, Brass Crosby, was then summoned before the House of Commons and committed to the Tower of London, where he remained until the prorogation of Parliament on 8 May. The House of Commons subsequently abandoned its attempt to prevent the publication of debates. Of Letter no. XLIV Junius wrote to Wilkes: 'The pains I took with that paper upon privilege were greater than I can express to you.' Private letter no. 71.

LETTER XLIV.

TO THE PRINTER OF THE PUBLIC ADVERTISER.

SIR, 22. *April* 1771.

TO write for profit without taxing the press;—to write for fame and to be unknown;—to support the intrigues of faction and to be disowned, as a dangerous auxiliary, by every party in the kingdom, are contradictions, which the minister must reconcile, before I forfeit my credit with the public. I may quit the service, but it would be absurd to suspect me of desertion. The reputation of these papers is an honourable pledge for my attachment to the people. To sacrifice a respected character, and to renounce the esteem of society, requires more than Mr. Wedderburne's resolution; and though, in him, it was rather a profession than a desertion of his principles, [I speak tenderly of this gentleman, for when treachery is in question, I think we should make allowances for a Scotchman,] yet we have seen him in the house of commons overwhelmed with confusion, and almost bereft of his faculties.[1] But in truth, Sir, I have left no room for an accommodation with the piety of St. James's. My offences are not to be redeemed by recantation or repentance. On one side, our warmest patriots would disclaim me as a burthen to their honest ambition. On the other, the vilest prostitution, if *Junius* could descend to it, would lose its natural merit and influence in the cabinet, and treachery be no longer a recommendation to the royal favour.

THE persons, who, till within these few years, have been most distinguished by their zeal for high church and prerogative, are now, it seems, the great assertors of the privileges of the house of commons. This sudden alteration of their sentiments or language carries with it a suspicious appearance. When I hear the undefined privileges of the popular branch of the legislature exalted by Tories and Jacobites, at the expence of those strict rights, which are known to the subject and limited by the laws, I cannot but suspect, that some mischievous scheme is in agitation, to destroy both law and privilege, by opposing them to each other. They who have uniformly denied the power of the whole legislature to alter the descent of the crown, and whose ancestors, in rebellion against his Majesty's family, have defended that doctrine at the hazard of their lives, now tell us that privilege of parliament is the only rule of

[1] Alexander Wedderburn was an able Scottish lawyer whose attitude towards the Middlesex election was somewhat equivocal. He was returned in 1768 for the borough of Richmond, under the patronage of Sir Lawrence Dundas, a government supporter: Wedderburn voted on 3 February 1769 with administration. But having been promised a seat by Lord Clive as an insurance, he spoke out against government on 8 May. Returned for Bishop's Castle in January 1770, he joined the government in January 1771 as Solicitor-General. His changes of front placed him at times in an awkward parliamentary situation. Horace Walpole wrote sourly of him that 'his politics, like his pleading, were at the service of whoever offered him most'; Walpole, iv. 174.

right, and the chief security of the public freedom.—I fear, Sir, that, while forms remain, there has been some material change in the substance of our constitution. The opinions of these men were too absurd to be so easily renounced. Liberal minds are open to conviction.—Liberal doctrines are capable of improvement.—There are proselites from atheism, but none from superstition.—If their present professions were sincere, I think they could not but be highly offended at seeing a question, concerning parliamentary privilege, unnecessarily started at a season so unfavourable to the house of commons, and by so very mean and insignificant a person as the minor *Onslow*.[1] They knew that the present house of commons, having commenced hostilities with the people, and degraded the authority of the laws by their own example, were likely enough to be resisted, *per fas & nefas*. If they were really friends to privilege, they would have thought the question of right too dangerous to be hazarded at this season, and, without the formality of a convention, would have left it undecided.

I HAVE been silent hitherto, though not from that shameful indifference about the interests of society, which too many of us profess, and call moderation. I confess, Sir, that I felt the prejudices of my education, in favour of a house of commons, still hanging about me. I thought that a question, between law and privilege, could never be brought to a formal decision, without inconvenience to the public service, or a manifest diminution of legal liberty;—that it ought therefore to be carefully avoided: and when I saw that the violence of the house of commons had carried them too far to retreat, I determined not to deliver a hasty opinion upon a matter of so much delicacy and importance.

THE state of things is much altered in this country, since it was necessary to protect our representatives against the direct power of the crown. We have nothing to apprehend from prerogative, but

[1] There were two George Onslows in Parliament at this time. The campaign against the printers was waged by George Onslow of Ockham, member for Guildford, usually known as Colonel Onslow or 'cocking George'. His cousin, George Onslow of Imber Court, sat for Surrey, was a Lord of the Treasury, and a more important political figure.

every thing from undue influence. Formerly it was the interest of the people, that the privileges of parliament should be left unlimited and undefined. At present it is not only their interest, but I hold it to be essentially necessary to the preservation of the constitution, that the privileges of parliament should be strictly ascertained, and confined within the narrowest bounds the nature of their institution will admit of. Upon the same principle, on which I would have resisted prerogative in the last century, I now resist privilege. It is indifferent to me, whether the crown, by its own immediate act, imposes new, and dispenses with old laws, or whether the same arbitrary power produces the same effects through the medium of the house of commons. We trusted our representatives with privileges for their own defence and ours. We cannot hinder their desertion, but we can prevent their carrying over their arms to the service of the enemy.—It will be said, that I begin with endeavouring to reduce the argument concerning privilege to a mere question of convenience;—that I deny at one moment what I would allow at another; and that to resist the power of a prostituted house of commons may establish a precedent injurious to all future parliaments.—To this I answer generally, that human affairs are in no instance governed by strict positive right. If change of circumstances were to have no weight in directing our conduct and opinions, the mutual intercourse of mankind would be nothing more than a contention between positive and equitable right. Society would be a state of war, and law itself would be injustice. On this general ground, it is highly reasonable, that the degree of our submission to privileges, which have never been defined by any positive law, should be considered as a question of convenience, and proportioned to the confidence we repose in the integrity of our representatives. As to the injury we may do to any future and more respectable house of commons, I own I am not now sanguine enough to expect a more plentiful harvest of parliamentary virtue in one year than another. Our political climate is severely altered; and, without dwelling upon the depravity of modern times, I think no reasonable man will expect that, as human nature is constituted, the enormous influence of the crown should cease to prevail over the virtue of individuals. The mischief lies too deep to be cured by any remedy, less than some great convulsion, which may either carry back the constitution to its original principles, or utterly destroy it.[1] I do not doubt that, in the first session after the next election, some popular measures may be adopted. The present house of commons have injured themselves by a too early and public profession of their principles; and if a strain of prostitution, which had no example, were within the reach of emulation, it might be imprudent to hazard the experiment too soon. But after all, Sir, it is very immaterial whether a house of commons shall preserve their virtue for a week, a month, or a year. The influence, which makes a septennial parliament dependent upon the pleasure of the crown, has a permanent operation, and cannot fail of success.—My premises, I know, will be denied in argument, but every man's conscience tells him they are true. It remains then to be considered, whether it be for the interest of the people that privilege of parliament (which*, in respect to the purposes, for which it has hitherto been acquiesced under, is merely nominal) should be contracted within some certain limits, or whether the subject shall be left at the mercy of a power, arbitrary upon the face of it, and notoriously under the direction of the crown.

I DO not mean to decline the question of *right*. On the contrary, Sir, I join issue with the advocates for privilege and affirm, that,

* "The necessity of securing the house of commons against the King's power, so that no interruption might be given either to the attendance of the members in parliament, or to the freedom of debate, was the foundation of parliamentary privilege; and we may observe, in all the addresses of new appointed Speakers to the Sovereign, the utmost privilege they demand is liberty of speech and freedom from arrests. The very word privilege, means no more than immunity, or a safeguard to the party who possesses it, and can never be construed into an active power of invading the rights of others."[2]

---

[1] Junius' gloom was no doubt partly rhetorical and adopted to point the danger and increase the literary tension. He seems also not to have anticipated that change in the balance of domestic politics brought about by the growth of an articulate and informed public opinion—of which he was himself a signal example. He was correct in arguing that there had been an increase in the influence of government since the Glorious Revolution through the growth of the armed forces and the administration. But at the time he was writing, the situation was beginning to change and the influence of the Crown, in patronage and electoral control, was on the wane.

[2] This is a quotation from a letter signed 'A Whig' printed in the *Public Advertiser*. See p. 490.

"excepting the cases, wherein the house of commons are a court of judicature; [to which, from the nature of their office, a coercive power must belong] and excepting such contempts as immediately interrupt their proceedings, they have no legal authority to imprison any man for any supposed violation of privilege whatsoever." —It is not pretended that privilege, as now claimed, has ever been defined or confirmed by statute; neither can it be said, with any colour of truth, to be a part of the common law of England, which had grown into prescription, long before we knew any thing of the existence of a house of commons. As for the law of parliament it is only another name for the privilege in question; and since the power of creating new privileges has been formally renounced by both houses,—since there is no code, in which we can study the law of parliament, we have but one way left to make ourselves acquainted with it;—that is, to compare the nature of the institution of a house of commons, with the facts upon record. To establish a claim of privilege in either house, and to distinguish original right from usurpation, it must appear that it is indispensably necessary for the performance of the duty they are employed in, and also that it has been uniformly allowed. From the first part of this description it follows clearly, that whatever privilege does of right belong to the present house of commons, did equally belong to the first assembly of their predecessors, was as compleatly vested in them, and might have been exercised in the same extent. From the second we must infer that privileges, which for several centuries, were not only never allowed, but never even claimed by the house of commons, must be founded upon usurpation. The constitutional duties of a house of commons, are not very complicated nor mysterious. They are to propose or assent to wholesome laws for the benefit of the nation. They are to grant the necessary aids to the King;—petition for the redress of grievances, and prosecute treason or high crimes against the state. If unlimited privilege be necessary to the performance of these duties, we have reason to conclude that, for many centuries after the institution of the house of commons, they were never performed. I am not bound to prove a negative, but I appeal to the English history when I affirm that, with the exceptions already stated, (which yet I might safely relinquish) there is no precedent, from the year 1265 to the death of Queen Elizabeth, of the house of commons having imprisoned any man (not a member of their house) for contempt or breach of privilege. In the most flagrant cases, and when their acknowledged privileges were most grossly violated, the *poor Commons*, as they then stiled themselves, never took the power of punishment into their own hands. They either sought redress by petition to the King, or, what is more remarkable, applied for justice to the house of lords; and when satisfaction was denied them or delayed, their only remedy was to refuse proceeding upon the King's business. So little conception had our ancestors of the monstrous doctrines, now maintained concerning privilege, that, in the reign of Elizabeth, even liberty of speech, the vital principle of a deliberative assembly, was restrained, by the Queen's authority, to a simple *aye* or *no*, and this restriction, though imposed upon three successive parliaments*, was never once disputed by the house of commons.[1]

I KNOW there are many precedents of arbitrary commitments for contempt. But, besides that they are of too modern a date to warrant a presumption that such a power was originally vested in the house of commons,—*Fact* alone does not constitute *Right*. If it does, general warrants were lawful.—An ordinance of the two houses has a force equal to law; and the criminal jurisdiction assumed by the Commons in 1621, in the case of Edward Loyd is a good precedent, to warrant the like proceedings against any man, who shall unadvisedly mention the folly of a King, or the ambition of a Princess.[2]—The truth is, Sir, that the greatest and most exceptionable part of the privileges now contended for, were introduced and asserted by a house of commons which abolished both

* In the years 1593—1597—and 1601.

[1] Junius's version of the situation at the end of Elizabeth's reign was unduly simple. The Queen's views in 1593 were put by the Lord Keeper and recorded by Sir Simonds D'Ewes in *The Journal of all the Parliaments during the reign of Queen Elizabeth* (1682), p. 460. Her main concern was to define the area of policy discussed. A commentary may be found in G. R. Elton, *The Tudor Constitution* (1960), pp. 254–7.

[2] Edward Lloyd or Floyd, a Roman Catholic barrister, was sentenced by the House of Commons in 1621 to a fine of £1,000 and the pillory for words disrespectful to the Elector Palatine and the Princess Elizabeth, daughter of James I. He was subsequently punished by the House of Lords.

monarchy and peerage, and whose proceedings, although they ended in one glorious act of substantial justice, could no way be reconciled to the forms of the constitution. Their successors profited by the example, and confirmed their power by a moderate or a popular use of it. Thus it grew by degrees, from a notorious innovation at one period, to be tacitly admitted as the privilege of parliament at another.

IF however it could be proved, from considerations of necessity or convenience, that an unlimited power of commitment ought to be intrusted to the house of commons, and that *in fact* they have exercised it without opposition, still, in contemplation of law, the presumption is strongly against them. It is a leading maxim of the laws of England (and, without it, all laws are nugatory) that there is no right without a remedy, nor any legal power without a legal course to carry it into effect. Let the power, now in question, be tried by this rule. The Speaker issues his warrant of attachment. The party attached either resists force with force, or appeals to a magistrate, who declares the warrant illegal, and discharges the prisoner. Does the law provide no legal means for inforcing a legal warrant? Is there no regular proceeding pointed out in our law books to assert and vindicate the authority of so high a court as the house of commons? The question is answered directly by the fact. Their unlawful commands are resisted, and they have no remedy. The imprisonment of their own members is revenge indeed, but it is no assertion of the privilege they contend for*. Their whole proceeding stops, and there they stand, ashamed to retreat, and unable to advance. Sir, these ignorant men should be informed that the execution of the laws of England is not left in this uncertain,

* Upon their own principles, they should have committed Mr. Wilkes, who had been guilty of a greater offence than even the Lord-Mayor or Alderman Oliver. But after repeatedly ordering him to attend, they at last adjourned beyond the day appointed for his attendance, and by this mean, pitiful evasion, gave up the point.— Such is the force of conscious guilt![1]

---

[1] Wilkes and Richard Oliver sat with Brass Crosby, the Lord Mayor, when the messenger of the House of Commons was sent into custody for assault. Crosby and Oliver attended the House of Commons and were imprisoned in the Tower. Wilkes refused to attend unless he could do so as the duly elected member for Middlesex. The House, learning prudence, overlooked his contumelious behaviour.

defenceless condition. If the process of the courts of Westminster-hall be resisted, they have a direct course, sufficient to inforce submission. The court of King's Bench commands the Sheriff to raise the *posse comitatûs*. The courts of Chancery and Exchequer issue a *writ of rebellion*, which must also be supported, if necessary, by the power of the county.—To whom will our honest representatives direct *their* writ of rebellion? The guards, I doubt not, are willing enough to be employed, but they know nothing of the doctrine of writs, and may think it necessary to wait for a letter from Lord Barrington.

IT may now be objected to me, that my arguments prove too much; for that certainly there may be instances of contempt and insult to the house of commons, which do not fall within my own exceptions, yet, in regard to the dignity of the house, ought not to pass unpunished. Be it so.—The courts of criminal jurisdiction are open to prosecutions, which the Attorney General may commence by information or indictment. A libel, tending to asperse or vilify the house of commons, or any of their members, may be as severely punished in the court of King's-bench, as a libel upon the King. Mr. De Grey thought so, when he drew up the information upon my letter to his Majesty, or he had no meaning in charging it to be a scandalous libel upon the house of commons. In *my* opinion, they would consult their real dignity much better, by appealing to the laws when they are offended, than by violating the first principle of natural justice, which forbids us to be judges, when we are parties to the cause*.

I DO not mean to pursue them through the remainder of their proceedings. In their first resolutions, it is possible they might

* "If it be demanded, in case a subject should be committed by either house, for a matter manifestly out of their jurisdiction, what remedy can he have? I answer, that it cannot well be imagined that the law, which favours nothing more than the liberty of the subject, should give us a remedy against commitments by the King himself, appearing to be illegal, and yet give us no manner of redress against a commitment by our fellow subjects, equally appearing to be unwarranted. But as this is a case, which I am persuaded will never happen, if seems needless over nicely to examine it.—*Hawkins* 2. 110."——*N.B. He was a good lawyer, but no prophet.*[1]

[1] William Hawkins, *A treatise of the pleas of the crown*, 3rd ed., 1739.

have been deceived by ill-considered precedents. For the rest, there is no colour of palliation or excuse. They have advised the King to resume a power of dispensing with the laws by royal proclamation*; and Kings we see are ready enough to follow such advice.[1] By mere violence, and without the shadow of right, they have expunged the record of a judicial proceeding†. Nothing remained, but to attribute to their own vote a power of stopping the whole distribution of criminal and civil justice.

THE public virtues of the chief magistrate have long since ceased to be in question. But it is said that he has private good qualities, and I myself have been ready to acknowledge them. They are now brought to the test. If he loves his people, he will dissolve a parliament, which they can never confide in or respect.—If he has any regard for his own honour, he will disdain to be any longer connected with such abandoned prostitution. But if it were conceivable, that a King of this country had lost all sense of personal honour, and all concern for the welfare of his subjects, I confess, Sir, I should be contented to renounce the forms of the constitution once more, if there were no other way to obtain substantial justice for the people.‡

JUNIUS.

* That their practice might be every way conformable to their principles, the house proceeded to advise the crown to publish a proclamation univerally acknowledged to be illegal. Mr. Moreton publicly protested against it before it was issued; and Lord Mansfield, though not scrupulous to an extreme, speaks of it with horror. It is remarkable enough that the very men, who advised the proclamation, and who hear it arraigned every day both within doors and without, are not daring enough to utter one word in its defence, nor have they ventured to take the least notice of Mr. Wilkes for discharging the persons apprehended under it.

† Lord Chatham very properly called this the act of a mob, not of a senate.[2]

‡ When Mr. Wilkes was to be punished, they made no scruple about the privileges of parliament; and although it was as well known as any matter of public

---

[1] On 4 March 1771 the deputy Serjeant-at-Arms reported that he had been unable to apprehend John Wheble and Roger Thompson, printers of the *Middlesex Journal* and *The Gazetteer and New Daily Advertiser* and the first objects of Colonel Onslow's campaign. The House then asked the King to issue a proclamation for their arrest, which was done on 9 March. It is printed in *Parl. Hist.* xvii. 75–6.

[2] The Lord Mayor's clerk was ordered to produce the book of recognizances and on 20 March, on Lord North's motion, the House voted to erase the reference to their messenger. Chatham's observations were made in the course of his speech of 1 May 1771 moving an address to the King to dissolve Parliament.

On 27 April 1771 Woodfall printed a reply to Junius by Mat. MOONSHINE, which taxed him with inconsistency in demanding a dissolution of Parliament, 'since you have already allowed, there is not much reason to expect that a new Parliament will be much more worthy of our Respect and confidence than the present'. The attack was repeated on 29 April by Brass Candlestick.

LETTER XLV.

TO THE PRINTER OF THE PUBLIC ADVERTISER.

SIR, 1. *May*, 1771.

THEY, who object to detached parts of Junius's last letter, either do not mean him fairly, or have not considered the general scope and course of his argument.—There are degrees in all the private vices.—Why not in public prostitution?—The influence of the crown naturally makes a septennial parliament dependent.—Does it follow that every house of commons will plunge at once into the *lowest depths* of prostitution?—Junius supposes that the present house of commons, in going such enormous lengths, have been *imprudent to themselves*, as well as wicked to the public;—

record and uninterrupted custom could be, *that the members of either house are privileged except in case of treason, felony, or breach of peace*, they declared without hesitation *that privilege of parliament did not extend to the case of a seditious libel*; and undoubtedly they would have done the same if Mr. Wilkes had been prosecuted for any other misdemeanor whatsoever. The ministry are of a sudden grown wonderfully careful of privileges, which their predecessors were as ready to invade. The known laws of the land, the rights of the subject, the sanctity of charters, and the reverence due to our magistrates, must all give way, without question or resistance, to a privilege of which no man knows either the origin or the extent. The house of commons judge of their own privileges without appeal:—they may take offence at the most innocent action, and imprison the person who offends them, during their arbitrary will and pleasure. The party has no remedy;—he cannot appeal from their jurisdiction; and if he questions the privilege, which he is supposed to have violated, it becomes an aggravation of his offence. Surely this doctrine is not to be found in Magna Charta. If it be admitted without limitation, I affirm that there is neither law nor liberty in this kingdom. We are the slaves of the house of commons, and, through them, we are the slaves of the King and his ministers. *Anonymous.*[1]

---

[1] This footnote, together with those on pp. 232 and 237, is taken from a letter signed A Whig, printed in the *Public Advertiser* of 9 April 1771. It is unlikely that Junius would have laid himself open to the charge of stealing other men's flowers and it may therefore be presumed to be his own composition. The matter is discussed in Appendix five, p. 489.

that their example is *not within the reach of emulation*;—and that, in the first session after the next election, *some* popular measures may probably be adopted. He does not expect that a dissolution of parliament will destroy corruption, but that at least it will be a check and terror to their successors, who will have seen that, *in flagrant cases*, their constituents *can* and *will* interpose with effect.—After all, Sir, will you not endeavour to remove or alleviate the most dangerous symptoms, because you cannot eradicate the disease? Will you not punish *treason* or *parricide*, because the sight of a gibbet does not prevent highway robberies? When the main argument of Junius is admitted to be unanswerable, I think it would become the minor critic, who hunts for blemishes, to be a little more distrustful of his own sagacity.—The other objection is hardly worth an answer. When Junius observes that Kings are ready enough to follow *such* advice, he does not mean to insinuate that, if the advice of parliament were good, the King would be so ready to follow it.

PHILO JUNIUS.

On 30 April 1771 the House of Lords negatived without a division a motion by the Duke of Richmond to expunge their resolution of 2 February 1771 on the Middlesex election. Nevertheless Junius continued to try to keep the issue alive.

In the collected edition, this letter was printed as a footnote to Letter XX in addition to appearing as Letter XLVI.

LETTER XLVI.

ADDRESSED TO THE PRINTER OF THE PUBLIC ADVERTISER.

SIR, 22. *May*, 1771.

VERY early in the debate upon the decision of the Middlesex election, it was well observed by *Junius*, that the house of commons had not only exceeded their boasted precedent of the expulsion and subsequent incapacitation of Mr. Walpole, but that they had not even adhered to it strictly as far as it went. After convicting Mr. Dyson of giving a false quotation from the journals, and having explained the purpose, which that contemptible fraud was intended to answer, he proceeds to state the vote itself, by which Mr. Walpole's supposed incapacity was declared,—viz. "Resolved, That Robert Walpole, Esq; having been this session of parliament committed a prisoner to the Tower, and expelled this house for a high breach of trust in the execution of his office, and notorious corruption when secretary at war, was and is incapable of being elected a member to serve in this present parliament."—And then observes that, from the terms of the vote, we have no right to annex the incapacitation to the *expulsion* only, for that, as the proposition stands, it must arise equally from the expulsion and the commitment to the Tower. I believe, Sir, no man, who knows any thing of dialectics, or who understands English, will dispute the truth and fairness of this construction. But *Junius* has a great authority to support him, which, to speak with the Duke of Grafton, I accidentally met with this morning in the course of my reading.[1] It contains an admonition, which cannot be repeated too often. Lord Sommers, in his excellent tract upon the rights of the people, after reciting the votes of the convention, of the 28th of January, 1689, viz.—"That King James the Second, having endeavoured to subvert the constitution of this kingdom by breaking the original contract between King and people; and by the advice of jesuits and other wicked persons having violated the fundamental laws, and having withdrawn himself out of this kingdom, hath abdicated the government, &c."—makes this observation upon it. "The word *abdicated* relates to *all* the clauses aforegoing, as well as to his deserting the kingdom, or else they would have been wholly in vain." And that there might be no pretence for confining the *abdication* merely to the *withdrawing*, Lord Sommers farther observes, *That King James, by refusing to govern us according to that law, by which he held the crown, did implicitly renounce his title to it.*

If *Junius*'s construction of the vote against Mr. Walpole be now admitted, (and indeed I cannot comprehend how it can honestly be

[1] This sarcasm, directed at the Duke's affectation of spontaneity, was originally made in a letter by Domitian, dated 8 December 1770. This was another of Junius' pseudonyms. See Appendix five.

disputed) the advocates of the house of commons must either give up their precedent entirely, or be reduced to the necessity of maintaining one of the grossest absurdities imaginable, viz. "That a commitment to the Tower is a constituent part of, and contributes half at least to the incapacitation of the person who suffers it."

I NEED not make you any excuse for endeavouring to keep alive the attention of the public to the decision of the Middlesex election. The more I consider it, the more I am convinced that, as a *fact*, it is indeed highly injurious to the rights of the people; but that, as a *precedent*, it is one of the most dangerous that ever was established against those who are to come after us. Yet I am so far a moderate man, that I verily believe the majority of the house of commons, when they passed this dangerous vote, neither understood the question, nor knew the consequence of what they were doing. Their motives were rather despicable than criminal in the extreme. One effect they certainly did not foresee. They are now reduced to such a situation, that if a member of the present house of commons were to conduct himself ever so improperly, and in reality deserve to be sent back to his constituents with a mark of disgrace, they would not dare to expel him; because they know that the people, in order to try again the great question of right, or to thwart an odious house of commons, would probably overlook his immediate unworthiness, and return the same person to parliament.—But, in time, the precedent will gain strength. A future house of commons will have no such apprehensions, consequently will not scruple to follow a precedent, which they did not establish. The miser himself seldom lives to enjoy the fruit of his extortion; but his heir succeeds to him of course, and takes possession without censure. No man expects him to make restitution, and no matter for his title, he lives quietly upon the estate.

PHILO JUNIUS.

LETTER XLVII.

TO THE PRINTER OF THE PUBLIC ADVERTISER.

SIR, 25. *May*, 1771.

I CONFESS my partiality to *Junius*, and feel a considerable pleasure in being able to communicate any thing to the public, in support of his opinions. The doctrine, laid down in his last letter, concerning the power of the house of commons to commit for contempt, is not so new as it appeared to many people, who, dazzled with the name of *privilege*, had never suffered themselves to examine the question fairly. *In the course of my reading this morning*,[1] I met with the following passage in the journals of the house of commons. (Vol. 1st. page 603.) Upon occasion of a jurisdiction unlawfully assumed by the house in the year 1621, Mr. Attorney-General *Noye* gave his opinion as follows. "No doubt but, in some cases, this house may give judgment;—in matters of returns, and concerning members of our house, or falling out in our view in parliament; but, for foreign matters, knoweth not how we can judge it.—Knoweth not that we have been used to give judgment in any case, but those beforementioned."

SIR Edward Coke, upon the same subject, says, (page 604) "No question but this is a house of record, and that it hath power of judicature in some cases;—have power to judge of returns and members of our house; one, no member, offending out of the parliament, *when he came hither and justified it*, was censured for it."

NOW, Sir, if you will compare the opinion of these great sages of the law with *Junius*'s doctrine, you will find they tally exactly.—He allows the power of the house to commit their own members; (which however they may grossly abuse.) He allows their power in cases where they are acting as a court of judicature, viz. elections, returns, &c.—and he allows it in such contempts as immediately interrupt their proceedings, or, as Mr. Noye expresses it, *falling out in their view in parliament.*

[1] See note on p. 240.

THEY, who would carry the privileges of parliament farther than *Junius*, either do not mean well to the public, or know not what they are doing. The government of England is a government of law. We betray ourselves, we contradict the spirit of our laws, and we shake the whole system of English jurisprudence, whenever we intrust a discretionary power over the life, liberty, or fortune of the subject, to any man, or set of men whatsoever, upon a presumption that it will not be abused.

PHILO JUNIUS.

LETTER XLVIII.

TO THE PRINTER OF THE PUBLIC ADVERTISER.

SIR, 28. *May*, 1771.

ANY man, who takes the trouble of perusing the journals of the house of commons, will soon be convinced, that very little, if any regard at all, ought to be paid to the resolutions of one branch of the legislature, declaratory of the law of the land, or even of what they call the law of parliament. It will appear that these resolutions have no one of the properties, by which, in this country, particularly, *law* is distinguished from mere *will* and *pleasure*; but that, on the contrary they bear every mark of a power arbitrarily assumed and capriciously applied:—That they are usually made in times of contest, and to serve some unworthy purpose of passion or party;—that the law is seldom declared until *after* the fact, by which it is supposed to be violated;—that legislation and jurisdiction are united in the same persons, and exercised at the same moment;—and that a court, from which there is no appeal, assumes an *original* jurisdiction in a criminal case;—in short, Sir, to collect a thousand absurdities into one mass, "we have a law, which cannot be known because it is *ex post facto*, the party is both legislator and judge, and the jurisdiction is without appeal.' Well might the judges say, *The law of parliament is above us.*

YOU will not wonder, Sir, that, with these qualifications, the declaratory resolutions of the house of commons should appear to be in perpetual contradiction, not only to common sense and to the laws we are acquainted with, (and which alone we can obey) but even to one another. I was led to trouble you with these observations by a passage, which, to speak in lutestring,[1] I *met with this morning in the course of my reading*, and upon which I mean to put a question to the advocates for privilege.—On the 8th of March 1704, (vide Journals, Vol. 14. p. 565.) the house thought proper to come to the following resolutions.—1. "That no commoner of England, committed by the house of commons for breach of privilege or contempt of that house, ought to be, by any writ of *Habeas Corpus*, made to appear in any other place, or before any other judicature, during that session of parliament, wherein such person was so committed".

2. "THAT the Serjeant at Arms, attending this house do make no return of or yield any obedience to the said writs of *Habeas Corpus*, and for such his refusal, that he have the protection of the house of commons"*.

WELBORE Ellis, What say you? Is this the law of parliament or is it not? I am a plain man, Sir, and cannot follow you through the phlegmatic forms of an oration. Speak out, Grildrig,—say yes, or no.[2]—If you say *yes*, I shall then inquire by what authority Mr. De Grey, the honest Lord Mansfield, and the Barons of the Exchequer,

* If there be in reality any such law in England, as the *law of parliament*, which, (under the exceptions stated in my letter on privilege) I confess, after long deliberation, I very much doubt, it certainly is not constituted by, not can it be collected from the resolutions of either house, whether *enacting or declaratory*. I desire the reader will compare the above resolution of the year 1704, with the following of the 3d of April, 1628.—"*Resolved*, That the writ of Habeas Corpus cannot be denied, but ought to be granted to *every* man, that is committed or detained in prison, or otherwise restrained, by the command of the King, the Privy Council, *or any other*, he praying the same."

---

[1] A phrase which baffles *OED*. It appears to mean to speak delicately or coyly.

[2] Welbore Ellis had taken a prominent part in the debates on the printers' case and moved that Oliver and the Lord Mayor be sent to the Tower. In his speech of 25 March 1771 he dealt very fully with the opposition assertion that 'parliamentary privilege is a monster which calls for immediate extermination'. *Parl. Hist.* xvii. 125–30. Grildrig (meaning Mannikin) was the name bestowed upon Gulliver in Brobdingnag by his child nurse Glumdalclitch, who was a mere 40 feet high. See Junius' note on p. 190.

dared to grant a writ of *Habeas Corpus* for bringing the bodies of the Lord Mayor and Mr. Oliver before them, and why the Lieutenant of the Tower made any return to a writ, which the house of commons had, in a similar instance, declared to be unlawful.[1]—If you say *no*, take care you do not at once give up the cause, in support of which you have so long and so laboriously tortured your understanding. Take care you do not confess that there is no test by which we can distinguish,—no evidence by which we can determine what is, and what is not the law of parliament. The resolutions I have quoted stand upon your journals, uncontroverted and unrepealed;—they contain a declaration of the law of parliament by a court, competent to the question, and whose decision, as you and Lord Mansfield say, must be law, because there is no appeal from it, and they were made, not hastily, but after long deliberation upon a constitutional question.—What farther sanction or solemnity will you annex to any resolution of the present house of commons, beyond what appears upon the face of those two resolutions, the legality of which you now deny. If you say that parliaments are not infallible, and that Queen Anne, in consequence of the violent proceedings of that house of commons, was obliged to prorogue and dissolve them, I shall agree with you very heartily, and think that the precedent ought to be followed immediately. But you, Mr. Ellis, who hold this language, are inconsistent with your own principles. You have hitherto maintained that the house of commons are the sole judges of their own privileges, and that their declaration does, *ipso facto*, constitute the law of parliament; yet now you confess that parliaments are fallible, and that their resolutions may be illegal, consequently that their resolutions *do not* constitute the law of parliament. When the King was urged to dissolve the present parliament, you advised him to tell his subjects, that *he was careful not to assume any of those powers, which the constitution had placed in other hands*, &c. Yet Queen Anne, it seems, was justified in exerting her prerogative to stop

[1] On 3 April 1771 the committee of the Common Council of the city of London instructed its legal advisers to move for habeas corpus in relation to the Lord Mayor and Richard Oliver. Brought before Lord Chief Justice de Grey and Mansfield on the 5th, they were returned to the Tower until Parliament was prorogued. *Gentleman's Magazine*, 1771, 188.

a house of commons, whose proceedings, compared with those of the assembly, of which you are a most worthy member, were the perfection of justice and reason.

IN what a labyrinth of nonsense does a man involve himself who labours to maintain falsehood by argument? How much better would it become the dignity of the house of commons to speak plainly to the people, and tell us at once, *that their will must be obeyed, not because it is lawful and reasonable, but because it is their will.* Their constituents would have a better opinion of their candour, and, I promise you, not a worse opinion of their integrity.

PHILO JUNIUS.

In the previous letters Junius was beating around old and worn themes. In June 1771 he returned to a more promising subject—the character of the Duke of Grafton, who rejoined the administration as Lord Privy Seal in succession to Lord Suffolk. 'I am strangely partial to the inclosed', Junius wrote to Woodfall in private letter no. 36. 'It is finished with the utmost Care. If I find myself mistaken in my judgement of this paper, I positively will never write again.'

LETTER XLIX.

TO HIS GRACE THE DUKE OF GRAFTON.

MY LORD, 22. *June*, 1771.

THE profound respect I bear to the gracious Prince, who governs this country with no less honour to himself than satisfaction to his subjects, and who restores you to your rank under his standard, will save you from a multitude of reproaches. The attention I should have paid to your failings is involuntarily attracted to the hand that rewards them; and though I am not so partial to the royal judgment, as to affirm, that the favour of a King can remove mountains of infamy, it serves to lessen at least, for undoubtedly it divides the burthen. While I remember how much is due to *his* sacred character, I cannot, with any decent appearance of propriety, call you the meanest and the basest fellow in the kingdom. I protest, my Lord, I do not think you so. You will have a dangerous rival, in that kind of fame to which you have hitherto so happily directed your ambition, as long as there is one man living, who thinks you worthy of his confidence, and fit to be trusted with any share in his government. I confess you have great intrinsic merit; but take care you do not value it too highly. Consider how much of it would have been lost to the world, if the King had not graciously affixed his stamp, and given it currency among his subjects. If it be true that a virtuous man, struggling with adversity, be a scene worthy of the gods, the glorious contention, between you and best of Princes, deserves a circle, equally attentive and respectable. I think I already see other gods rising from the earth to behold it.

BUT this language is too mild for the occasion. The King is determined, that our abilities shall not be lost to society. The perpetration and description of new crimes will find employment for us both. My Lord, if the persons, who have been loudest in their professions of patriotism, had done their duty to the public with the same zeal and perseverance that I did, I will not assert that government would have recovered its dignity, but at least our gracious Sovereign must have spared his subjects this last insult*, which, if there be any feeling left among us, they will resent more than even the real injuries they received from every measure of your Grace's administration. In vain would he have looked round him for another character so consummate as yours. Lord Mansfield shrinks from his principles;—his ideas of government perhaps go farther than your own, but his heart disgraces the theory of his understanding.—Charles Fox is yet in blossom; and as for Mr. Wedderburne, there is something about him, which even treachery cannot trust. For the present therefore, the best of Princes must have contented himself with Lord Sandwich.—You would long since have received your final dismission and reward; and I, my Lord, who do not esteem you the more for the high office you possess, would willingly have followed you to your retirement. There is surely something singularly benevolent in the character of

* The Duke was lately appointed Lord Privy Seal.

our Sovereign. From the moment he ascended the throne, there is no crime, of which human nature is capable, (and I call upon the Recorder to witness it) that has not appeared venial in his sight. With any other Prince, the shameful desertion of him, in the midst of that distress, which you alone had created,—in the very crisis of danger, when he fancied he saw the throne already surrounded by men of virtue and abilities, would have out-weighed the memory of your former services.[1] But his Majesty is full of justice, and understands the doctrine of compensations. He remembers with gratitude how soon you had accommodated your morals to the necessity of his service;—how chearfully you had abandoned the engagements of private friendship, and renounced the most solemn professions to the public. The sacrifice of Lord Chatham was not lost upon him. Even the cowardice and perfidy of deserting him may have done you no disservice in his esteem. The instance was painful, but the principle might please.

YOU did not neglect the magistrate, while you flattered the *man*. The expulsion of Mr. Wilkes predetermined in the cabinet;—the power of depriving the subject of his birthright, attributed to a resolution of one branch of the legislature;—the constitution impudently invaded by the house of commons;—the right of defending it treacherously renounced by the house of lords.—These are the strokes, my Lord, which, in the present reign, recommend to office, and constitute a minister. They would have determined your Sovereign's judgment, if they had made no impression upon his heart. We need not look for any other species of merit to account for his taking the earliest opportunity to recall you to his councils. Yet you have other merit in abundance.—Mr. Hine, —the Duke of Portland,—and Mr. Yorke.—Breach of trust, robbery, and murder. You would think it a compliment to your gallantry, if I added rape to the catalogue;—but the stile of your amours secures you from resistance. I know how well these several charges have been defended. In the first instance, the breach of

[1] In fact the King did resent Grafton's resignation in 1770 and eight years later wrote reproachfully to Lord North: 'Are you resolved, agreeable to the example of the Duke of Grafton, at the hour of danger to desert me?' Fortescue, iv, no. 2240.

trust is supposed to have been its own reward. Mr. Bradshaw affirms upon his honour, (and so may the gift of smiling never depart from him!) that you reserved no part of Mr. Hine's purchase-money for your own use, but that every shilling of it was scrupulously paid to governor Burgoyne.—Make haste, my Lord,—another patent, applied in time, may keep the OAKS* in the family.—If not, Birnham Wood, I fear, must come to the *Macaroni.*[1]

THE Duke of Portland was in life your earliest friend. In defence of his property he had nothing to plead, but equity against Sir James Lowther, and prescription against the crown. You felt for your friend; *but the law must take its course.* Posterity will scarce believe that Lord Bute's son-in-law had barely interest enough at the treasury to get his grant compleated before the general election.†

ENOUGH has been said of that detestable transaction, which ended in the death of Mr. Yorke,—I cannot speak of it without horror and compassion. To excuse yourself, you publicly impeach your accomplice, and to *his* mind perhaps the accusation may be flattery. But in murder you are both principals. It was once a question of emulation, and if the event had not disappointed the immediate schemes of the closet, it might still have been a hopeful subject of jest and merriment between you.

THIS letter, my Lord, is only a preface to my future correspondence. The remainder of the summer shall be dedicated to your amusement. I mean now and then to relieve the severity of your morning studies, and to prepare you for the business of the day. Without pretending to more than Mr. Bradshaw's sincerity, you may rely upon my attachment, as long as you are in office.

* A superb villa of Col. Burgoyne, about this time advertised for sale.

† It will appear by a subsequent letter, that the Duke's precipitation, proved fatal to the grant. It looks like the hurry and confusion of a young highwayman, who takes a few shillings, but leaves the purse and watch behind him.—And yet the Duke was an old offender![2]

---

[1] The name Macaroni, here applied to Burgoyne, became fashionable in the 1760s to mean fop, dandy, or lounger.

[2] See note on p. 315.

WILL your Grace forgive me, if I venture to express some anxiety for a man, whom I know you do not love? My Lord Weymouth has cowardice to plead, and a desertion of a later date than your own.[1] You know the privy seal was intended for him; and if you consider the dignity of the post he deserted, you will hardly think it decent to quarter him on Mr. Rigby. Yet he must have bread, my Lord;—or rather he must have wine. If you deny him the cup, there will be no keeping him within the pale of the ministry.

JUNIUS.

LETTER L.

TO HIS GRACE THE DUKE OF GRAFTON.

MY LORD, 9. *July*, 1771.

THE influence of your Grace's fortune still seems to preside over the treasury.—The genius of Mr. Bradshaw inspires Mr. Robinson*. How remarkable it is, (and I speak of it not as matter of reproach, but as something peculiar to your character) that you have never yet formed a friendship, which has not been fatal to the object of it, nor adopted a cause, to which, one way or other, you have not done mischief. Your attachment is infamy while it lasts, and which ever way it turns, leaves ruin and disgrace behind it. The deluded girl, who yields to such a profligate, even while he is constant, forfeits her reputation as well as her innocence,

* By an intercepted letter from the Secretary of the Treasury it appeared, *that the friends of government were to be very active* in supporting the ministerial nomination of sheriffs.[2]

[1] Lord Weymouth was Secretary of State for the Northern Department January–October 1768 and for the Southern October 1768–December 1770. He resigned during the Falkland Islands crisis, advocating a more belligerent attitude towards Spain. He continued to support administration, was discussed for Lord Privy Seal in 1771, and brought back as Secretary of State for the Southern Department in 1775. Fortescue, ii, nos. 852–4, 959, and 961.

[2] John Robinson, member for Westmorland, succeeded Bradshaw as Secretary to the Treasury in August 1770. A letter from him dated 25 June 1771 and intended for Benjamin Smith, a London merchant, was delivered by mistake to Mr. Smith of Budge Row, who published it together with an affidavit in the *Public Advertiser* of 26 June. It asked for support for Alderman Plumbe and Kirkman, the government candidates for the shrievalty, and urged Smith to liaise with Thomas Harley. Wade, ii. 357–8. Burke was of the opinion that, before the publication of Robinson's letter, the court candidates might have carried the election. *Burke Corr.* ii. 222.

and finds herself abandoned at last to misery and shame.—Thus it happened with the best of Princes. Poor Dingley too!—I protest I hardly know which of them we ought most to lament;—The unhappy man, who sinks under the sense of his dishonour, or him who survives it. Characters, so finished, are placed beyond the reach of panegyric. Death has fixed his seal upon Dingley, and you, my Lord, have set your mark upon the other.[1]

THE only letter I ever addressed to the King was so unkindly received, that I believe I shall never presume to trouble his Majesty, in that way, again. But my zeal for his service is superior to neglect, and like Mr. Wilkes's patriotism, thrives by persecution. Yet his Majesty is much addicted to useful reading, and, if I am not ill-informed, has honoured the *Public Advertiser* with particular attention. I have endeavoured therefore, and not without success, (as perhaps you may remember) to furnish it with such interesting and edifying intelligence, as probably would not reach him through any other channel. The services you have done the nation,—your integrity in office, and signal fidelity to your approved good master, have been faithfully recorded. Nor have his own virtues been intirely neglected. These letters, my Lord, are read in other countries and in other languages; and I think I may affirm without vanity, that the gracious character of the best of Princes is by this time not only perfectly known to his subjects, but tolerably well understood by the rest of Europe. In this respect alone, I have the advantage of Mr. Whitehead. His plan, I think, is too narrow. He seems to manufacture his verses for the sole use of the hero, who is supposed to be the subject of them, and, that his meaning may not be exported in foreign bottoms, sets all translation at defiance.[2]

[1] Charles Dingley, who had attempted to stand against Wilkes in March 1769, died on 13 November 1769. If the other rather obscure reference to a female 'abandoned at last to misery and shame' was meant for Nancy Parsons, it was wide of the mark. She flourished like the green bay tree and in 1776, when in her forties, married the 2nd Viscount Maynard, a young man of 23. She thus finished up as a peeress of the realm and died at a ripe old age in France in 1815.

[2] William Whitehead succeeded Colley Cibber as poet laureate in 1757. Perhaps it was the birthday ode published in the *Gentleman's Magazine* for June 1771 that set Junius' teeth on edge. The poet celebrated that happy month 'when the glad land her homage pays, to George, her Monarch and her Friend'. It seems rather hard to hold birthday odes against their author.

YOUR Grace's re-appointment to a seat in the cabinet was announced to the public by the ominous return of Lord Bute to this country. When that noxious planet approaches England, he never fails to bring plague and pestilence along with him. The King already feels the malignant effect of your influence over his councils. Your former administration made Mr. Wilkes an Alderman of London, and Representative of Middlesex. Your next appearance in office is marked with his election to the shrievalty. In whatever measure you are concerned, you are not only disappointed of success, but always contrive to make the government of the best of Princes contemptible in his own eyes, and ridiculous to the whole world. Making all due allowance for the effect of the minister's declared interposition, Mr. Robinson's activity, and Mr. Horne's new zeal in support of administration, we still want the genius of the Duke of Grafton to account for committing the whole interest of government in the city, to the conduct of Mr. Harley. I will not bear hard upon your faithful friend and emissary Mr. Touchet, for I know the difficulties of his situation, and that a few lottery tickets are of use to his œconomy.[1] There is a proverb concerning persons in the predicament of this gentleman, which however cannot be strictly applied to him. *They commence dupes, and finish knaves*. Now Mr. Touchet's character is uniform. I am convinced that his sentiments never depended upon his circumstances, and that, in the most prosperous state of his fortune, he was always the very man he is at present.—But was there no other person of rank and consequence in the city, whom government could confide in, but a notorious Jacobite? Did you imagine that the whole body of the Dissenters, that the whole Whig-interest of London would attend at the levy, and submit to the directions of a notorious Jacobite? Was there no Whig magistrate in the city, to whom the servants of George the Third could intrust the management of a business, so very interesting to their master as the election of sheriffs? Is there no room at St. James's, but for Scotchmen and Jacobites? My Lord, I do not mean to question the sincerity of Mr. Harley's attachment to his Majesty's government. Since the

[1] Sir Lewis Namier contributed a very full biography of Samuel Touchet, who had represented Shaftesbury 1761–8, to *The House of Commons, 1754–90*.

commencement of the present reign, I have seen still greater contradictions reconciled. The principles of these worthy Jacobites, are not so absurd, as they have been represented. Their ideas of divine right are not so much annexed to the person or family, as to the political character of the Sovereign. Had there ever been an honest man among the *Stuarts*, his Majesty's present friends would have been Whigs upon principle. But the conversion of the best of Princes has removed their scruples. They have forgiven him the sins of his Hanoverian ancestors, and acknowledge the hand of providence in the descent of the crown upon the head of a true *Stuart*. In you, my Lord, they also behold, with a kind of predilection, which borders upon loyalty, the natural representative of that illustrious family. The mode of your descent from Charles the Second is only a bar to your pretensions to the crown, and no way interrupts the regularity of your succession to all the virtues of the *Stuarts*.

THE unfortunate success of the reverend Mr. Horne's endeavours, in support of the ministerial nomination of sheriffs, will I fear obstruct his preferment. Permit me to recommend him to your Grace's protection.[1] You will find him copiously gifted with those qualities of the heart, which usually direct you in the choice of your friendships. He too was Mr. Wilkes's friend, and as incapable as you are of the liberal resentment of a gentleman. No, my Lord,— it was the solitary, vindictive malice of a monk, brooding over the infirmities of his friend, until he thought they quickened into public life; and feasting with a rancorous rapture, upon the sordid catalogue of his distresses. Now, let him go back to his cloister. The church is a proper retreat for him. In his principles he is already a Bishop.

THE mention of this man has moved me from my natural moderation. Let me return to your Grace. You are the pillow, upon

[1] John Horne had abandoned his clerical career. A moving spirit behind the Society of Supporters of the Bill of Rights, his proposal to divert £500 from its funds to assist William Bingley led to a breach with Wilkes. An acrimonious exchange between the two took place in the *Public Advertiser* during the early summer of 1771. At the election of sheriffs for the city of London, Horne supported Richard Oliver against Wilkes and his running-mate Frederick Bull. Oliver was badly beaten and an effigy of Horne was burned in front of the Mansion House by Wilkes's exuberant supporters.

which I am determined to rest all my resentments. What idea can the best of Sovereigns form to himself of his own government?—in what repute can he conceive that he stands with his people, when he sees, beyond the possibility of a doubt, that, whatever be the office, the suspicion of his favour is fatal to the candidate, and that, when the party he wishes well to has the fairest prospect of success, if his royal inclination should unfortunately be discovered, it drops like an acid, and turns the election. This event, among others, may perhaps contribute to open his Majesty's eyes to his real honour and interest. In spite of all your Grace's ingenuity, he may at last perceive the inconvenience of selecting, with such a curious felicity, every villain in the nation to fill the various departments of his government. Yet I should be sorry to confine him in the choice either of his footmen or his friends.

JUNIUS.

Horne's bitter exchanges with Wilkes during May and June were of little service to either man but a source of considerable pleasure to the supporters of government. Junius wrote to Woodfall in private letter no. 36: 'I think Wilkes has closed well. I hope he will keep his resolution not to write any more.' Horne was also satirized at the same time by Samuel Foote, the mimic and actor. He defended himself here against Junius' insinuations in a letter which is full of fine touches and all the better for being short.

LETTER LI.

FROM THE REVEREND MR. HORNE TO JUNIUS.

SIR, 13. *July* 1771.

FARCE, *Comedy*, and *Tragedy*,—*Wilkes*, *Foote*, and *Junius*, united at the same time, against one poor Parson, are fearful odds. The two former are only labouring in their vocation, and may equally plead in excuse, that their aim is a livelihood. I admit the plea for the *second*; his is an honest calling, and my clothes were lawful game; but I cannot so readily approve Mr. Wilkes, or commend him for making patriotism a trade, and a fraudulent trade. But what shall I say to *Junius?* the grave, the solemn, the didactic!

ridicule, indeed, has been ridiculously called the test of truth; but surely, to confess that you lose your *natural moderation* when mention is made of the man, does not promise much truth or justice when you speak of him yourself.

YOU charge me with "a new zeal in support of administration," and with "endeavours in support of the ministerial nomination of Sheriffs." The reputation which your talents have deservedly gained to the signature of *Junius*, draws from me a reply, which I disdained to give to the anonymous lies of Mr. Wilkes. You make frequent use of the word *Gentleman*; I only call myself a *Man*, and desire no other distinction: if you are either, you are bound to make good your charges, or to confess that you have done me a hasty injustice upon no authority.

I PUT the matter fairly to issue.—I say, that so far from any "new zeal in support of administration," I am possessed with the utmost abhorrence of their measures; and that I have ever shewn myself, and am still ready, in any rational manner, to lay down all I have—my life, in opposition to those measures. I say, that I have not, and never have had any communication or connexion of any kind, directly or indirectly, with any courtier or ministerial man, or any of their adherents: that I never have received, or solicited, or expected, or desired, or do now hope for, any reward of any sort, from any party or set of men in administration or opposition: I say, that I never used any "endeavours in support of the ministerial nomination of Sheriffs." That I did not solicit any one liveryman for his vote for any one of the candidates; nor employ any other person to solicit: and that I did not write one single line or word in favour of Messrs. Plumbe and Kirkman, whom I understand to have been supported by the ministry.——

YOU are bound to refute what I here advance, or to lose your credit for veracity: You must produce facts; surmise and general abuse, in however elegant language, ought not to pass for proofs. You have every advantage, and I have every disadvantage: you are unknown, I give my name: all parties, both in and out of administration, have their reasons (which I shall relate hereafter) for uniting in their wishes against me: and the popular prejudice is as strongly in your favour, as it is violent against the Parson.

SINGULAR as my present situation is, it is neither painful, nor was it unforeseen. He is not fit for public business who does not even at his entrance prepare his mind for such an event. Health, fortune, tranquility, and private connexions I have sacrificed upon the altar of the public; and the only return I receive, because I will not concur to dupe and mislead a senseless multitude, is barely, that they have not yet torn me in pieces. That this has been the only return, is my pride; and a source of more real satisfaction than honours or prosperity. I can practise before I am old, the lessons I learned in my youth; nor shall I ever forget the words of my ancient Monitor,[1]

"'Tis the last key-stone
That makes the arch: the rest that there were put,
Are nothing till that comes to bind and shut.
Then stands it a triumphal mark! then men
Observe the strength, the height, the why and when
It was erected; and still walking under,
Meet some new matter to look up and wonder!"

I am, SIR,
Your humble Servant,
JOHN HORNE.

Junius was rarely as effective in defence as in attack; nevertheless, his reply was a not unskilful exercise in evasion. He submitted it privately to Horne (private letter no. 37), who made no objection to its publication. In the *Public Advertiser* it was dated 17 July; the 24th was the date of publication.

LETTER LII.

TO THE REVEREND MR. HORNE.

SIR, 24. *July* 1771.

I CANNOT descend to an altercation with you in the news-papers. But since I have attacked your character, and you

[1] Ben Jonson, *Underwoods*: 'An epistle to Sir Edward Sackville, now Earl of Dorset'.

complain of injustice, I think you have some right to an explanation. You defy me to prove, that you ever solicited a vote, or wrote a word in support of the ministerial aldermen. Sir, I did never suspect you of such gross folly. It would have been impossible for Mr. Horne to have solicited votes, and very difficult to have written for the news-papers in defence of that cause, without being detected and brought to shame. Neither do I pretend to any intelligence concerning you, or to know more of your conduct, than you yourself have thought proper to communicate to the public. It is from your own letters I conclude that you have sold yourself to the ministry: or, if that charge be too severe, and supposing it possible to be deceived by appearances so very strongly against you, what are your friends to say in your defence? must they not confess that, to gratify your personal hatred of Mr. Wilkes, you sacrificed, as far as depended upon *your* interest and abilities, the cause of the country? I can make allowance for the violence of the passions, and if ever I should be convinced that you had no motive but to destroy Wilkes, I shall then be ready to do justice to your character, and to declare to the world, that I despise you somewhat less than I do at present.—But as a public man, I must for ever condemn you. You cannot but know,—nay you dare not pretend to be ignorant, that the highest gratification of which the most detestable —— in this nation is capable, would have been the defeat of Wilkes. I know *that man* much better than any of you. Nature intended him only for a good humoured-fool. A systematical education, with long practice, has made him a consummate hypocrite. Yet this man, to say nothing of his worthy ministers, you have most assiduously laboured to gratify. To exclude Wilkes, it was not necessary you should solicit votes for his opponents. We incline the balance as effectually by lessening the weight in one scale, as by increasing it in the other.

THE mode of your attack upon Wilkes (though I am far from thinking meanly of your abilities) convinces me, that you either want judgment extremely, or that you are blinded by your resentment. You ought to have foreseen, that the charges you urged against Wilkes could never do him any mischief. After all, when we expected discoveries highly interesting to the community, what a pitiful detail did it end in!—Some old cloaths—a Welsh poney—a French footman, and a hamper of claret. Indeed Mr. Horne, the public should, and *will* forgive him his claret and his footmen, and even the ambition of making his brother chamberlain of London, as long as he stands forth against a ministry and parliament, who are doing every thing they can to enslave the country, and as long as he is a thorn in the King's side. You will not suspect me of setting up *Wilkes* for a perfect character. The question to the public is, where shall we find a man, who, with purer principles, will go the lengths, and run the hazards that he has done? the season calls for such a man, and he ought to be supported. What would have been the triumph of that odious hypocrite and his minions, if *Wilkes* had been defeated! It was not *your* fault, reverend Sir, that he did not enjoy it compleatly.—But now I promise you, you have so little power to do mischief, that I much question whether the ministry will adhere to the promises they have made you. It will be in vain to say that I am a partizan of Mr. Wilkes, or personally your enemy. You will convince no man, for you do not believe it yourself. Yet, I confess, I am a little offended at the low rate, at which you seem to value my understanding. I beg, Mr. Horne, you will hereafter believe that I measure the integrity of men, by their conduct, not by their professions. Such tales may entertain Mr. Oliver, or your grandmother, but trust me, they are thrown away upon *Junius*.

YOU say you are a *man*. Was it generous, was it manly, repeatedly to introduce into a news-paper, the name of a young lady, with whom you must heretofore have lived on terms of politeness and good-humour?—but I have done with you.[1] In *my* opinion, your credit is irrecoverably ruined. Mr. *Townshend*, I think is nearly in the same predicament.—Poor *Oliver* has been shamefully duped by you. You have made him sacrifice all the honour he got by his imprisonment.—As for Mr. *Sawbridge*, whose character I really respect, I am astonished he does not see through your duplicity.

[1] The reference is to Wilkes's daughter Polly.

Never was so base a design so poorly conducted.—[1] This letter, you see, is not intended for the public, but if you think it will do you any service, you are at liberty to publish it.

JUNIUS.

⁂ This letter was transmitted privately by the Printer to Mr. Horne, by Junius's request. Mr. Horne returned it to the Printer, with directions to publish it.

The moderation and coolness of Horne's first letter gave him an advantage which he now pressed home. In particular he was able to exploit Junius' imprudent remark that he would continue to support Wilkes 'as long as he is a thorn in the King's side'. Making allowance for the occasional bombast and for Horne's reluctance to write tersely, public letter no. LIII remains the most effective criticism Junius received from any of his newspaper adversaries.

LETTER LIII.

FROM THE REVEREND MR. HORNE TO JUNIUS.

SIR, 31. *July*, 1771.

YOU have disappointed me. When I told you that surmise and general abuse, in however elegant language, ought not to pass for proofs, I evidently hinted at the reply which I expected; but you have dropped your usual elegance, and seem willing to try what will be the effect of surmise and general abuse in very coarse language. Your answer to my letter (which I hope was cool and temperate and modest) has convinced me that my idea of a *man* is much superior to yours of a *gentleman*. Of your former letters I have always said *materiem superabat opus*:[2] I do not think so of the present; the principles are more detestable than the expressions are mean and illiberal. I am contented that all those who adopt the one should for ever load me with the other.

[1] James Townsend, Richard Oliver, and John Sawbridge, all members of Parliament, were the most prominent of the Supporters of the Bill of Rights to resign with Horne and found a new Constitutional Society.

[2] Materiam superabat opus, Ovid, *Metamorphoses*, ii. 5: 'The craftsmanship was finer than the material.'

I APPEAL to the common-sense of the public, to which I have ever directed myself: I believe they have it, though I am sometimes half-inclined to suspect that Mr. Wilkes has formed a truer judgment of mankind than I have. However of this I am sure, that there is nothing else upon which to place a steady reliance. Trick, and low cunning, and addressing their prejudices and passions, may be the fittest means to carry a particular point; but if they have not common-sense, there is no prospect of gaining for them any real permanent good. The same passions which have been artfully used by an honest man for their advantage, may be more artfully employed by a dishonest man for their destruction. I desire them to apply their common-sense to this letter of *Junius*, not for my sake, but their own; it concerns them most nearly, for the principles it contains lead to disgrace and ruin, and are inconsistent with every notion of civil society.

THE charges which *Junius* has brought against me are made ridiculous by his own inconsistency and self-contradiction. He charges me positively with "a new zeal in support of administration;" and with "endeavours in support of the ministerial nomination of Sheriffs." And he assigns two inconsistent motives for my conduct: either that I have "*sold* myself to the ministry;" or am instigated "by the solitary, vindictive *malice* of a monk:" either that I am influenced by a sordid desire of *gain*; or am hurried on by "personal *hatred* and blinded by *resentment*.' In his letter to the Duke of Grafton he supposes me actuated by both: in his letter to me he at first doubts which of the two, whether interest, or revenge is my motive: however, at last he determines for the former, and again positively asserts that "the ministry have made me promises;" yet he produces no instance of corruption, nor pretends to have any intelligence of a ministerial connexion: he mentions no *cause* of personal hatred to Mr. Wilkes, nor any *reason* for my resentment, or revenge; nor has Mr. Wilkes himself ever hinted any, though repeatedly pressed. When *Junius* is called upon to justify his accusation, he answers, "he cannot descend to an altercation with me in the news papers." *Junius*, who *exists* only in the news papers, who acknowledges "he has attacked my character" *there*, and "thinks

I have some right to an *explanation*;" yet this *Junius* "cannot descend to an altercation in the news papers!" and because he cannot descend to an altercation with me in the news papers, he sends a letter of abuse by the printer, which he finishes with telling me— "I am at liberty to *publish* it." This to be sure is a most excellent method to avoid an altercation in the news papers!

THE *proofs* of his positive charges are as extraordinary, "He does not pretend to any intelligence concerning me, or to know more of my conduct than I myself have thought proper to communicate to the public." He does not suspect me of such gross folly as to have solicited votes, or to have written anonymously in the news papers; because it is impossible to do either of these without being detected and brought to shame. *Junius* says this! Who yet imagines that he has himself written two years under that signature, (and more under *others*) without being detected!—his warmest admirers will not hereafter add, without being brought to shame. But though he did never suspect me of such gross folly as to run the *hazard* of being detected and brought to shame by *anonymous* writing, he insists that I have been guilty of a much grosser folly of incurring the certainty of shame and detection by writings *signed* with my name! But this is a small flight for the towering *Junius*: "He is FAR from thinking meanly of my abilities," though he is "convinced that I want judgment extremely," and can, "really respect Mr. Sawbridge's character," though he declares him* to be

* I beg leave to introduce Mr. Horne to the character of the *Double Dealer*. I thought they had been better acquainted.—"Another very wrong objection has been made by some, who have not taken leisure to distinguish the characters. The hero of the play (meaning *Mellefont*) is a gull, and made a fool, and cheated.—Is every man a gull and a fool that is deceived?—At that rate, I am afraid the two classes of men will be reduced to one, and the knaves themselves be at a loss to justify their title. But if an open, honest-hearted man, who has an entire confidence in one, whom he takes to be his friend, and who (to confirm him in his opinion) in all appearance and upon several trials has been so; if this man be deceived by the treachery of the other, must he of necessity commence fool immediately, only because the other has proved a villain?"—YES, says parson *Horne*. No, says *Congreve*, and he, I think, is allowed to have known something of human nature.[1]

[1] The quotation from Congreve is taken from a letter of *c.* 7 December 1693 to Charles Montagu. It is reprinted in *William Congreve: Letters & Documents*, ed. J. C. Hodges (1964), 167.

so poor a creature as not to "see through the basest design conducted in the poorest manner!". And this most base design is conducted in the poorest manner, by a man whom he does not suspect of gross folly, and of whose abilities he is FAR from thinking meanly!

SHOULD we ask *Junius* to reconcile these contradictions, and explain this nonsense; the answer is ready; "he cannot descend to an altercation in the news papers." He feels no reluctance to attack the character of any man: the throne is not too high, nor the cottage too low: his mighty malice can grasp both extremes: he hints not his accusations as *opinion*, *conjecture*, or *inference*; but delivers them as *positive assertions:* Do the accused complain of injustice? He acknowledges they have some sort of right to an *explanation*; but if they ask for *proofs* and *facts*, he begs to be excused: and though he is no where else to be encountered—"he cannot descend to an altercation in the news papers."

AND this perhaps *Junius* may think "the *liberal resentment of a gentleman:*" this skulking assassination he may call courage. In all things as in this I hope we differ:

"I thought that fortitude had been a mean
'Twixt fear and rashness; not a lust obscene
Or appetite of offending; but a skill
And nice discernment between good and ill.
Her ends are honesty and public good,
And without these she is not understood."[1]

OF two things however he has condescended to give proof. He very properly produces a *young lady* to prove that I am not a man: and a good *old woman*, my grandmother, to prove Mr. Oliver a fool. Poor old soul! she read her bible far otherwise than *Junius!* she often found there that the sins of the fathers had been visited on the children; and therefore was cautious that herself and her immediate descendents should leave no reproach on her posterity: and they

[1] Jonson's 'Epistle to Sir Edward Sackville', incorrectly quoted.

left none: how little could she foresee this reverse of *Junius*, who visits my political sins upon my *grandmother!* I do not charge this to the score of malice in him, it proceeded intirely from his propensity to blunder; that whilst he was reproaching me for introducing in the most harmless manner, the name of *one* female, he might himself at the same instant, introduce *two*.

I AM represented alternately as it suits *Junius*'s purpose, under the opposite characters of a *gloomy Monk*, and a man of *politeness and good humour*. I am called "*a solitary Monk*," in order to confirm the notion given of me in Mr. Wilkes's anonymous paragraphs, that I *never laugh:* and the terms of *politeness* and *good humour* on which I am said to have lived heretofore with the *young lady*, are intended to confirm other paragraphs of Mr. Wilkes, in which he is supposed to have offended me by *refusing his daughter*. Ridiculous! Yet I cannot deny but that *Junius* has proved me *unmanly* and *ungenerous* as clearly as he has shewn me *corrupt* and *vindictive:* and I will tell him more; I have paid the present Ministry as many *visits*, and *compliments* as ever I paid to the *young lady*, and shall all my life treat them with the *same politeness and good humour*.

BUT *Junius* "begs me to believe that he measures the integrity of men by their *conduct*, not by their *professions*." Sure this *Junius* must imagine his readers as void of understanding, as he is of modesty! Where shall we find the standard of HIS integrity? By what are we to measure the *conduct* of this lurking assassin?—And he says this to me, whose conduct, wherever I could personally appear, has been as direct and open and public as my words; I have not, like him, concealed myself in my chamber to shoot my arrows out of the window; nor contented myself to view the battle from afar; but publicly mixed in the engagement, and shared the danger. To whom have I, like him, refused my name upon complaint of injury? what printer have I desired to conceal me? in the infinite variety of business I have been concerned, where it is not so easy to be faultless, which of my actions can he arraign? to what danger has any man been exposed, which I have not faced? *information*, *action*, *imprisonment*, or *death?* what labour have I refused? what expence have

I declined? what pleasure have I not renounced?—But *Junius, to whom no conduct belongs*, "measures the integrity of men by their *conduct*, not by their professions;" himself all the while being nothing but *professions*, and those too *anonymous!* the political ignorance or wilful falshood of this *declaimer* is extreme: his own *former* letters justify both my conduct and those whom his *last* letter abuses: for the public measures, which *Junius* has been all along defending, were ours, whom he attacks; and the uniform opposer of those measures has been Mr. Wilkes, whose bad actions and intentions he endeavours to screen.

LET *Junius* now, if he pleases, change his abuse; and quitting his loose hold of *interest* and *revenge*, accuse me of *vanity*, and call this defence *boasting*. I own I have a pride to see statues decreed, and the highest honours conferred for measures and actions which all men have approved: whilst those who counselled and caused them are execrated and insulted. The darkness in which *Junius* thinks himself shrouded, has not concealed him; nor the artifice of only *attacking under that signature* those he would pull down (whilst he *recommends by other ways* those he would have promoted) disguised from me whose partizan he is. When Lord Chatham can forgive the aukward situation in which for the sake of the public he was designedly placed by the thanks to him from the city:[1] and when *Wilkes's name* ceases to be necessary to Lord Rockingham to keep up a clamour against the *persons* of the ministry, without obliging the different factions now in opposition to bind themselves beforehand to some certain points, and to stipulate some precise advantages to the public; then, and not till then, may those whom he now abuses expect the approbation of *Junius*. The approbation of the public for our faithful attention to their interest by endeavours for those stipulations, which have made us as obnoxious to the factions in opposition as to those in administration, is not perhaps to be expected till some years hence; when the public will look back and see how shamefully they have been deluded; and by what arts they were made to lose the golden opportunity of preventing what they will surely experience,—a change of ministers, without a *material*

[1] See note 2, on p. 269.

change of measures, and without any security for a tottering constitution.

BUT what cares *Junius* for the security of the constitution? He has now unfolded to us his diabolical principles. *As a public man he must ever condemn* any measure which may tend accidentally to *gratify* the Sovereign: and Mr. Wilkes is to be supported and assisted in all his attempts (no matter how ridiculous and mischievous his projects) *as long as he continues to be a thorn in the King's side!*—The *cause of the country* it seems, in the opinion of *Junius*, is merely to vex the King; and any rascal is to be supported in any roguery, provided he can only thereby plant *a thorn in the King's side.*—This is the very extremity of faction, and the last degree of political wickedness. Because Lord Chatham has been ill-treated by the King and treacherously betrayed by the Duke of Grafton, the latter is to be "the pillow on which *Junius* will rest his resentment;" and the public are to oppose the measures of government from mere motives of personal enmity to the Sovereign!—These are the avowed principles of the man who in the same letter says, "if ever he should be convinced that I had no motive but to destroy Wilkes, he shall then be ready to do justice to my character, and to declare to the world that he despises me somewhat less than he does at present!" Had I ever acted from personal affection or enmity to Mr. *Wilkes*, I should justly be despised: But what does he deserve whose avowed motive is personal enmity to the Sovereign; the contempt which I should otherwise feel for the absurdity and glaring inconsistency of *Junius*, is here swallowed up in my abhorrence of his principle. The *right divine* and *sacredness* of Kings is to me a senseless jargon. It was thought a daring expression of Oliver Cromwell in the time of Charles the First, that if he found himself placed opposite to the King in battle, he would discharge his piece into his bosom as soon as into any other man's. I go farther: had I lived in those days, I would not have waited for chance to give me an opportunity of doing my duty; I would have sought him through the ranks, and without the least personal enmity, have discharged my piece into his bosom *rather* than into any other man's. The King, whose actions justify rebellion to his government, deserves death from the hand of every subject. And should such a time arrive, I shall be as free to act as to say. But till then, my attachment to the person and family of the Sovereign shall ever be found more zealous and sincere than that of his flatterers. I would offend the Sovereign with as much reluctance as the parent; but if the happiness and security of the whole family made it necessary, so far and no farther, I would offend him without remorse.

BUT let us consider a little whither these principles of *Junius* would lead us. Should Mr. Wilkes once more commission Mr. Thomas Walpole to procure for him a pension of *one thousand pounds* upon the Irish establishment for thirty years; he must be supported in the demand by the public—because it would mortify the King!

SHOULD he wish to see Lord Rockingham and his friends once more in administration, *unclogged by any stipulations for the people*, that he might again enjoy a *pension of one thousand and forty pounds* a year, viz. From the *First Lord of the Treasury* 500 l. From the *Lords of the Treasury* 60 l. each. From the *Lords of Trade*, 40 l. each, &c. The public must give up their attention to points of national benefit, and assist Mr. Wilkes in his attempt—because it would mortify the King!

SHOULD he demand the Government of *Canada*, or of *Jamaica*, or the embassy to *Constantinople*; and in case of refusal threaten to write them down, as he had before served another administration, in a year and a half; he must be supported in his pretensions and upheld in his insolence—because it would mortify the King!

JUNIUS may chuse to suppose that these things cannot happen! But that they have happened, notwithstanding Mr. Wilkes's denial, I do aver. I maintain that Mr. Wilkes did commission Mr. Thomas Walpole to solicit for him a pension of *one thousand pounds* on the *Irish* establishment for *thirty years*; with which and a pardon he declared he would be satisfied: and that, notwithstanding his letter to Mr. Onslow, he did accept a *clandestine*, *precarious* and *eleemosinary* pension from the Rockingham administration; which they paid in proportion to and out of their salaries; and so entirely was it ministerial, that as any of them went out of the ministry, their names were scratched out of the list, and they contributed no longer. I say, he did solicit the governments and the embassy, and threatened their refusal nearly in these words—"It cost me a year and a half to write down the last administration, should I employ as much time upon you, very few of you would be in at the death." When these threats did not prevail, he came over to England to embarrass them by his presence; and when he found that Lord Rockingham was something firmer and more manly than he expected, and refused to be bullied—into what he could not perform, Mr. Wilkes declared that he could not leave England without money; and the Duke of Portland and Lord Rockingham purchased his absence with *one hundred pounds a piece*; with which he returned to Paris. And for the truth of what I here advance, I appeal to the Duke of Portland, to Lord Rockingham, to Lord John Cavendish, to Mr. Walpole, &c.—I appeal to the hand-writing of Mr. Wilkes, which is still extant.[1]

SHOULD Mr. Wilkes afterwards (failing in this wholesale trade) chuse to dole out his popularity by the pound, and expose the city offices to sale to his brother, his attorney, &c. *Junius* will tell us, it is only an *ambition* that he has to make them *chamberlain*, *town-clerk*, &c. and he must not be opposed in thus robbing the ancient citizens of their birth-right—because any defeat of Mr. Wilkes would gratify the King!

SHOULD he, after consuming the whole of his own fortune and that of his wife, and incurring a debt of *twenty thousand pounds* merely by his own private extravagance, without a single service or exertion

[1] These allegations were substantially true. Cf. H. Bleackley, *Life of John Wilkes* (1917), 173–9. Wilkes first rejected the offer of a private pension with scorn, writing on 6 December 1765 to William Fitzherbert: 'I should despise myself as the most mean and abject wretch breathing, if I cou'd accept the offers made me. They are equally precarious, eleemosinary, and clandestine. I claim from the present ministers a full pardon under the Great Seal for having successfully served my country.' He repeated these phrases in a letter to George Onslow on 12 December. Both letters are given in full by W. P. Treloar, *Wilkes and the City* (1917), pp. 46–7. Wilkes's financial plight forced him subsequently to moderate his tone and accept the proposals.

all this time for the public, whilst his estate remained; should he, at length, being undone, commence patriot, have the good fortune to be illegally persecuted, and in consideration of that illegality be espoused by a few gentlemen of the purest public principles; should his debts, (though none of them were contracted for the public) and all his other incumbrances be discharged; should he be offered 600 l. or 1000 l. a year to make him independent for the future; and should he, after all, instead of gratitude for these services, insolently forbid his benefactors to bestow their own money upon any other object but himself, and revile them for setting any bounds to their supplies; *Junius* (who, any more than Lord Chatham, never contributed one farthing to these enormous expences) will tell them, that if they think of converting the supplies of Mr. Wilkes's private extravagance to the support of public measures —— they are as great fools as my *grandmother*; and that Mr. Wilkes ought to hold the strings of their purses—*as long as he continues to be a thorn in the King's side!*

UPON these principles I never have acted, and I never will act. In my opinion, it is less dishonourable to be the creature of a court than the tool of a faction. I will not be either. I understand the two great leaders of opposition to be Lord Rockingham and Lord Chatham; under one of whose banners all the opposing members of both houses, who desire to get places, enlist. I can place no confidence in either of them, or in any others, unless they will now engage, whilst they are OUT, to grant certain essential advantages for the security of the public when they shall be IN administration. These points they refuse to stipulate, because they are fearful lest they should prevent any future overtures from the court. To force them to these stipulations has been the uniform endeavour of Mr. Sawbridge, Mr. Townsend, Mr. Oliver, &c. and THEREFORE, they are abused by Junius. I know no reason but my zeal and industry in the same cause that should intitle me to the honour of being ranked by his abuse with persons of their fortune and station. It is a duty I owe to the memory of the late Mr. Beckford to say, that he had no other aim than this when he provided that sumptuous entertainment at the Mansion-house for the members of both houses in opposition.[1] At that time he drew up the heads of an engagement, which he gave to me with a request that I would couch it in terms so cautious and precise, as to leave no room for future quibble, and evasion; but to oblige them either to fulfil the intent of the obligation, or to sign their own infamy, and leave it on record; and this engagement he was determined to propose to them at the Mansion-house, that either by their refusal they might forfeit the confidence of the public, or by the engagement lay a foundation for confidence. When they were informed of the intention, Lord Rockingham and his friends flatly refused any engagement; and Mr. Beckford as flatly swore, they should then—"eat none of his broth;" and he was determined to put off the entertainment: But Mr. Beckford was prevailed upon by —— to indulge them in the ridiculous parade of a popular procession through the city, and to give them the foolish pleasure of an imaginary consequence, for the real benefit only of the cooks and purveyors.

It was the same motive which dictated the thanks of the city to Lord Chatham; which were expressed to be given for his declaration in favour of *short parliaments:* in order thereby to fix Lord Chatham at least to that one constitutional remedy, without which all others can afford no security.[2] The embarassment no doubt was cruel. He had his choice either to offend the Rockingham party, who declared *formally* against short parliaments, and with the assistance of whose numbers in both houses he must expect again to be minister; or to give up the confidence of the public, from whom finally all real consequence must proceed. Lord Chatham chose the latter: and I will venture to say, that, by his *answer* to those thanks, he has given up the people without gaining the friendship or cordial assistance of the Rockingham faction; whose little politics are confined to the making of matches, and extending their family connexions, and who think they gain more by

[1] In March 1770. See John Cannon, *Parliamentary reform, 1640–1832*, 64.

[2] The Common Council of the city of London resolved on 14 May 1770 to present its thanks to Chatham for his pledge to shorten the duration of Parliaments and to introduce a more full and equal representation. In his reply Chatham observed that there had been some 'misapprehension' of his attitude, that although he approved an addition of county members he could not support triennial Parliaments, and that he had thrown out his remarks 'with the just diffidence of a private man'.

procuring one additional vote to their party in the house of commons, than by adding their languid property and feeble character to the abilities of a *Chatham*, or the confidence of a public.

WHATEVER may be the event of the present wretched state of politics in this country, the principles of Junius will suit no form of government. They are not to be tolerated under any constitution. Personal enmity is a motive fit only for the devil. Whoever or whatever is Sovereign, demands the respect and support of the people. The union is formed for their happiness, which cannot be had without mutual respect; and he counsels maliciously who would persuade either to a wanton breach of it. When it is banished by either party, and when every method has been tried in vain to restore it, there is no remedy but a divorce: But even then he must have a hard and a wicked heart indeed who punishes the greatest criminal merely for the sake of the punishment; and who does not let fall a tear for every drop of blood that is shed in a public struggle, however just the quarrel.

JOHN HORNE.

Junius' reply was dated 10 August and appeared in the *Public Advertiser* on 13 August: the date printed on the letter in the collected edition is an error. To the printer, Junius wrote in private letter no. 38, 'If Mr. Horne answers this Letter handsomely and in point, he shall be my great Apollo.' But apart from some easy hits at Horne's foolish assertions of the terrible things he would have done to Charles I in battle, Junius was clearly on the defensive and admitted the 'single unguarded expression, in a letter not intended for the public'.

LETTER LIV.

TO THE PRINTER OF THE PUBLIC ADVERTISER.

SIR, 15. *Aug.* 1771.

I OUGHT to make an apology to the Duke of Grafton, for suffering any part of my attention to be diverted from his Grace to Mr. Horne. I am not justified by the similarity of their dispositions. Private vices, however detestable, have not dignity sufficient to attract the censure of the press, unless they are united with the power of doing some signal mischief to the community.—Mr. Horne's situation does not correspond with his intentions.—In my own opinion, (which I know, will be attributed to my usual vanity and presumption) his letter to me does not deserve an answer. But I understand that the public are not satisfied with my silence;—that an answer is expected from me, and that if I persist in refusing to plead, it will be taken for conviction. I should be inconsistent with the principles I profess, if I declined an appeal to the good sense of the people, or did not willingly submit myself to the judgment of my peers.

IF any coarse expressions have escaped me, I am ready to agree that they are unfit for Junius to make use of, but I see no reason to admit that they have been improperly applied.

MR. HORNE, it seems, is unable to comprehend how an extreme want of conduct and discretion can consist with the abilities I have allowed him; nor can he conceive that a very honest man, with a very good understanding, may be deceived by a knave. His knowledge of human nature must be limited indeed. Had he never mixed with the world, one would think that even his books might have taught him better. Did he hear Lord Mansfield, when he defended his doctrine concerning libels?—Or when he stated the law in prosecutions for criminal conversation?—Or when he delivered his reasons for calling the house of lords together to receive a copy of his charge to the jury in Woodfall's trial?—Had he been present upon any of these occasions, he would have seen how possible it is for a man of the first talents, to confound himself in absurdities, which would disgrace the lips of an ideot. Perhaps the example might have taught him not to value his own understanding so highly.—Lord Littleton's integrity and judgment are unquestionable;—yet he is known to admire that cunning Scotchman, and verily believes him an honest man.—I speak to facts, with which all of us are conversant,—I speak to men and to their experience, and will not descend to answer the little sneering sophistries of a collegian.—Distinguished talents are not necessarily connected with discretion. If there be any thing remarkable in the character of Mr. Horne, it is that extreme want of judgment should be united with his very moderate capacity. Yet I have not forgotten the acknowledgment I made him. He owes it to my bounty; and though his letter has lowered him in my opinion, I scorn to retract the charitable donation.

I SAID it would be *very difficult* for Mr. Horne to write directly in defence of a ministerial measure, and not be detected; and even that difficulty I confined to *his* particular situation. He changes the terms of the proposition, and supposes me to assert, that it would be *impossible* for *any* man to write for the news-papers and not be discovered.

HE repeatedly affirms or intimates at least, that he knows the author of these letters.—With what colour of truth then can he pretend *that I am no where to be encountered but in a news-paper?*—I shall leave him to his suspicions. It is not necessary that I should confide in the honour or discretion of a man, who already seems to hate me with as much rancour, as if I had formerly been his friend.—But he asserts that he has traced me thro' a variety of signatures. To make the discovery of any importance to his purpose, he should have proved, either that the fictitious character of *Junius* has not been consistently supported, or that the author has maintained different principles under different signatures.—I cannot recall to my memory the numberless trifles I have written; —but I rely upon the consciousness of my own integrity, and defy him to fix any colourable charge of inconsistency upon me.

I AM not bound to assign the secret motives of his apparent hatred of Mr. Wilkes: nor does it follow that I may not judge fairly of *his* conduct, though it were true *that I had no conduct of my own.*—Mr. Horne enlarges, with rapture, upon the importance of his services;—the dreadful battles which he might have been engaged in, and the dangers he has escaped.—In support of the formidable description, he quotes verses without mercy. The gentleman deals in fiction, and naturally appeals to the evidence of the poets.—Taking him at his word, he cannot but admit the superiority of Mr. Wilkes in this line of service. On one side we see nothing but imaginary distresses. On the other we see real prosecutions;—real penalties;—real imprisonment;—life repeatedly hazarded; and, at one moment, almost the certainty of death. Thanks are undoubtedly due to every man who does his duty in the engagement; but it is the wounded soldier who deserves the reward.

I DID not mean to deny that Mr. Horne had been an active partizan. It would defeat my own purpose not to allow him a degree of merit, which aggravates his guilt. The very charge of *contributing his utmost efforts to support a ministerial measure*, implies an acknowledgement of his former services. If he had not once been distinguished by his apparent zeal in defence of the common cause, he could not now be distinguished by deserting it.—As for myself, it is no longer a question *whether I shall mix with the throng, and take a single share in the danger*. Whenever *Junius* appears, he must encounter a host of enemies. But is there no honourable way to serve the public, without engaging in personal quarrels with insignificant individuals, or submitting to the drudgery of canvassing votes for an election? Is there no merit in dedicating my life to the information of my fellow-subjects?—What public question have I declined, what villain have I spared?—Is there no labour in the composition of these letters! Mr. Horne, I fear, is partial to me, and measures the facility of *my* writings, by the fluency of his own.

HE talks to us, in high terms, of the gallant feats he would have performed, if he had lived in the last century. The unhappy Charles could hardly have escaped him. But living princes have a claim to his attachment and respect. Upon these terms, there is no danger in being a patriot. If he means any thing more than a pompous rhapsody, let us try how well his argument holds together.—I presume he is not yet so much a courtier as to affirm that the constitution has not been grossly and daringly violated under the present reign. He will not say, that the laws have not been shamefully broken or perverted;—that the rights of the subject have not been invaded, or that redress has not been repeatedly solicited and refused.—Grievances like these were the foundation of the rebellion in the last century, and, if I understand Mr. Horne, they would, at that period, have justified him to his own mind, in deliberately attacking the life of his Sovereign. I shall not ask him to what political constitution this doctrine can be reconciled. But, at least, it is incumbent upon him to shew, that the present King has better excuses, than Charles the First, for the errors of his government. He ought to demonstrate to us that the constitution was better understood a hundred years ago than it is at present;—that the legal rights of the subject, and the limits of the prerogative were more accurately defined, and more clearly comprehended. If propositions like these cannot be fairly maintained, I do not see how he can reconcile it to his conscience, not to act immediately with the same freedom with which he speaks. I reverence the character of Charles the First as little as Mr. Horne; but I will not insult his misfortunes, by a comparison that would degrade him.

It is worth observing, by what gentle degrees, the furious, persecuting zeal of Mr. Horne has softened into moderation. Men and measures were yesterday his object. What pains did he once take to bring that great state criminal *Macquirk* to execution!—Today he confines himself to measures only.—No penal example is to be left to the successors of the Duke of Grafton.—To-morrow, I presume both men and measures will be forgiven. The flaming patriot, who so lately scorched us in the meridian, sinks temperately to the west, and is hardly felt as he descends.

I comprehend the policy of endeavouring to communicate to Mr. Oliver and Mr. Sawbridge, a share in the reproaches, with which he supposes me to have loaded him. My memory fails me, if I have mentioned their names with disrespect;—unless it be reproachful to acknowledge a sincere respect for the character of Mr. Sawbridge, and not to have questioned the innocence of Mr. Oliver's intentions.

IT seems I am a partizan of the great leader of the opposition. If the charge had been a reproach, it should have been better supported. I did not intend to make a public declaration of the respect I bear Lord Chatham. I well knew what unworthy conclusions would be drawn from it. But I am called upon to deliver my opinion, and surely it is not in the little censure of Mr. Horne to deter me from doing signal justice to a man, who, I confess, has grown upon my esteem. As for the common, sordid views of avarice, or any purpose of vulgar ambition, I question whether the applause of *Junius* would be of service to Lord Chatham. *My* vote will hardly recommend him to an increase of his pension, or to a seat in the cabinet. But if his ambition be upon a level with his understanding;—if he judges of what is truly honourable for himself, with the same superior genius, which animates and directs him, to eloquence in debate, to wisdom in decision, even the pen of Junius shall contribute to reward him. Recorded honours shall gather round his monument, and thicken over him. It is a solid fabric, and will support the laurels that adorn it.—I am not conversant in the language of panegyric.—These praises are extorted from me; but they will wear well, for they have been dearly earned.

MY detestation of the Duke of Grafton is not founded upon his treachery to any individual: though I am willing enough to suppose that, in public affairs, it would be impossible to desert or betray Lord Chatham, without doing an essential injury to this country. My abhorrence of the Duke arises from an intimate knowledge of his character, and from a thorough conviction, that his baseness has been the cause of greater mischief to England, than even the unfortunate ambition of Lord Bute.

THE shortening the duration of parliaments is a subject, on which Mr. Horne cannot enlarge too warmly; nor will I question his sincerity. If I did not profess the same sentiments, I should be shamefully inconsistent with myself. It is unnecessary to bind Lord Chatham by the written formality of an engagement. He has publicly declared himself a convert to Triennial Parliaments;[1] and

[1] In a speech of 1 May 1771; *Parl. Hist.* xvii, 223.

tho' I have long been convinced that this is the only possible resource we have left to preserve the substantial freedom of the constitution, I do not think we have a right to determine against the integrity of Lord Rockingham or his friends. Other measures may undoubtedly be supported in argument, as better adapted to the disorder, or more likely to be obtained.

MR. Horne is well assured, that I never was the champion of Mr. Wilkes. But tho' I am not obliged to answer for the firmness of his future adherence to the principles he professes, I have no reason to presume that he will hereafter disgrace them. As for all those imaginary cases, which Mr. Horne so petulantly urges against me, I have one plain, honest answer to make to him.—Whenever Mr. Wilkes shall be convicted of soliciting a pension, an embassy, or a government, he must depart from that situation, and renounce that character, which he assumes at present, and which, in *my* opinion, intitle him to the support of the public. By the same act, and at the same moment, he will forfeit his power of mortifying the King; and though he can never be a favourite at St. James's, his baseness may administer a solid satisfaction to the royal mind. The man, I speak of, has not a heart to feel for the frailties of his fellow-creatures. It is their virtues that afflict, it is their vices that console him.

I GIVE every possible advantage to Mr. Horne, when I take the facts he refers to for granted. That they are the produce of his invention, seems highly probable; that they are exaggerated I have no doubt. At the worst, what do they amount to, but that Mr. Wilkes, who never was thought of as a perfect pattern of morality, has not been at all times proof against the extremity of distress. How shameful is it, in a man who has lived in friendship with him, to reproach him with failings, too naturally connected with despair! Is no allowance to be made for banishment and ruin? Does a two years imprisonment make no atonement for his crimes?—The resentment of a priest is implacable. No sufferings can soften, no penitence can appease him.—Yet he himself, I think, upon his own system, has a multitude of political offences to atone for. I will not insist upon the nauseous detail, with which he so long disgusted the public. He seems to be ashamed of it. But what excuse will he make to the friends of the constitution for labouring to promote *this consummately bad man* to a station of the highest national trust and importance? Upon what honourable motives did he recommend him to the livery of London for their representative;—to the ward of Farringdon for their alderman;—to the county of Middlesex for their knight? Will he affirm that, at that time, he was ignorant of Mr. Wilkes's solicitations to the ministry?—That he should say so, is indeed very necessary for his own justification, but where will he find credulity to believe him?

IN what school this gentleman learned his ethics I know not. His *logic* seems to have been studied under Mr. Dyson. That miserable pamphleteer, by dividing the only precedent in point, and taking as much of it as suited his purpose, had reduced his argument upon the Middlesex election to something like the shape of a syllogism. Mr. Horne has conducted himself with the same ingenuity and candour. I had affirmed that Mr. Wilkes would preserve the public favour, "as long as he stood forth against a ministry and parliament, who were doing every thing they could to enslave the country, *and* as long as he was a thorn in the King's side." Yet, from the exulting triumph of Mr. Horne's reply, one would think that I had rested my expectation, that Mr. Wilkes would be supported by the public, upon the single condition of his mortifying the King. This may be logic at Cambridge or at the Treasury, but among men of sense and honour, it is folly or villainy in the extreme.[1]

I SEE the pitiful advantage he has taken of a single unguarded expression, in a letter not intended for the public. Yet is is only the *expression* that is unguarded. I adhere to the true meaning of that member of the sentence, taken separately as *he* takes it, and now, upon the coolest deliberation, reassert that, for the purposes I

[1] Horne was educated at St. John's College, Cambridge: Jeremiah Dyson was a Lord of the Treasury. Junius' accusation that the latter had deliberately suppressed part of a quotation was made in letter no. XX and repeated in no. XLVI.

referred to, it may be highly meritorious to the public, to wound the personal feelings of the Sovereign. It is not a general proposition, nor is it generally applied to the chief magistrate of this, or any other constitution. Mr. Horne knows as well as I do, that the best of princes is not displeased with the abuse, which he sees thrown upon his ostensible ministers. It makes them, I presume, more properly the objects of his royal compassion;—neither does it escape his sagacity, that the lower they are degraded in the public esteem, the more submissively they must depend upon his favour for protection. This, I affirm upon the most solemn conviction, and the most certain knowledge, is a leading maxim in the policy of the closet. It is unnecessary to pursue the argument any farther.

MR. Horne is now a very loyal subject. He laments the wretched state of politics in this country, and sees, in a new light, the weakness and folly of the opposition. *Whoever or whatever is Sovereign, demands the respect and support of the people*★, it was not so, *when Nero fiddled while Rome was burning.*[1] Our gracious Sovereign has had wonderful success, in creating new attachments *to his person and family*. He owes it, I presume, to the regular system he has pursued in the mystery of conversion. He began with an experiment upon the Scotch, and concludes with converting Mr. Horne.—What a pity it is, that the *Jews* should be condemned by Providence to wait for a Messiah of their own!

THE priesthood are accused of misinterpreting the scriptures. Mr. Horne has improved upon his profession. He alters the text, and creates a refutable doctrine of his own. Such artifices cannot long delude the understanding of the people; and without meaning an indecent comparison, I may venture to foretel, that the Bible

★ The very soliloque of Lord Suffolk, before he passed the Rubicon.[2]

---

[1] The remark attributed to Horne when the King received the remonstrance from the city of London. See p. 186 n. 1.

[2] Lord Suffolk strongly opposed Lord North's government in 1770, accusing it of delight 'in opposing the wishes of the people'. *Parl. Hist.* xvi. 972. But he accepted office the following year as Lord Privy Seal, subsequently becoming Secretary of State for the Northern Department.

and *Junius* will be read, when the commentaries of the Jesuits are forgotten.

JUNIUS.

The concluding remarks of public letter no. LIV provoked accusations of profanity from A North Briton and Vetus in the *Public Advertiser* of 21 and 24 August 1771. As usual, Philo Junius was sent to the rescue. Junius changed the chronological order of the letters when compiling the collected edition, thus, perhaps inadvertently, making it more difficult for the reader to follow the exchange with Horne.

LETTER LV.

TO THE PRINTER OF THE PUBLIC ADVERTISER.

SIR, 26. *August*, 1771.

THE enemies of the people, having now nothing better to object to my friend *Junius*, are at last obliged to quit his politics and to rail at him for crimes he is not guilty of. His vanity and impiety are now the perpetual topics of their abuse. I do not mean to lessen the force of such charges, (supposing they were true), but to shew that they are not founded. If I admitted the premises, I should readily agree in all the consequences drawn from them. Vanity indeed is a venial error, for it usually carries its own punishment with it;—but if I thought *Junius* capable of uttering a disrespectful word of the religion of his country, I should be the first to renounce and give him up to the public contempt and indignation. As a man, I am satisfied that he is a Christian upon the most sincere conviction. As a writer, he would be grossly inconsistent with his political principles, if he dared to attack a religion established by those laws, which it seems to be the purpose of his life to defend.—Now for the proofs.—*Junius* is accused of an impious allusion to the holy sacrament, where he says that, *if Lord Weymouth be denied the cup, there will be no keeping him within the pale of the ministry*. Now, Sir, I affirm that this passage refers intirely to a ceremonial in the Roman catholic church, which denies the cup to the laity. It has no manner of relation to the Protestant creed, and is in this country, as fair an object of ridicule as *transubstantiation*, or any other part of Lord *Peter*'s history in the Tale of the Tub.[1]

BUT *Junius* is charged with equal vanity and impiety, in comparing his writings to the holy scripture.—The formal protest he makes against any such comparison, avails him nothing. It becomes necessary then to shew that the charge destroys itself.—If he be *vain*, he cannot be *impious*. A vain man does not usually compare himself to an object, which it is his design to undervalue. On the other hand, if he be *impious*, he cannot be *vain*. For his impiety, if any, must consist in his endeavouring to degrade the holy scriptures by a comparison with his own contemptible writings. This would be folly indeed of the grossest nature, but where lies the vanity?—I shall now be told,—"Sir, what you say is plausible enough, but still you must allow that it is shamefully impudent in *Junius* to tell us that his works will live as long as the Bible." My answer is. *Agreed: but first prove that he has said so.* Look at his words, and you will find that the utmost he expects is, that the Bible and *Junius* will survive the commentaries of the Jesuits, which may prove true in a fortnight. The most malignant sagacity cannot shew that his works are, *in his opinion*, to live as long as the Bible. —Suppose I were to foretell that *Jack* and *Tom* would survive *Harry*.—Does it follow that *Jack* must live as long as *Tom?* I would only illustrate my meaning and protest against the least idea of profaneness.

YET this is the way in which *Junius* is usually answered, arraigned and convicted. These candid critics never remember any thing he says in honour of our holy religion; though it is true that one of his leading arguments is made to rest *upon the internal evidence which the purest of all religions carries with it.* I quote his words, and conclude from them, that he is a true and hearty Christian, in

[1] Jonathan Swift's *A Tale of a Tub*, his first major work, was published in 1704: the reference is to section iv. Junius' remark about Weymouth came at the end of letter no. XLIX.

substance, not in ceremony; though possibly he may not agree with my Reverend Lords the Bishops, or with the Head of the Church, *that prayers are morality, or that kneeling is religion.*

PHILO JUNIUS.

Horne's reply to public letter no. LIV in fact appeared in the *Public Advertiser* for Friday, 16 August 1771.

LETTER LVI.

FROM THE REVEREND MR. HORNE TO JUNIUS.

17. *August*, 1771.

I CONGRATULATE you, Sir, on the recovery of your wonted style, though it has cost you a fortnight. I compassionate your labour in the composition of your letters, and will communicate to you the secret of my fluency.—Truth needs no ornament; and, in my opinion, what she borrows of the pencil is deformity.

YOU brought a positive charge against me of corruption. I denied the charge, and called for your proofs. You replied with abuse and re-asserted your charge. I called again for proofs. You reply again with abuse only, and drop your accusation. In your fortnight's letter there is not one word upon the subject of my corruption.

I HAVE no more to say, but to return thanks to you for your *condescension*, and to a *grateful* public and *honest* ministry for all the favours they have conferred upon me. The two latter, I am sure, will never refuse me any grace I shall solicit; and since you have been pleased to acknowledge that you told a deliberate lye in my favour out of bounty, and as a charitable donation, why may I not expect that you will hereafter (if you do not forget you ever mentioned my name with disrespect) make the same acknowledgement for what you have said to my prejudice?—This second recantation will perhaps be more abhorrent from your disposition; but should you decline it, you will only afford one more instance how much easier it is to be generous than just, and that men are sometimes bountiful who are not honest.

AT all events I am as well satisfied with your panegyric as Lord Chatham can be. Monument I shall have none; but over my grave it will be said, in your own words, "*Horne's situation did not correspond with his intentions**."

JOHN HORNE.

Junius then resumed his attack upon Grafton, making use of assertions he had heard against the Duke's conduct in his capacity of Ranger of Whittlebury Forest in Northamptonshire.

LETTER LVII.

TO HIS GRACE THE DUKE OF GRAFTON.

28. *Sept.* 1771.

MY LORD,

THE people of England are not apprised of the full extent of their obligations to you. They have yet no adequate idea of the endless variety of your character. They have seen you distinguished and successful in the continued violation of those moral and political duties, by which the little, as well as the great societies of life, are collected and held together. Every colour, every character became you. With a rate of abilities, which Lord Weymouth very justly looks down upon with contempt, you have done as much mischief to the community as *Cromwell* would have done, if *Cromwell* had been a coward, and as much as *Machiavel*, if *Machiavel* had not known, that an appearance of morals and religion are useful in society.—To a thinking man, the influence of the crown will, in no view, appear so formidable, as when he observes to what

* The epitaph would not be ill suited to the character;—At the best, it is but equivocal.

enormous excesses it has safely conducted your Grace, without a ray of real understanding, without even the pretensions to common decency or principle of any kind, or a single spark of personal resolution. What must be the operation of that pernicious influence, (for which our Kings have wisely exchanged the nugatory name of prerogative) that, in the highest stations, can so abundantly supply the absence of virtue, courage, and abilities, and qualify a man to be the minister of a great nation, whom a private gentleman would be ashamed and afraid to admit into his family! Like the universal passport of an ambassador, it supersedes the prohibition of the laws, banishes the staple virtues of the country, and introduces vice and folly triumphantly into all the departments of the state. Other princes, besides his Majesty, have had the means of corruption within their reach, but they have used it with moderation. In former times corruption was considered as a foreign auxiliary to government, and only called in upon extraordinary emergencies. The unfeigned piety, the sanctified religion of *George the Third* have taught him to new model the civil forces of the state. The natural resources of the crown are no longer confided in. Corruption glitters in the van;—collects and maintains a standing army of mercenaries, and, at the same moment, impoverishes and inslaves the country.—His Majesty's predecessors, (excepting that worthy family, from which you, my Lord, are unquestionably descended,) had some generous qualities in their composition, with vices, I confess, or frailties in abundance. They were kings or gentlemen, not hypocrites or priests. They were at the head of the church, but did not know the value of their office. They said their prayers without ceremony, and had too little priestcraft in their understanding, to reconcile the sanctimonious forms of religion with the utter destruction of the morality of their people.—My Lord this is fact, not declamation.—With all your partiality to the house *of Stuart*, you must confess, that even *Charles the Second* would have blushed at that open encouragement, at those eager, meretricious caresses, with which every species of private vice and public prostitution is received at *St. James's*.—The unfortunate house of *Stuart* has been treated with an asperity, which, if comparison be a defence, seems to border upon injustice. Neither *Charles* nor his brother were qualified to support such a system of measures, as would be necessary, to change the government, and subvert the constitution of England. One of them was too much in earnest in his pleasures,—the other in his religion. But the danger to this country would cease to be problematical, if the crown should ever descend to a prince, whose apparent simplicity might throw his subjects off their guard,—who might be no libertine in behaviour,—who should have no sense of honour to restrain him, and who, with just religion enough to impose upon the multitude, might have no scruples of conscience to interfere with his morality. With these honourable qualifications, and the decisive advantage of situation, low craft and falsehood are all the abilities that are wanting to destroy the wisdom of ages, and to deface the noblest monument that human policy has erected—I know *such* a man;—My Lord, I know you both; and with the blessing of God (for I too am religious,) the people of England shall know you as well as I do. I am not very sure that greater abilities would not in effect be an impediment to a design, which seems at first sight to require a superior capacity. A better understanding might make him sensible of the wonderful beauty of that system he was endeavouring to corrupt. The danger of the attempt might alarm him. The meanness, and intrinsic worthlessness of the object (supposing he could attain it) would fill him with shame, repentance, and disgust. But these are sensations, which find no entrance into a barbarous, contracted heart. In some men, there is a malignant passion to destroy the works of genius, literature, and freedom. The *Vandal* and the *Monk* find equal gratification in it.

REFLECTIONS like these, my Lord, have a general relation to your grace, and inseparably attend you, in whatever company or situation your character occurs to us. They have no immediate connexion with the following recent fact, which I lay before the public, for the honour of the best of Sovereigns, and for the edification of his people.

A PRINCE (whose piety and self-denial, one would think, might secure him from such a multitude of worldy necessities,) with an annual revenue of near a million sterling, unfortunately *wants money*.—The navy of England, by an equally strange concurrence of unforeseen circumstances, (though not quite so unfortunately for his Majesty) is in equal want of timber. The world knows, in what a hopeful condition you delivered the navy to your successor, and in what a condition we found it in the moment of distress. You were determined it should continue in the situation in which you left it. It happened, however, very luckily for the privy purse, that one of the above wants promised fair to supply the other. Our religious, benevolent, generous Sovereign, has no objection to selling *his own* timber to *his own* admiralty, to repair *his own* ships, nor to putting the money into *his own* pocket. People of a religious turn naturally adhere to the principles of the church. Whatever they acquire falls into *mortmain*.—Upon a representation from the admiralty of the extraordinary want of timber, for the indispensable repairs of the navy, the surveyor general was directed to make a survey of the timber in all the royal chaces and forests in England. Having obeyed his orders with accuracy and attention, he reported, that the finest timber he had any where met with, and the properest in every respect for the purposes of the navy, was in *Whittlebury Forest*, of which your Grace, I think, is hereditary ranger. In consequence of this report, the usual warrant was prepared at the treasury, and delivered to the surveyor, by which he or his deputy were authorised to cut down any trees in *Whittlebury Forest*, which should appear to be proper for the purposes above-mentioned. The deputy being informed that the warrant was signed and delivered to his principal in London, crosses the country to Northamptonshire, and with an officious zeal for the public service, begins to do his duty in the forest. Unfortunately for him, he had not the warrant in his pocket. The oversight was enormous, and you have punished him for it accordingly. You have insisted that an active, useful officer should be dismissed from his place. You have ruined an innocent man, and his family.—In what language shall I address so black, so cowardly a tyrant;—thou worse than *one* of the *Brunswicks*, and all the *Stuarts!*—To them, who know Lord North, it is unnecessary to say, that he was mean and base enough to submit to you.—This however is but a small part of the fact. After ruining the surveyor's deputy, for acting without the warrant, you attacked the warrant itself. You declared it was illegal, and swore, in a fit of foaming, frantic passion, that it never should be executed. You asserted upon your honour, that in the grant of the rangership of *Whittlebury Forest*, made by *Charles the Second*, (whom, with a modesty that would do honour to Mr. Rigby, you are pleased to call your ancestor) to one of his bastards, (from whom I make no doubt of your descent,) the property of the timber is vested in the ranger.—I have examined the original grant, and now, in the face of the public, contradict you directly upon the fact. The very reverse, of what you have asserted upon your honour is the truth. The grant, *expressly, and by a particular clause*, reserves the property of the timber for the use of the crown.—In spite of this evidence,—in defiance of the representations of the admiralty,—in perfect mockery of the notorious distresses of the English navy, and those equally pressing, and almost equally notorious necessities of your pious Sovereign,—here the matter rests.—The lords of the treasury recal their warrant; the deputy-surveyor is ruined for doing his duty;—Mr. John Pitt, (whose name I suppose is offensive to you) submits to be brow-beaten and insulted;—the oaks keep their ground;—the King is defrauded, and the navy of England may perish for want of the best and finest timber in the island. And all this is submitted to—to appease the Duke of Grafton!—To gratify the man, who has involved the King and his kingdom in confusion and distress, and who, like a treacherous coward, deserted his Sovereign in the midst of it![1]

THERE has been a strange alteration in your doctrines, since you thought it adviseable to rob the *Duke of Portland* of his property, in order to strengthen the interest of Lord *Bute*'s son-in-law, before the last general election.[2] *Nullum tempus occurrit regi*, was then your

[1] A careful and apparently authoritative refutation of Junius' accusation was made by Philalethes in the *Public Advertiser* of 9 and 23 October and 1 November. It asserted that the deputy surveyor-general had undertaken the felling of the trees with unnecessary haste, damaging the underwood and infringing the rights of the local inhabitants. The refutation is printed in full by Wade, i. 403–5. Wade's guess that the letters came from John Pitt, surveyor-general, seems unlikely since they appear to blame the surveyor-general himself. Detailed information on Whittlebury Forest is in *Notes & Queries*, 3rd series, viii. 230–3.

[2] See p. 315 n. 1.

boasted motto, and the cry of all your hungry partizans. Now it seems a grant of *Charles the Second* to one of his bastards is to be held sacred and inviolable! It must not be questioned by the King's servants, nor submitted to any interpretation but your own.—My Lord, this was not the language you held, when it suited you to insult the memory of the glorious deliverer of England from that detested family, to which you are still more nearly allied in principle than in blood.—In the name of decency and common-sense, what are your grace's merits, either with King or ministry, that should intitle you to assume this domineering authority over both?—Is it the fortunate consanguinity you claim with the house of *Stuart?*—Is it the secret correspondence you have for so many years carried on with Lord Bute, by the assiduous assistance of your *cream coloured parasite?*[1]—Could not your gallantry find sufficient employment for him, in those *gentle* offices by which he first acquired the tender friendship of *Lord Barrington?*—Or is it only that wonderful sympathy of manners, which subsists between your Grace and one of your superiors, and does so much honour to you both?—Is the union of *Blifil* and *Black George* no longer a *romance?*[2]—From whatever origin your influence in this country arises, it is a phænomenon in the history of human virtue and understanding.—Good men can hardly believe the fact. Wise men are unable to account for it. Religious men find exercise for their faith, and make it the last effort of their piety, not to repine against providence.

JUNIUS.

The rift in the Society of Supporters of the Bill of Rights and the acrimonious exchanges between reformers gave the government an excellent opportunity to recover some of its influence in the city of London. Its support in the autumn election for Lord Mayor went to William Nash, a salter and the senior alderman. Wilkes attempted to obtain the re-election of Brass Crosby, one of his staunchest supporters. Two members of the anti-Wilkite Constitutional Society offered themselves—John Sawbridge and James Townsend.

[1] Junius' favourite epithet for Bradshaw.

[2] H. Fielding, *The history of Tom Jones* (1749). The reference is discussed in *Notes & Queries*, 1st series, vi. 341, 566, 588.

Junius' interest in the affairs of the city had grown throughout 1771. In August he opened a private correspondence with Wilkes, urging him to switch his support to Sawbridge. In Letter no. LVIII, dated 30 September but published in the *Public Advertiser* on Tuesday, 1 October, Junius begged the liverymen not to vote for Nash. His appeal was unsuccessful. Voting continued for a week and ended on 5 October: Nash gained 2,199 votes, Sawbridge 1,879, Crosby 1,795, Sir Thomas Hallifax 846, James Townsend 151, and Sir Henry Bankes 36. The court of Aldermen then exercised its right of selecting from the first two candidates in favour of Nash, much to the satisfaction of the King, who was convinced that the result would 'greatly tend to restore the tranquillity of this greatest Trading City in the world'. Fortescue, ii, no. 980.

LETTER LVIII.

ADDRESSED TO THE LIVERY OF LONDON.

GENTLEMEN, 30. *Sept.* 1771.

IF *you* alone were concerned in the event of the present election of a chief magistrate of the metropolis, it would be the highest presumption in a stranger, to attempt to influence your choice, or even to offer you his opinion. But the situation of public affairs has annexed an extraordinary importance to your resolutions. You cannot, in the choice of your magistrate, determine for *yourselves only*. You are going to determine upon a point, in which every member of the community is interested. I will not scruple to say, that the very being of that law, of that right, of that constitution, for which we have been so long contending, is now at stake. They, who would ensnare your judgment, tell you, it is a *common*, *ordinary* case, and to be decided by ordinary precedent and practice. They artfully conclude, from moderate peaceable times, to times which *are not* moderate, and which *ought not* to be peaceable.—While they solicit your favour, they insist upon a rule of rotation, which excludes all idea of election.

LET me be honoured with a few minutes of your attention.—The question, to those who mean fairly to the liberty of the people, (which we all profess to have in view) lies within a very narrow compass.—Do you mean to desert that just and honourable system of measures which you have hitherto pursued, in hopes of obtaining from parliament or from the crown, a full redress of past grievances, and a security for the future?—Do you think the cause desperate, and will you declare, that you think so to the whole people of England?—If this be your meaning and opinion, you will act consistently with it, in choosing Mr. *Nash*.—I profess to be unacquainted with his private character. But he has acted as a magistrate,—as a public man.—As such I speak of him,—I see his name in a protest against one of your remonstrances to the crown.—He has done every thing in his power to destroy the freedom of popular elections in the city by publishing the poll upon a former occasion;[1] and I know, in general, that he has distinguished himself, by slighting and thwarting all those public measures, which *you* have engaged in with the greatest warmth, and hitherto thought most worthy of your approbation.—From his past conduct, what conclusion will you draw, but that he will act the same part as *Lord Mayor*, which he has invariably acted as *Alderman* and *Sheriff*? He cannot alter his conduct, without confessing that he never acted upon principle of any kind.—I should be sorry to injure the character of a man, who perhaps may be honest in his intention, by supposing it *possible*, that he can ever concur with you in any political measure, or opinion.

If, on the other hand, you mean to persevere in those resolutions for the public good, which though not always successful, are always honourable, your choice will naturally incline to those men, who, (whatever they be in other respects,) are most likely to co-operate with you in the great purposes which you are determined not to relinquish:—The question is not, of what metal your instruments

[1] Nash had been sheriff at the time of the previous general election in 1768, subsequent to which a poll book was published. This was used against him in the campaign for the Lord Mayoralty, his opponents insisting that the publication of voting enabled pressure to be brought to bear. On 30 September 1771 A Liveryman in the *Public Advertiser* asked rhetorically, 'Was it to injure persons in trade, because they differed from you in opinion?' Wilkes declared that no poll book would be allowed while he was sheriff. *Annual Register*, 1771, 145. Nash's supporters replied that the poll book had been published at the request of the four members for the city of London.

are made, but *whether they are adapted to the work you have in hand?* The honours of the city, *in these times*, are improperly, because exclusively, called a *reward*. You mean not merely to *pay*, but to *employ*.—Are Mr. *Crosby* and Mr. *Sawbridge* likely to execute the extraordinary, as well as the ordinary duties of Lord Mayor?—Will they grant you common halls when it shall be necessary?[1]—Will they go up with remonstrances to the King?—Have they firmness enough to meet the fury of a venal house of commons?—Have they fortitude enough not to shrink at imprisonment?—Have they spirit enough to hazard their lives and fortunes in a contest, if it should be necessary, with a prostituted legislature?—If these questions can fairly be answered in the affirmative, your choice is made. Forgive this passionate language.—I am unable to correct it.—The subject comes home to us all.—It is the language of my heart.

JUNIUS.

This letter, dated 5 October, appeared on 8 October 1771, the day on which the choice of Nash as Lord Mayor testified to the damage done to the popular cause by dissensions. Junius made this the theme of his remarks and his letter was reprinted in the *Gentleman's Magazine* under the heading of 'Junius's Conciliatory Letter'. It is one of his least impressive compositions. The attack upon Lord Mansfield seems out of place, subjects introduced merely as illustrations are discussed at excessive length, and the whole letter is disjointed.

[1] A 'Common Hall' was the term used for an extraordinary meeting of the Liverymen of the city of London called, at the discretion of the Lord Mayor, to discuss public business. It could be used to bypass the Court of Aldermen and the Common Council, where government influence was stronger. In April 1769 Samuel Turner, as Lord Mayor, with the approval of the Common Council, refused to summon a Common Hall. The Liverymen were therefore obliged to wait until their regular meeting on 24 June to elect sheriffs, when they passed a strong resolution complaining of 'intolerable grievances'. This was presented to the King on 5 July but received no reply. It is referred to in public letter no. XV. William Beckford as Lord Mayor was sympathetic to the opposition and granted a Common Hall on 6 March 1770: this produced the remonstrance discussed by Junius in letter no. XXXVII.

The Lord Mayor's willingness to summon a Common Hall became part of the tug-of-war between radicals and moderates in city politics. In a letter reprinted in the *Gentleman's Magazine*, 1770, 113–14, Creon argued that Common Halls were illegal, and the Court treated them as of dubious standing.

Gentleman's Magazine, 1769, 266–7, 317, 329–31, 361–3; 1770, 91–3, 108–15, 139–40.

LETTER LIX.

TO THE PRINTER OF THE PUBLIC ADVERTISER.

SIR, 5. *October*, 1771.

NO man laments, more sincerely than I do, the unhappy differences, which have arisen among the friends of the people, and divided them from each other. The cause undoubtedly suffers, as well by the diminution of that strength, which union carries with it, as by the separate loss of personal reputation, which every man sustains, when his character and conduct are frequently held forth in odious or contemptible colours.——These differences are only advantageous to the common enemy of the country.—The hearty friends of the cause are provoked and disgusted.—The lukewarm advocate avails himself of any pretence to relapse into that indolent indifference about every thing that ought to interest an Englishman, so unjustly dignified with the title of moderation. ——The false, insidious partisan, who creates or foments the disorder, sees the fruit of his dishonest industry ripen beyond his hopes, and rejoices in the promise of a banquet, only delicious to such an appetite as his own.—It is time for those, who really mean the *Cause* and the *People*, who have no view to private advantage, and who have virtue enough to prefer the general good of the community to the gratification of personal animosities,—it is time for such men to interpose.—Let us try whether these fatal dissentions may not yet be reconciled; or, if that be impracticable, let us guard at least against the worst effects of division, and endeavour to persuade these furious partizans, if they will not consent to draw together, to be separately useful to that cause, which they all pretend to be attached to.—Honour and honesty must not be renounced, although a thousand modes of right and wrong were to occupy the degrees of morality between Zeno and Epicurus. The fundamental principles of Christianity may still be preserved, though every zealous sectary adheres to his own exclusive doctrine, and pious Ecclesiastics make it part of their religion to persecute one another.——The civil constitution too, that legal liberty, that general creed, which every Englishman professes, may still be supported, though Wilkes, and Horne, and Townsend, and Sawbridge, should obstinately refuse to communicate, and even if the fathers of the church, if Savil, Richmond, Camden, Rockingham, and Chatham, should disagree in the ceremonies of their political worship, and even in the interpretation of twenty texts in Magna Charta.—I speak to the people as one of the people.—Let us employ these men in whatever departments their various abilities are best suited to, and as much to the advantage of the common cause, as their different inclinations will permit. They cannot serve *us*, without essentially serving themselves.

IF Mr. *Nash* be elected, he will hardly venture, after so recent a mark of the personal esteem of his fellow-citizens, to declare himself immediately a courtier. The spirit and activity of the Sheriffs will, I hope, be sufficient to counteract any sinister intentions of the Lord-Mayor. In collision with *their* virtue, perhaps he may take fire.[1]

IT is not necessary to exact from Mr. Wilkes the virtues of a Stoic. They were inconsistent with themselves, who, almost at the same moment, represented him as the basest of mankind, yet seemed to expect from him such instances of fortitude and self-denial, as would do honour to an apostle. It is not however flattery to say, that he is obstinate, intrepid, and fertile in expedients.—That he has no possible resource, but in the public favour, is, in my judgment, a considerable recommendation of him. I wish that every man, who pretended to popularity, were in the same predicament. I wish that a retreat to St. James's were not so easy and open, as Patriots have found it. To Mr. Wilkes there is no access. However he may be misled by passion or imprudence, I think he cannot be guilty of a deliberate treachery to the public. The favour of his country constitutes the shield, which defends him against a thousand daggers. Desertion would disarm him.[2]

[1] The sheriffs were Wilkes and his ally, Frederick Bull.

[2] Junius redrafted this passage when preparing the collected edition. In the *Public Advertiser*, it ran: 'The favour of his country constitutes the shield which defends him against a thousand daggers. Desertion would disarm him. However he may be misled by passion or imprudence, I think he cannot be guilty of a deliberate treachery to the public.'

I CAN more readily admire the liberal spirit and integrity, than the sound judgment of any man, who prefers a republican form of government, in this or any other empire of equal extent, to a monarchy so qualified and limited as ours. I am convinced, that neither is it in theory the wisest system of government, nor practicable in this country. Yet, though I hope the English constitution will for ever preserve its original monarchical form, I would have the manners of the people purely and strictly republican.—I do not mean the licentious spirit of anarchy and riot.—I mean a general attachment to the common weal, distinct from any partial attachment to persons or families;—an implicit submission to the laws only, and an affection to the magistrate, proportioned to the integrity and wisdom, with which he distributes justice to his people, and administers their affairs. The present habit of our political body appears to me the very reverse of what it ought to be. The form of the constitution leans rather more than enough to the popular branch; while, in effect, the manners of the people (of those at least who are likely to take a lead in the country) incline too generally to a dependance upon the crown. The real friends of arbitrary power combine the facts, and are not inconsistent with their principles, when they strenuously support the unwarrantable privileges assumed by the House of Commons.—In these circumstances, it were much to be desired, that we had many such men as Mr. Sawbridge to represent us in parliament.—I speak from common report and opinion only, when I impute to him a speculative predilection in favour of a republic.—In the personal conduct and manners of the man, I cannot be mistaken. He has shewn himself possessed of that republican firmness, which the times require, and by which an English gentleman may be as usefully and as honourably distinguished, as any citizen of ancient Rome, of Athens, or Lacedæmon.

MR. Townsend complains, that the public gratitude has not been answerable to his deserts.—It is not difficult to trace the artifices, which have suggested to him a language, so unworthy of his understanding. A great man commands the affections of the people. A prudent man does not complain when he has lost them.

Yet they are far from being lost to Mr. Townsend. He has treated our opinion a little too cavalierly. A young man is apt to rely too confidently upon himself, to be as attentive to his mistress, as a polite and passionate lover ought to be. Perhaps he found her at first too easy a conquest.—Yet, I fancy, she will be ready to receive him, whenever he thinks proper to renew his addresses. With all his youth, his spirit, and his appearance, it would be indecent in the lady to solicit his return.

I HAVE too much respect for the abilities of Mr. Horne, to flatter myself that these gentlemen will ever be cordially re-united. It is not, however, unreasonable to expect, that each of them should act his separate part, with honour and integrity to the public.—As for differences of opinion upon speculative questions, if we wait until *they* are reconciled, the action of human affairs must be suspended for ever. But neither are we to look for perfection in any one man, nor for agreement among many.——When *Lord Chatham* affirms, that the authority of the British legislature is not supreme over the colonies, in the same sense in which it is supreme over Great Britain;——when *Lord Camden* supposes a necessity, (which the King is to judge of) and, founded upon that necessity, attributes to the crown a legal power (not given by the act itself) to suspend the operation of an act of the legislature,—I listen to them both with diffidence and respect, but without the smallest degree of conviction or assent. Yet, I doubt not, they delivered their real sentiments, nor ought they to be hastily condemned.—*I too* have a claim to the candid interpretation of my country, when I acknowledge an involuntary, compulsive assent to one very unpopular opinion. I lament the unhappy necessity, whenever it arises, of providing for the safety of the state, by a temporary invasion of the personal liberty of the subject.[1] Would to God it were practicable to reconcile these important objects, in every possible situation of public affairs!—I regard the legal liberty of the meanest man in Britain, as much as my own, and would defend it with the same

[1] This abrupt transition introduced Junius' sentiments on the pressing of seamen, a practice which Wilkes denounced. In private letter no. 76 of 16 October 1771 Junius wrote to Wilkes: 'I see, we do not agree about the strict right of pressing. If you are as sincere as I am, we shall not quarrel about a difference of Opinion.'

zeal. I know we must stand or fall together. But I never can doubt, that the community has a right to command, as well as to purchase, the service of its members. I see that right founded originally upon a necessity, which supersedes all argument. I see it established by usage immemorial, and admitted by more than a tacit assent of the legislature. I conclude there is no remedy, in the nature of things, for the grievance complained of; for, if there were, it must long since have been redressed. Though numberless opportunities have presented themselves, highly favourable to public liberty, no successful attempt has ever been made for the relief of the subject in this article. Yet it has been felt and complained of, ever since England had a navy.—The conditions, which constitute this right, must be taken together. Separately, they have little weight. It is not fair to argue, from any abuse in the execution, to the illegality of the power; much less is a conclusion to be drawn from the navy to the land service. A seaman can never be employed but against the enemies of his country. The only case in which the King can have a right to arm his subjects in general, is that of a foreign force being actually landed upon our coast. Whenever that case happens, no true Englishman will enquire, whether the King's right to compel him to defend his country be the custom of England, or a grant of the legislature. With regard to the press for seamen, it does not follow that the symptoms may not be softened, although the distemper cannot be cured. Let bounties be increased as far as the public purse can support them. Still they have a limit; and when every reasonable expence is incurred, it will be found, in fact, that the spur of the press is wanted to give operation to the bounty.

UPON the whole, I never had a doubt about the strict right of pressing, until I heard that Lord Mansfield had applauded Lord Chatham for delivering something like this doctrine in the house of lords. That consideration staggered me not a little. But, upon reflection, his conduct accounts naturally for itself. He knew the doctrine was unpopular, and was eager to fix it upon the man, who is the first object of his fear and detestation. The cunning Scotchman never speaks truth without a fraudulent design. In council, he generally affects to take a moderate part. Besides his natural timidity, it makes part of his political plan, never to be known to recommend violent measures. When the guards are called forth to murder their fellow-subjects, it is not by the ostensible advice of Lord Mansfield. That odious office, his prudence tells him, is better left to such men as Gower and Weymouth, as Barrington and Grafton. Lord Hillsborough wisely confines *his* firmness to the distant Americans.—The designs of Mansfield are more subtle, more effectual, and secure.—Who attacks the liberty of the press?—Lord Mansfield.—Who invades the constitutional power of juries?—Lord Mansfield.—What judge ever challenged a juryman, but Lord Mansfield?—Who was that judge, who, to save the King's brother, affirmed that a man of the first rank and quality, who obtains a verdict in a suit for criminal conversation, is entitled to no greater damages than the meanest mechanic?—Lord Mansfield.—Who is it makes commissioners of the great seal?—Lord Mansfield.—Who is it forms a decree for those commissioners, deciding against Lord Chatham, and afterwards (finding himself opposed by the judges) declares in parliament, that he never had a doubt that the law was in direct opposition to that decree?—Lord Mansfield.[1]—Who is he, that has made it the study and practice of his life, to undermine and alter the whole system of jurisprudence in the court of King's Bench?—Lord Mansfield. There never existed a man but himself, who answered exactly to so complicated a description. Compared to these enormities, his original attachment to the Pretender, (to whom his dearest brother was confidential secretary) is a virtue of the first magnitude. But the hour of impeachment *will* come, and neither he nor Grafton shall escape me. Now let them make common cause against England and the house of Hanover. A Stuart and a Murray should sympathise with each other.

WHEN I refer to signal instances of unpopular opinions delivered and maintained by men, who may well be supposed to have no

[1] Sir William Pynsent left the estate of Burton Pynsent in Somerset to Lord Chatham in 1765. The will was disputed by relatives and a legal action ensued. It was settled in Chatham's favour by a House of Lords judgement in 1771. J. Brown, *Reports of cases upon appeal and writs of error determined in the High Court of Parliament*, 2nd edn., vii. 453–60.

view but the public good, I do not mean to renew the discussion of such opinions. I should be sorry to revive the dormant questions of *Stamp-act*, *Corn-bill*, or *Press-warrant*. I mean only to illustrate one useful proposition, which it is the intention of this paper to inculcate;—*That we should not generally reject the friendship or services of any man, because he differs from us in a particular opinion.* This will not appear a superfluous caution, if we observe the ordinary conduct of mankind. In public affairs, there is the least chance of a perfect concurrence of sentiment, or inclination. Yet every man is able to contribute something to the common stock, and no man's contribution should be rejected. If individuals have no virtues, their vices may be of use to us. I care not with what principle the new-born patriot is animated, if the measures he supports are beneficial to the community. The nation is interested in his conduct. His motives are his own. The properties of a patriot are perishable in the individual, but there is a quick succession of subjects, and the breed is worth preserving.—The spirit of the Americans may be an useful example to us. Our dogs and horses are only English upon English ground; but patriotism, it seems, may be improved by transplanting.—I will not reject a bill, which tends to confine parliamentary privilege within reasonable bounds, though it should be stolen from the house of Cavendish, and introduced by Mr. Onslow.[1] The features of the infant are a proof of the descent, and vindicate the noble birth from the baseness of the adoption.—I willingly accept of a sarcasm from *Colonel Barrè*, or a simile from *Mr. Burke*. Even the silent vote of *Mr. Calcraft* is worth reckoning in a division.—What though he riots in the plunder of the army, and has only determined to be a patriot, when he could not be a peer?—Let us profit by the assistance of such men, while they are with us, and place them, if it be possible, in the post of danger, to prevent desertion. The wary *Wedderburne*, the pompous *Suffolk* never threw away the scabbard, nor ever went upon a forlorn hope. They always treated the King's servants as men, with whom, some time or other, they might possibly be in friendship.—

[1] 10 George III, c. 50 curtailed privilege of Parliament in respect of legal actions. Surriensis in the *Public Advertiser* of 12 October 1771 denied that Onslow filched the bill from the Cavendishes.

When a man who stands forth for the public, has gone that length, from which there is no practicable retreat,—when he has given that kind of personal offence, which a pious monarch never pardons, I then begin to think him in earnest, and that he never will have occasion to solicit the forgiveness of his country.—But instances of a determination so entire and unreserved are rarely met with. Let us take mankind, *as they are*. Let us distribute the virtues and abilities of individuals, according to the offices they affect, and when they quit the service, let us endeavour to supply their places with better men than we have lost. In this country, there are always candidates enough for popular favour. The temple of *fame* is the shortest passage to riches and preferment.

ABOVE all things, let me guard my countrymen against the meanness and folly of accepting of a trifling or moderate compensation for extraordinary and essential injuries. Our enemies treat us, as the cunning trader does the unskilful Indian. They magnify their generosity, when they give us baubles, of little proportionate value, for ivory and gold. The same house of commons, who robbed the constituent body of their right of free election, who presumed to *make* a law under pretence of *declaring* it, who paid our good King's debts, without once enquiring how they were incurred; who gave thanks for repeated murders committed at home, and for national infamy incurred abroad; who screened *Lord Mansfield*; who imprisoned the magistrates of the metropolis, for asserting the subjects right to the protection of the laws; who erased a judicial record, and ordered all proceedings in a criminal suit to be suspended;—this very house of commons have graciously consented, that their own members may be compelled to pay their debts, and that contested elections shall for the future be determined with some decent regard to the merits of the case.[1] The event of the suit is of no consequence to the crown. While parliaments are septennial, the purchase of the sitting member or of the petitioner makes but the difference of a day.—Concessions, such as these, are of little moment to the sum of things; unless it be to prove, that the

[1] The first act referred to is 10 George III, c. 50. Grenville's Act, 10 George III, c. 16, provided for a less partisan method of dealing with disputed elections.

worst of men are sensible of the injuries they have done us, and perhaps to demonstrate to us the imminent danger of our situation. In the shipwreck of the state, trifles float and are preserved; while every thing solid and valuable sinks to the bottom, and is lost for ever.

JUNIUS.

Junius' belated attempts to reconcile differences were singularly ill rewarded and he suffered the fate of most peacemakers. Truth objected on 12 October to his remarks about Calcraft, and An Old Correspondent on 14 October to his views on the pressing of seamen. A more persistent critic was Scaevola, who accused him on 12 October of misrepresenting Lord Camden's opinion on the proclamation for prohibiting the export of corn. The incident had taken place in the autumn of 1766: the ministry acted while Parliament was in recess and asked for an indemnity as soon as it reassembled. Scaevola argued that Camden's doctrine was perfectly proper since it preserved parliamentary supervision. The consequence was that an unnecessary illustration in Junius' previous letter involved him in fresh disputes. Philo Junius was once more employed in a minor skirmish.

Scaevola was identified in R. Chalmers, *Cyclopaedia of English Literature* as James Macpherson, author of *Ossian* and later member of Parliament for Camelford.

LETTER LX.

TO THE PRINTER OF THE PUBLIC ADVERTISER.

SIR, 15. *October*, 1771.

I AM convinced that *Junius* is incapable of wilfully misrepresenting any man's opinion, and that his inclination leads him to treat *Lord Camden* with particular candour and respect. The doctrine attributed to him by *Junius*, as far as it goes, corresponds with that stated by your correspondent *Scævola*, who seems to make a distinction without a difference. *Lord Camden*, it is agreed, did certainly maintain that, in the recess of parliament, the King, (by which we all mean the *King in council*, or the executive power) might suspend the operation of an act of the legislature; and he founded his doctrine upon a supposed necessity, of which the King, *in the first instance*, must be judge. The lords and commons cannot be judges of it in the first instance, for they do not exist.—Thus far *Junius*.

BUT, says *Scævola*, *Lord Camden* made *parliament*, and not the *King*, judges of the necessity.—That parliament may review the acts of ministers is unquestionable; but there is a wide difference between saying that the crown has a *legal* power, and, that ministers may act *at their peril*. When we say an act is *illegal*, we mean that it is forbidden by a joint resolution of the three estates. How a subsequent resolution of two of those branches can make it *legal ab initio*, will require explanation. If it could, the consequence would be truly dreadful, especially in these times. There is no act of arbitrary power, which the King might not attribute to *necessity*, and for which he would not be secure of obtaining the approbation of his prostituted lords and commons. If Lord *Camden* admits that the subsequent sanction of parliament was necessary to make the proclamation *legal*, why did he so obstinately oppose the bill, which was soon after brought in, for indemnifying all those persons, who had acted under it?—If that bill had not been passed, I am ready to maintain, in direct contradiction to Lord Camden's doctrine, (taken as *Scævola* states it) that a litigious exporter of corn, who had suffered in his property in consequence of the proclamation, might have laid his action against the custom-house officers, and would infallibly have recovered damages.[1] No jury could refuse them; and if I, who am by no means litigious, had been so injured, I would assuredly have instituted a suit in Westminster-hall, on purpose to try the question of right. I would have done it upon a principle of defiance of the pretended power of either or both houses to make declarations inconsistent with law, and I have no doubt, that, with an act of parliament of my side, I should have been too strong for them all. This is the way, in which an Englishman should speak and act, and not suffer dangerous precedents to be established, because the circumstances are favourable or palliating.

WITH regard to Lord *Camden*, the truth is, that he inadvertently over-shot himself, as appears plainly by that unguarded mention

[1] *Parl. Hist.* xvi. 245–313. The indemnity bill passed as 7 George III, c. 7.

of *a tyranny of forty days*, which I myself heard. Instead of asserting that the proclamation was *legal*, he *should* have said, "My lords, I know the proclamation was *illegal*, but I advised it because it was indispensably necessary to save the kingdom from famine, and I submit myself to the justice and mercy of my country."

SUCH language as this would have been manly, rational, and consistent:—not unfit for a lawyer, and every way worthy of a great man.

PHILO JUNIUS.

P.S. IF *Scævola* should think proper to write again upon this subject, I beg of him to give me a *direct* answer, that is, a plain affirmative or negative, to the following questions:—In the interval between the publishing such a proclamation (or order of council) as that in question, and it's receiving the sanction of the two houses, of what nature is it—is it *legal* or *illegal*; or is it neither one nor the other?—I mean to be candid, and will point out to him the consequence of his answer either way.—If it be *legal*, it wants no farther sanction. If it be *illegal*, the subject is not bound to obey it, consequently it is a useless, nugatory act, even as to it's declared purpose. Before the meeting of parliament, the whole mischief, which it means to prevent, will have been compleated.

Scaevola replied on 24 October, conceding that Camden's view of the matter seemed wrong: 'The shade between his erroneous doctrine and the true one being in sense and reason hardly distinguishable; both doctrines admit the proclamation to be illegal, and at the minister's peril till the meeting of Parliament—both doctrines admit the two Houses of Parliament (in this or that mode) sole judges of the necessity—both doctrines agree in exposing the minister to impeachment if the two Houses of Parliament should decide against his plea of necessity. Whether upon the declaration of necessity the act becomes good in law *ab initio*, or not, is the only question. Locke (no Tory) holds the affirmative. The law, in my opinion, strictly taken, is in the negative . . .'

The *Public Advertiser* on the 25th carried two questions to Scaevola, presumably from Junius:

'1st. In what part of Mr. Locke's writings is it maintained that the king may suspend an act of parliament, and that the subsequent approbation of the two Houses makes the suspension legal *ab initio*, or to that effect?

'2nd. Does Scaevola think that an act of the whole legislature is as easily obtained and completed as a vote of the Lords or Commons?—The rest is a dispute about words not worth continuing.'

Junius' letter no. LIX also prompted a defence of Lord Mansfield in the *Public Advertiser* of the 15th by Zeno. The address to 'Junius, alias Edmund the Jesuit of St Omer's' was an insinuation against Edmund Burke, believed by many to be Junius. 'Why', asked Zeno, 'in a letter professedly written to reconcile the patriots of the city do you make a digression to abuse Lord Mansfield? . . . Nothing more likely to reconcile rogues who rail at each other than railing at honest men.' Zeno's letter is printed in full in Wade, i. 421–5.

LETTER LXI.

TO ZENO.

SIR, 17. *Oct.* 1771.

THE sophistry of your letter in defence of *Lord Mansfield* is adapted to the character you defend. But *Lord Mansfield* is a man of *form*, and seldom in his behaviour transgresses the rules of decorum. I shall imitate his lordship's good manners, and leave *you* in the full possession of his principles. I will not call you *liar*, *jesuit*, or *villain*; but, with all the politeness imaginable, perhaps I may prove you so.

LIKE other fair pleaders in *Lord Mansfield*'s school of justice, you answer *Junius* by misquoting his words, and mistating his propositions. If I am candid enough to admit that this is the very logic taught at *St. Omer*'s, you will readily allow that it is the constant practice in the court of *King's Bench*.

—JUNIUS *does not say*, that he never had a doubt about the strict right of pressing, *till he knew Lord Mansfield was of the same opinion.* His words are, *until he heard that Lord Mansfield had applauded Lord Chatham for maintaining that doctrine in the house of lords.* It was not the accidental concurrence of Lord Mansfield's opinion, but the suspicious applause given by a cunning Scotchman to the man he detests, that raised and justified a doubt in the mind of *Junius*. The question is not, whether Lord Mansfield be a man of learning and abilities (which *Junius* has never disputed,) but whether or no he abuses and misapplies his talents.

Junius did *not* say that Lord Mansfield had advised the calling out the guards. On the contrary, his plain meaning is, that he left that odious office to men less cunning than himself.—Whether Lord Mansfield's doctrine concerning libels be or be not an attack upon the liberty of the press, is a question, which the public in general are very well able to determine. I shall not enter into it at present. Nor do I think it necessary to say much to a man, who had the daring confidence to say to a jury, "Gentlemen, you are to bring in a verdict *guilty* or *not guilty*, but whether the defendant be guilty or innocent is not matter for *your* consideration." Cloath it in what language you will, this is the sum total of Lord Mansfield doctrine. If not, let *Zeno* shew us the difference.

BUT it seems, *the liberty of the press may be abused*, and *the abuse of a valuable privilege is the certain means to lose it*. The *first* I admit,—but let the *abuse* be submitted to a jury, a sufficient and indeed the only legal and constitutional check upon the licence of the press. The *second*, I flatly deny. In direct contradiction to *Lord Mansfield* I affirm that "the abuse of a valuable privilege *is not* the *certain* means to lose it." If it were, the English nation would have few privileges left, for where is the privilege that has not, at one time or other, been abused by individuals. But it is false in reason and equity, that particular abuses should produce a general forfeiture. Shall the community be deprived of the protection of the laws because there are robbers and murderers?—Shall the community be punished, because individuals have offended. Lord Mansfield says so, consistently enough with his principles, but I wonder to find him so explicit. Yet, for one concession, however extorted, I confess myself obliged to him.—The liberty of the press is after all a *valuable privilege*. I agree with him most heartily, and will defend it against him.

YOU ask me, What *juryman* was challenged by Lord Mansfield?—I tell you, his name was *Benson*. When his name was called, Lord

Mansfield ordered the clerk to pass him by. As for his reasons, you may ask himself, for he assigned none. But I can tell you what all men thought of it. This *Benson* had been refractory upon a former jury, and would not accept of the law as delivered by Lord Mansfield; but had the impudence to pretend to think for himself.—But you it seems, honest *Zeno*, know nothing of the matter! You never read *Junius*'s letter to your patron! You never heard of the intended instructions from the city to impeach Lord Mansfield!—You never heard by what dexterity of *Mr. Paterson* that measure was prevented! How wonderfully ill some people are informed![1]

Junius did *never* affirm that the crime, of seducing the wife of a mechanic or a peer, is not the same, taken in a moral or religious view. What he affirmed in contradiction to the levelling principle so lately adopted by Lord Mansfield was, *that the damages should be proportioned to the rank and fortune of the parties*; and for this plain reason; (admitted by every other judge that ever sat in Westminster Hall) because, what is a compensation or penalty to one man is none to another. The sophistical distinction you attempt to draw between the person *injured*, and the person *injuring* is *Mansfield* all over. If you can once establish the proposition that the injured party is not intitled to *receive* large damages, it follows pretty plainly that the party *injuring* should not be compelled to *pay* them; consequently the King's brother is effectually screened by *Lord Mansfield*'s doctrine. Your reference to *Nathan* and *David* come naturally in aid of your patron's professed system of jurisprudence. He is fond of introducing into the *court of King's Bench* any law that contradicts or excludes the common law of England; whether it be *canon*, *civil*, *jus gentium*, or *levitical*. But, Sir, the Bible is the code of our religious faith, not of our municipal jurisprudence; and though it was the pleasure of God to inflict a particular punishment upon David's crime (taken as a breach of his divine commands) and to send his prophet to denounce it, an English jury have nothing to do either with David or the prophet. They consider the crime, only

[1] Junius referred to Benson in his letter to Mansfield of 14 November 1770. John Paterson was a well-known government supporter in the city and had been the member for Ludgershall 1761–8.

as it is a breach of order, an injury to an individual, and an offence to society, and they judge of it by certain positive rules of law, or by the practice of their ancestors. Upon the whole, the man, *after God's own heart* is much indebted to you for comparing him to the Duke of Cumberland. That his Royal Highness may be the man after *Lord Mansfield*'s own heart seems much more probable, and you I think *Mr. Zeno*, might succeed tolerably well in the character of *Nathan*. The evil deity, the prophet, and the royal sinner would be very proper company for one another.

YOU say Lord Mansfield did not *make* the commissioners of the Great Seal, and that he only advised the King to appoint. I believe *Junius* meant no more, and the distinction is hardly worth disputing.—

YOU say he *did not* deliver an opinion upon Lord Chatham's appeal.—I affirm that he *did*, directly in favour of the appeal. This is a point of fact, to be determined by evidence only. But you assign no reason for his supposed silence, nor for his desiring a conference with the judges the day before. Was not all Westminster-hall convinced that he did it with a view to puzzle them with some perplexing question, and in hopes of bringing some of them over to him?—You say the commissioners were *very capable of framing a decree for themselves*. By the fact, it only appears, that they were capable of framing an *illegal* one, which, I apprehend, is not much to the credit either of their learning or integrity.

WE are both agreed that *Lord Mansfield* has incessantly laboured to introduce new modes of proceeding in the court where he presides; but *you* attribute it to an honest zeal in behalf of innocence oppressed by quibble and chicane. I say that he has introduced *new law* too, and removed the landmarks established by former decisions. I say that his view is to change a court of common law into a court of equity, and to bring every thing within the *arbitrium* of a *prætorian* court. The public must determine between us. *But now for his merits. First* then, the establishment of the judges in their places for life, (which you tell us was advised by Lord Mansfield) was a concession merely to catch the people. It bore the appearance of a royal bounty, but had nothing real in it.[1] The judges were already for life, excepting in the case of a *demise*. Your boasted bill only provides that it shall not be in the power of the King's successor to remove them. At the best therefore, it is only a legacy, not a gift on the part of his present Majesty, since for himself, he gives up nothing.—That he did oppose *Lord Camden* and *Lord Northington* upon the proclamation against the exportation of corn, is most true, and with great ability. With his talents, and taking the right side of so clear a question, it was impossible to speak ill.—His motives are not so easily penetrated. They, who are acquainted with the state of politics, at that period, will judge of them somewhat differently from *Zeno*. Of the popular bills, which you say he supported in the house of lords, the most material is unquestionably that of *Mr. Grenville*, for deciding contested elections. But I should be glad to know upon what possible pretence any member of the upper house could oppose such a bill, after it had passed the *house of commons?*—I do not pretend to know what share he had in promoting the other two bills, but I am ready to give him all the credit you desire.[2] Still you will find that a whole life of deliberate iniquity is ill atoned for by doing now and then a laudable action upon a mixed or doubtful principle.—If it be unworthy of him, thus ungratefully treated, to labour any longer for the public, in God's name let him retire. His brother's patron, (whose health he once was anxious for) is dead, but the son of that unfortunate prince survives, and, I dare say, will be ready to receive him.[3]

PHILO JUNIUS.

The views Junius expressed on the pressing of seamen were attacked on 16 October 1771 by An Advocate in the cause of the People. Conceding that Junius was 'the greatest reformer of our political creed', An Advocate condemned him for resting his defence of pressing on 'necessity and usage immemorial'. An Advocate was John Hope, member for Linlithgowshire

[1] This was 1 George III, c. 23.

[2] Zeno's references were to the bill to curtail privilege of Parliament and the Nullum Tempus bill.

[3] The Old Pretender died in 1766; Prince Charles Edward survived until 1788.

1768–70. He reprinted his four letters on the subject in *Thoughts in prose and verse*, published 1780. His introduction claimed that 'though I pretend not to say that Junius thought himself in the argument foiled, certain it is, he deemed them not equally deserving of a republication with the letters of Sir William Draper and the Reverend Mr. Horne.'

LETTER LXII.

TO AN ADVOCATE IN THE CAUSE OF THE PEOPLE.

SIR, 18. *October*, 1771.

YOU do not treat *Junius* fairly. You would not have condemned him so hastily, if you had ever read *Judge Foster*'s argument upon the legality of pressing seamen.[1] A man who has not read that argument, is not qualified to speak accurately upon the subject. In answer to strong facts and fair reasoning, you produce nothing but a vague comparison between two things, which have little or no resemblance to each other. *General Warrants*, it is true, had been often issued, but they had never been regularly questioned or resisted, until the case of *Mr. Wilkes*. He brought them to trial, and the moment they were tried, they were declared *illegal*. This is not the case of *Press Warrants*. They have been complained of, questioned, and resisted in a thousand instances; but still the legislature have never interposed, nor has there ever been a formal decision against them in any of the superior courts. On the contrary, they have been frequently recognized and admitted by parliament, and there are judicial opinions given in their favour, by judges of the first character. Under the various circumstances, stated by *Junius*, he has a right to conclude, *for himself*, that there is no remedy. If you have a good one to propose, you may depend upon the assistance and applause of *Junius*. The magistrate, who guards the liberty of the individual, deserves to be commended. But let him remember that it is also his duty to provide for, or at least not to hazard the safety of the community. If, in the case of a foreign war and the expectation of an invasion, you would rather

[1] *A report of some proceedings on the commission for the trial of the rebels in the year 1746 and of other crown cases, by Sir Michael Foster*, ed. M. Dodson, 2nd edn. 1776, pp. 157–80, the case of Alexander Broadfoot.

keep your fleet in harbour, than man it by pressing seamen, who refuse the bounty, I have done.

YOU talk of disbanding the army with wonderful ease and indifference. If a wiser man held such language, I should be apt to suspect his sincerity.

AS for keeping up a *much greater* number of seamen in time of peace, it is not to be done. You will oppress the merchant, you will distress trade, and destroy the nursery of your seamen. He must be a miserable statesman, who voluntarily, by the same act increases the public expence, and lessens the means of supporting it.

PHILO JUNIUS.

A Barrister at Law joined in the defence of Lord Mansfield with a letter in the *Public Advertiser* of 19 October 1771. He denied that Mansfield could have challenged a juror without providing grounds for a retrial; Junius' own letters showed that the liberty of the press was still intact. The full text is given in Wade, i. 432–5.

LETTER LXIII.

22. *October*, 1771.

A FRIEND of *Junius* desires it may be observed, (in answer to *A Barrister at Law*)

1°. THAT the fact of Lord Mansfield's having ordered a juryman to be passed by (which poor *Zeno* never heard of) is now formally admitted. When *Mr. Benson*'s name was called, *Lord Mansfield* was observed to flush in the face, (a signal of guilt not uncommon with him) and cried out, *Pass him by*. This I take to be something more than a peremptory challenge. It is an *unlawful command*, without any reason assigned. That the council did not resist, is true; but this might happen either from inadvertence, or a criminal complaisance to Lord Mansfield.—You *Barristers* are too apt to be civil to my Lord Chief Justice, at the expence of your clients.

2°. *Junius* did never say that Lord Mansfield had *destroyed* the liberty of the press. "That his lordship has *laboured to destroy*,—that his doctrine is an *attack* upon the liberty of the press,—that it is an *invasion* of the right of juries," are the propositions maintained by *Junius*. His opponents never answer him in point, for they never meet him fairly upon his own ground.

3°. *Lord Mansfield*'s policy, in endeavouring to screen his unconstitutional doctrines behind an act of the legislature, is easily understood.—Let every Englishman stand upon his guard;—the right of juries to return a general verdict, in all cases whatsoever, is a part of our constitution. It stands in no need of a bill, either *enacting* or *declaratory*, to confirm it.[1]

4°. WITH regard to the *Grosvenor cause*, it is pleasant to observe that the doctrine attributed by *Junius* to Lord Mansfield, is admitted by *Zeno* and directly defended. The *Barrister* has not the assurance to deny it flatly, but he evades the charge and softens the doctrine by such poor, contemptible quibbles, as cannot impose upon the meanest understanding.

5°. THE quantity of business in the *court of King's Bench* proves nothing but the litigious spirit of the people, arising from the great increase of wealth and commerce. These however are now upon the decline, and will soon leave nothing but *law suits* behind them. When *Junius* affirms that Lord Mansfield has laboured to alter the system of jurisprudence, in the court where his lordship presides, he speaks to those, who are able to look a little farther than the vulgar. Besides that the multitude are easily deceived by the imposing names of *equity* and *substantial justice*, it does not follow that a judge, who introduces into his court new modes of proceeding, and new principles of law, intends, *in every instance*, to decide unjustly. Why should he, where he has no interest?—We say that Lord Mansfield is a bad *man*, and a worse *judge*;—but we do not say that he is a *mere devil*. Our adversaries would fain reduce us to

[1] A Barrister at Law had argued that Lord Mansfield stated the law on juries as clearly as possible so that those who objected could bring forward a bill. On 7 March 1771 William Dowdeswell moved for leave to bring in a bill 'for settling doubts and controversies concerning the right of jurors'. The opposition was divided on the subject, many members holding, with Junius, that no bill was necessary, and the motion was defeated by 218 votes to 72. *Parl. Hist.* xvii. 43–58.

the difficulty of proving too much.—This artifice however shall not avail him. The truth of the matter is plainly this. When *Lord Mansfield* has succeeded in his scheme of changing a court of *common law* to a court of *equity*, he will have it in his power to do injustice, *whenever he thinks proper*. This, though a wicked purpose, is neither absurd nor unattainable.

6°. THE last paragraph, relative to *Lord Chatham*'s cause cannot be answered. It partly refers to facts, of too secret a nature to be ascertained and partly is unintelligible. "Upon *one* point, the cause is decided against Lord Chatham.—Upon *another* point, it is decided for him."—Both the *law* and the *language* are well suited to a *Barrister!*—If I have any guess at this honest gentleman's meaning, it is, that, "whereas the commissioners of the Great Seal saw the question in a point of view unfavourable to *Lord Chatham*, and decreed accordingly,—Lord Mansfield, out of sheer love and kindness to Lord Chatham, took the pains to place it in a point of view more favourable to the *appellant*."—*Credat Judæus Apella.*—So curious an assertion would stagger the faith of *Mr. Sylva.*[1]

Nearly a month after its publication, Junius was still trying to extricate himself from the difficulties caused by his 'conciliatory' letter no. LIX.

LETTER LXIV.

2. *November*, 1771.

WE are desired to make the following declaration, in behalf of *Junius*, upon three material points, on which his opinion has been mistaken, or misrepresented.

1°. *Junius* considers the right of taxing the colonies, by an act of the British Legislature, as a *speculative* right merely, never to be

[1] The quotation is from Horace, *Satires*, I. v. 100: 'Let Apella the Jew believe that, if he will'—i.e. a likely story! Isaac Fernandes Sylva was a Jewish moneylender from whom Wilkes borrowed in 1761, giving him worthless guarantees. Horne raised the matter again in his newspaper exchanges with Wilkes in the summer of 1771, accusing him of cheating the Jew. Junius used Sylva as an extreme example of human credulity.

exerted, nor ever to be *renounced.* To *his* judgment it appears plain, "That the general reasonings, which were employed against that power, went directly to our whole legislative right, and that one part of it could not be yielded to such arguments, without a virtual surrender of all the rest."

2°. THAT, with regard to press-warrants, his argument should be taken in his own words, and answered strictly;—that comparisons may sometimes illustrate, but prove nothing; and that, in this case, an appeal to the passions is unfair and unnecessary. *Junius* feels and acknowledges the evil in the most express terms, and will shew himself ready to concur in any rational plan, that may provide for the liberty of the individual, without hazarding the safety of the community. At the same time, he expects that the evil, such as it is, be not exaggerated or misrepresented. In general, it is *not* unjust that, when the rich man contributes his wealth, the *poor* man should serve the state in person;—otherwise the latter contributes nothing to the defence of that law and constitution, from which he demands safety and protection. But the question does not lye between *rich* and *poor*. The laws of England make no such distinctions. Neither is it true that the poor man is torn from the care and support of a wife and family, helpless without him. The single question is, whether the *seaman**, in times of public danger, shall serve the merchant or the state, in that profession to which he was bred, and by the exercise of which alone he can honestly support himself and his family.—General arguments against the doctrine of *necessity*, and the dangerous use that may be made of it, are of no weight in this particular case. *Necessity* includes the idea of *inevitable*. Whenever it is so, it creates a law, to which all *positive* laws, and all *positive* rights must give way. In this sense the levy of *ship-money* by the King's warrant was not *necessary*, because the business might have been as well or better done by parliament. If the doctrine, maintained by *Junius*, be confined within this limitation, it will go but very little way in support of arbitrary power. That the King is to judge of the occasion, is no objection, unless we are told how it can possibly be

* I confine myself strictly to *seamen*;—if any others are pressed, it is a gross abuse, which the magistrate can and should correct.

otherwise. There are other instances, not less important in the exercise nor less dangerous in the abuse, in which the constitution relies entirely upon the King's judgment. The executive power proclaims war and peace, binds the nation by treaties, orders general embargoes, and imposes quarantines, not to mention a multitude of prerogative writs, which, though liable to the greatest abuses, were never disputed.

3°. IT has been urged, as a reproach to *Junius*, that he has not delivered an opinion upon the Game Laws, and particularly the late *Dog-act.*[1] But *Junius* thinks he has much greater reason to complain, that he is never assisted by those, who are able to assist him, and that almost the whole labour of the press is thrown upon a single hand, from which a discussion of *every* public question whatsoever is unreasonably expected. He is not paid for his labour, and certainly has a right to choose his employment.——[2] As to the *Game Laws*, he never scrupled to declare his opinion, that they are a species of the *Forest Laws*, that they are oppressive to the subject, and that the spirit of them is incompatible with legal liberty:—that the penalties, imposed by these laws, bear no proportion to the nature of the offence, that the mode of trial and the degree and kind of evidence necessary to convict, not only deprive the subject of all the benefits of a trial by jury, but are in themselves too summary, and to the last degree arbitrary and oppressive. That, in particular, the late acts to prevent dog-stealing, or killing game between sun and sun, are distinguished by their absurdity, extravagance, and pernicious tendency.[3] If these terms are weak, or ambigu-

[1] There is a long attack upon the Dog Act, 10 George III, c. 18, in the *Gentleman's Magazine*, 1770, 163–5. Philetymus in the *Public Advertiser* of 29 October 1771 criticized Junius' 'total silence' on the matter, and Philo-Patriae, the following day, defended Mansfield, arguing that he was absent when the act passed.

[2] Junius complained to Wilkes in private letter no. 80: 'No man writes under so many disadvantages as I do. I cannot consult the learned,—I cannot directly ask the opinion of my acquaintance, and in the newspapers I never am assisted.'

[3] The killing of game was prohibited, under an act of 1671, to all except owners of land worth £100 p.a., lessees worth £150 p.a., and persons of high degree. No fewer than thirty-two acts of Parliament were passed in George III's reign to regulate the preservation of game: the 'poaching war' was a constant irritant in country life. The Dog Act aimed at preventing the stealing of dogs, provided for a fine of up to £50 at the second offence, and allowed magistrates to issue warrants to search

ous, in what language can *Junius* express himself? —It is no excuse for *Lord Mansfield* to say that he *happened* to be absent when these bills passed the house of lords. It was his duty to be present. Such bills could never have passed the house of commons without his knowledge. But we very well know by what rule he regulates his attendance. When that order was made in the house of lords in the case of *Lord Pomfret*, at which every Englishman shudders, my honest *Lord Mansfield* found himself, *by mere accident*, in the court of king's bench.—[1] Otherwise, he would have done wonders in defence of law and property! The pitiful evasion is adapted to the character. But *Junius* will never justify himself, by the example of this bad man. The distinction between *doing wrong*, and *avoiding to do right* belongs to Lord Mansfield. *Junius* disclaims it.

For many months Junius had nursed the ambition of bringing Lord Mansfield to ruin and in October 1771 saw what he regarded as an opportunity. John Eyre, a man of considerable private means, was caught on 2 October stealing large quantities of paper from the Guildhall, which he attended on the plea that he was studying law. Alderman Hallifax and the Lord Mayor both refused bail on the grounds that Eyre had been taken in the act. Lord Mansfield granted bail on 19 October and despite reports that Eyre had fled, he duly presented himself for trial on 1 November, pleading guilty. He was sentenced to transportation. The matter had already been the subject of much newspaper comment when Junius entered the fray with his challenge to Mansfield: 'The above to that Scotchman should be printed conspicuously tomorrow', he told Woodfall on 1 November (private letter no. 40).

for stolen dogs. The act for the better preservation of game at night, 10 George III, c. 19, provided for six months' imprisonment at first offence and double, with a public whipping, for any subsequent offence. It was much criticized and was repealed in 1773 by 13 George III, c. 80. These matters are discussed in Chapter XII of E. W. Bovill, *English country life, 1780–1830* (1962), in Chapter 5 of *Albion's Fatal Tree*, ed. D. Hay, P. Linebaugh, and E. P. Thompson (1975), and in E. P. Thompson, *Whigs and Hunters: the origins of the Waltham Black Act* (1975). Critics pointed out that a countryman needed fifty times as much property to entitle him to kill game as he did to cast a vote as a forty-shilling freeholder.

[1] Lord Pomfret was party in a protracted legal action over the Beldy Hill lead-mine in Swaledale, Yorkshire. On 5 March 1771 the House of Lords allowed him a retrial, but the final verdict went against him. J. Brown, *Reports of cases*, iv. 700–8; vii. 169–76; *Gentleman's Magazine*, 1772, 148, 539, 595.

LETTER LXV.

TO LORD CHIEF JUSTICE MANSFIELD.

2. *November*, 1771.

AT the intercession of three of your countrymen, you have bailed a man, who, I presume, is also a *Scotchman*, and whom the Lord Mayor of London had refused to bail. I do not mean to enter into an examination of the partial, sinister motives of your conduct; but confining myself strictly to the fact, I affirm, that you have done that, which by law you were not warranted to do. The thief was taken in the theft;—the stolen goods were found upon him, and he made no defence. In these circumstances, (the truth of which You dare not deny, because it is of public notoriety) it could not stand indifferent whether he was guilty or not, much less could there be any presumption of his innocence; and, in these circumstances, I affirm, in contradiction to YOU, LORD CHIEF JUSTICE MANSFIELD, that, by the laws of England, he was *not bailable*. If ever *Mr. Eyre* should be brought to trial, we shall hear what You have to say for Yourself; and I pledge myself, before God and my country, in proper time and place to make good my charge against you.

JUNIUS.

When Junius wrote his first challenge he did not know that Eyre was coming up for trial so soon. On 6 November he wrote urgently to Wilkes for 'the most exact account' of the proceedings against Eyre and 'any Observations of your own that you think material' (private letter no. 80). Three days later, he acknowledged Wilkes's reply, adding: 'The facts are as I understood them, and, with the blessing of God, I will pull Mansfield to the ground' (private letter no. 83). He then repeated his public challenge.

LETTER LXVI.

TO THE PRINTER OF THE PUBLIC ADVERTISER.

9. *November* 1771.

JUNIUS engages to make good his charge against *Lord Chief Justice Mansfield*, some time before the meeting of parliament, in order that the house of commons may, if they think proper, make it one article in the impeachment of the said *Lord Chief Justice.*

While preparing the grand indictment of Mansfield, Junius resumed his campaign against the Duke of Grafton, which had been much interrupted by the skirmish with Horne and the incursion into city politics.

LETTER LXVII.

TO HIS GRACE THE DUKE OF GRAFTON.

27. *Nov.* 1771.

WHAT is the reason, my Lord, that, when almost every man in the kingdom, without distinction of principles or party, exults in the ridiculous defeat of Sir James Lowther, when good and bad men unite in one common opinion of that baronet, and triumph in his distress, as if the event (without any reference to vice or virtue) were interesting to human nature, your Grace alone should appear so miserably depressed and afflicted?[1] In such

[1] The long-standing dispute between the Duke of Portland and Sir James Lowther was decided before the Barons of the Exchequer on 20 November 1771. In 1767 the forest of Inglewood in Cumberland had been granted by the crown to Sir James Lowther in defiance of the claim by the Duke of Portland that it had been in the possession of his family since the reign of William III. The great public feeling about the transaction arose mainly from three considerations: the almost unique unpopularity of Sir James himself; the use of a crown prerogative, a year before a general election, to swing electoral influence from an opponent to a supporter; and the reputed danger to all private property if long and undisputed tenure could be set aside. 'The principle of this grant', wrote Mnemon in the *Public Advertiser* of 24 February 1768, 'has given a shock to the whole landed property of England.' The crown lawyers argued, in the words of an ancient maxim, that 'Nullum tempus

universal joy, I know not where you will look for a compliment of condoleance, unless you appeal to the tender, sympathetic sorrows of Mr. Bradshaw. That cream-coloured gentleman's tears, affecting as they are, carry consolation along with them. He never weeps, but, like an April shower, with a lambent ray of sunshine upon his countenance. From the feelings of honest men, upon this joyful occasion, I do not mean to draw any conclusion to your Grace. *They* naturally rejoice, when they see a signal instance of tyranny resisted with success;—of treachery exposed to the derision of the world;—an infamous informer defeated, and an impudent robber dragged to the public gibbet.—But, in the *other* class of mankind, I own I expected to meet the Duke of Grafton. Men, who have no regard for justice, nor any sense of honour, seem as heartily pleased with Sir James Lowther's well deserved punishment, as if it did not constitute an example against themselves. The unhappy Baronet has no friends, even among those who resemble him. You, my Lord, are not reduced to so deplorable a state of dereliction. Every villain in the kingdom is your friend; and, in compliment to such amity, I think you should suffer your dismal countenance to clear up. Besides, my Lord;—I am a little anxious for the consistency of your character. You violate your own rules of decorum, when you do not insult the man, whom you have betrayed.

THE divine justice of retribution seems now to have begun its progress. Deliberate treachery entails punishment upon the traitor. There is no possibility of escaping it, even in the highest rank, to which the consent of society can exalt the meanest and worst of men. The forced, unnatural union of Luttrell and Middlesex was an omen of another unnatural union, by which indefeasible infamy is attached to the house of Brunswick.[1] If one of those acts was

occurrit regi'—no length of tenure holds good against the crown. The matter was repeatedly raised in Parliament, and in 1769 the Nullum Tempus Act—9 George III, c. 16—was passed, limiting the crown's power of challenging possession. The decision in November 1771 went in favour of the Duke of Portland on a technicality.

[1] The reference is to the Duke of Cumberland's marriage with Mrs. Horton, sister of Colonel Luttrell. The ceremony took place on 4 October 1771. The news was given in the *Public Advertiser* of 8 November 1771 under the heading *Intelligence Extraordinary, though true.*

virtuous and honourable, the best of princes, I thank God, is happily rewarded for it by the other. —Your Grace, *it has been said*, had some share in recommending Colonel Luttrell to the King;—or was it only the gentle Bradshaw, who made himself answerable for the good behaviour of his friend? An intimate connexion has long subsisted between him and the worthy Lord Irnham. It arose from a fortunate similarity of principles, cemented by the constant mediation of their common friend Miss Davis*.

* There is a certain family in this country, on which nature seems to have entailed an hereditary baseness of disposition. As far as their history has been known, the son has regularly improved upon the vices of his father, and has taken care to transmit them pure and undiminished into the bosom of his successor. In the senate, their abilities have confined them to those humble, sordid services, in which the scavengers of the ministry are usually employed. But in the memoirs of private treachery, they stand first and unrivalled. The following story will serve to illustrate the character of this respectable family, and to convince the world that the present possessor has as clear a title to the infamy of his ancestors, as he has to their estate. It deserves to be recorded for the curiosity of the fact, and should be given to the public as a warning to every honest member of society.

The present Lord Irnham, who is now in the decline of life, lately cultivated the acquaintance of a younger brother of a family, with which he had lived in some degree of intimacy and friendship. The young man had long been the dupe of a most unhappy attachment to a common prostitute. His friends and relations foresaw the consequences of this connexion, and did every thing that depended upon them to save him from ruin. But he had a friend in Lord Irnham, whose advice rendered all their endeavours ineffectual. This hoary letcher, not contented with the enjoyment of his friend's mistress, was base enough to take advantage of the passions and folly of a young man, and persuaded him to marry her. He descended even to perform the office of father to the prostitute. He gave her to his friend, who was on the point of leaving the kingdom, and the next night lay with her himself.

Whether the depravity of the human heart can produce any thing more base and detestable than this fact, must be left undetermined, until the son shall arrive at his father's age and experience.[1]

---

[1] This footnote first appeared in the *Public Advertiser* of 7 April 1769 under the signature of Recens. The anecdote about Polly Davis is also given in Cumbriensis's letter of 13 November 1771: there are strong reasons for thinking that Cumbriensis was Junius. Simon, 1st Baron Irnham, was the father of Colonel Luttrell. It was not a popular family. Lady Louisa Stuart wrote that Lord Irnham was 'the greatest reprobate in England' and relates that when he once challenged Colonel Luttrell to a duel, the son replied that he was willing if his father could find any gentleman to act as second. *The Letters and Journals of Lady Mary Coke*, ed. J. A. Home (1889–96), i. p. xcv.

L. D. Campbell, *The miscellaneous works of Hugh Boyd* (1800), i. 18, 146, identified the young man as a younger brother of Cosby and Arnold Nesbitt. This would suggest William Nesbitt (1732–76), an army officer, though he is said to have married Mary Blackwood. C. and A. Nesbitt, *History of the family of Nisbet or Nesbitt in Scotland and Ireland* (1898), 58.

YET I confess I should be sorry that the opprobrious infamy of this match should reach beyond the family.—We have now a better reason than ever to pray for the long life of the best of princes, and the welfare of his royal *issue*.—I will not mix any thing ominous with my prayers;—but let parliament look to it.—A *Luttrell* shall never succeed to the crown of England.—If the hereditary virtues of the family deserve a kingdom, Scotland will be a proper retreat for them.

THE next is a most remarkable instance of the goodness of providence. The just law of retaliation has at last overtaken the little, contemptible tyrant of the North.[1] To this son-in-law of your dearest friend the Earl of Bute, you meant to transfer the Duke of Portland's property; and you hastened the grant, with an expedition unknown to the Treasury, that he might have it time enough to give a decisive turn to the election for the county. The immediate consequence of this flagitious robbery was, that he lost the election, which you meant to insure to him, and with such signal circumstances of scorn, reproach, and insult, (to say nothing of the general exultation of all parties) as, (excepting the King's brother-in-law Col. Luttrell, and old *Simon* his father-in-law) hardly ever fell upon a gentleman in this country.[2]—In the event, he loses the very property, of which he thought he had gotten possession; and after an expence, which would have paid the value of the land in question twenty times over.—The forms of villainy, you see, are necessary to its success. Hereafter you will act with greater circumspection, and not drive so directly to your object. To *snatch a grace*, beyond the reach of common treachery, is an exception, not a rule.

AND now, my good Lord, does not your conscious heart inform you, that the justice of retribution begins to operate, and that it

[1] Sir James Lowther.

[2] The best account of the Cumberland contest of 1768 is to be found in B. Bonsall, *Sir James Lowther and Cumberland & Westmorland elections, 1754–75* (1960), ch. X. The Lowther interest had held both seats for Cumberland since 1754. At the 1768 general election the poll was open for nineteen days and more than 4,000 freeholders voted. Humphrey Senhouse, standing with Lowther, came bottom of the poll, and, though Lowther was returned, he lost the seat to Henry Fletcher on petition. At the subsequent general election in 1774, Lowther succeeded in recapturing his own seat.

may soon approach your person?—Do you think that *Junius* has renounced the Middlesex election?—Or that the King's timber shall be refused to the Royal Navy with impunity?—Or that you shall hear no more of the sale of that patent to *Mr. Hine*, which you endeavoured to skreen by suddenly dropping your prosecution of *Samuel Vaughan*, when the rule against him was made absolute? I believe indeed there never was such an instance in all the history of negative impudence.—But it shall not save you. The very sunshine you live in is a prelude to your dissolution. When you are ripe, you shall be plucked.

JUNIUS.

P.S. I beg you will convey to our gracious master my humble congratulations upon the glorious success of peerages and pensions, so lavishly distributed as the rewards of Irish virtue.[1]

Junius took the greatest pains with the promised denunciation of Lord Mansfield, which was timed to coincide with the opening of Parliament. It was, he told the printer, 'in *my* opinion, of the highest Style of Junius and cannot fail to sell' (private letter no. 50). Special precautions for printing it in secret were taken and Junius sent proofs in advance to Lord Chatham, begging him to attend the debate and to be ready to move Mansfield's commitment to the Tower.

The result was almost total fiasco. Not a word was said in either House of Parliament on the subject and Chatham did not even bother to attend. The letter dropped like a stone. Most of the readers who followed Junius' lengthy exposition to its conclusion remained unconvinced. His newspaper opponents were jubilant at his evident discomfiture. Aper, on 30 January 1772, condemned the letter as 'legal slush' and a 'chilling string of quotations', a detailed refutation followed from Justinius on 5 February, and it was confidently asserted in the newspapers that even Lord Camden admitted Junius to be wrong.

The legal argument turned mainly on whether Lord Mansfield possessed a discretionary power in regard to bail. Junius was obliged to admit that he had, but argued that it had been improperly exercised in the case of Eyre. Had Eyre absconded, it is just possible that Junius could have succeeded in

[1] There were five promotions to earl and one new viscountcy in the list printed by the *Gentleman's Magazine*, 1771, 519. The pensions on the civil establishment for Ireland are given in the same volume, pp. 529–32.

making the question seem of real importance, but since Eyre had, in fact, presented himself for trial and had been sentenced before Junius' challenge appeared, it was difficult to make the matter seem urgent. Anti-Belial, who may have been Junius, writing in the *Public Advertiser* of 6 February 1772 conceded that 'Junius does not insist upon the case of Eyre so much on the score of its own enormity as because it establishes a dangerous doctrine.' It was unwise of Junius to challenge Mansfield over an action which, whatever the legality, was, as Scien pointed out on 7 February, a gesture of kindness and humanity. There was an enormous gulf between the importance of the case itself and the repercussions, including impeachment and the Tower, which Junius anticipated from it. But Junius' most signal blunder was that he had bored his readers. The *Gentleman's Magazine*, which had faithfully reprinted most of his previous letters in full, cut this one to a fragment of its length.

LETTER LXVIII.

TO LORD CHIEF JUSTICE MANSFIELD.

21. *January*, 1772.

I HAVE undertaken to prove that when, at the intercession of three of your countrymen, you bailed *John Eyre*, you did that, *which by law you were not warranted to do*, and that a felon, under the circumstances, *of being taken in the fact*, *with the stolen goods upon him*, *and making no defence*, is *not bailable* by the laws of England. Your learned advocates have interpreted this charge into a denial that the court of King's Bench, or the judges of that court during the vacation, have any greater authority to bail for criminal offences, than a justice of peace. With the instance before me, I am supposed to question your power of doing wrong, and to deny the existence of a power, at the same moment that I arraign the illegal exercise of it. But the opinions of such men, whether wilful in their malignity, or sincere in their ignorance, are unworthy of my notice. You, Lord Mansfield, did not understand me so, and, I promise you, your cause requires an abler defence.—I am now to make good my charge against you. However dull my argument, the subject of it is interesting. I shall be honoured with the attention of the public, and have a right to demand the attention of the legislature. Supported, as I am, by the whole body of the criminal law of England, I have no doubt of establishing my charge. If, on your part, you should have no plain, substantial defence, but should endeavour to shelter yourself under the quirk and evasion of a practising lawyer, or under the mere, insulting assertion of power without right, the reputation you pretend to is gone for ever;—you stand degraded from the respect and authority of your office, and are no longer, *de jure*, Lord Chief Justice of England. This letter, my Lord, is addressed, not so much to *you*, as to the public. Learned as you are, and quick in apprehension, few arguments are necessary to satisfy you, that you have done that, which by law you were not warranted to do. Your conscience already tells you, that you have sinned against knowledge, and that whatever defence you make contradicts your own internal conviction. But other men are willing enough to take the law upon trust. They rely upon your authority, because they are too indolent to search for information; or, conceiving that there is some mystery in the laws of their country, which lawyers only are qualified to explain, they distrust their judgment, and voluntarily renounce the right of thinking for themselves. With all the evidence of history before them, from *Tresillian* to *Jefferies*, from *Jefferies* to *Mansfield*, they will not believe it possible that a learned judge can act in direct contradiction to those laws, which he is supposed to have made the study of his life, and which he has sworn to administer faithfully. Superstition is certainly not the characteristic of this age. Yet some men are bigoted in politics, who are infidels in religion.—I do not despair of making them ashamed of their credulity.

THE charge I brought against you is expressed in terms guarded and well considered. They do not deny the strict power of the judges of the court of King's Bench to bail in cases, not bailable by a justice of peace, nor replevisable by the common writ, or *ex officio* by the Sheriff. I well knew the practice of the court, and by what legal rules it ought to be directed. But, far from meaning to soften or diminish the force of those terms I have made use of, I now go beyond them, and affirm,

I. THAT the superior power of bailing for felony, claimed by the court of King's Bench, is founded upon the opinion of lawyers, and the practice of the court;—that the assent of the legislature to this power is merely negative, and that it is not supported by any positive provision in any statute whatsoever.—If it be, produce the statute.

II. ADMITTING that the judges of the court of King's Bench are vested with a discretionary power to examine and judge of circumstances and allegations, which a justice of peace is not permitted to consider, I affirm that the judges, in the use and application of that discretionary power, are as strictly bound by the spirit, intent, and meaning, as the justice of peace is by the words of the legislature. Favourable circumstances, alledged before the judge, may justify a doubt whether the prisoner be guilty or not; and where the guilt is doubtful, a presumption of innocence should, in general, be admitted. But, when any such probable circumstances are alledged, they alter the state and condition of the prisoner. *He* is no longer that *all-but-convicted* felon, whom the law intends, and who by law is *not bailable at all*. If no circumstances whatsoever are alledged in his favour;—if no allegation whatsoever be made to lessen the force of that evidence, which the law annexes to a positive charge of felony, and particularly to the fact of *being taken with the maner*, I then say that the Lord Chief Justice of England has no more right to bail him than a justice of peace. The discretion of an English judge is not of mere will and pleasure;—it is not arbitrary;—it is not capricious; but, as that great lawyer, (whose authority I wish you respected half as much as I do) truly says*, "Discretion, taken as it ought to be, is, *discernere per legem quid sit justum*. If it be not directed by the right line of the law, it is a crooked cord, and appeareth to be unlawful"—If discretion were arbitrary in the judge, he might introduce whatever novelties he thought proper; but, says Lord Coke, "Novelties, without warrant of precedents, are not to be allowed; some certain rules are to be followed;—*Quicquid judicis authoritati subjicitur, novitati non subjicitur*;" and this sound doctrine is applied to the Star-chamber, a court confessedly arbitrary. If you will abide by the authority of

* *Inst*. 41. 66.[1]

[1] Sir Edward Coke, *Institutes of the laws of England.*

this great man, you shall have all the advantage of his opinion, wherever it appears to favour you. Excepting the plain, express meaning of the legislature, to which all private opinions must give way, I desire no better judge between us than Lord Coke.

III. I AFFIRM that, according to the obvious, indisputable meaning of the legislature, repeatedly expressed, a person positively charged with *feloniously stealing* and taken *in flagrante delicto*, with the stolen goods upon him, is *not bailable*. The law considers him as differing in nothing from a *convict*, but in the form of conviction, and (whatever a corrupt judge may do) will accept of no security, but the confinement of his body within four walls. I know it has been alledged in your favour, that you have often bailed for murders, rapes, and other manifest crimes. Without questioning the fact, I shall not admit that you are to be justified by your own example. If that were a protection to you, where is the crime that, as a judge, you might not now securely commit? But neither shall I suffer myself to be drawn aside from my present argument, nor *you* to profit by your own wrong.—To prove the meaning and intent of the legislature will require a minute and tedious deduction. To investigate a question of law demands some labour and attention, though very little genius or sagacity. As a practical profession, the study of the law requires but a moderate portion of abilities. The learning of a pleader is usually upon a level with his integrity. The indiscriminate defence of right and wrong contracts the understanding, while it corrupts the heart. Subtlety is soon mistaken for wisdom, and impunity for virtue. If there be any instances upon record, as some there are undoubtedly, of genius and morality united in a lawyer, they are distinguished by their singularity, and operate as exceptions.

I MUST solicit the patience of my readers. This is no light matter, nor is it any more susceptible of ornament, than the conduct of Lord Mansfield is capable of aggravation.

As the law of bail, in charges of felony, has been exactly ascertained by acts of the legislature, it is at present of little consequence to enquire how it stood at common law, before the statute of

Westminster. And yet it is worth the reader's attention to observe, how nearly, in the ideas of our ancestors, the circumstance of being taken *with the maner* approached to the conviction of the felon.* It "fixed the authoritative stamp of verisimilitude upon the accusation, and, by the common law, when a thief was taken *with the maner* (that is, with the thing stolen upon him, *in manu*) he might, so detected *flagrante delicto*, be brought into court, arraigned and tried, *without indictment*; as, by the Danish law, he might be taken and hanged upon the spot, without accusation or trial." It will soon appear that our statute law, in this behalf, tho' less summary in point of proceeding, is directed by the same spirit. In one instance, the very form is adhered to. In offences relating to the forest, if a man was taken with vert, or venison†, it was declared to be equivalent to indictment. To enable the reader to judge for himself, I shall state, in due order, the several statutes relative to bail in criminal cases, or as much of them as may be material to the point in question, omitting superfluous words. If I misrepresent, or do not quote with fidelity, it will not be difficult to detect me.

‡THE statute of Westminster the first, in 1275, sets forth that, "Forasmuch as Sheriffs and others, who have taken and kept in prison persons detected of felony, and incontinent have let out by replevin such as were *not replevisable* because they would gain of the one party and grieve the other; and, forasmuch as, before this time, it was not determined which persons were replevisable and which not, it is provided and by the King commanded that such prisoners, &c. as be *taken with the maner*, &c. or for *manifest* offences, shall be *in no wise* replevisable by the common writ, nor without writ."§—Lord Coke, in his exposition of the last part of this quo-

* *Blackstone*, 4. 303.

† 1 Ed. III. *cap*. 8—and 7 *Rich*. II. *cap*. 4.

‡ '*Videtur que le statute de mainprise nest que rehersall del comen ley*.' Bro. Mainp. 61.[1]

§ 'There are three points to be considered in the construction of all remedial statutes;—the old law, the mischief, and the remedy;—that is, how the common law stood at the making of the act, what the mischief was for which the common law did not provide, and what remedy the parliament hath provided to cure this mischief. It is the business of the judges, so to construe the act, as to suppress the mischief and advance the remedy.' *Blackstone*, 1. 87.

[1] Junius was quoting from Sir Robert Brooke, *La Graunde Abridgement*, a Tudor legal authority.

tation, accurately distinguishes between *replevy* by the common writ or ex officio, and *bail* by the King's Bench. The words of the statute certainly do not extend to the judges of that court. But, besides that the reader will soon find reason to think that the legislature, in their intention, made no difference between *bailable* and *replevisable*, Lord Coke himself (if he be understood to mean nothing but an exposition of the statute of Westminster, and not to state the law generally) does not adhere to his own distinction. In expounding the other offences, which, by this statute, are declared *not replevisable*, he constantly uses the words *not bailable.*—"That outlaws, for instance, are *not bailable at all*;—that persons, who have abjured the realm, are attainted upon their own confession, and therefore *not bailable at all by law*;—that provers are *not bailable*;[1] —that notorious felons are *not bailable.*" The reason, why the superior courts were not named in the statute of Westminster, was plainly this, "because antiently most of the business, touching bailment of prisoners for felony or misdemeanors, was performed by the Sheriffs, or special bailiffs of liberties, either by writ, or *virtute officii*★;" consequently the superior courts had little or no opportunity to commit those abuses, which the statute imputes to the Sheriffs.—With submission to Doctor Blackstone, I think he has fallen into a contradiction, which, in terms at least, appears irreconcileable. After enumerating several offences not bailable, he asserts, without any condition or limitation whatsoever,† "all these are clearly not admissible to bail." Yet in a few lines after he says, "*it is agreed* that the court of King's Bench may bail for any crime whatsoever, *according to circumstances of* the case." To his first proposition he should have added, *by Sheriffs or Justices*; otherwise the two propositions contradict each other; with this difference however, that the first is absolute, the second limited by a *consideration of circumstances.* I say this without the least intended disrespect to the learned author. His work is of public utility, and should not hastily be condemned.

★ 2 *Hale*, P. C. 128. 136.[2]

† *Blackstone*, 4. 296.

[1] Provers were persons who had turned King's evidence.

[2] Sir Matthew Hale, *Historia placitorum coronae: the history of the pleas of the crown* (1736).

THE statute of 17 *Richard* II. *cap.* 10. 1393, sets forth, that "forasmuch as thieves notoriously defamed, *and others taken with the maner*, by their long abiding in prison, were delivered by charters, and favourable inquests procured, to the great hindrance of the people, two men of law shall be assigned, in every commission of the peace, to proceed to the deliverance of such felons, &c." It seems by this act, that there was a constant struggle between the legislature and the officers of justice. Not daring to admit felons *taken with the maner* to bail or mainprize, they evaded the law by keeping the party in prison a long time, and then delivering him without due trial.

THE statute of 1 *Richard* III. in 1483, sets forth, that "forasmuch as divers persons have been daily arrested and imprisoned for *suspicion* of felony, sometime of malice, and sometime of *a light suspicion*, and so kept in prison without bail or mainprize, be it ordained that every justice of peace shall have authority, by his discretion, to let such prisoners and persons so arrested to bail or mainprize."—By this act it appears that there had been abuses in matter of imprisonment, and that the legislature meant to provide for the immediate enlargement of persons arrested on *light suspicion* of felony.

THE statute of 3 Henry VII. in 1486, declares, that "under colour of the preceding act of Richard the Third, persons, *such as were not mainpernable*, were oftentimes let to bail or mainprize, by justices of the peace, whereby many murderers and felons escaped, the King, &c. hath ordained, that the justices of the peace, or two of them at least (whereof one to be of the *quorum*) have authority to let any such prisoners or persons, mainpernable by the law, to bail or mainprize."

THE statute of 1st and 2d of Philip and Mary, in 1554, sets forth, that "notwithstanding the preceding statute of Henry the Seventh, *one* justice of peace hath oftentimes, by sinister labour and means, set at large the greatest and notablest offenders, *such as be not replevisable by the laws of this realm*, and yet, the rather to hide their affections in that behalf, have signed the cause of their apprehension to be but only for *suspicion* of felony, whereby the said offenders have escaped unpunished, and do daily, to the high displeasure of Almighty God, the great peril of the King and Queen's true subjects, and encouragement of all thieves and evil-doers;—for reformation whereof be it enacted, that no justices of peace shall let to bail or mainprize any such persons, which, for any offence by them committed, be declared *not* to be *replevised*, or *bailed*, or be forbidden to be *replevised* or *bailed* by the statute of Westminster the first; and furthermore that any persons, arrested for manslaughter, felony, *being bailable by the law*, shall not be let to bail or mainprize, by any justices of peace, but in the form therein after prescribed."—In the two preceding statutes, the words *bailable*, *replevisable*, and *mainpernable* are used synonymously*, or promiscuously to express the same single intention of the legislature, viz. *not to accept of any security but the body of the offender*; and when the latter statute prescribes the form, in which persons arrested on *suspicion* of felony (*being bailable by the law*) may be let to bail, it evidently supposes that there are some cases, *not* bailable by the law.—It may be thought perhaps, that I attribute to the legislature an appearance of inaccuracy in the use of terms, merely to serve my present purpose. But, in truth, it would make more forcibly for my argument to presume that the legislature were constantly aware of the strict legal distinction between *bail* and *replevy*, and that they always meant to adhere to it.† For if it be true that *replevy* is by the Sheriffs, and *bail* by the higher courts at Westminster, (which I think no lawyer will deny) it follows that, when the legislature expressly say, that any particular offence is by law *not bailable*, the superior courts are comprehended in the prohibition, and bound by it. Otherwise, unless there was a positive exception of the superior courts (which I affirm there never was in any statute relative to bail) the legislature would grossly contradict themselves, and the manifest intention of the law be evaded. It is an established rule

* 2 *Hale*, P. C. 2. 124.

† *Vide* 2 Inst. 150. 186.—"The word *replevisable* never signifies *bailable*. *Bailable* is in a court of record by the King's justices; but *replevisable* is by the Sheriff." *Selden*, State Tr. 7. 149.[1]

---

[1] *A complete collection of state trials*, 2nd edn., ed. Sollom Emlyn, 1730, 1735.

that, when the law is *special*, and reason of it general, it is to be *generally* understood; and though, by custom, a latitude be allowed to the court of King's Bench, (to consider circumstances inductive of a doubt whether the prisoner be guilty or innocent) if this latitude be taken as an arbitrary power to bail, when no circumstances whatsoever are alledged in favour of the prisoner, it is a power without right, and a daring violation of the whole English law of bail.

THE act of the 31st of Charles the Second (commonly called the *Habeas Corpus act*) particularly declares, that it is not meant to extend to treason or felony plainly and specially expressed in the warrant of commitment. The prisoner is therefore left to seek his *Habeas Corpus* at common law; and so far was the legislature from supposing that persons, (committed for treason or felony plainly and specially expressed in the warrant of commitment) could be let to bail by a single judge, or by the whole court, that this very act provides a remedy for such persons, in case they are not indicted in the course of the term or sessions subsequent to their commitment. The law neither suffers them to be enlarged before trial, nor to be imprisoned after the time, in which they ought regularly to be tried. In this case the law says, "It shall and may be lawful to and for the judges of the court of King's Bench and justices of oyer and terminer, or general goal delivery, and they are hereby required, upon motion to them made in open court, the last day of the term, session, or goal delivery, either by the prisoner or any one in his behalf, to set at liberty the prisoner upon bail; unless it appear to the judges and justices, upon oath made, that the witnesses for the King could not be produced the same term, sessions, or goal delivery,"—Upon the whole of this article I observe, 1. That the provision, made in the first part of it, would be, in a great measure, useless and nugatory, if any single judge might have bailed the prisoner *ex arbitrio*, during the vacation; or if the court might have bailed him immediately after the commencement of the term or sessions.—2. When the law says, *It shall and may be lawful* to bail for felony under particular circumstances, we must presume that, before the passing of that act, it was *not* lawful to bail under those circumstances. The terms used by the legislature are *enacting*, not *declaratory*.—3. Notwithstanding the party may have been imprisoned during the greatest part of the vacation, and during the whole session, the court are expressly forbidden to bail him from that session to the next, if oath be made that the witnesses for the King could not be produced that same term or sessions.

HAVING faithfully stated the several acts of parliament relative to bail in criminal cases, it may be useful to the reader to take a short, historical review of the law of bail, through its various gradations and improvements.

BY the ancient common law, before and since the conquest, all felonies were bailable, till murder was excepted by statute, so that persons might be admitted to bail, before conviction, almost in every case. The statute of Westminster says that, before that time, it had not been determined, which offences were replevisable, and which were not, whether by the common writ *de homine replegiando*, or *ex officio* by the Sheriff. It is very remarkable that the abuses arising from this unlimited power of replevy, dreadful as they were and destructive to the peace of society, were not corrected or taken notice of by the legislature, until the commons of the kingdom had obtained a share in it by their representatives; but the house of commons had scarce begun to exist, when these formidable abuses were corrected by the statute of Westminster. It is highly probable that the mischief had been severely felt by the people, although no remedy had been provided for it by the Norman Kings or Barons.* "The iniquity of the times was so great, as it even forced the subjects to forego that, which was in account a great liberty, to stop the course of a growing mischief." The preamble to the statutes, made by the first parliament of Edward the First, assigns the reason of calling it,† "because the people had been

* *Selden*, by *N. Bacon*. 182.[1]

† Parliamentary History. 1. 82.[2]

---

[1] The full reference is *An historical and political discourse of the laws and government of England . . . collected from some manuscript notes of John Selden, Esq.* by N. Bacon. 1682.

[2] Junius is not referring to Cobbett's *Parliamentary History*, which was not published until the nineteenth century, but to *The Parliamentary or constitutional history of England . . . By several hands*, 24 v., 1751–61. The full reference is in *British Museum Catalogue of Printed Books*, v. 63, column 756.

otherwise entreated than they ought to be, the peace less kept, the laws less used, and *offenders less punished* than they ought to be, by reason whereof the people feared less to offend;" and the first attempt to reform these various abuses was by contracting the power of replevying felons.

FOR above two centuries following it does not appear that any alteration was made in the law of bail, except that *being taken with vert or venison* was declared to be equivalent to indictment. The legislature adhered firmly to the spirit of the statute of Westminster. The statute of 27th of Edward the first directs the justices of assize to enquire and punish officers bailing such as were *not bailable*. As for the judges of the superior courts, it is probable that, in those days, they thought themselves bound by the obvious intent and meaning of the legislature. They considered not so much to what particular persons the prohibition was addressed, as what the *thing* was, which the legislature meant to prohibit, well knowing that in law, *quando aliquid prohibetur, prohibetur et omne, per quod devenitur ad illud.* "When anything is forbidden, all the means, by which the same thing may be compassed or done, are equally forbidden."

BY the statute of Richard the third, the power of bailing was a little enlarged. Every justice of peace was authorised to bail for felony; but they were expressly confined to persons arrested *on light suspicion*; and even this power, so limited, was found to produce such inconveniences that, in three years after, the legislature found it necessary to repeal it. Instead of trusting any longer to a single justice of peace, the act of 3d. Henry VIIth, repeals the preceding act, and directs "that no prisoner, (*of those who are mainpernable by the law*) shall be let to bail or mainprise, by less than *two* justices, whereof one to be of the quorum." And so indispensably necessary was this provision thought, for the administration of justice, and for the security and peace of society, that, at this time, an oath was proposed by the King to be taken by the knights and esquires of his household, by the members of the house of commons, and by the peers spiritual and temporal, and accepted and sworn to *quasi unâ* *voce* by them all, which, among other engagements, binds them "not to let any man to bail or mainprise, knowing and deeming him to be a felon, upon your honour and worship. So help you God and all saints.*"

IN about half a century however even these provisions were found insufficient. The act of Henry the seventh was evaded, and the legislature once more obliged to interpose. The act of 1st and 2d of Philip and Mary takes away intirely from the justices all power of bailing for offences declared *not bailable* by the statute of Westminster.

THE illegal imprisonment of several persons, who had refused to contribute to a loan exacted by Charles the first, and the delay of the *Habeas Corpus* and subsequent refusal to bail them, constituted one of the first and most important grievances of that reign. Yet when the house of commons, which met in the year 1628, resolved upon measures of the most firm and strenuous resistance to the power of imprisonment assumed by the King or privy-council, and to the refusal to bail the party on the return of the *Habeas Corpus*, they did expressly, in all their resolutions, make an exception of commitments, where the cause of the restraint was expressed, and did by law justify the commitment. The reason of the distinction is, that, whereas when the cause of commitment is expressed, the crime is then known and the offender must be brought to the ordinary trial; if, on the contrary, no cause of commitment be expressed, and the prisoner be thereupon remanded, it may operate to perpetual imprisonment. This contest with Charles the first produced the act of the 16th of that King, by which the court of King's Bench are directed, within three days after the return to the *Habeas Corpus* to examine and determine the legality of any commitment by the King or privy-council, and to do *what to justice shall appertain* in delivering, bailing, or *remanding* the prisoner.—*Now*, it seems, it is unnecessary for the judge to do what appertains to justice. The same scandalous traffic, in which we have seen the privilege of parliament exerted or relaxed, to gratify the present

* Parliamentary History. 2. 419.

humour, or to serve the immediate purpose of the crown, is introduced into the administration of justice. The magistrate, it seems, has now no rule to follow, but the dictates of personal enmity, national partiality, or perhaps the most prostituted corruption.

To compleat this historical inquiry, it only remains to be observed that, the *Habeas Corpus* act of 31st of Charles the second, so justly considered as another Magna Carta of the kingdom* "extends only to the case of commitments for such criminal charge, as can produce no inconvenience to public justice by a temporary enlargement of the prisoner."—So careful were the legislature, at the very moment, when they were providing for the liberty of the subject, not to furnish any colour or pretence for violating or evading the established law of bail in the higher criminal offences. But the exception, stated in the body of the act, puts the matter out of all doubt. After directing the judges how they are to proceed to the discharge of the prisoner upon recognisance and surety, having regard to the quality of the prisoner and nature of the offence, it is expressly added, "unless it shall appear to the said Lord Chancellor, &c. that the party, so committed, is detained for such matters, or offences, for the which, BY THE LAW THE PRISONER IS NOT BAILABLE."

When the laws, plain of themselves, are thus illustrated by facts, and their uniform meaning established by history we do not want the authority of opinions however respectable, to inform our judgment or to confirm our belief. But I am determined that you shall have no escape. Authority of every sort shall be produced against you, from *Jacob* to *Lord Coke*, from the dictionary to the classic.[1]—In vain shall you appeal from those upright judges, whom you disdain to imitate, to those whom you have made your example. With one voice, they all condemn you.

"To be taken with the *maner* is where a thief, having stolen any thing, is taken with the same about him, as it were in his hands,

* Blackstone. 4. 137.

---

1 The reference is to Giles Jacob, *A New Law-Dictionary*, first published in 1729.

which is called *flagrante delicto*. Such a criminal is *not bailable by law*."—*Jacob under the word Maner.*

"THOSE, who are taken with the *Maner*, are excluded, by the statute of Westminster, from the benefit of a replevin."—*Hawkins. P. C.* 2. 98.[1]

"OF such heinous offences no one, who is notoriously guilty, seems to be *bailable* by the intent of this statute."—*Dº*. 2. 99.

"THE common practice, and allowed general rule is, that bail is only then proper where it stands *indifferent* whether the party were guilty or innocent."—*Dº*. *Dº*.

"THERE is no doubt but that the bailing of a person, *who is not bailable by law*, is punishable, either at common law as a negligent escape, or as an offence against the several statutes relative to bail."—*Dº*. 89.

"IT cannot be doubted but that, neither the judges of this, nor of any other superior court of justice, are strictly within the purview of that statute, yet they will always, in their discretion, pay a due regard to it, and not admit a person to bail, who is expressly declared by it irreplevisable, *without some particular circumstance in his favour*; and therefore it seems difficult to find an instance, where persons, attainted of felony, or notoriously guilty of treason or manslaughter, &c. by their own confession, or *otherwise*, have been admitted to the benefit of bail, without some special motive to the court to grant it."—*Dº*. 114.

"IF it appears that any man hath injury or wrong by his imprisonment, we have power to deliver and discharge him;—if otherwise, *he is to be remanded* by us to prison again."—*Lord Ch. J. Hyde. State Trials*. 7. 115.

"THE statute of Westminster was especially for direction to the Sheriffs and others, but to say courts of justice are excluded from this statute, I conceive it cannot be."—*Attorney General Heath. Dº*. 132.

[1] William Hawkins, *A treatise of the pleas of the crown* (1716).

"THE court, upon view of the return, judgeth of the sufficiency or insufficiency of it. If they think the prisoner *in law* to be *bailable*, he is committed to the Marshal and bailed; if not, he is remanded."—Through the whole debate the objection, on the part of the prisoners, was, that no cause of commitment was expressed in the warrant; but it was uniformly admitted by their council that, if the cause of commitment had been expressed for treason or felony, the court would then have done right in remanding them.

THE Attorney General having urged, before a committee of both houses, that, in Beckwith's case and others, the lords of the council sent a letter to the court of King's Bench to bail; it was replied by the managers of the house of commons, that this was of no moment, "for that either the prisoner was *bailable by the law*, or *not bailable*;—if bailable by the law, then he was to be bailed without any such letter;—if not bailable by the law, then plainly the judges could not have bailed him upon the letter, without breach of their oath, which is, *that they are to do justice according to the law*, &c."—*State Trials*. 7. 175.

"SO that, in bailing upon such offences of the highest nature, a kind of discretion, rather than a constant law, hath been exercised, when it stands *wholly indifferent* in the eye of the court, whether the prisoner be guilty or not." *Selden. St. Tr.* 7. 230. I.

"I DENY that a man is always bailable, when imprisonment is imposed upon him for custody." *Attorney General Heath. d^o^*. 238.—By these quotations from the State Trials, though otherwise not of authority, it appears plainly that, in regard to *bailable* or *not bailable*, all parties agreed in admitting one proposition as incontrovertible.

"IN relation to capital offences there are especially these acts of parliament that are the common *landmarks** touching offences bailable or not bailable." *Hale*. 2. *P. C.* 127. The enumeration includes the several acts cited in this paper.

* It has been the study of Lord Mansfield to remove landmarks.

"PERSONS, taken with the *Manouvre*, are not bailable, because it is *furtum manifestum.*" *Hale.* 2. *P. C.* 133.

"THE writ of *Habeas Corpus* is of a high nature; for if persons be wrongfully committed, they are to be discharged upon this writ returned; or, if bailable, they are to be bailed;—*if not bailable, they are to be committed.*" *Hale.* 2. *P. C.* 143. This doctrine of Lord Chief Justice Hale refers immediately to the superior courts from whence the writ issues.—"After the return is filed, the court is either to discharge, or bail, or *commit* him, as the nature of the cause requires." *Hale.* 2. *P. C.* 146.

"IF bail be granted, *otherwise than the law alloweth*, the party that alloweth the same, shall be fined, imprisoned, render damages, or forfeit his place, as the case shall require." *Selden by N. Bacon.* 182.

"THIS induces an absolute necessity of expressing, upon every commitment, the reason, for which it is made; that the court, upon a *Habeas Corpus*, may examine into its validity, and *according to the circumstances of the case*, may discharge, admit to bail, or *remand* the prisoner." *Blackstone.* 3. 133.

"MARRIOT was committed for forging indorsements upon bank bills, and, upon a *Habeas Corpus*, was bailed, because the crime was only a great misdemeanor;—for though the forging the bills be felony, yet forging the indorsement is not." *Salkeld.* 1. 104.[1]

"APPELL de Mahem, &c. ideo ne fuit lesse a baille, nient plus que in appell de robbery ou murder; quod nota, et que in robry et murder le partie n'est baillable." *Bro. Mainprise.* 67.

"THE intendment of the law in bails is, *quod stat indifferenter* whether he be guilty or no; but, when he is convict by verdict or confession, then he must be deemed in law to be guilty of the felony, and therefore *not bailable at all.*" *Coke.* 2. *Inst.* 188.—4. 178.

[1] *Reports of cases adjudg'd in the Court of King's Bench . . . from the first year of K. William and Q. Mary to the tenth year of Queen Anne*, compiled by William Salkeld, 1717–18.

"BAIL is *quando stat indifferenter*, and *not* when the offence is open and manifest." 2. *Inst.* 189.

"IN this case *non stat indifferenter* whether he be guilty or no, being taken with the *Maner*, that is, with the thing stolen, as it were in his hand." *D°. D°.*

"IF it appeareth that this imprisonment be just and lawful, he *shall* be *remanded* to the former goaler; but, if it shall appear to the court that he was imprisoned against the law of the land, they ought, by force of this statute, to deliver him; if it be *doubtful*, and under consideration, he may be bailed." 2. *Inst.* 55.

IT is unnecessary to load the reader with any farther quotations. If these authorities are not deemed sufficient to establish the doctrine maintained in this paper, it will be in vain to appeal to the evidence of law-books, or to the opinions of judges. They are not the authorities, by which Lord Mansfield will abide. He assumes an arbitrary power of doing right; and, if he does wrong, it lies only between God and his conscience.

NOW, my Lord, although I have great faith in the preceding argument, I will not say, that every minute part of it is absolutely invulnerable. I am too well acquainted with the practice of a certain court, directed by your example, as it is governed by your authority, to think there ever yet was an argument, however conformable to law and reason, in which a cunning, quibbling attorney might not discover a flaw. But, taking the whole of it together, I affirm that it constitutes a mass of demonstration, than which nothing more compleat or satisfactory can be offered to the human mind. How an evasive, indirect reply will stand with your reputation, or how far it will answer in point of defence at the bar of the house of lords, is worth your consideration. If, after all that has been said, it should still be maintained, that the court of King's Bench, in bailing felons, are exempted from all legal rules whatsoever, and that the judge has no direction to pursue, but his private affections, or mere unquestionable will and pleasure, it will follow plainly, that the distinction between *bailable* and *not bailable*, uniformly expressed by the legislature, current through all our law-books, and admitted by all our great lawyers without exception, is in one sense a nugatory, in another a pernicious distinction. It is nugatory, as it supposes a difference in the bailable quality of offences, when, in effect, the distinction refers only to the rank of the magistrate. It is pernicious, as it implies a rule of law, which yet the judge is not bound to pay the least regard to, and impresses an idea upon the minds of the people, that the judge is wiser and greater than the law.

It remains only to apply the law, thus stated, to the fact in question. By an authentic copy of the *mittimus* it appears that John Eyre was committed for felony, plainly and specially expressed in the warrant of commitment. He was charged before Alderman Halifax by the oath of Thomas Fielding, William Holder, William Payne, and William Nash, for *feloniously stealing* eleven quires of writing-paper, value six shillings, the property of Thomas Beach, &c.—by the examinations, upon oath, of the four persons mentioned in the *mittimus*, it was proved, that large quantities of paper had been missed, and that eleven quires (previously marked from a suspicion that Eyre was the thief) were found upon him. Many other quires of paper, marked in the same manner, were found at his lodgings; and after he had been sometime in Wood-street Compter, a key was found in his room there, which appeared to be a key to the closet at Guildhall, from whence the paper was stolen. When asked what he had to say in his defence, his only answer was, *I hope you will bail me.* Mr. Holder, the Clerk, replied, *That is impossible. There never was an instance of it, when the stolen goods were found upon the thief.* The Lord Mayor was then applied to, and refused to bail him.—Of all these circumstances it was your duty to have informed yourself minutely. The fact was remarkable, and the chief magistrate of the city of London was known to have refused to bail the offender. To justify your compliance with the solicitations of your three countrymen, it should be proved that such allegations were offered to you, in behalf of their associate, as honestly and *bona fide* reduced it to a matter of doubt and indifference whether the prisoner was innocent or guilty.—Was any thing offered by the Scotch triumvirate that tended to invalidate the positive charge made against him by four credible witnesses upon oath?—Was it even insinuated to you, either by himself or his bail, that no felony was committed;—or that *he* was not the felon;—that the stolen goods were *not* found upon him;—or that he was only the receiver, not knowing them to be stolen?—Or, in short, did they attempt to produce any evidence of his insanity?—To all these questions, I answer for you, without the least fear of contradiction, positively NO. From the moment he was arrested, he never entertained any hope of acquittal; therefore thought of nothing but obtaining bail, that he might have time to settle his affairs, convey his fortune into another country, and spend the remainder of his life in comfort and affluence abroad. In this prudential scheme of future happiness, the Lord Chief Justice of England most readily and heartily concurred. At sight of so much virtue in distress, your natural benevolence took the alarm. Such a man as Mr. Eyre, struggling with adversity, must always be an interesting scene to Lord Mansfield.—Or was it that liberal anxiety, by which your whole life has been distinguished, to enlarge the liberty of the subject?—My Lord, we did not want this new instance of the liberality of your principles. We already knew what kind of subjects they were, for whose liberty you were anxious. At all events, the public are much indebted to you for fixing a price, at which felony may be committed with impunity. You bound a felon, notoriously worth thirty thousand pounds, in the sum of three hundred. With your natural turn to equity, and knowing, as you are, in the doctrine of precedents, you undoubtedly meant to settle the proportion between the fortune of the felon, and the fine, by which he may compound for his felony. The ratio now upon record, and transmitted to posterity under the auspices of Lord Mansfield, is exactly one to a hundred.—My Lord, without intending it, you have laid a cruel restraint upon the genius of your countrymen. In the warmest indulgence of their passions, they have an eye to the expence, and if their other virtues fail us, we have a resource in their œconomy.

BY taking so trifling a security from John Eyre, you invited and manifestly exhorted him to escape. Although in bailable cases, it be usual to take four securities, you left him in the custody of three Scotchmen, whom he might have easily satisfied for conniving at his retreat. That he did not make use of the opportunity you industriously gave him neither justifies your conduct, nor can it be any way accounted for, but by his excessive and monstrous avarice. Any other man, but this bosom-friend of three Scotchmen, would gladly have sacrificed a few hundred pounds, rather than to submit to the infamy of pleading guilty in open court. It is possible indeed that he might have flattered himself, and not unreasonably, with the hopes of a pardon. That he would have been pardoned seems more than probable, if I had not directed the public attention to the leading step you took in favour of him. In the present gentle reign, we well know what use has been made of the lenity of the court and of the mercy of the crown. The Lord Chief Justice of England accepts of the hundredth part of the property of a felon taken in the fact, as a recognizance for his appearance. Your brother *Smythe* brow-beats a jury, and forces them to alter their verdict, by which they had found a Scotch serjeant guilty of murder; and though the Kennedies were convicted of a most deliberate and atrocious murder, they still had a claim to the royal mercy.[1]—They were saved by the chastity of their connexions.—They had a sister; —yet it was not her beauty, but the pliancy of her virtue that recommended her to the King.—The holy author of our religion was seen in the company of sinners; but it was his gracious purpose to convert them from their sins. Another man, who in the ceremonies of our faith might give lessons to the great enemy of it, upon different principles keeps much the same company. He advertises for patients, collects all the diseases of the heart, and turns a royal palace into an hospital for incurables.—

[1] John Taylor, a sergeant in the 1st or Royal Scots Regiment of Foot, was tried for murder on 1 August 1770 before Sir Sidney Stafford Smythe. The victim was James Smith, landlord of the Wheatsheaf tavern, stabbed in a brawl after an exchange of insults between Scots and English. After the judge had insisted that the jury should return a verdict of manslaughter only, a relative of the dead man stepped forward to protest that by this juries were rendered unnecessary. *London Chronicle*, 2/4 and 7/9 August; *Public Advertiser*, 27 August 1770, 31 January 1771. The matter was referred to in the debate in the House of Commons of 6 December 1770, when Dunning defended the judge's action; *Parl. Hist.* xvi. 1217–18, 1237–8, 1276. For the Kennedy family, see n. 2 to public letter no. XXXIX, p. 203.

A man of honour has no ticket of admission at St. James's. They receive him, like a virgin at the Magdalen's; —*Go thou and do likewise.*[1]

MY charge against you is now made good. I shall however be ready to answer or to submit to fair objections. If, whenever this matter shall be agitated, you suffer the doors of the house of lords to be shut, I now protest, that I shall consider you as having made no reply. From that moment, in the opinion of the world, you will stand self-convicted. Whether your reply be quibbling and evasive, or liberal and in point, will be matter for the judgment of your peers;—but if, when every possible idea of disrespect to that noble house, (in whose honour and justice the nation implicitly confides) is here most solemnly disclaimed, you should endeavour to represent this charge, as a contempt of their authority, and move their lordships to censure the publisher of this paper, I then affirm that you support injustice by violence, that you are guilty of a heinous aggravation of your offence, and that you contribute your utmost influence to promote, on the part of the highest court of judicature, a positive denial of justice to the nation.

JUNIUS.

As if letter no. LXVIII had not been long enough, Junius then tacked on to it letter no. LXIX, explaining to Lord Chatham that he did so because 'the nation in general are not quite so secure of *his* [Lord Camden's] firmness as they are of Lord Chatham'. Private letter no. 89.

LETTER LXIX.

TO THE RIGHT HON. LORD CAMDEN.

MY LORD,

I TURN with pleasure, from that barren waste, in which no salutary plant takes root, no verdure quickens, to a character

[1] The Magdalen Hospital for penitent prostitutes was opened in Goodman's Fields in August 1758.

fertile, as I willingly believe, in every great and good qualification. I call upon you, in the name of the English nation, to stand forth in defence of the laws of your country, and to exert, in the cause of truth and justice, those great abilities, with which you were entrusted for the benefit of mankind. To ascertain the facts, set forth in the preceding paper, it may be necessary to call the persons, mentioned in the *mittimus*, to the bar of the house of lords. If a motion for that purpose should be rejected, we shall know what to think of Lord Mansfield's innocence. The legal argument is submitted to your lordship's judgment. After the noble stand you made against Lord Mansfield upon the question of libel, we did expect that you would not have suffered that matter to have remained undetermined. But it was said that Lord Chief Justice Wilmot had been *prevailed upon* to vouch for an opinion of the late Judge Yates, which was supposed to make against you; and we admit of the excuse. When such detestable arts are employed to prejudge a question of right, it might have been imprudent, at that time, to have brought it to a decision. In the present instance you will have no such opposition to contend with. If there be a judge, or a lawyer of any note in Westminster-hall, who shall be daring enough to affirm that, according to the true intendment of the laws of England, a felon, taken with the *Maner*, *in flagranti delicto*, is bailable; or that the discretion of an English judge is merely arbitrary, and not governed by rules of law,—I should be glad to be acquainted with him. Whoever he be, I will take care that he shall not give you much trouble. Your lordship's character assures me that you will assume that principal part, which belongs to you, in supporting the laws of England, against a wicked judge, who makes it the occupation of his life, to misinterpret and pervert them. If you decline this honourable office, I fear it will be said that, for some months past, you have kept too much company with the Duke of Grafton. When the contest turns upon the interpretation of the laws, you cannot, without a formal surrender of all your reputation, yield the post of honour even to Lord Chatham. Considering the situation and abilities of Lord Mansfield, I do not scruple to affirm, with the most solemn appeal to God for my sincerity, that, in *my* judgment, he is the very worst and most dangerous man in the kingdom. Thus far I have done my duty in endeavouring to bring him to punishment. But mine is an inferior, ministerial office in the temple of justice. —I have bound the victim, and dragged him to the altar.

JUNIUS.

After Junius and Wilkes had both engaged during 1771 in public controversy with John Horne, a friendly exchange of private letters began in August. These letters were not printed until Mason Good's edition of Junius came out in 1812. In his second letter Junius commented at length on the resolutions adopted by the Society of Supporters of the Bill of Rights on 23 July 1771, calling for a reform of Parliament. With Junius' approval, Wilkes read the letter to a meeting of the society on 24 September. Rumours were soon circulating that Junius had adopted a very moderate position and in private letter no. 45 he seems to have suspected Wilkes rather than Horne of misrepresenting his views. On 6 January 1772 a version of Junius' letter was published in the *Morning Chronicle* under circumstances discussed by Wilkes in his private letter no. 84 of 15 January 1772. Junius decided to print these extracts as an appendix to his collected edition. The full text, with a commentary, may be found as private letter no. 67, p. 404.

THE Reverend Mr. John Horne having with his usual veracity and honest industry, circulated a report that Junius, in a letter to the Supporters of the Bill of Rights, had warmly declared himself in favour of long parliaments and rotten boroughs, it is thought necessary to submit to the public the following extract from his letter to John Wilkes, Esq; dated the 7th of September 1771, and laid before the society on the 24th of the same month.

"WITH regard to the several articles, taken separately, I own I am concerned to see that the great condition, which ought to be the *sine quâ non* of parliamentary qualification,—which ought to be the basis (as it assuredly will be the only support) of every barrier raised in defence of the constitution, I mean *a declaration upon oath to shorten the duration of parliaments*, is reduced to the fourth rank in the esteem of the society; and, even in that place, far from being insisted on with firmness and vehemence, seems to have been particularly slighted in the expression.—*You shall endeavour to restore annual parliaments!*—Are these the terms, which men, who are in earnest, make use of, when the *salus reipublicæ* is at stake?—I expected other language from Mr. Wilkes.—Besides my objection in point of form, I disapprove highly of the meaning of the fourth article as it stands. Whenever the question shall be seriously agitated, I will endeavour (and if I live will assuredly attempt it) to convince the English nation, by arguments to *my* understanding unanswerable, that they ought to insist upon a triennial, and banish the idea of an annual parliament. . . . . I am convinced that, if shortening the duration of parliaments (which in effect is keeping the representative under the rod of the constituent) be not made the basis of our new parliamentary jurisprudence, other checks or improvements signify nothing. On the contrary, if this be made the foundation, other measures may come in aid, and, as auxiliaries, be of considerable advantage. Lord Chatham's project, for instance, of increasing the number of knights of shires, appears to me admirable. . . . . . As to cutting away the rotten boroughs, I am as much offended as any man at seeing so many of them under the direct influence of the crown, or at the disposal of private persons. Yet, I own, I have both doubts and apprehensions, in regard to the remedy you propose. I shall be charged perhaps with an unusual want of political intrepidity, when I honestly confess to you, that I am startled at the idea of so extensive an amputation.—In the first place, I question the power, *de jure*, of the legislature to disfranchise a number of boroughs, upon the general ground of improving the constitution. There cannot be a doctrine more fatal to the liberty and property we are contending for, than that, which confounds the idea of a *supreme* and an *arbitrary* legislature. I need not point out to you the fatal purposes, to which it has been, and may be applied. If we are sincere in the political creed we profess, there are many things, which we ought to affirm, cannot be done by King, Lords and Commons. Among these I reckon the disfranchising of boroughs with a general view of improvement. I consider it as equivalent to robbing the parties concerned of their freehold, of their birth-right. I say that, although this birth-right may be forfeited, or the exercise of it suspended in particular cases, it cannot be taken away, by a general law, for any real or pretended purpose of improving the constitution. Supposing the attempt made, I am persuaded you cannot mean that either King, or Lords should take an active part in it. A bill, which only touches the representation of the people, must originate in the house of commons. In the formation and mode of passing it, the exclusive right of the commons must be asserted as scrupulously, as in the case of a money-bill. Now, Sir, I should be glad to know by what kind of reasoning it can be proved, that there is a power vested in the representative to destroy his immediate constituent. From whence could he possibly derive it? A courtier, I know, will be ready to maintain the affirmative. The doctrine suits him exactly, because it gives an unlimited operation to the influence of the crown. But we, Mr. Wilkes, ought to hold a different language. It is no answer to me to say, that the bill, when it passes the house of commons, is the act of the majority, and not the representatives of the particular boroughs concerned. If the majority can disfranchise ten boroughs, why not twenty, why not the whole kingdom? Why should not they make their own seats in parliament for life?—When the septennial act passed, the legislature did what, apparently and palpably, they had no power to do; but they did more than people in general were aware of: they, in effect, disfranchised the whole kingdom for four years.

"FOR argument's sake, I will now suppose, that the expediency of the measure, and the power of parliament are unquestionable. Still you will find an insurmountable difficulty in the execution. When all your instruments of amputation are prepared, when the unhappy patient lies bound at your feet, without the possibility of resistance, by what infallible rule will you direct the operation?—When you propose to cut away the *rotten* parts, can you tell us what parts are perfectly *sound?*—Are there any certain limits, in fact or theory, to inform you at what point you must stop, at what point the mortification ends. To a man so capable of observation and reflection as you are, it is unnecessary to say all that might be said upon the subject. Besides that I approve highly of Lord Chatham's idea *of infusing a portion of new health into the constitution to enable it to bear its infirmities*, (a brilliant expression, and full of intrinsic wisdom) other reasons concur in persuading me to adopt it. I have no objection, &c."

THE man, who fairly and compleatly answers this argument, shall have my thanks and my applause.[1] My heart is already with him.—I am ready to be converted.—I admire his morality, and would gladly subscribe to the articles of his faith.—Grateful, as I am, to the GOOD BEING, whose bounty has imparted to me this reasoning intellect, whatever it is, I hold myself proportionably indebted to him, from whose inlightened understanding another ray of knowledge communicates to mine. But neither should I think the most exalted faculties of the human mind, a gift worthy of the divinity; nor any assistance, in the improvement of them, a subject of gratitude to my fellow creature, if I were not satisfied, that really to inform the understanding corrects and enlarges the heart.

JUNIUS.

FINIS.

[1] This paragraph was not, of course, in the original letter but was added by Junius in order to provide a more appropriate ending for the collected edition.

APPENDIX ONE

PRIVATE LETTERS BETWEEN JUNIUS AND HENRY SAMPSON WOODFALL

This collection of notes from Junius to the printer of the *Public Advertiser* remained in the hands of the Woodfall family and was first published in the edition of 1812, prepared by Mason Good for George Woodfall. It is of particular importance in any attempt to elucidate the authorship since Junius was more likely to have provided unwitting clues in private than in public correspondence. Junius' authorship of miscellaneous letters under the names of Veteran, Vindex, and Domitian is dependent upon the evidence contained in this appendix and it was the connection between Junius and Veteran that prompted John Taylor to suggest Sir Philip Francis as a candidate.

There can be no doubt that there were other notes from Junius—perhaps many—which have not survived. In letter no. 45, for example, he wrote that he had never questioned Woodfall's understanding: 'The Latin word *simplex* conveys to me an amiable character and never denotes folly.' The letter in which the *simplex* remark was made is missing. Similarly, in letter no. 44, while preparing the collected edition, Junius wrote that he could not proceed 'without answers to those seven queries'. We do not know what those queries were since they were in another letter that has not survived. The point is of importance because some controversialists have tried to identify Junius by noting the gaps in his correspondence with Woodfall: such a proceeding is fraught with uncertainty.

The dating of these notes is also a problem of some complexity. In only two letters did Junius himself provide a full dating (one of which was, ironically, incorrect):[1] most of the others are totally without date, though some give the day—'Friday' or 'Wednesday night'. Mason Good devoted much time and ingenuity to the dating of these letters but did considerable harm by printing his results with no indication to the reader that they were conjectural. John Wade, in the 1850 edition which became the standard version, reproduced Mason Good's attributions, again without any warning. Not until Charles Wentworth Dilke drew attention to the question in his reviews of Wade's edition did the reader learn that the original letters were not dated.[2] Some of Mason Good's attributions are demonstrably wrong and all are suspect. Since the correct dating is of more than common importance —e.g. in establishing where Junius was at a particular moment—I have

[1] Letter no. 45 which Junius dated 27 November 1770: it is clear from internal evidence that it was written in 1771. The other letter was no. 49, dated 6 January 1772.

[2] The *Athenaeum*, 14 September 1850, subsequently reprinted in *Papers of a critic*.

entered the dates in square brackets only where there is reasonable certitude and have summarized at the bottom of each letter the argumentation, so that readers may agree or disagree with it.[1] In many of these letters the dating depends upon their juxtaposition with the signals inserted by Woodfall in the *Public Advertiser*. These may be found in Appendix Seven.

A number of the letters were sent by penny post, though the majority were probably delivered by a servant or chairman. The triangular postmark includes the day of postage as well as the post-office, and where this has not been obliterated it is useful evidence. When Junius used a single sheet of paper, folding it over to form an envelope, we can be sure that postmark and note go together; but where he used a second piece of paper to form the envelope, it would be unwise to presume that the postmark necessarily fits the letter to which it is attached in the archives.[2]

The text of these notes is taken, in all but two cases, from the original manuscripts in the British Library, Add. MS. 27774. Letter no. 7 is missing, but has been corrected from the facsimile in E. Twisleton, *The handwriting of Junius professionally investigated by Mr. Charles Chabot, expert* (1871). Letter no. 33, from Woodfall to Junius, is Add. MS. 27777, f. 14. I have printed the letters in what I take to be the chronological order; it should be noted that the numbers given to them are not necessarily the same as those in previous editions.

LETTER NO. 1 [21 April 1769]

M^r. Woodfall

Sir.

I am preparing a paper, which you shall have on or before Saturday night. Advertise it for Monday—*Junius on Monday*

If any enquiry is made about these papers, I shall rely on y^r. giving me a hint.

C

Address: To M^r. Woodfall / Printer in / Paternosterrow
Postmark: On separate sheet, T FR / 5 o'clock
Endorsed 'Hay'. Seal intact.

EXPLANATION OF DATING

The formality of address suggests an early date. Only three Junius letters appeared in 1769 on a Monday: of these, only one was advertised in advance

[1] Dilke obtained from George Woodfall a note showing the basis for the suggestions made in his 1812 edition. Dilke's own copy is extant in his manuscripts in the Codrington Library at All Souls, volume one, 159–62.

[2] There can be no doubt, for instance, that the envelope attached to letter no. 41 is misplaced. The letter deals with the production of the collected edition and must have been composed during the late autumn of 1771: the envelope is dated 14 March. For the operation of London postal services, see J. G. Hendy, *The History of the early postmarks of the British Isles* (1905).

'JUNIUS on Monday'—that of 24 April, announced on Saturday, 22 April. Hence Friday, 21 April 1769 appears a reasonable suggestion.

LETTER NO. 2

[5 May 1769]

friday

Sir

it is essentially necessary that the inclosed should be published to morrow, as the great Question comes on on monday, & Lord Granby is already staggered.

if you shd. receive any answer to it, You will oblige me much by not publishing it, till after Monday.

C

Address: to Mr. Woodfall / to be opened by himself only.
No postmark.

EXPLANATION OF DATING

The 'great Question' was the debate of Monday, 8 May 1769 on the Middlesex election. On Saturday, 6 May the *Public Advertiser* printed a letter from Your Real Friend to the Marquis of Granby, begging him to abandon the government. Assuming 'the inclosed' to be Your Real Friend, this letter must be Friday, 5 May 1769. Granby subsequently resigned as Commander-in-Chief and admitted that he had been 'in error'.

LETTER NO. 3

[15 July 1769]

Saturday.

Sir.

I have recd. the favor of yr. note. from the Contents of it, I imagine you may have something to communicate to me. If that be the Case, I beg you will be particular; & also that you will tell me candidly whether you know or suspect who I am. direct a letter to Mr. William Middleton, to be left at the bar of the new exchange Coffee house on Monday, as early as you think proper.

I am, Sir, your most obedient & most humble Servant

C

On back: private
No postmark.

EXPLANATION OF DATING

The *Public Advertiser* of Thursday, 20 July 1769 carried a note, 'Mr. William Middleton's Letter is sent as desired'. This suggests Saturday, 15 July 1769 for this letter, with some unexplained delay in acknowledgement.

LETTER NO. 4 [17 July 1769]

private.

Sir. Mr. Newbery having thought proper to reprint my Letters, I wish at least he had done it correctly.

You will oblige me much by giving him the following hint, tomorrow.[1] The inclosed when you think proper.[2]

"Mr. Newbery having thought proper to reprint Junius's Letters might at least have corrected the Errata as we did constantly.

"Page 1st. line 13. for *national*, read *rational*
"page 3d. line 4. for *was* read *were*
"page 5. line 15. for *indisputable* read *indispensable*
"letter 7. line 4. for *in all mazes* read *in all the mazes*
"page 15. line 24. for *rightest* read *brightest*
"page 48. line 2. for *indiscreet* read *indirect*

I did not expect more than the life of a newspaper, but if this man will keep me alive, let me live without being offensive.

Speciosa quæro pascere tigres.[3]

On back: private
No postmark.

EXPLANATION OF DATING

The *Public Advertiser* of Tuesday, 18 July carried a note: 'Reasons why the Hint was not printed are sent to the last-mentioned Coffee house in the Strand, from whence our *old* Correspondent will be pleased to send for them.' This suggests that Junius' note was written on Monday, 17 July, which is confirmed by Junius' confusion about 'Monday'. Newbery's edition of the letters was entitled *The political contest*: Woodfall was already thinking of the possibility of bringing out his own edition.

LETTER NO. 5 [21 July 1769]

friday Night.

Sir.

i can have no manner of objection to your reprinting the Letters, if you think it will answer, which I believe it might, before Newbery appeared. if you determine to do it, give me a hint, & I will send you

[1] 'on Monday' is crossed out and 'tomorrow' written over the top.
[2] Presumably public letter no. XVI, printed 19 July 1769.
[3] Horace, *Odes*, III. xxvii. 55–6. The reference is rather a loose one: perhaps Junius meant 'I wish to be fed to the tigers while as beautiful as possible.'

more Errata (indeed they are innumerable.) & perhaps a preface. I really doubt whether I shall write any more under this Signature. I am weary of attacking a Set of Brutes, whose writings are too dull to furnish me even with the materials of Contention, & whose measures are too gross & direct to be the Subject of Argument or to require Illustration.

That Swinney is a wretched but a dangerous fool. he had the impudence to go to Lord G. Sackville, whom he had never spoken to, & to ask him, whether or no he was the Authour of of Junius—take care of him.[1]

Whenever you have any thing to communicate to me, let the hint be thus *C at the usual place* & so direct to Mr. John Fretley at the same Coffee house where it is absolutely impossible I shd. be known.

I did *not* mean the Latin to be printed.

I wish Lord Holland may acquit himself with honour. If his Cause be good, he shd. at once have published that Account, to which he refers in his letter to the Mayor.[2]

pray tell me whether George Onslow means to keep his word with you; about prosecuting.—*Yes* or *No* will be sufficient.[3] Your Lycurgus is a Mr. Kent a young Man of good parts, upon Town.[4] And so I wish you a good Night.

Yours

C

Address: to Mr. Woodfall. private

No postmark. Seal obliterated.

[1] Junius added an extra 'of' to the sentence.

[2] Henry Fox, 1st Baron Holland, held the lucrative post of Paymaster-General from 1757 until May 1765. He became very unpopular for the part he played in helping Lord Bute to get the Peace of Paris accepted by Parliament and on 5 July 1769, in an address to the King from the livery of the city of London, was denounced as *the public defaulter of unaccounted millions*. Holland at once protested to the Lord Mayor and on receiving no satisfactory answer published in the *Public Advertiser* of Saturday, 22 July a long defence and statement of account. He observed in passing that the accounts of Lord Chatham, Paymaster from 1746 to 1755, had not been cleared until 1768. The main documents are in Wade, ii. 7–14.

[3] In the *Public Advertiser* of 14 July 1769 Another Freeholder of Surrey accused George Onslow, member for that county, of being party to a corrupt bargain. Onslow retorted with a letter of 18 July threatening the printer with legal action if he did not divulge the name of his correspondent. John Horne then admitted authorship and defied Onslow. An action for defamation was heard in 1770, when Onslow was twice nonsuited on a technicality. Onslow, a Lord of the Treasury, had taken a prominent part in the proceedings against John Wilkes in the spring of 1769. Wade, ii. 14–20.

[4] Lycurgus contributed a series of letters to the *Public Advertiser* in the spring of 1769, most of them attacking Henry Lawes Luttrell.

EXPLANATION OF DATING

Onslow's letter appeared on Tuesday, 18 July and Holland's statement on Saturday, 22 July. Mason Good was therefore correct in suggesting Friday, 21 July 1769 for this letter.

LETTER NO. 6

Wednesday night

Sir.

I have been some days in the Country, & co[d.] not conveniently send for y[r.] Letter untill this night. Your correction was perfectly right. the sense required it, & I am much obliged to you. When I spoke of *innumerable* Blunders, I meant Newberry's pamphlet; for I must confess that upon the whole *your* papers are very correctly printed.

Do with my letters exactly what you please. I sh[d.] think that, to make a better figure than Newbery, some others of my letters may be added, & so throw out a hint, that you have reason to suspect that they are by the same Authour. If you adopt this plan, I shall point out those, which I wo[d.] recommend; for you know, I do not nor indeed have I time to give Equal Care to them all.

I know M[r.] Onslow perfectly. He is a false silly fellow. Depend upon it, he will get nothing but shame by contending with Horne.

I believe I need not assure you that I have never written in any other paper since I began with Yours. As to Junius, I must wait for fresh Matter, as this is a Character, which must be kept up with credit. Avoid prosecutions, if you can, but above all things avoid the Houses of Parl[t.]—there is no contending with them. At present you are safe; for this H[o.] of Cms has lost all dignity & dare not do any thing.—

adieu

C

Address: To M[r.] Woodfall. / Printer in / Paternoster row

Postmark: On separate sheet, obliterated.

Endorsed 'Halemand'? Seal intact.

EXPLANATION OF DATING

This letter is difficult to date. We can presume that Woodfall replied to letter no. 5, protesting that his paper did not carry 'innumerable' errata, and that this was the message signalled in the *Public Advertiser* of Saturday, 29 July

—'C. in the usual place.' Mason Good assumed letter no. 6 to be a very belated reply by Junius and suggested 16 August. To this there are objections. A delay of 18 days in collecting the letter demands more than 'some days' in the country. If Mason Good was correct in dating letter no. 7 as 6 August, Junius could have cleared up the misunderstanding about the errata in that letter, since he was usually careful not to offend Woodfall. Lastly, the Onslow affair had died down by the middle of August while at the beginning of the month angry letters were still being exchanged. My own suggestion is Wednesday, 2 August 1769, though the evidence is not strong.

LETTER NO. 7[1] [6 August 1769]

Sunday.

Sir

The Spirit of your letter convinces me that you are a much better writer than most of the people, whose works you publish. Whether you have guessed well or ill must be left to our future Acquaintance. For the matter of assistance, be assured that, if a question should arise upon any writings of mine, you shall not want it. Yet you see how things go, and I fear my Assistance would not avail you much. For the other points of printing etc. it does not depend upon us at present. My own works you you shall constantly have, & in point of money, be assured you never shall suffer.[2] I wish the inclosed to be announced tomorrow *conspicuously* for Tuesday. I am not capable of writing any thing more finished.

Your friend

C

Your Veridicus is Mr. Whitworth. I assure you I have not confided in him.[3]

No postmark.

EXPLANATION OF DATING

Mason Good attached the date 6 August 1769 to this letter. It is evidently subsequent to letter no. 3, which had invited Woodfall to guess at Junius'

[1] This letter is missing from Add. MS. 27774 and is reprinted from the facsimile in *The handwriting of Junius professionally investigated by Mr. Charles Chabot, expert.*

[2] Junius' error.

[3] Veridicus specialized in attacks upon Grafton. In a 'farewell letter' of 12 June 1769 he had referred to 'my friend Junius'. It is possible that Woodfall wanted to get in touch with him and believed that he and Junius were working together.

identity. The next four public letters to appear on a Tuesday were those of 1, 8, and 22 August and 19 September on pp. 91, 105, 111, 116.
The covering note for the last one is letter no. 9. The letters of 1 and 22 August are too slight to merit Junius' description. But the letter of 8 August is a substantial and informed composition and was announced on the 7th. Therefore I take Mason Good's attribution to be sound.

LETTER NO. 8

private.

Sir. The last letter you printed was idle & improper, & I assure you printed against my own opinion.[1] The Truth is, there are people about me, whom I wo[d.] wish not to contradict, & who had rather see Junius in the papers ever so improperly, than not at all. I wish it co[d]. be recalled. Suppose you were to say:—*We have some reason to suspect that the last Letter signed Junius in this paper was not written by the real Junius, tho' the Observation escaped us at the time*; or if you can hit off any thing yourself more plausible, you will much oblige me, but without a positive assertion. Don't let it be the same day with the inclosed.[2] —begging your pardon for this trouble, I remain, your friend & humble

Servant

C

Address: To / M[r.] Woodfall
No postmark.

EXPLANATION OF DATING

The reply to Junia was printed on Thursday, 7 September and the retraction on Monday, 11th. The 10th, the date assigned by Mason Good, seems rather a long time for Junius to wait before reacting. The phrase 'the last letter' seems to rule out the 7th or 8th (when 'today's letter' or 'yesterday's letter' would appear more natural). Saturday, 9 September 1769 looks the best guess.

[1] This refers to the reply to Junia, published on 7 September 1769. It is in Appendix Four, p. 457.

[2] The 'inclosed' cannot refer to a Junius letter, since the next one was not until the 19th, and was, in any case, the subject of a separate note. It might be a news item. If it was a miscellaneous letter, the choice seems between Augur on the 8th, Laelius attacking the Duke of Bedford on the 12th and 15th, and Artemidorus attacking Grafton on the 13th. The last seems most probable.

LETTER NO. 9

[15 September 1769]

friday night.

private

Sir.

I beg you will tomorrow advertise, *Junius to another Duke in our next*. If Monday's paper be engaged, then let it be for Tuesday, but not advertised till Monday. You shall have it some time tomorrow night. It cannot be corrected & copied sooner. I mean to make it worth printing.

Yours C

No postmark.

EXPLANATION OF DATING

Everett dated it 10 September 1769 for no very obvious reason: 10 September was not a Friday. Junius' letter to the Duke of Bedford appeared on Tuesday, 19 September and was announced the previous day. This letter is therefore 15 September. Woodfall was presumably worried about the contents and the *Public Advertiser* for 16 September carried a signal, 'C. in the usual place'.

LETTER NO. 10

Thursday night

I shall be glad to see the pacquet you speak of. It cannot come from the Cañdishes, tho there be no End of the family. They would not be so silly as to put their arms on the Cover. As to *me*, be assured that it is not in the Nature of Things that they, or you, or any body else should ever know me, unless I make myself known. All arts or Inquiries, or rewards would be equally ineffectual.

As to *you*, it is clearly my opinion, that you have nothing to fear from the D. of B—[1] I reserve some things expressly to awe him, in case he shd. think of bringing you before the Ho. of L.—I am sure I can threaten him privately with such a Storm, as wod. him tremble even his grave.[2]—You may send tomorrow to the same place without farther notice; & if you have any thing of your own to communicate, I shall be glad to hear it.

C

Address: to Mr. Printer Woodfall / in / Paternosterrow

No postmark. Seal broken.

[1] The Duke of Bedford.

[2] The words 'make' and 'in' were obviously omitted by oversight. It is possible that Junius' threat, if it meant anything, referred to the peace negotiations. See the introduction to public letter no. XXIV, p. 125.

EXPLANATION OF DATING

This letter is clearly subsequent to the attack upon Bedford in public letter no. XXIV, printed 19 September. Mason Good suggested the date 5 October. I see nothing to justify that. The phrase 'without farther notice' implies that this letter was in response to a signal. There were only two signals in this period—on 16 September and 19 October. If, as seems probable, this letter was a reply to the first signal, it must be dated Thursday, 21 September. In his notebooks (i. 160) Dilke recorded that George Woodfall had suggested Thursday, 19 October, to coincide with the second signal. This is a possibility. But in private letter no. 11, which can with certainty be dated 8 November, Junius remarked that he had been out of town for three weeks 'and tho' I got your last, could not conveniently answer it'. This implies that the message signalled on 19 October was not acknowledged until then. In which case letter no. 10 must be the reply to the earlier signal and should be dated 21 September 1769.

LETTER NO. 11 [8 November 1769]

Sir. I have been out of town these three weeks, &, tho' I got your last, could not conveniently answer it. Be so good as to signify to A.B.C., either by word of mouth or in your own hand, "that his papers are received, & that I sh$^{d.}$ have been ready to do him the service he desires but at present it wo$^{d.}$ be quite useless to the parties, & might offend some persons who must not be offended."[1]—As to M$^{r.}$ Mortimer, only make him some civil excuse.[2]

I should be much obliged to you if you wo$^{d.}$ reprint (& in the front page if not improper or inconvenient,) a letter in the London Evening Post of last night to the D. of G–n.[3] If it had not been anticipated, I sh$^{d.}$ have touched upon the subject myself. However it is not ill done, & it is very material that it sh$^{d.}$ spread.—The person alluded to is Lord Denbigh. I sh$^{d.}$ think you might venture him with a *D.* As it stands few people can guess who is meant.[4]

The only thing that hinders my pushing the subject of my last letter is really the fear of ruining that poor devil Gansel, & those

[1] This seems to have been a reference to Samuel Vaughan. Wade actually prints 'Vaughan' instead of 'A.B.C.', but he had no authority for doing so.

[2] Probably Thomas Mortimer. See biographical notes.

[3] The Duke of Grafton.

[4] A.B., in a letter which appears to be an imitation of Junius' style, attacked Grafton for appointing certain persons to the bench in Leicestershire on the advice of Lord Denbigh and without consulting the Duke of Rutland, who was Lord Lieutenant of that county. It is printed in full in Wade, ii. 277–80. On 17 November Woodfall assured his readers that the letter signed A.B. was not by Junius.

other Blockheads.[1]—But as soon as a good subject offers.—Your types really wanted mending.

C

Address: To Mr. Woodfall / Printer / Paternoster row
Postmark: On letter, W WE / 3 o'clock
Seal intact.

EXPLANATION OF DATING

A.B.'s letter appeared in the *London Evening Post* of 7 November 1769 and was reprinted in the *Public Advertiser* on 10 November. This letter is therefore Wednesday, 8 November 1769.

LETTER NO. 12 [12 November 1769]

Sir

I return you the letters you sent me yesterday. A man, who can neither write common English, nor spell, is hardly worth attending to. It is probably a trap for me. I shd. be glad however to know what the fool means. If he writes again, open his letter, & if it contains any thing worth my knowing send it. otherwise not.

Instead of C in the usual place—say only *a Letter*, when you have occasion to write to me again.—I shall understand you.

No postmark.

EXPLANATION OF DATING

The last signal '*C.* in the usual Place' appeared in the *Public Advertiser* on 11 November: the next signal 'A LETTER' was on 16 November. The reference to 'the letters you sent me yesterday' means that this note must have been written on Sunday, 12 November 1769.

LETTER NO. 13 [16 November 1769]

thursday.

as I do not choose to answer for any body's Sins but my own, I must desire you to say tomorrow, "We can assure the public that the Letter, signed A.B. relative to the Duke of Rutland, is not written by the Author of Junius".

[1] Referring to public letter no. XXX, published 17 October 1769.

I sometimes change my Signature, but could have no reason to change the paper, especially for one that does not circulate half so much as Yours.

C

for the future open all letters to me, & don't send them, unless of importance—I can give You light ab$^{t.}$ Veridicus.[1]

Address: To M$^{r.}$ Woodfall. printer in / Paternoster Row

No postmark. Seal obscured.

EXPLANATION OF DATING

Dated Thursday, 16 November 1769 by the retraction that appeared in the *Public Advertiser* on the 17th.

LETTER NO. 14

Sir,

You may tell M$^{r.}$ V.[2] that I did not receive his Letter 'till last night. & have not had time to look into the paper annext. I cannot at present understand what use I can make of it. it certainly shall not be an ungenerous one to him.—If he or his Council *know how to act*, I have saved him already and really without intending it.

The facts are all literally true.[3] M$^{r.}$ Hine's place is Customer at the port of Exeter. Col$^{o.}$ Burgoyne received £ 4000 for it.—to mend the Matter, the Money was raised by Contribution, & the subscribers quartered upon M$^{r.}$ Hine.—Among the rest, one Doctor Brook a Physician at Exeter has 100£ a y$^{r.}$ out of the salary.

I think you might give these particulars in your own way to the public.

As to yourself, I am convinced the Ministry will not venture to attack you. they dare not submit to such an Inquiry. If they do, shew no fear, but tell them plainly you will justify & subpaenâ M$^{r.}$ Hine,

[1] The last two words are badly blotted but appear to have been correctly identified by Mason Good. For Veridicus see n. 3 to letter no. 7. After a 'farewell letter' in June 1769 he resumed writing on 9 February 1770 with another attack on Grafton. Perhaps Woodfall had coaxed him back into action. Silurus, a government writer, kept bragging that he had put Veridicus down.

[2] Vaughan. He had been threatened with a prosecution by the government for attempting a corrupt transaction. See the introduction to public letter no. XXXIII. By 'saving' him, Junius meant that the ministry would not dare to press their charges against Vaughan in the light of the new revelations about Hine.

[3] Presumably as stated in Junius' public letter no. XXXIII.

Burgoyne & Bradshaw of the Treasury—that will silence them at once.—As to the H°· of C. there may be more danger. but even there I am fully Satisfied the Ministry will exert themselves to quash such an Inquiry, & on the other side, you will have friends.—but they have been so grossly abused on all Sides, that they will hardly begin with *you*.

tell Vaughan his paper shall be returned. I am now meditating a capital & I hope a final Piece;—You shall hear of it shortly.

Address:[1] To / Mr· Woodfall printer / in / Pater Noster row

No postmark. Seal broken.

EXPLANATION OF DATING

Mason Good dated this letter 12 December 1769, apparently because Woodfall had written 13 December 1769 on the back (Dilke's Notebook, i. 160). This is far from conclusive. Woodfall's jotting could have been made at any time subsequent to the receipt of the letter. There was a signal in the *Public Advertiser* of 12 December, but Junius' opening sentence implies some delay in collection.

There are further difficulties. 'The facts' were not given to the public by the printer as Junius suggested but were used by Junius himself in his public letter no. XXXIV of 12 December. Moreover the 'capital and final piece' was Junius' very long letter to the King, which appeared on 19 December: it is most unlikely that, as late as 12 December, he was still 'meditating' it. Another problem is that Mason Good placed this letter after no. 16, which can with certainty be dated 9 or 10 December. But this letter promises to return Vaughan's paper, while letter no. 16 hopes that he has got his papers again.

All one can say is that this letter appears to be subsequent to 29 November, when the Hine affair was first mentioned, but before 12 December, when the full facts were published. My guess is that Woodfall raised the possibility of a prosecution in the letter he signalled to Junius on 2 December and that this is Junius' comforting reply.

LETTER NO. 15

private

Sir. I desired Mr· . . . . .n[2] not to write to me untill I gave him notice. he must therefore blame himself, if the detention of his papers has been inconvenient to him. pray tell him this, & that he shall have

[1] On the back of the letter is a rough note, probably made by Woodfall: 'List of Colliers — Erroneous — Mr. S. — Close of the Election — Wednesday Dec. 13 1769'.

[2] Presumably Vaughan.

them in a day or two. I shall also keep my promise to him, but to do it immediately wo$^{d.}$ be useless to *him*, & unadviseable with respect to myself.

I believe you may banish your fears. The information will only be for a misdemeanour, and I am advised that no Jury, especially in these times, will find it. I suspect the Channel, thro' which you have your Intelligence. It will be carried on coldly. You must not write to me again, but be assured I will never desert you. I received your letters regularly, but it was *impossible* to answer them sooner. You shall hear from me again shortly.

C

Address: M$^{r.}$ Woodfall / Printer / Paternosterrow

Postmark: On separate sheet, T WE / 12 o'clock

Endorsed 'Emblin'. Seal broken.

EXPLANATION OF DATING

Mason Good suggested 12 January 1770 and George Woodfall observed (Dilke's Notebook, i. 160) that it was after the two signals on 23 and 27 December 1769. But 12 January was not a Wednesday, the day indicated by the postmark. There is very little to go on. It is not clear whether the prosecution Woodfall feared was concerned with public letter no. XXXIII about Hine or the famous Letter to the King. If the papers referred to are the same as those mentioned in letter no. 14, then this letter must be a few days before 10 December, when Junius asked if they had been received. There seems to be close continuity in the subject-matter of letters 14 and 15.

LETTER NO. 16

I wo$^{d.}$ wish the paper (N$^{o.}$ 2) might be advertised for tuesday.—

By way of intelligence, you may inform the public that M$^{r.}$ Delafontaine, *for his secret services in the Ally*,[1] is appointed Barrack Master to the Savoy.

I hope Vaughan has got his papers again

No postmark.

EXPLANATION OF DATING

The news item was printed in the *Public Advertiser* of Monday, 11 December 1769. Public letter no. XXXIV came out on Tuesday, 12th. Hence this letter must be 9 or 10 December 1769.

[1] i.e. on the Stock Exchange. 'Change Alley was famous for scenes of speculation during the South Sea crisis.

LETTER NO. 17

Sir

with the inclosed Alterations, I sh$^{d.}$ think our paper might appear. As to embowelling, do whatever you think proper, provided you leave it intelligible to vulgar Capacities.—but wo$^{d.}$ not it be the shortest way at once to print it in an anonymous pamphlet? judge for yourself.

I enter sincerely into the Anxiety of your Situation. At the same time I am strongly inclined to think that you will not be called upon.—They can not do it without subjecting Hine's affair to an Inquiry, which wo$^{d.}$ be worse than death to the Minister. As it is, they are more seriously stabbed with this last stroke, than all the rest.—At any rate, stand firm—(I mean with all the humble appearances of Contrition)—if you trim or faulter, you will lose friends without gaining others.

Vaughan has done right in publishing his letter. it defends him more effectually than all his nonsense.—I believe I shall give him a Lift, for I really think he has been punished infinitely beyond his merits.[1]—I doubt much whether I shall ever have the pleasure of knowing you; but if things take the turn I expect, you shall know me *by my works*.

C

No postmark.

EXPLANATION OF DATING

Mason Good dated this letter 26 December 1769 merely because he presumed that the signal of 27 December must be a reply. He was then obliged to assume that 'our paper' was totally suppressed.

It seems unlikely that a letter, substantial enough to be considered for pamphlet production and over which Junius and Woodfall had consulted, should not be used, and it may reasonably be presumed to be the Letter to the King, published on 19 December. The threatened prosecution was still for letter no. XXXIII, since Hine's affair could not be brought in as evidence in any trial on the Letter to the King. 'This last stroke' was the revelations of 12 December, which were undoubtedly more embarrassing to the ministers than insults thrown at the royal person.

The reference to Vaughan's letter is not as helpful as it might have been,

[1] On 10 October the Society of Supporters of the Bill of Rights, to which Vaughan belonged, had declared self-righteously that 'the conduct of Samuel Vaughan Esq. having been brought into Question' it would, unless he could justify himself, 'proceed to an Examination of his public Conduct'. *Public Advertiser*, 21 October 1769.

since there were spurious versions. But a 'genuine copy' appeared in the *Public Advertiser* of 15 December. Hence we may infer that letter no. 17 was written on 15 or 16 December 1769.

LETTER NO. 18 [19 December 1769]

for *material* affection, for god's sake read *maternal.* it is in the 6 Par. the rest is excellently done

Address: to / Mr. Woodfall, Printer / Pater Noster row

No postmark. Seal broken.

EXPLANATION OF DATING

This note refers to the Letter to the King, published on 19 December 1769. The correction appeared the following day. Hence it is Tuesday, 19 December 1769.

LETTER NO. 19

private

Sir

When you consider to what excessive enmities I may be exposed, you will not wonder at my caution. I really have not known how to procure your last. if it be not of any great moment, I would wish you to recall it. If it be, give me a hint.—If your Affair shd. come to a trial, and you shd. be found guilty, you will then let me know what Expence falls particularly on yourself; for I understand you are ingaged with other proprietors. Some way or other *you* shall be reimbursed. But seriously & bonâ fide, I think it is impossible.

C

Address: To Mr. Woodfall

No postmark.

EXPLANATION OF DATING

The weeks after the publication of the Letter to the King on 19 December were hectic. Woodfall was threatened with a prosecution and there was a hue and cry after Junius. Mason Good suggested early February. The only guide are the signals in the newspaper on 27 December, 20 February, and 5 March. There is a note in the *Public Advertiser* of 2 February 1770 which might refer to this letter: 'An Old Corrt. may banish his anxiety on the score he makes mention of. This the printer hopes will be sufficient.'

LETTER NO. 20

I have carefully perused the Infn. it is so loose & ill drawn, that I am persuaded Mr. De Grey cod. not have had a hand in it.—Their inserting the whole proves they had no strong passages to fix on. I still think it will not be tried. If it shd.—it is not possible for a Jury to find you guilty.[1]

No postmark.

EXPLANATION OF DATING

Mason Good suggested 'about 14 February' but offered no evidence. The information would be moved after Hilary Term had commenced on 20 January.

LETTER NO. 21 [17 March 1770]

Saturday.

tomorrow before 12 you shall have a Junius, it will be absolutely necessary that it should be published on Monday.

Would it be possible to give Notice of tonight or tomorrow, by a dispersing a few Handbills. Pray do what ever you think will answer this purpose best, for now is the Crisis.

C

Address: To— / Mr. Woodfall / Printer in / Paternoster Row

Postmark: On letter, W SA / 5 o'clock. Seal broken.

EXPLANATION OF DATING

Letters 21 and 22 stand together, the second showing it to be the spring of 1770. There were six Junius letters in 1770, of which two appeared on a Monday—19 March and 28 May. The reference to Lord Chatham in letter no. 22 indicates that it is March, when he was expected to attend the Westminster remonstrance. This letter is therefore Saturday, 17 March 1770.

LETTER NO. 22 [18 March 1770]

Sunday

this letter is written wide, & I suppose will not fill two Columns. for God's sake, let it appear to morrow.—

[1] Woodfall was charged with seditious libel in publishing the Letter to the King. When the case was heard on 13 June 1770, the jury returned its famous verdict that he was guilty of printing and publishing only. William De Grey was Attorney-General.

I hope you received my Note of yesterday.

Lord Chatham is determined to go to the Hall to support the Westminster Remonstrance. I have no doubt that we shall conquer them at last.[1]

C

No postmark.

EXPLANATION OF DATING

Public letter no. XXXVII, dated 19 March 1770, was not announced in advance and did not fill two columns. In conjunction with letter no. 21, this letter may be dated Sunday, 18 March 1770.

LETTER NO. 23 [19 October 1770]

friday morn.

private

by your affected silence you encourage an idle opinion that I am the Author of the *Whig*, etc. tho' you very well know the contrary. I neither admire the Writer nor his Idol. I hope you will soon set this Matter right.[2]

C

Postmark: obliterated, 5 o'clock

Endorsed 'Mullins'. Seal broken.

EXPLANATION OF DATING

The retraction in the newspaper of Saturday, 20 October 1770 confirms this note as Friday, 19 October 1770.

LETTER NO. 24 [12 November 1770]

Monday Evening. Sir. the inclosed, tho' begun within these few days, has been greatly laboured. It is very correctly copied, & I beg

[1] The Westminster remonstrance was agreed on 28 March. Lord Chatham did not attend but applauded from afar. *Pitt. Corr.* iii. 434.

[2] A letter signed A Whig and an Englishman was printed in the *Public Advertiser* on 11 October 1770. Two days later, Cinna accused Junius of being the author. It defended Lord Chatham's American policy. On Saturday, 20 October Woodfall published a statement that it was not by Junius and on 25 October he added, in notes to correspondents: 'The printer really did not AFFECT a silence on a CERTAIN OCCASION, with a View of encouraging his Readers or Correspondents in an idle Opinion: The Motives for his Conduct were, the Fear of being thought impertinent by declaring (without Direction) what he knew; and the Probability of rendering himself liable to incur the Displeasure of either of those who were pleased to favour him with their Correspondence.'

you will take Care that it be literally printed as it stands. I don't think you run the least Risque. We have got the Rascal down. Let us strangle him if it be possible. this paper sh$^{d.}$ properly have appeared tomorrow, but I co$^{d.}$ not compass it. so let it be announced tomorrow & printed Wednesday.—if you sh$^{d.}$ have any Fears, I intreat you to send it early enough to Miller, to appear tomorrow night in the London Ev$^{g.}$ Post.—In that Case, you will oblige me by informing the public tomorrow in *your own paper*, that a real Junius will appear at Night in the London.—Miller, I am sure, will have no Scruples.

Lord Mansfield has thrown Ministry into Confusion, by suddenly resigning the office of Speaker of the H. of L$^{ds.}$—[1]

On back: private

No postmark.

EXPLANATION OF DATING

The *Public Advertiser* of 13 November carried the news about Mansfield and public letter no. XLI to Mansfield came out the following day. This dates letter no. 24 as Monday, 12 November 1770.

LETTER NO. 25

Wednesday night.

I shall be very glad to hear from your friend at Guildhall.[2]—You may, if you think proper, give my Compliments to him, & tell him, if it be possible, I will make use of any Materials he gives me. I will never rest 'till I have destroyed or expelled that Wretch.—I wish you Joy of Yesterday.—The fellow truckles already.—[3]

C

the inclosed strikes deeper than you may imagine.[4]

No postmark.

[1] After the difficulties of finding a successor to Camden as Lord Chancellor in January 1770, the great seal had been put into commission. Lord Mansfield then acted as Speaker of the House of Lords.

[2] Mason Good assumed that Junius' correspondent was Wilkes, who had been elected an Alderman in January 1769. It is probably correct, yet it is strange that in September 1771 Wilkes had to ask how he was to communicate with Junius.

[3] Presumably a reference to Mansfield against whom public letter no. XLI of 14 November had been directed.

[4] Written on back of the note. Mason Good suggested that this referred to a letter under the name Testiculus. It was printed on 24 November and was an attack upon Lord Barrington, the Secretary-at-War.

EXPLANATION OF DATING

There is not much to go on. Mason Good dated it Wednesday, 21 November 1770 on the assumption that 'joy of yesterday' referred to Woodfall being granted a new trial.

LETTER NO. 26

friday 1 o'clock

I wish it were possible for you to print the inclosed tomorrow.—Observe the Italics strictly where they are marked.[1]

Why don't I hear from Guildhall.—If he trifles with me, he shall hear of it.

C

No postmark.

EXPLANATION OF DATING

Although it obviously stands with letter no. 25, this does not help much. Neither can be dated with confidence.

LETTER NO. 27

Sir.

i have rec^d. y^r. mysterious epistle. i dare say a Letter may safely be left at the same place; but you may change the direction to M^r. John Fretly. You need not advertise it.

Yours

C

Address: to / M^r. Woodfall / Printer in / Paternoster Row

Postmark: On letter, T FR / ? 12 o'clock

Endorsed 'Emblin'. Seal broken.

EXPLANATION OF DATING

There is no evidence to date this letter within months or years. Mason Good suggested 2 January 1771 on the assumption that it was a reply to Woodfall's signal 'THIS DAY' on the 1st. But the 2nd was a Wednesday, not a Friday, and there is no particular reason to connect it with that signal.

The reference to leaving the letter in the same place but changing the name to Fretly suggests that it may have followed closely after letter no. 3 which had mentioned the New Exchange Coffee House and suggested the name William Middleton.

[1] Mason Good identified the 'inclosed' as Domitian's letter of 8 December 1770. This was printed on a Saturday, had italics, and was not announced in advance.

LETTER NO. 28

N°. 2.

You may assure the public that a Squadron of four Ships of the Line is ordered to be got ready with *all possible expedition* for the East Indies. It is to be commanded by Commodore Spry.

With regarding the language of ignorant or interested people,[1] depend upon the Assurance *I* give you that every Man in Administration looks upon War as inevitable.

Address: To / Mr. Woodfall / Printer in / Paternoster Row

No postmark. Seal broken.

EXPLANATION OF DATING

The reference to Commodore Spry was carried by the *Public Advertiser* of 17 January 1771: Mason Good therefore suggested Wednesday, 16 January for this letter. But if this note was No. 2, what was No. 1? There is no public letter from Junius near this date but Domitian was printed on 17 January. Since Domitian was announced the previous day, it follows that if it was No. 1, this letter must have been written on the 15th.

LETTER NO. 29 [30 January 1771]

the paper is extremely well printed & has a great effect.[2]—it is of the utmost importance to the Public Cause that the Doors of the H°. of Lords sh$^{d.}$ be opened on Tuesday next.[3] perhaps the following may help to shame them into it—

We hear that the Ministry intend to move for opening the Doors of both Houses of parliam^{t}. on Tuesday next in the usual Manner,

[1] The sense requires 'without regarding . . .'

[2] The paper was public letter no. XLII, printed on Wednesday, 30 January 1771, accusing the ministry of feebleness over the dispute with Spain.

[3] The debate in the House of Lords took place on Tuesday, 5 February 1771. Junius' puffs were a rather naïve way of attempting to force the government's hand. It has been inferred from Junius' anxiety to have the doors open that he could not have been a member of Parliament and had to attend as one of the general public, but it may also have been that he wanted the greatest possible publicity for a debate which he thought would prove awkward to the government. Though Woodfall duly inserted the puffs, the public was not admitted. There are only the briefest reports of the discussion in the House of Lords, where Chatham moved to ask the judges whether the proposed settlement with Spain was legal. The motion was defeated. *Lords' Journals*, xxxiii. 54–5. Lord Camden wrote to Chatham on the morning of the debate disapproving of his initiative and concluding that the settlement was probably legal; *Pitt. Corr.* iv. 90–2.

being desirous that the Nation shd. be exactly informed of their whole Conduct in the Business of Falkland Island.

next Day

The Nation expect that, on Tuesday next at least, both Houses will be open as usual; otherwise there will be too much reason to suspect, that the proceedings of the Ministry having been such as will not bear a public Discussion.[1]

We hear that the Ministry intend to move that no Gentleman may be refused Admittance into either house on Tuesday next. Lord North in particular thinks it touches his character to have no part of his Conduct concealed from the Nation.

The Resolution of the Ministry to move for opening both Houses on Tuesday next does them great honour. If they were to do otherwise, it wod. raise & justify Suspicions, very disadvantageous to their own reputation & to the King's honour.

pray keep it up.[2]

C

Address: Mr. Woodfall / Printer / in / Paternoster Row

Postmark: On letter, T WE

Endorsed 'Pryer'. Seal intact.

EXPLANATION OF DATING

Junius' public letter no. XLII appeared on Wednesday, 30 January 1771. Puffs to persuade the ministry to open the doors were printed on 1, 2, and 4 February, the last using Junius' exact words. Mason Good dated this letter Thursday, 31 January, but the postmark makes it clear that it must have been written on Wednesday, 30 January 1771.

LETTER NO. 30

Tuesday noon.

Sir.

I did not receive your Letter untill this day. I shall be very glad to hear what you have to communicate.

C

You need not advertise any Notice

No postmark.

[1] Junius obviously wrote his instructions in a hurry and the grammar became contorted at this point. There are several changes in the manuscript.

[2] The second, third, and fourth paragraphs of this letter have been scratched through, presumably by the printer as he made use of them.

EXPLANATION OF DATING

Mason Good suggested 5 February 1771. This may be right, but I know of no evidence to support it. One may presume that Woodfall's communication, to which this is a reply, was signalled: there are no signals between 'THIS DAY' on 1 January and 'A LETTER' on 20 February. The signal on 20 February was acknowledged in letter no. 34.

LETTER NO. 31

Monday

private.

our Correspondence is attended with difficulties. Yet I sh[d.] be glad to see the paper you mention. Let it be left to morrow, *without farther notice.* i am seriously of Opinion that it will all end in smoke.

C

No postmark.

EXPLANATION OF DATING

Mason Good dated this Monday, 11 February 1771 and related it to a communication to Woodfall from the Attorney-General about public letter no. XLII on 2 February. It is true that Junius had difficulties in collecting the printer's letters during February 1771.

LETTER NO. 32

[18 February 1771]

Monday.

If you are not grown too ministerial in your politics, I shall hope to see the inclosed announced tomorrow, & published on Wednesday—[1]

No postmark.

EXPLANATION OF DATING

Woodfall replied to this letter, refuting the sneer, on 19 February. This was therefore written on Monday, 18 February 1771.

LETTER NO. 33[2]

[19 February 1771]

Sir,

To have *de*served any Portion of your good Opinion affords me no

[1] This was a letter signed Vindex, which was printed, in truncated form, on Friday, 22 February 1771. It is given in full in Appendix Five, p. 487.

[2] This is Woodfall's reply to Junius' letter no. 32. It was omitted in Everett's edition and printed as a footnote in Wade's. This seems illogical since they both printed Woodfall's letter of 7 March 1773.

It was addressed to M[r.] John Fretley at the New Exchange Coffee House, Strand. It is printed from the original letter in Add. MS. 27777, f. 14, which must have been recovered by Woodfall after Junius had found difficulty in obtaining it.

small Satisfaction—to *pre*serve it shall ever be my constant Endeavour. Always willing to oblige you as much as lies in my Power, I, with great Avidity, open your Letters; and sometimes, without reading the Contents, promise the Publication. Such is my present Situation, and I hope you will not be offended at my declining to publish your Letter as I am convinced the Subject of it must, if I was to publish it, render me liable to very severe reprehension.[1] That I am not grown ministerial in my [politics][2] every Day's Paper will I hope sufficiently evince, . . . [and I][2] rather hope some little regard to Prudence will not by you be deemed Squeamishness, or tend to lessen me in your Opinion, as I shall ever think myself,

Your very much obliged humble servant,

Feb. 19. 1771 Henry Sampson Woodfall

P.S. I shall wait your Directions what to do with the Paper in Question, as I did not chuse to trust it under Cover till I was further acquainted with your Pleasure.

No postmark.

EXPLANATION OF DATING

Dated on original.

LETTER NO. 34 [21 February 1771]

private.

Sir. it will be very difficult, if not impracticable, for me to get your Note. I presume it relates to V——x. I leave it to you to alter or omit as you think proper;—or burn it;—I think the argument about Gibraltar etc is too good to be lost. As to the Satyrical part, I must tell you, (& with positive Certainty) that our gracious ——is as callous as Stockfish to every thing but the Reproach of *Cowardice*.[3] That alone is able to set the humours afloat. After a paper of that kind he won't eat Meat for a Week.[4]

[1] It contained a direct accusation of cowardice against the King.

[2] The manuscript is torn, but Woodfall is replying to the taunt in letter no. 32.

[3] Stockfish is a gadoid fish such as cod. It is dried for keeping and beaten with staves or hammers before cooking. Hence the term is used to mean dry, dead, or unfeeling.

[4] In a note to public letter no. XXXVIII Junius wrote of the King during the spring of 1770 that 'he was obliged to live upon potatoes for three weeks, to keep off a malignant fever'.

You may rely upon it, the Ministry are sick of prosecutions. Those against Junius cost the Treasury above six thousand p$^{ds.}$ & after all they got nothing but Disgrace. After the paper you have printed today, (signed Brutus) one wo$^{d.}$ think you feared Nothing.[1] —For my own part, I can very truly assure you that nothing wo$^{d.}$ afflict me more than to have drawn you into a personal Danger, because it admits of no recompence. A little expence is not to be regarded, & I hope these papers have reimbursed you. I never will send you anything that *I* think dangerous, but the risque is yours & you must determine for yourself.

C

all the above is private

No postmark.

EXPLANATION OF DATING

The signal of 20 February suggests Thursday, 21 February for this note, which is confirmed by the reference to Brutus 'today'.

LETTER NO. 35

friday noon

I hope you will approve of announcing the inclosed *Junius* to morrow, & publishing it on Monday. If, for any reasons that do not occur to me, you should think it unadviseable to print it, as it stands, I must intreat the favour of you to transmit it to Bingley, & satisfy him that it is a real Junius, worth a North Briton Extraordinary. It will be impossible for me to have an opportunity of altering any part of it.

I am, very truly Your friend

C

No postmark.

EXPLANATION OF DATING

The tone of this letter is subdued and suggests that it was written after the disagreement about Vindex. There was only one subsequent Junius letter published on a Monday, that of 22 April. Therefore Friday, 19 April 1771 seems probable.

[1] Brutus' letter appeared on 21 February 1771 and was an attack upon Lord North, finishing 'Remember, my Lord, there is a very short period between a minister's imprisonment and his grave.' It is printed in full by Wade, ii. 36–7.

LETTER NO. 36 [20 June 1771]

I am strangely partial to the inclosed. It is finished with the utmost Care. if I find myself mistaken in my judgement of this paper, I positively will never write again.[1]

C

let it be announced tomorrow *Js. to the D. of G.* for Saturday. I think Wilkes has closed well. I hope he will keep his resolution not to write any more.[2]

thursday

Address: To / Mr. Woodfall, printer, in / Paternoster Row
No postmark. Seal broken.

EXPLANATION OF DATING

There were several letters to the Duke of Grafton but the reference to Wilkes makes it clear that it was public letter no. XLIX, printed on Saturday, 22 June. Consequently this note must be Thursday, 20 June 1771.

LETTER NO. 37 [17 July 1771]

to prevent any unfair use being made of the inclosed, I intreat you to keep a Copy of it. then seal & deliver it to Mr. Horne.—I presume you know where he is to be found.

C

No postmark.

EXPLANATION OF DATING

Horne's first letter was printed in the *Public Advertiser* on 13 July 1771. On the 23rd, a note announced: 'The Letter from JUNIUS having been transmitted by the Printer privately to Mr. HORNE, according to JUNIUS's orders, Mr. Horne has directed the Printer to publish it.' It appeared the following day.

This is therefore the covering note to public letter no. LII. That letter was dated 17 July (though printed on the 24th). This note is therefore 17 July 1771 and not 16 July as Mason Good suggested.

[1] Public letter no. XLIX addressed to the Duke of Grafton.

[2] Wilkes had been engaged in a lengthy altercation with John Horne. His final letter appeared in the *Public Advertiser* of 20 June 1771. It is printed in Wade, ii. 39.

LETTER NO. 38 [13 August 1771]

pray make an erratum for *ultimate* in the paragraph about the D. of G. it should be *intimate*. the rest is very correct.

If Mr. Horne answers this Letter handsomely & in point, he shall be my great Apollo.

No postmark.

EXPLANATION OF DATING

The reference is to public letter no. LIV, published 13 August 1771. The erratum appeared the following day. This note is therefore Tuesday, 13 August 1771. In his collected edition, Junius misdated Letter LIV.

LETTER NO. 39

Wednesday noon.

the inclosed is of such importance, so very material, that it *must* be given to the public immediately.

I will not advise;—tho' I think you perfectly safe.—all I say is that I *rely* upon your Care to have it printed either tomorrow in yr. own paper, or tonight in the Pacquet.

I have not been able to get yrs. from that place, but you shall hear from me soon.

No postmark.

EXPLANATION OF DATING

There is little to date this letter within months or years. Mason Good assumed that the item of such importance was Junius' letter to Grafton about Whittlebury Forest (p. 282) and therefore affixed the date 25 September 1771. To this there are many objections: (1) there is no obvious reason why letter no. LVII had to be published in a hurry; (2) letter no. LVII did not, in fact, appear until Saturday, 28th; (3) it ran to two columns and could hardly be inserted at short notice in that evening's paper; (4) Woodfall was unlikely to agree to a genuine Junius letter going to a rival paper.

The reference to the 'inclosed' sounds more like a news item than a letter, while 'you shall hear from me soon' sounds like a letter in preparation. If Mason Good was correct at all in placing it during September 1771, it could be a promise of letter no. LVII to come (after a gap since 13 August). In which case it might be a reply to the signal of 21 September and Woodfall's letter signalled on 27 September might be concerned with printing letter no. LVII. The *Public Advertiser* of Thursday, 19 September carried the kind of news item that Junius liked to contribute: 'We are told that Orders are issued from the War Office for all the officers belonging to the artillery companies at Portsmouth and Plymouth to join their respective corps with all expedition.' But it is mere conjecture.

LETTER NO. 40 [1 November 1771]

friday. the above to that Scotchman sh[d.] be printed conspicuously tomorrow. At last I have concluded my great Work, & I assure you with no small labour. I wo[d.] have you begin to advertise immediately & publish before the meeting of parl[t.] Let all *my* papers in defence of Jun[s.] be inserted. I shall now supply you very fast with Copy & Notes. The paper & type sh[d.] at least be as good as Whebles.[1] You must correct the press yourself, but I sh[d.] be glad to see corrected proofs of the 2 first sheets.

Shew the Dedication & preface to M[r.] Wilkes, and if he has any *material* Objection, let me know. I say *material* because of the difficulty of getting your letters.

C

secret beware of David Garrick. he was sent to pump you, & went directly to Richmond to tell the king I sh[d.] write no more.

the dedication must stand first[2]

Address: For M[r.] W[l.]
No postmark.

EXPLANATION OF DATING

Mason Good dated this note 8 November 1771, presuming that the enclosed letter was the short challenge to Mansfield which appeared in the *Public Advertiser* of 9 November. This cannot be correct since Wilkes, in a letter of 4 November, acknowledged receipt of the Dedication and Preface. Consequently this note must be Friday, 1 November and the enclosure was the longer challenge to Mansfield printed on the 2nd. It appeared conspicuously on the front page with a decorated initial letter.

LETTER NO. 41

your reasons are very just ab[t.] printing the preface etc. it is your own affair. Do whatever you think proper. I am convinced the book will

[1] John Wheble of Paternoster Row was the printer of the Piccadilly edition of the letters, published in 1771.

[2] This is written down the left side of the page.

sell, & I suppose will make two volumes, the type might be one size larger than Whebles. but of all this you are the best Judge. I think you shd. give money to the Waiters at that place, to make them more attentive.[1]—the Notes shd. be in a smaller type.
pray find out, if you can, upon what day, the late D. of Bedford, was flogged on the Course at Litchfield by Mr. Heston Homphrey.[2]

Address:[3]

No postmark. Seal broken.

EXPLANATION OF DATING

The discussion about the preparations for the collected edition places this letter somewhere about November 1771, when Junius was working on the notes. In private letter no. 44, which can be dated with some confidence around 15 November, Junius again mentioned the flogging of the Duke. This letter is obviously a reply to one from Woodfall, which must have been signalled in the *Public Advertiser*: there are signals on 5 and 8 November.

LETTER NO. 42 [8 November 1771]

print the following as soon as you think proper, & at the head of yr. paper.

I sent you three Sheets of Copy last night. When you send to me, instead of the usual signal, say, *Vindex shall be considered.* & keep the Alteration a Secret to every body.

Address: To Mr. Woodfall / printer / in Paternoster Row

Postmark: On letter, T FR / 12 o'clock

Endorsed 'Hay'. Seal broken.

EXPLANATION OF DATING

This note must be between 8 November 1771, when the signal 'C' was used, and 12 November, when 'Vindex shall be considered' appeared. Mason Good dated it 11 November, presuming that the enclosure was a reference to the Duke of Cumberland's marriage, printed on 12 November. But the 11th was not a Friday and the paragraphs on Cumberland were not strictly at the head of the paper, though they were at the head of a column. I think the enclosure was more probably the letter under the signature Cumbriensis, which appeared at the head of the paper on Wednesday, 13 November. Letter no. 42 should then be dated Friday, 8 November 1771.

[1] i.e. at the coffee-house where communications were left.

[2] See notes to public letter no. XXIII of 19 September 1769.

[3] In the archives this letter is related to a folder, addressed 'To the Printer of the Public Advertiser' and dated 14 March. It is clearly not the correct folder.

LETTER NO. 43 [10 November 1771]

To Mr. David Garrick

I am very exactly informed of your impertinent inquiries, & of the information you so busily sent to Richmond, & with what triumph & exultation it was received. I knew every particular of it the next day. Now mark me, vagabond.—keep to your pantomimes, or be assured you shall hear of it. Meddle no more, thou busy informer!—It is in *my* power to make you curse the hour, in which you dared to interfere with

Junius[1]

I wod. send the above to Garrick directly, but that I wod. avoid having this hand too commonly seen. Oblige me then so much as to have it copied in any hand, & sent by the penny post, that is, if you dislike sending it in your own writing.—I must be more cautious than ever. I am sure I shd. not survive a Discovery three days or if I did, they wod. attaint me by bill. Change to the *Somerset Coffee house*,[2] & let no mortal know the alteration. I am persuaded you are too honest a man to contribute in any way to my destruction. Act honorably by me, & at a proper time you shall know me.

I think the second page, with the widest lines, looks best.—What is your essential reason?—for the change. I send you some more sheets. —I think the paper is not so good as *Wheble's*.—but I may be mistaken—the type is good. The aspersions thrown upon my Lr to the Bill of Rts. shd. be refuted by publication. prevail upon Mr. Wilkes to let you have Extracts of my 2d. & 3d. Letter to him. It will make the book still more new.—I wod. see them before they are printed, but keep this last to yrself.[3]

Address: To / Mr. Woodfall

On back: private & particular

No postmark. Seal broken.

[1] Junius' anxiety on this occasion was reflected in the absurdly melodramatic language he wished to use to Garrick. It is clear from Garrick's reply, printed as a note to letter no. 44, that Junius had totally misunderstood the situation. The worst that had happened was that Woodfall himself had been a little indiscreet.

[2] For the Somerset Coffee House in the Strand, see B. Lillywhite, *London coffee houses*, 538–40.

[3] For the complications arising out of Junius' advice to the Supporters of the Bill of Rights, see notes to Public letter no. LXIX. Junius wanted to make sure that Wilkes had not altered the letters in any way but did not wish his suspicions to be known.

EXPLANATION OF DATING

The letter to Garrick, with alterations, appears to have been received by him on Monday, 18 November. Woodfall signalled a letter to Junius on 12 November, presumably giving his own explanation of what had occurred with Garrick. Hence Mason Good's suggestion of 10 November 1771 for letter no. 43 seems reasonable.

LETTER NO. 44

If you can find the date of the D. of B's flogging, insert it in the Note.—I think it was soon after the Westm^r.^ Election.[1]—The *philos* are not to be placed as notes, except where I mention it particularly.[2]

I have no doubt about what you say about D.G.—so drop the Note.[3] The truth is that in order to curry favor, he made himself a greater Rascal than he was. Depend upon what i tell you;—the king understood that he had found out the secret by his own cunning & activity;—As it is important to deter him from meddling, I desire you will tell him that I am aware of his practises, & will certainly be revenged, if he does not desist. An appeal to the public from J^s.^ wo^d.^ destroy him.

Let me know whether Mr. W. will give you the Extracts.[4]

I cannot proceed without answers to those 7 queries.

Think no more of Junius Americanus.—Let him reprint his Letters himself. he acts most dishonorably, in suffering Junius to be so traduced. but this falsehood will all revert upon Horne. In the meantime, I laugh at him.[5]

[1] The attack upon the Duke of Bedford at Lichfield races took place in September 1747. The general election of July 1747 had produced a bitter contest at Westminster where the Duke of Bedford's interest went to his brother-in-law, Lord Trentham; *The House of Commons, 1715–54*, i. 286–7. Junius may have become confused with the more ferocious by-election of 1750: this would account for his failure to find the exact date. See note to public letter no. XXIII.

[2] i.e. the letters written under the name of Philo Junius.

[3] David Garrick. The note was subsequently sent.

[4] The reference is to Wilkes and the extracts from Junius' letters to him mentioned in private letter no. 43.

[5] Dr. Arthur Lee, a member of the Society of Supporters of the Bill of Rights, contributed letters to the *Gazetteer* under the name Junius Americanus. He was also, according to Wilkes, the author of the Society's resolutions, criticized by Junius in private letter no. 67. Junius was much irritated by the misrepresentations of his position which had appeared in the press: *Lloyd's Evening Post* of 1/4 November carried a report that he had 'declared himself strenuously in favour of *long Parliaments*'. See also public letter no. LXIX and private letters nos. 45, 70, 75, and 84.

With submission, i think it is not y^{r}· interest to declare that I have done.

As to y^{r}·self, I really think you are in no danger. *You* are not the object, & punishing *you* (unless it answ^{d}· the purpose of stopping the press) wo^{d}· be no gratification to the king. If undesignedly I sh^{d}· send you any thing you may think dangerous, judge for yourself, or take any opinion you think proper. You cannot offend or afflict me but by hazarding y^{r}· own safety. They talk of farther informations, but they will always hold that language in terrorem.

Don't always use the same signal.—any absurd Latin verse will ans^{r}· the purpose. Let me know about what time you may want more Copy.

Upon reflection I think it absolutely necessary to send that Note to D.G.—only say *practises*, instead of *impert^{t}· Inq^{s}·* I think you have no measures to keep with a man, who co^{d}· betray a confidential letter, for so base a purpose as pleasing the odious hypocrite.[1]

1 'The odious hypocrite' was George III. Garrick's reply was as follows:

TO HENRY SAMPSON WOODFALL

Sir Novr 20th 1771

I am oblig'd to address this letter to You, & to appeal to your probity—in that, and my own, lies my defence against a most unprovok'd & illiberal attack made upon Me by your celebrated Correspondent Junius—had you not convinc'd Me, that the letter I receiv'd last Monday Night, was really written by that Gentleman, I could not have imagin'd, that such talents could have descended to such Scurrility: however Mighty the Power may be, wth Which he is Pleas'd to threaten Me, I trust, with truth on my side, & your assistance to be able to parry ye Vigor of his Arm, & oblige him to drop his point, not for want of force to overcome so feeble an adversary as I am, but from ye Shame & consciousness of a very bad Cause. in *one* particular I will be acknowledg'd his superiour, for how ever Easy & justifiable such a return may be, I will make Use of no foul language—my Vindication wants neither violence or abuse to support it: it would be as unmanly to give injurious names to Me, who *will* not, as to him who *can*not resent it. Now to ye fact, which till you had explain'd to Me, had made no impression upon my Mind. I am told in most outrageous terms, & near a Month after ye suppos'd crime was committed (for Junius was exactly inform'd of my practices ye day after) that if the Vagabond does not keep to his Pantomimes Every hour of his Life shall be curs'd for interfering with Junius—is not this rather too Inquisitorial for the great Champion of our Liberties!—now let us examine into ye dreadful Cause of this denunciation—Mr Woodfall, the first Informer, informs Me in a letter in no wise relative to ye Subject, without any previous impertinent enquiries on my part, or ye least desire of Secrecy on his, that *Junius would write no more*: two or three days after the receipt of yours, being oblig'd to write a letter upon the business of the theatre to one at Richmond, & after making my Excuses for not being able to obey his Majesty's Commands, I mention'd to him that Junius would write no more—but ye Triumphs y^{t} Succeeded this Intelligence never reach'd me, till I receiv'd Junius's letter—& so far was I from thinking there was a Crime in communicating what was sent to me without reserve, that I will freely confess, tell me how long it may be before you want more Copy.—I want rest most severely, & am going to find it in the Country for a few days.

Cumbriensis has taken greatly.[1]

Private

No postmark.

EXPLANATION OF DATING

It must fall between 13 November, when Cumbriensis appeared, and 18 November, when Garrick received Junius' note.

> that I wrote no letter to any of my friends without the mention of so remarkable an Event: I will venture to go farther, & affirm, that it would have been insensible & unnatural not to have done it.
>
> I beg You will assure Junius that I have as proper an abhorrence of an Informer, as he can have, that I have been honour'd with y[e] Confidence of men, of all Parties, & I defy my greatest Enemy to produce a Single instance of any one repenting of such Confidence—I have always declar'd that were I by any Accident to discover Junius, no consideration should prevail upon me to reveal a Secret productive of so much mischief, nor can his most undeserv'd treatment of me make me alter my Sentiments. One thing more I must observe, that Junius has given Credit to an *Informer* in prejudice of him, who was never in y[e] least suspected of being a Spy before: had any of our Judges condemn'd the lowest Culprit upon such Evidence without hearing the person Accus'd, & other Witnesses, the Nation would have rung with the Injustice! I shall say no more, but I beg you to tell all you know of this matter, and b[e] assur'd, that I am with great regard for Junius['s] Talents, but without y[e] least for his threatnings
>
> Your Wellwisher and humble Servant
>
> D Garrick.

Woodfall passed Garrick's letter on to Junius, the signal of 21 November presumably referring to that transaction. Junius' reply has not been preserved but that he was not much mollified may be inferred from his subsequent sneers at Garrick and from the account which Woodfall sent to Thomas à Becket, a friend of Garrick, on 23 November, *The private correspondence of David Garrick* (1831), i. 444–5:

> Dear Becket,
>
> I have just received a general letter from Junius upon private subjects, in which he had returned me Mr. G's letter, without the satisfactory answer I had wished to have received with it. I am of opinion some enemy of Mr. G's has endeavoured to excite Junius's resentment against Mr. G. and that it does not proceed merely from this little communication which Mr. G. was not enjoined to keep secret by me. The following passage I have extracted from this letter to Mr. G: 'If he attacks me again, I will appeal to the Public against him. If not, he may safely set me at Defiance.' I wish a more favourable construction of what I sent would have permitted me to have written to Mr. G., so as to have given him the fullest satisfaction: I am not without hopes of still accomplishing the matter to his mind . . .

[1] Cumbriensis' letter, at the expense of the Duke of Cumberland and his new Duchess, appeared in the *Public Advertiser* on 13 November. It is given in full by Wade, ii. 387–9.

LETTER NO. 45 [27 November 1771]

27 Nov. 1770[1]

the postcript to Titus must be omitted.[2]—I did never question your understanding. far otherwise. the Latin word *simplex* conveys to me an amiable character, & never denotes folly. Tho' we may not be deficient in point of Capacity, it is very possible that neither of us may be cunning enough for Mr. Garrick. But with a sound heart, be assured you are better gifted, even for worldly happiness, than if you had been cursed with the abilities of a Mansfield. After long experience of the world, I affirm, before God I never knew a rogue, who was not unhappy.

Your account of my letter to the Bill of rights astonishes me. I always thought the misrepresentation had been the work of Mr. Horne. I will not trust myself with suspecting. The remedy is in my own hands, but, for Mr. Wilkes's honour, I wish it to come freely and honorably from himself. publish nothing of mine, untill I have seen it.—in the meantime, be assured that nothing can be more express than my declaration against long parliaments.—try Mr. Wilkes once more.—speak for me in a most friendly but *firm* tone.—that I *will not* submit to be any longer aspersed.—Between ourselves, let me recommend it to you to be much upon your guard with patriots.[3]—I fear your friend Jerry Dyson will lose his irish pension.[4]
Say *Received.*
in page 25. it shd. be *the* instead of *your*. this is a woeful Mistake.—pray take care for the future—keep a page for Errata.[5]

[1] Dated on the original manuscript, apparently in Junius' hand. The year should, of course, be 1771.

[2] A postscript to public letter no. V of 21 February 1769 promised Titus an answer. None was forthcoming so Junius deleted the reference in the collected edition.

[3] Woodfall suspected Wilkes of leaking Junius' private letter no. 67. Wilkes exculpated himself in private letter no. 84. Woodfall passed on Junius' complaint in Add. MS. 30881, f. 13.

[4] Jeremiah Dyson was member for Weymouth and Melcombe Regis and a Lord of the Treasury. Just before the Duke of Grafton resigned, Dyson was given a pension of £1,000 p.a. on the Irish establishment. In a debate of 5 April 1770 Lord North defended the pension as a 'decent provision for an old servant of the crown'. But when the Irish Parliament met, a motion was carried on 25 November 1771 by 106 votes to 105 that the pension was 'an unnecessary charge upon the establishment of Ireland and ought not to be provided for'. It was subsequently agreed to. Wade's note that Dyson's pension was for resigning his seat in favour of Charles James Fox is a poetic invention. *Calendar of Home Office Papers*, *1770–2*, nos. 99, 252, 927, 931 1026, 1048, and 1073.

[5] The collected edition was then in proof stage.

D.G. has literally forced me to break my resolution of writing no more.

No postmark.

EXPLANATION OF DATING

The date on the original is confirmed by 'Received' in the *Public Advertiser* of 28 November 1771.

LETTER NO. 46 [5 December 1771]

These papers are all in their exact Order. take great care to keep them so. In a few days more I shall have sent you all the Copy. You must then take care of it yourself, except that I must see proof sheets of the Ded$^{n.}$ & pref. & these, if at all, I must see before the End of next week.—

You shall have the Extract to go into the second volume. it will be a short one.—Scaevola, I see, is determined to make me an Enemy to Lord Camden. If it be not wilful malice, I beg you will signify to him that when I originally mentioned Ld. C's Declaration ab$^{t.}$ the Corn bill it was without any view of discussing that Doctrine, & only as an instance of a singular Opinion maintained by a man of great learning & integrity.—Such an instance was necessary to the plan of my letter.—I think he has in effect injured the man whom he meant to defend.[1]

When you send the above men$^{d.}$ proof sheets, return my own copy with them.

No postmark.

EXPLANATION OF DATING

Mason Good suggested 5 December 1771, which seems correct. Scaevola published a letter that day; on the 6th the *Public Advertiser* carried the signal 'Received', and on the 7th Woodfall inquired in the newspaper how he could establish communication with Scaevola.

LETTER NO. 47

The inclosed compleats all the materials that I can give you. I have done *my* part. take care *you* do yours. There are still two

[1] See introduction to Letter no. LX of 15 October 1771, p. 299 above.

Letters wanting, which *I expect you will not fail* to insert in their places. One is from Ph°·J$^{s.}$ to Scaevola about L$^{d.}$ Camden, the other to a friend of the people about pressing. They must be in the Course of October.—I have no view but to serve you, & consequently have only to desire that Ded. & Pref. may be correct. Look to it. If you take it upon y^{r}·self, I will not forgive your suffering it to be spoiled. I weigh every word; & every Alteration, in my Eyes at least, is a blemish.

I sh$^{d.}$ not trouble you or myself, about that Blockhead Scaevola, but that his absurd fiction of *my* being L$^{d.}$ C·'s Enemy has done harm.—Every fool can do mischief.—therefore signify to him what I said.

Garrick has certainly betrayed himself, probably to the King, who makes it a Rule to betray every body that confides in him. That new Disgrace of Mansfield is true.[1]—What do you mean by affirming that the Dowager is better. I tell you she suckles toads from morning till night.[2] I think I have now done my duty by you, so farewell.

No postmark.

EXPLANATION OF DATING

Mason Good's suggestion was 10 December 1771. But the report on the Dowager Princess's health appeared in the *Public Advertiser* on 6 December and the reference to Scaevola indicates that it was soon after the previous communication. The most likely date is 7 December 1771, in reply to the signal on the 6th.

LETTER NO. 48 [17 December 1771]

Make your mind easy about me. I believe you are an honest man, and I never am angry.—say tomorrow "We are desired to inform Scaevola that his private note was received with the most profound indifference & Contempt." I see his design. The duke of Grafton has been long labouring to detach Camden. This Scaevola is the wretchedest of all fools; & dirty knave.—

[1] Lord Mansfield in the summer of 1771 heard an action for trespass brought by Meres and Shepley against Ansell. Verdict went to the defendant. Plaintiffs' counsel then moved for a new trial on the grounds of misdirection of the jury, and the Court of Common Pleas upheld their submission. It was reported in the *Public Advertiser* for 9 December 1771. See also, private letter no. 89.

[2] The Princess Dowager of Wales was dying from cancer of the throat. A treatment of the time was to hang toads in small bags round the neck in the hope that they would suck the poison from the infected areas. She died 8 February 1772.

Upon no account nor for any reason whatsoever are you to write to me, untill I give you notice.

When the Book is finished let me have a set bound in vellum, gilt & lettered Junius, as handsomely as you can,—the edges gilt. let the

I. 2.

Sheets be well dried before binding.—I must also have two Sets in blue paper Covers. This is all the fee I shall ever desire of you.—I think you ought not to publish before the second week in January.

the L$^{n.}$ packet is not worth our Notice. I suspect Garrick, & I wo$^{d.}$ have you hint so to him.[1]

No postmark.

EXPLANATION OF DATING

The note to Scaevola duly appeared in the *Public Advertiser* of 18 December 1771. This letter may be presumed to be 17 December in answer to the signal in that day's paper.

LETTER NO. 49 [6 January 1772]

6. January. 72.

I have a thing to mention to you in great Confidence. I expect your assistance, & rely upon your Secrecy.

There is a long paper ready for publication, but which must not appear until the morning of the meeting of parliament, nor be announced in any shape whatsoever.[2] Much depends upon its appearing unexpectedly. If you receive it on the 8th or 9th instant, can you in a day or two have it composed, & two proof sheets struck off & sent me,[3] & can you keep the press standing ready for the public Adv$^{r.}$ of the 21$^{st.}$ And can all this be done with such secrecy that none of y^{r} people shall know what is going forward except the Composer, & can you rely on *his* fidelity? Consider of it &, if it be possible, say *Yes* in your paper tomorrow.

I think it will take four full Columns at the least, but I undertake that it shall sell.—It is essential that I sh$^{d.}$ have a proof sheet, & correct it myself.

[1] Presumably the false letter, dated 13 December 1771, subsequently printed in *Barатariana* in 1773. See Appendix Four, p. 459.

[2] Letter no. LXVIII to Lord Mansfield.

[3] Junius intended to send an advance copy to Lord Chatham for his opinion. See Appendix Three.

Let me know if the are ready,[1] that I may tell you what to do with them.

Address: To / Mr. Woodfall / Printer, / in Paternosterrow
No postmark. Seal broken.

EXPLANATION OF DATING

The date 6 January 1772 is on the original and is confirmed by 'YES—CERTAINLY' in the *Public Advertiser* of the 7th.

LETTER NO. 50

[11 January 1772]

Saturday.

Your failing to send me the proofs, as you engaged to do, disappoints & distresses me extreamly. It is not merely to correct the press, (tho' even that is of Consequence) but for another *most material* purpose. This will be entirely defeated, if you do not let me have the two proofs on Monday morning.

The paper is, in *my* opinion, of the highest Stile of Js. & cannot fail to sell.—my reason for not announcing it was that the party might have no time to concert his measures with the Ministry. but, upon reflection, I think it may answer better (in order to excite Attention) to advertise it the day before. *Js. to L.C.J.M. tomorrow.*[2]

Quoting from memory, I have made a Mistake about Blackstone, where I say *that he confines the power to the Court, & does not extend it to the Judges separately.* those lines must be omitted.—the rest is right.—If you have any regard for me, or for the cause, let nothing hinder your sending the proofs on Monday.

Address: To Mr. H. S. Woodfall / Printer in / Paternoster Row
Postmark: On letter, ? SA / 3 o'clock
Endorsed 'Thrale'. Seal intact.

EXPLANATION OF DATING

The letter to Lord Chatham, enclosing the proofs, was dated 14 January 1772, a Tuesday. This must therefore be Saturday, 11 January. There was a signal in the newspaper on Monday, presumably that the proofs were ready for collection.

[1] i.e. 'if the *books* are ready'.
[2] i.e. Lord Chief Justice Mansfield.

LETTER NO. 51

I return you the proof, with the errata, which you will be so good as to correct carefully.

I have the greatest reason to be pleased with your care & attention, & wish it were in my power to render you some essential service.—

Announce it on Monday.

Address: Mr. Woodfall, Printer, in / Paternoster Row

Postmark: On separate sheet, missing, 3 o'clock. Seal intact.

EXPLANATION OF DATING

Assuming that this refers to the last letter to Mansfield, which was announced on Monday, 20 January 1772 and printed the following day, it must be between the 13th and the 18th. Mason Good's suggestion was Thursday, 16th. But the *Public Advertiser* of 15 January carried the signal '*RECEIVED*' and my inclination is to date it Tuesday, 14 January 1772.

LETTER NO. 52

[18 January 1772]

private

Saturday.

The gentleman, who transacts the conveyancing part of our Correspondence tells me there was much difficulty last night. for this reason, & because it cod. be no way material for me to see a paper on Saturday, which is to appear on Monday, I had resolved not to send for it.—Your hint of this Morning, I suppose, relates to this.—I am truly concerned to see, that the publication of the book is so long delayed.—It ought to have appeared before the meeting of Pt.—By no means wod. I have you insert this long letter, if it made more than the difference of two days in the publication.

Believe me, the delay is a real Injury to the Cause.—the letter to M. may come into a new Edition.[1]

Mr. W. seems not to know that Morris published that Letter. I think you should set him right.[2]

Address: To Mr. Woodfall / Printer in / Paternoster Row

Postmark: On letter, missing, 5 o'clock

Endorsed 'White'. Seal obscured.

[1] i.e. the letter to Mansfield.

[2] Junius' private letter to the Supporters of the Bill of Rights had been published without his permission. In his private letter of 15 January, below, p. 436, Wilkes blamed Patrick Cawdron: Junius' suggestion was that Robert Morris, a lawyer and former secretary to the society, was the person responsible.

EXPLANATION OF DATING

The reference to imminent publication establishes this note as during January 1772 and Wilkes's private letter to Junius was written on Wednesday, 15th. This must therefore be Saturday, 18 January 1772. 'Your hint of this morning' was the signal '*Mutare necessarium est*'. On Monday 20th, the *Public Advertiser* carried a note from Woodfall: 'Though the Printer knows the *usual Method* of CONVEYANCING is shut up, owing probably to the Intenseness of the Frost, yet another can surely be opened.'

There is one small complication. The paper 'which is to appear on Monday' cannot be public letter no. LXVIII attacking Mansfield. This came out on Tuesday to coincide with the opening of Parliament and it is unlikely that Junius would have made a mistake. Moreover he had already seen the proofs of that letter and returned them. The *Public Advertiser* for Monday, 20 January carried a long letter from Wilkes, which he referred to in his private letter to Junius on the 15th. It is possible that Wilkes sent it to Junius for approval: this might also account for Junius' apparent lack of interest in the matter.

LETTER NO. 53

having nothing better to do, I propose to entertain myself & the public, with torturing that bloody wretch Barrington. He has just appointed a french Broker his deputy, for no reason but his relation to Bradshaw. I hear from all quarters, that it is looked upon as a most impudent insult to the army.—Be careful not to have it known to come from me. Such an insignificant creature is not worth the generous rage of J^s.[1]

I am impatient for the Book.

No postmark.

EXPLANATION OF DATING

The *Public Advertiser* of Monday, 27 January 1772 carried the announcement 'VETERAN TO LORD BARRINGTON—Tomorrow.' That suggests that this note was probably written on Saturday, 25 January 1772.

[1] Lord Barrington, Secretary-at-War, appointed Anthony Chamier his deputy in succession to Christopher D'Oyly. His wife's sister was married to Thomas Bradshaw. The letters attacking Barrington appeared under the name of Veteran and are printed in full in Appendix Five. The case that Philip Francis was Junius rests heavily on the connection through these letters.

LETTER NO. 54

Monday.

I confess I do not see the use of the Table of Contents. I think it will be endless, & answer no purpose;—An index of proper names, & materials wo^d. in my opinion be sufficient. You may safely defy the malice of M^r. Wheble. Whoever buys such a book will naturally prefer the author's Edition, & I think it will always be a book for Sale.[1] I really am in no hurry about that Set.[2]

Purling, I hear, is to come in for Eastlow.—a sure proof of the connection between him & Government.[3]

I wo^d. have you open any thing that may be brought to you for me (except from M^r. W.)[4]—& not forward it, unless it be material.—That large Roll contained a pamphlet.

Address: To / M^r. Woodfall, printer / in / Paternosterrow

Postmark: On letter, W MO / 3 o'clock

Endorsed 'Thrale'. Seal broken.

EXPLANATION OF DATING

Mason Good gave the date Monday, 3 February 1772. I do not see any evidence to warrant such precision. It was presumably subsequent to letter no. 48 of 17 December 1771, asking for a 'set bound in vellum'. Yet the discussion about the table of contents suggests that it was still early in the production stage and by February Junius' correspondence with Wilkes seems to have petered out. Richard Leigh, the member for East Looe, did not die until 24 March 1772, but he had been ill for some time.

LETTER NO. 55

Monday. If you have any thing to communicate, you may send it to the original place for once, N.E.Co.—[5] & mention any new place

[1] T. H. Bowyer, *A bibliographical examination of the earliest editions of the letters of Junius* (1957), describes John Wheble as 'probably the most prolific pirate of The Letters of Junius'. A careful survey of Wheble's edition is on pp. 27–58. Woodfall had suggested a table of contents in order to make his edition more complete than Wheble's.

[2] The books referred to in private letter no. 48.

[3] John Purling was chairman of the East India Company. Returned to Parliament for New Shoreham in November 1770, he lost his seat on grounds of bribery. He came in for East Looe on 9 April 1772: the patron of the borough, John Buller, was a government placeman. The previous member, Richard Leigh, had been ill for some months.

[4] Wilkes.

[5] The New Exchange Coffee House.

you think proper, west of Temple Bar. The delay of the book spoils everything.

Address: To Mr. H. S. Woodfall / printer in / Paternoster Row

Postmark: On letter, W MO / 12 o'clock. Seal intact.

EXPLANATION OF DATING

Mason Good guessed at Monday, 10 February 1772. But the letter presupposes a signal from the printer that he had something to communicate: there is no signal on or near 10 February. The previous signals were on the 27 and 28 January: since the 27th was a Monday, it may be the one referred to.

LETTER NO. 56

Monday night.

Surely you have misjudged it very much about the Book.—I could not have conceived it possible that you could protract the publication so long.—At this time, particularly before Mr. Sawbridge's Motion, it wod. have been of singular use. You have trifled too long with the public Expectation.—At a certain point of time the appetite palls.—I fear you have already lost the season.—the Book, I am sure will lose the greatest part of the Effect I expected from it.—

But I have done.

Address: To Mr. Woodfall / printer in / Paternoster Row

Postmark: On letter, missing. Endorsed 'Bishop'? Seal intact.

EXPLANATION OF DATING

There is little more than Junius' rising temper to go on. John Sawbridge's motion for shorter parliaments was put on 4 March 1772. Monday, 17 February looks the most likely possibility. Woodfall would certainly reply to such an irritable attack and there is a signal in the *Public Advertiser* for 20 February. Letter no. 57, which can with some confidence be dated 21 February, is then Junius' reply, acknowledging that the printer was not to blame for the delay.

LETTER NO. 57

I do you the justice to believe that the Delay has been unavoidable. The expedient you propose, of printing the Ded. & pref. in the P.A. is unadvisable. The Attention of the public wod. then be quite lost to the book itself. I think your Rivals will be disappointed. Nobody will apply to *them*, when they can be supplied at the fountain head. I hope you are too forward, to have any room for that Letter of Dom^n.[1]—otherwise it is merely indifferent.

The Latin I thought much superior to the English.—The intended Bill, in consequence of the Message, will be a most dangerous innovation in the internal policy of this Country.[2] What an abandoned, prostituted Ideot is your Lord Mayor![3]—The shameful Mismanagement, which brought him into office, gave me the first, & an unconquerable Disgust.[4]—All I can now say is, make haste with the Book.—

C

The appointm^t. of this Broker, I am told, gives universal disgust.[5] That bloody Wretch wo^d. never have taken a step, apparently so absurd, if there were some wicked design in it, more than we are aware of.[6] At any rate, the Broker sh^d. be run down. That at least is due to his Master.

No postmark.

EXPLANATION OF DATING

The royal message was delivered on Thursday, 20 February 1772 and the bill introduced the following day. The Lord Mayor refused a Common Hall for the second time on 20 February. Therefore Friday, 21 February looks probable, in reply to the significant signal in the previous day's newspaper: '*quousque tandem*, ABUTERE *patientia nostra*?'—'how long will you abuse our patience?'

[1] The five letters signed Domitian are printed in Appendix Five. They were not included in the collected edition.

[2] A royal message sent to both Houses of Parliament on 20 February 1772 invited them to consider whether it would not be prudent to guard the royal family from marriages made 'without the approbation of His Majesty'. This was the outcome of the marriage of the Duke of Cumberland, which the King had learned about on 1 November 1771. Another brother, the Duke of Gloucester, was also secretly married, though the King did not find out until September 1772. The Royal Marriage Bill was introduced in the House of Lords on 21 February 1772.

[3] Alderman Nash, as Lord Mayor, had refused requests on 12 and 20 February for a Common Hall to discuss Sawbridge's motion; *Gentleman's Magazine*, 1772, 91–2. See p. 290, n. 1.

[4] Junius blamed Wilkes for the mismanagement. See the introduction to public letter no. LVIII and private letter no. 66.

[5] The Veteran letters, which Junius was producing, aimed at holding Anthony Chamier up to ridicule. The second was printed on 17 February.

[6] The 'bloody Wretch' was Lord Barrington. The sense requires 'if there were *not* some wicked design in it'.

LETTER NO. 58 [29 February 1772]

Saturday. 29. Feb. I am very glad to see that the Book will be out before Sawbridge's Motion.—there is no occasion for a Mark of Admiration at the End of the Motto.[1] but it is of no moment whatsoever. When you see Mr. W.[2] pray return him my thanks for the Trouble he has taken. I wish he had taken more.—I shd. be glad to have a set, sewed, left at the same place *to morrow* evening. let it be well sealed up.

C

Address: To Mr. Woodfall / Printer / Paternoster Row
Postmark: On letter, ? SA / 12 o'clock
Endorsed 'Thrale'. Seal broken.

EXPLANATION OF DATING

Dated 29 February on original and clearly 1772. Woodfall signalled a letter in his newspaper of 28 February.

LETTER NO. 59 [3 March 1772]

tuesday. your letter was twice refused last night, & the waiter as often attempted to see the person who sent for it.—I was impatient to see the book, & think I had a right to that Attention, a little before the general publication. When I desired to have two sets sewed, & one bound in vellum, it was not from a principle of Oeconomy. I despise such little savings, & shall still be a purchaser.—If I was to buy as many sets as I want, it wod. be remarked.

Pray let the *two* sets be well parcelled up & left at the bar of Munday's Coffee house, Maiden Lane, with the same Direction, & with orders to be Delivered to a Chairman who will ask for them in the Course of tomorrow Evening. farewell.

Address: To Mr. Woodfall, printer / in / Paternoster Row
Postmark: On letter, T TU / 5 o'clock.
Endorsed 'Hay'. Seal broken.

EXPLANATION OF DATING

Immediately prior to publication and therefore Tuesday, 3 March 1772. The *Public Advertiser* for Monday, 2nd carried a signal that a letter was ready

[1] More commonly a Note of Admiration—i.e. an exclamation mark.

[2] Wilkes had read the Dedication and Preface. See his letter of 4 November 1771 in Appendix Two.

or collection and on the 4th Woodfall wrote in his Answers to Correspondents: 'Received, and shall be *strickly* attended to'.

LETTER NO. 60 [5 March 1772]

Thursday.—Your letters with the books are come safe to hand. The difficulty of corresponding arises from Situation & Necessity to which we must submit. Be assured I will not give you more trouble than is unavoidable.—If the vellum books are not yet bound, I wo^d. wait for the Index.[1] If they are, let me know by a line in the P.A.—When they are ready, they may safely be left at the same place as last night.

On *your* account I was alarmed at the price of the book[2]—but of the Sale of books I am no Judge, & can only pray for your success.—What you say about the profits is very handsome. I like to deal with such men. As for myself, be assured that I am far above all pecuniary views; & no other person I think has any claim to share with you. Make the most of it therefore, & let all your views in life be directed to a solid, however moderate independence. Without it, no man can be happy, nor even honest.—

If I saw any prospect of uniting the City once more, I wo^d. readily continue to labour in the vineyard. Whenever M^r. W. can tell me that such a union is in prospect, he shall hear of me.[3]

Quod si quis existimat me aut voluntate esse mutatâ, aut debilitatâ virtute, aut animo fracto, vehementur errat.[4]

farewell.

in the preface p. 20. line 7 read unſeasonable
p. 26. 18 accura*c*y

Address: To / M^r. Woodfall printer / in / Paternoster Row

Postmark: On letter, missing.

Endorsed 'Thrale'.

[1] An index and a table of contents was compiled and published in a second edition in 1773.

[2] The complete edition, in two volumes, cost 10*s*. 6*d*. Wheble's first edition, a pocket version, sold at 3*s*.; Newbery's *The political contest*, which included only the early letters, cost one shilling.

[3] The quarrel between Wilkes and the other city radicals continued for some time. See private letter no. 65.

[4] Cicero, *Oratio Post Reditum ad Quirites*, 19. 'But if anyone thinks that I have changed my intention, or that my strength is failing, or my spirit broken, he is much in error.'

EXPLANATION OF DATING

Obviously immediately after publication and therefore Thursday, 5 March 1772. The *Public Advertiser* on the 6th carried a reply to the inquiry about the vellum books: 'They are not in hand therefore *Directions* shall be punctually complied with.'

LETTER NO. 61 [22 March 1772]

Sunday

I am in no manner of hurry about the books. I hope the Sale has answered.—I think it will always be a saleable book. The inclosed is fact, & I wish it co$^{d.}$ be printed to morrow. It is not worth announcing. The proceedings of this wretch are unaccountable. There must be some Mystery in it, which I hope will soon be discovered to his Confusion.—Next to the D. of G$^{n.}$ I verily believe that the blackest heart in the kingdom belongs to Lord B$^{n.}$[1]

Address: To / M^{r}. Woodfall, / Printer in / Paternoster Row

Postmark: On separate folder, blurred, 12 o'clock

Endorsed 'Emblin'. Seal broken.

EXPLANATION OF DATING

Mason Good dated this Sunday, 3 May 1772 and stated that the enclosed was the letter signed Scotus, printed on 4 May, and attacking Lord Barrington. This cannot be correct: (1) Scotus was announced in advance, on 2 May; (2) 'The inclosed is fact' suggests a news item rather than a letter: it does not fit Scotus; (3) the remark about the books and the inquiry about sales suggests some time in March.

The opening sentence reads like a reply to an apology by the printer. There is a signal on Saturday, 21 March: this note appears to be Junius' reply the following day. The 'inclosed' is then Veteran's short letter of Monday, 23 March, not announced in advance, and beginning: 'I desire you will inform the public that the worthy Lord Barrington, not contented with having driven Mr. D'Oyly out of the War Office, has at last contrived to expel Mr. Francis.' All the other Veteran letters were announced in advance.

The point is of some consequence since it means that some of the strongest language ever employed by Junius ('the blackest heart in the kingdom') was provoked by the resignation of a War Office clerk. It strengthens the case for Philip Francis as the author of the letters.

[1] The offensive comparison is between the Duke of Grafton and Lord Barrington.

LETTER NO. 62 [4 May 1772]

if pars pro toto be meant for me, I must beg the favour of you to recall it. At present it wo[d.] be difficult for me to receive it.—When the books are ready a Latin verse will be sufficient.

Address: To / M[r.] Woodfall, printer / in / Paternoster Row
Postmark: On letter, G MO / 12 o'clock. Seal intact.

EXPLANATION OF DATING

The signal 'PARS, PRO TOTO' appeared in the *Public Advertiser* on Saturday, 2 May 1772. This reply is presumably Monday, 4 May.

LETTER NO. 63

pray let this be announced, *Memoirs of Lord Barrington in our next.* keep the author a secret.

Address: To M[r.] Woodfall printer in / Paternoster Row
No postmark. Seal intact.

EXPLANATION OF DATING

The Memoirs, under the name of Nemesis, were announced in the *Public Advertiser* of Monday, 11 May 1772 and published next day. This letter may be either 9 or 10 May.

LETTER NO. 64 [19 January 1773]

19. Jan. i have seen the signals thrown out for y[r.] old friend & Correspondent. be assured that I have had good reason for not complying with them. In the present state of things, If I were to write again, I must be as silly as any of the horned Cattle, that run mad thro' the City, or as any of your wise Aldermen. I meant the Cause & the public. both are given up. I feel for the honour of this Country, when I see that there are not ten men in it, who will unite & stand together upon any one question. But it is all alike, vile & contemptible.

you have never flinched that I know of; & I shall always rejoice to hear of your prosperity. If you have any thing to communicate, (of moment to yourself) you may use the last address & give a hint.

Address: To / M[r.] Woodfall. printer / in Paternoster Row
Postmark: On letter, T WE
Endorsed 'Hay'. Seal obscured.

EXPLANATION OF DATING

19 January is given at the top of the letter and the context places it in 1773. It was in answer to repeated signals on 21 and 23 December and 2, 8, and 19 January. The *Public Advertiser* of 18 January carried an account of a bullock which did great damage in Fleet Market. Woodfall waited until the books were ready before attempting to contact Junius again; he acknowledged receipt of this letter in the newspaper of 8 March: 'The letter from AN OLD FRIEND AND CORRESPONDENT, dated Jan. 19, came safe to Hand, and his Directions are *strictly followed*.' 19 January 1773 was a Wednesday as shown on the postmark.

LETTER NO. 65 [7 March 1773]

Sir,

I have troubled you with the Perusal of two Letters, as that of the prior Date accounts for the Delay of not sending the Books sooner; and this acquaints you that I did not get them out of the Bookbinder's Hands till Yesterday; nor, tho' I desired them to be finished in the most elegant manner possible, are they done so well as I wished. But Sir if the manner of the Contents and Index are not agreeable to you they shall be done over again according to any Directions you shall please to favour me with. With respect to City Politics, I fear the Breach is too wide ever to be again closed, and even my Friend Mr. Wilkes lost some of his wonted coolness at the late Election, on Sawbridge, Oliver, etc., scratching against him.[1] I hope you will believe that however agreeable to me it must be to be honoured with your Correspondence, I should never entertain the most distant Wish that one Ray of your Splendour should be diminished by your continuing to write. Mr. Wilkes indeed mentioned to me the other Day that he thought the East India Company a proper Subject, and asked if I could communicate anything to You, to which my Reply was that I could not tell, (as I did not know whether you might chuse to be intruded upon).—You will perceive by the Papers that two Persons have obtruded themselves upon us who, without a Tythe of Mr. Wilkes's Abilities imagine the Public will look up to them as their Deliverers, but they are most egregiously mistaken, as every one who possesses a Grain of Common Sense holds them in

[1] At the election for Lord Mayor in October 1772 the following votes were cast: Wilkes 2,301, Townsend 2,278, Hallifax 2,126, Shakespear 1,912, Bankes 3. The court of Aldermen, contrary to its normal practice, then chose the second of the candidates. Sawbridge and Oliver voted for Townsend. Wilkes did not succeed in becoming Lord Mayor until 1774.

almost utter Contempt. You will probably guess that I mean Allen & Lewes, & were I capable of drawing a Parallel I should borrow some Part of it from Shakespare's Iago and Roderigo.[1]—Should it please the Almighty to spare your Life till the next General Election, and I should at that Time exist, I shall hope you will deign to instruct me for whom I should give my Vote, as my Wish is to be represented by the honestest and ablest, and I know there cannot be any one who is so fit to judge as Your self. I have no Connections to warp me nor am I acquainted with but one person who would speak to me on the Subject, and that Gentleman is, I believe, a true Friend to the real Good of his Country; I mean Mr. Glover, the Author of Leonidas.[2]

As I thought Serjeant Glyn deserving of something more than the mere Fees of his Profession, for the Pains he took upon my Tryal I have made a Purchase of a small Freehold at Brentford by way of Qualification, in order to convince him, if he should offer himself at the next Election whenever it should happen, that I hold his Services in grateful Remembrance, but I am since informed that it is not his Intention, and that Lord Percy is to be joined with Sir W. B. Proctor who is to be supported by the Duke of Northumberland's Interest.[3] —I have heard much of a most trimming Letter from Mr. Stewart to Lord Mansfield on the Douglas Cause, but cannot possibly get a Copy, which probably would be a good Letter to print.[4]

[1] In place of 'You will probably guess that I mean Allen & Lewes', Wade's edition had 'You will probably guess who I mean'. Captain Allen and Watkin Lewes had been active in London politics for some years as ardent supporters of Wilkes. A long autobiographical speech by Allen was reported in the *Public Advertiser* for 7 October 1771. Another speech in October 1772 is reported in the *Gentleman's Magazine*, 491, and a third speech, deploring the disunity of the radicals, may be found in the *Gentleman's Magazine*, 1773, 517–18. Watkin Lewes in January 1773 had challenged Oliver to a duel, though the matter was eventually settled peacefully; *Gentleman's Magazine*, 99. Lewes became an Alderman of London in 1772, sheriff the same year, and Lord Mayor in 1780.

[2] Richard Glover published his epic poem *Leonidas* in 1737 at the age of 25. He entered Parliament in 1761 but made no real mark in the House and did not stand again in 1768. There is something a little naïve about Woodfall's remark, as though he intended it as a sighting shot. Richard Duppa published in 1814 *An inquiry concerning the author of the Letter of Junius*, naming Glover as the man, but he has never been regarded as a serious contender.

[3] John Glynn acted as counsel for Wilkes on several occasions. He was returned for Middlesex at a by-election in December 1768, defeating Sir William Beauchamp Proctor in a fierce contest. His health was not good but he did stand again at the general election of 1774: the government, after considerable effort, found it impossible to put candidates into the field; *The House of Commons, 1754–90*, i. 331–5.

[4] Andrew Stuart took the leading part on behalf of the Hamilton family in the Douglas case, a *cause célèbre* which dragged on throughout the 1760s. Vast Scottish

If Sir, you should not disapprove of the Contents & Index I thought of advertising them in the Manner of the enclosed Form, if I may have your Permission so to do, but not otherwise.—May I beg the Favour of a Line in answer? Believe me Sir to be, with Gratitude and Respect,

Your much obliged
humble servant to command
Henry Sampson Woodfall

Sunday 7 March 1773

Address: For / Mr. / F.

No postmark. Seal intact.

EXPLANATION OF DATING

The date 7 March 1773 is on the original and is confirmed by the signal in the *Public Advertiser* for 8 March. Woodfall's letter reads like a resumé of political affairs in the previous six months for someone who has been out of touch with them.

estates were at stake and the pleadings were conducted with great animosity. In 1769 the House of Lords, on appeal, found against Stuart's client. Of his *Letters to Lord Mansfield*, circulated in January 1773, Horace Walpole wrote: 'A Scot dissects a Scot with ten times more address than Churchill and Junius.' Letter to Lady Ossory, 25 January 1773, *Yale Edition*, xxxii. 90.

APPENDIX TWO

PRIVATE LETTERS BETWEEN JUNIUS AND JOHN WILKES

Junius' early opinion of John Wilkes was not flattering. In his Letter to the King of 19 December 1769 he wrote:

> 'A man, not very honourably distinguished in the world, commences a formal attack upon your favourite . . . Mr. Wilkes brought with him into politics the same liberal sentiments by which his private conduct had been directed, and seemed to think, that as there are few excesses in which an English gentleman may not be permitted to indulge, the same latitude was allowed him in the choice of his political principles, and in the spirit of maintaining them. . . . Is this a contention worthy of a king?'

But in the split which occurred early in 1771 in the ranks of the Society of Supporters of the Bill of Rights, Junius took Wilkes's part, arguing that his personal idiosyncrasies should not obscure his service to the public cause. In reply to John Horne's strictures on Wilkes, he wrote, simply: 'You will not suspect me of setting up *Wilkes* for a perfect character. The question to the public is, where shall we find a man who, with purer principles, will go the lengths and run the hazards that he has done? the season calls for such a man, and he ought to be supported.'[1]

On 21 August 1771 Wilkes was sent from Junius a private letter, which he docketed: 'Received on Wednesday noon by a chairman, who said he brought it from a gentleman whom he saw in Lancaster Court, in the Strand.' This was followed by a second letter on 7 September and led to an exchange of views between the two men. One of Junius' first tasks was to palliate the sentiments he had previously expressed. 'Think no more of what is past', he wrote cheerfully; 'You did not then stand so well in my opinion; and it was necessary to the plan of that letter to rate you lower than you deserved. The wound is curable, and the scar shall be no disgrace to you.'[2]

The letters were preserved by Wilkes and first published in the edition of 1812, printed by George Woodfall and prepared by Mason Good. They destroyed the hypothesis, which had sometimes been advanced, that Wilkes himself was Junius. The text has been corrected from the original manuscripts in the British Library, Add. MS. 30881.

[1] Public letter no. LII of 24 July 1771.

[2] Private letter no. 71 of 18 September 1771. In his letter of 12 September Wilkes had written ruefully that Junius had 'poured balm into my wounds, the deepest of which, I sigh when I recollect, were made by that now friendly hand'.

LETTER NO. 66. JUNIUS TO JOHN WILKES

21 August 1771

John Sawbridge, whose claims to the Lord Mayoralty Junius tried to promote, had political connections with Chatham but preserved a reputation for independence. Junius' intention was to win him back to the Wilkite camp and split him from Horne, Oliver, and Townsend, whom he judged to be irreconcilable. Wilkes's plan was to secure the re-election of Brass Crosby by having him returned with William Bridgen: the latter was regarded as so unpopular that Wilkes assumed that the Aldermen would be forced to choose Crosby. Wilkes's scheme collapsed when, at a late stage, Bridgen refused to stand. The outcome was the election of a moderate government supporter, William Nash. See also public letter no. LVIII of 30 September 1771.

*To John Wilkes Esq*r.

London. 21st. August. 1771.

I presume, Sir, you are satisfied that I mean you well, & that it is not necessary to assure you that, while you adhere to the Resolution of depending only upon the public favour, (which, if you have half the understanding I attribute to you, you never can depart from) you may rely upon my utmost assistance. Whatever imaginary views may be ascribed to the Author, it must always make part of *Junius's* plan to support Mr. Wilkes, while *he* makes common cause with the people. I would engage your favourable attention to what I am going to say to you; and I intreat you not to be too hasty in concluding, from the apparent tendency of this letter, to any possible interests or Connexions of my own. It is a very common mistake in Judgement, & a very dangerous one in Conduct, first to look for nothing in the argument proposed to us, but the motive of the man who uses it, & then to measure the truth of his argument by the motive we have assigned to him. With regard to me, Sir, any refinement, in this way, would assuredly mislead you; and tho' I do not disclaim the Idea of some personal views to future honour & advantage, (you would not believe me if I did) yet I can truly affirm that, neither are they little in themselves, nor can they, by any possible Conjecture, be collected from my Writings.

Mr. Horne, after doing much mischief, is now, I think, compleatly defeated & disarmed. The Author of the late unhappy divisions in the City is removed.—Why should we suffer his Works to live after him? —In this view, I confess I am vindictive, & would visit his sins upon his Children. I would punish him in his Offspring, by repairing the breaches he has made.—Convinced that I am speaking to a man, who has spirit enough to act, if his Judgement be satisfied, I will not scruple to declare at once, that Mr. Sawbridge ought to be Lord Mayor, & that he ought to owe it to *your* first Motion, & to the Exertion of all your Credit in the City. I affirm, without a doubt, that political prudence, the Benefit of the Cause, your public Reputation, & personal Interest do all equally demand this Conduct of you. I do not deny that a Stroke, like this, is above the Level of vulgar policy, or that, if you were a much less considerable Man than you are, it would not suit you. But you will recollect, Sir, that the public Opinion of you rises every day, & that you must enlarge your plan as you proceed, since you have every day a new acquisition of Credit to maintain. I offer you the sincere Opinion of a man, who perhaps has more leisure to make reflections than you have, & who, tho' he stands clear of all business & intrigue, mixes, sufficiently for the purposes of Intelligence, in the Conversation of the World.

Whatever language you in prudence assume to the public, you cannot but be sensible, that the Separation of those Gentlemen, who withdrew from the Bill of Rights, was of considerable disservice to you. It required, in *my* Opinion, your utmost dexterity & resolution, & not a little of your good fortune, to get the better of it. But are you now really upon the *best* ground, on which Mr. Wilkes might stand in the City? Will you say that to separate Mr. Sawbridge from a Connexion every way hostile to you, & to secure him against the insidious Arts of Mr. Horne, & the Fury of Mr. Townshend, (if it could be done without embarassing your leading measures, & much more if it promoted them) would not give you a considerable personal gratification?—Will you say that a public declaration of Mr. Sawbridge in your favour, & the Appearance of your acting together, (I do not speak at present of a hearty Coalition or Confidence) would not contribute to give you a more secure, a more permanent, and, without offence to any man, a more honourable Hold upon the City, than you have at present? What Sensations do you conceive a Union between you and Mr. Sawbridge would excite in the breast of Mr. Horne?—Would it not amount to a decisive Refutation of all the invidious Arguments he has drawn from your being deserted by so many of the considerable figures of the party? The Answer to these Questions is too obvious to be mistaken. But you will say to yourself what you would not confess to Junius. 'Mr. Sawbridge is a man of unquestionable Probity, & the Concurrence of his Reputation would undoubtedly be of Service to me; but he has not pliancy enough to yield to persuasion, and I, Wilkes, am determined not to suffer another to reap the harvest of my Labours; that is, to take the Lead of me in the City'.—Sir, I do not mean, or expect, that you should make such a Sacrifice to any man. But, besides the essential Difference in point of Conduct between leading & going foremost, I answer your Thoughts when I say, that, altho' Mr. Sawbridge is not to be directed, (and even this perhaps is not so literally & compleatly true as he himself imagines,) on the other hand, he does not mean to direct. His disposition, as you well know, is not fitted for that active Management & Intrigue, which acquire an operating popularity, and direct the people by their passions. I attribute to you both the most honorable Intentions for the public, but you travel different Roads, and never can be Rivals. It is not that Mr. Sawbridge does not wish to be popular; but, if I am not greatly mistaken, his virtues have not ostentation enough for the ordinary uses of party, and *that* they lead rather to the Esteem of Individuals than to popular Opinion. This, I conceive, is exactly the man you want. You cannot always support a Ferment in the Minds of Men. There will necessarily be Moments of Languor & Fatigue; & upon these occasions, Mr. Sawbridge's reputed Firmness and Integrity may be a capital Resource to you. You have too much Sagacity not to perceive how far this Reasoning might be carried.

In the very Outset, you reap a Considerable Advantage either from his Acceptance or Refusal.—What a Copious Subject of Ostentation!—what rich Colours to the public! Your Zeal to restore Tranquillity to the City—The sacrifice of all personal Recollections in favour of a man whose general Character you esteem;—the public good preferred to every private or interested Consideration, with a long *et cætera* to your own Advantage.—Yet I do not mean to persuade you to so simple a part, as that of contributing to gratify Mr. Sawbridge, without a reciprocal Assurance from him that, upon fair & honourable Occasions, he will in return promote your Advantage. Your own Judgement will easily suggest to you such terms of Acknowledgement, as may be binding upon him in point of Gratitude, & not offensive to his Delicacy. I have not entered into the Consideration of any Objections drawn from the fertile field of provocation & Resentment. Common Men are influenced by common Motives;—but you, Sir, who pretend to lead the people, must act upon higher principles. To make our passions subservient to you, you must command your own. The Man, who, for any personal Indulgence whatsoever, can sacrifice a great purpose to a little one, is not qualified for the Management of great Affairs.

Let me suppose then, that every material difficulty, on Your part, is removed; & that, as far as you alone are concerned, you would be ready to adopt the plan I propose to you. If you are a Man of honour, you will still have a powerful Objection to oppose to me. Admitting the apparent Advantage to your own purposes, & to the Cause you are engaged in, you will tell me 'that you are no longer at Liberty to choose;—that the Desertion of those persons, who once professed a warm Attachment to you, has reduced you to a Situation, in which you cannot do that, which is absolutely *best*;—that Mr. Crosby has deserved everything from *you* & from the City, & that you stand engaged to contribute your whole Strength to continue him another Year in the Mayoralty.'—My reply to this very just Objection is addressed rather to Mr. Crosby than to Mr. Wilkes. *He* ought, at all Events to be satisfied; &, if I cannot bring him over to my Opinion, there's an End of the Argument; for I do agree with you most heartily, that it is as gross a Breach of policy as of morals, to sacrifice the man, who has deserved well of us, to any temporary Benefit whatsoever. Far from meaning to separate you from Mr. Crosby, it is essential to the Measure I recommend, that it should be your joint Act. Nay, it is *he*, who, in the first instance, should open the Communication with Mr. Sawbridge; nor is it possible for *you* to gain any Credit by the Measure, in which he will not of necessity be a considerable Sharer. But now for Considerations, which immediately affect Mr. Crosby.

Your plan, as I am informed, is to engage the Livery to return him with Mr. Bridgen. In my own Opinion, the Court of Aldermen will choose Bridgen; consequently the Sacrifice I require of Mr. Crosby would in effect be nothing. That he will be defeated, is, to *my* Judgement, inevitable. It is for him to consider, whether the idea of a Defeat be not always attended with some Loss of Reputation. In that case too, he will have forced upon the Citizens, (whom he professes to love & respect) a Magistrate, upon whose odious & contemptible Character he at present founds his only hopes of Success.—Do you think that the City will not once, in the Course of a Twel'month, be sensible of the Displeasure you have done them?—or that it will not be placed in strong Terms to your Account?—I appeal to Miss Wilkes, whose Judgement I hear highly commended. Would she think herself much indebted to her favourite Admirer, if he forced a most disagreeable partner upon her for a long Winter's night, because he could not dance with her himself?

You will now say,—'Sir, we understand the Politics of the City better than you do, & are well assured that Mr. Crosby will be chosen Lord Mayor;—otherwise, we allow that, upon *your* plan, he might acquire Credit; without forfeiting any real Advantage.' Upon this ground I expect you, for I confess it is incumbent upon me to meet your Argument, where it lies strongest against me.—Taking it for granted then that Mr. Crosby may be Lord Mayor, I affirm that it is not his Interest, because it is not his greatest Interest. The little profit of the Salary cannot possibly be in Contemplation with him.—I do not doubt that he would rather make it an expensive Office to himself. His View must be directed then to the flattering distinction of succeeding to a second Mayoralty, &, what is still more honorable, to the being thought worthy of it by his fellow Citizens. Placing this Advantage in its strongest light, I say that every purpose of Distinction is as compleatly answered by his being known to have had the employment in his power, (which may well be insisted upon in Argument, & never can be disproved by the fact,) as by his accepting it. To this I add the signal Credit he will acquire with every honest Man by renouncing, upon motives of the clearest & most disinterested Public Spirit, a personal honour, which you may fairly tell the World was unquestionably within his reach.—But these are Trifles.—I assert that, by now accepting the Mayoralty, (which he may take hereafter whenever he pleases) he precludes himself from soliciting, with any Colour of Decency, a real & solid reward from the City.—I mean that he should be returned for London in the next parliament.—I think his Conduct intitles him to it, & that he cannot fail of succeeding, if he does not furnish his opponents with too just a pretence for saying that the City have already rewarded him. On the Contrary, with what force & Truth may he tell his fellow Citizens at the next Election;—'For your sakes I relinquished the honour you intended me. The common good required it. But I did not mean to renounce my hopes that, upon a proper Occasion, you would honour me with a public mark of your Approbation.'

You see I do not insist upon the good Effects of Mr. Sawbridge's Gratitude, yet I am sure it may be depended upon. I do not say that he is a man to go all lengths with Mr. Wilkes; but you may be assured that it is not danger that will deter him, and that, wherever you have the Voice of the people with you, he will, upon principle, support their Choice, at the hazard of his life & fortune.

Now, Sir, supposing all Objections are removed, & that you & Mr. Crosby are agreed, the question is, in what manner is the business to be opened to Mr. Sawbridge. Upon this point too, I shall offer you my opinion, because the plan of this letter would not otherwise be compleat. At the same Time, I do, very unaffectedly, submit myself to your Judgement.

I would have my Lord Mayor begin by desiring a private Interview between him, Mr. Crosby, & yourself.[1] Very little preface will be necessary. You have a man to deal with, who is too honorable to take an unfair Advantage of you. With such a man you gain every thing by Frankness & Candour, & hazard nothing by the Confidence you repose in him. Notwithstanding any passages in this letter, I would shew him the whole of it;—in a great business, there is nothing so fatal as cunning management; and I would tell him, it contained the plan, upon which Mr. Crosby & you were desirous to act, provided he would engage to concur in it, *bonâ fide*, so far forth as he was concerned. There is one Condition, I own, which appears to me a *sine quâ non*; & yet I do not see how it can be proposed in terms, unless his own good Sense suggests the Necessity of it to him—I mean the total & absolute renunciation of Mr. Horne. It is very likely indeed that this gentleman may do the business for himself, either by laying aside the Masque at once, or by abusing Mr. Sawbridge for accepting the Mayoralty upon any Terms whatsoever of Accommodation with Mr. Wilkes.[2]

This Letter, Sir, is not intended for a correct or polished Composition; but it contains the very best of Junius's understanding. Do not treat me so unworthily, or rather do not degrade yourself so much as to suspect me of any interested view to Mr. Sawbridge's particular Advantage.—By all that's honorable I mean nothing but the Cause; & I may defy your keenest penetration to assign a satisfactory reason, why Junius, whoever he be, shd. have a personal interest in giving the Mayoralty to Mr. Sawbridge rather than to Mr. Crosby.

I am heartily weary of writing, & shall reserve another subject, on which I mean to address you, for another Opportunity. I think that

[1] Crosby here is Junius' mistake for Sawbridge: Crosby was, of course, already Lord Mayor.

[2] Junius' motives seem a little transparent here and one can hardly help suspecting that his enthusiasm for Sawbridge was explained by his dislike of Horne.

this letter, if you act upon it, should be a secret to everybody, but Mr. Sawbridge & my Lord Mayor.

Junius

LETTER No. 67. Junius to John Wilkes

7 September 1771

The more prominent reformers having left the Society of Supporters of the Bill of Rights in April 1771 to form the Constitutional Society, the remainder felt the need to reassert their own belief in reform. On 23 July 1771, at a meeting in the London Tavern, they issued a long declaration of grievances and advised all electors to insist on the following pledges from parliamentary candidates:

'1. You shall consent to no supplies without a previous redress of grievances.

2. You shall promote a law, subjecting each candidate to an oath, against having used bribery, or any other illegal means of compassing his election.

3. You shall promote, to the utmost of your power, a full and equal representation of the people in parliament.

4. You shall endeavour to restore annual parliaments.

5. You shall promote a pension and place-bill, enacting, That any member who receives a place, pension, contract, lottery ticket, or any other emolument whatsoever from the Crown, or enjoys profit from any such place, pension, &c., shall not only vacate his seat, but be absolutely ineligible during his continuance under such undue influence.

6. You shall impeach the ministers who advised the violating the right of the freeholders in the Middlesex election; and the military murders in St. George's Fields.

7. You shall make strict inquiry into the conduct of judges touching juries.

8. You shall make strict inquiry into the application of the public money.

9. You shall use your utmost endeavours to have the resolution of the House of Commons expunged by which the magistrates of the city of London were arbitrarily imprisoned for strictly adhering to their charter and their oaths; and also that resolution by which a judicial record was erased to stop the course of justice.

10. You shall attend to the grievances of our fellow-subjects in Ireland, and second the complaints they may bring to the throne.

11. You shall endeavour to restore to America the essential right of taxation, by representatives of their own free election; repealing the acts passed in violation of that right since the year 1763, and the universal excise, so notoriously incompatible with every principle of British liberty, which has been lately substituted, in the colonies, for the laws of customs.'

Many opponents of the radicals maintained that the demand for pledges was an unwarrantable encroachment upon the freedom of judgement of a member of Parliament: the classic statement of this point of view was Burke's speech at Bristol on 3 November 1774. The full text of the Society's declaration is printed in Wade, ii. 71–4.

*To John Wilkes, Esq*r. London 7th. Septr 1771.

As this letter, Sir, has no relation to the Subject of my last, the Motives, upon which you may have rejected one of my Opinions, ought not to influence your Judgement of another. I am not very sanguine in my expectations of persuading, nor do I think myself intitled to quarrel with any man, for not following my Advice. Yet this, I believe, is a Species of Injustice you have often experienced from your friends. From you, Sir, I expect in return, that you will not remember how unsuccessfully I have recommended one measure to your Consideration, least you should think yourself bound to assert your Consistency, and, in the true Spirit of persecution, to pass the same sentence indifferently upon all my Opinions. Forgive this Levity, & now to the business.

A man, who honestly engages in a public cause, must prepare himself for Events, which will at once demand his utmost patience, & rouse his warmest indignation. I feel myself, at this Moment, in the very Situation I describe. Yet from the Common Enemy I expect nothing but hostilities against the people. It is the Conduct of our friends, that surprises & afflicts me. I cannot but resent the Injury done to the Common Cause by the Assembly at the London Tavern, nor can I conceal from you my own particular disappointment. They had it in their power to perform a real, effectual Service to the Nation, & we expected from them a proof, not only of their Zeal, but of their Judgement. Whereas the Measure they have adopted is so shamefully injudicious with regard to its declared object, that, in my own opinion, it will, and reasonably ought to make their Zeal very questionable with the people they mean to serve. When I see a Measure, excellent in itself, & not absolutely unattainable, either not made the principal Object, or extravagantly loaded with Conditions palpably absurd or impracticable, I cannot easily satisfy myself, that the man, who proposes it, is quite so sincere as he pretends to be. *You* at least, Mr. Wilkes, should have shewn more temper & prudence, & a better Knowledge of Mankind. No personal Respects whatsoever should have persuaded you to concur in these ridiculous Resolutions. But my own Zeal, I perceive, betrays me.—I will endeavour to keep a better guard upon my temper, & apply to your Judgement in the most cautious & measured language.

I object, in the first place, to the Bulk, & much more to the Stile of your Resolutions of the 23^{d} of July; tho' some part of the preamble is as pointed as I could wish. You talk of yourselves with too much Authority & Importance. By assuming this false Pomp and Air of Consequence, you either give general Disgust, or, what is infinitely more dangerous, you expose yourselves to be laughed at.[1] The English are a fastidious people, & will not submit to be talked to, in so high a Tone, by a Set of private Gentlemen, of whom they know nothing, but that they call themselves *Supporters of the Bill of Rights*. There are questions, which, in good policy, you should never provoke the people in general to ask themselves. At the same time, Sir, I am far from meaning to undervalue the Institution of this Society. On the contrary, I think the plan was admirable,—that it has already been of signal Service to the public, & may be of much greater; and I do most earnestly wish, that you would consider of & promote a plan for forming constitutional Clubs all thro' the Kingdom.[2] A Measure of this kind would alarm Government more, & be of more essential Service to the Cause, than any thing that can be done relative to new modelling the House of Commons. You see then, that my objections are directed to the particular measure & not to the general Institution.

In the Consideration of this Measure, my first Objection goes to the declared Purpose of the resolutions, in the Terms & Mode, in which you have described it;—viz *the Extermination of Corruption.* In *my* opinion, you grasp at *the impossible*, & *lose the really attainable.* Without plaguing you or myself with a logical argument upon a speculative question, I willingly appeal to your own Candour & Judgement. Can any man, in his Senses, affirm, that, as things are

[1] 'It is corruption that has engendered, nursed and nourished the monster. Against such corruption, then, all men, who value the preservation of their dearest rights, are called upon to unite. Let us remember that we ourselves, our children, and our posterity, must be freemen or slaves as we preserve or prostitute the noble birthright our ancestors bequeathed us: for should this corruption be once firmly rooted, we shall be an undone people. . . . Impressed with these ideas, the gentlemen who compose the Society of the Bill of Rights, have determined to use their utmost endeavours to exterminate this corruption . . . It is their great wish to render the House of Commons what it constitutionally ought to be, the temple of liberty.'

[2] For a discussion of the spread of clubs and societies, which made it easier to mobilize public opinion, see E. C. Black, *The Association: British extra-parliamentary political organization, 1769–1793* (1963).

now circumstanced in this Country, it is possible to *exterminate Corruption*? Do you seriously think it possible to carry, thro' both Houses, such a place-Bill, as you describe in the fifth Article; or, supposing it carried, that it would not be evaded? When you talk of Contracts & Lottery Tickets, do you think that any human Law can really prevent their being distributed & accepted; or do you only intend to mortify *Townshend & Harley*? In short, Sir, would you, *bonâ fide*, and as a man of honour, give it for your Expectation & Opinion, that there is a single County or Borough in the Kingdom, that will form the Declaration recommended to them in these Resolutions, & inforce it upon the Candidates. For myself, I will tell you freely not what I *think*, but what I *know*. The Resolutions are either totally neglected in the Country, or, if read, are laughed at, & by people, who mean as well to the Cause as any of us.

With regard to the Articles, taken separately, I own I am concerned to see that the great Condition, which ought to be the *sine quâ non* of parliamentary Qualification, which ought to be the Basis, as it assuredly will be the only Support, of every Barrier raised in Defence of the Constitution,—I mean *a Declaration upon Oath to shorten the Duration of parliaments*, is reduced to the fourth Rank in the Esteem of the Society, and, even in that place, far from being insisted on with Firmness & Vehemence, seems to have been particularly slighted in the Expression. *You shall endeavour to restore annual parliaments*!—Are these the Terms, which men, who are in earnest, make use of, when the *salus reipublicae* is at Stake! I expected other language from Mr. Wilkes.—Besides my objection in point of form, I disapprove highly of the meaning of the fourth Article as it stands.—Whenever the question shall be seriously agitated, I will endeavour (&, if I live, will assuredly attempt it,) to convince the English Nation, by Arguments, to *my* Understanding unanswerable, that they ought to insist upon a triennial, & banish the Idea of an annual Parliament.

Article 1. . . . The terms of the first Article would have been very proper a Century or two ago, but they are not adapted to the present State of the Constitution. The King does not act *directly*, either in imposing or redressing *grievances*. We need not *now* bribe the Crown to do us Justice; and, as to the refusal of Supplies, we might punish ourselves indeed, but it would be no way compulsory upon the King. With respect to his Civil List, he is already independant, or might be so, if he had common Sense, or common Resolution; and as for refusing to vote the Army or Navy, I hope we shall never be mad enough to try an Experiment, every way so hazardous. But, in fact, the Effort would be infinitely too great for the Occasion. All we want is an honest Representative, or at least such a one, as will have some respect for the Constituent Body. Formerly the House of Commons were compelled to *bargain* with the Sovereign. At present they may prescribe their own Conditions.—So much, in general, for grievances. As to particular grievances, almost all those we complain of are, apparently, the Acts either of the Lords or the Commons. The Appointment of unworthy Ministers is not strictly a Grievance, (that is, a legal Subject of Complaint to the King) until those Ministers are arraigned & convicted in due Course of Law. If, after that, the King should persist in keeping them in Office, it would be a *grievance* in the strict, legal Sense of the Word, & would undoubtedly justify Rebellion according to the forms, as well as the Spirit of the Constitution.—I am far from condemning the late Addresses to the Throne. They ought to be incessantly repeated. The people, by the singular Situation of their Affairs, are compelled to do the Duty of the House of Commons.

Article 2. . . . I object to the second Article, because I think that multiplying Oaths is only multiplying perjury. Besides this, I am satisfied that, with a triennial parliament, (& without it all other provisions are nugatory,) Mr. Grenville's Bill is, or may be made, a sufficient guard against any gross, or flagrant Offences in this Way.[1]

Article 3. . . . The terms of the third Article are too loose & indefinite to make a distinct or serious Impression.—That the people are not equally & fully represented is unquestionable. But let us take care what we attempt. We may demolish the venerable Fabric we intend to repair, & where is the Strength & Virtue to erect a better in its stead? I should not, for my own part, be so much moved at the corrupt & odious practises by which inconsiderable Men get into Parliament, nor even at the want of a perfect Representation, (& certainly nothing can be less reconcilable to the Theory, than the present practise of the Constitution), if Means could be found to compel such Men to do their Duty (in essentials at least) when they *are* in parliament. Now, Sir, I am convinced that, if shortening the Duration of parliaments (which in effect is keeping the representative under the Rod of the Constituent) be not made

[1] Grenville's Act, 10 George III, c. 16, attempted to avoid the partisan treatment of election petitions by transferring the hearing from the whole House to a small committee, specially selected to remove the zealots on either side.

the Basis of our new parliamentary Jurisprudence, other Checks or Improvements signify nothing. On the contrary, if this be made the Foundation, other Measures may come in aid, and, as auxiliaries, be of considerable Advantage. Lord Chatham's project, for instance, of increasing the Number of Knights of Shires, appears to me admirable, & the moment we have obtained a triennial parliament, it ought to be tried.[1] As to cutting away the rotten Boroughs, I am as much offended as any man, at seeing so many of them under the direct Influence of the Crown, or at the Disposal of private persons, yet, I own I have both doubts & apprehensions, in regard to the Remedy you propose. I shall be charged perhaps with an unusual Want of political Intrepidity, when I honestly confess to you, that I am startled at the Idea of so extensive an Amputation. In the first place, I question the power, *de jure*, of the Legislature to disfranchise a number of Boroughs upon the general Ground of improving the Constitution. There cannot be a Doctrine more fatal to the Liberty & Property we are contending for, than that, which confounds the Idea of a *supreme* and an *arbitrary* Legislature. I need not point out to you the fatal purposes, to which it has been, & may be applied. If we are sincere in the political Creed we profess, there are many Things, which, we ought to affirm, cannot be done by King, Lords, & Commons. Among these I reckon the disfranchising a Borough with a general View to Improvement. I consider it as equivalent to robbing the parties concerned, of their freehold, of their Birthright.[2] I say that, altho' this Birthright may be forfeited, or the Exercise of it suspended in particular Cases, it cannot be taken away by a general Law, for any real or pretended purpose of improving the Constitution. I believe there is no power in this Country to make such a Law.—Supposing the Attempt made, I am persuaded you cannot mean, that either King, or Lords, should take an active part in it. A Bill, which only touches the Representation of the People, must originate in the House of Commons. In the Formation & Mode of passing it, the exclusive Right of the Commons must be asserted as scrupulously as in the case of a Money Bill. Now, Sir, I should be glad to know by what kind of reasoning it can be proved, that there

[1] It is a sign of Junius' moderation that he approved so highly of a project which was certain to add substantially to the representation of the landed gentry—a group which could hardly claim to be under-represented in the unreformed House of Commons.

[2] This argument was repeatedly heard in the debates on the Great Reform Bill during 1831 and 1832.

is a power vested in the Representative to destroy his immediate Constituent. From whence could he possibly derive it? A Courtier, I know, will be ready enough to maintain the Affirmative. The Doctrine suits him exactly, because it gives an unlimited Operation to the Influence of the Crown. But *We*, Mr. Wilkes, must hold a different Language.—It is no answer to me to say, that the Bill, when it passes the House of Commons, is the Act of the Majority, & not of the Representatives of the particular Boroughs concerned. If the Majority can disfranchise ten Boroughs, why not twenty—why not the whole Kingdom? Why should not they make their own Seats in parliament, for Life? When the Septennial Act passed, the Legislature did what apparently & palpably they had no power to do; but they did more than people in general were aware of.—They disfranchised the whole Kingdom for four Years.

For Argument's Sake, I will now suppose, that the Expediency of the Measure & the power of Parliament were unquestionable. Still you will find an insurmountable difficulty in the Execution. When all your Instruments of Amputation are prepared,—when the unhappy patient lies bound at your feet, without the possibility of Resistance, by what infallible Rule will you direct the Operation? When you propose to cut away the rotten parts, can you tell us what parts are perfectly sound? Are there any, certain, Limits, in fact or theory, to inform you at what point you must stop,—at what point the Mortification ends?—To a man, so capable of Observation & Reflection as you are, it is unnecessary to say all that might be said upon the Subject.

Besides that I approve highly of Lord Chatham's Idea 'of infusing a portion of new health into the Constitution to enable it to bear its Infirmities,'—(a brilliant Expression, & full of intrinsic Wisdom!) other reasons concur in persuading me to adopt it. I have no Objection to paying him such Compliments as carry a Condition with them, & either bind him firmly to the Cause, or become the bitterest Reproach to him if he deserts it. Of this last, I have not the most distant Suspicion. There is another man indeed, with whose Conduct I am not so compleatly satisfied.[1] Yet even *he*, I think, has not Resolution enough to do anything flagrantly impudent in the face of his Country. —At the same time that I think it good policy to pay those Compli-

[1] Presumably Lord Camden. In letter no. 89 to Chatham, Junius remarked of Camden that 'the nation in general are not quite so secure of *his* firmness as they are of Lord Chatham'.

ments to Lord Chatham, which, in truth, he has nobly deserved, I should be glad to mortify those contemptible Creatures, who call themselves Noblemen, whose worthless importance depends intirely upon their Influence over Boroughs, & cannot be safely diminished but by increasing the power of the Counties at large. Among these men, I cannot but distinguish the meanest of the human Species, the whole Race of the *Conways*.[1] I have but one word to add.—I would not give Representatives to those great trading Towns, which have none at present.—If the Merchant & the Manufacturer must be *really* represented, let them become freeholders by their Industry, and let the Representation of the County be increased. You will find the Interruption of Business in those Towns, by the triennial Riot & Cabals of an Election, too dear a price for the nugatory privilege of sending Members to Parliament.[2]

4. 5. Art. The remaining Articles will not require a long discussion. —of the 4th. and 5th. I have spoken already.

6th. Art. The Measures recommended in the sixth are unexceptionable. My only doubt is, how can an act *apparently* done by the House of Commons, be fixed, by sufficient legal Evidence, upon the Duke of Grafton, or Lord North, of whose guilt I am nevertheless compleatly satisfied. As for Lord Weymouth & Lord Barrington, their own letters are a sufficient ground of Impeachment.[3]

7th. Art. . . . . The seventh Article is also very proper & necessary. The Impeachment of Lord Mansfield, upon his own paper, is indispensable. Yet suffer me to guard you against the seducing Idea of concurring in any Vote, or encouraging any Bill, which may pretend to ascertain, while in reality it limits the Constitutional power of Juries. I would have their Right, to return a general Verdict in all Cases whatsoever, considered as a part of the Constitution, funda-

[1] Francis Seymour Conway, 1st Earl of Hertford, was Lord Chamberlain. He was patron of the borough of Orford and had considerable influence in Warwickshire. Of his seven sons, six entered Parliament, the last going into the Church. His brother, Henry Seymour Conway, represented Thetford and was a politician of importance. Of Lord Hertford it was written that he had 'a constant appetite for all preferments'. *The House of Commons, 1754–90*, iii. 424.

[2] Mrs. Arbuthnot made the same objection to the Reform Bill sixty years later: 'nothing can exceed the folly of giving members to these populous towns. It causes riots and loss of lives and property at every election.' *The journal of Mrs. Arbuthnot, 1820–32* (1950), ii. 173.

[3] The reference is to their letters concerning the St. George's Field riots of May 1768. Weymouth's letter to the magistrates is commented on in note 1 on p. 31; Barrington's letter thanking the troops for devotion to duty is printed in the *Annual Register*, 1768, 111.

mental, sacred, & no more questionable by the Legislature, than whether the Government of the Country shall be by King, Lords, & Commons. Upon this point, an enacting Bill would be pernicious;—a declaratory Bill, to say the best of it, useless.

8th. Art. . . . I think the eighth Article would be more properly expressed thus. *You shall grant no Money unless for Services known to & approved of by Parliament.* In general the Supplies are appropriated, & cannot easily be misapplied. The House of Commons are indeed too ready in granting large Sums under the Head of *Extraordinaries incurred & not provided for;* but the Accounts lie before them;—it is their own fault, if they do not examine them.—The Manner, in which the late debt upon the Civil List was pretended to be incurred & really paid, demands a particular Examination.[1] Never was there a more impudent Outrage offered to a patient people.

9th. Art. . . . The ninth is indispensable; but I think the matter of it rather fitter for Instructions, than for the Declaration you have in view. I am very apprehensive of clogging the Declaration, & making it too long.

10th. & 11th. Art. In the tenth and eleventh you are very civil to Ireland and America; & if you mean nothing but ostentation, it may possibly answer your purpose.—Your Care of Ireland is much to be commended. But, I think, in good policy, you may as well compleat a Reformation at home, before you attempt to carry your Improvements to such a distance. Clearing the Fountain is the best & shortest way to purify the Stream. As to taxing the Americans by their own Representatives, I confess I do not perfectly understand you. If you propose that, in the Article of Taxation, they should hereafter be left to the Authority of their respective Assemblies, I must own I think you had no business to revive a question, which should, & probably would, have lain dormant for ever. If you mean that the Americans should be authorised to send their Representatives to the British parliament, I shall be contented with referring you to what Mr. Burke has said upon this Subject, & will not venture to add anything of my own, for fear of discovering an offensive disregard of your Opinion.[2] Since the repeal of the Stamp Act, I know of

[1] A debt of £513,000 on the civil list was declared in 1769; it was freely suggested that it had been incurred in corrupting the House of Commons. The matter is discussed in J. Brooke, *King George III*, 200–11.

[2] Burke objected that the distance involved and the hazards of communication rendered the proposal quite impracticable. The clearest statement of his opinion is in *Observations on a late publication, intitled The Present State of the Nation* published in 1769.

no Acts, tending to tax the Americans, except that which creates the Tea duty, & even that can hardly be called *internal*. Yet it ought to be repealed, as an impolitic Act, not as an oppressive one. It preserves the Contention between the Mother Country & the Colonies, when everything worth contending for, is in reality given up. When this Act is repealed, I presume you will turn your Thoughts to the postage of Letters, a Tax imposed by Authority of Parliament, & levied in the very heart of the Colonies. I am not sufficiently informed upon the Subject of that Excise, which you say is substituted in North America to the Laws of Customs, to deliver such an opinion upon it, as I would abide by. Yet I can easily comprehend that, admitting the necessity of raising a Revenue for the Support of Government there, any other Revenue Laws, but those of Excise, would be nugatory in such a Country as America. I say this with great Diffidence as to the point in question, and with a positive protest against any Conclusion from America to Great Britain.

If these Observations shall appear to deserve the Attention of the Society, it is for *them* to consider what use may be made of them. I know how difficult & irksome it is, to tread back the Steps we have taken. Yet, if any part of what I have submitted to you carries Reason & Conviction with it, I hope that no false shame will inflence our friends at the London Tavern. I do not deny that I expect my Opinions upon these points should have some degree of weight with you. I have served Mr. Wilkes, & am still capable of serving him. I have faithfully served the public, without the possibility of a personal Advantage. As *Junius* I can never expect to be rewarded.—The Secret is too important to be committed to any great man's discretion. If views of interest or Ambition could tempt me to betray my own Secret, how could I flatter myself that the Man I trusted would not act upon the same principles, & sacrifice me at once to the King's Curiosity & Resentment? Speaking therefore as a disinterested Man, I have a Claim to your Attention. Let my Opinions be fairly examined.

Junius

P.S. As you will probably never hear from me again, I will not omit this Opportunity of observing to you, that I am not properly supported in the Newspapers. One would think that all the Fools were of the other side of the question. As to myself it is of little moment. I can brush away the swarming Insects, whenever I think proper. But it is bad policy to let it appear, in any instance, that we have not Numbers as well as Justice of our side.

I wish you would contrive that the Receipt of this letter & my last might be barely acknowledged by a hint in the Public Advertiser.

LETTER NO. 68. JOHN WILKES TO JUNIUS

9 September 1771

Wilkes replied to the postscript with the following insertion in the *Public Advertiser*. It was a good deal less discreet than Junius had intended. The entry followed immediately after a paragraph referring to Junius.

Prince's Court. Monday Sept. 9.

Mr. Wilkes has the Honour of receiving from the same Gentleman two excellent letters on important subjects, one dated Aug. 21st, the other Sept. 7th. He begs the Favour of the Author to prescribe the Mode of Mr. Wilkes's communicating his Answer.

LETTER NO. 69. JUNIUS TO JOHN WILKES

10 September 1771

Junius' reply was endorsed by Wilkes: 'Received by the Penny Post. Sept. 10. 1771.'

You may intrust Woodfall with a letter for me. Leave the rest to his managem[t]. I expect that you will not enter into any explanations with him whatsoever.—

LETTER NO. 70. JOHN WILKES TO JUNIUS

12 September 1771

Junius' unsolicited advice may have placed Wilkes in some difficulty. He could not afford to offend so powerful an ally and it enhanced his reputation to have it known that he was in correspondence with Junius. But on neither the Lord Mayoralty nor the London Tavern resolutions did his opinions coincide with those of Junius. His reply appears candid and may have been so.

Sept. 12. 1771.

Sir,

I do not mean to indulge the impertinent curiosity of finding out the most important secret of our times, the author of Junius. I will not attempt with profane hands to tear the sacred veil of the Sanctuary; I am disposed with the inhabitants of Attica to erect *an altar to the unknown god* of our political idolatry, and will be content to worship him in clouds and darkness.

This very circumstance however, deeply embarrasses me. The first letter, with which I was honoured by Junius, called for a thousand anecdotes of Crosby, Sawbridge, and Townsend, too tedious, too minute to throw upon paper, which yet must be acted upon, and, as he well knows, mark the character of men. Junius has in my idea too favourable sentiments of Sawbridge. I allow him honest, but think he has more mulishness than understanding, more understanding than candour. He is become the absolute dupe of Malagrida's gang.[1] He has declared that if he was chosen Mayor this year, he would not serve the office, but fine, because Townsend ought to be Mayor. Such a declaration is certain, and, in my opinion, it borders on insanity. To me Sawbridge complained the last year, that his Sheriffalty passed in a continued secret cabal of Beckford, Townsend, and Horne, without the communication of any thing to him till the moment of execution. Sawbridge has openly acted against us. Our troops will not be brought at present to fight his battles. M^rs. Macaulay has warmly espoused the common cause, and severely condemns her brother.[2] Any overtures to Sawbridge I believe would have been rejected, perhaps treated with contempt by not the best-bred man in the island. How could I begin a negotiation, when I was already pledged to Crosby, who has fed himself with the hope of that, and the Membership, by which I overcame his natural timidity? Junius sees the confidence I place in him. Could there be a prospect of any cordiality between Sawbridge and the popular party, at least so soon as his Mayoralty? I should fear the Mansion House would be besieged and taken by the banditty of the Shelburnes. But what I am sure will be decisive to Junius, I was engaged to Crosby before I received the letter of Aug. 21st. and I have not since found in him the least inclination to yield the favourite point. The Membership of the

[1] Lord Shelburne was known by the nickname of Malagrida, a Jesuit priest executed in Portugal in 1761 for conspiracy against the life of the King. Many persons believed that Malagrida's reputation for duplicity was undeserved: hence, Goldsmith's famous *gaffe* when conversing with Shelburne—'I wonder they should call your Lordship *Malagrida*, for Malagrida was a very good man.' Boswell, *Life of Johnson*, ed. G. B. Hill, iv. 174.

[2] Mrs. Catherine Macaulay, the historian, was Sawbridge's sister. In 1770 she had written a sharp answer to Burke's *Thoughts on the cause of the present discontents*, dismissing the Rockinghams as a mere aristocratic faction.

City is a security to the Public for his steadiness in the cause. Surely then it would have been imprudent to have wished a change. My duty to the people only makes me form a wish for Crosby. To make Crosby Mayor it is necessary to return to the Court of Aldermen another man so obnoxious, that it is impossible for them to elect him. Bridgen I take to be this man. While he presided in the City, he treated them with insolence, was exceedingly rude and scurrilous to them personally, starved them at the few entertainments he gave, and pocketed the City cash.[1] As he has always voted on the popular side, we are justified to the Livery in the recommendation of him, and the rest will be guessed. Crosby will probably be the Locum tenens of Bridgen, if Bridgen is elected. I wrote the letter on this subject in the Public Advertiser of Sept. 5.[2] The argument there is specious, altho' my private opinion is, the House of Commons will not again fall into that snare. Into another I am satisfied they will. The House of Lords too will I think furnish a most interesting scene in consequence of the powers they usurp, and the Sheriffs mean the attack. I wish this great business, as I have projected it, could be unravelled in a letter or two to Junius, but the detail is too long and intricate.[3] How greatly is it to be lamented that the few real friends of the Public have so little communication of counsels, so few, and only distant means, of a reserved intercourse?

I have no where met with more excellent and abundant political matter than in the letter of Junius respecting the Bill of Rights. He ought to know from me, that the American Dr. Lee (the Gazetteer's Junius Americanus) was the author of the too long Preamble, Articles, &c. They were indeed, submitted to me on the morning of the day on which they passed, but I made few corrections. I disliked the extreme verbiage of every part, and wished the whole put again on the anvil. Sir Joseph Mawbey and I were of opinion to adjourn the business for a reconsideration, but the Majority of the members were too impatient to have something go forth in their names to the Public. It would have been highly imprudent in Sir Joseph or me to thwart them in so favourite a point, and the sub-

[1] Bridgen had been Lord Mayor in 1763/4.

[2] Under the name of A Liveryman.

[3] Wilkes's plan, which was never put into operation, was to goad the House of Lords into a second encounter over the printers by publishing an offensive letter about Lord Pomfret, a Lord of the Bedchamber. If the Lords then attempted to commit the printer, the city authorities would act as they had done over Wheble and Miller. See Dayrell to Temple, *Grenville papers*, iv. 535–7.

stance I indeed greatly approve. At all times I hate taking in other people's foul linnen to wash. The Society of the Bill of Rights have been called my Committee, and it has been said that they were governed entirely by me. This has spread a jealousy even among my friends. I was therefore necessitated to act the most cautious and prudent part. You cannot always do all the good you wish, and you are sometimes reduced to the necessity of yielding in a particular moment to conciliate the doubtfull, the peevish, or the refractory.

Junius may be assured that I will warmly recommend the formation of constitutional clubs in several parts of the kingdom. I am satisfied that nothing would more alarm the Ministry.

I agree that the shortening the duration of Parliaments is the first and most important of all considerations, without which all the rest would be nugatory, but I am unhappy to differ with Junius in so essential a point as that of triennial Parliaments. They are inadequate to the cure of destroying dependance in the Members on the Crown. They only lessen, not root out corruption, and only reduce the purchase money, for an annuity of three instead of seven years. I have a thousand arguments against triennial, and in favour of annual, Parliaments. The question was fairly agitated at the London Tavern, and several of your friends owned that they were convinced. The subject is too copious for a letter. I hope to read Junius's mature and deliberate thoughts on this subject. I own that in the House of Commons sound policy would rather favour triennial Parliaments as the necessary road to annual, but the constitutional question is different.

I am sorry likewise to differ with Junius as to the power, *de jure*, of the Legislature to disfranchise any boroughs. How originated the right, and why was it granted? Old Sarum and Gatton, for instance, were populous places when the right of representation was first given them. They are now desolate, and therefore in every thing should return to their former state. A barren mountain, or a single farm-house, can have no representatives in Parliament. I exceedingly approve Lord Chatham's idea of increasing the number of Knights of Shires. If Parliaments are not annual, I should not disapprove of a third part of the legislative body going out every year by ballot, and of consequence an annual reelection in part.

I am so much harrassed with business at present that I have not time to mention many particulars of importance, and these three days I have had the shivering fits of a slow, lurking fever, a strange disorder for Wilkes, which makes writing painfull to me. I could plunge the patriot dagger in the heart of the tyrant of my country, but my hand would now tremble in doing it. In general I enjoy settled confirmed health, to which I have for some years paid great attention, chiefly from public views.

I am satisfied that Junius now means me well, and I wish to merit more than his regard, his friendship. He has poured balm into my wounds, the deepest of which I sigh when I recollect were made by that now friendly hand, I am always ready to kiss his rod, but I hope its destination is changed, and that it will never again fall as heavy upon me as towards the conclusion of the year 1769, when Thurloe said sneeringly, the government prosecuted Junius out of compliment to Wilkes. I warmly wish Junius my friend. As a public man, I think myself secure of his support, for I will only depend on popular favour, and pursue only the true constitutional points of liberty. As a private person, I figure to myself that Junius is as amiable in the private, as he is great in the public, walk of life. I now live very much at home, happy in the elegant society of a sensible daughter, whom Junius has noticed in the most obliging manner.

I have not had a moment's conversation with Woodfall on the subject of our correspondence, nor did I mean to mention it to him. All he can guess will be from the following card, which I shall send by my servant with this letter. 'Mr. Wilkes presents his compliments to Mr. Woodfall, and desires him to direct and forward the enclosed to Junius.'

After the first letter of Junius to me, I did not go to Woodfall to pry into a secret I had no right to know. The letter itself bore the stamp of Jove. I was neither doubting nor impertinent. I wish to comply with every direction of Junius, to profit by his hints, and to have the permission of writing to him on any important occasion. I desire to assure him that in all great public concerns I am perfectly free from every personality, either of dislike or affection. The stoic apathy is then really mine.

Lord Chatham said to me ten years ago, 'the King is the falsest hypocrite in Europe.' I must hate the man as much as even Junius can, for thro' his whole reign almost it has been *the King versus Wilkes*. His conduct will probably make it *Wilkes versus the King*. Junius must imagine that no man in the island *feels* what he writes on that occasion more than I do.

This letter is an emanation of the heart, not an effort of the head. It claims indulgence from the honest zeal and sincerity of the writer, whose affection for his country will end only with his life.

John Wilkes

LETTER NO. 71. JUNIUS TO JOHN WILKES

18 September 1771

Junius' judgement on city affairs was better than Wilkes's. Bridgen threw up his nomination, Sawbridge and Crosby cancelled each other, and William Nash was elected. His conduct as Lord Mayor during 1771/2 was a source of irritation to the radicals. Wilkes endorsed this letter: 'Received Wednesday afternoon, Sept. 18. 1771.'

London. 18th. September. 1771.

Sir,

Your letter of the 12th. instant was carefully conveyed to me. I am much flattered, as you politely intended I should be, with the worship you are pleased to pay to the unknown God of Politics. I find I am treated, as other Gods usually are by their Votaries, with Sacrifice and Ceremony in Abundance, & very little obedience. The profession of your Faith is unexceptionable; but I am a modest Deity, & should be full as well satisfied with good Works and Morality.

There is a Rule in business, that would save much time & trouble, if it were generally adopted. *A question, once decided, is no longer a Subject of Argument.* You have taken your Resolution about the Mayoralty. What I have now to say is not meant to alter it, but, in perfect good humour, to guard you against some Inconveniences, which may attend the Execution. It is your own Affair, & tho' I still think you have chosen injudiciously, both for youself & for the public, I have no right to find fault or, to teize you with Reflections, which cannot divert you from your purpose.

I cannot comprehend the reason of Mr. Crosby's Eagerness to be Lord Mayor, unless he proposes to disgrace the office & himself by pocketing the Salary. In that Case, he will create a disgust among the Citizens, of which you & your party will feel the bad effects; & as for himself, he may bid adieu to all hopes of being returned for the City. That he should live with unusual Splendor is essentially your interest, and his own; and even then, I do not perceive that his Merits are so distinguished, as to intitle him to a double reward.—Of the dignity or Authority of a *Locum tenens*, I know nothing; nor can I conceive what Credit Mr. Crosby is likely to derive from representing Mr. Bridgen. But suppose Bridgen should be Lord Mayor, & should keep his word in appointing Crosby his Lieutenant, I should be glad to know who is to support the Expence and Dignity of the Office? It may suit such a fellow as Bridgen to shut up the Mansion house, but I promise you his œconomy will be of no Service to Mr. Wilkes. If you make him Mayor, you will be made answerable for his Conduct; & if he & Crosby be returned, you may depend upon it the Court of Aldermen will choose him.

With regard to Mr. Sawbridge, since I cannot prevail with you to lay the foundation of a closer Union between you, by any positive Sacrifice in his favour, at least let me intreat you to observe a moderate & guarded conduct towards him. I should be much concerned to see his Character traduced, or his person insulted. He is *not* a Dupe to any Set of Men whatsoever, nor do I think he has taken any violent or decided part against you. Yet to be excluded from those *honours*, which are the only rewards he pretends to, & to which he is so justly intitled, & to see them bestowed upon such men as *Crosby & Bridgen* is enough to excite & justify his Resentment. All this, Sir, is Matter of Convenience, which I hope you will consider. There is another point, upon which I must be much more serious & earnest with you. You seem to have no Anxiety or Apprehension, but least the friends of Lord Shelburne should get Possession of the Mansion house. In *my* Opinion they have no Chance of Success whatsoever. The real danger is from the interest of Government;—from Harley, & the Tories.[1] If, while you are employed in counteracting Mr. Townshend, a ministerial Alderman should be returned, you will have ruined the Cause,—you will have ruined yourself, and for ever. To say that *Junius* could never forgive you is nothing;—you could never forgive yourself. Junius, from that Moment, will be compelled to consider you as a Man, who has sacrificed the public to views which were every way unworthy of you. If, then, upon a fair Canvass of the Livery, you should see a probability that *Bridgen* may not be returned, let that point be given up at once, & let *Sawbridge* be returned with *Crosby*;—a more likely way, in *my* Judgement, to make *Crosby* Lord Mayor.

Nothing can do you more honour, nor be of greater benefit to the Community, than your intended Attack upon the unconstitutional powers assumed by the House of Lords. You have my warmest Applause; and, if I can assist, command my assistance. The arbitrary

[1] Lord Shelburne supported Townsend and Oliver: Harley supported Nash.

power of fine & Imprisonment, assumed by these men, would be a disgrace to any form of legal government, not purely *aristocratical.* Directly, it invades the Laws—Indirectly, it saps the Constitution. Naturally phlegmatic, these questions warm me.—I envy you the Laurels you will acquire. Banish the Thought that *Junius* can make a dishonourable, or an imprudent use of the Confidence you repose in him. When you have Leisure, communicate your Plan to me, that I may have time to examine it, & to consider what part I can act with the greatest Advantage to the Cause. The constitutional Argument is obvious. I wish you to point out to me, where you think the Force of the *formal*, *legal* Argument lies. In pursuing such Inquiries, I lie under a singular Disadvantage. Not venturing to consult those, who are qualified to inform me, I am forced to collect every thing from Books or common Conversation. The pains I took with that paper upon privilege were greater than I can express to you.[1] Yet, after I had blinded myself with poring over Journals, Debates, and parliamentary history, I was at last obliged to hazard a bold assertion, which I am now convinced is true (as I really then thought it) because it has not been disproved or disputed.—There is this material difference upon the face of the two Questions. We can clearly show a time, when the lower House had *not* an unlimited power of Commitment for Breach of Privilege.—Whereas, I fear, we shall not have the same Advantage over the House of Lords. It is not that Precedents have any weight, with *me*, in Opposition to Principles; but, I know, they weigh with the Multitude.

My opinion of the several Articles of the proposed Declaration remains unaltered. I cannot pretend to answer those Arguments, in favor of annual parliaments, by which you say the Friends of *Junius* were convinced. The question is not, what is best in Theory, (for there, I should undoubtedly agree with you,) but, what is most expedient in practise. You labour to carry the Constitution to a point of perfection, which it can never reach to, or at which it cannot long be stationary. In this idea, I think I see the Mistake of a speculative Man, who is either not conversant with the World, or not sufficiently persuaded of the Necessity of taking Things, *as they are.* The Objection, drawn from the purchase of an Annuity for *three* years instead of *seven*, is defective, because it applies, in the same proportion, to an Annuity for one year. This is not the question. The point is to keep the Representative as much under the Check &

[1] Public letter no. XLIV.

Controul of the Constituent, as can be done, consistently with other great & essential objects. But, without entering farther into the Debates, I would advise that this part of the Declaration be expressed in general Terms; viz. *to shorten the Duration of Parliaments*. This mediating Expedient will, for the present, take in both opinions, and leave open the *quantum of Time* to a future Discussion.

In answer to a general Argument, by which the uncontroulable Right of the people to form the third part of the Legislature is defended, you urge against me two gross Cases, which undoubtedly call for Correction. These Cases, you may believe, did not escape me, and, by and by, admit of a particular answer. But it is not treating me fairly, to oppose general principles with particular Abuses. It is not in human Policy to form an institution, from which no possible Inconvenience shall arise. I did not pretend to deliver a Doctrine, to which there could be no possible Objection. We are to choose between better & worse. Let us come fairly to the point.—Whether is it safer to *deny* the Legislature a power of disfranchising all the Electors of a Borough; (which, if denied, entails a Number of rotten Boroughs upon the Constitution)—or to *admit* the power, and so leave it with the Legislature to disfranchise, *ad arbitrium*, every Borough & County in the Kingdom. If you deny the consequence, it will be incumbent upon you to prove, by *positive* reasoning, that a Power which holds in the Case of Aylsbury or New Shoreham, *does not* hold in the Case of York, London, or Middlesex. To this question I desire a direct Answer; and when we have fixed upon our principles, we may regularly descend to the detail.—The cases of *Gatton* and *Old Sarum* do not embarass me. Their right to return Members to Parliament has neither fact nor Theory to support it. They have, *bonâ fide*, no Electors.' Consequently, there is no man to be dispossessed of his Freehold, no man to be disfranchised of his right of Election. At the worst, supposing the Annihilation of these pretended Boroughs could no way be reconciled to my own principles, I shall only say, 'Give me a healthy, vigorous constitution, & I shall hardly consult my Looking glass to discover a Blemish upon my Skin.'

You ask me, from whence did the right originate, & for what purpose was it granted? I do not see the Tendency of these Questions, but I answer them without Scruple. 'In general it arose from the King's Writs, & it was granted with a view to balance the power of the Nobility, & to obtain Aids from the People.'—But, without looking back to an obscure Antiquity, from which no certain information can be collected, you will find that the Laws of England have much greater Regard to *Possession* (of a certain length) than to any other Title whatsoever; and that in every kind of property, which savours of the *Realty*, this Doctrine is, most wisely, the Basis of our English Jurisprudence. Tho' I use the terms of art, do not injure me so much as to suspect I am a Lawyer.—I had as lief be a Scotchman.—It is the Encouragement given to Disputes about *Titles*, which has supported that iniquitous Profession at the Expence of the Community.—As to this whole Argument about rotten Boroughs, if I seem zealous in supporting my Opinion, it is not from a Conception, that the Constitution can possibly be relieved from them—I mean only to reconcile you to an Evil, which cannot safely be removed.

Now, Mr. Wilkes, I shall deal very plainly with you. The subject of my first Letter was private & personal, & I am content it should be forgotten.—Your letter to *me* is also sacred. But my second Letter is of public Import, & must not be suppressed. I did not mean that it should be buried in Prince's Court. It would be unfair to embarass you with a new question, while your City Election is depending. But if I perceive that, within a reasonable Time after that Business is concluded, no steps are taken with the Bill of Rights to form a new, short, & rational Declaration, (whether by laying my Letter before the Society, or by any other Mode that you shall think advisable), I shall hold myself obliged, by a Duty, paramount to all other Considerations, to institute an amicable Suit against the Society before the Tribunal of the public;—without asperity, without petulance or disrespect,—I propose to publish the second letter, & to answer or submit to argument. The necessity of taking this Step will indeed give me pain; for I well know, that Differences between the Advocates are of no Service to the Cause. But the Lives of the best of us are spent in choosing between Evils. As to you, Sir, you may as well take the Trouble of directing that Society, since whatever they do is placed to *your* Account.

The domestic society you speak of is much to be envied. I fancy I should like it still better than you do.—I too am no Enemy to good Fellowship, & have often cursed that canting parson, for wishing to deny you your Claret.[1] It is for *him*, & men like *him*, to beware of Intoxication. Tho' I do not place the little pleasures of Life in Competition with the glorious Business of instructing & directing the

[1] The reference is to John Horne's newspaper controversy with Wilkes in the summer of 1771.

people, yet I see no reason why a wise man may not unite the public Virtues of Cato, with the Indulgence of Epicurus.

Continue careful of your health. Your head is too useful to be spared, & your hand may be wanted. Think no more of what is past.—You did not then stand so well in my opinion; and it was necessary to the plan of that letter to rate you lower than you deserved. The wound is curable, & the Scar shall be no disgrace to you.[1]

I willingly accept of as much of your friendship, as you can impart to a man, whom you will assuredly never know.—Besides every personal Consideration, if I were known, I could no longer be a useful servant to the public. At present, there is something oracular in the delivery of my Opinions. I speak from a Recess, which no human Curiosity can penetrate; & Darkness, we are told, is one Source of the Sublime.—The Mystery of *Junius* increases his Importance.

Junius

LETTER NO. 72. JOHN WILKES TO JUNIUS

19 September 1771

Prince's Court, Thursday Sept. 19.

Mr. Wilkes thanks Mr. Woodfall for the care of the former letter, and desires him to transmit the enclosed to Junius.

Sept. 19. 1771.

Sir,

I had last night the honour of your letter of yesterday's date. I am just going to the Common Hall, but first take up the pen to thank you for the kindness you express to me, and to say that the Bill of Rights meet next tuesday. I thought it necessary not to lose a moment in giving you this information, that whatever you judge proper, may be submitted to that Society as early as possible. Junius may command me in every thing. When he says, 'my second letter is of public import, and must not be suppressed. I did not mean that it should be buried in Prince's Court,' does he wish it should be communicated to the Society, and in what manner? The beginning of the second letter refers to a first letter, and some other expressions may be improper for the knowledge of the Society. I wait Junius's directions.

[1] See the introduction to this appendix, p. 397.

I beg his free sentiments on all occasions. I mean next week to state a variety of particulars for his consideration, and in answer to his letter. I had now only a moment to mention a point of business, and a feeling of gratitude.

John Wilkes

LETTER NO. 73. JUNIUS TO JOHN WILKES

21 September 1771

Endorsed by Wilkes: 'Received Sept. 21 1771.'

21st. September. 1771.

Since you are so obliging as to say you will be guided by my Opinion, as to the manner of laying my Sentiments before the Bill of Rights, I see no reason why the whole of the 2d. Letter may not be read there next Tuesday, except the Postscript, which has no connexion with the rest;—the word *ridiculous*, which may naturally give offence;—& I mean to persuade & soften, not to irritate or offend. Let that word be expunged.[1] The prefatory part you may leave or not, as you think proper. You are not bound to satisfy any man's curiosity upon a *private* matter, & upon *my* Silence you may, I believe, depend intirely. As to other passages, I have no favour or affection—so let it all go.—It should be copied over in a better hand.

If any objections are raised, which are answered in my third Letter, you will, I am sure, answer for me, so far forth, *ore tenus*.

Js.

By all means let it be copied—This Manuscript is for private use only.

LETTER NO. 74. JUNIUS TO JOHN WILKES

23 September 1771

Endorsed by Wilkes: 'Received Sept. 23, 1771.'

Monday.

Sir,

When I wrote to you on Saturday, it did not occur to me that your own Advertisement had already informed the public of your receiving *two* letters; your omitting the preamble to the 2d. letter would therefore be to no purpose.

[1] This reference was to the 'ridiculous resolutions' of 23 July.

In *my* opinion you should not wish to decline the appearance of being particularly addressed in that Letter. It is calculated to give you *dignity* with the public. There is more in it than perhaps you are aware of. depend upon it, the perpetual Union of *Wilkes & Mob* does you no service. Not but that I love & esteem the Mob.—It is your interest to keep up dignity and gravity besides. I would not make myself cheap, by walking the Streets so much as you do.—*verbum sat.*

LETTER NO. 75. JOHN WILKES TO JUNIUS

25 September 1771

Wednesday Sept. 25

Sir,

Yesterday I attended the Meeting of the Society of the Bill of Rights, and laid before them the letter, which I had the honour of receiving from you on the 7th of September. The few lines of the Preamble I omitted, the word *ridiculous* according to your directions, and a very few more lines chiefly towards the conclusion. All the rest was a faithfull transcript, the exact *tenor.*[1] The season of the year occasioned the Meeting to be ill attended. Only eleven Members were present. The following Resolution passed unanimously, 'that Mr. Wilkes be desired to transmit to Junius the thanks of this Society for his letter, and to assure him that it was received with all the respect due to his distinguished character and abilities.' Soon after my fever obliged me to return home, and I have not heard of anything farther being done, but Mr. Lee told me he thought the letter capable of a full answer, which he meant on a future day to submit to the Society, and would previously communicate to me. The letter is left in the hands of Mr. Reynolds, who has the care of the other papers of the Society, with directions to permit every Member to peruse and even transcribe it, on the promise of non-publication. Some particular expressions appeared rather too harsh and grating to the ears of some of the members. Surely, Sir, nothing in the advertisement I inserted in the Public Advertiser could lead to the idea of the

[1] In 1764, when Wilkes was tried for publishing No. 45 of the *North Briton* and the Essay on Woman, Lord Mansfield permitted the prosecution to substitute the word 'tenor' for the word 'purport' in the indictment. His critics claimed that this was to Wilkes's disadvantage. H. Bleackley, *Life of John Wilkes*, 151; R. Postgate, *That devil Wilkes* (1930), 98.

two letters I mentioned coming from *Junius*. I intreat him to peruse once more that guarded advertisement.[1] I hope that Mr. Bull's and my address of saturday was approved where I most desire it should be thought of favourably. I know it made our enemies wince in the most tender part.[2]

I am too ill to-day to add more.
John Wilkes

LETTER NO. 76. JUNIUS TO JOHN WILKES

16 October 1771

16th. October. 1771.

I cannot help expressing to you my Thanks, & approbation of your Letter of this day.[3] I think it proper, manly, & to the purpose. In these Altercations, nothing can be more useful than to preserve Dignity, & *sang froid.*—fortiter in re, suaviter in modo, increases both the force & the severity. Your Conduct to Mr. Sawbridge is every thing I could wish.[4] Be assured you will find it both honourable and judicious. Had it been adopted a little sooner, you might have returned him & Crosby, and taken the whole merit of it to yourself. If I am truly informed of Mr. S.'s behaviour on the hustings, I must confess it does not satisfy me.[5] But perseverance, management, & determined good humour, will set every thing right, and, in the end, break the heart of Mr. Horne. Nothing can be more true than what you say about *great men*. They are indeed a worthless, pitiful race.[6]—

[1] The juxtaposition of Wilkes's acknowledgement in the *Public Advertiser* of 9 September (letter no. 68) made it perfectly clear that both letters were from Junius.

[2] Frederick Bull and Wilkes were sheriffs of London 1771/2. Their statement of 21 September declared that they would not call upon the military to assist the civil government of the city in the performance of its duties, particularly at executions.

[3] The animosities arising from the campaign for the Lord Mayoralty led to angry exchanges on the hustings. In the *Public Advertiser* of 16 October Wilkes published a letter to the livery.

[4] 'No man', Wilkes had written, 'can honour Mr. Sawbridge more than I do, for *every public* and private *virtue* which constitutes *a great* and amiable *character*.'

[5] Sawbridge had launched a powerful attack upon Wilkes, whom he accused of circulating insinuations and aspersions in the newspapers.

[6] Wilkes asserted that Townsend had been reluctant to move in the printers' case without the support of some great men. 'The *prudent* Mr. Townsend may wait the consent of *great men*. I will, on a national call, follow instantly the line of my duty, regardless of their applause or censure. Public spirit and virtue are seldom in the company of his Lordship or his Grace.'

Chatham has gallantly thrown away the Scabbard, & never flinched. —From that moment I began to like him.—

I see, we do not agree about the strict right of pressing.[1] If you are as sincere as I am, we shall not quarrel about a difference of Opinion. I shall say a few Words to morrow on this Subject, under the signature of Philo Junius.—The Letters under that name have been hastily drawn up, but the principles are tenable.—I thought your letter about the military very proper & well drawn.[2]

J$^{s.}$

LETTER NO. 77. JOHN WILKES TO JUNIUS

17 October 1771

October 17$^{th.}$ 1771.

I am not yet recovered, and to-day have been harassed with complaints against the greatest villains out of hell, the Bailiffs; but so very polite and friendly a letter as Junius's of yesterday, demands my earliest and warmest acknowledgments. I only take up the pen to say, that I think myself happy in his approbation, that a line of applause from him gives the same brisk circulation to my spirits as a kiss from Chloe, and that I mean soon to communicate to him a project of importance.

I will skirmish with the *great* almost every day in some way or other. Does Junius approve the following manœuvre instead of going in a gingerbread chariot to yawn thro' a dull sermon at St. Paul's?

Old Bailey, Oct. 24. 1771.

'Mr. Sheriff Wilkes presents his duty to the Lord Mayor, and asks his Lordship's leave to prefer the real service of his country to-morrow in the administration of justice here to the vain parade on the anniversary of the Accession of a Prince, under whose inauspicious government an universal discontent prevails among the people, and who still leaves the most intolerable grievances of his subjects unredressed.'[3]

[1] A newspaper controversy over pressing for the navy had broken out after the publication of Junius' letter of 5 October. Junius refused to condemn the practice. Letter no. LXII, in reply to An Advocate in the cause of the People, appeared in the *Public Advertiser* on 18 October.

[2] The statement referred to on p. 427 n. 2 to Letter no. 75.

[3] The thanksgiving service for the accession of George III.

This card to be published at length. Will Junius suggest any alteration or addition? It is a bold step. The sessions will not be ended on the 25th, and it is the duty of the Sheriffs to attend.

I will follow all your hints about Mr. Sawbridge. I am sorry to differ so much from you about Press Warrants. I own that I have warmly gone thro' that opposition, upon the clear conviction that every argument alleged for the legality of the Press Warrant would do equally well for Ship-Money. I believe Junius as sincere as myself. I will therefore be so far from quarrelling with him for any difference of opinion, that when I find we disagree, I will act with double caution, and some distrust of the certainty of my being clearly in the right.

I hope the Sheriff's letter to Mr. Akerman has your approbation.[1] Does Junius wish for the dinner or ball tickets for the Lord Mayor's day, for himself, or friends, or a favourite, or Junia? The day will be worth observation, whether, *cretâ an carbone notandus*, I do not know, but the *people*, *Sir*, *the people are the sight*.[2] How happy should I be to see my Portia here[3] dance a gracefull minuet with Junius Brutus! but Junius is inexorable, and I submit. I would send your tickets to Woodfall.

To-morrow I go with the Lord Mayor and my brother Sheriff to Rochester to take up our freedoms. We return on sunday night.

I entreat of Junius to favour me with every idea, which occurs to him for the common cause in every particular relative to my conduct. He shall find me no less gratefull than ductile.

John Wilkes

[1] This letter from Bull and Wilkes to the Keeper of Newgate was published in the *Public Advertiser* of 18 October 1771. It is reprinted in W. P. Treloar, *Wilkes and the City*, pp. 124–5. It instructed him to see that prisoners for trial were no longer presented in irons and to ensure that the public was admitted free of charge to the Old Bailey to see justice done. The experiment of opening the doors was a doubtful success: the *Gentleman's Magazine*, 1771, 471 reported that on the first day the crowds were so great that the business of the court was often brought to a standstill. C. P. in the *Gazetteer and New Daily Advertiser* of 14 January 1772 complained that Wilkes's orders had been disregarded and that doorkeepers still expected a shilling tip.

[2] Quorsum abeant, sani ut creta, an carbone notati? Horace, *Satires*. II. iii. 246: 'Into which list should they go, marked with chalk as sane, or with charcoal?' Wilkes meant that the sight would be worth seeing, one way or the other.

[3] Wilkes's daughter.

LETTER NO. 78. JUNIUS TO JOHN WILKES

21 October 1771

London. 21st. October. 1771.

Many thanks for your obliging offer;—but alas! my Age & figure would do but little credit to my partner.—I acknowledge the relation between Cato and Portia, but in truth I see no connexion between Junius and a Minuet.

You shall have my Opinion whenever you think proper to ask it, freely, honestly, & heartily. If I were only a party-man, I should naturally concur in any enterprise, likely to create a Bustle without risque or trouble to myself. But I love the Cause independant of persons, and I wish well to Mr. Wilkes independant of the cause. Feeling, as I really do for others where my own safety is provided for, the danger, to which I expose a simple printer, afflicts & depresses me. It lowers me to myself to draw another into a hazardous situation, which I cannot partake of with him. This Consideration will account for my abstaining from the King so long, & for the undeserved Moderation, with which I have treated him. I know my ground thoroughly when I affirm, that *he alone* is the Mark. It is not Bute, nor even the Princess Dowager. It is the odious hypocrite himself whom every honest Man should detest, and every brave man should attack. Some measures of dignity & prudence must nevertheless be preserved for our own sakes. I think your intended Message to the Lord Mayor is more spirited than judicious, and that it may be attended with Consequences, which (compared with the single purpose of insulting the King) are not worth hazarding.—*Non est tanti.*—Consider it is not Junius, or Jack Wilkes, but a grave sheriff (for *grave* you should be) who marks his Entrance into office with a direct outrage to the Chief Magistrate;—that it is only an Outrage, & leads to nothing. Will not Courtiers take advantage? Will not Whigs be offended? And, whether offended or not, will not all parties pretend to condemn you? If *measures & not men* has *any* Meaning (& I own it has very little), it must hold particularly in the case of the King; and if truth and reason be on one side, & all the common place Topics on the other, can you doubt to which side the Multitude will incline? Besides that it is too early to begin this kind of attack, I confess I am anxious for your safety. I know that, in the ordinary Course of Law, they cannot hurt you; but did the Idea of a Bill of Banishment never occur to you? And don't you think a demonstration of this kind, on your part, might furnish government with a specious pretence for destroying you at once, by a summary proceeding? Consider the Measure coolly, & then determine.

If these loose Thoughts should not weigh with you as much as I could wish, I would then recommend a little Alteration in the Message. I would have it stand thus:—

'Prince's Court. 24. October 1771

'Mr. Wilkes presents his duty to the Lord Mayor, & flatters himself he shall be honored with his Lordship's Approbation, if he prefers the real service of his Country tomorrow, in the administration of justice at the Old Bailey, to the vain parade of a procession to St. Paul's. With the warmest attachment to the House of Hanover, & the most determined allegiance to the chief magistrate, he hopes it will not be thought incumbent on him to take an active part, in celebrating the accession of a prince, under whose inauspicious reign the English Constitution has been grossly & deliberately violated, the civil rights of the people no less daringly invaded, & their humble petitions for Redress rejected with Contempt.'

In the first part, *to ask a man's Leave to prefer the real service of our Country to a vain parade*, seems, *if serious*, too servile;—*if jest*, unseasonable, & rather approaching to burlesque. The rest appears to me not less strong than your own Words, & better guarded in point of safety, which you neglect too much. I am now a little hurried, & shall write to you shortly upon some other topics.[1]

Junius

LETTER NO. 79. JOHN WILKES TO JUNIUS

4 November 1771

In November 1771 Junius was engaged in preparing his letters for the collected edition. On Friday, 1 November he wrote to Woodfall in private letter no. 40: 'Shew the Dedication & preface to Mr. Wilkes, and if he has any *material* Objection, let me know. I say *material* because of the difficulty of getting your letters.'

Letter no. 79 was endorsed by Wilkes: 'On returning Junius the *Dedication* and *Preface* he sent me.' He had obviously read them through in some haste and returned them with minor comments, if any. When the book was ready

[1] Wilkes did not proceed with his dramatic confrontation though, according to *Lloyd's Evening Post* of 23/5 October 1771, he did not attend the service.

for publication, Junius told Woodfall to thank Wilkes for the trouble he had taken, and added, laconically: 'I wish he had taken more.'

Prince's Court
Monday morning. Nov. 4.

On my return home last night I had the very great pleasure of reading the *Dedication* and *Preface* which Mr. Woodfall left for me. I am going with the City Officers to invite the *little great* to the custard on Saturday. *Perditur haec inter misero lux.*[1] I shall only add, *accepi, legi, probavi.* I am much honoured by the polite attention of Junius.

LETTER NO. 80. JUNIUS TO JOHN WILKES

6 November 1771

On 2 November Junius had issued his challenge to Lord Mansfield, insisting that the granting of bail to John Eyre had been illegal. He belatedly began gathering evidence to support his conclusion.

6. November. 1771.

I intreat you to procure for me Copies of the informations against Eyre before the Lord Mayor. I presume they were taken in writing. If not, I beg you will favour me with the most exact Account of the Substance of them, & any Observations of your own that you think material. If I am right in my facts, I answer for my Law, and mean to attack Lord Mansfield as soon as possible.

My American namesake is plainly a man of abilities, tho' I think a little unreasonable, when he insists upon more than an absolute surrender of the fact. I agree with him, that it is a hardship on the Americans to be taxed by the British Legislature; but it is a hardship, inseparable in theory from the Condition of Colonists, in which they have voluntarily placed themselves. If Emigration be no crime to deserve punishment, it is certainly no virtue to claim Exemption; & however it may have proved eventually beneficial, the Mother Country was but little obliged to the intentions of the first Emigrants. But, in fact, change of place does not exempt from Subjection. The members of our factories settled under foreign governments, & whose voluntary banishment is much more laudable with regard to

1 'Amid such trifling, alas, I waste my day', Horace, *Satires*, II. vi. 59. Saturday, 9 November was the occasion of the Lord Mayor's Ball at the Guildhall: Wilkes's diary shows that he dined at the Sheriffs' table (Add. MS. 30866, f. 21).

the Mother Country, are taxed by the Laws of Consulage. Au reste, I see no use in fighting this question in the newspapers, nor have I time.—You may assure Doctor Lee that to *my* heart & understanding the names of American & Englishman are synonymous, & that as to any future taxation of America, I look upon it as near to impossible, as the highest improbability can go.[1]

I hope that, since he has opposed me where he thinks me wrong, he will be equally ready to assist me when he thinks me right. Besides the Fallibility natural to us all, no man writes under so many disadvantages as I do. I cannot consult the learned,—I cannot directly ask the opinion of my acquaintance, and in the Newspapers I never am assisted. Those, who are conversant with books, well know how often they mislead us, when we have not a living monitor at hand to assist us in comparing practise with theory.—

LETTER NO. 81. JOHN WILKES TO JUNIUS

6 November 1771

In this letter Wilkes made a rather half-hearted attempt to induce Junius to abandon his anonymity. For the Eyre case, see the introduction to public letter no. LXV, p. 313.

Prince's Court
Wednesday Nov. 6.

Sir,

I do not delay a moment giving you the information you wish. I inclose a copy of Eyre's commitment. Nothing else in this business has been reduc'd to writing. The examination was before the sitting Justice, Alderman Halifax, at Guildhall; and it is not usual to take it in writing, on account of the multiplicity of business there. The paper was found upon him. He was ask'd what he had to say in his defence, his answer was, I hope you will bail me. Mr. Holder, the clerk, answer'd, that is impossible, there never was an instance of it, when the person was taken in the fact, or the goods found upon him. I believe Holder's law is right. Alderman Halifax likewise granted a search warrant prior to the examination. At Eyre's lodgings many

[1] Dr. Arthur Lee contributed letters to the *Gazetteer*. Despite the admiration Junius expressed here, he reacted sharply to Woodfall's suggestion that Lee's letters might also form a volume. 'Think no more of Junius Americanus,' he wrote in private letter no. 44; 'Let him reprint his Letters himself. he acts most dishonorably, in suffering Junius to be so traduced.'

more quires of paper were found, all mark'd on purpose from a suspicion of Eyre. After Eyre had been some time at Wood Street Compter, a key was found in his room there, which appears to be a key to the closet at Guildhall, from whence the paper was stolen. The Lord Mayor refus'd to bail Eyre, but I do not find that any fresh examination was taken at the Mansion House. The circumstances were well known. I was present at the examination before Halifax, but as Sheriff could not interfere, only I whispered Halifax he cou'd not bail Eyre. *Anglus* in to-day's Public Advertiser told some particulars I had mention'd. I did not know of that letter. It is Mr. Bernard's of Berkley Square. As to the Americans, I declare I know no difference between an inhabitant of Boston in Lincolnshire, and of Boston in New England. I honour the Americans; but our ancestors who staid and drove out the tyrant, are justly greater in merit and fame than those who fled and deserted their countrymen. Their future conduct has been a noble atonement, and their sons have much surpass'd them. I will mention to Dr. Lee what you desire. You shall have every communication you wish from me—yet I beg Junius to reflect a moment. To whom am I now writing? I am all doubt & uncertainty, tho' not mistrust or suspicion. I should be glad to canvass freely every part of a great plan. I dare not write it to a man I do not know, of whose connexions I am totally ignorant. I differ with Junius on one point: I think by being conceal'd he has infinite advantages which I want. I am on the Indian coast, where, from the fire kindled round me, I am mark'd out to every hostile arrow, which knows its way to me. Those who are in the dark, are safe from the want of direction of the pointless shaft. I follow'd Junius's advice about the Card on the anniversary of the King's Accession. I dropp'd the idea. I wish to know his sentiments about certain projects against the usurp'd powers of the House of Lords. The business is too vast to write, too hazardous to communicate, to an unknown person. Junius will forgive me. What can be done? Alas! where is the man after all Wilkes has experienc'd, in whose friendly bosom he can repose his secret thoughts, his noble but most dangerous, designs? The person most capable he can have no access to, & all others he will not trust. I stand, alone, *isolé* as the French call it, a single column, unpropp'd, and perhaps nodding to its fall.

John Wilkes

LETTER NO. 82. JUNIUS TO JOHN WILKES

6 November 1771

The following letter by Junius was written before he had received Wilkes's letter of the 6th. It is in Add. MS. 30881, f. 30. It has been suppressed by previous editors, presumably because of its unpleasant references to the royal family, though it is, in fact, far more damaging to Junius than to anyone else. Wilkes endorsed the letter: 'Received thursday morning Nov. 7. 1771.'

Since my note of this Morning, I know for certain that the Duke of Cumberland is married to Luttrell's sister.[1] The princess Dr. and the D of Glr. cannot live, & the odious hypocrite is *in profundis*.[2] Now is your time to torment him with some demonstration from the City.—Suppose an address from some proper number of Liverymen to the Mayor for a Common Hall, to consider of an Address of Congratulation.[3] then have it debated in Common Council.—think of something. You see you need not appear yr.self.

LETTER NO. 83. JUNIUS TO JOHN WILKES

9 November 1771

This letter is Junius' acknowledgement of Letter no. 81.

9. November. 1771

I am much obliged to you for your Information about *Eyre*. The facts are as I understood them, &, with the blessing of God, I will pull Mansfield to the ground.—Your offer to communicate your plan against the Lords was voluntary. Do now as you think proper. I have no resentments but against the common Enemy, & will assist you in any way that you will suffer yourself to be assisted. When you have satisfied your understanding that there may be reasons, why Junius shd. attack the King, the Minister, the Court of King's Bench, & the House of Commons, in the way that I have done, & yet should desert or betray the man who attacks the House of Lords, I wd. still

[1] This news was given in the *Public Advertiser* of 8 November under the heading 'Intelligence Extraordinary, though true.'

[2] George III's mother, the Princess Dowager, was gravely ill with cancer of the throat and died on 8 February 1772. Junius' intelligence was good. On 12 November the King wrote that his mother 'I am sorry to say visibly loses ground'. William, Duke of Gloucester, the King's favourite brother, had been taken ill in Italy: he recovered and died in 1805. J. Brooke, *King George III*, 266–7, 272.

[3] i.e. on the marriage.

appeal to your heart. Or if you have[1] any scruples about that kind of Evidence, ask that amiable daughter, whom you so implicitly confide in—*Is it possible that Junius should betray me?* Do not conceive that I solicit new Employment. I am overcome with the slavery of writing. Farewell.—

LETTER NO. 84. JOHN WILKES TO JUNIUS

15 January 1772

Junius' relations with Wilkes were soured by reports that, in his letter to the Supporters of the Bill of Rights, he had declared himself in favour of long parliaments. On 4 November 1771 Woodfall asked Wilkes, in Junius' name, to contradict 'that silly account' (Add. MS. 30881, f. 25). At the end of November Junius wrote to the printer in private letter no. 45: 'Your account of my letter to the Bill of rights astonishes me. I always thought the misrepresentation had been the work of Mr. Horne. I will not trust myself with suspecting. The remedy is in my own hands, but, for Mr. Wilkes's honour, I wish it to come freely and honorably from himself. . . . in the meantime, be assured that nothing can be more express than my declaration against long parliaments.—try Mr. Wilkes once more.—speak for me in a most friendly but *firm* tone.—that I *will not* submit to be any longer aspersed.—Between ourselves, let me recommend it to you to be much upon your guard with patriots.'

Woodfall's rendering of Junius' complaint is in Add. MS. 30881, f. 13. Early in 1772 extracts from Junius' letter to the Supporters were printed in the *Morning Chronicle*. Wilkes then wrote to explain what had happened.

Prince's Court, near Storey's Gate,
Westminster. Wednesday Jan. 15. 1772

A necessary attention to my health engrossed my time entirely in the few holydays I spent at Bath, and I am rewarded with being perfectly recovered. The repairs of the clay-cottage, to which I am tenant for life, seem to have taken place very successfully; and the building will probably last a few more years in tolerable condition.

Yesterday I met the Supporters of the Bill of Rights at the London Tavern. Much discourse passed about the publication of Junius's letter. Dr. Lee & Mr. Watkin Lewes, who were both suspected, fully exculpated themselves. I believe the publication was owing to the indiscretion of Mr. Patrick Cawdron, a linnen drapier in Cheapside, who showed it to his partner on the saturday. The partner copied it on the sunday, and the monday following it appeared in the Morning Chronicle. The Gazetteer only copied it from thence. The

[1] Junius wrote 'you have' twice by mistake.

Society directed a disavowal of their publication of it to be sent to you, and are to take the letter into consideration at the next meeting. I forgot to mention that Mr. Cawdron keeps the papers of the Society.[1]

The winter campaign will begin with the next week.[2] I believe that the Sheriffs will have the old battle renewed with the Commons, and I suppose the Lord Mayor and the Courtly Aldermen will commit the printers, for us to release. Another scene will probably open with the Lords. Junius has observed, 'the arbitrary power they have assumed of imposing fines, & committing during pleasure, will now be exercised in its fullest extent.' The progress of the business I suspect will be this. A bitter libel against Pomfret, Denbigh, or Talbot, attacking the Peer personally, not in his legislative or judicial capacity, will appear. His Lordship, passion's slave, will complain to the House. They will order the printer into custody, and set a heavy fine. The Sheriffs the next morning will go to Newgate, examine the Warrant of Commitment, and, like the angel to Peter, take the prisoner by the hand, and conduct him out of prison. Afterwards they will probably make their appeal to the public against the usurpation of their Lordships, and their entirely setting aside the power of juries in their proceedings. Are there more furious wild beasts to be found in the upper den than the three I have named? Miller, the printer of the London Evening Post, at No. 2, Queen's head passage, Paternoster Row, is the best man I know for this business. He will print whatever is sent him. He is a fine Oliverian soldier. I intend a manifesto with my name on monday to give spirit to the printers, and to show them, who will be their protector. I foresee it will make the two houses more cautious, but it is necessary for our friends, and the others shall be baited till they are driven into the snare. Adieu.[3]

John Wilkes

[1] I have not traced a copy of the *Morning Chronicle*, but the *Gazetteer* printed the extracts on Tuesday, 7 January 1772: it may be inferred that the first publication was on the 6th. Junius appears to have known more about the circumstances of publication than Wilkes did. On 18 January 1772, in private letter no. 52, he wrote to Woodfall: 'Mr. W. seems not to know that Morris published that Letter. I think you should set him right.' Robert Morris was a young barrister and is the subject of a biography *Radical adventurer*, by J. E. Ross.

[2] Parliament met on 21 January 1772.

[3] The two Houses of Parliament had learned from the events of 1771 and the planned confrontation did not take place.

APPENDIX THREE

PRIVATE LETTERS TO LORD CHATHAM AND GEORGE GRENVILLE

There are five letters in the Grenville and Chatham MSS. which have been attributed to Junius. The provenance of the letters to Grenville is of particular interest since in them the writer lays claim to many other contributions to the *Public Advertiser*, discussed in Appendix Five. The letters are as follows:

Anonymous to Lord Chatham	2 January 1768
C. to George Grenville	6 February 1768
C. to George Grenville	3 September 1768
Anonymous to George Grenville	20 October 1768
Junius to Lord Chatham	14 January 1772

The last letter constitutes no difficulty as it was signed by Junius. With it he forwarded the proofs of his public letter to Lord Mansfield of 21 January 1772, timed to appear on the morning of the meeting of Parliament. It is perhaps not too unkind to suggest that, in asking Chatham to attend the House of Lords and move to commit Mansfield to the Tower, Junius' judgement had given way to *folie de grandeur*.

The first letter to Chatham, dated 2 January 1768, is the most difficult to accept. There is no signature. The only evidence is therefore subject-matter and handwriting. The subject-matter is of the most general political character, furnishing no clues to the author and demanding no particularly detailed knowledge of events. Facsimiles of the handwriting in this letter and in that of 14 January 1772 are given at the beginning of volume four of the *Pitt Correspondence*. Handwriting is notoriously a difficult matter to judge, and experts disagree: readers must therefore draw their own conclusions.[1] It should also be noted that, if this letter is accepted as by Junius, difficulties are raised in also ascribing to Junius the letter to Grenville of 6 February 1768. It is hard to understand how the same man, in the space of one month, could commend with such enthusiasm the policies of Chatham, still regarded as the head of the ministry, and of George Grenville, the effective leader of the opposition. The famous reconciliation of the brothers did not take place until after Chatham's resignation in October 1768. The writer of the letter to Chatham assured him that he was convinced that 'if this Country can be

[1] My own impression, for what it is worth, is that though the two hands are very similar, the case is not proven. There appear to be differences (how significant I do not know) in the treatment of the words 'London', 'warmth', 'for your Character', 'private', and 'Chatham', which occur in both letters. Chabot conceded that the handwriting of the first letter was the 'most disguised' but accepted it as by Junius: *The handwriting of Junius professionally investigated.*

saved, it must be saved by Lord Chatham's spirit, by Lord Chatham's abilities': C., writing to Grenville, professed 'an esteem for your spirit and understanding which has, and will for ever, engage me in your cause'. Moreover, Chatham's correspondent used as a reproach to General Conway that he was 'very ready to acknowledge Mr. Grenville's merit as a Financier'.[1]

Alvar Ellegård's examination of the subject is not particularly helpful.[2] The anonymous letter to Chatham has a positive/negative ratio of 15/7, which makes it rather more Junian than the letters to Grenville at 60/45. But the margin is by no means decisive and it may be that the subject-matter of the first letter to Grenville—a detailed exposition of taxation policy—serves to conceal Junian expressions.

The evidence to associate the letters to Grenville with Junius is stronger. The first letter, of 6 February 1768, is signed C. It is true, as Dilke insisted, that, in itself, this proves nothing, but it is at least coincidental that Junius, in his private notes to Woodfall, should also use the letter C. The handwriting appears to me to be that of Junius:[3] in particular, the signature C.—with a dash above and below—is almost identical.

Nor is there the same difficulty in reconciling the sentiments of respect for Grenville with the known opinions of Junius. From the very beginning, Junius' attitude towards Grenville was friendly. In his first public letter of January 1769,[4] he gave a sympathetic account of Grenville's American policy (accusing Chatham at the same time of purely factious opposition). In 1771 Scaevola wrote as a matter of public knowledge of Junius' 'uncommon malignity, except as to Mr. Grenville' and accused Junius of being 'that gentleman's attached and partial friend'.[5]

The first letter to Grenville was not of much consequence. It offered advice on a taxation project and laid claim to 'a number of late publications'

[1] Of course one possible explanation is that the writer was hedging his bets. This is not as absurd as it might at first appear. In Francis's fragment of autobiography, printed in Parkes & Merivale, he wrote that Calcraft had during this period 'carefully kept up an interest and secret correspondence with them both' and laboured to bring them together.

Junius does not appear to have been an admirer of Chatham at the beginning. Setting aside such writings as Poplicola, which are disputable, we find him writing in October 1770, apropos of a newspaper letter in praise of Chatham, 'I neither admire the Writer nor his Idol.' (Private letter no. 23.) After the death of Grenville in November 1770 Chatham was clearly the opposition's mainstay and Junius' attitude changed. In August 1771 he admitted publicly that Chatham had 'grown upon my esteem. . . . These praises are extorted from me, but they will wear well, for they have been dearly earned.' Public letter no. LIV.

[2] *A statistical method for determining authorship: the Junius letters, 1769–72* (1962).

[3] Facsimile specimens are at the beginning of volume four of the *Grenville papers*. Specimens of the private letters to Woodfall may be found in the Routledge single-volume edition of 1874. Compare the signature C. in private letter no. 2 with that in the letter to Grenville of 6 February 1768. Chabot accepted that the handwriting of the letter to Grenville was that of Junius.

[4] Setting aside the letter of 21 November 1768 which Junius did not include in his collected edition.

[5] Quoted *Grenville papers*, iii, pp. xciv and xcv.

without specifying them. The second, dated 3 September 1768, is of greater interest. But there was a rather odd preliminary. On 10 August Thomas Whately wrote to Grenville, for whom he acted as man-of-business:[1]

'I was in town for a few hours on Monday: a friend of mine, who is always there, showed me the two enclosed publications, one without signature in the beginning of the second page of the *Public Advertiser* of the 6th of August, and the other signed *L. L.* of the 5th of August.[2] Surprised that I had not seen them, he asked whether you also missed of those which appeared only in the morning papers, and whether it would be agreeable to you to send such as might seem to him worth your perusal. I told him you would certainly be amused by any well-written papers sent to you in the country: you are not to know from whom they come, though you may easily guess. . . .

'That without a signature, he told me was evidently from a hand who had written on the same subject about ten days before, but I could not get that former paper: I could only get that one of his opponent's signed Tandem, to whom the turn of his answer seems masterly; but who this good writer is I cannot guess. . . .'

Whately added that there were strong reports that Grenville 'must be minister'.

It seems stretching coincidence a good deal to assume that, without further prompting, the unknown author surfaced three weeks later, writing to Grenville with details of the public letters he had composed. The probability is that Whately dropped a hint to the unknown author that Grenville thought highly of the public letters and would look kindly upon a private communication. But that implies either that Whately's friend knew how to contact the unknown author or that he was himself the author. If, as seems probable, the unknown author was also Junius,[3] then we should look for him among Whately's acquaintances. There is certainly no political difficulty involved in such a surmise since Whately's policy at this time was to construct a united opposition on the basis of the Middlesex election issue:[4] this was precisely the line Junius was to follow.

There is one further point. On the death of Grenville, Whately abandoned opposition with indecent haste, taking office within two months as a Lord of Trade. He was then bitterly attacked as an apostate in a paragraph entitled *Intelligence Extraordinary*, which has been attributed to Junius:[5]

'Indeed, Tom! you have betrayed yourself too soon. Mr. Grenville, your friend, your patron, your benefactor, who raised you from a depth compared to which even Bradshaw's family stands on an eminence, was hardly cold in his grave when you solicited the office of go-between to

[1] *Grenville papers*, iv. 337–8.

[2] These letters are discussed in Appendix Five.

[3] No letters under the name of Junius had at that time appeared.

[4] See the biography by John Brooke in *The House of Commons, 1754–90*, iii. 627.

[5] Printed in the *Public Advertiser* of 9 January 1771. The reference to Bradshaw suggests Junius at work: so does the technique of insulting two persons at once.

Lord North. You could not, in my eyes, be more contemptible, though you were convicted (as I dare say you might be) of having constantly betrayed him in his lifetime... be assured I shall watch you attentively.... Tom Whately, take care of yourself!'

The third letter to Grenville reveals something of the author's motives (and therefore perhaps something of Junius').[1] On 20 October 1768 he assured Grenville that 'untill you are Minister, I must not permit myself to think of the honour of being known to you. When that happens, you will not find me a needy or a troublesome dependant.' Only the most inexperienced eighteenth-century politician would have taken the last remark at its face value: the rest would have braced themselves for heavy demands. The body of work to which C. laid claim in his letter was substantial. 'Some late papers, in which the cause of this country, and the defence of your character and measures have been thought not ill maintained' probably referred to the anonymous letters of 19 December 1767, 30 July 1768, and 6 August 1768: there was one more to come on 15 December 1768; the Lucius series ran to eight letters; 'one or two upon the new Commission of Trade' referred to letters by C. on 19 and 23 July 1768; Atticus ran to four letters; in addition there were the Grand Council, L.L. of 5 August 1768, 'with a multitude of others'. It is clear that Grenville's correspondent was a major contributor to the *Public Advertiser* and that he was justified in asserting that his letters had attracted some attention. It is unlikely that he would have given up his activities during 1769, when Grenville's chances of returning to power seemed good. There is therefore a reasonable case for believing that C. was, in fact, Junius at his apprenticeship.[2]

Considerable inquiry has failed to reveal the whereabouts of the three letters to George Grenville, once in the possession of John Murray Ltd. They have therefore been checked against the facsimiles reproduced in Chabot's volume. The two letters to Lord Chatham are in the Public Record Office (P.R.O. 30/8/3 part ii, ff. 357–8 and P.R.O. 30/8/4 part i, ff. 136–7).

[1] The third letter is unsigned. Its author does not refer to any previous letters and the assumption that it was also by C. must depend upon handwriting and general probability. Specimens of the handwriting are reproduced in the *Grenville papers*.

[2] If my check is correct, Lucius and Atticus disappeared when Junius began writing. The last Lucius was on 20 September 1768 and the last Atticus on 14 November: the first Junius appeared on 21 November. When Atticus and Lucius reappeared in the spring of 1769 and the summer of 1770 respectively, the printer pointed out that they were not the previous writers (*Public Advertiser*, 19 March 1769, 13 September 1770). John Almon published in 1769 a collected edition of the letters of Atticus, Lucius, Junius, and others; he did not assert that they were all by the same author, but it may be another slight indication in favour of such a supposition.

LETTER NO. 85. ANONYMOUS TO LORD CHATHAM

2 January 1768

London. 2^d. January. 1768.

My Lord.[1]

If I were to give way to the sentiments of respect & veneration which I have always entertained for your character or to the warmth of my attachment to your person I should write a longer letter than your Lordship would have time or inclination to read. But the information, which I am going to lay before you, will, I hope, make a short one not unworthy your Attention. I have an opportunity of knowing something, & you may depend on my veracity.

During your absence from administration, it is well known that not one of the ministers has either adhered to you with firmness, or supported, with any degree of steadiness, those principles, on which you engaged in the King's service. From being their Idol at first, their veneration for you has gradually diminished, untill at last they have absolutely set you at defiance. The Chancellor, on whom you had particular reasons to rely, has played a sort of fast & loose game, and spoken of your Lordship with submission or indifference, according to the reports he heard of your health; nor has he altered his language until he found you were really returning to town.—Many circumstances must have made it impossible for you to depend much upon Lord Shelburne or his friends; besides that, from his youth & want of knowledge, he was hardly of weight, by himself, to maintain any Character in the Cabinet. The best of him is, perhaps, that he has not acted with greater insincerity to your Lordship than to former Connections.

Lord Northington's Conduct & Character need no observation. A singularity of manners, added to a perpetual affectation of discontent, has given him an excuse for declining all share in the support of government, & at last conducted him to his great object, a very high title, considering the species of his merit, and an opulent retreat. Your Lordship is best able to judge of what may be expected from this nobleman's gratitude.

Mr. Conway, as your Lordship knows by experience, is every thing to every body, as long as by such conduct he can maintain his ground. We have seen him, in one day, the humble prostrate admirer of Lord Chatham; the dearest friend of Rockingham & Richmond;

[1] Endorsed: '*private & secret.* to be opened by Lord Chatham only.'

fully sensible of the weight of the Duke of Bedford's Party; no irreconcileable Enemy to Lord Bute; and, at the same time, very ready to acknowledge Mr. Grenville's merit as a Financier. Lord Hertford is a little more explicit than his brother, & has taken every opportunity of treating your Lordship's name with indignity. But these are facts of little moment. The most considerable remains. It is understood by the publick that the plan of introducing the Duke of Bedford's Friends entirely belongs to the Duke of Grafton, with the secret concurrence, perhaps of Lord Bute, but certainly without your Lordship's consent, if not absolutely against your Advice. It is also understood, that if you should exert your influence with the King to overturn this Plan, the Duke of Grafton will be strong enough, with his new friends, to defeat any attempt of that kind; or if he should not, your Lordship will easily judge to what quarter his Grace will apply for assistance.

My Lord. The man, who presumes to give your Lordship these hints, admires your Character without servility, and is convinced that, if this Country can be saved, it must be saved by Lord Chatham's spirit, by Lord Chatham's abilities.

To The Earl of Chatham,
&c. &c. &c. &c.
At Hayes, near Bromley, Kent.

LETTER NO. 86. C. TO GEORGE GRENVILLE

6 February 1768

London, 6. February 1768.

Sir.

The observations contained in the inclosed paper are thrown together and sent to you upon a supposition that the Tax therein referred to will make part of the budget. if Lord North should have fallen upon any other scheme, they will be useless. but if the case happens, & they shall appear to have any weight, the author is satisfied, that no man in this Country can make so able a use of them, or place them in so advantageous a light as Mr. Grenville.

It is not, Sir, either necessary or proper to make myself known to you at present. hereafter I may perhaps claim that honour. in the mean Time be assured that it is a voluntary disinterested attachment to your person, founded on an esteem for your Spirit and Understanding, which has, & will for ever engage me in your Cause. A number of late publications, (falsely attributed to men of far greater talent)[1] may convince you of my Zeal, if not of my Capacity to serve you.

The only Condition, which I presume to make with you, is that you will not only not shew these papers to any body, but that you will never mention your having received them.

C.

It is a melancholy consideration that, when every commodity, which can admit of a Tax, is loaded to the last point, it shd. still be necessary for Government to contrive new taxes. The necessity of doing so in time of peace makes our situation still more alarming. But if we saw ourselves at the mercy of Bunglers, who might recommend Taxes, without the smallest conception of the manner in which they are to operate, or even of the first principles of taxation, we shd. be really reduced to a state of despair. In such unskilful hands, every drug is a poison, every weight an oppression. It is now generally known that the Ministry will be obliged to borrow one million eight or nine hundred thousand pounds for the service of the year, & that a new Fund, to be appropriated for part of the interest of this sum, or in aid of the whole, is to arise from a tax or duty of 3d. in the pound on every species of thing sold in this country by publick Auction with a very unreasonable exception in favour of the East India Company's sales. This I am well assured, (and if I were not well assured I cod. hardly believe it) is the main foundation of the intended tax, tho' I may not be exact in minuter particulars. Now, Sir, without entering into the merits of the Contriver, permit me to state to you some objections to the scheme itself, which tho' not less obvious than important, I presume have never once occurred to his mind. The publication of this paper may perhaps come time enough to rouse him from his dream, & to prevent his doing a national mischief in his Sleep.—

I believe it will be admitted that to lay a new tax indiscriminately & equally upon almost all saleable Commodities, which have been severally taxed before, some heavily some lightly, shows a great want of Judgement as well as a poverty of Contrivance in the first formation of the tax. To make no distinction between things, which have already different burthens laid upon them, & to distribute the

[1] The first bracket was omitted in error by the writer.

new burthen indifferently upon them all, may be short work indeed, but it is a sign of a bungling confused plan, and just as absurd as if a waggoner, who had a hundred weight of goods to carry more than he expected, were never to examine which of his waggons were laden before, & which not, but to divide the last load equally among them all, & so let some break down, while the rest travelled empty. So much for the generality of the Tax.—The next thing to be considered, particularly by gentlemen of landed estates, is that, as the mode of selling estates by auction is become very general, a tax on that mode is in effect an additional land-tax, & will be found a heavy Clog upon a most eligible way of alienating landed property. It is unnecessary to say that every impediment of this kind ought to be strongly discouraged in a commercial Country, whose welfare depends on the number of moderate fortunes engaged in trade. Whether the landed gentlemen, who thought it necessary to take off one shilling in the pound last year, will submit to this indirect reimposition of a part of it, is a point, which I shall leave to them to consider. Permit me only to observe that this method of encreasing the land tax will be particularly grievous, as it must fall chiefly on persons, who may be compelled by distress of Circumstances, or the call of some sudden Emergence, to part with their Estates.

My third Objection is that this tax will fall heaviest upon that part of the people, who stand most in need of ease & relief from the legislature & whose distresses, if they cannot be relieved, certainly require no aggravation. It must fall upon the creditors of Bankrupts, whose effects, tho' they may not produce half a crown in the pound, are to be liable to a farther defalcation; as if the loss of a considerable part of the debt were not sufficiently severe, or as if it were the office of the legislature to encrease the load of Misfortune, and to combine with the bankrupt in compleating the Creditor's destruction. But this is not the only blow levelled at the poor. Let it be considered that it is chiefly the lower rank of mechanicks & tradesmen, who, to raise ready money, have recourse to auctions, where their goods find a quick, if not a profitable vent. If you deprive them of this resource, by laying a new tax upon their labour (the materials of which have probably been taxed in various shapes before), what can be the consequence, but that their goods will perish in their shops, or be seised by their Creditors, or be sold at such a loss as Necessity & despair may force them to submit to; besides that, in many instances it may be more advantageous to sell a thing for two thirds of its value to-day, than for its full value six months hence. But I suppose the Chancellor of the Exchequer has never once considered what the addition of three pence in the pound to the present exorbitant demands made by Auctioneers, will amount to, nor how the industry of a poor man can bear such an accumulated oppression. I have often heard it said & by judicious people, that the suffering a number of small auctions in this town is a perpetual Source of Fraud, & an impediment to trade. perhaps it may be so; but I fear it is an inconvenience we must submit to, untill some other method of raising ready money upon the produce of their industry, be laid open to the poor. at all events the Tax in question will rather confirm and sanctify this fraudulent mode of traffick, by placing that which was only connived at before, under the immediate notice and protection of the legislature; or if it should operate as a prohibition, the tax will defeat itself as a fund of revenue, & the deficiency fall on the sinking fund, which we are told it is the object of Governm^t.^ to relieve.

A fourth objection, which appears to me more considerable than any of the former, arises from the method, in which all auctions are & must be conducted. When the Seller finds that there is less bidden for his property than he can afford to take for it, he is of course obliged to buy it in himself; so that, besides the Auctioneer's profits, he must pay a tax to Government, on account of a supposed sale of goods which never were sold; nor do I see a possibility of framing a Clause to relieve such a Case, without giving occasion to a multitude of frauds & perjuries. These are matters however, which it is no wonder great folks should be unacquainted with. Exempt as they are from the wants and distresses of life, they know nothing of the shifts, to which the poor man & his poverty are reduced. But there is another point, which I am astonished that the great persons, who frame & recommend this tax, should not understand. I am astonished that a Chancellor of the Exchequer sh^d.^ know so little of the laws relative to buying & selling as to attempt an act which directly invades this whole branch of the common Statute law of England, & forms a Contradiction, no less daring than absurd, to all the wisdom of our Ancestors. Untill this day it has been a Maxim of the English Legislature to give every possible encouragement to the most open & publick methods of disposing of property by bargain & sale. to this End fairs and markets have from time to time been Established, with grants of particular immunities & of exclusive privileges. Perhaps our Ancestors were mistaken, but it has been the prejudice of more than a thousand years, that the more publick and notorious the transaction of Sales was made, the more likely it would be to prevent Collusions & Frauds in traffick & consequently the more deserving of *favour & indulgence* from the legislature. Now, Sir, it cannot be denied that an auction, next to established fairs & markets, is the most open & publick method of sale that can be imagined. At least if Frauds are committed in this way, they ought to be corrected by regulations, not the thing itself restrained or suppressed by a tax, which, in many instances must amount to a prohibition, & when that happens, will at once defeat itself & injure the publick.

LETTER NO. 87. C. TO GEORGE GRENVILLE

3 September 1768

London. 3[d.] September. 1768.

Sir.

It may not be improper you should know that the publick is entirely mistaken with respect to the Author of some late publications in the Newspapers. Be assured that he is a man quite unknown & unconnected. He has attached himself to *your* cause and to *you* alone, upon motives, which, if he were of Consequence enough to give weight to his Judgement, would be thought as honourable to you, as they are truly satisfactory to himself. At a proper time he will solicit the honour of being known to you: he has present important reasons for wishing to be concealed.

Some late papers, in which the cause of this country, and the defence of your Character and measures have been thought not ill maintained;—others, signed Lucius, and one or two upon the new Commission of trade, with a multitude of others, came from this hand. They have been taken notice of by the Publick.

May I plead it as a merit with you, Sir, that no motives of vanity shall ever discover the author of this Letter. If an earnest wish to serve you gives me any claim, let me entreat you not to suffer a hint of this Communication to escape you to *any body*.

C.

LETTER NO. 88. ANONYMOUS TO GEORGE GRENVILLE
20 October 1768

London. 20th. October. 1768.

Sir.

I beg leave to offer you a letter, reprinted in the inclosed paper under the signature of Atticus, as finished with more care than I have usually time to give to these productions. The town is curious to know the author. Every body guesses, some are quite certain, and all are mistaken. Some, who bear your character, give it to the Rockinghams; (a policy I do not understand;) and Mr. Bourke denies it, as he would a fact, which he wished to have believed.

It may be proper to assure you that no man living knows or even suspects the Author. I have no connection with any party, except a voluntary attachment to *your* cause & Person. It began with amusement, grew into habit, was confirmed by a closer attention to your Principles & Conduct, & is now heated into Passion. The *Grand Council* was mine, & I may say, with truth, almost every thing that, for two years past, has attracted the attention of the publick. I am conscious these papers have been very unequal; but you will be candid enough to make allowances for a man, who writes absolutely without materials or instruction. For want of hints of this kind, I fear I frequently mistake your views, as well as the true point, whereon you would choose to rest the questions, in which your name is concerned. But this is an inconvenience without a remedy. I must continue to argue for you, as I would for myself in the same circumstances, as far as I understand yours. Untill you are Minister, I must not permit myself to think of the honour of being known to you. When that happens, you will not find me a needy or a troublesome dependant. In the mean time, I must console myself with reflecting, that, by resisting every temptation of vanity, & even the great desire I have of being honoured with your notice, I give you some assurance, that you may depend upon my firmness and fidelity hereafter.

LETTER NO. 89. JUNIUS TO LORD CHATHAM

14 January 1772

Most secret

London. 14th. January. 1772.

My Lord,

Confiding implicitly in your Lordship's Honour, I take the Liberty of submitting to you the inclosed paper, before it be given to the Public. It is to appear on the Morning of the Meeting of Parliament. Lord Mansfield flatters himself, that I have dropped all Thoughts of attacking him, and I would give him as little Time as possible to concert his Measures with the Ministry.—The address to Lord Camden will be accounted for, when I say, that the Nation in general are not quite so secure of *his* Firmness as they are of Lord Chatham.

I am so clearly satisfied that Lord Mansfield has done an Act not warranted by Law, & that the inclosed Argument is not to be answered, (besides that I find the Lawyers concur with me,) that I am inclined to expect he may himself acknowledge it as an oversight, & endeavour to whittle it away to Nothing. For this possible event, I would wish your Lordship & the Duke of Richmond to be prepared to take down his words, & thereupon to move for committing him to the Tower. I hope that proper steps will also be taken in the House of Commons.—If he makes no Confession of his guilt, but attempts to defend himself by any legal Argument, I then submit it to your Lordship, whether it might not be proper to put the following questions to the Judges. In fact, they answer themselves; but it will embarass the Ministry, and ruin the Character which Mansfield pretends to, if the House should put a direct Negative upon the Motion.

1°. "Whether, according to the true Meaning & Intendment of the Laws of England, relative to Bail for criminal Offences, a person positively charged with felony,—taken *in flagranti delicto*,—with the *mainœuvre*, & not making any defence, nor offering any evidence to induce a doubt whether he be guilty or innocent,—is *bailable* or *not bailable?*

2°. "Whether the power, exercised by the Judges of the Court of King's Bench, of bailing for Offences, not bailable by a Justice of Peace, be an absolute power, of mere Will & Pleasure in the Judge, —or a discretionary power, regulated & governed, in the application of it, by the true Meaning & Intendment of the Law relative to Bail?"

Lord Mansfield's constant Endeavour, to misinterpret the Laws of England is a sufficient general Ground of Impeachment.—The specific Instances may be taken from his Doctrine concerning Libels,—the Grosvenor Cause;—his pleading Mr. De Grey's Defence upon the Bench, when he said, *idem fecerunt alii, et multi et boni;*—his suffering an Affidavit to be read, in *the King against Blair*, tending to inflame the Court against the Defendant when he was brought up to receive Sentence;—his direction to the Jury, in the cause of Ansell, by which he admitted parol Evidence against a written agreement, & in consequence of which the Court of Common Pleas granted a new Trial; and, lastly, his partial & wicked motives for bailing Eyre.—There are some material Circumstances relative to this last, which I thought it right to reserve for your Lordship alone.

It will appear by the Evidence of the Goaler and the City Solicitor's Clerk, that Lord Mansfield refused to hear the return read, & at first ordered Eyre to be bound only in £200. with two Sureties, until his Clerk, Mr. Platt, proposed £300. with three Sureties. Mr. King, Clerk to the City Solicitor, was never asked for his Consent, nor did he ever give any. From these facts, I conclude, either that he bailed, without knowing the Cause of Commitment; or, which is highly probable, that he knew it extrajudicially from the Scotchmen, & was ashamed to have the Return read.

I will not presume to trouble your Lordship, with any Assurances, however sincere, of my respect & esteem for your Character, and Admiration of your Abilities. Retired & unknown, I live in the Shade, & have only a speculative Ambition.—In the warmth of my imagination, I sometimes conceive, that, when Junius exerts his utmost Faculties in the Service of his Country, he approaches in Theory to that exalted Character, which Lord Chatham alone fills up, and uniformly supports in Action.

JUNIUS.

APPENDIX FOUR

ADDITIONAL AND FALSE JUNIUS LETTERS

This appendix is concerned with those public letters unquestionably by Junius which were not included in his collected edition of 1772 and with other publications signed Junius which have been attributed to him. I have discussed them in chronological order. They range from the first of Junius' letters to appear in the *Public Advertiser*, which was almost certainly genuine, to letters signed Junius in the *Crisis* of 1775, which were almost certainly spurious. I have not investigated the many obvious derivatives, such as Junius Americanus, Junius Asiaticus, and Junius—not the first, which did not claim to be authentic.

June 1768	Harry & Nan, a poem	*Political Register*
21 November 1768	Junius, letter	*Public Advertiser*
12 April 1769	Junius, reply to Monody	*Public Advertiser*
7 September 1769	Junius, reply to Junia	*Public Advertiser*
March 1770	A Junius, letter	*Gentleman's Magazine*
24 March 1770	The Titans, a poem	*Public Advertiser*
7 February 1771	Philo Junius, letter	*Public Advertiser*
13 December 1771	Junius, letter	*London Packet*
March 1772	Letter to Lord North	*Gentleman's Magazine*
1772	Political poems	Published Crowder
24 August 1773	Junius, letter	*London Evening Post*
27 August 1774	Junius, letter	*Morning Chronicle*
18 February 1775	Letter to Lord Apsley	*Crisis*
25 March 1775	Junius, letter	*Crisis*
12 August 1775	Letter	*Crisis*
1778	*A serious letter to the public*	Pamphlet
1779/80	Three letters	Pamphlets
1779/80	The Whig	*Biographical anecdotes*, ed John Almon
1783	*The Ministerialist*	Pamphlet
1828	The Vices, a poem	Published H. Phillips

HARRY & NAN June 1768

The printed version of this poem, celebrating the liaison between the Duke of Grafton and Nancy Parsons, appeared in John Almon's *Political Register* for June 1768. It was unsigned. There is a manuscript version in the Woodfall papers, Add. MS. 27777, f. 12, in Junius' handwriting. The inference is that Junius sent it first to Woodfall, who refused to print it but passed it on to Almon. It was a subject that fascinated Junius. The poem is printed from the manuscript version.

An Elegy in the Manner of TIBULLUS

1.

Can Apollo resist, or a Poet refuse,
When Harry and Nancy solicit the Muse;
A Statesman, who makes a whole Nation his care,
And a Nymph, who is almost as chaste as she's fair.

2.

Dear Spousy had led such a damnable life,
He determin'd to keep any whore but his wife.
So Harry's Affairs, like those of the State,
Have been pretty well handled and tickled of late.

3.

From fourteen to forty our provident *Nan*
Had devoted her life to the Study of Man;
And thought it a natural change of her station,
From riding St. George, to ride over a nation.

4.

Secret service had wasted the national wealth,
But now—'tis the price of the Minister's health;—
An expence which the Treasury well may afford,
She who serves him in bed should be paid at the board.

5.

So lucky was Harry, that nothing could mend
His choice of a mistress, but that of a friend;—
A Friend so obliging, and yet so sincere,
With pleasure in one eye, in t'other a tear.

6.

My Friend holds the Candle——the Lovers debate,
And among them, God knows how they settle the State.
Was there ever a Nation so govern'd before,
By a Jockey and Gambler, a Pimp and a whore!

LETTER 21 November 1768

There seems to be no difficulty in accepting this letter, which appeared in the *Public Advertiser*, as a genuine production of Junius. It has the air of authority which he liked to cultivate, was signed Junius at a time when no impostors could be in the field, and scores high on Ellegård's linguistic test.

One can only speculate why Junius decided not to include it in his collected edition of 1772. Presumably he thought that the letter of 21 January 1769, with its systematic survey of the ministry and the reply from Sir William Draper, made a more suitable beginning to the series.

Sir,

It will soon be decided by the highest Authority, whether the Justice of our Laws, and the Liberty of our Constitution have been essentially violated in the Person of Mr. Wilkes. As a public Man, his Fate will be determined, nor is it safe or necessary at present to enter into the Merits of his Cause. We are interested in this Question no farther than as he is a Part of a well-regulated Society. If a Member of it be injured, the Laws and Constitution will defend him. But where is the Law to inforce the Engagements of private Faith, or to punish the Breach of them? Where shall *he* apply for Redress with whom all Ties of Honour, Professions of Friendship, and Obligations of Party have been violated or betrayed? A Man so injured has no Redress or Consolation, but what he finds in the Resentment and generous Sympathy of Mankind.

The Violation of Party Faith is of itself too common to excite Surprize or Indignation. Political Friendships are so well understood that we can hardly pity the Simplicity they deceive; and if Mr. Wilkes had only been deserted, he would but have given us one Example more of the Folly of relying on such Engagements. But his, I conceive, is a singular Situation. There is scarce an Instance of Party Merit so great as his, or so ill rewarded. Other Men have been abandoned by their Friends;—Mr. Wilkes alone is oppressed by them. One would think that the First Lord of the Treasury and the Chancellor might have been contented with forgetting the Man, to whom they principally owed their Elevation;—but Hearts like theirs are not so easily satisfied. They left him unsupported, when they ceased to want his Assistance, and, to cover the Reproach of Passive Ingratitude, they pursue him to Destruction. The Bounds of human Science are still unknown, but this assuredly is the last Limit of human Depravity. Notorious Facts speak for themselves, and in this Case an honest Man will want no Spur to rouse his Indignation. Men of a different Character would do well to consider what their Security is with a Minister, who breaks without Scruple through all Engagements of Party, and is weak enough to set all public Shame at Defiance. There is a Firmness of Character which will support a Minister, even against his Vices; but where is the Dependance of his Friends, when they have no Hold either on his Heart or his Understanding. Detested by the better Part of Mankind, he will soon be suspected by the worst; for no Man relies securely on another, whom he thinks less honest and less wise than himself.

In the present Instance the Duke of Grafton may possibly find that he has played a foolish Game. He rose by Mr. Wilkes's Popularity, and it is not improbable that he may fall by it.

JUNIUS

REPLY TO MONODY 12 April 1769

There is no doubt that this fragment was by Junius, though considered too trivial to be worth including in the collected edition. Poetikastos, identified as John Macpherson, published in the *Public Advertiser* of 10 April a Monody on the supposed death of Junius. One verse ran:

> Impossible!—then hear me, fiends of Hell,
> This dark event, this mystery unfold:
> Poison'd was Junius? No; 'Alas, he fell
> Midst arrows dipp'd in ministerial gold.'

Junius replied on 12 April and Poetikastos retorted on the 17th. The complete Monody is printed in Wade, ii. 263–4. Woodfall included the Reply to Monody as letter no. X in his draft for the collected edition, but Junius replied 'Omit this.' Add. MS. 27776.

I find this brief letter one of Junius' most effective. It is all the better for being even-tempered and the change from banter to seriousness is well done.

Mr. Woodfall,

The Monody on the supposed Death of *Junius* is not the less poetical for being founded on a Fiction. In some Parts of it, there is a Promise of Genius, which deserves to be encouraged. My letter of Monday will, I hope, convince the Author that I am neither a Partisan of Mr. Wilkes, nor yet bought off by the Ministry. It is true that I have refused Offers, which a more prudent or a more interested Man would have accepted. Whether it be Simplicity or Virtue in me, I can only affirm that *I am in earnest*; because I am convinced, as far as my Understanding is capable of judging that the present Ministry are driving this Country to Destruction; and you, I think, Sir, may be satisfied that my Rank and Fortune place me above a common Bribe.

JUNIUS

REPLY TO JUNIA 7 September 1769

This letter, in conjunction with private letter no. 8 to Woodfall, is one of the most intriguing Junius wrote. On 5 September Caleb Whitefoord published in the *Public Advertiser* a letter under the name of Junia. It contained some good hits. Junius was described as 'Calumniator-general to the opposition', and Junia observed that 'of all kinds of abuse, *private* scandal seems to be his *favourite* morsel'. The full text is given in Wade, ii. 272–4.

Junius' retort, a cheerful piece of salacious innuendo, appeared two days later. But he almost immediately repented of it, writing to Woodfall that it was 'idle and improper and I assure you printed against my own opinion'. He added that there were 'people about me, whom I would wish not to contradict, and who had rather see Junius in the papers ever so improperly, than not at all'. This is the only reference Junius made to others being involved, save for a remark in private letter no. 52 about 'the gentleman, who transacts the conveyancing part of our Correspondence'. Woodfall printed a disavowal in the *Public Advertiser* of 11 September and the letter was not, of course, included in the collected edition.

Sir,

I Find myself unexpectedly married in the Newspapers, without my Knowledge or Consent. Since I am fated to be a Husband, I hope at least the Lady will perform the principal Duty of a Wife. Marriages, they say, are made in Heaven, but they are consummated upon Earth; and since *Junia* has adopted my Name, she cannot, in common matrimonial Decency, refuse to make me a Tender of her Person. Politics are too barren a Subject for a new-married Couple. I should be glad to furnish her with one more fit for a Lady to handle, and better suited to the natural Dexterity of her Sex. In short, if *Junia* be young and handsome, she will have no Reason to complain of my Method of conducting an Argument. I abominate all Tergiversation in Discourse, and she may be assured that whatever I advance, whether it be weak or forcible, shall, at any Rate, be directly in Point. It is true I am a strenuous Advocate for Liberty and Property, but when these Rights are invaded by a pretty Woman, I am neither able to defend my Money nor my Freedom. The Divine Right of Beauty is the only one an Englishman ought to acknowledge, and a pretty Woman the only Tyrant he is not authorised to resist.

JUNIUS

A JUNIUS March 1770

Printed in the *Gentleman's Magazine*, 105–6. A rather desultory survey of the political scene, advising the King to dissolve Parliament, it reads like a dull imitation. Junius did not include it in the collected edition and even the *Gentleman's Magazine* had its doubts, since it was not indexed with the genuine Junius letters.

THE TITANS 24 March 1770

An attack upon Beckford and Chatham as noisy patriots, signed 'JUNIUS *himself*' and printed in the *Public Advertiser*. Apart from the inherent improbability of Junius breaking into verse, Beckford and Chatham were, at this time, his most reliable allies. Beckford's speech is parodied:

> That these here Grievances, more worser
> Than them of James or Charles the First are,
> By that there Scroll should be redress'd,
> He said and thump'd his hollow Breast,
> Which groan'd, *because as how* his Friends
> Had not *as yet* obtain'd their Ends—
> But LIBERTY! was all he spoke,
> His Negroes heard and shook their Yoke.

PHILO JUNIUS 7 February 1771

Anti-Junius wrote in the *Public Advertiser* of 4 February 1771 attacking Junius' argument about the Falkland Islands dispute. Junius took up the challenge on 6 February as Philo Junius in public letter no. XLIII. On the same day Anti-Junius published a second letter, to which Philo Junius briefly replied. It was too insignificant to be included in the collected edition. A third letter from Anti-Junius appeared on Friday, 22 February, but Junius made no further retort.

The first letter of *Anti Junius* did not promise a second, or at least it escaped me. I shall reserve my Observations upon his second till I see the whole.

In the third paragraph of *my* Letter (Line 29) it should have been printed Common *Course* not Common *Cause*.

LETTER 13 December 1771

John Taylor, *The identity of Junius established* (1816), 115–16, wrote that a false Junius was printed in the *London Packet* of 13 December 1771 and that Junius referred to this when he wrote to Woodfall in private letter no. 48: 'The *London Packet* is not worth our Notice. I suspect Garrick, and I would have you hint so to him.'

I have not succeeded in finding a copy of the *London Packet*, but there can be little doubt that the letter was identical with that to Lord North, printed in *Baratariana, a select collection of fugitive political pieces published during the administration of Lord Townshend in Ireland*, 2nd edn., Dublin, 1773. In that volume the letter, no. 29, is dated 14 December 1771, but has an accompanying note to the effect that it is 'not the production of the celebrated Junius'.

The point is of some substance because if Junius did choose to disregard false letters, it weakens the argument advanced by Fraser Rae that the letters of 24 August 1773 and 27 August 1774 must be genuine because they were not disavowed.

LETTER TO LORD NORTH March 1772

The text of this letter, reproaching North with indifference to the fate of the King's sister, the Queen of Denmark, may be found in the *Gentleman's Magazine*, 130–3. Fraser Rae, who reprinted it in the *Athenaeum*, no. 3957 of 29 August 1903, believed that it was a genuine Junius and 'not unworthy of him'. My own feeling is that it is a dreary imitation. I would not like to think that Junius had written the following:

> 'Are *you*, my Lord, quite devoid of feeling? Have you no warm blood that flows around your heart, that gives your frame a thrilling soft sensation, and makes your bosom glow with affection ornamental to man as a social creature.'

One might conjecture that the *Gentleman's Magazine* would not have found room for such rubbish had it not been signed 'Junius'.

I have been unable to ascertain where the letter first appeared. It was not printed in the *Public Advertiser*, which is in itself grounds for suspicion.

POLITICAL POEMS: A COMPILATION 1772

This shilling pamphlet, published in the summer of 1772, was said to have been compiled by Junius. It included poems by Addison, Goldsmith, Churchill, and a few anonymous ones. The pamphlet was sold by Stanley Crowder, who may also have been the printer. Fraser Rae in the *Athenaeum*, no. 3964, 17 October 1903, was inclined to believe that Junius might have had a hand in it, but it seems much more likely that it was a piece of hackwork, cashing in on Junius' reputation. The *Monthly Review*, xlvi. 455 dismissed it as a catchpenny touch.

LETTERS 24 August 1773
27 August 1774

These letters, printed in the *London Evening Post* and the *Morning Chronicle* respectively, were discussed by Fraser Rae in the *Athenaeum*, 1895, nos. 3520, 3523, and 3525. He was convinced that they were genuine and that they therefore disproved the case for Francis's authorship, since he left for India in April 1774. The first is an attack upon the priesthood, the second an attack upon Lord Mansfield.

Before accepting them, however, there are several points to be considered. (1) Appearances suggest that Junius felt he had completed his work with the publication of the collected edition: he was extremely proud of it and was unlikely to spoil the effect with isolated and fugitive pieces at a later date. (2) There was no reason for Junius to change his newspaper but every reason for an impostor to avoid the *Public Advertiser*. (3) We have seen that letters and pamphlets were not infrequently attributed to Junius in order to attract attention. (4) The subject of the priesthood is one in which Junius never showed the slightest interest, nor is it characteristic of him to pad out his arguments with a two-column quotation from another author. (5) On 12 September 1774, as Rae pointed out, William Woodfall, editor of the *Morning Chronicle*, wrote that 'Junius to Super Legale Meritum is under consideration'. It did not appear. It is most improbable that William Woodfall would suppress a genuine Junius, and Junius was certainly never treated in that fashion by Henry Sampson Woodfall. But it is quite likely that William Woodfall came to the conclusion that the letters were neither genuine nor interesting.

LETTERS 18 February 1775
25 March 1775
12 August 1775

These letters appeared in the *Crisis*, an opposition newspaper. The character of the paper, which started on 20 January 1775 and sold weekly at 2½*d*. may be judged from the second issue, headed, 'A BLOODY COURT, A BLOODY MINISTRY and a BLOODY PARLIAMENT'.

The first of these letters, addressed to the Lord Chancellor, Lord Apsley, was tacked on to an edition of Junius' letters first printed by John Wheble in 1771: presumably the intention was to get rid of old stock by pretending to bring the work up to date. This very odd publication is discussed by T. H. Bowyer, *A bibliographical examination of the earliest editions of the letters of Junius*, 43–7.

There is little doubt that all three letters were written by Philip Thicknesse. They comment on a legal action in which he was involved. Though the first two were signed Junius, the third (promised in the second) was signed Philip Thicknesse. Presumably he made use of the name Junius to attract a little more attention to his complaints.

A SERIOUS LETTER TO THE PUBLIC ON THE LATE TRANSACTION BETWEEN LORD NORTH AND THE DUKE OF GORDON 1778

Copies of this brief pamphlet are in the British Library and the Codrington Library at Oxford. Edmands and Cordasco in their bibliographies list it erroneously as 'Duke of Grafton'. It was a defence of Lord North against the charge made by Lord George Gordon that he had attempted by a 'corrupt bargain' to oust him from the House of Commons.

Though it is signed 'Junius', no effort is made to suggest any connection and there is no reason to believe there was. The *Monthly Review*, lviii. 474 observed that it could 'not discern the least resemblance of style or language' to the celebrated writer.

THREE LETTERS 1779/80

These letters from the MSS. of Sir Thomas Phillipps, Bart., at Middle Hill, are catalogued in the British Library under Tab. 436 a 5 as 'letters of Junius believed to be unpublished'.

They are all concerned with the loss of Rhode Island and may presumably be dated late 1779 or early 1780. The first is a brief statement of the loss of the base; the second, signed Veritas, is a garrulous attack upon Commodore Arbuthnot; the third, signed Junius, is addressed to Mr. Woodfall and predicts disaster. It contains a charmingly un-Junian sentence on Rhode Island: 'The French have now got it, and we shall rue the day it was abandoned.'

There is no reason whatever to connect them with Junius and they are of little interest.

THE WHIG 1779/80

A series of six letters, said to have been published in late 1779 and early 1780 and reprinted in John Almon's *Biographical, literary and political anecdotes of several of the most eminent persons of the present age*, iii. 1–36 (1797). On the title-page they are attributed to Junius but the claim is not made in the letters themselves and Almon's intention was presumably to lay hold of one more Eminent Person for his collection. They offer a routine commentary, from an opposition point of view, on constitutional theory.

THE MINISTERIALIST 1783

Printed by J. Stockdale and sold at a shilling. A 40-page tract satirically defending Charles Fox from a charge of dereliction of principle. Though it is printed 'By Junius' there is nothing whatever to connect it with the author of the letters.

THE VICES: A POEM IN THREE CANTOS 1828

This appears to have been composed during the 1780s and was printed for Horatio Phillips. The publisher wrote that it had been found among the papers of John Almon and that it was 'believed to be in the hand-writing of the unknown author of the Letters of Junius'. The poem itself is a turgid vision of Hell with desultory comments on leading political figures. It is totally devoid of interest, and the printer's motives for connecting it with Junius were presumably to promote what would otherwise have been an unsaleable work.

APPENDIX FIVE

MISCELLANEOUS LETTERS

By Miscellaneous Letters is meant those letters, printed in the *Public Advertiser* between 1767 and 1772 inclusive, signed under names other than Junius, which have been attributed to Junius. It is possible, of course, that Junius may have submitted letters under other names before 1767 and after 1772, but the chances of identifying them accurately are so remote that it did not seem worth the considerable effort needed to unearth them. Another possibility which I have not pursued is that Junius may have published under different names in other newspapers. But he assured Woodfall in August 1769 that he had 'never written in any other paper since I began with Yours', and in November he repeated that, though he sometimes changed his signature, he 'could have no reason to change the paper, especially for one that does not circulate half so much as Yours'.[1]

The great majority of these miscellaneous letters were first attributed to Junius in the 1812 edition, prepared by Mason Good. Though some of his suggestions were supported by signals in the *Public Advertiser* or by references in the private letters to the printer, most were made on grounds of style and subject-matter. They were reproduced in the Bohn edition of 1850, which established itself as the standard version of the letters. Joseph Parkes in his *Memoirs of Sir Philip Francis*, published in 1867, laid claim to dozens of other letters on behalf of Junius. These I have not discussed because in hardly any case is there evidence to support the attribution.[2]

The miscellaneous letters have been much used by authors trying to establish the true identity of Junius, since, if correctly attributed, they add substantially to our knowledge of his political attitude. But the attributions are in many cases so dubious that they have proved a quicksand to build upon. This appendix is therefore divided into two sections. In section A, I have printed those letters which are almost certainly by Junius: I have refused to accept the unsupported evidence of style because it is almost impossible to distinguish with total confidence between one piece of political vituperation and another. In section B, I have described and commented on the other letters which have been claimed as the work of Junius. These allocations remain a matter of judgement and conjecture. Even in section A—which I regard as the probables and for which a high level of verification is forthcoming—there

[1] Private letters nos. 6 and 13.

[2] Joseph Parkes's volumes were uncompleted at his death and were finished by Herman Merivale, who was evidently embarrassed at Parkes's enthusiasm for discovering secret Junius letters. Certainly he refused to continue the search beyond 1768, the point Parkes had reached.

are letters that cannot be proved beyond doubt to be by Junius.[1] In the same way, it is more than likely that in section B, which are merely possibles, there are letters genuinely written by Junius, but for which adequate proof is not available.[2]

The letters in section A are reprinted from the *Public Advertiser*: I have not given the text of the letters in section B, but have indicated where it may conveniently be found.

One of the questions with which Alvar Ellegård was concerned in his *Statistical method for determining authorship* was whether his technique of linguistic analysis could distinguish between miscellaneous letters rightly and wrongly attributed to Junius. Though his findings are of the greatest interest, he would not, I think, claim that they are more than indications—sometimes because the letters are too brief for adequate sampling but mainly because it remains a matter of judgement where, among results produced as ratios, the line should be drawn. If, for example, the letters of Sir William Draper, who was certainly not Junius, show a positive/negative ratio of 118/68, while Veteran (text 64), who certainly was Junius, yields only 38/24, there is an area of overlap that makes for uncertainty. In order to give some idea of the probability Ellegård attributes to the miscellaneous letters, I have summarized the findings of his Table 4a. The items at the top of the list show the most favourable positive/negative ratio and are most likely to have been by the author of Junius: those at the bottom are least likely.[3]

[1] I have, for example, presumed that when Junius in his collected edition incorporated the whole or part of a miscellaneous letter, he was the author. Recens and Phalaris are cases in point. I do not think that a man as proud and punctilious as Junius would lay himself open to the charge of plagiarism. But Charles Wentworth Dilke, a most learned critic, objected that this was not proof and observed that, though Junius quoted from Blackstone, it did not follow that he wrote the *Commentaries*. The reader must decide for himself.

[2] e.g. Testis and Testiculus. Even Dilke accepted these as Junius letters. But the standard of proof seems to me to fall short of that required for admission to section A.

[3] I am greatly obliged to Dr. Ellegård for discussing his findings with me and suggesting ways in which they might be presented. He emphasizes the importance of the length of the text examined: the shorter it is the less reliable is the indication. Table 4a should be studied in conjunction with Table 5, based on his final programme, and Table 11, discussed in his pp. 71–6.

ABSTRACT from Table 4a in A. Ellegård, *A statistical method for determining authorship*, showing miscellaneous letters in order of probable Junian origin

The first column indicates the length of the text item in hundreds of words. The number in brackets identifies the text according to the lists in Ellegård, pp. 81–90.

★ Asterisks before a text indicate that it is included in section A and may be regarded as almost certainly by Junius.

5	An Englishman (110)	16–2
7	L.L. (267)	31–4
4	Anonymous (89)	15–2
1	An Innocent Reader (98)	5–1
4	★Your Real Friend (79)	14–3
15	Poplicola (85)	60–14
3	Juniper (111)	8–2
6	★Phalaris (101)	16–4
8	Anonymous (106)	27–7
3	Intelligence Extraordinary (96)	7–2
20	★Domitian (59)	58–17
20	★Domitian (60)	57–17
9	X.X. (100)	10–3
26	Anonymous (104)	93–28
20	Atticus (74)	59–18
11	Anonymous (88)	32–10
6	Anti-sejanus, jr (107)	22–7
3	★Vindex (62)	12–4
20	Lucius (69)	71–24
8	★First Junius letter (57)	29–10
3	★Scotus (66)	14–5
13	★Nemesis (65)	36–13
14	Lucius (72)	47–17
9	Brutus (92)	44–16
20	★Domitian (58)	63–23
5	★Moderatus (61)	16–6
20	Atticus (73)	67–27
5	★Junius to Chatham (67)	22–9
11	A Labourer (109)	40–17
20	Lucius (71)	55–25
22	C. (78)	67–31
4	Fiat Justitia (90)	15–7
5	Anonymous to Chatham (84)	15–7
6	Testiculus (81)	14–7
10	Anonymous (105)	28–14
5	A member (124)	16–8
19	Atticus (75)	71–13
22	★A Whig (83)	82–16
6	Simplex (93)	20–4
48	Lusitanicus (248)	130–68
20	C. (77)	64–34
20	Lucius (70)	54–29
5	Anti-W (97)	13–7
18	Grand Council (68)	53–30
20	★Veteran (63)	46–26
6	Augur (123)	10–6
22	★Veteran (64)	38–24
10	Correggio (87)	19–12
28	Y.Z. (257)	67–46
21	Anonymous to Grenville (76)	60–45
9	Amicus Curiae (99)	27–16
5	Pomona (91)	14–9
5	Anti-Belial (103)	12–8
3	Anti-Fox (102)	3–2
28	Valerius (120)	72–50
30	Henricus (126)	72–52
12	Q in the Corner (94)	28–22
100	Vindex (244)	209–166
4	Temporum Felicitas (108)	5–4
5	Cumbriensis (82)	7–6
31	G.W. (125)	43–40
9	Anti-Stuart (118)	17–16
6	Why? (122)	9–9
3	Testis (80)	5–5
25	Mnemon (117)	57–62
12	A Chapter of Facts (95)	17–21
11	Bifrons (119)	17–23
3	Arthur Tell-Truth (112)	6–9
4	A Faithful Monitor (113)	4–7
3	N.L. (268)	4–7
12	Moderator (114)	15–29
1	Downright (116)	1–3

SECTION A

In this section are printed, in chronological order, those miscellaneous letters for which the evidence of authorship by Junius is strongest. The best authenticated is Vindex of 22 February 1771, which was the subject of an exchange between Junius and the printer and the manuscript of which, in Junius' hand, is extant in the Woodfall papers. The least well authenticated is probably the second letter of Phalaris, dated 20 December 1770, which is carried largely by the first letter, which is itself identified only by inference. On the first occasion of a name being used, I have explained my reasons for attributing the letter to Junius: I have not repeated the argument for subsequent letters unless there are special difficulties. I have not reprinted those letters which were incorporated by Junius, without alteration, into the collected edition of 1772.

7 April 1769	Recens	6 March 1771	Vindex
6 May 1769	Your Real Friend	9 April 1771	A Whig
12 June 1769	Philo Junius	1 May 1771	Philo Junius
22 June 1769	Philo Junius	22 May 1771	Philo Junius
1 August 1769	Philo Junius	25 May 1771	Philo Junius
14 August 1769	Philo Junius	28 June 1771	Domitian
4 September 1769	Philo Junius	26 August 1771	Philo Junius
19 October 1769	Philo Junius	15 October 1771	Philo Junius
14 November 1769	Moderatus	17 October 1771	Philo Junius
5 March 1770	Domitian	18 October 1771	Philo Junius
10 March 1770	Moderatus	22 October 1771	A Friend of Junius
8 December 1770	Domitian	28 January 1772	Veteran
17 December 1770	Phalaris	17 February 1772	Veteran
20 December 1770	Phararis	27 February 1772	Veteran
24 December 1770	Domitian	10 March 1772	Veteran
17 January 1771	Domitian	23 March 1772	Veteran
6 February 1771	Philo Junius	4 May 1772	Scotus
22 February 1771	Vindex	12 May 1772	Nemesis

RECENS 7 April 1769

A scurrilous attack upon the Luttrell family, reprinted by Junius in the collected edition as a footnote to Letter no. LXVII of 27 November 1771, p. 317. Presumed by Junius on the evidence of its adoption.

YOUR REAL FRIEND 6 May 1769

In private letter no. 2, Junius wrote to the printer: 'It is essentially necessary that the inclosed should be published tomorrow, as the great Question comes on on monday, & Lord Granby is already staggered.' The private letter was written on a Friday: on Monday, 8 May 1769 the House of Commons debated the Middlesex election. Your Real Friend was printed on Saturday, 6 May. Since Junius had already launched one attack upon Granby, it was necessary to find another name. The letter scores very high on Ellegård's test. Granby voted with the government on the 8th, but subsequently recanted.

TO THE MARQUIS OF GRANBY.

MY LORD, May 6, 1769.

You were once the Favourite of the Publick. As a brave Man you were admired by the Army, as a generous Man you were beloved. The Scene is altered; and even your immediate Dependants, who have profited most by your Good-nature, cannot conceal from you how much you have lost, both in the Affections of your Fellow-Soldiers and the Esteem of your Country. Your Character, once spotless, once irreproachable, has been drawn into a public Question—; attacked with Severity, defended with Imprudence, and, like the Seat of War, ruined by the Contention. Profligate as we are, the Virtues of the Heart are still so much respected, that even the Errors and Simplicity of a good Man are sacred against Censure or Derision. To a Man of your Lordship's high Rank and Fortune, is there anything in the Smiles of a Court, that can balance the Loss of that Affection (for surely it was something more cordial than Esteem) with which you were universally received upon your Return from Germany? You were then an independent gallant Soldier. As far as you thought proper to mix in Politics, you were the Friend and Patron of the People. Believe me, my Lord, the highest Rate of Abilities could never have given you a more honourable Station. From the Moment you quitted that Line, you have, perhaps, been better able to gratify some interested Favourites, but you have disgraced yourself;—and, to a Man of your Quality, Disgrace is Ruin.

You are now in the lowest Rank of ministerial Dependants. Your Vote is as secure to Administration, as if you were a Lord of Trade, or a Vice Treasurer of Ireland, and even Conway, at your Lordship's Expence, has mended his Reputation. I will not enter into a Detail of your past Conduct. You have Enemies enough already, and I would not wish you to despair of recovering the public Esteem. An Opportunity will soon present itself. The People of England are good-natured enough to make Allowances for your Mistakes, and to give you Credit for correcting them. One short Question will determine your Character for ever. Does it become the Name and Dignity of Manners, to place yourself upon a Level with a venal Tribe, who vote as they are directed, and to declare upon your Honour, in the Face of your Country, that Mr. Luttrell is, or ought to be the Sitting Member for the County of Middlesex?—I appeal, bonâ fide, to your Integrity as an honest Man;—I even appeal to your Understanding.

PHILO JUNIUS 12 June 1769
22 June 1769
1 August 1769
14 August 1769
4 September 1769
19 October 1769

Philo Junius was invented as an auxiliary in Junius' exchanges with other writers, enabling Junius to explain and defend his observations without being dragged too openly into the arena. All the letters under this name were included in the collected edition. Junius acknowledged them in his preface, adding: 'The fraud was innocent, and I always intended to explain it.' They are printed in full on pp. 75–80, 91–3, 98–105, 112–15, 139–42.

MODERATUS 14 November 1769

This letter, dealing with the case of General Gansell, was included in the collected edition under the name of Philo Junius on pp. 148–51.

DOMITIAN 5 March 1770

In private letter no. 57, when the collected edition was in preparation, Junius wrote to the printer: 'I hope you are too forward, to have any room for that Letter of Dom$^{n.}$' The five Domitian letters are all on subjects Junius treated elsewhere and score high on Ellegård's test. Lord Chatham commended this letter to his son William as a specimen of eloquence. Lord Stanhope, *Life of Pitt*, i. 7.

SIR,

There is a certain Set of Men who, upon almost every Action of their Lives, are insulted with the Pity both of their Enemies and their Friends. They seem to have discovered the Art of doing whatever is base and detestable, without forfeiting their Claim to the public Compassion. A bad Man, with Resolution and Abilities, is a formidable Being. His great Qualities compensate for the Absence of good ones, and tho' not intitled to Esteem, secure him from Contempt. The Persons I speak of are not in this Predicament: They have nothing elevated in their Vices. In vain do they labour to distinguish themselves by the Violation of all public Duties and private Engagements. They still preserve their natural Mediocrity of Character, and have as little chance of being honoured with the Detestation, as with the Esteem of their Country.

I cannot mention the Name of Sir Edward Hawke without Concern. How unfortunate it is, that a Heart, unacquainted with Fear should have so little sense of Propriety and Decorum! I should be sorry to puzzle him with intricate Questions either of Policy or Morals, but there are some Distinctions within the Reach even of *his* Understanding. In his Situation, it particularly became him to regulate his Conduct by the Judgment of the Public. Tho' not expected to think for himself, he might have taken a generous Part with the Friends of his Country, and still have been respected for the Integrity of his Intentions. To what a poor insignificant Condition has he now reduced himself! Behold him, at such a Conjuncture as the present, meanly keeping Possession of an Office, which he owes to Lord Chatham's Friendship, and distinguished as the only surviving Minister [of those introduced into the Cabinet by Lord Chatham] who supports the present Administration. What Opinion can he deliver in the House of Commons? What Measures can he maintain in the Cabinet? Instead of the Dignity of thundering out Secrets of State from the Gallery, we see the first Lord of the Admiralty skulking into the House, just before a Division, as if he thought that everybody had heard the peremptory Message sent him by Mr. Bradshaw.

As to his Opinions in Council, he must either adopt a new Set of Ideas, or, if he presumes to differ from his Colleagues, must silently submit to be over-ruled. On these Terms, he may be permitted to keep an Employment which, since he sold his Stock in the Beginning of the Winter, produces nothing, in Addition to the Salary, but the Means of providing for his Friends. The Choice of Commodore Hill and Admiral Geary proves that he can discover latent Merit in the most unpromising Subjects. By this Disposition of the Command at Chatham and Portsmouth, he seems to aim at encouraging *future* Services, rather than in rewarding the past; and as to his œconomy, was it possible to give a better Proof of it, than by turning adrift a Multitude of poor Artificers to Idleness and Beggary, on Purpose to make up four Pounds a Day for the Use of Mr. Geary?

Admiral Holburne's Services in America have also been very properly considered. When so many Englishmen vacate their Places, it would be strange indeed if a Scot of such distinguished Merit had been left unprovided for. Sir Percy Brett resigns,—Mr. Holburne succeeds him, and Sir Edward Hawke is still first lord of the Admiralty! Proceed, Sir Edward, in this honourable Line. Be a

Spendthrift of your good Name. We shall not quarrel with your Prodigality, for you have a Right to waste the Reputation you had acquired. You once contributed largely to save this Country, and have a Creditor's Claim to contribute to its Destruction.

The indigent circumstances of Lord Hertford's Family account for and justify their Conduct. The same Spirit of œconomy which animated the Father to the Sale of public Employments in Ireland, revives in the Son, and finds the best Market for the Ammunition of the Warwickshire Militia*. Lord Hertford, General Conway, and Lord Beauchamp are the very Quintessence of Courtesy and Candour. Undecided in their Opinions, disengaged from all Attachments, they support no Measures without leaving Room for Explanation, and can reconcile the coldest Indifference about the Interests of others, with the warmest Anxiety for their own. It is unluckily the Fate of these moderate, candid Persons to be despised by all Parties. In vain does the gentle Beauchamp give the Treasury Bench the negative Assistance of his Oratory; in vain does his honest Father beg an Audience for personal Solicitation in the Closet. General Howard and the Secretary at War have still Spirit to resist†. The Promotion goes in the Regiment, and the military Achievements of the younger Conway are left for future Consideration. Poor Lord Hertford! What is this but a Continuation of the Duke of Grafton's Tyranny? From one Minister we see him regularly kicked down to another. His Nephew treats him like a Footman, and Lord North, with still greater Severity, yoaks him with General Græme‡.

My sincere Compassion for Lord Cornwallis arises not so much from his Quality as from his Time of Life. A young Man, by a spirited Conduct, may atone for the Deficiences of his Understanding. Where was the Memory of this noble Lord, or what Kind of Intellects must he possess, when he resigns his Place, yet continues in the Support of Administration, and, to show his Independance, makes a Parade of attending Lord North's levy, and pays a public Homage to the Deputy of Lord Bute! Where is now his Attachment; where are now his Professions to Lord Chatham;—his Zeal for the Whig interest of England, and his Detestation of Lord Bute, the Bedfords,

* This Youth goes by the Name of Gunpowder Beauchamp thro' the whole County.

† Lord Hertford not long ago had the Modesty to desire that his Son, a Youth of twenty years old, might be put over the Heads of all General Howard's Officers.

‡ Lord Hertford and this worthy Scotchman are Spies in Ordinary to the Minister for the Time being.

and the Tories? Since the Time at which these were the only Topics of his Conversation, I presume he has shifted his Company, as well as his Opinions. Will he tell the World to which of his Uncles, or to what Friend, to Philipson, or a Tory Lord, he owes the Advice which has directed his Conduct? I will not press him farther. The young Man has taken a wise Resolution at last, for he is retiring into a voluntary Banishment, in Hopes of recovering the Ruin of his Reputation.

These loose sketches are sufficient to mark to you the Kind of Character which, with every Quality that ought to make it odious, still continues pitiful, and is never important enough in Mischief to excite Indignation. I would not waste a Thought in contriving the Punishment or Correction of such Men; but it may be useful to the Public to see by what Sort of Creatures the present Administration is supported. It is unnecessary to enlarge the Catalogue. Without Name or Description, they are distinguished by a certain Consciousness of Shame, which accompanies their actions. After deserting one Party, they dare not engage heartily with the other; and having renounced their first Sentiments and Connexions, are forced to proceed in the humble Track of voting as they are ordered, without Party, Principle, or Friends.

MODERATUS 10 March 1770

This letter followed the previous Moderatus sufficiently closely to make it unlikely that a new writer had intervened to take over the pseudonym. It deals with a subject in which Junius was interested and scores high on Ellegård's test. James Townsend, representing the city of London as Sheriff, was told by the King on 7 March that he would 'take time' to consider whether to receive its petition, and the following day Lord Weymouth asked 'what the nature of the assembly was in which this measure was adopted?' The Sheriffs insisted upon their right of audience with the King and of petition.

SIR,

No Man is more warmly attached to the best of Princes than I am. I reverence his personal Virtues, as much as I respect his Understanding, and am happy to find myself under the Government of a Prince, whose Temper and Abilities do equal Honour to his Character. At the same Time, I confess, I did not hear, without astonishment, of the Answer which some evil-minded Councillors advised him to return to the Sheriffs of the City of London. For a King of Great Britain to take Time to consider, whether he will or will not receive a Petition from his Subjects, seems to me to amount to this, that he will take Time to consider whether he will or will not adhere to the fourth Article of the Declaration of Rights. One would think that this could never have been a Question in the Mind of so gracious a Prince, if there were not some very dangerous Advice given in the Closet. I now hear that it has been signified to the Sheriffs, that his Majesty cannot receive the Petition, untill he is informed of the Nature of the Assembly, in which it was composed. A King indeed is not obliged to understand the political Forms and Constitution of every Corporation in his Dominions, but his Ministers must be uncommonly ignorant who could not save him the Embarrassment of asking such a Question concerning the first Body Corporate perhaps in the World. The Sheriffs, I presume, will hardly venture to satisfy so unusual an Inquiry upon their own bare Authority. They will naturally move the Lord-Mayor to summon another Common Hall, to answer for themselves; and then, I doubt not the Corporation of the City of London will fully explain, to those whom it may concern, *who they are, and what is the Nature of their Assembly.* After all, Sir, I do not apprehend that the Propriety of the King's receiving a Petition from any of his Subjects depends in the least upon *their* Quality or Situation. He is bound by the Declaration and subsequent Bill of Rights to receive all Petitions from his Subjects. What Notice or Answer the Contents of them may deserve, must be considered afterwards. To refuse the Petition itself is against Law. I am persuaded, however, that nothing can be farther from the Intention of our gracious Sovereign, than to offer a gross Affront to the whole City of London. It is evident that the Ministry either mean to gain time for carrying some poor Counter-Measure, by Means of the wretched Dependants of the Court, or to intimidate the City Magistrates, and deter them from doing their Duty. I think it therefore absolutely necessary for us to rouse in Defence of the Honour of the City, and demonstrate to the Ministry, by the Spirit and Vigour of our Proceedings, that we are not what *they* are pleased to represent us, the Scum of the Earth, and the vilest and basest of Mankind.

DOMITIAN 8 December 1770

A further attack upon the Duke of Grafton provoked by rumours that he was to rejoin the ministry. When he did so in June 1771 it was as Lord Privy Seal.

SIR,

A Report prevails that the late Premier is very soon to be placed at the Head of the Admiralty.—I thought Junius had fairly hissed him off the Stage. But since he adventures again to appear before the Public, let me do justice to his Modesty, and commend him for his Discretion in sinking to an inferior Character. I should be sorry to interrupt so natural a Descent. By dropping gradually from Part to Part, he may in Time arrive at something that will suit his Capacity. Besides the moral Fitness of reducing all Men to their proper Level, there will be a Novelty in the public Entertainment, when we see the same wretched Stroller, who strutted Yesterday in Othello, creeping upon the Stage to day in the shape of a Candle-Snuffer.

In the Article of Firmness, I think this young Man's character is universally given up; but I observe there is still an Opinion maintained by some People, that, in Point of Ability, he is not deficient. For my own part, Sir, I never could discover upon what Foundation that Opinion rested. Let it be fairly tried by the two great, decisive Tests of the human Understanding—*Conduct*, and *Discourse*. These, I know, are sometimes at variance with each other. An ingenious Man may act very absurdly, and we frequently see a dull Fellow conduct himself with Firmness and Propriety. It is the Duke's Misfortune that he fails equally in both Articles—that he neither acts with Judgment, nor speaks with Ability. Look at his Conduct from the Outset; I mean with a Reference not to the Treachery, but to the Folly of the Man. His earliest personal attachment in Life was to the Duke of Portland; that Friendship he has foolishly dissolved, without succeeding in his Purpose, to oblige Sir James Lowther.—His first public Connexion was with Lord Rockingham. That too is lost, together with the Friendship of Lord Chatham, for which he sacrificed the Marquis. For the Solidity of his Union with Lord Chatham, he pledged himself to the Public, by some very uncommon Declarations both abroad and in Parliament. Yet from this Union, and his subsequent Friendship with Lord Granby and Lord Camden, the Cajolery of the Closet soon seduced him. His easy Virtue is not made for Resistance. To support his last Plan, we have seen him renounce not only all these successive Connexions, but every political

Idea, Opinion, and Principle of his former Life, and throw himself, Body and Soul, into the Arms of the Bedfords. Here, at least, he might have stopped, since there was not another Party in the Kingdom, to which it was possible for him to transfer his Affections. He had gone resolutely through the whole Drudgery of the Middlesex Election. He had paid Governor Burgoyne's Expences very handsomely by the Sale of that Patent to Mr. Hine, which the right honourable the House of Commons have not yet thought proper to inquire into. He had shewn Fortitude enough to drop the Prosecution of Mr. Vaughan, though urged, insulted, braved to it by every *Stimulus*, that could touch the Feelings of a Man; and, in Conclusion, he had made himself *Accessory* to the untimely Death of Mr. Yorke;—I say *accessory*, because he was certainly not the principal Actor in that most Atrocious Business. After all, Sir, when it was impossible for him to add to his Guiltiness;—a Panic seizes him, he begins to measure his Expectations by the Sense of his Deserts, a visionary Gibbet appears before his Eyes, he flies from his Post, surrenders to another the Reward due to his honourable Services, and leaves his King and country to extricate themselves, if they can, from the Distress and Confusion in which he had involved them.

The Danger, as he conceives, being now pretty well over, what Plan do you think this worthy, resolute young Man pursues at present? While he was First Lord of the Treasury, it is well known, (and I speak from Knowledge when I assert), that he never treated Lord North even with the common Civility due to his Clerk. I appeal to Lord North himself, and to every Clerk in the Treasury (particularly to Grey Cooper), whether it was not known to be a difficult Matter for the Chancellor of the Exchequer to obtain an Audience even of Mr. Thomas Bradshaw. Would you believe it possible, Sir, that, after these Facts, this very Duke of Grafton can be so degraded, so lost to every Sensation of Pride, of Dignity, and Decorum, as to be a suppliant Beggar for Employment to this very Lord North? Yet so it is; and, if I were to tell you with what Circumstances of Humiliation he accompanies his Suit to the Minister, the Narrative would be nauseous and fulsome. He is so very impatient to be First Lord of the Admiralty, that Lord North can hardly keep the fawning Creature from under his Feet. Now, Sir, let any man living, I care not whether Friend or Foe, review this Summary of his Life, and tell us in what Instance he has discovered a single Ray of Wisdom, Solidity, or Judgment?

As to the other Test of his Abilities, I mean his Talent for talking in Public, I can speak with greater Precision, for I have often had the Honour of hearing him. With a very solemn and plausible Delivery, he has a Set of Thoughts, or rather of Words resembling Thoughts, which may be applied indifferently, and with equal Success, to all possible Subjects. There is this singular Advantage in his Grace's Method of Discourse, that, if it were once admitted that he spoke well upon any one given Topic, it would inevitably follow that he was qualified to deliver himself happily upon every Subject whatsoever. He would be *ipso facto*, an universal Orator. Accept of the following Specimen of his Grace's Eloquence, and I promise you you will be as well able to judge of his oratorial Powers, as if you had heard him a thousand Times.

"My Lords,

"When I came into the House this Day, I protest I did not think it possible—indeed I had formed in my own Breast a Resolution to the Contrary—but, my Lords, I really thought it impossible that I should be compelled to trouble your Lordships with *my* poor Thoughts upon the Question before your Lordships.—I never do presume to trouble your Lordships at any Time, without always feeling a pain—an internal Regret—a Degree of Uneasiness, which I can with Truth assure your Lordships, (and I flatter myself that I shall find credit with every noble Lord, who hears me), it is not easy for me to have the Honour of describing to your Lordships. My Lords, I am called upon, as I humbly conceive, and I appeal boldly not only to the Candour of noble Lords, but to your Lordships' severest Judgment, whether I am not compelled to declare my Sentiments, as explicitly as I now do, upon the Motion upon your Lordships' Table. Upon this Ground, my Lords, I meet the noble Lord without Fear, though I respect his superior Abilities, and I pledge *my*self to your Lordships for the Truth of what I assert. Otherwise, my Lords, if facts were not as I have stated them, where will your Lordships draw the Line? My Lords, I am really *as*tonished:—yet indeed, my Lords, I ought not to be *as*tonished. The Question has been handled with so much Ability by other noble lords, that I shall content *my*self with this simple, unadorned Declaration of *my* opinion. Yet I could quote Cases, my Lords, which I accidentally met with this Morning in the Course of *my* readings, which, I doubt not, would convince your Lordships, if Conviction were in Question. But I fear I have troubled your Lordships too long. I shall therefore return to the leading

Proposition, which I had the Honour of setting out with, and move for an immediate adjournment."

This style, I apprehend, Sir, is what the learned Scriblerus calls *Rigmarol* in Logic, *Riddlemeree* among Schoolboys, and in vulgar Acceptation, *Three blue Beans in a blue Bladder*. It is the perpetual Parturience of a Mountain and the never-failing delivery of a Mouse.

PHALARIS 17 December 1770

The penultimate paragraph of this letter was used by Junius, with some slight alterations, as a footnote to his preface, where he described it as part of a speech by Lord Chatham. The editor of the Bohn edition was under the impression that he had inadvertently omitted the introduction to the paragraph, whereas, in fact, he had omitted the whole thing (Wade, i. 95; ii. 324). Phalaris scores high on Ellegård's test.

Junius had already attacked Lord Mansfield in a letter of 14 November 1770. Phalaris wrote in reply to Nerva of 14 December 1770 (quoted in full by Wade, ii. 320–2), who accused Chatham of showing gross ignorance of the law in the debate in the House of Lords of 10 December.

SIR,

As far as Assertion goes, no Man argues better than your Correspondent *Nerva*. If we are contented to take his Word for Proof, Lord Chatham is a hare-brained, desperate old Fellow, and Lord Mansfield the very Quintessence of Integrity, Wisdom, Moderation, and Firmness. I wonder he did not assure us on the same Foundation that this worthy Judge *never* drank the Pretender's Health upon his Knees; or that his Brother was not Secretary to that most Catholic Prince; or that Peg Trentham's father had not his Left Foot in the Stirrup in the Year 1715, to go off to what he thought the best Side of the Question: All this too I suppose we shall be told is mere Fiction, mere inference of Law, and the Suggestion of the Devil; but, setting aside Ornament, let us look a little to matters of Fact.

For what Reason Lord Mansfield laid his paper upon the Table, *he* best knows. He gave none to the House of Lords, except that he thought calling them together was the most compendious Way of informing them where each Lord might, if he pleased, procure a Copy of his Charge to the Jury in Woodfall's cause. This was the whole, for he made no Motion whatsoever, nor did he pretend to say that, in their corporate Capacity as a House of Peers, they could take the least Notice of the Paper. Now, Sir, it remains with Lord Mansfield to give us an Example, if he can, of any respectable Peer having ever moved for a Call of the House for so trifling, so nugatory, so ridiculous a Purpose. I think it strongly deserves these Epithets, and after much Consideration I can find but one possible way of reconciling the fact with the cunning Understanding of the Man. When he summoned the House, he never meant to do what he afterwards did: Some Qualm, some Terror intervened, and forced him hastily to alter his Design, and to substitute a silly, absurd Measure in the Place of a dangerous one. As for his having *dared* Lord Chatham to a *trial* of his Doctrines, I should be glad to know by *whom* the Combat was refused. Lord Chatham attacked him directly upon the Spot, and on the very next Day it is known to the whole World, that the great Lord Camden addressed him in the following Words: "I consider the Paper delivered in by the noble Lord upon the Woolsack as a Challenge directed personally to *me*, and I accept of it;—he has thrown down the Glove, and *I* take it up. In direct Contradiction to him. I maintain that his Doctrine is not the Law of England. I am ready to enter into the Debate whenever the noble Lord will fix a Day for it. I desire, and insist, that it may be an early one." The Devil's in it if this be declining the Trial; But what was the Consequence? Lord Mansfield, after an Hour's shuffling and Evasion, finding himself pushed to the last Extremity, cried out in an Agony of Torture and Despair, *No, I will not fix a day—I will not pledge myself.*

As to Lord Chatham's Declaration concerning the irregular Production of Lord Mansfield's Opinion in the Court of King's Bench, I am sorry to say that your correspondent *Nerva* neither knows the Fact, nor understands the Argument. He talks of a *Judgment* in a cause where no *Judgment* was ever given. Leaving therefore this poor Man to his own unhappy Reveries, let me state briefly to the Public what *was* the Fact, and what *was* the Irregularity of the Proceeding upon it.

The verdict given at *Nisi Prius* in the King and Woodfall was, *Guilty of printing and publishing only*. A Motion in Arrest of Judgment was made by the Defendant's Council, grounded upon the Ambiguity of the Verdict. At the same Time a Motion was made by the Council for the Crown, for a Rule upon the Defendant to show cause why the Verdict should not be entered up according to the *legal* Import of the Words. On both Motions a Rule to show Cause was granted, and soon after the Matter was argued before the Court of

King's Bench. Lord Mansfield, when he delivered the Opinion of the Court upon the Verdict, went regularly thro' the whole of the Proceedings at *Nisi Prius*, as well the Evidence that had been given, as his own Charge to the Jury. This Proceeding would have been very proper had a Motion been made of either side for a new Trial, because either a Verdict given contrary to *evidence*, or an improper charge by the Judge at *Nisi Prius*, is held to be a sufficient Ground for granting a new Trial; but when a Motion is made in Arrest of Judgment, or for establishing the Verdict, by entering it up according to the *legal* Import of the Words, it must be on the Ground of something appearing *on the Record*; and the Court, in considering whether the Verdict shall be established or not, are so confin'd to the Record that they cannot take Notice of any Thing that does not appear on the Face of it; to make use of the legal Phrase, *they cannot travel out of the Record.* Lord Mansfield did travel out of the Record. I affirm therefore with Lord Chatham, that his conduct was IRREGULAR, EXTRAJUDICIAL and UNPRECEDENTED; and I am sure there is not a Lawyer in England that will contradict me. His real Motive for doing what he knew to be wrong was, that he might have an Opportunity of telling the Public *extrajudicially*, that the other three Judges agreed with him in the Doctrine laid down in his Charge.

When you have read this Paper, I am sure you will join with me in Opinion, that to support an uniform System of Falsehood, requires greater Parts than even those of Lord Mansfield.

PHALARIS 20 December 1770

This is one of the most baffling of all the miscellaneous letters. It raises a totally new subject and the persons referred to appear to have no political significance. But if the first Phalaris letter is correctly attributed to Junius, the second must follow. The printer always discouraged writers from taking each other's pseudonyms and would not have allowed a new Phalaris to enter so soon after the other: the handwriting would indicate whether the writer was the author of the first Phalaris letter.

Lady Williams I take to be the elderly widow of Sir Charles Hanbury Williams. She died in December 1781 and was buried in Westminster Abbey. The 'country seat near Hereford' was, I presume, Hampton Court, some eight miles to the north. I can only surmise that Phalaris thought he knew the identity of Nerva and hoped to irritate him with this piece of family scandal.

The Latin, a reference from Horace, *Odes*, I. xiii. 17–18, may be rendered thus:

Thrice happy they and more than thrice
Unbroken joined in love's sweet vice.

A CARD.

Phalaris presents his Compliments to Sir —— ——, is preparing for the Press a faithful account of Mr. Justice's Amours with the Lady Williams; and, as he wishes not to give a plain Narrative too much the Air of a Romance, would be very glad to be furnished with any material Facts which Mr. Justice may think proper to have inserted; But in order not to give Mr. Justice any unnecessary Trouble, *Phalaris* thinks it proper to apprise him of those Circumstances, in which he (*Phalaris*) is already particularly instructed, viz., How Mr. Justice was distressed for Want of Practice; how he was impatient at trying a long Cause in a hot Day at Hereford; how he made a Declaration at a public Dinner, confirmed by Execrations, that he would marry the Devil with Money, rather than practice the Law without it; how he was introduced to Lady Williams; how, upon sufficient Deliberation, he preferred her Ladyship to the Devil; how he explained his tender Passion; how, with a gallant Impatience, he hastened the Marriage Ceremony before he saw the Writings of her Estate; how he stepped into a Hackney Coach, one fine Morning, in a Suit of white Cloth lined with green Velvet; how he had a Levee of Visitors at his Gate the Day after his auspicious Nuptials; how Lady Williams complained next Morning; how she retired to her Country Seat near Hereford; how Mr. Justice pursued her in Company with a certain strong Lady with a strait Waistcoat; how both Parties, with great Cordiality, signed Articles of Separation; and how Mr. Justice retired to Ireland, without taking Leave of his Friends.

Phalaris hopes Mr. Justice will have no Objection to the following motto:

Felices ter, et amplius,
Quos irrupta tenet Copula.

DOMITIAN 24 December 1770

This is one of the most audacious of the miscellaneous letters, prophesying revolution.

SIR,

Without attempting to account for *all* the political Changes which have happened since his Majesty's auspicious Accession to the throne, it requires but little Sagacity to observe that the general Principle, from which they have arisen, is uniform and consistent with itself. A Prince of the House of Brunswick searches for the Consolation and Endearments of private Sociality and Friendship in the loyal Hearts of Jacobites, Tories, and Scotchmen:—a devout Prince, whose sincere, unaffected Piety would have done Honour even to Charles the First, intrusts the public Government of his Affairs to Grafton, North, Halifax, and Sandwich. The first Choice naturally led to the second. The private convivial Hours of Jonathan Wild were happily unbent in the Company of the lower Adepts in pilfering and petty Larceny. In public he resumed his State, and never appeared without an attendant Knot of Highwaymen and Assassins.

I congratulate this country upon the return of the Earl of Sandwich to a Station, in which he has heretofore given compleat Satisfaction to his Royal Master. It is the more pleasing, because it was unexpected. A gracious and a truly religious Prince had often declared that this was the only Man in his Dominions, whom he never would suffer to enter the Cabinet. He was tender of the Morals of his Ministers, and the Bedfords had Delicacy enough to acquiesce in the Truth of the Objection. I feel for his Majesty's Distress. To what a melancholy Condition must he be reduced, when he is forced to apply to the Earl of Sandwich as the last Resource, the only Prop remaining to stop the Fall of Government? Lord Weymouth it seems retires perfectly satisfied, and determined to support Men and Measures as vigorously, as if he had continued in Employment. Good humoured Creature! What a Pity it is, that he cannot submit to the Drudgery of receiving Seven Thousand Pounds a Year! The King presses him to accept of some other Post, where there is neither Labour nor Responsibility,—anything, in short, provided he will not fling the public Mortification upon his royal Master of quitting his Service at so critical a Conjuncture. Still he resists;—still he refuses; but though he quits all Connexion with Ministers and their Practices, it is impossible to interrupt his Complacency and Good-humour.—

By this Nobleman's Retreat, the Nation has made some capital Acquisitions. To say nothing of my Lord Sandwich, what do you think of the amiable Mr. Bamber Gascoyne, and that well-educated, genteel young broker, Mr. Chamier? The first is to thunder in the Senate;—the second, in Quality of Secretary, is to direct the most secret and important Manœuvres of Government. Well done, my Lord Sandwich! Your company, I'll be sworn, will be no Reproach to you. But was there no Employment to be found for Tommy Bradshaw's Sister as well as his Brother-in-law? She too understands the Disposal of Places;—at least his fraternal Affection has given her the Credit of it.—

Give me leave, Mr. Woodfall, to ask you a serious Question. How long do you think it possible for this Management to last? How long is this great Country to be governed by a Boot and a Petticoat?—by the infamous Tools of a Scotch exile, and her Royal Highness the Princess Dowager of Wales?—by North, Ellis, Barrington, Jenkinson, Hillsborough, Jerry Dyson, and Sandwich? I will answer you with Precision. It will last until there is a general Insurrection of the English Nation, or until the House of Bourbon have collected their Strength and strike you to the Heart.

P.S. Tell the Duke of Grafton, that, if he should dare to entertain the most distant Thought of the Admiralty, the whole Affair of *Hine's patent* shall be revived and published, with an Accumulation of Evidence. *He* at least shall be kept under. His Ciceronian Eloquence shall not save him.

DOMITIAN 17 January 1771

One of the strongest attacks upon the reputed influence of the Princess Augusta, widow of Frederick, Prince of Wales and mother of George III. Junius seems to have nursed an obsessive hatred of this unfortunate woman, gloating over the details of her final illness with sickening malignancy. Horace Walpole shared his suspicion of her influence: his *Memoirs of the reign of King George III* began with a reference to her and concluded with her death. There is no evidence that she was of political importance nor that she had improper relations with the Earl of Bute.

Lord Bristol was First Lord of the Bedchamber and Groom of the Stole. From the laboured joke at his expense it is clear that the word was pronounced 'stool'.

SIR,

If Sir Edward Hawke had followed the Advice and Example of his

Friends, he would not have been reduced to the dishonourable Necessity of quitting the Direction of the English Navy, at the very Moment it is going to be employed against the foreign Enemies of England. To be left in employment after Chatham, Granby, and Camden had retired; to continue in it in company with Grafton, North, Gower, and Hillsborough;—and at last to be succeeded by Lord Sandwich, are Circumstances too disgraceful to admit of Aggravation. It is natural to sympathise in the Distresses of a brave Man, and to lament that a noble Estate of Reputation should be squandered away in Debts of Dishonour contracted with Sharpers.

His Majesty, God bless him, has now got rid of every Man whose former Services or present Scruples could be supposed to give Offence to her ROYAL HIGHNESS THE PRINCESS DOWAGER OF WALES. The Security of our civil and religious Liberties cannot be more happily provided for, than while Lord Mansfield pronounces the Law, and Lord Sandwich represents the Religion of St. James's. Such Law and such Religion are too closely united, to suffer even a momentary Intervention of common Honesty between them. Her Royal Highness's Scheme of Government, formed long before her Husband's Death, is now accomplished. She has succeeded in disuniting every Party, and dissolving every Connexion; and, by the mere Influence of the Crown, has formed an Administration, such as it is, out of the Refuse of them all. There are two leading Principles in the Politics of St. James's, which will account for almost every Measure of Government, since the King's Accession. The first is, that the Prerogative is sufficient to make a Lackey a Prime Minister, and to maintain him in that Post, without any Regard to the Welfare or to the Opinion of the People.—The second is, that none but Persons insignificant in themselves, or of tainted Reputation, should be brought into Employment. Men of greater Consequence and Abilities will have Opinions of their own, and will not submit to the meddling, unnatural Ambition of a Mother, who grasps at unlimited Power, at the Hazard of her Son's Destruction. They will not suffer Measures of public Utility, which have been resolved upon in Council, to be checked and controlled by a secret Influence in the Closet. Such Men consequently will never be called upon, but in Cases of extreme Necessity. When that ceases, they find their Places no longer tenable. To answer the Purposes of an ambitious Woman, an Administration must be formed of more pliant Materials;—of Men, who, having no Connexion with each other, no personal Interest, no Weight or

Consideration with the People, may separately depend upon the Smiles of the Crown alone for their Advancement to high Offices, and for their Continuance there. If such Men resist the Princess Dowager's Pleasure, his Majesty knows that he may dismiss them without risking anything from their Resentment. His Wisdom suggests to him that, if he were to choose his Ministers for any of those Qualities which might entitle them to public Esteem, the Nation might take Part with them, and resent their Dismission. As it is, whenever he changes his Servants, he is sure to have the People, in that instance, of his Side.

I love and respect our gracious Sovereign too much to suppose it possible that *He* should be anything more than passive in forming and supporting such a System of Government; and even this Acquiescence of the best of Princes I am ready to attribute to a most amiable Quality implanted in him by Nature, and carefully cultivated by Art—unlimited Duty and Obedience to his dear Mother. Few Nations are in the Predicament that we are, to have nothing to complain of but the filial Virtues of our Sovereign. Charles the First had the same implicit Attachment to his Spouse; but his worthy Parent was in her grave. It were to be wished that the Parallel held good in all the Circumstances.

In respect to her Royal Highness, I shall deliver my sentiments without any false Tenderness or Reserve. I consider her not only as the original creating Cause of the shameful and deplorable Condition of this Country, but as a Being whose Operation is uniform and permanent; who watches, with a kind of providential Malignity, over the Work of her Hands, to correct, improve, and preserve it. If the strongest Appearances may be relied on, this lady has now brought her Schemes to Perfection. Every Office in Government is filled with Men, who are known to be her Creatures, or by mere Cyphers incapable of Resistance. Is it conceivable that anything, less than a determined Plan of drawing the whole Power of the Crown into her own Hands, could have collected such an Administration as the present? Who is Lord North? The son of a poor unknown Earl;—who four years ago was a needy Commissioner of the Treasury for the Benefit of a Subsistence, and who would have accepted a Commission of Hackney Coaches upon the same Terms. The Politics of Carlton House,—Finances picked up in Mr. Grenville's Anti-chamber, and the Elocution of a Demosthenes, endeavouring to speak plain with Pebbles in his Mouth, form the Stuffing of that Figure, that calls itself Minister, that does Homage to the Princess Dowager, and says, *Madam, I am your Man.*

The Stage was deprived of a promising Actor when poor Lord Hillsborough gave his Mind to Politics. Yet his theatrical Talents have been of Use to his Fortune. The Princess Dowager saw what Part this Man was capable of acting; and with regard to himself, it signified but little whether he represented *Prince Volscius* at Drury-lane, or Secretary of State at St. James's.

It is not pretended that Lord Rochford's Abilities are of the *explicit* kind. Yet from a *Chargé d'affaires* at Turin, the all-powerful guiding Hand has raised him to be Secretary of State. The Princess Dowager knows, better than we do, what positive good Qualities this Nobleman possesses. The Public only knows that he is a Mute in the House of Lords, and that he is destitute of Fortune, Interest, and Connexions. To do him Justice, he has all the negative Qualifications that constitute Merit at Carlton House.

The Character of third Secretary is not yet disposed of. Public suspicion gives Lord Hillsborough a formidable Rival. At the opening of the Theatre, young *Suffolk* is to be produced. Prince *Prettyman* can cant very near as well as Prince *Volscius*. Such a Pair of Actors make Tragedy ridiculous. Our Enemies at least will laugh at the Catastrophe. But this young Man shall be left for abler Hands. It requires no vulgar Pen to do Justice to such a Strain of monstrous Prostitution.

Why is that wretched creature Lord *Townshend* maintained in Ireland? Is it not universally known that the Ignorance, Presumption, and Incapacity of that Man have ruined the King's Affairs in Ireland?—that he has, in a great measure, destroyed the political Dependance of that Country upon Great Britain? But he too is an unconnected Being, without any Hope of Support but in the Protection of Lord Bute and the Princess Dowager.

Why is not a Commander in Chief appointed? Because there is an insignificant Secretary at War, who has no Chance of continuing in the Receipt of 2500*l.* a year, but by making himself the Instrument thro' which the Princess Dowager disposes of every valuable Commission in the Army.

Why have we not a Master General of the Ordnance? Because the gentle *Conway* knows how to be as pliant as Lord Barrington.

Why is there no Chancellor? Partly because there is a Convenience in bribing four of the Judges with the Emoluments of that Office, and partly because no Man of Credit in the Profession will submit to act with the present infamous Administration.

What merit has Lord Halifax?—The Issue of General Warrants; the Opposition of his Privilege for Years together to the Laws of his Country;—Prostitution in private Life, and Poverty in the Extreme.

Why is the King so fond of having Lord Bristol *about his Person?* If the Duties of the noble Lord's Office had a closer Connexion with the Title of it, as usually pronounced, I should understand his Majesty, and admire his Attention in paying so delicate a Compliment to his Lordship's Amours. The last Question I would ask is, by what Kind of Service or Ability the Earl of Sandwich is distinguished? Prostitution and Poverty may be found in other Subjects, and Appearances saved by a decent Formality of Behaviour. The Choice and Preference of the most profligate Character in the Kingdom may suit well enough with the substantial Purposes of Carlton House, but how does it consist with the hypocritical Decorum of Saint James's? What opinion are we to entertain of the Piety, Chastity, and Integrity of the best of Princes, when, in the face of England and of all Europe, he takes such a man as Sandwich to his Bosom! Let us hear no more of the Piety of Saint James's. To talk of Morals or Devotion in such Company is a scandalous Insult to Common Sense, and a still more scandalous Mockery of Religion.

The Princess Dowager having now carried her Plan of Administration into Effect, it is not to be wondered that she should be very unwilling to expose herself and her Schemes to the uncertain Events of a foreign War. She knows that a Disaster abroad would not only defeat the cunning Plan of Female Avarice and Ambition, but that it might reach Farther.—The Mothers of our Kings have heretofore been impeached; and if the precedents are not so compleat as they should be, they require and will admit of Improvement.

To maintain this Lady in her present State of Power and Security, there is no Insult, no Indignity, to which the King of Britain must not submit—no Condition, however humiliating, which the King and the Nation must not accept of without Resentment.—At this point, however, her Cunning forsakes her. Both she and her Ministers deceive themselves grossly, if they imagine that any Concessions can secure Peace with an Enemy determined upon War.—She may disgrace the English Nation. She may dishonour her Son, and persuade him to forfeit his Right to Precedence among the Sovereigns of Europe. The man who receives a Blow, and does not return it (whether he be a King or a private Person), from that Moment stands degraded from his natural Rank and Condition. If he be a young Man, his Infamy is immortal.—Yet I am ready to confess that where two Nations upon the Whole are peaceably disposed, there is a Degree of Slight, and ill Humour, and even of Injury, which, for the Sake of Peace, may and ought to be dissembled; But a direct, positive, intended Insult must always be resented. To flatter ourselves that the Moderation of the Spaniards will be proportioned to our Forbearance, or that, because we have submitted tamely to one Affront, they will therefore avoid offering us a second, would be arguing in Contradiction to all Reason and Experience. If Falkland Island had never existed, the Rancour of the Spaniards would not have failed to discover itself in some other Mode of Hostility. Their whole History, since the Accession of Philip the Vth., is a continued Proof of a rooted Antipathy to the Name of Englishman; and I am justified, by a series of indisputable Facts, in affirming that, from the Treaty of Utrecht to this Hour, there has never been a single Instance of common Justice or Decency, much less of Cordiality or Friendship, in the Conduct of the Court of Madrid towards this Country. Lord Sandwich declared a Month ago, in full Parliament, that Gibraltar was a Place of no Consequence, and immediately afterwards the Princess Dowager makes him Secretary of State. Whoever compares the Sale of Dunkirk with this Nobleman's Character, must be very much of a Sceptic, if he entertains any Doubt about the Fate of Gibraltar. But neither this Sacrifice, nor even that of Jamaica, would be sufficient to produce a solid, permanent Union with Spain. They may despise us more, but they will never hate us less.

By the Princess Dowager's Management, instead of avoiding a War, we make it certain. A little Spirit at first might perhaps have intimidated the Spaniards. Our notorious Weakness and shameful Submission have only served to encourage and confirm them in their Resolution. In point of Honour, we have let the proper Moment of Resentment pass away. The royal and national Honour is so irretrievably stained, that it cannot now be recovered by the most vigorous Measures of Revenge.—From her Royal Highness's Government in Time of Peace, we may well conclude in what Manner she will conduct a War. Gifted as she is, she could hardly fail of Success, if the Quarrels of Nations bore any Resemblance to domestic Feuds, or could be conducted upon the same Principles. The

Genius of Queen Elizabeth united the Nation, collected the Strength of the People, and carried it forward to Resistance and Victory. When the Demon of Discord sits at the Helm, what have we to expect but Distraction and Civil War at home, Disgrace and Infamy abroad?

PHILO JUNIUS 6 February 1771

Included in the collected edition as letter no. XLIII. A short addendum, published the following day, is printed in Appendix four, p. 458.

VINDEX 22 February 1771

The attribution of this letter is established by private letters nos. 33 and 34 and by the full text in Junius' handwriting in Add. MS. 27777, f. 13. The two Vindex letters score high on Ellegård's test. A pro-government pamphleteer called Vindex was very active in 1769 and early 1770, specializing in attacks on false patriots and factious opposition. Some of his letters were tested by Ellegård (text item 244) and scored low. Another Vindex intervened on 19 March 1770, causing the printer to beg his correspondents to employ different names.

In February 1771 Woodfall was threatened with a further prosecution for publishing Junius' letter of 30 January, which accused the government of accepting an ignominious settlement with Spain. He therefore told Junius that he was not prepared to print Vindex as it stood 'as I am convinced the Subject of it must . . . render me liable to very severe reprehension'. Junius replied authorizing the printer to 'alter or omit' at his own discretion. Woodfall then printed the first part of the letter as follows:

SIR,

The advocates of the Ministry are, in point of Ignorance, upon a Level with the People whose Conduct they defend. The Questions they ask are Suicide to their own cause. Gibraltar and Minorca were yielded to England by the Treaty of Utrecht, to which Treaty Spain acceded; and, admitting that they have never given up in Form their Claim to Jamaica, it is also true, that, since the Treaty of Utrecht, they have never asserted such a Claim, much less have *we* allowed it to be inserted in any Treaty between the two Crowns. But, Sir, the real Question is, not what Declarations or Pretensions Spain may have thought proper to advance, but, what Declarations or Pretensions on their Part *have we admitted and accepted?* To support a fair Comparison between the Terms on which we hold the above Places, and those on which Port Egmont is restored, it should be proved that Spain, in some Treaty, between us and them, have asserted their Claim of prior Right to Jamaica, Gibraltar, and Minorca, and that *we* have, with equal Formality, accepted a Treaty containing such an express Reservation, and declared ourselves *satisfied with it*. The Ministry would then have an Example in point.

Of the paragraph which Woodfall suppressed, Junius wrote privately: 'As to the Satyrical part, I must tell you, (and with positive Certainty) that our gracious —— is as callous as Stockfish to every thing but the Reproach of *Cowardice*. That alone is able to set the humours afloat. After a paper of that kind he won't eat Meat for a Week.' (Private letter no. 34.) The postscript was yet another reminder that Grafton had Stuart blood in his veins.

The rest of Vindex's letter was as follows:

Our Gracious Sovereign, who, sympathizing with Jerry Dyson, delights in Precedents of this kind, might say to himself, with heartfelt Satisfaction; "It is true, as a King I am degraded;—as a Man I am dishonoured;—as a young Man, I am branded for ever; but, Thanks to the Genius of Cowardice, I have not descended lower than some of my Predecessors."

This, Sir, you see, is mere matter of Supposition, for, in reality, his Majesty could not with Truth administer such Consolation to himself. There is no Precedent in the English history, that comes home to the present Case; his Majesty's reputation, in this instance, stands unrivalled. He has all the Glory & all the Merit of establishing a singular Example, which, when his royal posterity shall have occasion to surrender the Rights & honour of the Crown of England, they will look back to with pleasure. Neither is the best of Sovereigns left destitute of all Resources, if, in the melancholy Moments of Reflection, he should look round him for Consolation. He may find it in abundance in the *magnitudo infamiae*, the Excess of Infamy by which his faithful Servants (to say nothing of his own royal Inclinations) have successfully laboured to make their Friend immortal.

I am, Sir,

(With all possible Contempt for a *stigmatised* Coward)

Your humble servant

Vindex

P.S. When a certain young Duke ran away & left his Mistress in distress, we thought that such an instance of cowardly baseness in a young man & a lover, co^d. not be parallelled;—neither could it, Sir,—*out of the family*.—

VINDEX *6 March 1771*

Lauchlin Macleane, M.P. for Arundel, an erstwhile supporter of Lord Shelburne, spoke in favour of government in the debate of 13 February 1771 on the Falkland Islands dispute. He was rewarded three months later with a sinecure post and resigned his seat: hence Vindex's sarcastic reference to his disinterestedness. 'Unbroken melodious eloquence' is a jeer at his stammer. J. N. M. Maclean, *Reward is secondary* argues that Macleane was really Junius and that this was no more than a false wound.

SIR,

Pray tell that ingenious Gentleman, Mr. Laughlin Macleane, that when the King of Spain writes to the King of Great-Britain, he omits four-fifths of his Titles, and when our King writes to him, his Address is always *Carolo, dei gratia, Hispaniarum, utriusque Siciliæ, et Indiarum Regi Catholico.* It was reserved for his present Majesty to say, in a public Instrument, "Falkland Island is one of my Possessions, and yet I allow the King of Spain to reserve a Claim of prior Right, and I declare myself *satisfied* with that Reservation." In spite of Mr. Laughlin's disinterested, unbroken, melodious Eloquence, it is a melancholy Truth that the Crown of England was never so insulted, never so shamefully degraded, as by this Declaration, with which the best of Sovereigns assures his People he is perfectly, entirely, compleatly satisfied.

A WHIG *9 April 1771*

The argument for attributing this letter to Junius is that he quoted extensively from it in his collected edition, using it as footnotes to letter no. XLIV. It also scores very high on Ellegård's test. But there are two other letters of 15 and 26 January signed A Whig, both attacking the King.

This is a classic statement of the opposition belief that there had been a sustained and deliberate attempt in the early years of George III's reign to increase the influence of the crown. For a modern commentary on this, see I. R. Christie, 'Was there a "New Toryism" in the earlier part of George III's reign?', printed in *Myth and reality in late eighteenth century British politics*.

SIR,

The Arguments, used in Defence of the late Proceedings of the House of Commons, would have a considerable Weight with me, if I could persuade myself, that the present House of Commons were really in that independent State, in which the Constitution meant to place them. If I could be satisfied that their Resolutions were not previously determined in the King's Cabinet, that no personal Resentment was to be gratified, nor any ministerial Purpose to be answered, under Pretence of asserting their Privileges, I own I should be very unwilling to raise or encourage any Question between the strict Right of the Subject, and that discretionary Power, which our Representatives have assumed by Degrees, and which, until of late Years, they have very seldom abused. While the House of Commons form a real Representation of the People, while they preserve their Place in the Constitution, distinct from the Lords, and independent of the Crown, I think to contend with them about the limits of their Privileges would be contending with ourselves*. But the Question will be materially altered, if it should appear that, instead of preserving the due Balance of the Constitution, they have thrown their whole Weight into the same Scale with the Crown, and that their Privileges, instead of forming a Barrier against the Encroachments of the other Branches of the Legislature, are made subservient to the Views of the Sovereign, and employed, under the Direction of the Minister, in the Persecution of Individuals, and the Oppression of the People. In this case it would be the Duty of every honest Man to stand strictly to his Right; to question every Act of such a House of Commons with Jealousy and Suspicion, and wherever their pretended Privileges trenched upon the known Laws of the Land, in the minutest instance, to resist them with a determined and scrupulous Exactness. To ascertain the Fact, we need only consider in what Manner Parliaments have been managed since his Majesty's Accession.

He found this Country in that state of perfect Union and Happiness which good Government naturally produces, and which a bad one has destroyed. He promised to abolish all Distinctions of Party, and kept his Word by declaring Lord Bute his Favourite and Minister, by proscribing the whole Whig Interest of England, and by filling every Place of Trust and Profit under his Government, with profest Tories, notorious Jacobites, and Scotchmen of all Denomina-

* The Necessity of securing the H. of C. against the King's Power, so that no Interruption might be given either to the Attendance of the Members in Parliament, or to the Freedom of Debate, was the Foundation of Parliamentary Privilege; and we may observe, in all the Addresses of newly-appointed Speakers to the Sovereign, the utmost Privilege they demand is Liberty of Speech and Freedom from Arrests. The very Word Privilege means no more than Immunity, or a Safeguard to the Party who possesses it, and can never be construed into an active Power of invading the Rights of others.

tions. He abolished no Distinctions, but those, which are essential to the Safety of the Constitution. King, Lords, and Commons, which should for ever stand clear of each other, were soon melted down into one common Mass of Power, while equal Care was taken to draw a Line of Separation between the Legislature and the People, and more particularly between the representative and the constituent Body of the Commons. The Lower House distinguished themselves by an eager Compliance with every Measure that could be supposed to gratify the King personally, or to humour the vindictive Passions of his Royal Mother. When Mr. Wilkes was to be punished, they made no Scruple about the Privileges of Parliament; and altho' it was as well known as any Matter of public Record and uninterrupted Custom could be, *that the Members of either House are privileged except in cases of Treason, Felony, or Breach of the Peace*, they declared without Hesitation *that Privilege of Parliament did not extend to the Case of a seditious Libel;* and undoubtedly they would have done the same if Mr. Wilkes had been prosecuted for any other misdemeanor whatsoever. It was upon that occasion that Sir Fletcher Norton, the Patron of Privilege, declared in the House, that, if he were a Judge in Westminster Hall, he should regard a Vote of the House of Commons no more than a Resolution of a Company of drunken Porters.—To show us his Politeness, he preserves his Style;—to show us his Morality, he changes his Opinion.

The House of Lords have not been less pliant in surrendering the Rights of the Peerage, whenever it has suited the Purposes of the Cabinet. They joined heartily in the Vote above-mentioned, and when they were called upon to support that enormous Violation of all Law, Truth, and Reason, which was perpetrated by the House of Commons in the Case of the Middlesex election, they gave up that reciprocal Check and Controul, by which the Balance between the three Estates can alone be preserved, and were content to bury their own Privileges under the Ruins of the Constitution.—The Influence of the Crown over the Resolutions of both Houses continues to operate with equal Force, tho' now it assumes a different Appearance. The Liberty of the Press, besides giving a daily personal Offence to the Princess of Wales, must always be formidable, therefore always odious to such a Government as the present. Prosecutions had been attempted without Success. The Privilege of Parliament, which had been so shamefully surrendered to answer one ministerial Purpose, must now be as violently asserted to answer another. The ministry are of a sudden grown wonderfully careful of Privileges, which their Predecessors were as ready to invade. The known Laws of the Land, the Rights of the Subject, the Sanctity of Charters, and the Reverence due to our Magistrates, must all give way, without Question or Resistance, to a Privilege of which no Man knows either the Origin or the Extent. The House of Commons judge of their own Privileges without appeal;—They may take offence at the most innocent Action, and imprison the Person who offends them, during their arbitrary Will and Pleasure. The Party has no Remedy; he cannot appeal from their Jurisdiction; and if he questions the Privilege, which he is supposed to have violated, it becomes an Aggravation of his Offence. Surely, Sir, this Doctrine is not to be found in Magna Charta. If it be admitted without Limitation, I affirm that there is neither Law nor Liberty in this Kingdom. We are the Slaves of the House of Commons, and thro' them we are the Slaves of the King and his Ministers.

The Mode, in which the House have proceeded against the City Magistrates, can neither be reconciled to natural Justice, nor even to the common Forms of Decency. They begin with shutting the Doors against all *Strangers*, the usual name by which they describe their Constituents. Some of their Debates appear in the public Papers. The Offence, if any, is certainly not a new one. We have the Debates as regularly preserved as the Journals of Parliament*; nor can there be any honest Reason for concealing them. Mr. Onslow, however, thinks it necessary to prosecute the Press, and the House of Commons is mean enough to take Part in his Caprices. Lord North, who had so lately rewarded the Reverend Mr. Scot with the best Living in the King's Gift for heaping Invectives equally dull and virulent upon some of the most respectable Characters in the Kingdom, is now shameless enough to support a Motion against the Liberty of the Press, with the whole Influence of the Crown. That their Practice might be every Way conformable to their Principles, the House proceeded to advise the Crown to publish a Proclamation universally acknowledged to be illegal. Mr. Moreton publicly protested against it before it was issued; and Lord Mansfield, though not scrupulous to an Extreme, speaks of it with Horror. It is remarkable enough that the very Men, who advised the Proclamation, and who hear it arraigned every Day both within Doors

* Grey's Collection of Debates, in ten Volumes, was published under the Direction of the late Arthur Onslow, Esq.

and without, are not daring enough to utter one Word in its defence, nor have they ventured to take the least notice of Mr. Wilkes for discharging the Persons apprehended under it.

The pretended Trial of the Lord Mayor and Mr. Oliver resembled the dark Business of a Spanish Inquisition, rather than the fair Proceedings of an English Court of Judicature. These gentlemen, as Magistrates, had nothing to regard, but the Obligation of their Oaths, and the Execution of the Laws. If they were convinced that the Speaker's Warrant was not a legal Authority to the Messenger, it necessarily followed that, when he was charged upon Oath with a Breach of the Peace, they *must* hold him to Bail. They had no Option. Yet how have they been treated? Their Judges had been partially summoned by Treasury Mandates, pressing Attendance, and demanding a Vote of Condemnation. They were tried and condemned at Midnight, without being heard by themselves or their Counsel, on the only point on which their Justification could possibly depend.— In short, Sir, a Question, strictly of Jurisdiction, was referred to Numbers, and carried like a common ministerial Measure. Their next Step was to force the Lord Mayor's Clerk, by the Terror of a Prison, to erase the Record of a judicial Proceeding, held regularly before the Chief Magistrate of the City. Lord North himself made the Motion, and declared that the Constitution could not be safe, until it was carried into Effect. They then resolved that all Prosecutions for the Assault (which, though charged upon Oath, they call a pretended one) should be stopped. I wish that grave and sober Men would consider, independently of the other Questions before us, how far this particular Precedent may extend. If the House of Commons may interpose in a single Instance, between the subject, who complains, and the Laws, which ought to protect, I see no Reason why they may not, at any Time, by their Vote, stop the whole Course of Justice through the Kingdom. Besides the Injury done to the Subject, their granting a *Noli prosequi* is in effect an Incroachment upon the royal Prerogative.

Many Circumstances of Insult have been mixed with these Measures of Violence.—Their pretended Lenity to the Lord Mayor, which he nobly refused to accept of, amounted only to an Offer of the Garrets of the House for the Place of his Confinement instead of the Tower; and, though it be of less Moment, it is still worth observing, that the Indignity offered to the city is aggravated by the Time expressly chosen for imprisoning their Chief Magistrate.

Not content with interrupting all City Business, they fixed upon Easter, because it is the chief City Festival, and found a contemptible Gratification in putting a Stop to the Amusements usual at this Season, and depriving a public Charity of the customary Collections, which they knew must be reduced to nothing by the Absence of the Lord Mayor.

Nothing remained but to keep up a Terror and Alarm through the Kingdom by appointing Committees of Inquiry. This double Star Chamber was moved for long after Midnight, and Lists partially sent round by the Messengers of the Treasury.—Where will these arbitrary, iniquitous Proceedings end? The Ministry, I doubt not, have a Plan prepared, but it is such a one, as they neither dare openly avow, nor uniformly adhere to. One Day they appoint Committees of Inquisition to sit *de Die in diem;*—the next Thing we hear is that the Committees are adjourned, and the Members of them dispersed into the Country. After advising the King, very unnecessarily, to go to Parliament, they come to him, while his Equipage is in waiting, contradict their own Advice, and endeavour to stagger his Resolution at the Moment when he has most Occasion for it. They alone are answerable for all the Indignities heaped upon the King's person, since they could not but forsee, that the People would take the earliest Opportunity of resenting the Imprisonment of their Magistrates.

When the Princess of Wales was named in the House of Commons, where was that Zeal, which some People boast of, for their Royal Master? The Mother of their Sovereign was branded by Name, as the Authoress of all our Calamities, and the Assertion passed without Censure or Contradiction.

Sir, I most truly lament the Condition, to which we are reduced, and the more so, because there is but one Remedy for it, and that Remedy has been repeatedly refused.—A Dissolution of the Parliament would restore Tranquillity to the People, and to the King the Affections of his Subjects: The present House of Commons have nothing to expect but Contempt, Detestation, and Resistance. This violent State of Things cannot long continue. Either the Laws and Constitution must be preserved by a dreadful Appeal to the Sword; or (what probably is intended by the present System of Measures) the people will grow weary of their Condition, and surrender every Thing into the King's Hands, rather than submit to be trampled upon any longer by Five Hundred of their Equals.

PHILO JUNIUS 1 May 1771
22 May 1771
25 May 1771

These letters are printed in full on pp. 238–43.

DOMITIAN 28 June 1771

Domitian was challenged in the *Public Advertiser* of 19 June to fulfil the promise made in his letter of 24 December 1770 to revive the Hine affair 'with an accumulation of evidence' should Grafton become First Lord of the Admiralty. In June 1771 Grafton rejoined the government as Lord Privy Seal. This is Domitian's somewhat ineffective retort.

SIR,

In answer to the Card repeatedly addressed to *Domitian*, he desires it may be observed that although he has not altered his Sentiments with regard to the Duke of Grafton, the Case has not happened, in which he thinks himself bound either by the Letter or the Spirit of his Promise, to the Public. The Duke *is not* First Lord of the Admiralty, nor is he actually in any Post in which Patents can immediately be sold by himself, or by Tommy Bradshaw, or by Miss Polly Bradshaw, who, like the moon, lives upon the Light of her Brother's Countenance, and robs him of no small Part of his Lustre.—The Fact was notorious. The Sale of that Patent to Mr. Hine (the only Man of Merit whom the Duke of Grafton ever provided for), so far from being denied, was publicly defended. Yet the House of Commons, who pretend to be the Grand Inquest of the Nation, suffered this infamous Breach of Trust to pass by without Censure or Examination. For the present, therefore, it would answer no good Purpose for *Domitian* to produce his Evidence. But perhaps the Day of Inquiry is not far off. In the meantime, to show the Duke that *Domitian* does not speak at random, he begs Leave to remind his Grace that there are three such Persons in the World as *Ross*, the Agent;—*Taylor*, the House-builder;—and *Taylor's little boy.—Verbum sat.*

Domitian, upon the whole, thinks he may venture to leave the Duke of Grafton, or, if there be one more odious, more base, and more contemptible Person of Rank in the Kingdom, that he may safely leave them both to the Care of *Junius.*

PHILO JUNIUS 26 August 1771
15 October 1771
17 October 1771
18 October 1771

These letters are printed in full on pp. 279–81, 299–308.

A FRIEND OF *JUNIUS* 22 October 1771

This letter, answering one by A Barrister at Law on 19 October (printed Wade, i. 432–5), was included in the collected edition of 1772 as letter no. LXIII. Philo Junius having appeared three times in quick succession, Junius presumably thought that the time had come to ring the changes.

VETERAN 28 January 1772

In private letter no. 53, Junius wrote to Woodfall: 'Having nothing better to do, I propose to entertain myself & the public, with torturing that bloody wretch Barrington. He has just appointed a french Broker his deputy, for no reason but his relation to Bradshaw. . . . Be careful not to have it known to come from me.' This may reasonably be presumed to be Junius' attack. Its comparatively low score on Ellegård's test may reflect that the style is much more colloquial than in most of Junius' compositions.

Anthony Chamier, of Huguenot descent, was appointed Deputy Secretary-at-War in succession to Christopher D'Oyly. His wife's sister was married to Thomas Bradshaw, M.P. for Saltash, man-of-business to Lord Barrington and a close associate of the Duke of Grafton. Chamier later represented Tamworth in the House of Commons. Jonathan's Coffee House, Exchange Alley, Cornhill had been a haunt of stockbrokers since the 1690s.

MY LORD,

It is unlucky for the Army, that you should be so thoroughly convinced as you are, how extremely low you stand in their Opinion. The Consciousness that you are despised and detested by every Individual in it, from the Drummer (whose Discipline might be of Service to you) to the General Officer, makes you desperate about your Conduct and Character. You think that you are arrived at a State of Security, and that, being plunged to the very Heels in Infamy, the Dipping has made you invulnerable. There is no other Way to account for your late frantic Resolution of appointing *Tony Shammy* your Deputy-Secretary at War. Yet I am far from meaning to impeach his Character as a Broker. In that Line he was qualified to get forward by his Industry, Birth, Education, and Accomplishments. I make no Sort of Doubt of his cutting a mighty pretty figure at *Jonathan's*. To this Hour, among Bulls and Bears, his Name is mentioned with Respect. Every Israelite in the Alley is in Raptures. *What, our old Friend, little Shammy!—Ay, he was always a tight, active little Fellow, and would wrangle for an Eighth as if he had been born in Jerusalem. Who'd ha' thought it! Well, we may now look out for the rebuilding of the Temple.* My Lord, if I remember right, you are partial to the Spawn of Jonathan's. Witness the Care you took to provide for Mr. Delafontaine in the Military Department. He limped a little when he left the Alley, but your Lordship soon set him upon his Legs again. This last Resolution, however, approaches to Madness. Your Cream-coloured *Mercury* has over-reached both you and himself; and remember what I seriously tell you, this Measure will, sooner or later, be the Cause, not of your Disgrace (that Affair's settled), but of your Ruin. What Dæmon possessed you to place a little gambling Broker at the Head of the War Office, and in a Post of so much rank and confidence as that of Deputy to the Secretary at War? (I speak of your Office, not of your Person.) Do you think that his having been useful, in certain Practices to *Lord Sandwich* gives any great Relief to his Character, or raises him in point of Rank? My Lord, the rest of the World laugh at your Choice; but we soldiers feel it as an Indignity to the whole Army, and be assured we shall resent it accordingly. Not that I think you pay much Regard to the Sensations of any Thing under the Degree of a General Officer, and even that Rank you have publicly stigmatised in the most opprobrious Terms. Yet still some of them, though in your wise Opinion not qualified to command, are entitled to Respect. Let us suppose a Case, which every Man, acquainted with the War Office, will admit to be very probable. Suppose a Lieutenant General, who perhaps may be a Peer, or a Member of the House of Commons, does you the Honour to wait upon you, for Instructions relative to his Regiment. After explaining yourself to him with your usual Accuracy and Decision, you naturally refer him to your Deputy for the Detail of the Business. *My dear General, I'm prodigiously hurried. But do me the Favour to go to Mr. Shammy; go to little Waddlewell; go to my Duckling; go to little Three per cents reduced; you'll find him a mere Scrip of a secretary; an* OMNIUM *of all that's genteel; the Activity of a Broker; the Politeness of a Hair-dresser; the— the— the— &c.*

Our General Officer, we may presume, being curious to see this wonderful *Girgashite*, the following Dialogue passes between them:—

Lieut.-General. Sir, the Secretary at War refers me to you for an Account of what was done—

Waddlewell. Done, Sir! Closed at Three-eighths! Looked flat, I must own; but To-morrow, my dear Sir, I hope to see a more lively Appearance.

Lieut.-General. Sir, I speak of the Non-effective Fund.

Waddlewell. Fund, my dear Sir! In what Fund would you wish to be concerned? Speak freely: you may confide in your humble Servant—I'm all Discretion.

Lieut.-General. Sir, I really don't understand you. Lord Barrington says that my Regiment may possibly be thought of for India—

Waddlewell. India, my dear Sir! strange Fluctuation! From Fourteen and an Half to Twenty-two—never stood a Moment, but ended chearful;—no Mortal can account for it! *Lieut.-General.* Damn your Stocks, Sir! tell me whether the Commission—*Waddlewell.* As for Commission, my dear Sir, I'll venture to say that no Gentleman in the Alley does Business upon easier Terms. I never take less than an Eighth, except from Lord Sandwich and my Brother-in-law; but they deal largely, and you must be sensible, my dear Sir, that when the Commission is extensive, it may be worth a Broker's while to content himself with a Sixteenth.

The General Officer, at last, fatigued with such Extravagance, quits the Room in Disgust, and leaves the intoxicated Broker to settle his Accounts by himself.

After such a Scene as this, do you think that any Man of Rank or Consequence in the Army will ever apply to you or your Deputy again?—Will any Officer of Rank condescend to receive Orders from a little, whiffling Broker, to whom he may formerly perhaps have given Half a Crown for negotiating an Hundred Pound Stock, or Sixpence for a Lottery Ticket? My Lord, without a Jest, it is indecent, it is odious, it is preposterous.—Our gracious Master, it is said, reads the News-papers. If he does, he shall know minutely in what Manner you treat his faithful Army. This is the first of sixteen Letters addressed to your Lordship, which are ready for the Press, and shall appear as fast as it suits the Printer's Convenience.

VETERAN 17 February 1772

Lord Barrington, an Irish peer, held office continuously from 1746 until 1778 and again for a few months in 1782: for eighteen of these years he was Secretary-at-War. He served each administration in turn and in 1761 wrote cheerfully to a friend: 'The same strange fortune which made me Secretary of War five years and a half ago, has made me Chancellor of the Exchequer; it may perhaps at last make me Pope. I think I am equally fit to be head of the church as of the exchequer.' *Pitt. Corr.* ii. 99.

MY LORD,

In my last Letter I only meant to be jocular. An Essay, so replete with good Humour could not possibly give Offence. You are no Enemy to a Jest, or at least you would be thought callous to Reproach. You profess a most stoical Indifference about the Opinion of the World and, above all Things make it your Boast, that you can set the News-papers at Defiance. No Man indeed, has received a greater Share, of Correction in this Way, or profited less by it, than your Lordship. But we know you better. You have one Defect less than you pretend to. You are not insensible of the Scorn and Hatred of the World, tho' you take no Care to avoid it.—When the bloody Barrington, that silken fawning Courtier at St. James's—that stern and insolent Minister at the War Office, is pointed out to universal Contempt and Detestation, you smile indeed, but the last Agonies of the hysteric Passion are painted in your Countenance. Your Cheek betrays what passes within you, and your whole Frame is in Convulsions.—I now mean to be serious with you, but not to waste my Time in proving that you are an Enemy to the Laws and Liberties of this Country. The very Name of Barrington implies everything that is mean, cruel, false and contemptible. The Duke of Newcastle's Livery was the first Habit you put on.—What an indefatigable Courtier at his Levee!—What an assiduous Parasite at his Table!—Was there a dirty Job to be performed—*away went Barrington.*—Was a Message to be carried—*Who waits there?—My Lord Barrington.* After ruining that brave and worthy Man, General Fowke under the Auspices of the Duke of Newcastle, who saved you from Destruction, you deserted to Mr. Pitt the Moment he came into Power. Before the late King's Death, you secured a footing at Carlton House; and were prepared to abandon your last Patron, the Moment Lord Bute assumed the Reins of Government.—From Lord Bute to Mr. Grenville there was an easy Transfer of your Affections. You are the common Friend of all Ministers, but it is not in your Policy to engage in overt Acts of Hostility against those, who may perhaps be next in Turn to patronise Lord Barrington. *My dear Lord*, or, *my dear Sir*, are Titles, with which you have occasionally addressed every Man, who ever had an Office, or the Chance of an Office in this Kingdom. Even the proscribed *John Wilkes*, the Moment he was Sheriff, had a Claim upon your Politeness. Your Character was a little battered by the Frequency of your political Amours, when Lord Rockingham took you into Keeping.—While you existed by *his* Protection, you intrigued with the Duke of Grafton.—Another Change succeeded.—Your Mind was open to new Lights, and, *without a Doubt, Lord Chatham was the only Man in the Kingdom fit to govern a great Empire.* Still however your Opinions of Men and Things were not perfectly settled. When the Duke of Grafton took the Lead, the pliant Barrington of course saw Things in a different Point of View. There is Nothing in your Attachments, that savours of Obstinacy. When his Grace resigned, you soon discovered that to establish Government upon a solid Footing, the Minister's Presence was indispensable in the House of Commons.—Lord North was then the Man after your Lordship's own Heart.—In *your* Ideas, the First Lord of the Treasury, for the Time being, is always perfect:—*But every Change is for the better.*—With all your Professions of Attachment to this temporary Minister, I tell him, and I tell the Public, that at this very Hour, you are caballing with the Duke of Grafton and the Bedfords to obtain the Recall of Lord Townshend, and to drive Lord North from the Treasury.—But they all know you.—In the Inventory of the discarded Minister's Effects, Lord Barrington is always set down as a fixture.

By garbling and new modelling the War Office, you think you have reduced the Army to Subjection. *Walk in, gentlemen! Business done by Chamier and Co.*—To make your Office compleat, you want nothing now, but a Paper-Lanthorn at the Door, and the Scheme of a Lottery pasted upon the Window. With all your Folly and Obstinacy, I am at a Loss to conceive, what Countenance you assumed, when you told your royal Master, that you had taken a little frenchified Broker from Change Alley, to intrust with the Management of all the Affairs of his Army.—Did the following Dialogue leave no Impression upon your disordered Imagination? You know where it passed.

K.—Pray, my Lord, who have you appointed to succeed Mr. D'Oyly?

B. Please your M—, I believe I have made a Choice, that will be highly acceptable to the Public and to the Army.

K. Who is it?

B. Sire, il s'appelle Ragosin. Born and educated in Change Alley, he glories in the Name of Broker; and, to say nothing of Lord Sandwich's Friendship, I can assure your M— he has always kept the best Company at Jonathan's.

K. My Lord, I never interfere in these Matters. But I cannot help telling your Lordship, that you might have consulted my Honour and the Credit of my Army a little better. Your Appointment of so mean a Person, tho' he may be a very honest Man in the Mystery he was bred to, casts a reflection upon ME, *and is an Insult to the Army. At all Events, I desire it may be understood that I have no Concern in this ill judged, indecent Measure, and that I do not approve of it.*

I suppose, my Lord, you thought this Conversation might be sunk upon the Public. It does Honour to his Majesty, and therefore you concealed it.—In my next I propose to shew what a faithful Friend you have been to the Army, particularly to old worn out Officers.

VETERAN 27 February 1772

In a debate on 13 November 1770, Lord Barrington had declared incautiously that there were no general officers at that moment capable of acting as Commander-in-Chief. He was at once attacked in the newspapers by Testis and Testiculus (Wade, ii. 310–12), who may have been Junius, for a gross affront to the army. A version of Barrington's speech is in *Parl. Hist.* xvi. 1043–4 and a private explanation of his remarks is offered in a letter to Lord Albemarle in *Memoirs of the Marquis of Rockingham*, ed. Albemarle, ii. 192–3. Veteran returned to the incident before embarking upon the imaginary conversation in which Chamier appears as Waddlewell.

My Lord,

The Army now, according to your own Account of the Matter, is under a very creditable Sort of Direction. If we may rely upon the Secretary at War's Opinion, solemnly and deliberately expressed before the House of Commons, there is not a single Man in the Profession who is in any Shape qualified for Commander in chief; at least none, whom you would think it safe to recommend to his Majesty. If your Judgment upon this Subject had been better founded than it is, I do not understand that a Secretary at War has any Right to pass so disgraceful and precipitate a Sentence upon so many of his Superiors. Believe me, my good Lord, there is not one of those Officers, whom you dared to stigmatise in that infamous Manner, who is not qualified to be your Master in the Art Military, notwithstanding all the Experience you got in St. George's Fields, when you urged and exhorted the Guards to embrue their Hands in the Blood of their Fellow-Subjects.—While that bloody Scene was acting, where was the gentle Barrington?—Was he sighing at the Feet of antiquated Beauty?—Was he dreaming over the Loo-Table, or was he more innocently employed in combing her Ladyship's Lap-dog? —But, my Lord, when you paid that pretty Compliment to the Body of General Officers, had you no particular Apologies to make to *General Conway*, to *Lord Albemarle*, or to *Sir Jeffery Amherst*? Did *General Harvey* deserve nothing better of you, than a ridiculous Nickname, which, like Lord Mansfield's Secret, he must carry with him to his Grave? In lieu of a Commander-in-chief, you have advised the King, to put the Army into Commission.—*A Graduate in Physic, an old Woman, and a Broker from 'Change Alley.*—The Doctor prescribes,—the old Gentlewoman administers,—and little *Syringe*, the Apothecary, stands by the Glisterpipe. This, you tell the King, is making himself Commander in Chief, and the surest Way to preserve the Affections of the Army.—It may be so, my Lord, but I see no Right you had to give the Nickname of *Doctor Radcliffe* to so brave a Man as General Harvey. Though his natural Sweetness of Temper may induce him to pass it by, it must always be mortifying to a brave Adjutant General, when he marches into St. James's Coffee House, to hear the Ensigns of the Guards whisper to one another—*here comes the Doctor;*—or when he marches out, *there goes the Doctor.*—I dare say, he has furnished Work enough for the Surgeons; but, until you so politely pointed it out, I cannot say I ever saw any thing medical in his Appearance.

After treating the most powerful People in the Army with so much unprovoked Insolence, it is not to be supposed that Field officers, Captains, and Subalterns have any Chance of common Justice at your Hands. But that Matter shall be the Subject of another Letter, and every Letter shall be concluded with a Conversation Piece. The following Dialogue is not imaginary.

SCENE—WAR OFFICE.

Enter Barrington, *meeting* Waddlewell.

B. My dear Friend, you look charmingly this Morning.

W. My dearest Lord—the Sight of your Lordship—!—*Here they embrace, Waddlewell's Thoughts being too big for Utterance.*

B. When did you see my *Pylades*, our dear *Bradshaw?*

W. Ay, my Lord,—there is a Friend indeed—Firmness without Resistance,—Sincerity without Contradiction,—and the milky Way painted in his Countenance. If I could ever reconcile my Mind to the distracting Prospect of losing your Lordship, where else should we look for a Successor! But that Event, I hope, is at a great Distance. *Late, very late, Oh may he rule us!*

B. Ay, my dearest Waddlewell, but we are sadly abused, notwithstanding all our Virtues.

W. Merit, my dear Lord, Merit will for ever excite Enmity.—I found it so in the Alley. I never made a lucky Hit in my Life, that it did not set all Jonathan's in an Uproar. If an *Idea* succeeded, my best Friends turned against me, Judas and Levi, Moses and Issachar—People with whom I have been connected by the tenderest Ties—could not endure the Sight of my Prosperity. The ten Tribes of Israel united to destroy me, and for two Years together were malicious enough to call me *the lucky little Benjamin.* Friendship, among the best of Men, is little better than a Name.

B.—Why, my dear Deputy, it is not that I regard the Contempt and Hatred of all Mankind.—I never knew it otherwise. No Man's Patience has been better exercised. But what if the King should hear of it.—

W.—Ay, there's the Rub!

B.—If the best of Princes, who pretends to be his own Commander in Chief, should hear that the Name of Barrington is opprobrious in the Army;—that even he himself is not spared for supporting me—

W. Weeping—Oh, fatal Day!—Compared with this, what is a *Riscounter*!—Alas, my dearest Lord, you have unmanned your Deputy.—I feel myself already at Ten per Cent. Discount, and never shall be at Par again.

B.—Something must be done.—Let us consider.—

W.—Ay, my dear Lord, for Heaven's Sake let us speculate.

Exeunt, disputing about Precedence.

VETERAN 10 March 1772

Novalis's letter defending Lord Barrington was printed in the *Public Advertiser* on 3 March 1772. He accused Veteran of being author of Expositor on 13 February and of a card signed Several Officers on 22 February. Of Lord

Barrington he made the odd remark: 'I can say he is of longer standing in the War Office than most of his Clerks.'

MY LORD,

I am at a Loss for Words to express my Acknowledgment of the signal Honour you have done me. One of the principal Purposes of these Addresses, was to engage you in a regular public Correspondence. You very justly thought it unnecessary to sign your Name to this last, elegant Performance. *Novalis* answers as well as Barrington. We know you by your Stile. This is not the first of your Epistles, that has been submitted to the Criticism of the Public. While yet, like poor *Waddlewell*, you were young in Office, your letters to General Fowke were considered as the Standard of Perspicuity. You are now *very old* in Office, and continue to write exactly as you did in your Infancy. I do not wonder that the Extremes of your Capacity should meet in the same Point, but I should be glad to know at what Period you reckoned yourself in the Prime and Vigour of your official Understanding.—Was it when you signified to the Third Regiment of Guards his Majesty's Gratitude and your own, for their Alacrity in butchering their innocent Fellow-Subjects in St. George's Fields?—Was it when you informed the House of Commons, that *you* and the *Doctor* were equivalent to a Commander in Chief? Or when you declared that there was not a Man in the Army fit to be trusted with the Command of it? Or when you established that wise and humane Regulation that no Officer, let his Age and Infirmities be ever so great, and his Services ever so distinguished, should be suffered to sell out, unless he had bought all his former Commissions? Or, in short, was it when you dived into *Jonathan's* for a Deputy, and plucked up *Waddlewell* by the Locks? When you answer these Questions, I shall be ready to meet your Lordship upon that Ground, on which you think you stand the firmest. In the mean time, give me Leave to say a few Words to *Novalis*.

You are pleased to observe that my three first Letters are filled with low Scurrility upon hackneyed Topics collected from the Newspapers. Have a little Patience, my dear Lord;—I shall soon come to closer Quarters with you. As for those Dialogues, which you are pleased to say have neither Wit nor Humour in them, I can only observe that there are many Scenes, which pass off tolerably well upon the Stage, and yet will not bear the Examination of the Closet. You and *Waddlewell* are excellent Performers. Between a Courtier and a Broker, *Words* are the smallest part of the Conversation.

Shrugs and Smiles, Bows and Grimaces, the Condescension of St. James's, and the pliant Politeness of 'Change Alley, stand in the Place of Repartee, and fill up the Scene.

You intimate, without daring directly to assert, that *you did not* fix that odious Stigma upon the Body of General Officers. Have you forgot the Time when you attempted the same Evasion in the House of Commons, and forced General Howard to rise and say he was ashamed of you?—These mean, dirty, pitiful Tricks are fitter for Jonathan's than the War Office.

You have more Experience than any of your Clerks, and your GREAT ABILITIES *are acknowledged on all Sides.*—As for your Experience, we all know how much your Conduct has been improved by it. But pray who informed you of this *universal Acknowledgment* of your Abilities? The Sycophants, whose Company you delight in, are likely enough to fill you with these flattering Ideas. But if you were wise enough to consult the good Opinion of the World, you would not be so eager to establish the Credit of your Understanding. The Moment you arrive at the Character of a Man of Sense you are undone. You must then relinquish the only tolerable Excuse that can be made for your Conduct.—It is really unkind of you to distress the few Friends you have left.

To your Lordship's Zeal to discover and patronise *latent* Merit, the Public is indebted for the Services of *Mr. Bradshaw*.—Pray, my Lord, will you be so good as to explain to us, of what Nature were those services, which he first rendered to your Lordship?—Was he winged like a Messenger, or stationary like a Centinel?

— "Like Maia's Son he stood
And shook his Plumes;"—videlicet,

at the Door of Lady ——n's Cabinet.—His Zeal in the Execution of this honourable Office promoted him to another Door, where he also stands Centry,

—"Virgâque levem coercet
Aureá turbam."

That he has ably served the State, may be collected from the public Acknowledgments the Ministry have made him. Fifteen Hundred Pounds a Year, well secured to himself and his Family, will acquit the King of any Ingratitude to *Mr. Bradshaw*. It is by mere Accident that Sir Edward Hawke and Sir Jeffery Amherst are no better provided for.

But we are indebted to your Lordship for another Discovery of Merit equally latent with *Mr. Bradshaw*'s.—You have a Phœnix of a Deputy, tho' yet he is but young in his Nest.—He has hardly had Time to clear his Wings from the Ashes that gave him Birth.—This too, was your Lordship's Apology for ruining General Fowke. You gave it in Evidence, that you had been but four Months in Office; and now you tell us that your Deputy also is in the same unfledged State of Noviciate;—tho' for Abilities and Knowledge of the World, neither *Jew* nor *Gentile* can come up to him! For Shame, my Lord Barrington, send this whiffling Broker back to the Mystery he was bred in. Tho' an Infant in the War Office, the Man is too old to learn a new Trade.—At this very Moment they are calling out for him at the Bar of Jonathan's—Shammy!—Shammy!—Shammy!—The House of *Israel* are waiting to settle their last Account with him.—During his Absence, Things may take a desperate Turn in the Alley, and you never may be able to make up to the Man what he has lost in Half Crowns and Six-pences already.

VETERAN 23 March 1772

Christopher D'Oyly, the Deputy Secretary-at-War, and Philip Francis, the first clerk at the War Office, were on close terms. D'Oyly resigned on 21 December 1771, telling Francis: 'My request was readily and, which is mortifying, without one civil speech granted. I am persuaded whenever you please you may obtain the same permission on as easy terms.' It was his replacement by Anthony Chamier that provoked Veteran's ire and indignation. Francis claimed to have been offered the post by Barrington but to have refused: three months later he resigned from the clerkship. The matter is of critical importance in relation to the case for Francis's authorship of the letters and is discussed further in Appendix eight.

Though the first Veteran letter promised a series of sixteen, this, the fifth, was the last to appear. Two more letters signed Veteran, on 12 and 26 October 1772, seem to be by a new author; they are concerned with the prevalence of clubs and lodges and there is no connection with Lord Barrington.

SIR,

I desire you will inform the Public that the worthy Lord Barrington, not contented with having driven *Mr. D'Oyly* out of the War Office, has at last contrived to expel *Mr. Francis*. His Lordship will never rest 'till he has cleared his Office of every Gentleman, who can either be serviceable to the Public, or whose Honour and Integrity are a Check upon his own dark Proceedings. Men, who do their Duty with

Credit and Ability, are not proper Instruments for Lord Barrington to work with.—He must have a Broker from 'Change-Alley for his Deputy, and some raw, ignorant Boy for his first Clerk. I think the Public have a Right to call upon *Mr. D'Oyly* and *Mr. Francis* to declare their Reasons for quitting the War Office. Men of their unblemished Character do not resign lucrative Employments without some sufficient Reasons. The Conduct of these Gentlemen has always been approved of, and I know that they stand as well in the Esteem of the Army, as any Persons in their Station ever did. What then can be the Cause that the Public and the Army should be deprived of their Service?—There must certainly be something about Lord Barrington, which every honest Man dreads and detests. Or is it that they cannot be brought to connive at his Jobs and underhand Dealings?—They have too much Honour, I suppose, to do some certain Business *by Commission*.—They have not been educated in the Conversation of Jews and Gamblers;—they have had no Experience at *Jonathan's*;—they know nothing of the *Stocks*; and therefore Lord Barrington drives them out of the War Office.—The army indeed is come to a fine Pass, with a gambling Broker at the Head of it!—What signifies Ability, or Integrity, or Practice, or Experience in Business. Lord Barrington feels himself uneasy, while Men with such Qualifications are about him. He wants nothing in his Office but Ignorance, Impudence, Pertness, and Servility. Of these Commodities he has laid in a plentiful Stock, that ought to last him as long as he is Secretary at War. Again I wish that *Mr. Francis* and *Mr. D'Oyly* would give the Public some Account of what is going forward in the War Office. I think these Events so remarkable, that some Notice ought to be taken of them in the House of Commons. When the Public loses the Service of two able and honest Servants, it is but reasonable that the Wretch, who drives such Men out of a public Office, should be compelled to give some Account of himself and his Proceedings.

SCOTUS 4 May 1772

The original of this letter, in Junius' handwriting, is in the Woodfall papers, Add. MS. 27777, f. 16. It scores high on Ellegård's test. It is addressed to Lord Barrington.

My Lord,

I am a Scotchman, and can assure your Lordship, that I do not esteem my Country, or the Natives of it, the less because we are not so happy as to be honoured with *Lord Barrington's* favourable Opinion.—From a Pamphlet, which lately fell in my Way, I perceive that there is something in the Temper of the Scots, that does not suit the manly, sterling Virtue, which distinguishes your own worthy Character. We are too insolent to those beneath us, and too obsequious to our Superiors; and with such a Disposition must never hope to find Favour with *Lord Barrington*! "*And Cockburne*, LIKE MOST OF HIS COUNTRYMEN, *is as abject to those above him, as he is insolent to those below him.*" These are your Words, given under your Hand, as the solemn, deliberate Opinion of his Majesty's Secretary at War. Such a Censure, coming from a Man of Honour, good Sense, or Integrity, might, perhaps, have some Weight with the Thoughtless or Uncandid. But when it comes from a Man, whose whole Life has been employed in acting the Part of a false, cringing, fawning, Time-serving Courtier—from a Man, who never had a different Opinion from the Minister for the Time being, and who has always contrived to keep some lucrative Place or other under twenty different Administrations, I am not so much offended at the Reproach itself, which you have thought proper to throw upon the Scots, as I am shocked at the unparallelled Impudence of applying your own individual Character to a whole Nation.—It seems my Countrymen *are abject to those above them.* Pray, my good Lord, by what system of Conduct have you recommended yourself to every succeeding Minister for these last twenty Years?—Was it by maintaining your Opinion upon all Occasions, with a blunt, firm Integrity, or was it by the basest and vilest Servility to every Creature that had Power to do you either Good or Evil?—*But we are insolent to those below us.* Indeed, my Lord, you paint from your own Heart. There is Courage at least in *our* Composition. It is the Coward, who fawns upon those above him. It is the Coward, that is insolent, wherever he dares be so. You have had some *Lessons*, which have made you more cautious than you used to be. You have Reason to remember that modest, humble Merit will not always bear to be insulted by an Upstart in Office. For the future, my little Lord, be more sparing of your Reflections upon the Scots. We pay no Regard to the Calumny of anonymous Writers, and despise the Malignity of *John Wilkes.* But when a Man, so high in Office, as you are, pretends to give an odious Character of a whole Nation, and sets his Name to it, we should deserve the Reproach, if we did not resent it. You are so detested and despised by all Parties (because all Parties know you), that England, Scotland, and Ireland have but one Wish concerning you, and that is, that, as you have shown yourself a fawning Traitor to every Party and Person, with which you ever were connected, so all Parties may unite in loading you with Infamy and Contempt.

NEMESIS 12 May 1772

In private letter no. 63 Junius wrote: 'Pray let this be announced, *Memoirs of Lord Barrington in our next*. Keep the author a secret.' The notice was duly inserted on 11 May and Nemesis appeared the following day. It scores high on Ellegård's test. For a rather more favourable account of Barrington's career, see the biography by Sir Lewis Namier in *The House of Commons, 1754–90*, ii. 55–9.

SIR,

I am just returned from a Visit in a certain Part of Berkshire, near which I found Lord Barrington had spent his Easter Holidays. His Lordship, I presume, went into the Country to indulge his Grief; for whatever Company he happened to be in, it seems his Discourse turned intirely upon the Hardship and Difficulty of his Situation. The Impression which he would be glad to give of himself is that of an old faithful Servant of the Crown, who on one Side is abused and vilified for his great Zeal in Support of Government, and at the same Time gets no Thanks or Reward from the King or the Administration. He is modest enough to affirm in all Companies, that *his* Services are unrewarded; that *he* bears the Burthen; that other People ingross the Profits; and that *he* gets nothing. Those who know but little of his History may perhaps be inclined to pity him; but he and I have been old Acquaintance, and, considering the size of his Understanding, I believe I shall be able to prove, that no Man in the kingdom ever sold himself and his Services to better Advantage than Lord Barrington. Let us take a short Review of him from his political Birth.

On his Entrance into the House of Commons, he declared himself a Patriot; but he soon found Means to dispose of his Patriotism for a Seat at the Admiralty Board. This worthy Man, before he obtained his Price, was as deeply engaged in Opposition to Government, as any Member of the *Fountain Club*, to which he belonged. He then thought it no Sin to run down *Sir Robert Walpole*, though now he has altered his Tone. To oppose the Measures of Government, however dangerous to the Constitution, or to attack the Persons of Ministers, however justly odious to the Nation, is now *rank Faction*, in the Opinion of the pliant Lord Barrington. His Allegiance follows the Descent of Power, nor has he ever been known to dispute the Validity of the Minister's Title, as long as he continued in Possession.

His Lordship remained at the Admiralty, until long Servility and a studious Attachment to the Duke of Newcastle had engaged his Grace to recommend him for Secretary at War. When the Duke resigned in the year 1756, he of course expected that Lord Barrington would have followed him. But his Lordship's Gratitude to his Patron was not quite heavy enough to weigh against Two Thousand Five Hundred a Year. He knew the Value of his Place and kept it by making the same Professions to Mr. Pitt and Lord Temple by which he had deceived the Duke of Newcastle. Before the late King's Death, he had taken early Measures to secure an Interest at Carlton House; and when his present Majesty could no longer bear him as Secretary at War, he found Means to ingratiate himself so far with Lord Bute, that for some time he was suffered to be Chancellor of the Exchequer; and when that Post appeared to be not tenable, he still had Art and Contrivance enough to secure himself in the lucrative Office of Treasurer of the Navy. In 1762, he was the most humble Servant of Mr. Fox. In 1763 and 1764, he was no Enemy to Mr. Grenville. In 1765, he gave himself back, body and soul, to the late Duke of Cumberland and Lord Rockingham. This last Manœuvre restored him to the War Office, where he has continued ever since, with equal Fidelity to Mr. Pitt, the Duke of Grafton, and Lord North; and now he modestly tells the World *that he gets nothing* by his Services.

Besides the singular good Fortune of never being himself a Moment out of Place, he has had extraordinary Success in providing for every Branch of his Family. One Brother was a General Officer, with a Regiment and Chief Command at Guadaloupe. A second is high in the Navy, with a Regiment of Marines. A third is a Judge, and the fourth is a Bishop. Yet this is the Man who complains *that he gets nothing*. At the same Time his parliamentary Interest is so inconsiderable that, ever since his canting Hypocrisy and pretended Attachment to the Dissenters was discovered at Berwick, he has been obliged to the Influence of Government for a Seat in the House of Commons, which he holds without its costing him a Shilling.

Having given you a short Account of the Emoluments he has received from Government, I should be very glad to see as faithful an Account of his Services. Some of them are probably of a secret Nature, of which we can form no Judgment. His ostensible Services, in the public Opinion at least, have been considerably overpaid. At his very Outset, the blundering Orders he sent to Gibraltar might have occasioned the Loss of that important Place. When the Fate of Gibraltar was at Stake, we had a Secretary at War who could neither write plain English nor Common-sense. But he compensated for his own Blunder by ruining the worthy General Fowke, whom he and a certain Countess (taking a base Advantage of the unhappy Man's Distress) prevailed upon to write a Letter, the Recollection of which soon after broke his Heart. In the House of Commons, I think, the noble Lord was never reckoned an able Debater. *Poor B—ch*, for many years was his Nickname. His Time-serving Duplicity is now so well known, that he seldom speaks without being laughed at. Sometimes his Folly exceeds all Bounds; as, for Instance, when he traduced the whole Body of general Officers, which, I presume, they will not readily forget. In the War Office he has made it his Study to oppress all the lower Part of the Army by a Multitude of foolish Regulations, by which he hoped to gain the Reputation of great Discipline and Œconomy, but which have only served to make him as odious to the Military, as he is to every other Rank of People in the Kingdom.—With respect to the Public in general, I presume there never was a Man so generally or so deservedly detested as himself. The People of this Country will never forget nor forgive the inhuman Part he took in the Affair of St. George's Fields. Other Secretaries at War have ordered out Troops to assist the Civil Magistrate. For this Man it was reserved, to give it under his Hand, that he rejoiced and exulted in the Blood of his Fellow-Subjects. This Stroke alone would be sufficient to determine his Character. Yet so far from having done the King any Service by his officious Zeal upon this Occasion, I am convinced that no one Circumstance has so much contributed to throw an Odium upon the present Reign. I will not suppose it possible, that the best of Princes could be pleased with the Treason, but I am sure he has Reason enough to hate the Traitor.

Such are the Services which, in his Lordship's Opinion, can never be sufficiently rewarded. He complains that he gets nothing, although upon a moderate Computation, he has *not* received less of the public Money than Fifty-three Thousand Pounds, viz.

Ten Years Lord of the Admiralty	£8,000
Eighteen Years either Secretary at War, Chancellor of the Exchequer, or Treasurer of the Navy, at 2500 per Annum	45,000
	£53,000

It is not possible to ascertain what further Advantages he may have made by Preference in Subscriptions, Lottery Tickets, and the Management of large Sums lying in his Hands as Treasurer of the Navy. *Mr. Chamier*, if he thought proper, might give us some tolerable account of the Matter. When a Secretary at War chooses a Broker for his Deputy, it is not difficult to guess what Kind of Transactions must formerly have passed between them. I don't mean to question the Honour of *Mr. Chamier*. He always had the Reputation of as active a little Fellow as any in Jonathan's. But putting all Things together, I think we may affirm that, when Lord Barrington complains of getting nothing from Government, he must have conceived a most extravagant Idea of his own Importance, or that the inward Torture he suffers, from knowing how thoroughly he is hated and despised, is such as no pecuniary Emoluments can repay.

SECTION B

In this section I have briefly considered those letters attributed to Junius by some other editors but which do not seem to be conclusively supported by the evidence. Those with the highest degree of probability are Testis and Testiculus of November 1770 which dealt with subjects in which Junius was particularly interested;[1] among the least probable is A Faithful Monitor of 25 August 1767 which contains one sentence that would have caused Junius stylistic agony—'I find you and your brother printers have got greatly into a sort of knack of stuffing your papers with flummery upon two certain brothers who are labour-in-vain endeavouring to force themselves out of the world's contempt.' I have indicated where the text of the letters may be found.

2 January 1767	Lusitanicus	24 June 1767	Anti-Sejanus, jr.
13 January 1767	Lusitanicus	25 August 1767	A Faithful Monitor
24 January 1767	Lusitanicus	16 September 1767	Correggio
28 April 1767	Poplicola	12 October 1767	Moderator
28 May 1767	Poplicola	22 October 1767	Grand Council

[1] They are severe attacks upon Lord Barrington. Testis is too brief to provide an adequate sample for Ellegård's method, though it does not score high; Testiculus was attributed by Mason Good to Junius on the strength of a covering note. But one cannot be certain that the note referred to that letter.

31 October 1767	Anonymous
5 December 1767	Y.Z.
19 December 1767	Anonymous
22 December 1767	Downright
16 February 1768	Anonymous
24 February 1768	Mnemon
4 March 1768	Mnemon
24 March 1768	Anti-Stuart
5 April 1768	C.
5 April 1768	Q in the Corner
12 April 1768	C.
23 April 1768	Anonymous
23 April 1768	Bifrons
6 May 1768	C.
12 May 1768	Valerius
19 May 1768	Fiat Justitia
1 July 1768	Pomona
19 July 1768	C.
23 July 1768	C.
30 July 1768	Anonymous
5 August 1768	L.L.
6 August 1768	Anonymous
10 August 1768	Lucius
19 August 1768	Atticus
23 August 1768	Valerius
29 August 1768	Lucius
1 September 1768	Lucius
6 September 1768	N.L.
7 September 1768	Lucius
9 September 1768	Lucius
10 September 1768	Lucius
15 September 1768	Lucius
20 September 1768	Lucius
6 October 1768	Atticus
12 October 1768	Temporum Felicitas
15 October 1768	Brutus
19 October 1768	Atticus
26 October 1768	Why?
27 October 1768	Brutus
12 November 1768	Brutus
14 November 1768	Atticus
15 December 1768	Anonymous
20 April 1769	Crito
27 April 1769	Crito
6 June 1769	Simplex
10 June 1769	Amicus Curiae
16 August 1769	Q in the Corner
8 September 1769	Augur
10 November 1769	A.B.
17 November 1769	X.X.
20 November 1769	X.X.
25 November 1769	X.X.
2 December 1769	X.X.
26 June 1770	Q in the Corner
27 June 1770	A Labourer in the same cause
30 June 1770	Q in the Corner
7 July 1770	Q in the Corner
7 July 1770	A Labourer in the same cause
19 November 1770	Testis
24 November 1770	Testiculus
13 December 1770	Chapter of Facts
14 December 1770	Second Chapter of Facts
9 January 1771	Intelligence Extraordinary
11 January 1771	Anti-W
13 February 1771	A Member of one House
16 February 1771	A.B.
12 March 1771	Cumbriensis
25 March 1771	An Englishman
29 March 1771	G.W.
8 April 1771	G.W.
15 April 1771	Henricus
21 May 1771	Henricus
4 June 1771	Q in the Corner
5 July 1771	An Innocent Reader
16 October 1771	Anti-Fox
5 November 1771	A.B.
8 November 1771	Intelligence Extraordinary
13 November 1771	Cumbriensis
19 November 1771	Anti-Belial
4 December 1771	Juniper
10 January 1772	News item
6 February 1772	Anti-Belial
8 May 1772	Arthur Tell-Truth

LUSITANICUS
2 January 1767
13 January 1767
24 January 1767

This series of letters on Portuguese trade was almost certainly by Philip Francis, who had acted as secretary to the embassy in Portugal in 1760 and was an authority on Portuguese affairs. They are discussed in some detail in A. Ellegård, *Who was Junius?*, 127–31. Whether they may also be claimed for Junius depends upon the strength of the Francis case: they score moderately well on Ellegård's linguistic test. They have not been reprinted.

POPLICOLA 28 April 1767
28 May 1767

Two letters attacking Lord Chatham for a career of intrigue and hypocrisy and threatening him with the gibbet. If they are by Junius it seems rather unlikely that the same man could have been responsible for the letter to Chatham seven months later expressing 'the veneration which I have always entertained for your character'. Poplicola scores high on Ellegård's test and there is perhaps an echo of the argument about the prohibition of corn in the second letter in Philo Junius of 15 October 1771. Printed Wade, ii. 108–17.

ANTI-SEJANUS, JR. 24 June 1767

There is no very obvious reason why this letter should have been reprinted in Mason Good's edition nor why it was attributed to Junius. Anti-Sejanus was a frequent contributor to the *Public Advertiser* in 1766 and 1767 and has been identified as James Scott, a follower of Lord Sandwich. *Pitt. Corr.* iv. 66. This was a routine attack upon Lord Bute, who was accused of leading Chatham into 'base apostacy'. Ellegård's linguistic test does, however, produce a high score. Wade, ii. 118–20.

A FAITHFUL MONITOR 25 August 1767

It seems improbable that this, an attack upon Lord Townshend and his brother Charles, was by Junius. There is no signal to provide any connection, it does not read like Junius, and it scores very low on Ellegård's test. Wade, ii. 120–1.

CORREGGIO 16 September 1767

A strong attack upon the ministers, referring to Chatham as 'a lunatic brandishing a crutch'. Mason Good presumed that the following note in the *Public Advertiser* of 16 September referred to this letter and therefore identified it as by Junius: 'Our correspondent C. will observe that we have obeyed his directions in every particular, and we shall always pay the utmost attention to whatever comes from so masterly a pen.' This note probably did refer to Correggio, which had many italicized passages, requiring careful attention. But the connection with Junius is merely that he signed his letters C. when corresponding with Woodfall. Dilke pointed out that it would be natural enough for Correggio to use the letter C. and that there were other replies to C. which Mason Good did not connect with Junius. The score on Ellegård's test is rather low and does not lend much support to the suggestion that Correggio was Junius. Mason Good suppressed the two final paragraphs, which are coarse rather than indecent; Wade resorted to asterisks. The offending words are 'posteriors' and 'backsides'. Wade, ii. 121–4.

MODERATOR 12 October 1767

The style of this piece, which is heavily jocular, does not seem particularly Junian and it scores very low on Ellegård's test. There is no other evidence. Wade, ii. 125–8.

GRAND COUNCIL UPON THE AFFAIRS OF IRELAND 22 October 1767

Mason Good connected this with the printer's note on 21 October that 'our friend and correspondent C. will always find the utmost attention paid to his favours', and inferred that it was by Junius. It is a burlesque account of a ministerial consultation. Ellegård's test yields a low score, yet it is claimed by the anonymous writer to Grenville on 20 October 1768 (private letter no. 88) as one of his productions, along with Atticus which returns a high score. The low score on the Grand Council may be a reflection of the colloquial style of writing. Wade, ii. 128–34.

ANONYMOUS 31 October 1767

Defending the Grand Council from a counter-attack on 27 October. Perhaps one may detect a Junian touch in the threat to produce more evidence. Ellegård included it with the Grand Council for test purposes. Wade, ii. 135–7.

Y.Z. 5 December 1767

This is merely the covering note to a report of a speech in Parliament by Edmund Burke. Mason Good presumed that a note in the *Public Advertiser* of 1 December referred to this letter: the printer asked his 'valuable correspondent C.' to agree to some modifications being made. It seems quite possible that Woodfall, anxious not to run foul of the House of Commons over privilege, suggested the formula whereby the speech was said to have been made 'in a kind of political club'. The letter does not score particularly high on Ellegård's test but not low enough to rule it out. Wade, ii. 137–44.

ANONYMOUS 19 December 1767

A defence of George Grenville, complaining that a feeble ministry is encouraging resistance in America. Mason Good linked it with a note of 18 December: 'C's favour is come to hand.' Ellegård tested it with the anonymous letter of 30 July 1768 on the same subject and found a high positive score. Wade, ii. 145–8.

DOWNRIGHT 22 December 1767

A very brief attack upon an 'idol', Lord Chatham. Mason Good identified it with Junius by means of a note in the *Public Advertiser* of 21 December: 'C's favour is come to hand.' It is too short to permit a satisfactory linguistic test, but Ellegård's evidence suggests that it is not by Junius. The closeness of this letter chronologically with the private letter to Chatham, a mere ten days later, raises considerable difficulty in attributing them both to Junius. Another letter by Downright on 26 October 1767 was not claimed by Mason Good. Wade, ii. 148.

ANONYMOUS 16 February 1768

A letter, hostile to Chatham, on the privy seal being held in commission. There is no direct connection with Junius though it scores very high on Ellegård's test. Wade, ii. 149–52.

MNEMON 24 February 1768
4 March 1768

Two attacks on the ministry, mainly over the affair of the Portland estates. They score very low on Ellegård's test and there is no other evidence to connect them with Junius. Ross Hoffman, *The Marquis* (1973), 213, n. 20, suggests that Burke may have been the author. Mnemon was a rather popular name with newspaper writers and there appear to have been several at work. A prolific Mnemon early in 1769 wrote against Wilkes and in favour of law and order; another in the spring of 1771 wrote a series of letters defending the freedom of the press. A third Mnemon wrote on 24 March 1770 attacking Lord Chatham. Wade, ii. 153–60.

ANTI-STUART 24 March 1768

Mnemon of 4 March was attacked by Anti Van Teague, who was in turn attacked in this letter by Anti-Stuart. It disparages the Duke of Grafton. Anti-Stuart scores low on Ellegård's test. It is very possibly by the author of Mnemon, but there is no strong reason to attribute it to Junius. Wade, ii. 161–3.

C. 5 April 1768

The link with Junius was made by Mason Good on the strength of Junius signing himself C. in his letters to Woodfall. The letter is a strong attack upon the ministers for allowing 'Mr. Wilkes and his banditti' to defy the law with impunity. At its face value it is a right-wing criticism and fits rather uneasily into Junius' general political attitude. Ellegård tested it with C. of 12 April 1768: they returned a lowish score but could be within the Junian range. Wade, ii. 163–7.

Q IN THE CORNER 5 April 1768

This letter, printed the same day as C., makes substantially the same point. One may perhaps presume that most authors would have been content with one letter on the subject and that these are therefore from different hands. Q in the Corner was tested by Ellegård with three subsequent letters under that name and scored rather low. Wade, ii. 167–8.

C. 12 April 1768

A detailed investigation of the question of the Portland estates. It seems a little flat to be the work of Junius. See comment on C. of 5 April, above. Wade, ii. 168–71.

ANONYMOUS 23 April 1768

A severe attack, in Junian style, on the private life of the Duke of Grafton. It adds, for good measure, a sneer at Thomas Bradshaw, for whom Junius appears to have had a special distaste. It scores extremely high on Ellegård's test and may be regarded as very probably by Junius. The author remarked that 'even Lord B—e prefers the simplicity of seduction to the poignant pleasures of a rape'. Wade associated this with Lord Bute, who was blameless: it was a reference to Lord Baltimore, who was acquitted on 26 March on a charge of rape. Wade, ii. 171–3.

BIFRONS 23 April 1768

A dull attack upon the Duke of Grafton. Bifrons has attracted much attention since the author declared that he had been witness to the burning of Jesuit books in Paris, presumably in 1761: commentators have used this evidence in attempts to identify Junius. There is, however, little reason to believe that Bifrons was Junius. Ellegård's test suggested strongly that he was not. Surprisingly Ellegård chose to disregard his own statistical evidence and accepted, with hesitation, the letter as Junian. His argumentation is not, however, up to its usual high standard, because it is obviously dangerous to base the identification on the assumption that Philip Francis was Junius. Wade, ii. 173–7.

C. 6 May 1768

Pursues the theme of C. of 5 April that the ministers are feebly providing for Wilkes's triumphs. The tone is that of a staunch supporter of the dignity of the crown. Ellegård tested it together with letters by C. on 19 July and 23 July: it scored well within the Junian range. Wade, ii. 177–8.

VALERIUS 12 May 1768

Another long letter on the question of the Portland estates. There is nothing to connect it with Junius and it scores low on Ellegård's linguistic test. Wade, ii. 178–82.

FIAT JUSTITIA 19 May 1768

Attacking Lord Barrington, the Secretary-at-War, over the riots in St. George's Fields on 10 May. It is rather a short letter for Ellegård's test but yields positive results. Wade, ii. 182–4.

POMONA 1 July 1768

A satirical attack upon Grafton with side sallies at Bradshaw. The only evidence is Ellegård's test, which does not yield a very high score. But the interest in Bradshaw and Nancy Parsons may reveal Junius. Wade, ii. 184–5.

C. 19 July 1768
23 July 1768

Two attacks upon the government over the commission of trade. The first produced a reply from Insomnis on 21 July. The author of the private letter to Grenville signed C. on 3 September 1768 claimed, among other letters, 'one or two upon the new Commission of Trade'. We may presume that these were the letters referred to. They are competent but unremarkable performances. Ellegård tested them with C. of 6 May (which also commented upon an item in the *Gazette*): the score, though not high, was well within the Junian range. Wade, ii. 186–91.

ANONYMOUS 30 July 1768

A long letter on American affairs, defending George Grenville and calling for a firm policy. The author linked it with a previous letter 'not many months since', which may be presumed to be that of 19 December 1767. Ellegård tested them together and found that they scored high. It is probably one of the letters in which the author of the private letter to Grenville signed C. claimed that 'the defence of your character and measures have been thought not ill maintained'. Wade, ii. 191–5.

L.L. 5 August 1768

Deals with the dismissal of Sir Jeffery Amherst from his governorship of Virginia. There is no direct evidence to connect it with Junius but it scores very high indeed on Ellegård's linguistic test. Thomas Whately referred to it in *Grenville papers*, iv. 337–8. Wade, ii. 195–7.

ANONYMOUS 6 August 1768

The Anonymous letter of 30 July produced replies from Moderator and Tandem on 3 and 4 August. This is the retort to them. It is treated separately by Ellegård and scores moderately. Thomas Whately's comments are in *Grenville papers*, iv. 337–8. Wade, ii. 197–200.

LUCIUS 10 August 1768

A short letter exchanging blows with Virginius of 6 August, who had defended the government's actions over Amherst. It is the first of a series of letters under this name. A long account of the controversy over Amherst is given in *Grenville papers*, iv. 347–54. The Lucius letters were claimed by C. when he wrote privately to Grenville on 3 September 1768. Lucius was a favourite pseudonym and it is difficult to disentangle all the writers who employed it. An anti-government Lucius was active in the summer of 1770, but on 13 September the printer noted that he was *not* the Lucius of two years before. A Lucius of 4 February 1771 wrote on the state of the Navy, and another in the summer of 1772 was interested mainly in East Indian matters. Ellegård found the Lucius letters of 1768 well within the Junian range. Wade, ii. 201–2.

ATTICUS 19 August 1768

Predicting commercial disaster and attacking the ministers. This letter was claimed by the anonymous correspondent of Grenville on 20 October 1768, together with the Grand Council and others. Ellegård assumed that the handwriting of the anonymous letter was unquestionably that of Junius and therefore ascribed Atticus to him as well. It scores high on the linguistic test. It is, however, not one of Junius' favourite subjects and is not particularly vituperative. The Atticus letters attracted some attention and are referred to in *Grenville papers*, iv. 391. There were many other writers in this period using the same name. The printer remarked of an Atticus of 15 March 1769 on the Middlesex election that it was not by the previous writer. There are at least another twelve Atticus letters in 1772, most of them attacking Lord Bute. Wade, ii. 202–6.

VALERIUS 23 August 1768

Comments on the Amherst affair. It scores low on Ellegård's test. Wade, ii. 206–9.

LUCIUS 29 August 1768

Continues the Amherst issue and attacks Lord Hillsborough. It is remarkable for its description of Chatham as a 'miserable, decrepid, worn-out old man'. Wade, ii. 210–13.

LUCIUS 1 September 1768

Lucius' third letter on the Amherst affair, replying to one by Cleophas on 30 August. Wade, ii. 216–20.

N.L. 6 September 1768

This letter, a reply to Cleophas, junior of 5 September, was printed by Mason Good under the erroneous impression that it was signed L.L. and was therefore by the author of the letter of 5 August. Though it is too brief to permit a conclusive test, it scores very low on Ellegård's analysis and there is no particular reason to attribute it to Junius. Wade, ii. 220–1.

LUCIUS 7 September 1768

A reply to Cleophas, junior of 5 September. The fact that this and the previous letter are both replies to the same writer makes it improbable that N.L. was by Junius. He was not likely to send in two letters and Lucius' was the more effective retort. Wade, ii. 221–2.

LUCIUS 9 September 1768

A fifth letter replying to Cleophas of 7 September. Wade, ii. 225–8.

LUCIUS 10 September 1768

Replying to Scrutator of 8 September. Wade, ii. 229–32.

LUCIUS 15 September 1768

The controversy over Sir Jeffery Amherst ground on, with contributions from Misopseudologos, Independent Country Gentleman, Chrononhotonthologos, Corrector, and others. This letter from Lucius attempted to broaden out the discussion into some consideration of American policy. Wade, ii. 233–5.

LUCIUS 20 September 1768

The last letter by Lucius in this series. A strong attack upon Lord Hillsborough. Wade, ii. 236–8.

ATTICUS 6 October 1768

A second letter prophesying doom unless a great and able minister can be found to replace the present weak and distracted administration. Wade, ii. 238–41.

TEMPORUM FELICITAS 12 October 1768

Returning to the theme of Amherst and supporting Lucius. On Ellegård's test Temporum Felicitas scores low, though it is too brief to be at all conclusive. Wade, ii. 241–2.

BRUTUS 15 October 1768

Replying to A Friend to Public Credit of 11 October 1768, Brutus deplores the feebleness of British policy and declares that the Bourbon powers are waiting only for Britain to become embroiled in American troubles before attacking. There are of course many other letters signed Brutus and it is difficult to disentangle the different authors. Junius, by inference, disclaimed the Brutus of 21 February 1771 in his private letter no. 34. The Brutus letters of 15 and 27 October 1768 score high on Ellegård's test. Wade, ii. 242–3.

ATTICUS 19 October 1768

A very long letter replying to A Friend to Public Credit of 11 October 1768 and attacking the ministers in turn. Unless there is evidence in the Grenville MSS. to the contrary, I think that it is more probable that this was the letter Charles Lloyd referred to on 20 October 1768 (*Grenville papers*, iv. 383) than the one identified by W. J. Smith. Wade, ii. 243–50.

WHY? 26 October 1768

Asking why Lord Rochford was appointed Secretary of State for the *Northern* Department when his expertise was in Southern Europe and hinting at some secret understanding with the French. It was intended, apparently, as a follow-up to Atticus of 19 October, which is mentioned. It scores low on the linguistic test. Wade, ii. 250–1.

BRUTUS 27 October 1768

Replies to Truth and Justice of 25 October and commends Atticus. Wade, ii. 252–3.

BRUTUS 12 November 1768

This letter was overlooked by Mason Good and is not included in his edition. It forecasts disaster from the dissensions of the state and attacks Amherst in passing as encouraging faction.

ATTICUS 14 November 1768

A concluding letter cataloguing the misdeeds of the ministry and the inadequacy of the ministers. Wade, ii. 254–7.

ANONYMOUS 15 December 1768

A sustained panegyric on George Grenville, probably by the author of the previous anonymous letters on his behalf. Ellegård tested this letter separately and found that it scored very high. Wade, ii. 259–61.

CRITO 20 April 1769
27 April 1769

Mason Good insisted that these letters, supporting the attack upon Edward Weston, were '*obviously from the pen of Junius*'. For the reputation of Junius, one hopes not. The first ends: 'Let Junius be the dirty rascal you call him, I know, you know, and all the world knows, *what* You *are*.' I do not find this a very sophisticated exchange of insults. Junius took up the attack under his own name on 21 April and is not likely to have wasted so many shots. Ellegård does not discuss them. Wade, i. 144–5.

SIMPLEX 6 June 1769

An attack upon Sir William Blackstone over the pardon to MacQuirk. It is rather a brief specimen for test purposes but Ellegård scores it extremely high. Wade, ii. 267–8.

AMICUS CURIAE 10 June 1769

Supporting Junius' letters on Grafton and replying to Anti-Malagrida. It does not score very high on Ellegård's test. Another Amicus Curiae on 13 December 1770 dealt with the dispute with Spain. Wade, ii. 269–71.

Q IN THE CORNER 16 August 1769

Mason Good reprinted four letters under this name, ranging from 5 April 1768 to 4 June 1771. But he seems to have missed this letter and Ellegård did not test it. The other four score rather low but Ellegård inclined to accept them.

AUGUR 8 September 1769

An unsubtle letter complaining of the activities of the ministerial writers Poetikastos, Silurus, and Pericles and threatening Grafton with the block. It has, in my judgement, little of the urbanity of Junius. Dilke pointed out that, since Junius in private letter no. 8 on p. 354 referred to the answer to Junia as 'the last letter you printed', by inference Augur on the 8th cannot be his composition. But it is a delicate argument depending upon more precision in the dating of private letter no. 8 than one can guarantee. Augur does not score high on the linguistic test and Ellegård was inclined to reject it. Wade, ii. 276–7.

A.B. 10 November 1769

Junius was accused by Messala on 17 November of being the author of A.B., but asked the printer in private letter no. 13 of 16 November to deny it. Wade, ii. 277–80.

X.X. 17 November 1769
20 November 1769
25 November 1769
2 December 1769

The first of these letters was no more than a covering note to a letter from George Onslow to Wilkes, dated 21 November 1763. Its publication was intended to embarrass Onslow by revealing the terms of close friendship on which he had been with Wilkes. The other three take issue with Modestus and Y.Y. over the case of General Gansell, first raised by Junius on 17 October. Modestus accused X.X. of being Junius in disguise and, in my view, the letters read like the work of Junius. Ellegård tested them together: they score very high. I do not understand why Ellegård wrote that they scored 'rather low', since the positive/negative ratio places them well above certain Juniuses, such as Scotus, Nemesis, Domitian, and Moderatus. Wade, ii. 281–4; 287–8; 292.

Q IN THE CORNER 26 June 1770

A detailed accusation against Thomas Bradshaw alleging a corrupt transaction. The tone is similar to that of Junius' letter of 29 November 1769 about the Hine affair. *Notes & Queries*, 3rd series, xi. 100 prints Treasury minutes on the subject. The Q series score rather low on the linguistic test and they could be imitations of Junius' style. Wade, ii. 299–301.

A LABOURER IN THE SAME CAUSE 27 June 1770

Taking up A Fellow Labourer in the public cause of 26 June and advising Wilkes not to abandon Middlesex and stand for the city of London. There is nothing to connect it directly with Junius. Though it scores high on Ellegård's test, he is inclined to exclude it on the ground of negative expressions. Wade, ii. 301–4.

Q IN THE CORNER 30 June 1770
7 July 1770

Combating Grey Cooper's statement on Bradshaw's behalf. A later Q in the Corner of 4 June 1771, deploring the dissoluteness and extravagance of the younger generation, seems to be by a different author. Wade, ii. 305–6.

A LABOURER IN THE SAME CAUSE 7 July 1770

Replying on the Wilkes question to Another Labourer in the same cause of 28 June and A Fellow Labourer in the public cause of 5 July. Wade, ii. 307–9.

TESTIS 19 November 1770

An attack upon Lord Barrington for a remark in the House of Commons that he would find difficulty in suggesting a suitable Commander-in-Chief. The matter is discussed in section A under Veteran of 27 February 1772 on p. 501. The subject and style seem to indicate Junius but there is no direct evidence and the score on the linguistic test is low: Ellegård is inclined to reject it. Wade, ii. 310.

TESTICULUS 24 November 1770

Insinuating that Lord Barrington was acting under royal orders in disparaging the army. Testiculus scores more positively on the linguistic test than Testis, yet they are presumably by the same author. Mason Good assumed that it was the enclosure referred to in private letter no. 25, but there is little to go on. Wade, ii. 311–12.

CHAPTER OF FACTS, OR MATERIALS FOR HISTORY 13 December 1770
SECOND CHAPTER OF FACTS, OR MATERIALS FOR HISTORY 14 December 1770

Miscellaneous squibs at the expense of the ministers. For the authenticity of the first letter, Wade referred the reader to the second: of the second he wrote merely that it was unquestionably from Junius. The repetition adds nothing to the argument. Ellegård tested them together: they score very low. Wade, ii. 316–20.

INTELLIGENCE EXTRAORDINARY 9 January 1771

Noting the ministerial changes and attacking Thomas Whately, once man-of-business to George Grenville. It is too brief for the linguistic test to be particularly helpful: nevertheless it scores high. Wade, ii. 328–9.

ANTI-W 11 January 1771

Defends Junius from an attack by W on 9 January over Mansfield's handling of the Grosvenor case. It scores moderately on Ellegård's test. Wade, ii. 329–31.

A MEMBER OF ONE HOUSE OF PARLIAMENT 13 February 1771

This letter, the full signature of which is A member of one House of Parliament in mourning for the honour of his King and Country, accuses the ministers of a craven surrender to Spain in the dispute over the Falkland Islands. It is in the middle range on Ellegård's test but he is inclined to exclude it on grounds of negative expressions. Wade, ii. 337–44.

A.B. 16 February 1771

Concerned with the election of Lord Gower as a Knight of the Garter. Mason Good reprinted another A.B. for 5 November 1771. But, in fact, A.B.s are ten a penny. Junius disavowed one for 10 November 1769 and the printer disavowed another, on his behalf, for 12 October 1772. A rather dreary A.B. wrote through the spring and summer of 1769 on Indian affairs and the danger to the constitution; another A.B. (possibly the same man, judging by the banality of his observations) wrote repeatedly in 1772 on a variety of trivial subjects. Ellegård does not appear to have tested the A.B. letters. Wade, ii. 345–6.

CUMBRIENSIS 12 March 1771

An attack upon the ministry over the Portland estates. This letter is not included by Mason Good. But a strong case can be offered for a second Cumbriensis of 13 November 1771 and therefore this letter should be considered.

AN ENGLISHMAN, AND ENEMY TO THE CABINET THEREFORE 25 March 1771

The title of this letter, which declares the constitution to be in danger, does not convey Junian briskness. Yet the positive/negative ratio is the most conclusive for any letter Ellegård tested. Perhaps the letter is too short for the sampling to be reliable. Ellegård sets aside the strict statistical evidence and is of the opinion that An Englishman is probably not by Junius. Wade, ii, 348–51.

G.W. 29 March 1771
8 April 1771

Two very long and closely argued letters dealing with the legal implications of the clash between the House of Commons and the city of London over the printers. A third letter, promised in the second, does not appear to have been published—at least not under those initials. Junius had a taste for legal disputation, but these letters score low on Ellegård's test and his advice is to reject them. Wade, ii. 351–61.

HENRICUS 15 April 1771
21 May 1771

Two long letters attacking Lord Suffolk. The author remarks, possibly truthfully, that these are the first productions he has ventured to give to the public. They read to me like a deliberate imitation of Junius' style with little of his vivacity. Dilke pointed out that the publication of the first letter had been delayed a month by the printer losing it, which is unlikely to have happened, at this time, to a genuine Junius letter. The Henricus letters score rather low on the linguistic test. Wade, ii. 368–81.

Q IN THE CORNER 4 June 1771

This letter is not printed by Mason Good. It is a tedious lamentation on the dissipation of modern youth.

AN INNOCENT READER 5 July 1771

A short squib at the expense of the King and the Princess Dowager. It is really too brief to support the linguistic test though it scores very high indeed. The subject was, of course, one which fascinated Junius. Wade, ii. 383.

ANTI-FOX 16 October 1771

Defending Junius against the attacks of An Old Correspondent of 14 October. Anti-Fox remarks: 'I know nothing of Junius but I see plainly that he has designedly spared Lord Holland and his family.' Since Junius does seem to have had some respect for Holland (who would otherwise have made a splendid target) it seems strange that he should deliberately have called attention to it. Wade commented that 'it was doubtless intended . . . to divert any suspicion that the author . . . was in any way connected with his Lordship's family': it seems an odd way of setting about it. Anti-Fox is very short; it scores low on the linguistic test and Ellegård suggests that it should be rejected. Wade, ii. 384.

A.B. 5 November 1771

Junius accused Lord Mansfield on 2 November of having broken the law of the land by admitting bail to John Eyre. He was attacked by One of the three who bailed Mr. Eyre and by Anti-Junius. A.B.'s reply was to assert a Scottish conspiracy: 'If the devil himself . . . were taken up for felony, I do not doubt that all Scotland, to a *mon*, would readily be his security.' Ellegård did not test the A.B. letters. Wade, ii. 385–7.

INTELLIGENCE EXTRAORDINARY, THOUGH TRUE 8 November 1771

A short paragraph communicating the news of the Duke of Cumberland's marriage to Mrs. Horton. The dragging-in of Grafton and Bradshaw may suggest Junius at work. Junius wrote to Wilkes on 6 November in private letter no. 82 on p. 435: 'Since my note of this Morning, I know for certain that the Duke of Cumberland is married to Luttrell's sister.' Wade, ii. 387–8.

CUMBRIENSIS 13 November 1771

Henry, Duke of Cumberland, brother of the King, married in October 1771 Mrs. Horton, sister of Colonel Luttrell, who had replaced Wilkes as the member for Middlesex. Cumbriensis congratulated the Duke ironically on finding so suitable a spouse. In private letter no. 44 Junius wrote to Woodfall: 'Cumbriensis has taken greatly.' This falls short of proof but, together with Junius' known interest in the subject, is a strong presumption of authorship. It should be noted, however, that Cumbriensis does not score at all high on Ellegård's test. The words, coyly omitted by Wade in his edition were 'with her father' and 'consummate with your spouse'. Wade, ii. 387–9.

ANTI-BELIAL 19 November 1771

Anti-Belial is a short appeal to other writers to let Junius deal with Mansfield in his own way. Junius had already committed himself in the most deliberate fashion to 'make good his charge' against Mansfield and may have been impatient at seeing his thunder stolen by bit-players. This letter is too brief to be tested satisfactorily: though it scores low, it is presumably from Junius. Wade, ii. 389–90.

JUNIPER 4 December 1771

Anti-Junius on 30 November complained that Junius had become stale and repetitive. Juniper came to Junius' defence. Wade declared that Juniper and Anti-Belial were 'doubtless from the varied and prolific pen of Junius'. Juniper, though short, scores very high on the linguistic test: Ellegård's advice, however, is to disregard it. My own guess is that it is by Junius though there is no hard evidence. Wade, ii. 390–1.

NEWS ITEM 10 January 1772

A detailed account of the resignation of Christopher D'Oyly from his post as Deputy Secretary-at-War. The reference to Bradshaw as 'the cream-coloured cherub' suggests Junius. It may conveniently be found in the *Quarterly Review*, xc. 98.

ANTI-BELIAL 6 February 1772

This was the second letter under that pseudonym. Junius' long-awaited indictment of Lord Mansfield had appeared on 21 January and had unquestionably misfired. Among others, Justinius of 5 February attacked his reasoning. Anti-Belial replied on Junius' behalf. In surmising Junius' motives, Anti-Belial seems to come very close to admitting that he is Junius. Wade, ii. 395–6.

ARTHUR TELL-TRUTH 8 May 1772

An unremarkable attack upon Thomas Bradshaw, who had recently been appointed to the Board of Admiralty. Though Bradshaw was one of Junius' favourite targets, there is little zest in this letter and it scores exceptionally low on Ellegård's test. Wade, ii. 407–8.

APPENDIX SIX

COMPARISON OF THE 1772 COLLECTED EDITION WITH THE LETTERS AS FIRST PRINTED IN THE *PUBLIC ADVERTISER*

It would not have been easy for Junius to have made substantial alterations when preparing his letters for the collected edition without his political opponents accusing him of distorting evidence: since he had been heavily sardonic at the expense of Jeremiah Dyson for editing a quotation to his own advantage, Junius was in no position to be other than scrupulous.[1] There are, in fact, few changes and most of them are of a routine nature. In the collected version he abandoned the somewhat excessive capitalization and punctuation which Woodfall employed in his newspaper. Names which had been expressed merely with capitals were spelt out in full: hence D. of G—— was changed to Duke of Grafton, and so on. Obvious misprints were corrected: in letter no. LIX 'single instances of unpopular opinions' is altered to 'signal instances'.

Junius also took the opportunity to give further polish to his already shining prose. In letter no. XIII the original version of the third remark about Grafton ran: 'The idea of his death is only prophetic; and what is prophecy but a narrative preceding the fact, which may be History To-morrow.' Junius decided that the last five words were laborious and deleted them, to advantage. In letter no. LIX he came to the conclusion that 'gentle' was too insipid an adjective for Lord Suffolk and changed it to 'pompous'. Not every alteration was an improvement. In letter no. XXIX he originally made fun of Rigby's brashness, observing that he was 'certainly the Reverse of *Modestus*'; the change to 'certainly not *Modestus*' weakens the remark and makes it easier for the reader to miss the point.[2]

The way in which Junius prepared his collected edition may be worked out from the evidence surviving in the Woodfall papers. The Dedication and Preface were, of course, new and were drafted in October 1771: the originals, in Junius' handwriting, are in Add. MS. 27775. Woodfall prepared a specimen version of the book, which Junius returned to him with corrections, alterations, and footnotes: this is Add. MS. 27776. The print used was much smaller than in the final version: in private letter no. 43 Junius favoured a specimen with 'widest lines'. Junius then pointed out to Woodfall where the Philo Junius letters should be placed and corrected them from newspaper cuttings: these are in Add. MS. 27785.[3] Junius insisted that the printer should

[1] Public letters nos. XX, XXII, XLVI, and LIV.

[2] Other instances are commented on in the text: see public letters nos. XXXVI and LIX, pp. 175, 292.

[3] The short Reply to Monody of 12 April 1769 was inserted by Woodfall as letter no. X, but Junius wrote back, 'Omit this'.

proof-read the letters of Draper and Horne himself and Woodfall's working copy is Add. MS. 27788.

The most substantial additions to the original text, apart from the Dedication and Preface, were the footnotes, some of which were lengthy. One note, not finally printed, shows Junius at his least agreeable. In the newspaper version of his letter of 30 January 1771 he had written of the Princess Dowager: 'It would indeed be happy for this Country, if the Lady I speak of were obliged to prepare herself for a different Situation.' See note on p. 220. By the late autumn of 1771 newspapers were full of reports that the Princess was dying of cancer of the throat. Junius then proposed to substitute the following note: 'The Lady herself is now preparing for a different Situation. Nothing keeps her alive, but the horrible Suction of Toads:—Such an instance of divine Justice would convert an Atheist.'[1] Both the original passage and the proposed note were omitted from the final edition—whether because the Princess had died in the meantime or because Woodfall was more squeamish than Junius, it is impossible to say.

[1] Add. MS. 27776, f. 139. See n. 2 to private letter no. 47.

APPENDIX SEVEN

LIST OF SIGNALS

In the considerable correspondence between Junius and Henry Sampson Woodfall, lasting more than four years and involving the exchange of proofs, documents, and letters forwarded from other persons, the difficulty lay in Woodfall contacting Junius. It was obviously undesirable that letters and packages should be left longer than necessary at coffee-houses, where they might be opened or tampered with. The problem was overcome by the use of a system of signals, placed by the printer in the Answers to Correspondents section of his newspaper. It was a method which he also made use of to establish contact with other writers and, even if detected by government agents, conveyed little to outsiders. Three pick-up points we can be sure were used were the New Exchange Coffee House, the Somerset Coffee House, and Munday's Coffee House in Maiden Lane. Among the names employed by Junius were William Middleton and John Fretley. From private letter no. 5 it appears that Junius first collected the letters himself, but in private letter no. 52 he refers to a go-between.

The signals are of importance in helping to date the correspondence between Junius and Woodfall. They may also be used, though with great caution, to explore the authorship controversy. The advocates for certain candidates have attempted to relate their movements to those of Junius as inferred from his private letters, but the dating of those letters is so conjectural that the attempt is fraught with danger. The signals are, in some ways, a better guide, provided that it is remembered that it does not follow that letters advertised were also collected. The signals must also be interpreted in conjunction with the published letters. There is, for example, a gap in the signals for more than six months between March and October 1770, but it should not be inferred that Junius was absent during that period: he printed letters under his own name in March, April, May, and August, probably a Moderatus in March, and possibly letters in the summer from Q in the Corner and A Labourer in the same cause.

Remarks in parentheses are messages in the private letters from Junius about the signals. In November 1771 Junius and Woodfall adopted a system based upon Latin tags and quotations. These are reproduced exactly as they appeared in the *Public Advertiser*, though they were sometimes inaccurate or garbled versions. Mr. S. J. Tester of the Department of Classics in the University of Bristol has traced the sources of these quotations and suggested translations. I am much indebted to him for his assistance.

1769

18 July	Reasons why the Hint was not printed are sent to the last-mentioned Coffee-house in the Strand, from whence our *old* Correspondent will be pleased to send for them.
20 July	Mr. *William Middleton*'s Letter is sent as desired. (21 July: Whenever you have any thing to communicate to me, let the hint be thus *C at the usual place* and so direct to Mr. John Fretley at the same Coffee house where it is absolutely impossible I should be known. Letter no. 5.)
29 July	C. *in the usual Place.*
16 September	C. in the usual Place.
19 October	C. in the usual Place.
2 November	C. *in the usual Place.*
11 November	*C.* in the usual Place. (12 November: Instead of C in the usual place—say only *a Letter*, when you have occasion to write to me again.—I shall understand you. Letter no. 12.)
16 November	A LETTER.
24 November	A LETTER.
2 December	A LETTER.
12 December	A LETTER.
23 December	A LETTER.
27 December	A LETTER.

1770

20 February	A LETTER.
5 March	A LETTER.
25 October	The Printer really did not AFFECT a Silence on a CERTAIN OCCASION, with a View of encouraging his Readers or

Correspondents in an idle Opinion: The Motives for his Conduct were, the Fear of being thought impertinent by declaring (without Direction) what he knew; and the Probability of rendering himself liable to incur the Displeasure of either of those who were pleased to favour him with their Correspondence.

16 November	A LETTER.	
8 December	THIS DAY.	
1771		
1 January	THIS DAY.	
20 February	A LETTER.	
12 August	A Correspondent may rest assured that his directions ever have been and ever will be strictly attended to.	
13 September	C.	
17 September	C.	
21 September	C.	
27 September	C.	
17 October	C. in the *usual* Place.	
19 October	C.	
5 November	C.	
8 November	C.	
	(8 November: When you send to me, instead of the usual signal, say, *Vindex shall be considered.* and keep the Alteration a Secret to every body. Letter no. 42.)	
12 November	VINDEX shall be considered.	
	(?15 November: Don't always use the same signal.—any absurd Latin verse will answer the purpose. Letter no. 44.)	
21 November	*Dic quibus in terris, et eris mihi magnus* APOLLO.	Tell me where in the world and you will be my great Apollo. Virg. *Ecl.* iii. 104.
26 November	*Quid rides? de* TE *fabula narratur.*	What are you smiling for? The tale is told of you. Hor. *Sat.* I. i. 69/70.
	(27 November: Say *Received.* Letter no. 45.)	
28 November	*Received.*	

30 November	*dicere* VERUM *Quid vetat?*	What forbids (us) telling the truth? Hor. *Sat.* I. i. 24/5.
5 December	*Jam* NOVA *progenies caelo demittitur alto.*	Now a new-born child is sent down from high heaven. Virg. *Ecl.* iv. 7.
6 December	*Received. Quis te,* MAGNE CATO *Tacitum?*	Who would leave you, great Cato, unspoken with? Virg. *Aen.* vi. 841.
17 December	*Infandum,* REGINA, *jubes renovare dolorem*	You bid me, Queen, to revive a grief not to be told. Virg. *Aen.* ii. 3.
1772		
	(6 January: Consider of it and, if it be possible, say *Yes* in your paper tomorrow. Letter no. 49.)	
7 January	YES—CERTAINLY.	
8 January	RECEIVED.	
13 January	ILLE *ego, qui quondam gracili modulatus avena*	I am he who once played to the modest pipe. Virg. *Aen.* i. 1ª (a disputed text now usually omitted).
15 January	RECEIVED.	
17 January	*Consurgunt venti; atque in nubem cogitur aer*	The winds rise and the air is piled thick into a cloud. Virg. *Aen.* v. 20.
18 January	MUTARE *necessarium est*	Presumably Woodfall's own remark—'it is necessary to change'.
20 January	Though the Printer knows the *usual Method* of CONVEYANCING is shut up, owing probably to the Intenseness of the Frost, yet another can surely be opened—*Sat verbum* SAPIENTI.	A commonplace tag—'a word is enough for the wise'.
27 January	*Tentanda Via est certe;*—sed *quo modo?*	Woodfall's adaptation of Virg. *Georg.* iii. 8: 'The way must be attempted, surely, but how?'

28 January	*Cultrixque foci secura patella est.*	(You have) a snug dish for fireside service—i.e. you're well off. Persius, *Sat.* iii. 26.
20 February	*Quousque tandem* ABUTERE, *patientia nostra?*	How long will you abuse our patience? Cic. *Oratio in Catilinam*, i. 1.
28 February	MUNERA, LAETITIAMQUE DEI	The gifts and joy of the god. Virg. *Aen.* i. 636. An obscure text.
2 March	PERGE, SEQUAR.	Go on, I'll follow. Virg. *Aen.* iv. 114.
4 March	RECEIVED; and shall be *strickly* attended to. (5 March: If the vellum books are not yet bound, I would wait for the Index. If they are, let me know by a line in the P.A. Letter no. 60.)	
6 March	They are not in hand, therefore *Directions* shall be punctually complied with.	
21 March	*Per* VARIOS *casus, per* TOT *discrimina rerum.*	(We have come to Latium) through so many misfortunes and so many dangers. Virg. *Aen.* i. 204.
4 April	*Non* OMNES *arbusta juvant, humilieque myricae.*	The hazel copse and lowly tamarisk do not always please. Virg. *Ecl.* iv. 2.
2 May	PARS, PRO TOTO (4 May: If pars pro toto be meant for me, I must beg the favour of you to recall it. At present it would be difficult for me to receive it.—When the books are ready a Latin verse will be sufficient. Letter no. 62.)	The part for the whole.
5 May	*Received*—SAT VERB. SAP.	

21 December	HIC murus aheneus *esto*!—*mens conscia recti.*	Let this be a brazen wall! Hor. *Ep.* I. i. 60. A mind sure of its rightness. Virg. *Aen.* i. 604.
23 December	SIC *transit Gloria* MUNDY.	Commonplace tag. Since the previous collecting-point was Munday's Coffee house, it looks as though a pun was intended.
1773		
2 January	ITERUMQUE, ITERUMQUE MONEBO.	Again and again I'll warn (you). Virg. *Aen.* iii. 436.
8 January	SAT VERBUM SAPIENTI.	
19 January	ITERUMQUE, ITERUMQUE MONEBO (19 January: I have seen the signals thrown out for your old friend and Correspondent. Be assured that I have had good reason for not complying with them. Letter no. 64.)	See 2 January above.
8 March	The letter from AN OLD FRIEND AND CORRESPONDENT, dated Jan. 19, came safe to Hand, and his Directions are *strictly followed.* Quod, si quis existimat, aut, etc.	Refers to private letter no. 64. Junius had used the Latin quotation at the end of private letter no. 60. But if anyone thinks that (I) have changed my intention, or that my strength is failing, or my spirit broken, he is much in error. Cic. *Oratio Post Reditum ad Quirites.* 19.
20 March	AUT VOLUNTATE, ESSE MUTATA.	Reminiscence from the Cicero quotation on 8 March.
29 March	AUT DEBILITATA VIRTUTE.	Continued.
7 April	DIC QUIBIS IN TERRIS—	See 21 November 1771.

APPENDIX EIGHT

A NOTE ON AUTHORSHIP

'But who is this Devil Junius,' wrote Dr. Philip Francis to his son on 11 February 1769; 'is it not B——k's pen dipp'd in the Gall of Sa——lle's heart?'[1] Though at that time Junius had written no more than two letters,[2] his formidable retort to Sir William Draper had already attracted public attention. With the attacks upon Grafton, Bedford, and the King in the course of 1769, speculation about the identity of the author became intense.

Dr. Francis's guess, among the first put forward, may be quickly dismissed. Edmund Burke, as one of the ablest literary men on the side of opposition, was suspected by many. Oxoniensis, writing in the *Public Advertiser* of 6 November 1771, declared his conviction that the letters were produced by 'Edmund the Jesuit of St. Omer's'.[3] The Piccadilly edition of Junius' letters, published in 1771, impudently printed 'Anecdotes of the Author' as an introduction, positively identifying him as the man who had written *Origin of our ideas of the sublime and beautiful* and *Considerations on the causes of the present discontents*. These allegations certainly caused Burke uneasiness and he wrote repeatedly to his friends to deny them. But few people today would take them seriously. Though literary comparisons are notoriously treacherous, no one who has read Burke and Junius is likely to believe that they were the same man: where Burke is lofty, broad and general, Junius is mundane and specific; where Burke is reflective and philosophical, Junius is analytical, pointed, and sardonic. In addition, Burke's denial was categorical, and, in my view, decisive: to Charles Townshend he wrote, 'I now give you my word and honour that I am not the author of Junius.'[4]

[1] Parkes and Merivale, i. 228–9. Francis senior was at Bath and in contact with Draper. His suggestion was Edmund Burke, assisted by Sir George Savile, the member for Yorkshire.

[2] Setting aside the letter of 21 November 1768, which was not particularly noticed by the public and which Junius excluded from his collected edition.

[3] For other newspaper references, see A. Ellegård, *Who was Junius?*, 25–6. Later attempts to construct a case for Burke were made by John Roche, *An inquiry concerning the author of the letters of Junius* (1813) and P. Kelly, *Junius proved to be Burke* (1826).

[4] *Burke Corr.* ii. 288–9. There are further denials on pp. 249–86. There is also the remarkable tribute made by Burke to Junius in his speech of 27 November 1770.

In the early years of the nineteenth century, as the Junius controversy became a kind of cottage industry, the list of candidates lengthened until it was fifty or more, many of them supported by substantial pamphlets or books.[1] *Junius discovered* was followed in quick succession by *Junius identified*, *Junius elucidated*, *Junius revealed*, and *Junius unveiled*.[2] He was also repeatedly 'unmasked'—first in

[1] The total depends upon how seriously some candidatures are entertained. I have not felt under the obligation of investigating minutely the suggestion that Richard Suett, the comedian, was the real author, though his name is put forward in an odd publication of 1819 entitled *Junius with his vizor up* by Oedipus Oronoko. Nor have I examined the claims of George III, despite John Roche's solemn report in *An inquiry* (1813), 6–7, that 'he was considered in his own family as the author of the Letters'. Everett, Junius' previous editor, provided a list of candidates on pp. 382–7, characteristically counting William Henry Cavendish Bentinck and the Duke of Portland as rival contenders. I append a list of persons who have been suggested, though the evidence in support of such candidates as Charles Wolfran Cornwall, George Dempster, Sir George Jackson, and John Smith is trifling.

1 James Adair
2 Miles Allen
3 Claudius Amyand
4 Isaac Barré
5 Hugh Macaulay Boyd
6 Edmund Burke
7 William Burke
8 Dr. John Butler
9 Lord Camden
10 Sir Henry Cavendish
11 Lord Chatham
12 Lord Chesterfield
13 Lt.-Col. Robert Clerk
14 Charles Wolfran Cornwall
15 Jean Louis de Lolme
16 George Dempster
17 John Dunning
18 Samuel Dyer
19 Thady Fitzpatrick
20 Henry Flood
21 Philip Francis, sr.
22 Philip Francis, jr.
23 Edward Gibbon
24 Richard Glover
25 Henry Grattan
26 William Greatrakes
27 George Grenville
28 James Grenville
29 William Gerard Hamilton
30 James Hollis
31 Thomas Hollis
32 John Horne
33 Revd. Robert Hort, Canon of Windsor
34 Sir George Jackson
35 Sir William Jones
36 John Kent
37 General Charles Lee
38 Charles Lloyd
39 Lord Lyttelton
40 Catherine Macaulay
41 Lauchlin Macleane
42 Thomas Mante
43 Edmund Marshal
44 William Mason
45 Thomas Paine
46 Duke of Portland
47 Thomas Pownall
48 Sir Robert Rich
49 John Roberts
50 Philip Rosenhagen
51 Lord George Sackville
52 Lord Shelburne
53 John Smith, fa. of Sir Sydney Smith
54 George Steevens
55 Dr. Gilbert Stuart
56 Lord Temple
57 Horace Walpole
58 Alexander Wedderburn
59 John Wilkes
60 Dr. James Wilmot
61 Daniel Wray

[2] The first *Junius discovered* in 1789 was by Philip Thicknesse on behalf of John Horne; the second in 1821 was in favour of Lord Chesterfield; the third in 1854, by

1819 as Edward Gibbon the historian, again in 1828 as Lord George Sackville, and once more in 1872 as Tom Paine, author of *The Rights of Man.*[1]

This literary warfare was carried on without quarter and certainly without false modesty: indeed, one of the joys of Junian scholarship is the confidence placed by participants in the most unlikely propositions. *The authorship of Junius ascertained from a concatenation of circumstances amounting to a moral demonstration* was the title of George Chalmers's tract in 1817 in favour of Hugh Macaulay Boyd. J. B. Blakeway was convinced that his attribution of the letters to John Horne established 'an historical fact which will not hereafter be disputed',[2] while James Falconar buttressed a distressingly shaky case on behalf of Daniel Wray with the reproof that anyone who doubted 'would still be doubting though one rose from the dead for his conviction'.[3] Seldom did enthusiasts allow any nice regard for evidence to stand in their way. The author of *Junius unmasked*, proposing Gibbon, pointedly drew attention to the absence of evidence as proof of the lengths the historian had been prepared to go in order to conceal his guilty secret.[4] William Cramp, whose assertions in favour of Lord Chesterfield were disappointingly received, was by no means nonplussed at the reasonable objection that his lordship, when Junius ceased to write, was 79 years of age, almost totally incapacitated, half-blind, deaf, and bedridden: it was, explained Cramp, an elaborate subterfuge.[5]

A solemn examination of the pretensions of all these candidates would be neither sensible nor welcome. Fortunately, many of them

F. Griffin, advanced the claims of Thomas Pownall. *Junius identified* in 1818 was by John Taylor and advocated Philip Francis, junior; *Junius elucidated* by John Britton in 1848 argued in favour of a group, including Shelburne, Barré, and Dunning; *Junius revealed* in 1894 was by H. R. Francis in favour of his grandfather; *Junius unveiled* in 1909 was by James Smith and proposed Gibbon.

[1] The first tract was anonymously published by Effingham Wilson; the second was by J. B. Manning and the third by Joel Moody.

[2] *An attempt to ascertain the author of the letters published under the signature of Junius.*

[3] Connoisseurs of lunatic scholarship who cannot face his *The secret revealed of the authorship of Junius' letters* may find the argument confidently asserted in *Notes & Queries*, 2nd series, ii. 164 and disposed of on p. 212.

[4] p. 44.

[5] Chesterfield died on 24 March 1773. Cramp's book was *Junius and his works compared with the character and writings of the Earl of Chesterfield.* The reference is page v. Chesterfield's health was so bad in his declining years that he turned it to witty advantage: 'Tyrawley and I', he told an inquirer, 'have been dead these two years, but we do not choose to have it known.'

may be disposed of peremptorily. The case for James Wilmot rests upon a hilariously implausible forgery.[1] Next come the candidates who died before Junius' last letter of 19 January 1773 was written: this eliminates George Grenville (who must otherwise be supposed to have written secret advice to himself), Samuel Dyer, John Roberts, and Charles Lloyd.[2] A second group who can be ruled out are persons who are known to have been away from London or abroad while the letters were being produced.[3] This removes Lord Shelburne, the favourite of the previous editor,[4] Lord Lyttelton,[5] William Mason,[6] Charles Lee,[7] Horace Walpole,[8] Edward Gibbon,[9] and Philip Rosen-

[1] Published in 1813 by his niece Olivia Wilmot Serres. Her trump card was a facsimile, allegedly in her uncle's handwriting, on a spare piece of paper: 'I have this day completed my last letter of Ju——s and sent the same to L—d S———ne. J. W. 17 March 1767'. Unfortunately this was two years before any letter by Junius appeared. She later claimed to be the rightful Princess of Cumberland.

[2] George Grenville died 13 November 1770; Dyer 15 September 1772, Roberts 13 July 1772. Charles Lloyd did not die until 22 January 1773, so that it is theoretically possible that Junius' last letter was written on his death-bed, but he is said to have been a long time dying. John Kent is also said by the *Dictionary of anonymous and pseudonymous English literature*, iii. 329, to have died on 22 January 1773 'after a lingering illness'.

[3] More important to this line of argument than the public letters are the private letters to the printer, many of which contain scraps of gossip and news available only to someone residing in London.

[4] Lord Fitzmaurice, *Life of William Earl of Shelburne* (2nd edn., 1912), i. 424 shows that Shelburne left England with Barré on 11 May 1771 and spent the summer in France. Everett argued cheerfully: 'What safer way was there to throw off suspicion than to go abroad, making arrangements for Junius to continue his appearance in the *Public Advertiser*?' But during this time not only were there at least seven public letters, which show no traces of prefabrication, but also private letters nos. 36 and 38, which can only have been written by someone in London.

[5] The case for Thomas, Lord Lyttelton was advanced by D. T. Coulton in *Quarterly Review*, xc. 91–163 and attacked, largely on character grounds, by Dilke in the *Athenaeum*, 17 January 1852. R. Blunt, *Thomas, Lord Lyttelton*, 74–7, makes it clear than he was on the Continent from June 1769 until January 1772.

[6] Mason was discussed by Dilke, partly in jest, in the *Athenaeum* of 17 May 1851. But Mason wrote to Walpole from Yorkshire on 21 September 1771 while the exchange between Junius and Wilkes was being conducted at close quarters.

[7] Lee was advocated by T. Girdlestone, *Reasons for rejecting the presumptive evidence of Mr. Almon that Mr. Hugh Boyd was the writer of Junius*. But the *Dictionary of American biography* shows that Lee was in Poland during the year 1769.

[8] Walpole's *Paris Journals* show him in France from 18 August 1769 until 10 October 1769 and again from 8 July 1771 until 5 September 1771.

[9] Gibbon was at Beriton, Hants, on 12 November 1770, the day his father died. Junius wrote that same evening to Woodfall (private letter no. 24) with information about Mansfield that had only just become known in London and was used in the next day's *Public Advertiser*. There are further difficulties in reconciling Gibbon's known movements with private letters nos. 37, 40, 42, 43, 44, 49, 50, 51, and 52.

hagen.[1] In this group may also be included Sir William Jones, the orientalist, whose claims have been revived as recently as November 1973,[2] but who was in fact travelling on the Continent from the autumn of 1769 to the summer of 1770.[3] During that time Junius wrote at least nine public and twelve private letters.

Another small group of candidates who may be eliminated includes John Wilkes, Lord Chatham, and John Horne. Their claims are worth consideration only if it can be explained satisfactorily why they should have engaged themselves in correspondence.[4]

The number of absurd publications issued in the course of the controversy makes it necessary to insist that a serious candidature must depend, not on one remarkable anecdote or coincidence, but on a careful examination of the candidate's known political opinions, some evidence that he possessed the necessary literary talents, and a demonstration that there is nothing in his life history to render the claim impossible. Sensational revelations abound in Junian mythology. A favourite story is how Junius 'gave himself away' by quoting from a letter not then in print. In view of the precautions Junius is known to have taken to prevent discovery, the story is self-evidently unlikely. In its first form, William Gerard Hamilton betrayed himself to the Duke of Richmond; the revised version has Lord Shelburne and his friends blurting out the truth to Dr. Popham; yet another account has Lauchlin Macleane revealing all: 'Raphael West, son of the painter Benjamin West, once heard Macleane repeat a passage in one of the letters, which was not then published . . . A more correct and veracious man than Mr. R. West could not be.'[5]

[1] A clergyman with political and literary interests, Rosenhagen was forced by debt to spend several years on the Continent after 1770. He seems to have cultivated the impression that he was Junius.

[2] By Francesco Cordasco in *Notes & Queries*, drawing attention to an exchange in the *Gentleman's Magazine* for 1817.

[3] *The letters of Sir William Jones*, ed. G. Cannon, i. 40–58. In a letter of 29 January 1770 Jones wrote that he had been in Nice for three months.

[4] The case for Wilkes must explain why he disparaged himself, then complained to himself, and finally soothed himself with an apology. Junius' letter to Chatham can be explained as an attempt to put people off the scent only had it been published. Philip Thicknesse, the author of *Junius discovered*, did try to overcome the awkward fact of Horne's exchanges with Junius by arguing that Junius' attacks were 'so easily wiped off' that they must have been designed to give Horne a public triumph.

[5] *The letters of Junius*, 1812 edition, i. *118–19; *Walpoliana*, i. 69; J. Britton, *The authorship of the letters of Junius elucidated*, 9; *Notes & Queries*, 1st series, iii. 378. Raphael West may indeed have been veracious, but since he was only three when Junius ceased to write, the evidence is not strong. An elegant variation on the same theme may be found in John Roche, *An inquiry*, 292: 'During the time that the

Another story which originated with William Jackson, the printer, was that he once saw 'a tall gentleman, dressed in a light coat, with bag and sword' throw a Junius letter into the doorway of the *Public Advertiser* office. Why Junius should choose to deliver his letters in this rather theatrical way when he could and did use the penny post is not easy to explain. Nevertheless, the anecdote served to sustain a host of Junius candidates. Richard Duppa pointed out that the description fitted Richard Glover remarkably well;[1] John Jaques observed that 'in person Lord Sackville was full six feet high. He always wore a bag and invariably a sword'.[2] After being used to assist Lord Lyttelton ('he alluded himself to his skinny shape'[3]), and Sir Philip Francis ('answers very well to the portrait preserved of his person'),[4] it made an expected reappearance in J. N. M. MacLean's biography of Lauchlin Macleane, 'who was a very tall man'.[5]

The candidature of Macleane, described as 'the most spectacular of the Irish and Scottish adventurers of his day',[6] deserves more than summary rejection. In 1771 the Marquis of Rockingham thought that he detected some similarity between Junius' letter of 30 January and a letter to Wilkes from Macleane, which appeared in the same copy of the *Public Advertiser*.[7] In recent years Macleane's case has been presented in a book of remarkable ingenuity.[8] The author attempts to deal with one of the more obvious difficulties, viz. that Junius attacked Macleane in a letter of 6 March 1771, by suggesting that it was a slight wound given to 'escape suspicion'. This clearly will not do. Since the letter was published not under the name of Junius but of Vindex, and at that time only the printer knew that Vindex was Junius, it could not serve to mislead anyone. There are further objections. In January 1770, when Dr. Musgrave was examined

letters appeared in the *Public Advertiser* Mr. Burke's son was a scholar at Westminster school; *and it is remembered by some of those, who were at Westminster school at the same time, that his private tutor was sometimes able to tell, before hand, when a Junius was to appear.*'

[1] *An inquiry concerning the author of the letters of Junius*, 29–30.

[2] *The history of Junius and his works*, 345.

[3] *Quarterly Review*, December 1851, 160.

[4] Wade, ii, p. xlii.

[5] *Reward is secondary: the life of a political adventurer and an inquiry into the mystery of 'Junius'*, 395.

[6] L. S. Sutherland, writing in *The House of Commons, 1754–90*, iii. 94.

[7] Rockingham wrote to Burke, 3 February 1771: 'The Junius upon conciliation is a well wrote performance and carries daggers with it. Surely a letter in the same paper by way of challenge to Wilkes is wrote much in the same manner?' *Burke Corr.* ii. 191–2. The challenge to Wilkes is known to have come from Macleane.

[8] J. N. M. MacLean, *Reward is secondary*, 1963.

before the House of Commons, Macleane took a prominent part in the hostile questioning and protested that 'as our story differs materially in point of fact, the House will weigh whether I could have ever had any inducement to frame this tale'.[1] Yet Junius went out of his way to defend Musgrave, who 'with no other support but truth . . . resisted and overcame the whole House of Commons'.[2]

J. N. M. MacLean's general argument was that the letters were the work of a 'Celtic mafia' of disgruntled Jacobites: he draws attention to the 'purely pro-Scottish feeling' of Lauchlin Macleane and the overweening pride in his ancestry felt by his 'co-adjutor', Andrew Stuart.[3] One can only say that, if they wrote the letters, they chose a very odd way of demonstrating their Scottish pride, for Junius can scarcely resist any occasion to sneer at the Scots, whether relevant or not. 'Scottish sincerity', he remarked, 'is such that when they smile, I feel an involuntary emotion to guard myself against mischief.' In his letter to the King, George's supposed fondness for the Scots is said to be ill-judged and foolish, excusable only by his youth and inexperience and he is warned to beware their 'fawning treachery against which no prudence will guard'. In the preface composed for the collected edition Junius included a wholly gratuitous attack upon the Scottish nation—'the characteristic prudence, the selfish nationality, the indefatigable smile, the persevering assiduity'. To counter the surprise one might feel at the suggestion that an active Jacobite cause was still operating in the 1770s, MacLean explains that 'they were far too obsessed to see that it was pointless'. But to discover the truth they had only to consult Junius himself, who dismissed the Jacobite cause as 'desperate' and the name of Stuart as 'only contemptible'.[4]

[1] *Parl. Hist.* xvi. 783. [2] Public letter no. XXXIX. [3] pp. 382–4.

[4] Further criticism of the Macleane case, as put by Francesco Cordasco, may be found in the *Philological Quarterly*, 1950, 284–5.

It is perhaps necessary to warn the reader that Mr. MacLean's handling of evidence is inclined to be cavalier. His account of the Giles letter and the resignation of Francis omits critical pieces of information. His description of the evidence on Coxe the printer is not confirmed by the reference he gives to *HMC 4th report*, appendix 1, 402, which makes it clear that, far from being a 'cryptic entry', it was merely the address to which Dr. Dodd suggested Wilkes should send any news items. Contrary to MacLean's statement, there is no difficulty whatever in discovering the present whereabouts of the document: it is Add. MS. 30875, f. 111.

It is a serious misrepresentation of the evidence of Kemp Knott in *Notes & Queries*, 2nd series, vii. 310 to summarize it as 'Junius . . . had been drowned coming from or going to India. This was, of course, an indirect identification of Lauchlin Macleane.' What Kemp Knott is reported to have said is that Junius had been drowned in the

Among the more interesting of the other contenders is Jean Louis de Lolme, a native of Geneva. The evidence on his behalf, though slight, is intriguing. Junius concluded his preface with a quotation from 'a foreign writer', whose performance he commended as 'deep, solid and ingenious'. This was de Lolme, whose *Constitution de l'Angleterre* had been published in Amsterdam in 1771. When an English translation appeared in 1775 the passage quoted was rendered exactly in Junius' words. Thomas Busby used this evidence to support de Lolme's claims, while W. J. Smith argued that it strengthened the case for Lord Temple.[1] There is, however, no very obvious reason why the translator should not have made use of Junius' rendering, which was well known, and it is hard to understand why de Lolme, if he were Junius, should take the most elaborate precautions to defy detection, only to conclude by drawing attention so pointedly to himself. According to de Lolme's own evidence, he did not come to England until 1769.[2] He could not therefore have composed the Junius letter of 21 November 1768, which has all the appearances of genuineness. Moreover the fact that his work on the English constitution should be published first in French suggests a fairly limited command of the English language. The case for de Lolme also demands that we accept that a foreigner, in his first two years in a strange country, could produce not only the constitutional treatise—a substantial work in its own right—but the sixty-nine public letters of Junius as well.

Another theory, suggesting that the letters were the work of a group, came from John Britton in his *Junius elucidated*, which named Barré, Dunning, and Shelburne as the persons responsible. Some readers will feel that a careful study of the letters, public and private, leaves a powerful impression of one mind at work. Nevertheless, the possibility of a group cannot be ruled out, particularly in the light of Junius' strange private letter no. 8, which refers to 'people about

Aurora, which would identify him as Henry Vansittart. MacLean is far too indulgent to Kift, whose testimony seems to have been taken from *Notes & Queries*, 1st series, iii. 378. According to his own admission, Kift held on to vital evidence for eight years, until the witness had died, explaining that 'the subject escaped my memory'.

[1] *Arguments and facts*, 1816; *Grenville papers*, vol. iii.

[2] In the introduction to the English translation, de Lolme wrote that he was 27 when he came to England: 'after being in it only a year, I began to write my work which I published about nine months afterwards'. In Book Two, chapter xv, he noted that 'a little after I came to England for the first time an action was brought in a court of justice against a prince, very nearly related to the Crown'. This refers to Lord Grosvenor's action against the Duke of Cumberland in July 1770.

me . . . who had rather see Junius in the newspapers ever so improperly than not at all'. This, in itself, is difficult to reconcile with the proud assertion in the *Dedication* that 'I am the sole depositary of my own secret and it shall perish with me'. If Dunning had a hand in the letters, Junius must be convicted of a deliberate falsehood in maintaining in the preface 'I am no lawyer by profession', and in assuring Wilkes privately that he would 'as lief be a Scotchman'.[1] On general grounds it is difficult to accept that several people could have preserved so tightly such an important secret and since all three were well-known politicians it would have been hard for them to have conducted 'the conveyancing part of the operations'.

Britton's case also involves considerable political difficulties. The first is that until January 1770 Dunning was Solicitor-General in that administration which Junius was assailing with such vigour. Secondly, in his dealings with Wilkes, Junius, though not sharing Wilkes's contempt for the Shelburnites, dismissed them as of little consequence. The letter to Chatham of 2 January 1768 would have to be abandoned since in it the author remarked of Shelburne that 'the best of him is, perhaps, that he has not acted with greater insincerity to your Lordship than to former connections'. The letters to Grenville must also be given up since in them C. claimed the authorship of Atticus of 19 October 1768, which referred to Shelburne's 'fawning baseness' and declared that his conduct was 'a satire upon mankind'. Nor, if the triumvirate was responsible for the letters, is it easy to account for the respect Junius habitually showed towards George Grenville, whose American policy had been repeatedly denounced by Shelburne and Barré.[2]

* * *

Out of the mass of starters a front runner ultimately emerged. In 1812 a new edition, published by George Woodfall, son of the printer of the *Public Advertiser*, provided important fresh evidence in the shape of the private letters which had passed between Junius and the printer and which had survived in the possession of the Woodfall family. Though some of the value of the letters was destroyed by the questionable dates fixed to them by the editor, Mason Good, it was

[1] Private letter no. 71. Less easy to explain would be the errors in law of which Junius has been accused—e.g. in his exposition of the law of bail or in his use of the term 'fee simple' in the Dedication. See Lord Campbell, *Lives of the Lord Chancellors*, vi. 344.

[2] *Parl. Hist.* xvi. 38–40, 165–6.

clear that any clue to the authorship was much more likely to be found in these hasty jottings and notes than in the formal letters carefully prepared for publication. In particular, by providing proof that Junius had also contributed public letters as Domitian, Vindex, Veteran, and so on, the 1812 edition substantially extended the area in which clues might be sought. It also provided, for the first time, facsimiles of Junius' handwriting.[1]

The most significant piece of new evidence was the revelation that Junius was the author of the attacks upon Lord Barrington, Secretary-at-War, under the name of Veteran. Junius had shown little interest in Barrington in his main writings: as Veteran he had launched repeated assaults. Of particular interest was a letter of 23 March 1772 which began:

> I desire you will inform the public that the worthy Lord Barrington, not contented with having driven Mr. D'Oyly out of the War Office, has at last contrived to expel Mr. Francis. His Lordship will never rest till he has cleared his office of every gentleman who can either be serviceable to the public or whose honour and integrity are a check upon his own dark proceedings.

In a covering note to the series, Junius wrote to the printer: 'Be careful not to have it known to come from me. Such an insignificant creature is not worth the generous rage of Junius.'[2]

The Veteran letters raised several questions. Why should Junius, who had struck at Grafton and Bedford, Lord North and the King, be so concerned with the affairs of a War Office clerk? Why, if the person attacked was genuinely insignificant, was Junius bothering? Why was he anxious that the letters should not be traced to him?

[1] The question of handwriting is expert and contentious. It is not even agreed whether the hand in which the private letters were written was genuine or feigned. The handwriting has been attributed, with equal assurance, to Lady Temple, John Horne, Charles Lee, Mrs. Dayrolles, William Gerard Hamilton, Charles Lloyd, James Wilmot, Hugh Macaulay Boyd, J. L. de Lolme, William Greatrakes, and many others. The most massive study, conducted by Charles Chabot in 1871 on behalf of Edward Twisleton, resulted in a volume entitled *The handwriting of Junius professionally investigated*. Chabot achieved at least one spectacular conversion: the *Quarterly Review*, cxxx. 349, which had supported the case for Lyttelton and ridiculed that of Francis, recanted at once. A later investigation by C. A. Mitchell in *Discovery*, July 1929, 217–20, though by no means thorough, confirmed Chabot's conclusions. But the subject is not one for lay opinions. A useful summary is in Ellegård, *Who was Junius?*, 76–84, though he is perhaps overcritical of Chabot's methodology.

[2] Private letter no. 53. The 'insignificant creature' was Anthony Chamier, appointed Deputy Secretary-at-War by Lord Barrington.

These queries prompted John Taylor to develop a new theory in *A discovery of the author of the letters of Junius*, issued in 1813. Since the Veteran, Scotus, and Nemesis letters were all concerned with the War Office, might not Junius be found there, or connected with someone who worked there? Taylor ruled out Philip Francis, the senior clerk, under the mistaken impression that he was only nineteen years of age when the letters first appeared. But there was no reason why he could not have passed on information to his father, the Revd. Dr. Francis, an experienced polemicist, and it was the father whom Taylor displayed to the world as the main author. He attempted to buttress the case with stylistic parallels and comparisons.[1]

On discovering the error about Francis's age, Taylor produced a new edition of his work under the title *The identity of Junius with a distinguished living character established* (1816). This argued the case for Philip Francis, junior, as the sole author of the letters. But Taylor's earlier assertion that there was unmistakable evidence of two hands at work was bound to weaken the authority of the revised version.

Sir Philip Francis was 73 when Taylor's first book appeared in 1813. His attitude towards it was curiously ambivalent. When asked by the editor of the *Monthly Magazine* for a comment, he replied: 'Whether you will assist in giving currency to a silly malignant falsehood is a question for your own discretion.'[2] It should be noted that this reproof was in response to Taylor's argument that Francis's father was the chief author. In relation to Francis's own position, it has been very differently interpreted. Opponents of the Francis candidature have remarked that the use of the words silly and malignant in referring to letters of which the author was inordinately proud scarcely suggests parental fondness: supporters have pointed out that the reply was evasive and conditional and that, had Francis wished to put the matter beyond doubt, he could have issued a blunt denial, on his honour, as Burke had done.

One might be inclined to take this retort as a categorical disclaimer were it not that in many other ways Francis encouraged the belief that he was indeed the author. In particular, he bombarded his second wife, whom he married at the age of 74, with hints and suggestions. According to her testimony, the first gift he put into her hands after their wedding was a volume of the letters, and on 1 April 1818, nine

[1] Discussed A. Ellegård, *Who was Junius?*, 39–42.

[2] xxxv. 533.

months before his death, he wrote the following inscription on the flyleaf of a copy of *The identity of Junius established*: 'I give this book, in fee simple, to my most learned lady and future widow. P.F.'[1] Lady Francis was convinced that her husband had been Junius: 'I am certain he would not have allowed me to continue in error . . . had Sir Philip once said to me, "I am not the writer of Junius," I should have given up the belief immediately.'

The case for Francis, as expounded by John Taylor, became the bastion to be stormed by every controversialist who had a rival theory to propose. Charles Wentworth Dilke, while editor of the *Athenaeum* in the 1840s and 1850s, reviewed a number of publications on the subject of Junius and devoted his remarkable powers to the exposure of loose and credulous scholarship. He was particularly scathing about Lady Francis's testimony and hinted strongly that Philip Francis was one of many people who wished to pass as Junius and had planted evidence in his declining years. It was perhaps the memory of Dilke's criticisms that persuaded Herman Merivale, when completing the *Memoirs of Sir Philip Francis*, to concede that Lady Francis was 'one of the most garrulous, credulous, inaccurate, and in every way perplexing of reminiscents'.[2]

Though he refrained from putting forward a candidate himself, Dilke had nothing but contempt for the suggestion that Philip Francis was the author, summarizing his objections in a passage more remarkable for its splendid rhetoric than close argument:[3]

> Was there ever a more improbable conjecture than that this clerk in the War Office was the writer of the Letters of Junius? . . . there remains the astounding assumption that this office-bred boy, this office-fed man, this clerk who had married early . . . should hazard everything . . . that he might indulge his public spirit or private hatred, week after week, month after month, year after year, in a series of outrageous attacks on those above him . . . without a chance in his favour of conciliating thereby any person or party, or winning even empty fame.

[1] Lady Francis's testimony was given in a letter to Edward Dubois and printed by Lord Campbell in his *Lives of the Lord Chancellors*, vi. 344. Of the inscribed volume she merely remarked that it was a posthumous present. In view of the doubts that have been expressed about the value of her evidence, it is worth remarking that the British Library copy of *The identity of Junius established* has a note by Joseph Parkes that he had collated Francis's comments from the copy given to Lady Francis. He adds that he later purchased the gift volume from Lady Francis's grandson, J. G. Francis. The British Library copy has the inscription quoted above but I am not certain whether it is Parkes's copy or the original gift volume.

[2] Vol. i, p. xii, 'Preliminary remarks'.

[3] The *Athenaeum*, 1850, 939, subsequently reprinted in *Papers of a critic*.

Taylor had insisted that Francis's quarrel with Lord Barrington and subsequent resignation explained why, under the name of Veteran, he had launched his attacks and that, in doing so, he had given himself away. Dilke and subsequent critics of the Francis case[1] retorted that there never had been a quarrel and that, since Veteran was clearly misinformed about the circumstances of Francis's resignation, the two could not be identified. This interpretation certainly seemed to be corroborated by Francis's letter of 24 January 1772 to his cousin, Philip Baggs. It referred to the resignation of Francis's close friend, Christopher D'Oyly, Deputy Secretary-at-War, and continued: 'Immediately upon my return, Lord Barrington was so good as to make me the offer, with many obliging and friendly expressions. I had, however, solid reasons for declining.'[2] Furthermore, it was undoubtedly through the good offices of Lord Barrington, the following year, that Francis was appointed to the Supreme Council in India at the princely salary of £10,000 p.a.

Dilke also drew attention to Junius' sarcasms at the expense of Welbore Ellis and John Calcraft—men to whom Francis was greatly indebted. Taylor's use of the miscellaneous letters and the private letters to the printer was challenged by Dilke, who demonstrated, for the first time, how little evidence there was for the attribution to Junius of most of the miscellaneous letters or for the dates Mason Good had affixed to the private correspondence. Indeed, it was extraordinary, concluded Dilke, that thirty-two years after Francis's own death, despite 'his hints and all but confession—and with the zealous good wishes of his widow and family—we could not get hold of a single date or incident . . . to help us to even a plausible conjecture'.[3]

The closely packed volumes on the Junius question preserved in the Codrington Library testify to Dilke's indefatigability. But there is no doubt that his zeal caused him seriously to overreach himself. His criticisms of the standard of Junian editorship were much more penetrating than his attack on the Francis candidature. Indeed, every one of his objections to the case for Francis can not only be met but turned to Dilke's disadvantage.

[1] Notably Gustave Simonson, Charles Everett, and Francesco Cordasco, each of whom leaned heavily on Dilke's work. Simonson's unpublished manuscript, 'A history of the letters of Junius', is in the British Library, 11857 d. 34.

[2] Parkes and Merivale, i. 275.

[3] The *Athenaeum*, 1850, 969. I have postponed any discussion of the reporting of debates by Francis, a matter to which Dilke devoted much attention, until later in this appendix.

In the first place, Dilke's insinuation that *The identity of Junius established* had been composed not by Taylor, but by Edward Dubois, a close friend of Sir Philip Francis, and was therefore totally suspect as an 'inspired' version, was staunchly denied by the author himself. 'It is fortunate', wrote John Taylor mildly, 'that I am still living to vindicate my title to the authorship of my own book, which seems otherwise in danger of being taken from me.' Though the point was not one of great importance, it served as a reminder that Dilke was fallible and his reply was neither generous nor convincing.[1]

Secondly, though the greater part of Lady Francis's testimony was obviously hearsay, not all of it could safely be disregarded. An interesting new piece of evidence appeared in the shape of some polite verses, written to a Miss Giles at Bath in 1771, with a covering note in a hand remarkably similar to that of Junius. In 1852 Lady Francis had sent to H. R. Francis copies of the verses in Sir Philip's own handwriting, explaining that he had given them to her at the time of their marriage as examples of his early poems. In 1871 Charles Chabot, expert in the subject, identified the handwriting in the verses to Miss Giles as that of Richard Tilghman, Francis's cousin, and further evidence was produced to show that Francis himself was almost certainly the author. Though the connection with Junius still depended on the validity of Chabot's identification, the coincidence seemed remarkable.[2]

Dilke's trump card had been the argument that Veteran, who was unquestionably Junius, had misunderstood the circumstances of Francis's resignation from the War Office. But as more of Francis's correspondence became available, it was apparent that Dilke's account was not wholly adequate. A phrase in Francis's letter to Baggs—'all this I should be glad you would communicate to anyone that is willing to hear it'—suggests to a suspicious mind that this was the version Francis wished to have put around.[3] For there can be no

[1] The *Athenaeum*, 1850, 1021–2, 1071.

[2] *The handwriting of Junius professionally investigated*. Tilghman wrote to Francis, 29 September 1773: 'I am yet ready to allow you can weave originals, because "in the School of the Graces, by Venus attended, Belinda improves every hour".' This was the beginning of the second stanza of the verses.

J. N. M. MacLean argued that the verses were sent by Joseph King, whom Miss Giles subsequently married, and complained that John Wade had 'distorted the evidence out of all recognition in order to bolster up an already shaky contention that the true Junius was Francis'. But MacLean himself omits to mention the vital evidence of Tilghman's letter which confirms that Francis was the author of the verses.

[3] Francis's letter to Baggs conveyed the impression that he had at once been

doubt that there had been difficulties between Francis and Lord Barrington prior to his resignation. In a memoir of Francis printed in 1810 in the *Monthly Mirror* it was stated that he had left the War Office 'in consequence of a difference with Lord Barrington by whom he thought himself injured'.[1] This version is confirmed by several contemporary accounts. Christopher D'Oyly, Francis's friend, sent him in December 1771 news of his own resignation in a letter that makes it clear that the two men disliked their chief, Lord Barrington: 'My request', wrote D'Oyly sardonically, 'was readily and, which is mortifying, without one civil speech granted. I am persuaded whenever you please you may obtain the same permission on as easy terms.'[2] Lord Barrington himself, in a letter of February 1772, asked Francis to compose his own account of his resignation since the affair could not remain a secret: 'I have no objection to your mentioning any of those things which have given you uneasiness heretofore if you add (what I hope you may add with sincerity) that I have since made you easy as to those points.'[3]

An independent confirmation that there had been bad feeling comes from the correspondence of John Calcraft, Francis's closest patron. On 13 January 1772 he wrote to John Almon, the bookseller:[4]

> If you put in paragraphs, put, that Mr. Francis is appointed Deputy at War, and continues his present employment also. It will teaze the worthy Secretary, as I well know and oblige me. . . . you will find more folly in that noble lord than ever you thought him capable of.

Almon must have replied that Chamier was to be appointed because on the 18th, Calcraft wrote:

> I was not misinformed. I knew Francis was not Deputy, but wished him so; and to cram the newspapers with paragraphs that he was so. For he is very deserving.

offered the post of Deputy in succession to D'Oyly. But D'Oyly's letter of 21 December 1771 suggests that this was not so: 'He [Barrington] mentioned Smith as the proper successor, but upon my saying I believed he would not like the place he instantly took to his friend Bradshaw, and in full possession of that idea, I left him' (Parkes and Merivale, i. 274–5).

[1] The *Monthly Mirror* was edited by Dubois, a friend of Francis, and the memoir can therefore be regarded as reliable. Simonson tried to dismiss this evidence as planted by Francis to lend support to his bogus claim. Yet one can hardly argue that evidence could be planted in 1810 in case the private letters should be published in 1812.

[2] Parkes and Merivale, i. 274.

[3] Ibid. 275.

[4] *Memoirs of a late eminent bookseller*, 83–4.

These remarks tell us several things. First it is apparent that the succession to D'Oyly had not gone as Calcraft (and presumably Francis) wanted. Secondly, it hints at a possible difficulty—that the Deputy's place being worth only £400 p.a., Francis would have liked to keep the senior clerkship as well. Thirdly, it establishes a good deal of common ground between Calcraft and Junius. Each was interested in the affairs of the War Office. On 13 January, Calcraft intended to 'teaze' Lord Barrington: on 27 January, Junius declared his intention of 'torturing that bloody wretch Barrington'. Calcraft found in Barrington 'more folly than you ever thought him capable of':[1] Junius believed that 'next to the Duke of Grafton . . . the blackest heart in the kingdom belongs to Lord Barrington'.[2]

We have now arrived at two apparently conflicting hypotheses—that Francis was discontented at the treatment he had received from Barrington, yet it was to Barrington that he owed his place in India the following year. It seems hardly to be straining conjecture to suggest that Francis could not afford to quarrel publicly with so influential a patron yet could find an outlet for his resentments through the Veteran letters. In which case it was a matter of elementary prudence to make use of a name other than Junius. Thus the evidence which the most recent editor of the letters regarded as the 'fundamental basis' of the case against Francis's candidature may legitimately be interpreted in favour of it.[3]

Dilke's other objections, which looked so weighty when first made, are no more insuperable. His rejection of large numbers of the miscellaneous letters did nothing to weaken the Francis case and the removal of so much dubious evidence made it easier to construct a plausible candidature. Though it was remiss of Mason Good not to explain that his dating of the private correspondence was from internal evidence only, his suggestions were for the most part informed and intelligent. The amendments which have to be made do nothing to rule out Francis: indeed, one amendment, which Dilke himself noted, brings the argument closer to Francis than before.[4]

[1] *Memoirs of a late eminent bookseller*, 84.

[2] Private letters nos. 53 and 61. A further example of Calcraft's hostility towards Barrington is contained in a letter of July 1772 to Almon, when he wrote of a certain peer that 'his delight is a place at court. Et tu, Barrington! What is twenty, nay thirty years friendship?'

[3] Charles Everett made no attempt to deal with the complications of the resignation issue and was content to accept the argument as Dilke left it in 1850.

[4] See pp. 562–3.

Nor, in the light of Francis's autobiographical fragment, does Dilke's suggestion that he could not be Junius because of the attacks on Welbore Ellis and Calcraft present much difficulty. Francis and his father were undoubtedly under obligations to Henry Fox and Calcraft, yet he wrote of them, coldly: 'There was not virtue enough in either of them to justify their quarrelling. If either of them had had common honesty, he could never have been the friend of the other.' Francis was not the only man in the eighteenth century to chafe under the system of patronage. The note of cynicism struck in the autobiographical fragment carries echoes of Junius: each was at heart an outraged moralist of the Swift variety. 'Lasting enmities', observed Francis, 'are much upon the same footing with lasting friendships in the breast of a statesman.' 'Political friendships', wrote Junius, 'are so well understood that we can hardly pity the simplicity they deceive.'[1]

The question of motivation raised by Dilke is an extremely complex one and a thorough investigation, in political and psychological terms, would take us outside the limits of an appendix. It should first be noted that the picture Dilke painted of the young Francis as a kind of Dickensian clerk, scribbling away on a high stool, is most misleading. At the time of the Junius letters Francis was, in modern terms, a senior civil servant: the fact that he could be appointed to the Council in India indicates that he was a man of standing and experience. It has often been argued that his official duties would have left him no time to compose the letters. But we find him writing in June 1771 of the 'uninteresting indolence' of his official position.[2] His private letters are evidence that he took a keen interest in political affairs. He was without question extremely ambitious and he had, in addition, a taste for good living which he found difficulty in gratifying.

A summary of Junius' political attitude would be that he strove to bring down first the Grafton ministry and then that of Lord North, that he laboured to persuade the opposition to work in harmony, and that after the death of George Grenville he seems to have drawn closer to Lord Chatham. Francis described his own position in his fragment of autobiography:

I had no hope of advancement but on the line of Opposition. I was sincere tho' mistaken in my politics and was convinced the ministry could never

[1] Parkes and Merivale, i. 362; public letter of 21 November 1768.

[2] Parkes and Merivale, i. 263.

stand the consequences of the Middlesex election. . . .[1] The interest of all parties evidently required a coalition and Calcraft was again the mediator; at least he told me so. To his industry and activity the Opposition were in some measure indebted for the formidable appearance they made in the beginning of the year 1770, when Chatham, Camden and Granby resigned, when Yorke put an end to his life, when Grafton abandoned the government, and North succeeded to what I believe he himself and every man in the kingdom at that time thought a forlorn hope. It is not easy to say by what means all these flattering expectations were disappointed. . . .

Calcraft and I soon saw that the game was lost with respect to opposition in general, but we still thought it possible that Chatham might be sent for alone. . . . If Chatham had come in, I might have commanded anything, and could not but have risen under his protection.'[2]

After the death of Calcraft in August 1772, Francis wrote that he was plunged into despair and saved only by the friendship of D'Oyly: 'We agreed that all former schemes or views, in the political line, were to be buried in oblivion.'

Even in detail, the parallels between Francis's autobiographical fragment and the known interests of Junius seem remarkable. Francis thought that Granby's reluctance to resign 'with spirit' may have been the fatal stroke to opposition: Junius had written a letter to Granby urging him to resign.[3] Francis thought that the opposition in 1770 was bound to succeed: 'I have no doubt that we shall conquer them at last', wrote Junius. Francis devoted a considerable part of his fragment to a detailed account of the trial of Woodfall for publishing Junius' letter to the King. Francis deplored the fact that the opposition chiefs quarrelled among themselves: Junius complained that there were not ten men in the country who would 'unite and stand together'.[4]

In the dispute over the Falkland Islands Francis and Junius seem very close. Junius appeared in his letters to Woodfall to be more than commonly excited about the issue. 'Depend upon the assurance *I* give you that every man in administration looks upon war as inevitable,' he wrote. When war was averted by a negotiated settlement,

[1] Junius had warned Grafton in public letter no. XI that 'there never yet was a minister in this country who could stand the issue of such a conflict'.

[2] Parkes and Merivale, i. 361–3. Readers will remember that Junius had written to Chatham in January 1772, perhaps somewhat unnecessarily. His letter concluded: 'I will not presume to trouble your Lordship with any assurances, however sincere, of my respect and esteem for your character, and admiration of your abilities.'

[3] Your Real Friend, 6 May 1769. See Appendix five, p. 466.

[4] Private letters nos. 22 and 64.

he attacked it as craven and humiliating. In private letter no. 29 he insisted that Woodfall insert hints to ensure that the House of Lords would be open when the matter came up for debate: 'It is of the utmost importance to the public cause', he declared. In subsequent letters he showed strong dislike for the Stock Exchange and its members, attacking Anthony Chamier as 'a little whiffling broker' and 'poor Waddlewell'.[1] Compare Francis's view of the same events:

> Chatham came forward again and attacked the ministry with wonderful eloquence. . . . It had a great effect abroad and alarmed or offended the ministry so much, that they determined to shut the doors of the House of Lords against all strangers . . . The stroke was fatal to the Opposition. It was in vain to make speeches, when there was no audience to be informed or inflamed, nor any means of dispersing them among the people. Still however we thought a Spanish war inevitable and that Chatham must be employed. Lord Weymouth, on that occasion, resigned the Secretary of State's office; and I lost five hundred pounds in the stocks. By that loss however I gained knowledge enough of the mode of transacting business in the Alley, to deter me into entering into such traffic again. The convention with Spain sunk me and my hopes to a lower state than ever.

The problem of motivation cannot be left without at least a brief discussion of Junius' personality. Though his concern for the public good, as he saw it, may be conceded, one cannot ignore a less amiable side—a willingness to hurt, to ridicule, and to torment. His writing is at its most vigorous not when he is debating some great political or legal cause but when he is flaying Grafton, Bedford, or the Luttrells. The author of the letter signed Junia scored a direct hit when he wrote:[3]

> Junius lays hold of a scandalous anecdote with as much keenness as a *spider* seizes an unfortunate fly; he crawls forth from the dark hole where he lay concealed; how eagerly he clutches it; with what a malicious pleasure he drags it along; his eyes gloat upon it with cruel delight.

Leslie Stephen, in his *English thought in the eighteenth century*, agreed that 'the invective suggests rancorous ill-will rather than virtuous indignation'.[4]

[1] Private letters nos. 28, 29, and 34; Vindex, 22 February 1771; public letter no. XLII; Veteran, 28 January 1772, 17 February, 27 February, 10 March, 23 March 1772.

[2] Parkes and Merivale, i. 363.

[3] *Public Advertiser*, 5 September 1769. It was claimed by Caleb Whitefoord.

[4] 3rd edition (1902), ii. 200.

There is nothing in the character of Philip Francis to rule him out. By and large he appears as a sour and embittered man, more than commonly prone to disparage his associates and contemporaries. A sneer came easily to him. Of Edward Young, a poor curate, who married Holland's natural daughter and was made an Irish bishop, Francis remarked: 'I have often seen that worthy prelate and his wife at breakfast and dinner with his patron's servants. Such Christian humility entitled him to a mitre.'[1] Of Charles Fox he wrote that 'the essential defect in his character was that he had no heart . . . he *hated* very little, because in general he loved nobody'.[2] Herman Merivale finished the biography of Francis by drawing attention to 'that unhappy nature' which

> made him quarrel with one friend and benefactor after another, and leave on record the most cutting memorials of his displeasure against them. . . . One friend, supporter, patron and colleague after another—Kinnoul, Chatham, Robert Wood, Calcraft, D'Oyly, Clavering, Fowke, Coote, Fox, the Prince of Wales—those who had wished well to him, defended him, showered benefits on him—appear at last, in his written records, branded with some unfriendly or contemptuous notice, some insinuated or pronounced aspersion . . .

Nor did he ever change. Sir James Mackintosh dined with him in the last year of his life and noted in his diary: 'The vigorous hatreds which seem to keep Francis alive were very amusing.'[3]

It must be admitted that all the evidence brought forward to support Francis's candidature is of a circumstantial nature. It carries conviction, if at all, by its cumulative effect. But this must be true of any candidate. Direct implication, after 1773, is not to be obtained. Even a signed and sealed confession would be suspect on the grounds that it might be a forgery or a plant.[4] But the evidence of the pre-

[1] Parkes and Merivale, i. 360–1. [2] Ibid. ii. 451, 459.

[3] *Memoirs of the life of the Rt. Hon. Sir James Mackintosh*, ed. R. J. Mackintosh (1835), ii. 342.

[4] In 1949 Francesco Cordasco announced a major discovery—a hand-sewn manuscript by Shelburne naming Macleane as Junius. This was said to have been found in some papers that had belonged to Sir David Brewster, a nineteenth-century antiquarian and which Cordasco had purchased. It was a remarkable claim since it had always been understood that Shelburne had died before recording his opinion. It also presumed that Sir David Brewster, an inveterate Junius enthusiast over many years, had failed to notice that he had in his own collection such a vital document. There are points of confusion in Cordasco's two accounts of the acquisition of the manuscript and it has not yet been made available. Why Cordasco should continue, in 1973, to write articles drawing attention to the claims of persons like Sir William Jones if he has finally unlocked the secret is a mystery in its own right. I understand, however, from Professor Cordasco that the document is to be published imminently

vious pages is enough to suggest that it was rather wilful of Gustave Simonson to declare so categorically that the case for Francis had 'not the slightest merit' or for Francesco Cordasco to insist that it was a 'bankrupt hypothesis'.[1]

* * *

The evidence to which I have referred in the preceding section seems to me to establish a respectable, if not a conclusive case in favour of Francis's candidature. The last section of this appendix is devoted to material that has become available in recent years and which reinforces that contention.

From the very commencement of the controversy about authorship, attempts have been made to identify Junius by means of stylistic comparisons. In the nineteenth century this method became the mainstay of most candidatures and the books and tracts on the subject groaned with examples of remarkable similarities between the style of Junius and that of Burke, Glover, Portland, Gibbon, or Chesterfield. This approach was bound to be inconclusive. Often the examples quoted were subsequent to Junius, and, since his writings were greatly admired, it was impossible to rule out direct imitation. But in any case, the language of political vituperation in a given period is too limited to permit identifications to be made with much confidence.

In the 1950s a Swedish philologist, Alvar Ellegård, tried a new approach to the problem. Working on the assumption that every author has certain literary habits, favourite words and phrases, of which he may be totally unaware but which serve as his hallmark, Ellegård fed large portions of the writings of Junius and forty of his contemporaries into a computer. Though on purely literary grounds he felt that the case for Francis was not strong, the stylo-linguistic evidence, in Ellegård's judgement, offered the most conclusive identification. In his book, *Who was Junius?*, published in 1962, he claimed that 'the statement that Sir Philip Francis was Junius may henceforth be allowed to stand without a question-mark'.[2]

in a history of the Junius controversy when, no doubt, all these difficulties will be cleared up. F. Cordasco, *A Junius bibliography*; *Journal of English Literary History*, December 1949; Fitzmaurice, op. cit. ii. 434; *Notes & Queries*, November 1973.

[1] For Simonson, see section 3 of the Bibliography. Professor Cordasco's comment is in the *American book collector*, v. 20 (1969), 7.

[2] p. 119. The detailed evidence on which Professor Ellegård's findings were based is in *A statistical method for determining authorship: the Junius letters, 1769–72*. Discussion of the methodology may be found in the *Times Literary Supplement*, 25 January 1963,

New and important evidence was also discovered in the Archives Nationales in Paris.[1] It has often been pointed out that no one appears to have mentioned or suspected Francis in connection with the letters until the publication of George Woodfall's edition in 1812.[2] But a report to Louis XVI in the 1770s attributed the letters to a 'Mr. Fitzpatrick . . . a private friend to one Mr. Francis, a man of parts, who was a clerk in the court offices and from him Mr. Fitzpatrick got his best informations'. It added that this was the opinion of Garrick and others who knew Fitzpatrick.

Thady Fitzpatrick, a man about town and a contributor to newspapers, was undoubtedly a boon companion of Philip Francis. He was certainly not the author of the letters since he died in September 1771, before the series had been completed. But in several other respects the new information linked up with that already available. Charles Butler in his *Reminiscences* in 1822 had referred to a belief that Fitzpatrick was Junius, though his account was a confused one and he apologized for offering it on such slender grounds.[3] Secondly, Fitzpatrick had been involved in a brush with Lord Mansfield in 1763, when, after the 'half-price' theatre riots, he had been severely warned as to his future conduct. Thirdly, there are in Francis's letters references to jolly and convivial evenings spent in Fitzpatrick's company and it is possible that he was one of the 'people about me' to whom Junius referred when asking Woodfall to disavow the reply to Junia.[4]

The main confirmatory evidence concerns David Garrick. The theatre riots had led to a noisy and protracted feud between Garrick and Fitzpatrick. It will be remembered how agitated Junius became early in November 1771 when he believed that Garrick had prised

1 March 1963; *Language*, xl (1964), 85–90; *Studia Neophilologica*, xxxvi (1964), 203–6; *English Studies*, 44. 376–81; *English Historical Review*, lxxix. 862–3; *Journal of English and Germanic Philology*, lxii. 688–9; *Modern Language Review*, lviii. 412–13. No fundamental criticisms are offered of either Ellegård's method or his statistical accuracy.

[1] L. S. Sutherland, W. Doyle, and J. M. J. Rogister, 'Junius and Philip Francis: new evidence', *Bulletin of the Institute of Historical Research*, xlii (1969), 158–72.

[2] The only evidence to the contrary was George Woodfall's assertion that he had once heard his father declare that Francis was certainly not Junius. But George Woodfall admitted that it was a recollection 'more than forty years since' and if the incident happened at the time he stated, he was no more than fifteen years of age. Add. MS. 27783, ff. 16–18.

[3] Fitzpatrick had also been hinted at as 'Fitzgerald, an accomplished Irishman' in a garbled account submitted to the *Scots Magazine*, November 1799 by An Old Magistrate.

[4] Private letter no. 8 and note to Reply to Junia in Appendix four.

secrets out of Woodfall and had assured the King that Junius would write no more. Junius at once dispatched a ferocious letter to Garrick, warning him to cease his 'impertinent enquiries', and later he remarked to Woodfall that Garrick had forced him to break his resolution to write no more.[1] Garrick's interest in the matter was shown in the month following Fitzpatrick's death. It does not seem a fanciful surmise to suggest that Garrick might have associated Fitzpatrick with the letters and that Junius found the conjectures too close for comfort.

In the earlier part of this appendix we have seen examples of attempts to support or disqualify candidates according to a comparison of their known movements with those of Junius. All such arguments need to be examined with the greatest caution.[2] In some cases, as of lengthy absence abroad, a candidate may sometimes be ruled out in this way. But when it is a matter of movements within the country the method is much less reliable. John Wade put forward the over-dramatic claim that 'as Francis moves Junius moves, like substance and shadow . . . Siamese twins were not more closely conjoined.'[3] But this kind of argument was based upon the private letters, and the extent to which the dates affixed by Mason Good were merely conjectures was not always appreciated. There is little point in labouring to establish Francis's movements to within hours or days if some of the letters can hardly be dated within weeks or months.

[1] Private letters nos. 43, 44, and 45.

[2] To give but one example, in an article advancing the claims of Lauchlin Macleane in the *Journal of English Literary History*, December 1949, 281, Francesco Cordasco wrote that 'in January 1772, he was appointed Collector of Customs of Philadelphia. His absence from England agrees *exactly* with the interval in the correspondence between Junius and Woodfall . . . Macleane returned to England in 1773 . . . and Junius reappeared from his occultation of eight months.' In fact the appointment was a sinecure and Macleane never left England. J. N. M. MacLean, *Reward is secondary*, refers to letters to Burke in July and August 1772 from Macleane's London address and he was sworn in for another appointment at India House in December 1772.

[3] Wade, ii, pp. xxxviii–xxxix. Opponents of the Francis candidature draw attention to the fact that he was apparently at Oxford on Friday, 10 August 1771 at the end of a fortnight's tour and intended to reach his London home on the night of Sunday, 12th. They argue that Francis could not have had time to send letter no. LIV to Woodfall and have it published on the 13th. But the letter was dated 10 August. It was not a composition demanding painstaking research and there is no very obvious reason why it should not have been written on tour and posted from Oxford. In his reply Horne noted that there had been some delay in answering and congratulated Junius on the recovery of his wonted style 'though it has cost you a fortnight'.

But a source of information which does not suffer from the same defect are the signals inserted by Woodfall in the *Public Advertiser*. It is true that they do not tell us where Junius was—merely that Woodfall wished to communicate with him. Nevertheless, one sequence of signals does repay close attention.[1]

In 1772, after the collected edition of the letters had been published, Woodfall signalled to Junius on 5 May: after a gap of seven months he signalled again on 21 December and then, at brief intervals, on 23 December, 2 January 1773, 8 January, and 19 January. The repetition of the later signals suggests that Woodfall was anticipating a reply and was puzzled at its absence. On 19 January Junius at last answered, writing: 'I have seen the signals thrown out for your old friend and correspondent. Be assured that I have had good reason for not complying with them.'[2] Woodfall replied with private letter no. 65 which included comments on the political events of the previous months, as though the printer knew that Junius had been away and was in need of briefing.[3]

We know precisely what Francis's movements were for most of this period since he travelled on the Continent and kept a diary, which is extant. He left on 8 July and returned home on 14 December. This was a week before Woodfall resumed signalling. Moreover, in a memorandum in the summer of 1772, Calcraft wrote of Francis, 'He will be home about Christmas.'[4] No doubt there were hundreds of gentlemen who took continental holidays in 1772 and returned in time for Christmas, but there are very few of the serious Junius contenders for whom this can be demonstrated. Taken in isolation, the matter is of no consequence; placed in the balance along with the other evidence, it acquires significance.

A similar argument may be applied to the re-dating of private letter no. 61. In it Junius remarked that 'Next to the Duke of Grafton . . . the blackest heart in the kingdom belongs to Lord Barrington.' Wade and Everett followed Mason Good in dating this 3 May 1772,

[1] See Appendix seven.

[2] Private letter no. 64. Private letter no. 63 may with confidence be dated either 9 or 10 May 1772, which narrows Junius' movements further.

[3] 'Even my friend Mr. Wilkes lost some of his wonted coolness at the late election, on Sawbridge, Oliver, etc. scratching against him.' This was a reference to the election for Lord Mayor in October 1772. 'You will perceive by the papers that two persons have obtruded themselves upon us who, without a tythe of Mr. Wilkes's abilities, imagine the public will look up to them as their deliverers . . . You will probably guess that I mean Allen & Lewes . . .'

[4] Parkes and Merivale, i. 318.

presuming that 'the inclosed' referred to a letter signed Scotus. From internal evidence, however, it can be shown that letter no. 61 must have been written on 22 March and that the enclosed letter was that of Veteran for 23 March. Veteran's letter begged the printer to inform the public that among his other misdeeds Lord Barrington had dismissed Philip Francis from the War Office. In other words, some of the most violent language ever employed by Junius was provoked by Francis's resignation. Those who maintain that Francis had nothing to do with the letters are under some obligation to explain why Junius should think his dismissal of such overwhelming interest and consequence.

A line of inquiry begun by John Taylor attempted to establish connections between certain speeches by Chatham in 1770, apparently reported by Francis, and expressions in them employed by Junius.

The first task was to confirm that Francis had attended the House of Lords and reported debates. In a manuscript note in his own copy of Belsham's *History* Francis claimed: 'I wrote this speech for Lord Mansfield as well as all those of Lord Chatham on the Middlesex election.' By this he obviously meant that he had written them up for publication.[1] In addition to this, the editor of volume xvi of the *Parliamentary History* noted that Chatham's speeches of 9 and 22 January and 22 November 1770 had been taken 'by a gentleman who afterwards made a distinguished figure in the House of Commons'. When approached by Taylor he identified this gentleman as Francis and subsequently confirmed the identification in volume xxxiv. The speeches in question had originally been printed in John Almon's *Anecdotes of Chatham*, published in 1792, where it was claimed that they were in print for the first time, having been submitted by 'a gentleman of strong memory, now a member of the House of Commons'.[2] Moreover, in publications in 1810 and 1811, Francis remarked that he had heard Chatham's speeches of 9 and 22 January 1770.[3] Taylor proceeded to argue that certain passages were to be found also in the writings of Junius. If Almon was correct in saying that the speeches had not been printed before 1792, Junius must either have borrowed notes on the debates from Francis, or they must have been the same person.

[1] This is not quite such a grandiose claim as might appear at first sight. Chatham was out of politics during 1769 and missed many of the earlier debates on the Middlesex election. There were five debates in 1770 in which Chatham took part and the subject was raised.

[2] ii. 236, 270.

[3] *Essay on the Regency; Essay on paper currency.*

Charles Dilke, in the *Athenaeum*, turned with his usual gusto to destroying this part of the Francis case. He insinuated that Francis had laid a false claim to have reported the debates at a time when he was anxious to be taken for Junius. Dilke was able to show that reports of *some* of the 1770 debates had appeared in contemporary newspapers and he inferred that Junius could have borrowed his passages from these publications. In tones of heavy irony, Dilke implied that Francis had never reported the debates: 'Not one of his contemporaries, as far as we know, ever heard of this clerk in the war office as a reporter at all.' It was not, observed Dilke, until forty-three years had elapsed that the editor of the *Parliamentary History* dragged 'the modest and retiring gentleman' from his concealment.[1]

Dilke's argument was, to say the least, forced. He was obliged to assume that Francis had hoodwinked not only John Taylor but the editor of the *Parliamentary History* as well. It was necessary to ignore the fact that Francis had mentioned in 1810 and 1811 having heard Chatham's speeches, since it would be straining credulity to assert that he was even then—before he had been suggested as a possible candidate—laying false clues. The publication of the *Memoirs of Sir Philip Francis* in 1867 disposed of Dilke's remaining objections. First, the authors were able to print, as an appendix, notes on the debate of 2 February 1770 in Francis's own hand. Next, in the autobiographical fragment composed during the 1770s, Francis had observed that he 'took down from memory' Chatham's famous speech of 22 November 1770 and 'had it published in a few days'. He also noted that he had been present at a debate of 10 December 1770 in the House of Lords, and there was a long letter the following day to his cousin Philip Baggs to confirm his evidence. Consequently, none but the most determined sceptic could deny that Francis had, in 1770, attended debates and reported them and that therefore his later claim to have reported Chatham's speeches was by no means improbable.

But once this is admitted, the case for Francis as Junius is considerably strengthened. In the debate of 9 January 1770, which Francis claimed to have attended and reported, Chatham had offered a defence of his proclamation of 1766. Dilke had been unable to say more than that his speech had 'probably' been reported in a newspaper which had subsequently been lost. But Junius, writing as

[1] 21 September 1850.

Philo Junius on 15 October 1771, quoted Chatham's words: 'I advised it because it was indispensably necessary to save the kingdom from famine, and I submit myself to the justice and mercy of my country.'[1]

For Chatham's speech of 22 January 1770, Dilke was unable to suggest any report at all. Francis wrote that he had heard the speech delivered. Junius quoted from it in a private letter to Wilkes on 7 September 1771: 'I approve highly of Lord Chatham's idea of "infusing a portion of new health into the constitution to enable it to bear its infirmities".'

In relation to Chatham's speech of 22 November 1770 about the Falkland Islands, Dilke's ingenuity did positive harm to his own cause. He demonstrated with some triumph that the speech had unquestionably been reported at the time. But since Francis in his autobiographical fragment had written, 'I had it published in a few days', Dilke's search merely confirmed that Francis was probably telling the truth.

Chatham's speech of 10 December 1770 provides the most interesting evidence. He launched an attack upon Lord Mansfield, asserting that his directions to the jury in the Woodfall case had been improper. Subsequently the proceedings turned into a shouting-match and the opposition peers withdrew, protesting at an 'indecent and unprecedented uproar'. Francis wrote that he had been present at 'that ridiculous scene of riot and confusion'. But he also claimed that, overhearing some days before in a tavern a hint that Mansfield's charge had been 'extra judicial and improper', he had sent to Calcraft a brief note for Chatham: 'within three days after, I heard the great Earl of Chatham repeat my letter verbatim in the House of Lords . . . following the argument exactly.'[2] That this was not mere bombast on Francis's part was proved in 1840 when the editors of the *Chatham Correspondence* printed the anonymous note, dated 9 December 1770.[3]

A week after the debate, Phalaris, writing in the *Public Advertiser*, gave an account of Chatham's speech. This version was subsequently used by Junius and printed as a footnote to his preface in the

[1] Junius quotes the passage as what Lord Camden *should* have said in defence of the proclamation. But it is clearly based upon what Lord Chatham *had* said. The version given to Chatham in *Parl. Hist.* xvi. 648 is 'he had recommended it as a measure of necessity, to save a starving people from famine, and had submitted to the judgement of his country.'

[2] Parkes and Merivale, i. 364.

[3] iv. 48–9.

collected edition, with the remark that it was 'taken with exactness'. This, in itself, strictly implies that Junius must have heard the debate.[1] But the argument can be pushed even closer. Dilke's explanation was that a report of Chatham's speech had appeared in the *London Evening Post* of 11 December 1770 and that Phalaris's version could have been taken from this. But there is so remarkable a similarity between the words employed by Chatham's anonymous correspondent and the version given by Phalaris that it is very difficult not to believe that one was based on the other.[2] The *London Evening Post* version, while making the main point, is quite different in wording.[3]

A further example of conjunction between Junius and Francis which appears to have gone unnoticed concerns the debate of 10 December 1766 on the proclamation to forbid the export of wheat. Lord Mansfield made a severe attack upon Lord Camden for asserting that this use of the royal prerogative was 'but forty days tyranny at the outside'. In a letter of 15 October 1771 Philo Junius commented: 'With regard to Lord Camden, the truth is that he inadvertently overshot himself, as appears plainly by that unguarded mention of a *tyranny of forty days*, which I myself heard.'[4] Merivale and Parkes in their *Memoirs of Sir Philip Francis*, while not connecting the information with Junius in any way, noted that Francis had a copy of a pamphlet version of Mansfield's speech, to which he had made typographical corrections. They inferred that he might have been the

[1] Junius' public letter no. LIV, in reply to Horne Tooke, also implies that he heard the debate of 10 December 1770. 'Did he hear Lord Mansfield . . . when he delivered his reasons for calling the House of Lords together to receive a copy of his charge to the jury in Woodfall's trial?' Junius asked: 'Had he been present upon any of these occasions he would have seen how possible it is for a man of the first talents to confound himself in absurdities which would disgrace the lips of an idiot.'

[2] The anonymous letter wrote of Mansfield as follows: 'His reason for this proceeding was, that he might have an opportunity of saying what he had no right to say on that occasion, that the three other judges concurred with him in the doctrine laid down in his charge to the jury.' The Phalaris version was: 'His real motive for doing what he knew to be wrong was, that he might have an opportunity of telling the public extrajudicially, that the other three judges agreed with him in the doctrine laid down in his charge.' It may also be significant that, in the version Junius used in his preface, he reverted to the original ending—'that the other three judges *concurred* in the doctrine'.

[3] Quoted by Dilke in the *Athenaeum*, 21 September 1850. There is no reference at all in the *London Evening Post* version to any motive imputed to Mansfield. The evidence is carefully discussed by Leslie Stephen in 'Chatham, Francis and Junius', *English Historical Review*, 1888. But Stephen misdated Phalaris's letter.

[4] There was presumably little danger to Junius in confessing that he had witnessed a debate five years earlier.

reporter and almost certainly attended the debate.[1] Though the evidence is, in itself, of no great weight, it is yet another instance which must be explained away as pure coincidence if the case for Francis is to be dismissed.

The last area to be explored is that of Francis's own letters in the period when Junius was writing. This is more than commonly necessary since Alvar Ellegård, in an otherwise lucid and reliable summary of the controversy, gives a misleading impression when he observes that another difficulty in the way of Francis's candidature is 'the extremely non-political nature of Francis' private correspondence during the Junian period'.[2]

It does not, fortunately, require vast researches to demonstrate that Francis was, at that time, a keen politician. First, it must be remembered that almost all of his correspondence with John Calcraft, his chief patron, was destroyed.[3] Nevertheless, three of his letters to Calcraft have survived, two of them because they were forwarded to Chatham and preserved among his papers. That of 21 April 1770 gave news of the Boston massacre; the letter of 9 December 1770, which has already been referred to, suggested legal arguments against Lord Mansfield. The third letter, of 1 December 1770, was a long tactical discussion of the best method of attack upon Mansfield in the House of Lords.[4] We have also seen that Francis attended debates, that he made abstracts of some of the speeches, and that he reported some in the newspapers. This was really rather strange conduct for a man said not to be much interested in political affairs. In addition, his autobiographical fragment for this period is totally political in character, and further evidence of his leanings may be found in the large number of political tracts and pamphlets in his library.[5]

[1] i. 126–7.

[2] *Who was Junius?*, 93.

[3] It may be thought of some significance that Francis made a point of recovering all his letters after Calcraft's death in 1772 and was, presumably, responsible for their destruction.

[4] It is printed as appendix vii in Parkes and Merivale, vol. i. Curiously enough, Merivale misidentified it, confusing it with the letter of advice of 9 December 1770. He acknowledged the error in the *Fortnightly Review* of March 1868.

[5] Parkes and Merivale printed the sale catalogue of Francis's library as appendix i of volume two. Among the dozens of pamphlets are the following:

Conduct of the late administration, 1767
Collection of letters of Atticus, Lucius and Junius, 1769
Controversy between Great Britain and the colonies, 1769
Case of the Duke of Portland, 1768

[*continued overleaf*

Ellegård's remark that in Francis's private letters before 1774 'political affairs are hardly ever touched on' is very odd. The corrective is to read the letters. Parkes and Merivale printed at least twenty-three letters written between 1769 and 1772 to his brother-in-law Alexander Mackrabie or his cousin Philip Baggs in which there is substantial political content. The letter of 7 June 1769, for example, is exclusively political in character, discussing Corsica, the Middle East, American policy, and Wilkes. On 11 December 1770 Francis sent Baggs a long description of the previous day's debate in the House of Lords. Indeed, Francis's zest for political controversy was well enough established for Mackrabie to taunt him about it. 'The Devil take politics', he wrote in his letter of 9 June 1770; 'I'll never debate with either you or Dick. You both have too much to say.'[1]

A close examination of Francis's private correspondence reveals more than a general interest in politics. It may first be noted that there are five references to Junius in his letters and he devoted in addition considerable space in the autobiographical fragment to the Woodfall trial. These five references occur in thirty-two letters written between January 1769 and January 1772.[2] This may be contrasted with one reference by Gibbon in eighty letters of the same period, four references by Burke out of eighty-four letters, and no references at all by Chatham in seventy-one letters. Statistically Francis showed seven times more interest in Junius than the other three politicians put together. But if one examines the references, the point becomes

A short view of the political life of a commoner
Speech on behalf of the constitution by Mansfield, 1767
A vindication of the Duke of Grafton against Junius
Interesting letters from Wilkes, Horne, Beckford & Junius
An address to Junius
Dr. Musgrave's reply to D'Eon, 1769
3 pamphlets concerning Wilkes, 1769
Fearne, Answer to Junius, 1770
S. Johnson, *The False Alarm*, 1770
Miller's trial for printing Junius, 1770
Trial of J. Almon for selling Junius, 1770
S. Johnson, *The Falkland Islands*, 1771
Answer to Junius, 1771
A letter to Dr. Blackstone, 1770

[1] Parkes and Merivale, i. 444–5. Dick was Richard Tilghman, another cousin, referred to above, p. 552, in connection with the verses to Miss Giles.

[2] I have excluded a few brief letters from Francis to his wife, which are totally domestic. I need hardly say that this comparison is meant to be thought-provoking rather than scientific.

sharper. Three of Burke's references were, in fact, denials of authorship. Francis's references, on the other hand, are mainly laudatory. On 12 June 1770 he told Mackrabie: 'Junius is not known and that circumstance is perhaps as curious as any of his writings. I have always suspected Burke . . .' On 25 June 1771 he noted that Junius had written Grafton 'a peppering letter'. The following month he told Baggs that Junius had given Horne 'a most severe correction'—though Francis must have been one of the few people who thought so. On 20 August 1771 he declared that Junius' letter was a masterpiece and that 'poor Horne is drubbed till he screeches for mercy'. Two days later he sent Baggs a copy of the 'famous Junius' letter.

Francis's reference on 26 July 1771 is particularly interesting:

> Junius has given Horne a most severe correction. The best on't is, that Junius, under pretence of writing Horne a *private* letter, makes him the *editor* of the grossest and most infamous libel that ever was printed. This I take to be a *coup* d'état. Wouldn't you laugh if you saw the parson in the pillory for publishing a letter, in which he himself is virulently abused?

Merivale's comment was unhelpful: 'I am not able to explain the particular course of reasoning in the writer's mind.' But a reference to Junius' letter of 24 July 1771 shows that, along with ridicule of Horne, he mixed abuse of the King: 'Nature intended him only for a good-humoured fool. A systematical education, with long practice, has made him a consummate hypocrite.' Junius concluded by advising Horne that the letter was not intended for the public, 'but if you think it will do you any service, you are at liberty to publish it'. But by instructing Woodfall to publish it, Horne made himself actionable at law. It is a complex thought to occur to a casual reader and one wonders whether Francis's gleeful appreciation of Junius' ingenuity does not betray him.

It is difficult within the limits of an appendix to do justice to the argument based upon parallels between Francis's correspondence and Junius' interests, since that argument must depend upon repeated instances. Occasional parallels are to be found in the correspondence of other politicians, such as William Gerard Hamilton, Thomas Whately, and Lord Temple: it is the number of examples in Francis's letters that gives rise to suspicion. This is particularly true if one includes references from Calcraft's letters, which seems permissible since we know that he and Francis worked closely together.

In a letter of 5 July 1769 Francis referred to Grafton's election as Chancellor of the University of Cambridge and to the presentation of the London petition to the King: both subjects are developed in Junius' next public letter on 8 July. On 6 September 1769 Francis noted the Duke of Bedford's election setback—'never was there a more disgraceful defeat'. Junius' next letter on 19 September taunts the Duke with the 'disgrace of a mortifying defeat'. On 17 March 1770 Calcraft wrote that 'the fright at court continues' and Junius told Woodfall in confidence, 'Now is the crisis.' The following day Calcraft wrote that 'Lord Chatham's proposal about Westminster adds to their alarm' and Junius told Woodfall that 'Lord Chatham is determined to go to the hall to support the Westminster remonstrance.' On 11 November 1770 Calcraft told Chatham of the news that Mansfield was to resign the speakership of the House of Lords: the following day Junius told Woodfall, 'Lord Mansfield has thrown the ministry into confusion by suddenly resigning the office of speaker of the House of Lords.' In the same letter Calcraft hinted that the King had made several army appointments 'all . . . without any communication with ministers': Testiculus, who was probably Junius, wrote on 24 November that it appeared to be the King's intention to 'govern the army himself'. On 11 December 1770 Francis wrote a long account of the previous day's debate in the House of Lords, which Junius had apparently attended. A copy of Lord Rochford's dispatch of 22 January 1771, which Junius ridiculed in public letter no. XLII for its 'barbarous French', is preserved in the Francis papers.[1]

Often it is not merely that Francis and Junius should be interested in the same things but that they should be misinformed together. On 14 January 1771 Calcraft wrote that war 'according to my intelligence is more and more certain': two days later Junius assured Woodfall that every man regarded war as inevitable. On 1 May 1771 Francis told Mackrabie that he would not wonder at a dissolution of Parliament: on the same day, in a hasty letter, Philo Junius discussed the dissolution of Parliament. On 30 May 1771 Francis confided to Baggs the absurd suspicion that Horne was bribed by the government: in his letter of 9 July 1771 Junius ridiculed Horne's 'new zeal in support of administration'.

A few more examples must suffice. Junius remarked privately in letter no. 45 that Jeremiah Dyson was to lose his pension: a week later, Francis passed on the news to Baggs. On 6 November Wilkes confided to Junius that he entertained 'certain projects against the

[1] Add. MS. 40759, ff. 77–8.

House of Lords': 'Wilkes meditates an attack upon the House of Lords', wrote Francis in December.[1] Junius was much concerned with the Princess Dowager's health and told Wilkes on 7 November 1771 that she could not live: Calcraft touched on the same subject on 11 November and Francis on 24 January 1772. And finally, on 20 March 1772, Francis wrote, 'at the end of this quarter I leave the war office'; three days later, Junius, writing as Veteran, informed the public that Francis was to leave the War Office.

Perhaps I may be allowed to finish this appendix on a personal note. I began my work on the authorship controversy in a state of splendid ignorance, many traces of which no doubt remain. This had at least the advantage that I was not wedded to the claims of a particular candidate. I postponed the writing of this appendix until the last possible moment so that I could continue sifting the evidence without having to commit myself. In some ways it would have been entertaining to have become convinced of the claims of a rank outsider and I have always felt a sense of anticlimax when confessing to inquirers that Philip Francis did, after all, seem the most probable contender.

I do not propose to say how decisive the case for Francis is, since the object of this appendix is to place the reader in a position to form his own conclusion. It is in the nature of circumstantial evidence that one never feels that there is quite enough to convict. In addition there must always remain the possibility, however slight, of contradictory evidence becoming available. Nevertheless, the coincidence between Francis's political views and those of Junius appears remarkable. There is much in Junius' letters about Draper, General Gansell, and Lord Barrington to suggest a close acquaintance with and a deep interest in the affairs of the War Office. The most thorough investigation of the question of handwriting produced an answer pointing to Francis; the only stylo-linguistic study that has been attempted also pointed to him. There is nothing of which I am aware in the personal and private life of Francis to make his claim untenable and there are several pieces of evidence, such as the Giles letters, the Fitzpatrick reference, and the Chatham debate reports, which can be explained away only by pleading coincidence to an excessive degree.

[1] This specimen provides a good example of how carefully the evidence must be weighed. Wilkes appeared to entrust it to Junius as a matter of the utmost confidence, leaving one to ponder how Francis could have got to know it. It seems, however, to have been an open secret. E. Dayrell told Temple in September that Wilkes planned an attack upon the Lords. *Grenville papers*, iv. 536.

If a cautious conclusion is unacceptable to some readers, they are at liberty to be as dogmatic as they wish: it would certainly have pleased the author himself, who wrote 'The mystery of Junius increases his importance.'[1]

[1] Private letter no. 71.

BIOGRAPHICAL NOTES

A short biographical note is included here for each person referred to in the public letters, in the private letters to Woodfall, Wilkes, Chatham, and Grenville, and in those miscellaneous letters printed in section A of Appendix Five.

The main abbreviations used are as follows:

AR	*Annual Register*
Beaven	A. B. Beaven, *The Aldermen of the City of London*
DNB	*Dictionary of National Biography*
Foss	E. Foss, *The Judges of England*
GM	*Gentleman's Magazine*
HoP	*The History of Parliament: The House of Commons, 1715–54*, ed. R. R. Sedgwick; *The House of Commons, 1754–90*, ed. Sir Lewis Namier & John Brooke
N & Q	*Notes and Queries*
Plomer	H. R. Plomer, G. H. Bushnell, and E. R. McC. Dix, *A dictionary of printers and booksellers, 1726–75*
Venn	J. A. Venn, *Alumni Cantabrigienses*

Peers are listed under their titles, thus:

Bedford, John Russell, 4th Duke of

AKERMAN, RICHARD (1722–92)

Private letter no. 77.
Keeper of Newgate prison; Wilkes's letter referred to him in terms of respect and Johnson and Burke paid tribute to his humanity; he died in November 1792 a comparatively wealthy man. *GM*, 1792, ii. 1062, 1150; Boswell, *Life of Johnson.*

ALBEMARLE, George Keppel, 3rd Earl of (1724–72)

Veteran, 27 Feb. 1772.
Army officer; ensign 1738; col. 20 Ft. Guards 1749; maj.-gen. 1756; lt.-gen. 1759; gen. 1772; Governor of Jersey 1761-d.; M.P. Chichester 1746–54; supporter of Cumberland, then of Rockingham. *GEC*, *HoP.*

ALLEN, MILES (d. 1791)

Private letter no. 65.
Captain; radical supporter of Wilkes; of Sidcup, Kent; trying in 1787 to borrow money from Wilkes; d. in King's Bench prison Dec. 1791. *N & Q*, 1st ser. xi. 302; *GM*, 1791, 1165; Add. MS. 30873, ff. 68, 71, 73, 74.

ALMON, JOHN (1737–1805)

Preface; public letters nos. XXXIX and XLI.
Pamphleteer, publisher, and bookseller; fined June 1770 for selling Junius' letter to the King; in his 1806 edition of the letters argued the case for Boyd. *DNB; State Trials*, xx. 802–68; *Plomer; Memoirs of a late eminent bookseller*.

AMHERST, SIR JEFFERY (1717–97)

Public letters nos. III and XXXVI; Veteran, 27 Feb. and 10 Mar. 1772.
Army officer; ensign 1731; lt.-col. 1745; maj.-gen. 1757; lt.-gen. 1765; gen. 1778; f.m. 1796; K.B. 1761; cr. 1st Baron Amherst 1776; his replacement as governor of Virginia 1768 brought protests. *DNB*, *GEC*.

ANNE, QUEEN (1665–1714)

Public letter no. XLVIII.
2nd da. of James, Duke of York, later James II, by Anne, da. of Edward Hyde, 1st Earl of Clarendon; passing reference to her dissolving Parliament. *DNB*.

ANNE OF AUSTRIA (1601–66)

Public letter no. XXXV.
Da. of Philip III of Spain, wife of Louis XIII of France, mother of Louis XIV; Regent during the Frondes, sharing power with Mazarin; used by Junius as parallel for Bute and Princess Augusta.

ANSELL

Private letter no. 89.
Legal action referred to by Junius. *English Reports*, xcv. 1053–4.

ANSON, George Anson, 1st Baron (1697–1762)

Public letter no. XLII.
Naval officer; entered Navy 1712; lt. 1716; capt. 1724; r.-adm. 1744; v.-adm. 1746; adm. 1748; adm. and C. in C. of Fleet 1761; M.P. Hedon 1744–7; cr. Baron Anson 1747; Lord of Admiralty 1744–51; First Lord of Admiralty 1751–6, 1757–d.; became a national hero after his voyage round the world in the 1740s. *DNB*, *GEC*, *HoP*.

ARBUTHNOT, JOHN (1667–1735)

Public letter no. XXVI.
Physician, poet, and satirist; close friend of Swift and Pope; political opponent of Walpole. *DNB*.

ASTON, SIR RICHARD (d. 1778)
Public letter no. XLI.
Judge; K.C. 1759; Lord Chief Justice of Common Pleas, Ireland 1761; Justice of King's Bench and knighted 1765; Joint Commissioner for Great Seal 1770–1. *Foss*, *DNB*.

AUGUSTA, PRINCESS (1719–72)
Public letters nos. XXIII, XXXV, and XL; private letters nos. 47, 78, and 82; Domitian, 24 Dec. 1770, 17 Jan. 1771; A Whig, 9 Apr. 1771.
Da. of Frederick of Saxe-Gotha, wife of Frederick Lewis, Prince of Wales, mother of George III; it was an article of opposition creed that, with Bute, the Princess Dowager exercised a baneful influence on the young king. Walpole, *Memoirs of George III*; J. Brooke, *King George III*.

BALDWIN, HENRY
Public letter no. XLI.
Printer of the *St. James's Chronicle*; of Britannia Printing Office, White Fryers, Fleet St.; brother of Robert Baldwin, publisher, of Paternoster Row; prosecuted for reprinting Junius' letter to the King but acquitted. *State Trials*, xx; *Plomer*.

BARRÉ, ISAAC (1726–1802)
Public letter no. LIX.
Army officer and politician; s. of Huguenot parents who settled in Ireland; ensign 1746; lt. 1755; capt. 1758; lt.-col. 1761; M.P. Chipping Wycombe 1761–74, Calne 1774–90; joint Vice-Treasurer (I) 1766–8; Treasurer of Navy Apr.–July 1782; Paymaster-General 1782–3; Clerk of the Pells 1784–d.; powerful and vigorous speaker, supporter of Chatham and associate of Shelburne. *DNB*, *HoP*.

BARRINGTON, William Wildman, 2nd Viscount (I.) (1717–93)
Preface; public letters nos. XXXVIII, XLIV, LVII, and LIX; private letters nos. 53, 57, 61, 63, 67; Domitian, 24 Dec. 1770, 17 Jan. 1771; Veteran, 28 Jan. 1772, 17 Feb. 1772, 27 Feb. 1772, 10 Mar. 1772, 23 Mar. 1772; Scotus, 4 May 1772; Nemesis, 12 May 1772.
M.P. Berwick 1740–54, Plymouth 1754–78; Lord of Admiralty 1746–54; Master of the Great Wardrobe 1754–5; Secretary-at-War 1755–61 and 1765–78; Chancellor of the Exchequer 1761–2; Treasurer of the Navy 1762–5; Joint Postmaster-General Jan.–Apr. 1782; one of the most remarkable office-holders in the eighteenth century; his position as Secretary-at-War brought him into prominence during the Wilkite riots through the use of the military and he was repeatedly attacked by Junius, particularly in the miscellaneous letters of 1772. *DNB*, *GEC*, *HoP*.

BEACH, THOMAS (1720–88)
Public letter no. LXVIII.
Referred to as the owner of paper stolen by John Eyre; attorney in Lord Mayor's court and coroner of London. *GM*, 1788, 661.

BEALE, RICHARD and WILLIAM
Public letter no. VIII.
Witnesses at the trial of Edward MacQuirk for murder.

BEAUCHAMP, Francis Seymour Conway, Viscount (1743–1822)
Domitian, 5 Mar. 1770.
Son of Francis, 1st Earl of Hertford; succ. fa., as 2nd Marquess of Hertford 1794; M.P. Lostwithiel 1766–8, Orford 1768–94; Constable of Dublin Castle 1766–d.; Lord of Treasury 1774–80; Cofferer of the Household 1780–2; Master of the Horse 1804–6; Lord Chamberlain 1812–21; K.G. 1807; the family's possessions in Warwickshire gave it considerable influence in that county. *GEC*, *HoP*.

BECKFORD, WILLIAM (1709–70)
Public letters nos. XXXIX and LIII; private letter no. 70.
M.P. Shaftesbury 1747–54, London 1754–70; Alderman of London 1752; sheriff 1755–6; Lord Mayor 1762–3 and 1769–70; Jamaican planter of vast fortune; a supporter of William Pitt and a power in city politics, urging parliamentary reform in the 1760s; died shortly after remonstrating with the King at a public audience in May 1770; statue in Guildhall. *DNB*, *HoP*.

BECKWITH, RICHARD
Public letter no. LXVIII.
Case of 1614 cited by Junius in support of his contention about the law of bail. *State Trials*, iii. 47, 56, 101, 138.

BEDFORD, Gertrude Russell, 4th Duchess of (1719–94)
Public letters nos. XII and XXIX.
Da. of John Leveson-Gower, 1st Earl Gower, 2nd wife of John Russell, 4th Duke of Bedford and mother of Lord Tavistock. *GEC*.

BEDFORD, John Russell, 4th Duke of (1710–71)
Public letters nos. IV, XII, XIV, XXIII, XXVI, XXVII, XXVIII, XXIX, XXXVI, XL; private letters nos. 9, 10, 41, 44, 85; Domitian, 8 Dec. 1770, 24 Dec. 1770; Veteran, 17 Feb. 1772.
First Lord of Admiralty 1744–8; Secretary of State for South 1748–51; Lord Lieutenant of Ireland 1756–61; Lord Privy Seal 1761–3; Ambassador to France to negotiate peace 1762–3; Lord President of the Council 1763–5; at

the time of Junius' stinging attacks, Bedford was coming to the end of his long political career and going blind; his unpopularity was mainly due to the opinion that the peace settlement was inadequate. *DNB*, *GEC*.

BENSON

Public letters nos. XLI, LXI and LXIII.

Juryman said to have been put aside by Mansfield; the case was referred to in a Commons debate of 27 Nov. 1770. *Parl. Hist.* xvi. 1135.

BERNARD, JOHN (d. 1784)

Private letter no. 81.

Identified by Wilkes as author of Anglus in *Public Advertiser* of 6 Nov. 1771; only son of Sir John Barnard, Alderman and M.P. London. H. Bleackley, *Life of John Wilkes*, 294–6, *sub* Barnard; *GM*, 1785, 155.

BINGLEY, WILLIAM (d. 1799)

Public letters nos. VII and XLI; private letter no. 35.

Printer and bookseller opposite Durham Yard, Strand, and at 34 Newgate St.; publisher of the revived *North Briton*; imprisoned for refusing to answer questions. W. Bingley, *A sketch of English liberty*; R. R. Rea, *The English press in politics, 1760–74; Plomer.*

BLACKSTONE, SIR WILLIAM (1723–80)

Public letters nos. XIV, XVII, XVIII, XIX, XXII, LXVIII; private letter no. 50.

Lawyer and jurisprudent; author of the *Commentaries*; M.P. Hindon 1761–8, Westbury 1768–70; Recorder of Wallingford 1749; Vinerian professor of English law, Oxford, 1758–66; Principal of New Inn Hall 1761–6; Sol.-Gen. to the Queen 1763–70; Justice of Common Pleas 1770–d.; knighted 1770; took a prominent though uneasy part in the debates on the Middlesex election. *DNB*, *HoP*.

BRADSHAW, JOHN (1602–59)

Public letter no. XIV.

Regicide; lawyer and leading Parliamentarian during the Commonwealth period; judge of sheriff's court in London 1643; Chief Justice of Chester 1646–7; President of Council of State 1648–9; Chancellor of Duchy of Lancaster 1649; presided over court which tried Charles I but subsequently quarrelled with Cromwell. *DNB*.

BRADSHAW, POLLY

Domitian, 24 Dec. 1770, 28 June 1771.

Sister of Thomas Bradshaw; accused by Q in the Corner of 26 June 1770 of selling posts.

BRADSHAW, THOMAS (1733–74)

Public letters nos. XIV, XXXIV, XXXVI, XLIX, L, LVII, LXV, and LXVII; private letters nos. 14 and 53; Domitian, 5 Mar. 1770, 8 Dec. 1770, 24 Dec. 1770, 28 June 1771; Veteran, 28 Jan. 1772, 27 Feb. 1772, 10 Mar. 1772.
M.P. Harwich 1767–8, Saltash 1768–74; clerk in War Office 1757–61; at Treasury 1761–3; commissioner of taxes 1763–7; Secretary to the Treasury 1767–70; Lord of Admiralty 1772–d.; man-of-business to Grafton and under patronage of Barrington; said to have committed suicide when heavily in debt; favourite butt for Junius' ridicule. *HoP.*

BRETT, SIR PIERCY (1709–81)

Domitian, 5 Mar. 1770.
Naval officer; lt. 1734; capt. 1743; r.-adm. 1762; v.-adm. 1770; adm. 1778; knighted 1753; M.P. Queenborough 1754–74; Lord of Admiralty 1766–70. *DNB, HoP.*

BRIDGEN, WILLIAM (d. 1779)

Private letters nos. 66, 70, and 71.
Alderman of the city of London 1754; sheriff 1756–7; Lord Mayor 1763–4; he did not take an active part in city affairs in his later years. *Beaven*; *GM*, 1779, 519.

BRISTOL, George William Hervey, 2nd Earl of (1721–75)

Domitian, 17 Jan. 1771.
Army officer 1739–42; envoy to Turin 1755–8; Ambassador at Madrid 1758–61; Lord Lieutenant of Ireland 1766–7; Lord Privy Seal 1768–70; Groom of the Stole and First Lord of Bedchamber 1770–d. *GEC.*

BROMFIELD, WILLIAM (1712–92)

Public letter no. VIII.
Surgeon who examined the body of George Clarke and declared he did not die as the result of a blow; he held the position of surgeon to the Princess Dowager and there had been a baronetcy in his family; published 1773 *Chirurgical observations and cases*. *Proc. R.S. of Medicine* 1915; *Lancet* 1915; *DNB.*

BROOKE, DR.

Public letter no. XXXIV; private letter no. 14.
Physician at Exeter alleged to be sharing in Hine's post; *Public Advertiser*, 20 Dec. 1769 denied he was 'the physician to St. Luke's Hospital'.

BUCARELI Y URSUA, ANTONIO MARIA (1717–79)

Public letter no. XLII.
Soldier and colonial administrator; Governor of Cuba 1760; Governor of Buenos Aires; Viceroy of New Spain 1771–d.

BULL, FREDERICK (*c.* 1714–84)

Private letter no. 75.
Sheriff of London 1771; Alderman 1772; Lord Mayor 1773–4; M.P. London 1773–84; wealthy tea merchant who became an ardent supporter of Wilkes; treasurer of the Society of Supporters of the Bill of Rights. *HoP.*

BURGOYNE, JOHN (1723–92)

Public letters nos. XXXIII, XXXIV, XXXVI, XXXIX, XLIX; private letter no. 14; Domitian, 8 Dec. 1770.
Playwright, soldier, and politician; cornet 1744; lt. 1745; capt. 1745; lt.-col. 1758; col. 1762; maj.-gen. 1772; lt.-gen. 1777; Governor of Fort William 1769–79; C.-in C. Ireland 1782–4; M.P. Midhurst 1761–8, Preston 1768–92; in the 1760s he was known as a sharp card player; in 1777 he commanded the army forced to surrender at Saratoga. *DNB*, *HoP.*

BURKE, EDMUND (1729–97)

Public letter no. LIX; private letters nos. 67 and 88.
M.P. Wendover 1765–74, Bristol 1774–80, Malton 1780–94; Paymaster-General Mar.–July 1782, Apr.–Dec. 1783; at the time of Junius' letters Burke was building a reputation as the ablest debater and pamphleteer among the Rockinghams. *DNB*, *HoP.*

BUTE, John Stuart, 3rd Earl of (1713–92)

Public letters nos. XII, XV, XXIII, XXXV, XXXVI, XL, XLIX, L, LIV, LVII, LXVII; private letters nos. 78 and 85; Domitian, 5 Mar. 1770, 24 Dec. 1770, 17 Jan. 1771; A Whig, 9 Apr. 1771; Veteran, 17 Feb. 1772; Nemesis, 12 May 1772.
Lord of Bedchamber to Prince of Wales 1750–1; Groom of the Stole to Prince of Wales 1756–60 and to the King 1760–1; Secretary of State for North 1761–2; First Lord of the Treasury 1762–3; though by Junius' time Bute no longer took a prominent part in public life he was believed to wield great influence through his friendship with the Dowager Princess of Wales. *DNB*, *GEC.*

CALCRAFT, JOHN (1726–72)

Public letter no. LIX.
M.P. Calne 1766–8, Rochester 1768–72; clerk in Pay Office *c.* 1745–57; clerk in War Office 1747–56; paymaster of widows' pensions 1757–62; dep. commissary of musters 1756–63; in the 1760s Calcraft transferred his support from Fox to Chatham; patron to Philip Francis, he left instructions in his will to bring him into Parliament. *DNB*, *HoP.*

CAMDEN, Charles Pratt, 1st Earl (1714–94)

Public letters nos. I, XXXVI, LIX, LX, LXI, LXIX; private letters nos. 46, 47, 48, 85, and 89; Junius, 21 Nov. 1768; Domitian, 8 Dec. 1770, 17 Jan. 1771; Phalaris, 17 Dec. 1770.

Lawyer; M.P. Downton 1757–62; Att.-Gen. to Prince of Wales 1756–7; Att.-Gen. 1757–62; Lord Chief Justice of Common Pleas 1762–6; Lord Chancellor 1766–70; cr. Baron Camden 1765; Lord President of the Council 1782–3 and 1784–d.; his decision in favour of Wilkes on general warrants gave him great popularity; in Junius' demonology Camden was the righteous judge in juxtaposition to Mansfield. *DNB*, *GEC*, *HoP*.

CAVENDISH, LORD JOHN (1732–96)

Public letters nos. LIII and LIX; private letter no. 10.

M.P. Weymouth and Melcombe Regis 1754–61, Knaresborough 1761–8, York 1768–84, Derbyshire 1794–6; Lord of Treasury 1765–6; Chancellor of the Exchequer Mar.–July 1782 and Apr.–Dec. 1783; prominent member of the Rockingham party. *DNB*, *HoP*.

CAWDRON, PATRICK

Private letter no. 84.

Linen-draper of Cheapside and member of Society of Supporters of Bill of Rights; the da. of a Mr. Cawdron of Enfield, Middlesex—a sheriff's officer—was reported married in *GM*, 1806, 873.

CHAMIER, ANTHONY (1725–80)

Private letters nos. 53 and 57; Domitian, 24 Dec. 1770; Veteran, 28 Jan. 1772, 17 Feb. 1772, 27 Feb. 1772, 10 Mar. 1772; Nemesis, 12 May 1772.

M.P. Tamworth 1778–80; Secretary to C.-in-C. 1763–72; Deputy Secretary-at-War 1772–5; Under Secretary of State 1775–d.; descendant of Huguenot refugees and a leading London financier; despite Junius' sneers as a parvenu he was a man of cultivated taste. *HoP*.

CHARLES I, KING (1600–49)

Preface; public letters nos. IX, XII, XIV, XXXV, XXXVII, XXXVIII, LIII, LIV, LXVIII; Domitian, 24 Dec. 1770, 17 Jan. 1771.

Junius' references to him are usually as a scheming hypocrite or to hint that his fate might be repeated. *DNB*.

CHARLES II, KING (1630–85)

Public letters nos. XII, XXXV, XXXVII, L, LVII.

Usually brought in as a taunt to Grafton whose great-grandfather was the son of Barbara, Lady Castlemaine by the King. *DNB*.

CHARLES III, KING OF SPAIN (1716–88)

Vindex, 6 Mar. 1771.
Succeeded half-brother Ferdinand VI as King of Spain in 1759; an enlightened ruler, he was king during the dispute over the Falkland Islands.

CHARLOTTE SOPHIA, QUEEN (1744–1818)

Public letter no. XIV.
Da. of Charles Lewis, brother of Frederick, 3rd Duke of Mecklenburg-Strelitz; wife of George III. *DNB.*

CHATHAM, William Pitt, 1st Earl of (1708–78)

Preface; public letters nos. I, XI, XII, XIII, XIV, XV, XXXVI, XLIV, XLIX, LIII, LIV, LVI, LIX, LXI, LXIII, LXIX; private letters nos. 22, 67, 70, 76, 85, 89; Domitian, 5 Mar. 1770, 8 Dec. 1770, 17 Jan. 1771; Phalaris, 17 Dec. 1770; Veteran, 17 Feb. 1772; Nemesis, 12 May 1772.
M.P. Old Sarum 1735–47, Seaford 1747–54, Aldborough 1754–6, Buckingham 1756, Okehampton 1756–7, Bath 1757–66; cr. Earl 1766; Groom of Bedchamber to Prince of Wales 1737–45; Joint Vice-Treasurer of Ireland 1746; Paymaster-General 1746–55; Secretary of State for South 1756–7 and 1757–61; Lord Privy Seal 1766–8; at the time of the Junius letters, Chatham was a strange and disturbing political figure, with something of the great war leader clinging to him but overlaid by the memory of his disastrous administration and extraordinary illness; he had quarrelled with his former colleague Grafton and was moving into avowed opposition, wooing the urban radicals with references to parliamentary reform; it still seemed possible that he might have a political future should war come or the administration fold up. *DNB, GEC, HoP.*

CHESTERFIELD, Philip Dormer Stanhope, 4th Earl of (1694–1773)

Public letter no. XXIII.
M.P. St. Germans 1715–22, Lostwithiel 1722–3; Lord of Bedchamber to Prince of Wales 1715–27; Lord of Bedchamber to the King 1727–30; Lord Steward 1730–3; Lord Lieutenant of Ireland 1745–6; Secretary of State for North 1746–8; by the later 1760s he was elderly, in poor health, and of no political consequence. *DNB, GEC, HoP.*

CHOISEUL, Étienne François de Choiseul, Duke of (1719–85)

Public letter no. I.
French diplomat and statesman; after service as ambassador he was in charge of foreign affairs from 1758 to 1770; advocated a forward policy over the Falkland Islands dispute.

CLARKE, GEORGE

Public letter no. VIII.

Victim of the riot at Brentford on 8 December 1768.

CLIVE, Robert Clive, 1st Baron (1725–74)

Public letter no. IV.

Soldier and administrator; M.P. Mitchell 1754–5, Shrewsbury 1761–74; on his return to England in 1767, at the end of his second spell in India, Clive built up an important parliamentary interest and took a prominent part in the affairs of the East India Company; Junius himself made no mention of Clive's activities. *DNB*, *GEC*, *HoP*.

COCKBURN, SIR JAMES (1729–1804)

Preface; Scotus, 4 May 1772.

Conjectural identification; M.P. Linlithgow burghs 1772–84; commissary-general to army in Germany 1762–3; succeeded as 8th Bt. 1745; his post might have brought him into contact with Barrington. An alternative possibility is John Cockburn, M.P. Haddingtonshire 1708–41. *HoP*.

COKE, SIR EDWARD (1552–1634)

Preface; public letters nos. XLVII and LXVIII.

Lawyer and jurisprudent; Speaker 1592; Sol.-Gen. 1592; Att.-Gen. 1593; Chief Justice of Common Pleas 1613–16; M.P. Aldeburgh 1589, Norfolk 1592, Liskeard 1620, Coventry 1624, Norfolk 1625, Bucks. 1628. *DNB*, *Foss*.

COMYNS, SIR JOHN (*c.* 1667–1740)

Public letter no. XIX.

Lawyer and jurisprudent; M.P. Maldon 1701–8, 1710–15, 1722–6; Baron of Exchequer 1726; knighted 1726; Justice of Common Pleas 1736; Lord Chief Baron of Exchequer 1738–d.; ousted on petition in 1715 for want of property qualification. *DNB*, *Foss*.

CONWAY, HENRY SEYMOUR (1719–95)

Public letters nos. XI, XII, XIV; private letters nos. 67 and 85; Your Real Friend, 6 May 1769; Domitian, 5 Mar. 1770, 17 Jan. 1771; Veteran, 27 Feb. 1772.

Army officer and politician; lt. 1737; capt. 1740; col. 1746; maj.-gen. 1756; lt.-gen. 1759; gen. 1772; f.m. 1793; M.P. Higham Ferrers 1741–7, Penryn 1747–54, St. Mawes 1754–61; Thetford 1761–74, Bury St. Edmunds 1775–84; Groom of Bedchamber 1757–64; Secretary of State for South 1765–6; Secretary of State for North 1766–8; Lt.-Gen. of the Ordnance 1767–72; C. in C. 1782–3; a member of the cabinet until Nov. 1770, he was rather aloof from all groups. *DNB*, *HoP*.

COOPER, GREY (*c.* 1726–1801)

Domitian, 5 Dec. 1770.

Politician and administrator; M.P. Rochester 1765–8, Grampound 1768–74, Saltash 1774–84, Richmond 1786–90; Secretary to Treasury 1765–82; Lord of Treasury Mar.–Dec. 1783; lawyer and useful man-of-business. *DNB*, *HoP*.

CORNISH, SIR SAMUEL (*c.* 1715–70)

Public letters nos. IV and XXIV.

Naval officer; lt. 1739; capt. 1742; r.-adm. 1759; v.-adm. 1762; cr. Bt. 1766; M.P. New Shoreham 1765–70; commanded the naval force at the capture of Manila in 1762. *HoP*.

CORNWALLIS, Charles Cornwallis, 2nd Earl (1738–1805)

Domitian, 5 Mar. 1770.

Army officer; ensign 1756; capt. 1759; lt.-col. 1761; col. 1764; maj.-gen. 1775; lt.-gen. 1777; gen. 1793; Lord of Bedchamber July–Aug. 1765; Chief Justice in Eyre south of Trent 1766–9; Joint Vice-Treasurer Ireland 1769–70; Constable of Tower of London 1770–84; envoy to Prussia 1785; Governor-General of Bengal 1786–93; Master-General of Ordnance 1795–1801; Lord Lieutenant of Ireland 1798–1801; Governor-General of Bengal 1805; M.P. Eye 1760–2; his surrender at Yorktown marked the end of the American war; cr. Marquess 1792. *DNB*, *GEC*, *HoP*.

CROMWELL, OLIVER (1599–1658)

Public letters nos. XIV, XLIII, LIII, LVII.

Leader of the parliamentary forces against the King and Lord Protector 1653–d.; M.P. Huntingdon 1628, Cambridge 1640. *DNB*.

CROSBY, BRASS (1725–93)

Public letter no. LVIII; private letters nos. 66, 70, 71, 76; A Whig, 9 Apr. 1771.

Attorney and politician; sheriff of London 1764–5; Alderman 1765; Lord Mayor 1770–1; M.P. Honiton 1768–74; a devoted follower of Wilkes, he was sent to the Tower in 1771 for his part in the printers' dispute. *Beaven*, *HoP*.

CUMBERLAND, William Augustus, 3rd Duke of (1721–65)

Public letters nos. IV and XII; Nemesis, 12 May 1772.

2nd son of George II, he made a career in the army and was in command at Culloden; resigned his position as Captain General in 1757 after the convention of Klosterseven was repudiated; political patron of Henry Fox and one of the spectres at Leicester House during George III's adolescence; political broker to the Rockingham ministry in 1765. *DNB*, *GEC*.

CUMBERLAND, Henry Frederick, 4th Duke of (1745–90)

Public letters nos. XLI, LXI, LXVII; private letter no. 82.
4th son of Frederick, Prince of Wales and yo. brother to George III; married in October 1771 Anne, da. of Simon Luttrell, 1st Lord Irnham and widow of Christopher Horton; this marriage led to the passing of the Royal Marriage Act of 1772; *GEC* remarks that he was 'probably the most foolish of Frederick's sons'—a harsh judgement considering the competition. *DNB*, *GEC*.

CUNINGHAME, ROBERT (*c.* 1728–1801)

Public letter no. XL.
Soldier; ensign 1746; capt. 1752; lt.-col. 1757; col. 1762; maj.-gen. 1772; lt.-gen. 1777; gen. 1793; Governor of Kinsale Fort 1770–d.; C.-in-C. Ireland 1793–6; cr. Baron Rossmore (I.) 1796; M.P. East Grinstead 1788–9. *GEC*, *HoP*.

DAVENANT, CHARLES (1656–1714)

Public letter no. XXXIX.
Prolific writer on trade and politics; M.P. St. Ives 1685, Great Bedwyn 1698 and 1700; his collected works were published in 1771, which probably jogged Junius' memory. *DNB*.

DAVIS, POLLY

Public letter no. LXVII; Recens, 7 Apr. 1769.
Described by Junius as a 'common prostitute': see his note to public letter no. LXVII.

DE GREY, WILLIAM (1719–81)

Preface, public letters nos. XIV, XLI, XLIV, XLVIII; private letters nos. 20 and 89.
Lawyer; Sol.-Gen. to the Queen 1761–3; Sol.-Gen. 1763–6; Att.-Gen. 1766–71; Lord Chief Justice of Common Pleas 1771–80; knighted 1771; cr. Baron Walsingham 1780; M.P. Newport (C.) 1761–70, Cambridge University 1770–1. *DNB*, *GEC*, *HoP*.

DE LA FONTAINE, ELIAS

Private letter no. 16; Veteran, 28 Jan. 1772.
Universal Director, 1763, gives 'Delafontain, E. Benjamin. General Merchant, Leadenhall St.'; Baldwin's *New Complete Guide*, 1770, gives 'Delafontaine & Brymer, brokers, 14, Lombard St.'

DE LOLME, JEAN LOUIS (1745–1807)

Preface.
Author; Junius quoted with approval from his *Constitution de l'Angleterre*; claimed by Thomas Busby to be Junius himself. *N & Q*, 2nd ser. vii. 136.

DENBIGH, Basil Feilding, 6th Earl of (1719–1800)
Private letters nos. 11 and 84.
Courtier; Master of the Royal Harriers 1761–82; Lord of Bedchamber 1763–d. *GEC.*

DINGLEY, CHARLES (d. 1769)
Public letters nos. IX and L.
Saw-mill proprietor at Limehouse; took a prominent part in favour of administration in spring of 1769; clashed with Wilkes's attorney on 8 March and tried to stand as candidate for Middlesex on 16 March; d. at Hampstead 13 Nov. 1769. *Pitt. Corr.* iii. 352.

DODD, CAPTAIN JOHN
Public letters nos. XXX and XXXI.
Officer commanding the guard which rescued General Gansell; lt. and capt. in 1st Ft. Guards 1763; capt. and lt.-col. 1775; no reference after 1776. *Army lists.*

D'OYLY, CHRISTOPHER (*c.* 1717–95)
Veteran, 17 Feb. 1772, 23 Mar. 1772.
Lawyer, administrator, and politician; First Clerk in War Office 1761–2; Deputy Secretary-at-War 1763–72; Under-Secretary Colonial Department 1776–8; commissary-general of the musters 1776–80; M.P. Wareham 1774–80, Seaford 1780–84; close friend of Philip Francis and his colleague in the War Office. *HoP.*

DRAPER, LADY CAROLINE (d. 1769)
Public letter no. V.
1st wife of Sir William Draper and da. of Lord William Beauclerk, son of 1st Duke of St. Albans. *DNB.*

DRAPER, SIR WILLIAM (1721–87)
Preface; public letters nos. II, III, IV, V, VI, VII, XXIV, XXV, XXVI, XXVII, and XXIX.
Army officer; ensign 1744; capt. 1749; col. 1762; maj.-gen. 1772; lt.-gen. 1777; after service in India during the Seven Years War he took charge of the expedition against the Philippines; knighted for his services 1766; his defence of Lord Granby led to an exchange with Junius; lived at Clifton and buried in Bath Abbey. *DNB.*

DYSON, JEREMIAH (?1722–76)
Public letters nos. XX, XXII, XXXVIII, XLVI, LIV; private letter no. 45; Domitian, 24 Dec. 1770; Vindex, 22 Feb. 1771.
Politician, pamphleteer, and man-of-business; Clerk of the House of Commons

1748–62; Secretary to Treasury 1762–4; Lord of Trade 1764–8; Lord of Treasury 1768–74; Cofferer of the Household 1774–d.; M.P. Yarmouth I.o.W. 1762–8, Weymouth and Melcombe Regis 1768–74, Horsham 1774–6; his biography in the *History of Parliament* is particularly good. *DNB*, *HoP*.

EDWARD II, KING (1284–1327)
Public letter no. XXXIX.
Murdered at Berkeley Castle; his fate used as an example for George III to contemplate. *DNB*.

EDWARD III, KING (1312–77)
Public letter no. XXXV.
The story of Edward's overthrow of the adulterous partnership of his mother Isabella and Mortimer was a favourite opposition device for taunting the Princess Dowager and Bute. *DNB*.

EGLINTOUN, Alexander Montgomerie, 10th Earl of (1723–69)
Public letter no. XXIII.
Lord of the Bedchamber 1760–7 and Scottish representative peer; killed in a quarrel. *DNB*.

EGMONT, John Perceval, 2nd Earl of (1711–70)
Public letter no. XLII.
M.P. Westminster 1741–7, Weobley 1747–54, Bridgwater 1754–62; Lord of Bedchamber to Prince of Wales 1748–51; Joint Postmaster-General 1762–3; First Lord of Admiralty 1763–6; cr. Baron Lovel and Holland 1762. *DNB*, *GEC*, *HoP*.

EGREMONT, Charles Wyndham, 2nd Earl of (1710–63)
Public letters nos. IV and XXIII.
M.P. Bridgwater 1735–41, Appleby 1742–7, Taunton 1747–50; Secretary of State for South 1761–3. *DNB*, *GEC*, *HoP*.

ELIZABETH, QUEEN (1533–1603)
Public letters nos. XLIII and XLIV; Domitian, 17 Jan. 1771.
Used by Domitian as a reproach to the Princess Dowager. *DNB*.

ELLIS, WELBORE (1713–1802)
Public letters nos. XXXVIII and XLVIII; Domitian, 24 Dec. 1770.
M.P. Cricklade 1741–7, Weymouth and Melcombe Regis 1747–61, Aylesbury 1761–8, Petersfield 1768–74, Weymouth and Melcombe Regis 1774–90, Petersfield 1791–4; cr. Baron Mendip 1794; Lord of Admiralty 1747–55;

Joint Vice-Treasurer Ireland 1755–62; Secretary-at-War 1762–5; Joint Vice-Treasurer Ireland 1770–7; Treasurer of the Navy 1777–82; Secretary of State for America Feb.–Mar. 1782. *DNB*, *GEC*, *HoP*.

EWER, JOHN (*c.* 1706–74)
Public letter no. II.
Cleric; Fellow of King's, Cambridge 1727; rector of Bottesford, Lincs. 1735–52; Canon of Windsor 1737; rector of Dengie, Essex 1749; Bishop of Llandaff 1761, of Bangor 1768. *DNB*, *Venn*.

EYRE, SIR JAMES (1734–99)
Public letter no. VIII.
Lawyer; Deputy Recorder of London 1761; Recorder of London 1763; Baron of Exchequer 1772; President of Court of Exchequer 1787; Chief Commissioner for Great Seal 1792–3; Chief Justice of Common Pleas 1793. *DNB*, *Foss*.

EYRE, JOHN
Public letters nos. LXV and LXVIII; private letters nos. 80, 81, 83, 89.
Sentenced to transportation in November 1771 for stealing paper from the Guildhall; Junius used his case in an attempt to discredit Lord Mansfield. *GM*, 1771, 517, 520; *AR*, 1771, 146, 152.

FERDINAND, PRINCE, DUKE OF BRUNSWICK (1721–92)
Public letter no. IV.
Soldier; fought with Frederick the Great in the War of the Austrian Succession; C.-in-C. allied forces in Germany 1757; victor at Minden 1757; retired from Prussian service 1766.

FIELDING, THOMAS
Public letter no. LXVIII.
Witness at the trial of John Eyre; possibly landlord of the Carolina coffee-house, Cornhill. *GM*, 1791, 974.

FOOT, JOHN
Public letter no. VIII.
Surgeon; examined the body of George Clarke and gave evidence at MacQuirk's trial. *GM*, 1769, 135–40, 161; *An appeal to the public touching the death of Mr. George Clark*, 1769.

FOOTE, SAMUEL (1720–77)
Public letter no. LI.
Actor, mimic, and dramatist; he had caricatured Horne on the stage. *DNB*.

FOSTER, SIR MICHAEL (1689–1763)

Public letter no. LXII.

Judge; Recorder of Bristol 1735; Justice of King's Bench 1745; in 1743 at the trial of Alexander Broadfoot he delivered a long opinion in support of the legality of pressing seamen. *DNB*, *Foss*.

FOWKE, THOMAS (d. 1765)

Veteran, 17 Feb. 1772, 10 Mar. 1772; Nemesis, 12 May 1772.

Soldier; cornet 1704; capt. 1707; maj. 1716; lt. col. 1720; col. 1741; brig.-gen. 1745; maj.-gen. 1747; lt.-gen. 1754; appointed Governor of Gibraltar 1753; court-martialled and dismissed service 1756; restored to rank and appointed Adjutant-General in Ireland 1761; at Gibraltar involved in the loss of Minorca to the French; pleaded that his orders were conflicting; the editorial note in Wade, ii. 397 is totally inaccurate. D. Pope, *At 12 Mr. Byng was shot*; Sir J. Fortescue, *History of the British Army; Burke's Landed Gentry*, 12th edn.

FOX, CHARLES JAMES (1749–1806)

Public letter no. XLIX.

M.P. Midhurst 1768–74, Malmesbury 1774–80, Westminster 1780–4, Tain burghs 1784–5, Westminster 1785–1806; Lord of Admiralty 1770–2; Lord of Treasury 1773–4; Secretary of State for Foreign Affairs Mar.–July 1782, Apr.–Dec. 1783, Feb. 1806–d.; at the time of the Junius letters, Fox was a rising young politician on the side of firm government and authority. *DNB*, *HoP*.

FRANCIS, PHILIP (1740–1818)

Veteran, 23 Mar. 1772.

M.P. Yarmouth I.o.W. 1784–90, Bletchingley 1790–6, Appleby 1802–7; knighted 1806; the single reference in Junius' letters is to his resignation from the post of First Clerk in the War Office in March 1772; the following year he was appointed to the Supreme Council in India; on his return in 1781 he became a prominent member of the Foxite opposition. *DNB*, *HoP*.

FRASER, SIMON (d. 1777)

Public letter no. XL.

Soldier; capt. 1759; maj. 1761; brig.-gen. 1776; Quartermaster-General in succession to Gisborne in Ireland; killed in action in America 19 Sept. 1777. *DNB*.

GANSELL, WILLIAM (d. 1774)

Public letters nos. XXX, XXXI, XXXII; private letter no. 11.

Soldier; ensign 1734; lt. 1739; lt.-col. 1749; col. 1761; maj.-gen. 1762; lt.-gen. 1772; reported to be a connoisseur of painting on which he spent extravagantly; after the incident in 1769 when he was arrested for debt, he was once more arrested in August 1773 (with another affray); d. in Fleet Prison 28 July 1774. *AR*, 1769, 132; 1774, 139; *GM*, 1774, 335; note to 1783 edn. of Junius, i. 228; *Apology for the life of George Ann Bellamy*, ii. 122–4, 172–89.

GARRICK, DAVID (1717–79)

Private letters nos. 40, 43, 44, 45, 47, 48.
Actor and dramatist; Garrick had passed on to the court a hint received from Woodfall that Junius in October 1771 would write no more; Junius' alarm on this occasion may have arisen in part from the fact that Garrick was a part-proprietor of the *Public Advertiser* and on close terms with Woodfall. *DNB*.

GARTH, CAPTAIN GEORGE

Public letters nos. XXX and XXXI.
Involved with Capt. Dodd in rescue of General Gansell; ensign 1st Ft. Guards 1755; capt. 1758; lt.-col. 1772; col. 1779; maj.-gen. 1782; lt.-gen. 1796; gen. 1801; Army list of 1819 in Inst. Hist. Research has name crossed out and 'dead'. *Army lists*.

GASCOYNE, BAMBER (1725–91)

Domitian, 24 Dec. 1770.
M.P. Maldon 1761–3, Midhurst 1765–8, Weobley 1770–4, Truro 1774–84, Bossiney 1784–6; Lord of Trade 1763–5 and 1772–9; Lord of Admiralty 1779–82; Receiver-General of Customs 1786–d. *HoP*.

GEARY, SIR FRANCIS (?1710–96)

Domitian, 5 Mar. 1770.
Naval officer; entered navy 1727; lt. 1734; commanded the *Squirrel* 1742; r.-adm. 1759; v.-adm. 1762; adm. 1775; cr. Bt. 1782. *DNB*.

GEORGE II, KING (1683–1760)

Public letters nos. XII and XXIII; Nemesis, 12 May 1772.
DNB; C. Chevenix Trench, *George II*.

GEORGE III, KING (1738–1820)

Dedication; preface; public letters nos. I, IV, V, VI, VIII, XI, XV, XXXIV, XXXV, XXXVI, XXXVII, XXXVIII, XXXIX, XLII, XLIII, XLIV, XLV, XLVIII, XLIX, L, LII, LIII, LIV, LVII, LXI; private letters nos. 34, 44, 47, 67, 70, 78, 82; Moderatus, 10 Mar. 1770; Domitian, 24 Dec. 1770, 17 Jan. 1771; Vindex, 22 Feb. 1771, 6 Mar. 1771; A Whig, 9 Apr. 1771; Veteran, 17 Feb. 1772; Nemesis, 12 May 1772.
Though Junius in his public letters treats the King for the most part with respect, in his private letters he refers to him as 'the odious hypocrite'. *DNB*; J. Brooke, *King George III*; S. Ayling, *George III*.

GISBORNE, JAMES (d. 1778)
Public letters nos. III, IV, V, XL.
Soldier; maj. 1755; col. 1762; maj.-gen. 1770; lt.-gen. 1777; Quartermaster-General of Ireland 1761. *Army lists.*

GLOUCESTER, William Henry, 1st Duke of (1743–1805)
Private letter no. 82.
Brother of George III; severe illness mentioned. *DNB*, *GEC.*

GLOVER, RICHARD (?1712–85)
Private letter no. 65.
Politician and writer; M.P. Weymouth and Melcombe Regis 1761–8; became well known at age of 25 for his poem *Leonidas* in 1737. *DNB*, *HoP.*

GLYNN, JOHN (1722–79)
Public letter no. IX; private letter no. 65.
Lawyer and politician; M.P. Middlesex 1768–79; Recorder of London 1772–9; acted on behalf of Wilkes and other radicals and was returned for Middlesex in December 1768 as a supporter of opposition. *DNB*, *HoP.*

GOWER, Granville Leveson Gower, 2nd Earl (1721–1803)
Public letters nos. XXIII, XXXVI, XXXVIII, LIX; Domitian, 17 Jan. 1771.
M.P. Bishop's Castle 1744–7, Westminster 1747–54, Lichfield Apr.–Dec. 1754; Lord of Admiralty 1749–51; Lord Privy Seal 1755–7; Master of the Horse 1757–60; Master of the Wardrobe 1760–3; Lord Chamberlain 1763–5; Lord President of the Council 1767–79 and 1783–4; Lord Privy Seal 1784–94; styled Viscount Trentham 1746–54; cr. Marquess of Stafford 1786; a leading member of the Bedford group. *DNB*, *GEC*, *HoP.*

GRAEME, DAVID (1716–97)
Domitian, 5 Mar. 1770.
Soldier and politician; capt. 1745; lt.-col. 1752; col. 1761; maj.-gen. 1762; lt.-gen. 1772; gen. 1783; M.P. Perthshire 1764–73; Secretary to the Queen 1761–74; Comptroller of the Queen's Household 1765–74. *HoP.*

GRAFTON, Augustus Henry Fitzroy, 3rd Duke of (1735–1811)
Public letters nos. I, III, IV, VIII, IX, XI, XII, XIII, XIV, XV, XX, XXIII, XXX, XXXII, XXXIII, XXXIV, XXXVI, XXXVIII, XXXIX, XL, XLVI, XLIX, L, LIII, LIV, LVII, LIX, LXVII, LXIX; private letters nos. 11, 36, 38, 48, 61, 67, 85; Harry and Nan; Junius 21 Nov. 1768; Domitian, 5 Mar. 1770, 8 Dec. 1770, 24 Dec. 1770, 17 Jan. 1771, 28 June 1771; Veteran, 17 Feb. 1772; Nemesis, 12 May 1772.
M.P. Bury St. Edmunds 1756–7; Lord of Bedchamber 1756–8; Secretary of State for North 1765–6; First Lord of the Treasury 1766–70; Lord Privy

Seal 1771–5 and 1782–3; first minister when Junius' letters began and his chief victim. *DNB*, *GEC*, *HoP*.

GRANBY, John Manners, Marquess of (1721–70)

Public letters nos. I, II, III, IV, V, VII, XXVII, XXXVI; private letter no. 2; Your Real Friend, 6 May 1769; Domitian, 8 Dec. 1770, 17 Jan. 1771.
Soldier and politician; col. 1745; maj.-gen. 1755; lt.-gen. 1759; Lt.-Gen. of the Ordnance 1759–63; Master-Gen. of the Ordnance 1763–70; C.-in-C. 1766–70; M.P. Grantham 1741–54, Cambridgeshire 1754–70; a popular hero of the Seven Years War. *DNB*, *GEC*, *HoP*.

GRENVILLE, GEORGE (1712–70)

Public letters nos. I, IV, XV, XVIII, XIX, XXIII, LXI; private letters nos. 67, 85, 86, 87, 88; Domitian, 17 Jan. 1771; Veteran, 17 Feb. 1772; Nemesis, 12 May 1772.
M.P. Buckingham 1741–70; Lord of Admiralty 1744–7; Lord of Treasury 1747–54; Treasurer of the Navy 1754–5, 1756–7 and June 1757–62; Secretary of State May–Oct. 1762; First Lord of the Admiralty 1762–3; First Lord of the Treasury 1763–5; when Junius' letters began, Grenville was in open opposition to the Grafton ministry; he was one of the few persons of whom Junius invariably wrote with respect. *DNB*, *HoP*.

GROSVENOR, Richard Grosvenor, 1st Baron (1731–1802)

Public letters nos. XLI and LXIII.
M.P. Chester 1754–61; cr. Earl Grosvenor 1784; brought an action against the Duke of Cumberland in 1770 for criminal conversation with Lady Grosvenor. *DNB*, *GEC*, *HoP*.

HALE, MATTHEW (1609–76)

Public letter no. LXVIII.
Judge; Justice of Common Pleas 1654; Chief Baron of the Exchequer 1660–71; Chief Justice of King's Bench 1671–6; M.P. Gloucestershire 1654, Oxford University 1659, Gloucestershire 1660; quoted by Junius in his argument about the law of bail. *DNB*, *Foss*.

HALIFAX, George Montagu Dunk, 2nd Earl of (1716–71)

Public letter no. XXIII; Domitian, 24 Dec. 1770, 17 Jan. 1771.
Col. 1745; maj.-gen. 1755; lt.-gen. 1759; Lord of Bedchamber to Prince of Wales 1742–4; Master of the Buckhounds 1744–6; Chief Justice in Eyre south of Trent 1746–8; President of the Board of Trade 1748–61; Lord Lieutenant of Ireland 1761–3; First Lord of the Admiralty June–Oct. 1762; Secretary of State for North 1762–3; Secretary of State for South 1763–5; Lord Privy Seal 1770–Jan. 1771; Secretary of State for North Jan.–June 1771. *DNB*, *GEC*.

HALLIFAX, SIR THOMAS (1721–89)
Public letter no. LXVIII; private letter no. 81.
Banker and politician; Alderman of London 1766; sheriff 1768–9; Lord Mayor 1776–7; knighted 1773; M.P. Coventry 1780–1, Aylesbury 1784–9. *Beaven, DNB, HoP.*

HAMPDEN, JOHN (1594–1643)
Public letter no. XXXIX.
M.P. Grampound 1621, Wendover 1623, 1625, 1629, Buckinghamshire 1640; opponent of Charles I and of ship-money, mortally wounded at Chalgrove Field. *DNB.*

HARLEY, THOMAS (1730–1804)
Public letter no. L; private letters nos. 67 and 71.
Banker and politician; Alderman of London 1761; sheriff 1763–4; Lord Mayor 1767–8; M.P. London 1761–74, Herefordshire 1776–1802; a stalwart of the court party in the city of London. *Beaven, DNB, HoP.*

HARVEY, EDWARD (1718–78)
Public letters nos. II and XL; Veteran, 27 Feb. 1772.
Soldier and politician; cornet 1741; capt. 1747; maj. 1751; lt.-col. 1754; col. 1760; maj.-gen. 1762; lt.-gen. 1772; M.P. Gatton 1761–8, Harwich 1768–78; Adjutant-General to the Forces 1765–d.; Governor of Portsmouth 1773–d. *HoP.*

HAWKE, SIR EDWARD (1710–81)
Public letters nos. I, XXIII, XXXVI; Domitian, 5 Mar. 1770, 17 Jan. 1771.
Sailor and politician; entered navy 1720; lt. 1729; cdr. 1733; capt. 1734; r.-adm. 1747; v.-adm. 1748; adm. 1757; Admiral of the Fleet 1768; M.P. Portsmouth 1747–76; First Lord of the Admiralty 1766–71. *DNB, GEC, HoP.*

HAWKINS, WILLIAM (1673–1746)
Public letter no. LXVIII.
Lawyer and jurisprudent; published 1716 a *Treatise on the pleas of the Crown*, quoted by Junius in his controversy over bail. *DNB.*

HEATH, SIR ROBERT (1575–1649)
Public letter no. LXVIII.
Lawyer and politician; M.P. London 1620, East Grinstead 1623, 1625; Sol.-gen. 1621–5; Att.-Gen. 1625–31; Chief Justice of Common Pleas 1631–4; Justice of King's Bench 1641–3; Chief Justice of King's Bench 1643–9; quoted by Junius on subject of bail. *DNB, Foss.*

HENRY VIII, KING (1491–1547)

Dedication; public letter no. XLIII.

Regarded by Junius as an absolute prince. *DNB.*

HERTFORD, Francis Seymour Conway, 1st Earl of (1718–94)

Private letter no. 85; Domitian, 5 Mar. 1770.

Lord of Bedchamber 1751–64; Ambassador to Paris 1763–5; Lord Lieutenant of Ireland 1765; Master of Horse 1766; Lord Chamberlain 1766–82 and Apr.–Dec. 1783; cr. Marquess of Hertford 1793. *DNB, GEC.*

HILL, CHRISTOPHER (d. 1778)

Domitian, 5 Mar. 1770.

Naval officer; lt. 1740; capt. 1747; r.-adm. 1778. *GM*, 1778, 335.

HILLSBOROUGH, Wills Hill, 1st Earl of (1718–93)

Public letters nos. I, III, LIX; Domitian, 24 Dec. 1770, 17 Jan. 1771.

M.P. Warwick 1741–56; cr. Earl of Hillsborough (I.) 1751; Baron Harwich (G.B.) 1756; Earl of Hillsborough (G.B.) 1772; Marquess of Downshire (I.) 1789; Comptroller of Household 1754–5; Treasurer of Chamber 1755–6; Lord of Trade 1763–5 and 1766; Joint Postmaster-General 1766–8; Secretary of State for American Dept. 1768–72; Secretary of State for South 1779–82; in charge of policy towards America at this critical juncture. *DNB, GEC, HoP.*

HINE, ROBERT

Public letters nos. XXXIII, XXXIV, XXXVI, XXXIX, XLIX, LXVII; private letters nos. 14, 17; Domitian, 8 Dec. 1770, 24 Dec. 1770, 28 June 1771.

More properly Hinde; admitted Lincoln's Inn 1738, 2nd son of Peter Hinde of Red Lyon Square, Middlesex; appointed Collector of Customs at Exeter by patent dated 22 Jan. 1768; described by Junius as 'the only man of merit whom the Duke of Grafton ever provided for'; author of *The modern practice of the High Court of Chancery*, 1785; *Lincoln's Inn Register*, i. 417; P.R.O./T 11/28/p. 467.

HODGES, SIR JAMES (d. 1774)

Public letter no. XXXVIII.

Appointed Town Clerk of London 1757; knighted 1759; said by Walpole to have started life as a tradesman on London Bridge. Walpole, *Memoirs of George III*, iv. 65; *AR*, 1774, 198.

HOLBURNE, FRANCIS (1704–71)

Domitian, 5 Mar. 1770.

Sailor and politician; entered navy 1720; lt. 1727; capt. 1740; r.-adm. 1755; v.-adm. 1757; adm. 1768; M.P. Stirling burghs 1761–8, Plymouth 1768–71; Lord of Admiralty Feb. 1770–Jan. 1771. *DNB, HoP.*

HOLDER, WILLIAM (d. 1790)

Public letter no. LXVIII; private letter no. 81.
Clerk to the court at Guildhall and witness against Eyre. *GM*, 1790, 958.

HOLLAND, Henry Fox, 1st Baron (1705–74)

Private letter no. 5; Nemesis, 12 May 1772.
M.P. Hindon 1735–41, Windsor 1741–61, Dunwich 1761–3; cr. Baron Holland 1763; Surveyor-General of Works 1737–43; Lord of Treasury 1743–6; Secretary-at-War 1746–55; Secretary of State for South 1755–6; Paymaster-General 1757–65; by the time of the letters, Holland had ceased to be of political importance but was still attacked in the press for corruption; Junius' private reference to him was unusually charitable. *DNB*, *GEC*, *HoP*.

HOMPHREY, JESTON

Public letter no. XXIII; private letter no. 41.
Country attorney who assaulted the Duke of Bedford at Lichfield races in 1747; of Egglesfield, Yorks.; d. 1772. *N & Q*, 11th ser. iii. 375 is painfully inaccurate but corrects the name; see *Burke's Landed Gentry* under Homfray.

HORNE, JOHN (1736–1812)

Preface; public letters nos. XXIII, XXXVII, XXXVIII, L, LI, LII, LIII, LIV, LVI, LIX, LXIX; private letters nos. 6, 37, 38, 44, 45, 66, 70, 71, 76.
M.P. Old Sarum 1801–2; took holy orders 1760 and presented to living at Brentford; became acquainted with Wilkes 1765; founder-member of Society of Supporters of the Bill of Rights but quarrelled with Wilkes and led breakaway group; later well known as a philologist and parliamentary reformer; added the name Tooke in 1782. *DNB*.

HORTON, MRS. ANNE (1743–1808)

Private letter no. 82.
Da. of Simon Luttrell, 1st Lord Irnham and sister of Henry Lawes Luttrell, Wilkes's opponent in the Middlesex election; she married, first, Christopher Horton, who died; then, in October 1771, Henry Frederick, 4th Duke of Cumberland. *GEC*; Walpole, *Memoirs of George III*, iv. 237–41.

HOWARD, SIR GEORGE (1718–96)

Domitian, 5 Mar. 1770; Veteran, 10 Mar. 1772.
Army officer; ensign 1725; lt. 1736; capt. 1737; lt.-col. 1744; col. 1749; maj.-gen. 1750; lt.-gen. 1760; gen. 1777; knighted 1774; M.P. Lostwithiel 1761–6, Stamford 1768–96; Governor of Minorca 1766–8; Governor of Chelsea Hospital 1768–95; Governor of Jersey 1795–d. *DNB*, *HoP*.

HYDE, SIR NICHOLAS (d. 1631)
Public letter no. LXVIII.
Lawyer; M.P. Andover 1601, Christchurch 1603; Lord Chief Justice of King's Bench 1627–31; quoted by Junius in connection with argument about bail. *Foss*, *DNB*.

IRNHAM, Simon Luttrell, 1st Baron (I.) (1713–87)
Public letters nos. XL and LXVII.
M.P. Mitchell 1755–61, Wigan 1761–8, Weobley 1768–74, Stockbridge 1774–80; cr. Baron Irnham (I.) 1768; Viscount Carhampton (I.) 1781; Earl of Carhampton (I.) 1785; fa. of Henry Lawes Luttrell, who stood against Wilkes in the Middlesex election, and of Anne who, as a widow, married the young Duke of Cumberland. *DNB*, *GEC*, *HoP*.

JACOB, GILES (1686–1744)
Public letter no. LXVIII.
Author; quoted by Junius in his discussion of the law on bail. *DNB*.

JAMES I, KING (1566–1625)
Public letter no. XLIV.
DNB.

JAMES II, KING (1633–1701)
Preface; public letters nos. XX, XXXVII, XLVI, and LVII. *DNB*.

JEFFREYS, GEORGE (1645–89)
Public letters nos. I and LXVIII.
Judge; Sol.-Gen. to Duke of York 1677; Recorder of London 1675–80; Chief Justice of Chester 1680; Lord Chancellor 1685–8; Lord High Steward 1685–6; cr. Bt. 1681; cr. Baron Jeffreys 1685; famous for his part in the Bloody Assizes. *DNB*, *Foss*, *GEC*.

JENKINSON, CHARLES (1729–1808)
Domitian, 24 Dec. 1770.
M.P. Cockermouth 1761–6, Appleby 1767–72, Harwich 1772–4, Hastings 1774–80, Saltash 1780–86; cr. Baron Hawkesbury 1786; Earl of Liverpool 1796; Under-Secretary of State 1761–2; Treasurer of Ordnance 1762–3; Joint Secretary to the Treasury 1763–5; auditor to the Princess Dowager 1765–72; Lord of Admiralty 1766–7; Lord of Treasury 1767–73; Joint Vice-Treasurer (I.) 1773–5; Clerk of the Pells 1775–d.; Secretary-at-War 1778–82; Member of the Board of Trade 1784; President of Board of Trade 1786–1804; Chancellor of Duchy of Lancaster 1786–1803; one of the most hard-working and efficient men-of-business of the period. *DNB*, *GEC*, *HoP*.

JONSON, BEN (?1573–1637)
Public letters nos. XXXIX, LI, and LIII.
Dramatist; quoted by Junius and Horne. *DNB*.

JUSTICE, MR.
Phalaris, 20 December 1770.
There is no firm evidence on which to base an identification. The name might be fictitious or ironic, though the details about Lady Williams appear precise enough. William Justice of Burlingham Hall, Norfolk, is mentioned in the diary of Sylas Neville and a Shropshire family of that name had a house at Hinstock: there is nothing to connect them with the anecdote Phalaris relates. Efforts to follow up the legal clues have been unsuccessful.

KENNEDY, KITTY
KENNEDY, MATTHEW
KENNEDY, PATRICK
Public letters nos. XXXIX and LXVIII.
The two brothers were convicted of murdering a night-watchman; sentence of death was mitigated, it was said at the intervention of their sister, a well-known prostitute: see note to Letter no. XXXIX; Kitty Kennedy of Newman St., is not to be confused with two of her competitors Polly Kennedy of Gt. Russell St. and another Polly Kennedy of Piercy St. *English Reports*, xcviii. 398–402; H. Bleackley, *Ladies fair and frail: sketches of the demi-monde during the eighteenth century*.

KENT, JOHN (d. 1773)
Private letter no. 5.
Junius identified him as the author of letters signed Lycurgus, printed in the *Public Advertiser* during 1769. S. Halkett & J. Laing, *Dictionary of anonymous and pseudonymous English literature*, iii. 329.

KING
Private letter no. 89.
Clerk to the city solicitor.

KIRKMAN, JOHN (1741–80)
Public letter no. LI.
London merchant; M.P. London 1780; Alderman of London 1768–d.; candidate for shrievalty 1771; d. 1780 during the poll. *Beaven*, *HoP*.

LEE
Preface.
Publisher of letter to Lord Melcombe; I have not succeeded in identifying

him; among possibilities are Arthur Lee (below), John Lee the actor (*DNB*), and John Lee the lawyer (*DNB*).

LEE, ARTHUR (1740–92)

Private letters nos. 44, 70, 75, 80, 81, 84.
Born in Virginia but educated in Britain; acted as agent for Massachusetts; author of newspaper letters signed Junius Americanus; responsible for draft of resolutions of Supporters of Bill of Rights; doctor of medicine (Edinburgh). *Dict. Amer. Biog.*

LEGGE, HENRY BILSON (1708–64)

Public letter no. XXXV.
M.P. East Looe 1740–1, Orford 1741–59, Hampshire 1759–64; Secretary to Treasury 1741–2; Surveyor of Woods and Forests south of Trent 1742–5; Lord of Admiralty 1745–6; Lord of Treasury 1746–9; Treasurer of Navy 1749–54; Chancellor of Exchequer 1754–5, 1756–7, 1757–61; dismissed by George III at outset of reign. *DNB*, *HoP*.

LEIGH, RICHARD (1727–72)

Public letter no. XLI.
M.P. East Looe 1770–2; lawyer. *HoP*.

LEWES, WATKIN (?1740–1821)

Private letters nos. 65 and 84.
M.P. London 1781–96; educated as a lawyer, became a keen parliamentary reformer and contested Worcester four times as a radical; Alderman of London 1772–d.; sheriff 1772–3; Lord Mayor 1780–1; knighted 1773. *Beaven*, *HoP*.

LIDDELL, ANNE (1739–1804)

Public letters nos. XII and XIV.
Da. of Henry Liddell, 1st Lord Ravensworth; married first in 1756 to Duke of Grafton, from whom she was separated, then divorced; secondly in March 1769 John Fitzpatrick, 2nd Earl of Upper Ossory. *GEC*.

LIGONIER, JOHN LOUIS (1680–1770)

Public letters nos. II and III.
Soldier; capt. 1703; maj. 1706; lt.-col. 1712; col. 1720; brig.-gen. 1735; maj.-gen. 1739; lt.-gen. 1743; gen. 1746; f.m. 1757; M.P. Bath 1748–63; cr. Viscount (I.) 1757; Baron Ligonier (G.B.) 1763; Earl Ligonier (G.B.) 1766; Lt.-Gen. of the Ordnance 1749–57; C.-in-C. 1757–66; Master-Gen. of the Ordnance 1759–63; naturalized Huguenot refugee. R. Whitworth, *Lord Ligonier*; *DNB*, *GEC*, *HoP*.

LINDSEY, Robert Bertie, 3rd Earl of (*c.* 1630–1701)
Dedication.
M.P. Boston 1661–6; Gentleman of Bedchamber 1674–85. *GEC.*

LITTLETON, see LYTTELTON

LLOYD, EDWARD
Public letter no. XLIV.
Otherwise known as Floyd; heavily punished 1621 for slandering the da. of James I; d. ?1648. *DNB.*

LOUIS XIV (1638–1715)
Public letters nos. XXXV and XLIII.
King of France 1643–1715. J. B. Wolf, *Louis XIV.*

LOWTHER, SIR JAMES, 5th Bt. (1736–1802)
Public letters nos. IX, XLIX, LVII, LXVII; Domitian, 8 Dec. 1770.
M.P. Cumberland 1757–61, Westmorland 1761–2, Cumberland 1762–8, Cockermouth 1769–74, Cumberland 1774–84; cr. Earl of Lonsdale 1784; very wealthy and unpopular; his struggle with Portland for electoral supremacy in Cumberland led to the Nullum Tempus agitation. *DNB, GEC, HoP.*

LUTTRELL, HENRY LAWES (?1737–1821)
Public letters nos. XI, XIII, XIV, XV, XVI, XVII, XVIII, XIX, XXII, XXXVI, XXXVII, XXXIX, XL, LXVII; Your Real Friend, 6 May 1769.
Soldier and politician; succeeded as 2nd Earl of Carhampton 1787; ensign 1757, lt. 1759; capt. 1759; maj. 1762; lt.-col. 1765; col. 1777; maj.-gen. 1782; lt.-gen. 1793; gen. 1798; M.P. Bossiney 1768–9, Middlesex 1769–74, Bossiney 1774–84, Plympton Erle 1790–4, Ludgershall 1817–21; Adjutant-general (I) 1770–83; Lt.-Gen. of the Ordnance (I.) 1787–97; C.-in-C. (I.) 1796–7; Master-Gen. of the Ordnance (I.) 1797–1800; famous as Wilkes's opponent at the Middlesex by-election in April 1769; his sister married the Duke of Cumberland, younger brother to the King. *DNB, GEC, HoP.*

LYTTELTON, George Lyttelton, 1st Baron (1709–73)
Public letter no. LIV.
M.P. Okehampton 1735–56; Lord of Treasury 1744–54; Cofferer of the Household 1754–5; Chancellor of Exchequer 1755–6; cr. Baron Lyttelton 1756; a politician of some importance in George II's reign but of no consequence by Junius' time. *DNB, GEC, HoP.*

MACAULAY, CATHERINE (1731–91)
Private letter no. 70.
Historian and radical polemicist; sister of John Sawbridge, M.P.; in the 1760s she was producing, by instalments, a History of England from Stuart times. *DNB.*

MACHIAVELLI or MACHIAVEL, NICCOLO (1469–1527)

Public Letter no. LVII.
Statesman and author of *Il Principe*; used here in his familiar role as demon and debaucher of public morality.

MACKENZIE, see STUART MACKENZIE

MACLEANE, LAUCHLIN (?1727–78)

Vindex, 6 Mar. 1771.
M.P. Arundel 1768–71; Governor of St. Vincent Mar.–Oct. 1766; Under-Secretary of State 1766–8; Superintendent of Lazarettos 1771; Collector at Philadelphia 1772; comptroller of army accounts in Bengal 1772–3; commissary of musters in Bengal 1773; drowned at sea returning from India; persistently put forward as author of letters of Junius. *HoP*; J. N. M. Maclean, *Reward is secondary*.

MACQUIRK, EDWARD

Public letters nos. VIII, IX, LIV.
Also spelt M'Quirk, Kirk and Quirk; convicted of murder after a riot at Middlesex by-election of December 1768 but given royal pardon. *GM*, 1769, 52, 135–40, 161; *Sessions Papers*, 1769.

MANSFIELD, William Murray, 1st Baron (1705–93)

Preface; public letters nos. I, III, XXXIV, XLI, XLIV, XLVIII, XLIX, LIV, LIX, LXI, LXIII, LXIV, LXV, LXVI, LXVIII, LXIX; private letters nos. 24, 40, 45, 47, 50, 52, 65, 67, 80, 83, 89; Phalaris, 17 Dec. 1770; Domitian, 17 Jan. 1771; A Whig, 9 Apr. 1771; Veteran, 27 Feb. 1772.
Lawyer and politician; M.P. Boroughbridge 1742–56; cr. Baron Mansfield 1756; Earl of Mansfield 1776; Sol.-Gen. 1742–54; Att.-Gen. 1754–6; Lord Chief Justice of King's Bench 1756–88; his position placed him in the middle of the struggle between the government and its newspaper critics in the 1760s and he was regarded by Junius as a determined advocate of royal power. An assessment of his judicial career is C. H. S. Fifoot, *Lord Mansfield*; *DNB*, *Foss*, *GEC*, *HoP*.

MARLBOROUGH, John Churchill, 1st Duke of (1650–1722)

Public letter no. XXIX.
Victor at Blenheim (1704), Ramillies (1706), Oudenarde (1708), and Malplaquet (1709). *DNB*, *GEC*.

MARRIOT

Public letter no. LXVIII.
Case cited by Junius in reference to law of bail. *English Reports*, XCI.96.

MAWBEY, SIR JOSEPH, 1st Bt. (1730–98)

Private letter no. 70.

Vinegar manufacturer and radical politician; M.P. Southwark 1761–74, Surrey 1775–90; cr. Bt. 1765; member of Society of Supporters of Bill of Rights. *DNB, HoP.*

MAZARIN, JULES (1602–61)

Public letter no. XXXV.

Cardinal and statesman; effective ruler of France after the death of Richelieu; used by Junius as a parallel for Bute's influence over George III.

MELCOMBE, George Bubb Dodington, 1st Baron (1691–1762)

Preface.

M.P. Winchelsea 1715–22, Bridgwater 1722–54, Weymouth and Melcombe Regis 1754–61; took name of Dodington in 1717; Envoy to Spain 1715–17; Clerk of the Pells (I.) 1720–d.; Lord of Treasury 1724–40; Treasurer of Navy 1744–9; Treasurer of Chamber to Prince of Wales 1749–51; Treasurer of Navy 1755–6; cr. Baron Melcombe 1761; celebrated as diarist and place-hunter. *DNB, GEC, HoP.*

MEREDITH, SIR WILLIAM, 3rd Bt. (?1725–90)

Public letters nos. XVIII, XX, XXII.

M.P. Wigan 1754–61, Liverpool 1761–80; Lord of Admiralty 1765–6; Comptroller of Household 1774–7; succeeded as 3rd Bt. 1752. *DNB, HoP.*

MILLER, JOHN (d. 1809)

Public letter no. XLI; private letters nos. 24 and 84.

Printer; of 2 Queen's Head Passage, Paternoster Row; tried July 1770 for publishing Junius' letter to the King but acquitted; his arrest 1771 led to the clash between the Lord Mayor and the Commons; subsequently emigrated to America. *State Trials*, xx. 869–96; *Plomer; N & Q*, cxcv. 319.

MONSON, GEORGE (1730–76)

Public letter no. XXIV.

Soldier and politician; ensign 1750; lt. and capt. 1753; maj. 1757; lt.-col. 1760; brig.-gen. (India) 1763; col. 1769; M.P. Lincoln 1754–68; Groom of Bedchamber to Prince of Wales 1756–60, to the King 1760–3; member of Supreme Council in India 1773–d.; served with Draper in expedition against the Philippines. *DNB, HoP.*

MONTESQUIEU, Charles Louis de Secondat, Baron de (1689–1755)

Public letter no. VIII.

French philosopher; his *De l'esprit des lois* (1748) was a major contribution to political and constitutional theory.

MOORE, SIR JOHN (d. 1790)

Public letters nos. XII, XIII, XIV.
Probably the 5th Bt., who succeeded his brother in 1738; sold family estate at Fawley, Berks. in 1765 and d. 1790 'at his seat near Bury, Suffolk, at an advanced age'; Junius says he was an old Newmarket friend of Grafton who obtained a pension for him. *Complete baronetage; VCH Berks.* iv.

MORETON, JOHN (?1714–80)

Public letter no. XLIV; A Whig, 9 Apr. 1771.
Lawyer and politician; more commonly spelt Morton; M.P. Abingdon 1747–70, New Romney 1770–4, Wigan 1775–80; Recorder of Woodstock 1743; Chief Justice of Chester 1762–d.; Att.-Gen. to the Queen 1770–d. *HoP.*

MORRIS, ROBERT (1743–93)

Public letter no. XLI; private letter no. 52.
Barrister; secretary to the Society of Supporters of the Bill of Rights 1769–70; eloped 1772 with a 12-year-old heiress. *Radical adventurer*, ed. J. E. Ross.

MORTIMER, ROGER DE (?1287–1330)

Public letter no. XXXV.
8th Baron of Wigmore and 1st Earl of March; lover of Isabella, Queen of Edward II and in effective control of the country until hanged by order of Edward III; used by Junius to taunt Bute and the Princess Dowager. *DNB, GEC.*

MORTIMER, MR.

Private letter no. 11.
Identified by Wade, ii. 24, as 'employed by Mr. Woodfall to procure intelligence for the *Public Advertiser*'; probably Thomas Mortimer, dismissed his post as vice-consul at Ostend 1768; he claimed that this was because he was too friendly towards Wilkes and that he was the victim of ministerial oppression; it seems that he was trying to interest Junius in his case; edited a large number of tracts and dictionaries on commercial matters. *Political Register*, July 1769; *The remarkable case of T. Mortimer, late Vice-Consul for the Austrian Netherlands*, 1770.

MURRAY, JAMES (*c.* 1690–1770)

Public letter no. XLI.
M.P. Dumfriesshire 1711–13, Elgin burghs 1713–15; elder brother of Lord Mansfield; active Jacobite; Secretary of State to the Pretender 1727–47; cr. Earl of Dunbar in the Jacobite peerage. *GEC, HoP.*

MUSGRAVE, SAMUEL (1732–80)

Public letter no. XXXIX.
Physician of Exeter; visited Lord Halifax in 1765 and asserted that while in France he had obtained proof that the peace settlement had been procured by bribes to Bute, Fox, and the Princess Dowager; when Halifax ignored the allegations, Musgrave accused him of obstructing justice and published an *Address to the Gentlemen of Devon*; after an inquiry in January 1770 the House of Commons voted his information 'frivolous and unworthy of credit'. *DNB; Parl. Hist.* xvi. 763–85; *GM*, 1769, 429–34, 585–7 and 1770, 44, 93; W. Munk, *Roll of the Royal College of Physicians*, ii. 312–16.

NASH, WILLIAM (d. 1772)

Public letters nos. LVIII and LIX; private letters nos. 57, 77, 78, 80, 81.
Government supporter in the city of London; Alderman 1766; Sheriff 1767–8; Lord Mayor 1771–2. *Beaven.*

NEWBERY, FRANCIS

Private letters nos. 4, 5, 6.
Printer; published the first collection of Junius' letters under title *The political contest*; either (1) s. of Francis Newbery; succeeded to father's business at St. Paul's Churchyard 1767; bookseller 1743–1818; or (2) nephew of John Newbery and cousin of (1); publisher of 20 Ludgate St.; d. 1780. *DNB, Plomer.*

NEWCASTLE, Thomas Pelham Holles, 1st Duke of (1693–1768)

Veteran, 17 Feb. 1772; Nemesis, 12 May 1772.
Politician; succeeded as Baron Pelham 1712; cr. Earl of Clare 1714; Duke of Newcastle 1715; Lord Chamberlain 1717–24; Secretary of State for South 1724–48; Secretary of State for North 1748–54; First Lord of the Treasury 1754–6 and 1757–62; Lord Privy Seal 1765–6. *DNB, GEC.*

NORTH, Frederick North, Lord (1732–90)

Public letters nos. I, III, XII, XXXVI, XXXVIII, XXXIX, XL, XLII, LVII; private letters nos. 29, 67, 86; Domitian, 5 Mar. 1770, 8 Dec. 1770, 24 Dec. 1770, 17 Jan. 1771; A Whig, 9 Apr. 1771; Veteran, 17 Feb. 1772; Nemesis, 12 May 1772.
Politician; M.P. Banbury 1754–90; succeeded father as 2nd Earl of Guilford 1790; Lord of Treasury 1759–65; Joint Postmaster-General 1766–7; Chancellor of Exchequer 1767–82; First Lord of Treasury 1770–82; Home Secretary Apr.–Dec. 1783; in his earlier letters Junius ridiculed North's ability but his resolute defence after Grafton's resignation prevented an opposition triumph. *DNB, GEC, HoP.*

NORTHINGTON, Robert Henley, 1st Earl of (1708–72)
Public letters nos. XXXVI and LXI; private letter no. 85.
Lawyer and politician; M.P. Bath 1747–57; Sol.-Gen. to Prince of Wales 1751–4; Att.-Gen. to Prince of Wales 1754–6; Att.-Gen. 1756–7; Lord Keeper 1757–61; Lord Chancellor 1761–6; Lord President of the Council 1766–7; cr. Baron Henley 1760, Earl of Northington 1764. *DNB*, *GEC*, *HoP*.

NORTHUMBERLAND, Hugh Smithson, 1st Duke of (1715–86)
Private letter no. 65.
Added name Percy on marriage to heiress of 7th Duke of Somerset; cr. Earl of Northumberland 1756; Duke of Northumberland 1766; Lord of Bedchamber 1753–63; Lord Chamberlain to the Queen 1762–8; M.P. Middlesex 1740–50; considerable influence in Middlesex, of which he was Lord Lieutenant 1762–d. *DNB*, *GEC*, *HoP*.

NORTON, SIR FLETCHER (1716–89)
Public letters nos. XI, XIV, XIX, XXXIX; A Whig, 9 Apr. 1771.
Lawyer and politician; M.P. Appleby 1756–61, Wigan 1761–8, Guildford 1768–82; cr. Baron Grantley 1782; Att.-Gen. to Duchy of Lancaster 1758–63; Sol.-Gen. 1762–3; Att.-Gen. 1763–5; Chief Justice in Eyre south of Trent 1769–d.; Speaker of House of Commons 1770–80. *DNB*, *GEC*, *HoP*.

NOYE, WILLIAM (1577–1634)
Public letter no. XLVII.
Lawyer; M.P. Grampound 1604, 1614, Helston 1621, Fowey 1623, St. Ives 1625, Helston 1628; Att.-Gen. 1631; quoted by Junius on a point of law. *DNB*.

OLIVER, RICHARD (1735–84)
Public letters nos. XLIV, XLVIII, LII, LIII, LIV: private letter no. 65; A Whig, 9 Apr. 1771.
M.P. London 1770–80; Alderman 1770–8; Sheriff 1772–3; founder-member of the Society of Supporters of Bill of Rights but quarrelled with Wilkes and seceded with Horne. *Beaven*, *DNB*, *HoP*.

ONSLOW, GEORGE (1731–92)
Public letter no. XLIV; A Whig, 9 Apr. 1771.
Army officer and politician; M.P. Guildford 1760–84; ensign 1748; capt. 1750; maj. 1757; lt.-col. 1759; Out Ranger of Windsor Great Park 1765–d.; usually referred to as Colonel Onslow or cocking George; initiated the campaign against the printers in 1771. *HoP*.

ONSLOW, GEORGE (1731–1814)
Public letters nos. XXXVI, XXXVIII, LIII, LIX: private letters nos. 5 and 6.
Cousin of the above; M.P. Rye 1754–61; Surrey 1761–74; succeeded as 4th

Baron Onslow 1776; cr. Earl of Onslow 1801; Out Ranger of Windsor Great Park 1754–63; Surveyor of the King's gardens 1761–3; Lord of Treasury 1765–77; Comptroller of the Household 1777–9; during the time of Junius' letters he was considerably embarrassed by the closeness of his former friendship with Wilkes. *GEC, HoP.*

PARSONS, ANN [otherwise NANCY] (d. 1815)
Public letters nos. XI, XII, XIII, XIV; Harry and Nan.
Mistress of the Duke of Grafton; reputed to be the da. of a Bond St. tailor; married first a West Indian merchant named Horton; after being discarded by Grafton married 1776 2nd Viscount Maynard; d. in France 1815. H. Bleackley, *Ladies fair and frail; GEC.*

PATERSON, JOHN (?1705–89)
Public letter no. LXI.
Solicitor; M.P. Ludgershall 1761–8; common councillor of city of London 1759–71; chairman of ways and means 1765–8; clerk to the commissioners of land tax for London 1772–d. *HoP.*

PAYNE, WILLIAM
Public letter no. LXVIII.
Witness in Eyre case.

PERCY, HUGH (1742–1817)
Public letters nos. III, IV, V; private letter no. 65.
Army officer and politician; ensign 1759; capt. 1759; lt.-col. 1762; col. 1764; maj.-gen. 1775; lt-gen. 1777; M.P. Westminster 1763–76; known as Lord Percy after his father created Duke of Northumberland 1766; succeeded mother as Baron Percy 1776; succeeded as 2nd Duke of Northumberland 1786. *GEC, HoP.*

PHILIP V, KING OF SPAIN (1683–1746)
Domitian, 17 Jan. 1771.
First of the Bourbon dynasty in Spain; his succession in 1700 led to European conflict.

PHILLIPSON, RICHARD (?1723–92)
Domitian, 5 Mar. 1770.
Soldier and politician; born Burton, took the name Phillipson in 1766; cornet 1744; lt. 1746; capt. 1751; maj. 1759; lt.-col. 1761; col. 1775; maj.-gen. 1779; lt.-gen. 1787; M.P. Eye 1762–8, 1770–92; close friend of Lord Cornwallis for whose borough he sat. *HoP.*

PITT, JOHN (*c.* 1706–87)
Public letter no. LVII.
M.P. Wareham 1734–47, 1748–50, Dorchester 1751–61, Wareham 1761–8; Lord of Trade 1744–55; Lord of Admiralty Nov.–Dec. 1756; Surveyor-General of Woods and Forests 1756–63, 1768–86; cousin of William Pitt, Earl of Chatham; a civil servant, his appearance in the letters is incidental to the Whittlebury Forest dispute. *HoP.*

PLATT, S.
Private letter no. 89.
Clerk to King's Bench; Cryer at Nisi Prius in London and Middlesex 1762–73. *The Royal Kalendar*, 1771, 108.

PLUMBE, SAMUEL (d. 1784)
Public letter no. LI.
Sugar refiner; 23 Foster Lane; Alderman of London 1767; defeated as candidate for sheriff 1769, receiving a derisory vote; in 1771 ran fourth to Wilkes, Bull, and Kirkman; d. Feb. 1784 in Golden Square. *Beaven.*

POMFRET, George Fermor, 2nd Earl of (1722–85)
Public letter no. LXIV; private letter no. 84.
Lord of Bedchamber 1763–81; Ranger of the little park of Windsor 1763. *GEC.*

POPE, ALEXANDER (1688–1744)
Public letter no. XXVI.
Poet; Junius quoted approvingly Pope's view that satire should sting individuals. *DNB.*

PORTLAND, William Henry Cavendish-Bentinck, 3rd Duke of (1738–1809)
Public letters nos. XXXVI, XXXVII, XLIX, LIII, LVII, LXVII; Domitian, 8 Dec. 1770.
M.P. Weobley 1761–2; succeeded as 3rd Duke 1762; Lord Chamberlain 1765–6; Lord Lieutenant of Ireland Apr.–Aug. 1782; First Lord of the Treasury Apr.–Dec. 1783; Home Secretary 1794–1801; Lord President 1801–5; First Lord of the Treasury 1807–9; a member of the Rockingham party; well known in the 1760s because of his struggle with Lowther for Cumberland influence. *DNB*, *GEC*, *HoP.*

PROCTOR, SIR WILLIAM BEAUCHAMP, 1st Bt. (1722–73)
Public letter no. IX; private letter no. 65.
M.P. Middlesex 1747–68; cr. Bt. 1745; defeated for Middlesex at general election of 1768 and again at by-election in December 1768. *HoP.*

PURLING, JOHN (?1722–1800)

Private letter no. 54.

M.P. New Shoreham Nov.–Dec. 1770, East Looe 1772–4, Weymouth and Melcome Regis 1774–90; Director of East India Company 1763–7, 1768–70, 1777–80; Deputy Chairman 1770–1; Chairman 1771–2. *HoP.*

RADCLIFFE, JOHN (1650–1714)

Veteran, 27 Feb. 1772.

Physician; M.P. Bramber 1690, Buckingham 1713–15; benefactor to Oxford University; his reputation as a physician was equivocal and Veteran used him as a figure of fun; see also Testis, 19 Nov. 1770. *DNB.*

RAVENSWORTH, Henry Liddell, 1st Baron (1708–84)

Public letter no. XLI.

M.P. Morpeth 1734–47; cr. Baron Ravensworth 1747. *GEC, HoP.*

REYNOLDS, JOHN

Private letter no. 75.

Attorney; frequently acted on behalf of Wilkes; mentioned as custodian of papers of the Society of Supporters of Bill of Rights; born 1728, lived at Southbarrow, Bromley; involved in financial difficulties in 1780s and spent rest of life in France. *Life and times of Frederick Reynolds by himself.*

RICHARD II, KING (1367–1400)

Public letter no. XXXIX.

Employed as a warning to George III. *DNB.*

RICHMOND, Charles Lennox, 3rd Duke of (1735–1806)

Public letter no. LIX; private letters nos. 85 and 89.

Soldier and politician; ensign 1751; capt. 1753; lt.-col. 1756; col. 1758; maj.-gen. 1761; lt.-gen. 1770; gen. 1782; f.m. 1792; Lord of Bedchamber Nov.–Dec. 1760; Ambassador to Paris 1765–6; Secretary of State for South May–Aug. 1766; Master-Gen. of the Ordnance Mar. 1782–Apr. 1783, Dec. 1783–95. *DNB, GEC.*

RIGBY, RICHARD (1722–88)

Public letters nos. XIV, XXIII, XXVII, XXIX, XXXIV, XXXVI, XXXVIII, XLIX, LVII.

M.P. Castle Rising 1745–7, Sudbury 1747–54, Tavistock 1754–88; Lord of Trade 1755–60; Secretary to Lord Lieutenant of Ireland 1757–61; Master of Rolls (I.) 1759–d.; Joint Vice-Treasurer of Ireland 1762–5, 1768; Paymaster-General 1768–82; bluff, aggressive, and self-seeking, he was man-of-business to the Duke of Bedford. *DNB, HoP.*

ROBINSON, JOHN (1727–1802)
Public letter no. L.
M.P. Westmorland 1764–74, Harwich 1774–1802; Joint Secretary to the Treasury 1770–82; Surveyor-General of Woods and Forests 1786–d.; one of the most reliable administrators in Lord North's government. *DNB*, *HoP*.

ROCHFORD, William Henry Nassau de Zuylestein, 4th Earl of (1717–81)
Public letters nos. I, VIII, X, XLII; Domitian, 17 Jan. 1771.
Lord of Bedchamber 1738–55; Envoy to Turin 1749–55; Groom of the Stole and First Lord of Bedchamber 1755–60; Ambassador to Madrid 1763–6; Ambassador to Paris 1766–8; Secretary of State for North 1768–70; Secretary of State for South 1770–5. *DNB*, *GEC*.

ROCKINGHAM, Charles Watson-Wentworth, 2nd Marquess of (1730–82)
Public letters nos. I, IV, XII, XIII, XIV, XV, XXIII, XXXVI, LIII, LIV, LIX; private letter no. 85; Domitian, 8 Dec. 1770; Veteran, 17 Feb. 1772; Nemesis, 12 May 1772.
Lord of Bedchamber 1751–62; First Lord of the Treasury 1765–6, Mar. 1782–d.; nominal leader of the old Newcastle party. *DNB*, *GEC*.

ROSS, GEORGE (1700–86)
Public letter no. XXXIV; Domitian, 28 June 1771.
M.P. Cromartyshire 1780–4, Tain burghs Mar.–Apr. 1786; army agent, he also represented the convention of royal burghs in London. *HoP*.

RUTLAND, John Manners, 3rd Duke of (1696–1779)
Private letter no. 13.
M.P. Rutland 1719–21; succeeded as 3rd Duke 1721; Lord of Bedchamber 1721–7; Chancellor of Duchy of Lancaster 1727–36; Lord Steward 1754–61; Master of the Horse 1761–6; Groom of the Stole 1761. *GEC*, *HoP*.

SACHEVERELL, HENRY (?1674–1724)
Public letter no. XIX.
Clergyman; High Tory demagogue impeached 1710 for treasonable sermon. *DNB*; G. Holmes, *The trial of Dr. Sacheverell*.

SACKVILLE, LORD GEORGE (1716–85)
Private letter no. 5.
Army officer and politician; capt. 1737; lt.-col. 1740; col. 1745; maj.-gen. 1755; lt.-gen. 1758; C.-in-C. British forces in Germany 1758; dismissed the service 1759 after battle of Minden; M.P. Dover 1741–61, Hythe 1761–8, East Grinstead 1768–82; changed name to Germain 1769; cr. Viscount Sackville 1782; Ranger of Phoenix Park 1736–d.; Chief Secretary in Ireland 1751–5;

Joint Vice-Treasurer (I.) 1765–6; First Lord of Trade 1775–9; Secretary of State for America 1775–82. *DNB*, *GEC*, *HoP*.

SALKELD, WILLIAM (1671–1715)

Public letter no. LXVIII.

Legal authority; Chief Justice of Carmarthen, Cardigan, and Pembrokeshire 1713. *DNB*.

SANDWICH, John Montagu, 4th Earl of (1718–92)

Public letters nos. XIV, XXIII, XXXVI, XXXVIII, XLIX; Domitian, 24 Dec. 1770, 17 Jan. 1771; Veteran, 28 Jan. 1772, 17 Feb. 1772.

Army officer and politician; col. 1745; maj.-gen. 1755; lt.-gen. 1759; gen. 1772; succeeded as 4th Earl 1729; Lord of Admiralty 1744–6; Minister Plenipotentiary 1746–9; First Lord of the Admiralty 1749–51; Joint Vice-Treasurer (I.) 1755–63; First Lord of the Admiralty 1763; Secretary of State for North 1763–5; Joint Postmaster-General 1768–70; Secretary of State for North 1770–1; First Lord of the Admiralty 1771–82; Ranger of St. James's and Hyde Park 1783–4. *DNB*, *GEC*.

SAVILE, SIR GEORGE, 8th Bt. (1726–84)

Public letters nos. XXXIX and LIX.

M.P. Yorkshire 1759–83; one of the most respected and independent of the supporters of Rockingham. *DNB*, *HoP*.

SAWBRIDGE, JOHN (1732–95)

Public letters nos. LII, LIII, LIV, LVIII, LIX; private letters nos. 56, 58, 65, 66, 70, 71, 76, 77.

M.P. Hythe 1768–74, London 1774–80, Nov. 1780–95; Alderman of London 1769; sheriff 1769–70; Lord Mayor 1775–6; independent-minded radical; seceded from Society of Supporters of Bill of Rights with Horne, Oliver, and others. *DNB*, *HoP*.

SCIPIO (d. 211 B.C.)

Public letter no. III.

Roman general; full name Publius Cornelius Scipio; adversary of Hannibal, by whom he was defeated.

SCOTT, JAMES (1733–1814)

A Whig, 9 Apr. 1771.

Cleric and author; D.D. 1775; frequent writer in the *Public Advertiser* under names of Anti-Sejanus, Old Slyboots, and others; rector of Simonburn, Northumberland 1771; follower of Lord Sandwich. *DNB*; Walpole, *Memoirs of George III*, ii. 191; *BM prints & drawings*, no. 4426.

SELDEN, JOHN (1585–1654)
Public letter no. LXVIII.
Jurist; M.P. Lancaster 1623, Great Bedwyn 1626, Ludgershall 1628, University of Oxford 1640; quoted by Junius in his argument about law of bail. *DNB*.

SHELBURNE, William Petty, 2nd Earl of (1737–1805)
Public letters nos. IV, XII, XXIV; private letters nos. 70, 71, 85.
M.P. Wycombe 1760–1; succeeded as 2nd Earl 1761; cr. Marquis of Lansdowne 1784; lt. 1757; col. 1760; maj.-gen. 1765; gen. 1783; First Lord of Trade Apr.–Sept. 1763; Secretary of State for South 1766–8; Secretary of State for Home Affairs Mar.–July 1782; First Lord of the Treasury July 1782–Apr. 1783; at the time of Junius' letters, he had resigned from the ministry and was building up his city interest in connection with Sawbridge and Townsend. *DNB*, *GEC*, *HoP*.

SMYTHE, SIR SYDNEY STAFFORD (1705–78)
Public letter no. LXVIII.
M.P. East Grinstead 1747–50; knighted 1750; Baron of the Exchequer 1750; Chief Baron of the Exchequer 1772–7. *Foss*, *HoP*.

SOMERS, John Somers, 1st Baron (1651–1716)
Public letter no. XLVI.
Lawyer; M.P. Worcester 1689–93; Sol.-Gen. 1689–92; Att.-Gen. 1692–3; cr. Baron 1697; Lord Chancellor 1697–1700; Lord High Steward 1689; Lord President of the Council 1708–10; great Whig lawyer. *DNB*, *GEC*.

SPRY, RICHARD (1715–75)
Private letter no. 28.
Naval officer; entered navy 1733; lt. 1740; commander 1744; capt. 1745; commodore 1762; r.-adm. 1770; knighted 1773. *DNB*.

STARLING, SOLOMON
Public letter no. VIII.
Apothecary; gave evidence concerning death of George Clarke; of Princess St., Hanover Square.

STEELE, SIR RICHARD (1672–1729)
Public letter no. XXII.
Author and politician; M.P. Stockbridge 1713–14, Boroughbridge 1715–22, Wendover 1722–7; spent early years in army; Commissioner of Stamps 1710–13; Surveyor of stables at Hampton Court 1714–17; Commissioner for Forfeited Estates 1716–25. *DNB*, *HoP*.

STUART, ANDREW (1725–1801)
Private letter no. 65.
Lawyer and politician; M.P. Lanarkshire 1774–84, Weymouth and Melcombe Regis 1790–1801; Writer to the Signet 1759; King's Remembrancer in Exchequer 1770–1; joint Remembrancer 1771–86; Joint Keeper of the Signet 1777–9; Lord of Trade 1779–82; Keeper of Register of Sasines 1781–99; Joint Keeper 1799–d.; represented the Hamilton case in the dispute over the Douglas estates; the decision against him by the Lords in Feb. 1769 led to great bitterness. *HoP.*

STUART MACKENZIE, JAMES (?1719–1800)
Public letters nos. XII, XXIII, XXXVI.
M.P. Argyllshire 1742–7, Buteshire 1747–54, Ayr burghs 1754–61, Ross-shire 1761–80; Envoy extraordinary at Turin 1758–61; Lord Privy Seal (Scotland) 1763–5, 1766–d.; his dismissal in 1765 was regarded as a crucial demonstration that his brother Lord Bute no longer influenced the King. *HoP.*

SUFFOLK, Henry Howard, 12th Earl of (1739–79)
Public letters nos. LIV and LIX; Domitian, 17 Jan. 1771.
Succeeded as 12th Earl 1757; Deputy Earl Marshal 1763–5; Lord Privy Seal Jan.–June 1771; Secretary of State for North 1771–d.; one of the Grenville group who went over to administration soon after George Grenville's death. *DNB, GEC.*

SWINNEY, SIDNEY (*c.* 1724–83)
Private letter no. 5.
Cleric and author; educated at Eton and Clare, Cambridge; son of Matthew Swinney of Pontefract, Yorks.; married da. of John Zephaniah Holwell, Governor of Bengal; chaplain to embassy at Constantinople and chaplain in army at Minden; rector of Barton-le-Street from 1775; D.D. 1763; F.R.S. 1764; F.S.A. 1767; miscellaneous writings include *Ninth satire of Horace* 1767; *Tour through some parts of the Levant* 1769; *Fugitive pieces* 1768; *The battle of Minden, a poem* 1769. *Venn; GM*, 1783, ii. 982.

SYLVA, ISAAC FERNANDES
Public letter no. LXIII.
Jewish moneylender from whom Wilkes borrowed £3–4,000 in 1761; d. Pimlico 1810. *Lloyd's Evening Post*, 7/9 & 23/6 Aug. 1771; *GM*, 1810, 499.

TALBOT, William Talbot, 1st Earl (1710–82)
Private letter no. 84.
M.P. Glamorgan 1734–7; succeeded as 2nd Baron 1737; cr. Earl Talbot 1761; Lord Steward of the Household 1761–d.; Lord High Steward at George III's coronation; fought a duel with Wilkes in Oct. 1762. *GEC, HoP.*

TAVISTOCK, Elizabeth Russell, Marchioness of (1739–68)

Public letter no. XXIX.
Da. of William Keppel, 2nd Earl of Albemarle. *GEC.*

TAVISTOCK, Francis Russell, Marquess of (1739–67)

Public letters nos. XXIII, XXVI, XXVII, XXIX.
Son of John, Duke of Bedford; M.P. Bedfordshire 1761–7; thrown from horse and died after fracturing skull. *HoP.*

TAYLOR, ROBERT (1714–88)

Public letter no. XXXIV; Domitian, 28 June 1771.
Architect; knighted 1782; sheriff of London 1782–3; bequest provided funds for Taylorian Institute at Oxford. *DNB.*

TAYLOR, SAMUEL (1668–1727)

Public letters nos. XVI, XIX, XX, XXII.
Walpole's opponent at King's Lynn; son of Sir Simon Taylor, M.P. (*c.* 1633–89). *CJ* xvii. 105, 128; *Supplement to Blomefield's Norfolk*; H. L. Bradfer-Lawrence, *The Merchants of Lynn*, 161–4.

TEMPLE, Richard Grenville, 2nd Earl (1711–79)

Nemesis, 12 May 1772.
M.P. Buckingham 1734–41, Buckinghamshire 1741–7, Buckingham 1747–52; succeeded 1752 as 2nd Earl; First Lord of Admiralty 1756–7; Lord Privy Seal 1757–61. *DNB, GEC, HoP.*

THURLOW, EDWARD (1731–1806)

Private letter no. 70.
Lawyer and politician; M.P. Tamworth 1765–78; cr. Baron Thurlow 1778; Sol.-Gen. 1770–1; Att.-Gen. 1771–8; Lord Chancellor 1778–83, Dec. 1783–92; Teller of the Exchequer 1786–d. *DNB, GEC, HoP.*

TORCY, Jean-Baptiste Colbert, Marquis de (1665–1746)

Public letter no. XXVII.
His *Mémoires, pour servir à l'histoire des négociations depuis le Traité de Riswick jusqu'à la Paix d'Utrecht* was translated in 1757.

TOUCHET, SAMUEL (*c.* 1705–73)

Public letter no. L.
Contractor; M.P. Shaftesbury 1761–8; for the last ten years of his life he was in financial difficulties and is said to have hanged himself. *HoP.*

TOWNSEND, JAMES (1737–87)

Public letters nos. LII, LIII, LIX: private letters nos. *66*, *67*, *70*, *71*.
M.P. West Looe 1767–74, Calne 1782–7; Alderman of London 1769; sheriff 1769–70; Lord Mayor 1772–3; a follower of Shelburne, he seceded with Horne from the Society of Supporters of the Bill of Rights. *Beaven*, *HoP*.

TOWNSHEND, CHARLES (1725–67)

Public letters nos. XII and XIV.
M.P. Great Yarmouth 1747–56, Saltash 1756–61, Harwich 1761–7; Treasurer of the Chamber 1756–61; Secretary-at-War 1761–2; First Lord of Trade Feb.–Apr. 1763; Paymaster-General 1765–6; Chancellor of the Exchequer 1766–d.; author of the duties to raise a revenue in America. *DNB*, *HoP*.

TOWNSHEND, George Townshend, 4th Viscount (1724–1807)

Public letters nos. IV, XXXV, XL; Domitian, 17 Jan. 1771; Veteran, 17 Feb. 1772.
M.P. Norfolk 1747–64; succeeded as 4th Viscount 1764; cr. Marquis 1787; joined army 1743; capt. 1745; lt.-col. 1748; col. 1758; maj.-gen. 1761; lt.-gen. 1770; gen. 1782; f.m. 1796; Lt.-Gen. of the Ordnance 1763–7; Lord Lieutenant of Ireland 1767–72; Master-Gen. of the Ordnance 1772–82, Apr.–Dec. 1783. *DNB*, *GEC*, *HoP*.

TRECOTHICK, BARLOW (?1718–75)

Public letter no. XXXIX.
M.P. London 1768–74; Alderman 1764; sheriff 1766–7; Lord Mayor 1770; his political connections were with the Rockinghams. *Beaven*, *HoP*.

TRENTHAM, Granville Leveson-Gower, Viscount (1721–1803)

Public letter no. XXIII.
See under GOWER.

TRESILIAN, ROBERT (d. 1388)

Public letter no. LXVIII.
M.P. Cornwall 1368; Justice of King's Bench 1378; Chief Justice 1381–8; executed as a traitor 1388. *DNB*, *Foss*.

UPPER OSSORY, John Fitzpatrick, 2nd Earl of (1745–1818)

Public letters nos. XII and XIV.
M.P. Bedfordshire 1767–94; succeeded as 2nd Earl 1758; cr. Baron Upper Ossory (G.B.) 1794; married the divorced wife of the Duke of Grafton; nephew of 4th Duke of Bedford. *GEC*, *HoP*.

VAUGHAN, SAMUEL (1720–1802)

Public letters nos. XXXIII, XXXIV, XXXVI, LXVII; private letters nos. 11, 14, 15, 16, 17; Domitian, 8 Dec. 1770.
Jamaican merchant of Mincing Lane; an active radical, prosecuted for an attempt to obtain office by bribery; see Introduction to public letter no. XXXIII, p. 153; *GM*, 1769, 579–80; 1802, 1169; J. Burrows, *Law Reports*, iv. 2494; *A refutation of a false aspersion upon Samuel Vaughan, Esq.; An appeal to the public on behalf of Samuel Vaughan; BM prints and drawings*, nos. 4304 and 4305.

VERRES, GAIUS (*c.* 115–43 B.C.)

Public letter no. XXIII.
Roman administrator prosecuted by Cicero for corruption while governor of Sicily 73–71 B.C.

WALPOLE, SIR ROBERT (1676–1745)

Public letters nos. XV, XVI, XIX, XX, XXI, XXII, XLVI; Nemesis, 12 May 1772.
M.P. Castle Rising 1701–2, King's Lynn 1702–12, 1713–42; knighted 1725; cr. Earl of Orford 1742; Secretary-at-War 1708–10; Treasurer of the Navy 1710–11; Paymaster of the Forces 1714–15, 1720–1; First Lord of the Treasury 1715–17, 1721–42. *DNB, GEC, HoP.*

WALPOLE, THOMAS (1727–1803)

Public letter no. LIII.
M.P. Sudbury 1754–61, Ashburton 1761–8, King's Lynn 1768–84; Director East India Company 1753–4. *HoP.*

WEDDERBURN, ALEXANDER (1733–1805)

Public letters nos. XLIV, XLIX, LIX.
Lawyer and politician; M.P. Ayr burghs 1761–8, Richmond 1768–9, Bishop's Castle 1770–4, Okehampton 1774–8, Bishop's Castle 1778–80; cr. Baron Loughborough 1780; Earl of Rosslyn 1801; Sol.-Gen. 1771–8; Chancellor to the Queen 1771–80; Att.-Gen. 1778–80; Lord Chief Justice of Common Pleas 1780–93; First Commissioner of Great Seal Apr.–Dec. 1783; Lord Chancellor 1793–1801. *DNB, Foss, GEC, HoP.*

WESTON, EDWARD (1703–70)

Public letters nos. IX and X.
Civil servant and writer; Comptroller of the Salt Office *c.* 1735–d.; Under-Secretary of State 1730–46, 1761–4; Chief Secretary in Ireland 1746–51; Writer to the *London Gazette* 1741–d.; Clerk of the Signet. *DNB; Venn; H.M.C. 10th report*, app. 1.

WEYMOUTH, Thomas Thynne, 3rd Viscount (1734–96)

Public letters nos. I, III, XI, XXIII, XXVIII, XLIX, LV, LVII, LIX; private letter no. 67; Domitian, 24 Dec. 1770.

Succeeded as 3rd Viscount 1751; cr. Marquis of Bath 1789; Lord of Bedchamber 1760–3; Master of Horse to the Queen 1763–5; Lord Lieutenant of Ireland 1765; Secretary of State for the North Jan.–Oct. 1768; Secretary of State for the South 1768–70, 1775–9; Groom of the Stole Mar.–Nov. 1775, 1782–d. *DNB*, *GEC*.

WHEBLE, JOHN (1746–1820)

Private letters nos. 40, 41, 43, 54.

Bookseller and publisher; of 24 Paternoster Row; printer of the *Middlesex Journal*. *Plomer*.

WHITEHEAD, WILLIAM (1715–85)

Public letter no. L.

Successor to Colley Cibber as poet laureate in 1757. *DNB*.

WHITWORTH, RICHARD (?1734–1811)

Private letter no. 7.

M.P. Stafford 1768–80; voted and spoke at first with opposition but went over to government 1772; Junius identified him as Veridicus, a writer in the *Public Advertiser*. *HoP*.

WILD, JONATHAN (1682–1725)

Domitian, 24 Dec. 1770.

Celebrated criminal, eventually hanged; became something of a folk hero and used by Fielding in the *Life of the late Jonathan Wild the great*. *DNB*.

WILKES, JOHN (1725–97)

Preface; public letters nos. I, III, VIII, IX, XI, XII, XIII, XIV, XV, XVI, XVII, XVIII, XIX, XXXV, XXXVII, XXXIX, XLIV, XLIX, L, LI, LII, LIII, LIV, LIX, LXII, LXIX; private letters nos. 25, 26, 36, 40, 43, 44, 45, 52, 54, 58, 60, 65 and 66–84; Junius, 21 Nov. 1768; Reply to Monody, 12 Apr. 1769; A Whig, 9 Apr. 1771; Veteran, 17 Feb. 1772; Scotus, 4 May 1772.

M.P. Aylesbury 1757–64, Middlesex 1768–9, 1774–90; Alderman of London 1769; sheriff 1771–2; Lord Mayor 1774–5; City Chamberlain 1779–d. *DNB*, *HoP*.

WILKES, MARY (1750–1802)

Public letters nos. LII and LIII; private letters nos. 66, 77 and 78.

Otherwise known as Polly; only legitimate child of John Wilkes. H. Bleackley, *Life of John Wilkes*.

WILLIAMS, LADY FRANCES (d. 1781)
Phalaris, 20 Dec. 1770.
Yo. da. of Thomas, 1st Earl Coningsby and widow of Sir Charles Hanbury Williams; heiress of Hampton Court, Herefordshire. *GEC.*

WILMOT, JOHN EARDLEY (1709–92)
Public letter no. LXIX.
Justice of King's Bench 1755; Chief Justice of Common Pleas 1766–71. *DNB, Foss.*

WOLLASTON, RICHARD (d. ?1728)
Public letters nos. XX, XXI, XXII.
Otherwise Woolaston; M.P. Whitchurch 1698–9, 1699–1710; expelled the House of Commons 1699. *CJ* xii. 519; *Musgrave's obituary.*

WOODFALL, HENRY SAMPSON (1739–1805)
Preface; Public letters nos. XLI and LIV; private letters nos. 1–65; 69, 70, 72, 77, 78, 79; Phalaris, 17 Dec. 1770.
Printer of the *Public Advertiser*; prosecuted June 1770 for printing Junius' letter to the King but found guilty of printing and publishing only. *DNB.*

WROTTESLEY, ELIZABETH (1745–1822)
Public letters nos. XII and XIV.
Da. of Revd. Sir Richard Wrottesley, 7th Bt.; married the Duke of Grafton 1769. *GEC.*

YATES, SIR JOSEPH (1722–70)
Public letters nos. XLI and LXIX.
Judge; knighted 1763; Justice of King's Bench 1764; Justice of Common Pleas 1770–d. *DNB, Foss.*

YORKE, CHARLES (1722–70)
Public letters nos. XXXVI, XXXVIII, XLIX; Domitian, 8 Dec. 1770.
Lawyer and politician; M.P. Reigate 1747–68, Cambridge University 1768–70; clerk of the crown in Chancery 1747–d.; Sol.-Gen. to Prince of Wales 1754–6; Att.-Gen. 1762–3, 1765–6; Lord Chancellor 1770; connected with the Rockinghams, he d. 20 Jan. 1770, three days after accepting the seals as Lord Chancellor, in circumstances that suggested suicide; it was asserted that the King had employed uncommon pressure to induce him to take office. *DNB, HoP.*

BIBLIOGRAPHY

There is an enormous number of publications on the subject of Junius. Since many of them are worthless, some eccentric, and a few lunatic, a select bibliography seems most suitable.

1. BIBLIOGRAPHIES

A preliminary list was in W. T. Lowndes, *The bibliographer's manual of English literature*, first published in 1834. John Edmands printed a fuller version in the *Bulletin of the Mercantile Library of Philadelphia* between 1890 and 1892. This was used and expanded by F. Cordasco, *A Junius bibliography*, 1949, a second and revised edition appearing in 1973. Professor Cordasco has also contributed a number of articles, largely on textual and bibliographical points, to recent volumes of *Notes and Queries*. *The new Cambridge bibliography of English literature*, ii: *1660–1800*, ed. George Watson, published 1971, has a section on Junius. An excellent brief bibliography, with comments, is appended to A. Ellegård, *Who was Junius?*, 1962. Another detailed and scholarly study is T. H. Bowyer, *A bibliographical examination of the earliest editions of the letters of Junius*, 1957.

2. ORIGINAL TEXTS

The letters of Junius first appeared in the *Public Advertiser* between 1768 and 1772: good runs are available in the Burney collection in the British Library and in the London Library. The collected edition, prepared by Junius himself, was published in March 1772 by Henry Sampson Woodfall in two volumes.

Junius' private notes to the printer are preserved in Add. MS. 27774. Woodfall's letter to Junius of 19 February 1771 about Vindex was recovered by the printer and is Add. MS. 27777, f. 14. The same volume of manuscripts also includes, in Junius' handwriting, the originals of Harry and Nan, Vindex of 22 February 1771, and Scotus (ff. 12, 13, and 16).

The correspondence between Junius and Wilkes is in Add. MS. 30881. Junius' letter to Chatham of 14 January 1772 and the anonymous letter of 2 January 1768 (attributed by some to Junius) are in the Chatham MSS. (P.R.O. 30/8/3 part ii, f. 357 and P.R.O. 30/8/4 part i, f. 136). The whereabouts of the three letters to George Grenville, once in the possession of John Murray Ltd., publishers, is not known. They were not in the additional Grenville papers deposited in the British Library in 1972 and further inquiries have failed to trace them.

The Woodfall papers in the British Library also include the original draft, in Junius' handwriting, of the Preface and Dedication for the collected edition and many pages of his proof corrections (Add. MS. 27775 and 27776). These are of interest since some commentators have claimed to detect similarities between the proof markings of Junius and of certain candidates for the authorship.

The only other specimen of Junius' handwriting (if accepted) is the covering note to the verses to Miss Giles, preserved in Add. MS. 27457, f. 22. These verses are discussed above on p. 552.

3. SPECIAL COLLECTIONS

There are several special collections of Junius material. Lord Carlingford's notes are in the Strachie MSS. in the C.R.O., Taunton, but are of little interest. Of greater value is the part of the Joseph Parkes collection preserved in the Heslop Room in the University of Birmingham: it includes some useful pamphlets. The Codrington Library at All Souls has a splendid number of early tracts on the authorship controversy, and of particular interest are the notebooks of Charles Wentworth Dilke. A small collection of research notes by H. Dodwell has recently been deposited with the Codrington Library. Gustave Simonson's typewritten manuscript, 'A History of the Letters of Junius', was deposited in the British Library on his death in 1930 and is catalogued as 11857. d. 34. It has interesting comments, particularly on the miscellaneous letters.

4. MAIN PRINTED SOURCES UP TO 1950

1772 *The letters of Junius*, 2 vols. Published by Henry Sampson Woodfall. Prepared for the press by the author and used as the basis for this edition.

1802 *The letters of Junius*, 2 vols. Edited by Robert Heron with comprehensive notes.

1812 *The letters of Junius*, 3 vols., ed. J. Mason Good. A new edition published by George Woodfall and including, for the first time, Junius' private letters to Henry Sampson Woodfall and John Wilkes.

1813 John Taylor, *A discovery of the author of the letters of Junius*. Suggested the Revd. Dr. Philip Francis as the main author.

1816 John Taylor, *The identity of Junius with a distinguished living character established*. The revised version in favour of Philip Francis, junior.

1838 *The correspondence of William Pitt, Earl of Chatham*, 4 vols., ed. W. S. Taylor and J. H. Pringle. Printed two letters to Chatham, one undoubtedly by Junius.

1843 John Jaques, *The history of Junius and his works*. A review of the authorship controversy.

1850 *The letters of Junius*, 2 vols., ed. John Wade. The Bohn edition, with a long editorial commentary supporting the claims of Sir Philip Francis.

1852–3 *The Grenville papers*, 4 vols., ed. W. J. Smith. The third volume included a lengthy exposition in support of Lord Temple; printed three letters to George Grenville, possibly by Junius.

1867 J. Parkes and H. Merivale, *The memoirs of Sir Philip Francis*, 2 vols. Heavy argumentation in favour of the Francis case; printed the autobiographical fragment.

1871 *The handwriting of Junius professionally investigated by Mr. Charles Chabot, expert, with preface and collateral evidence by Hon. Edward Twisleton.* The only really detailed study of the handwriting evidence.

1875 C. W. Dilke, *The papers of a critic*, 2 vols. Posthumous reprint of many of his articles on Junius for the *Athenaeum*. Hostile to the case for Francis.

1888 L. Stephen, 'Chatham, Francis and Junius', *English Historical Review*, vol. iii. Examined the question of the reports of debates.

1894 H. R. Francis, *Junius revealed.* Important for new evidence concerning the verses to Miss Giles.

1927 *The letters of Junius*, ed. C. W. Everett. The editorial introduction urged the claims of Lord Shelburne. The edition was criticized by L. B. Namier in *The Nation & Athenaeum*, 4 February 1928, and the *Observer*, 5 February 1928. Another hostile review was in the *Times Literary Supplement*, 8 March 1928.

5. RECENT PRINTED SOURCES

1955 S. Maccoby, *English Radicalism, 1762–1785.*

1960 R. L. Haig, *The Gazetteer, 1735–1797: a study in the eighteenth-century English newspaper.*

1961 Edward A. Bloom, 'Neoclassic "Paper Wars" for a Free Press', *Modern Language Review*, vol. lvi.

1962 A. Ellegård, *Who was Junius?*

1962 A. Ellegård, *A statistical method for determining authorship: the Junius letters, 1769–1772.*

1963 R. R. Rea, *The English press in politics, 1760–74.*

1963 J. T. Boulton, *The language of politics in the age of Wilkes and Burke.*

1963 J. N. M. Maclean, *Reward is secondary: the life of a political adventurer and an inquiry into the mystery of 'Junius'.*

1964 R. D'O. Butler, review of *Correspondance secrète du comte de Broglie avec Louis XV (1756–74)*, *English Historical Review*, vol. lxxix.

1968 J. N. M. Maclean, 'Grant of Blairfindy, Junius and Francis', *Bulletin of the Institute of Historical Research*, vol. xli.

1969 L. S. Sutherland, W. Doyle, and J. M. J. Rogister, 'Junius and Philip Francis: new evidence', *Bulletin of the Institute of Historical Research*, vol. xlii.

1973 J. Wardroper, *Kings, Lords and Wicked Libellers: Satire and Protest, 1760–1837*.

1976 J. Brewer, *Party Ideology and Popular Politics at the Accession of George III*.

INDEX

N.B. A short biographical note on each person referred to in the public letters, in the private letters to Woodfall, Wilkes, Chatham, and Grenville, and in those miscellaneous letters printed in section A of Appendix five, will be found between pp. 573 and 615.

Peers are listed under their titles, thus: Holland, Henry Fox, 1st Baron.